SIGPLAN
NOTICES
Volume 27
Number 7
July 1992

ACM PRESS

Proceedings of the

ACM

SIGPLAN '92 Conference on

Programming Language Design and Implementation

San Francisco, California
June 17-19, 1992

Sponsored by the
Special Interest Group on Programming Languages,
Association for Computing Machinery

The Association for Computing Machinery
1515 Broadway
New York, New York 10036

Soft Cover ISBN: 0-89791-475-9
Series Hard Cover ISBN: 0-89791-476-7

Additional copies may be ordered prepaid from:

ACM Order Department
P.O. Box 64145
Baltimore, MD 21264

1-800 342-6626
1-410 528-4261 (Outside US, MD and AK)

ACM Order Number: 548920

ACM SIGPLAN'92 Conference on
Programming Language Design and Implementation
San Francisco, California, June 17-19, 1992

Wednesday, June 17, 1992

Thursday, June 18, 1992

Friday, June 19, 1992

AUTHOR INDEX

TUTORIAL PROGRAM

Tutorials Chair: William Pugh (University of Maryland)

Track I: Strategies for Code Improvement

Optimization Techniques for Imperative Languages

Ken Zadeck (Brown University)

Instruction Scheduling

Monica Lam, Michael Smith (Stanford University)

Dependence Analysis and Reordering Transformations

Randy Allen (Kubota Pacific Computer)

Post-Compiler Code Transformation

David Wall (DEC WRL)

Track II: Strategies for Non-Traditional Problems

Implementing Object-oriented Languages

David Ungar (Sun Microsystems Laboratories), Craig Chambers (University of Washington)

Compiler Toolkits

Tim Teitelbaum (Cornell University), Peter Lee (CMU), Bill Waite (University of Colorado)

Compilers and Runtime Systems for Languages with Garbage Collection

Andrew W. Appel (Princeton University)

Visual Programming Languages: Programming Paradigms and Design Issues

Allen Ambler (University of Kansas), Margaret Burnett (Michigan Technological University)

A New Approach to Debugging Optimized Code

Gary Brooks, Gilbert J. Hansen, Steve Simmons

Convex Computer Corporation
P.O. Box 833851
Richardson, TX 75083-3851
gbrooks@convex.com, hansen@convex.com, ssimmons@convex.com

ABSTRACT

Debugging optimized code is a desirable capability not provided by most current debuggers. Users are forced to debug the unoptimized code when a bug occurs in the optimized version. Current research offers partial solutions for a small class of optimizations, but not a unified approach that handles a wide range of optimizations, such as the sophisticated optimizations performed by supercomputer compilers.

The trend with current research is to make the effects of optimization transparent, i.e., provide the same behavior as that of the unoptimized program. We contend that this approach is neither totally feasible nor entirely desirable. Instead, we propose a new approach based on the premise that one should be able to debug the optimized code. This implies mapping the current state of execution back to the original source, tracking the location of variables, and mapping compiler-synthesized variables back to user-defined induction variables. To aid the user in understanding program behavior, various visual means are provided, e.g., different forms of highlighting and annotating of the source/assembly code. While this unavoidably requires the user to have a basic understanding of the optimizations performed, it permits the user to see what is actually happening, infer the optimizations performed, and detect bugs. An example illustrates the effectiveness of visual feedback.

To support conventional debugger functionality for optimized code, the compiler must generate additional information. Current compiler-debugger interfaces (CDIs) were neither designed to handle this new information nor are they extensible in a straight forward manner. Therefore, a new CDI was designed that supports providing visual feedback and the debugging of optimized code. This paper specifies the details of a new CDI and relates each feature back to the debugger functionality it supports.

ACM SIGPLAN '92 PLDI-6/92/CA
© 1992 ACM 0-89791-476-7/92/0006/0001...$1.50

1. INTRODUCTION

The traditional approach to developing production code is to compile and debug the program without optimization, and then compile it with optimizations to get performance enhancements. There are cases when the ability to debug optimized code is a necessary and desirable capability. For example,

- Some logic errors only materialize in the presence of optimization. This includes programs with timing or instability problems, or programs with explicit compiler directives that force code to be wrongly vectorized or parallelized.
- A program may need to be optimized in order to be runnable or fully testable because of time or size constraints. For example, optimization may considerably reduce the execution time to reach a point of failure.
- By observing the behavior of the optimized code, a user can identify what logic may be causing performance problems.
- Production code is usually fully optimized. Should a customer submit a bug report involving a core file, the core dump can be analyzed.
- To find a bug in optimized code requires recompiling without optimization. This extra compilation step can be eliminated.
- Compiler bugs can involve optimizations being performed incorrectly. By observing program behavior, a compiler developer can identify what optimizations caused the bug.

Without debugger support, debugging an optimized program can be very tedious and time consuming, if not impractical. The user must be able to correlate the optimized code with the original source code. This is undesirable because it requires expert optimization knowledge and can be a challenging process even for a compiler developer. The compiler optimizations reorder, replicate, factor, fuse, delete, and transform source constructs, thereby destroying the direct mapping between object and source code. Furthermore, the use of variables may be eliminated (e.g., constant propagation), synthesized (e.g., induction variables), or assigned to registers. Values at a stop point may be different from that in the unoptimized program.

Providing support for the debugging of optimized code is a difficult problem. Some of the complications that arise are:

- The behavior of the optimized code must be conveyed in terms of the original source code. Conveying execution state in terms of source code unparsed from the optimized code is generally not possible for the optimized code is generally not expressible using the constructs of the source language.
- The mapping of object code to source code is no longer 1-to-1. Code fragments will be replicated, fused, eliminated, or reordered.
- The location of a variable may alternate between a register and memory. The use of a variable may even be eliminated.
- The usage of an induction variable may be replaced by compiler-synthesized variables.
- The compiler-debugger interface must incorporate information about the transformations performed by the compiler.
- Collecting the necessary debugger information requires extensive modifications to the compiler(s) to track each optimization performed

This paper presents the design of a new CDI that permits a debugger to handle the mapping from optimized object code to source code, to make certain optimizations transparent, to provide visual feedback of the effect of control flow optimizations on program behavior, and to display the correct value of a variable. Our approach is a combination of, and departure from, current research efforts. Section 2 briefly surveys other approaches taken to debugging optimized code. Section 3 describes the new approach we have taken. Section 4 discusses the design of the new CDI and Section 5 presents a debugging example. Section 6 discusses compilation times and space requirements using the new CDI compared to an existing CDI. Section 7 describes future enhancements.

2. PREVIOUS WORK

2.1 Current Work on Debugging Optimized Code

The current approach to debugging optimized code is exemplified by the work of Hennessy [Henn82, WaSr85], Zellweger [Zell83, Zell84], Coutant et al [CoMe88], and Zurawski and Johnson[ZuJo90]. Each effort is concerned with making the effects of the optimizations transparent to the programmer and providing *expected behavior.* Hennessy's research deals with the problem of providing the values of noncurrent variables that are consistent with the order of evaluation and assignment in the original unoptimized program. Closely related is the work of Coutant et al. They too can provide the value of noncurrent variables, but also handle global optimizations and track a variable's value from memory through registers. Zellweger's work addresses the problems of making the effect of inlining and cross-jumping optimizations transparent to the programmer. Zurawski and Johnson take an approach different from Zellweger's. Their debugger is based on a context-oriented model. Providing expected behavior transparently may involve switching between the optimized and unoptimized program and placing restrictions on some optimizations. The capability to recover the value of noncurrent variables is also provided.

Each of the prototypes [Zell83, CoMe88] utilized multiple windows, in particular, a command and source window. However, none took advantage of available graphical capabilities to provide visual feedback on the effects of optimizations.

2.2 Current Status of Debugger Technology

Most current debuggers, such as the UNIX debuggers (gdb, dbx, and CONVEX csd), VAX DEBUG [Bean83], and the CONVEX Ada debugger, a.db, usually use a line-oriented compiler-debugger interface. The debugging information usually conveys the name, type, and location for variables and the starting address of a statement or basic block, and the associated source code line.

Statement-oriented debugging information has inherent limitations that prohibit it from being extended to support the debugging of optimized code. For example,

- The granularity is too coarse. Many optimizations involve expressions that cannot be conveyed at the statement level.
- There is only a 1-to-1 mapping between source lines and object code addresses which is insufficient in the presence of optimization. Optimizations require both mapping multiple source codes to a singular object code (e.g., common subexpression elimination) and mapping a singular source code to multiple object codes (e.g., inlining and dynamic selection).
- The implementation is a non-variant record/structure which is too restrictive for optimized debugging information. For example, UNIX stabs (symbol table structures) have a fixed number of fields of fixed size

Despite the narrow scope of current research on debugging optimized code and the problems incurred, much useful support for debugging optimized code can be provided. This paper discusses an alternate approach based on a new compiler-debugger interface (CDI). Instead of trying to provide expected behavior, highlighting and animation (via repetitive stepping) is used to convey the effects of optimizations on the behavior of a program.

3. AN ALTERNATE APPROACH TO DEBUGGING OPTIMIZED CODE

The premise of our approach to debugging optimized code is that it is better to depict what is actually happening than to always make the effects of optimizations transparent. We contend that making the effects of optimizations transparent is both undesirable and intractable. It is undesirable because transparent debugging maintains a facade of what is actually happening, thereby inhibiting the user from debugging the actual optimized code. It is intractable because it is not possible to supply the information necessary to invert the effects of all the optimizations applied to each code section. Optimizations are cascaded and reapplied an arbitrary number of times in various orders. It is unrealistic to propagate and maintain information needed to unravel the effects of each optimization, especially when many of the optimizations are very complex in nature.

One major goal was to convey the effects of optimizations on a program's behavior. This was achieved by providing effective visual feedback in the form of highlighted program text using a finer source granularity than the statement level. This process of debugger interaction with the user is referred to as *visual debugging*. Text sections may be highlighted by boxing, using reverse video, grey-scale shading, underlining, multiple fonts and icons. Highlighting can be used for:

- Currently executing code — Whenever a program is stopped, the text sections of the program which correspond to the current point in the executable are highlighted.
- Previously executed code — Within a basic block, previously executed expressions can be highlighted to distinguish them from other expressions yet to be executed.
- Eventpoints — Source lines on which an eventpoint has been set can be annotated appropriately.
- Compiler optimizations — For example, loop invariant code executed prior to the loop can be highlighted prior to loop entry, but the loop construct is not highlighted, indicating the invariants were hoisted out of the loop.
- Animating program behavior — As a user steps through source, the expressions currently being executed are highlighted. Repetitive stepping will give rise to animation as successive sections of the program are highlighted while execution proceeds through the program.

Based on this visual feedback, a user can make intelligent queries about program state and deduce expected behavior (e.g., deduce the value of a variable), and gain insight into a program's actual behavior. Also, visual feedback of abnormal behavior can indicate to a compiler developer there is an optimizer bug.

Another major goal was to always provide the correct value of a variable. Two situations were addressed. First, the location of a variable can be allocated to a register and/or memory over different regions of code [CoMe 88]. This requires keeping track of the liveness of each variable over various instruction ranges. Second, usages of induction variables are replaced by compiler-synthesized variables. This requires maintaining the linear function relating the two.

Additional design goals were to:

- Support standard debugger functionality
- Provide visual debugging for optimizations performed by the CONVEX compilers
- Make the compiler collection of debugging information non-intrusive, i.e., compiling for debugging would not affect either the optimizations performed or the code generated
- Design the debugging information to be extensible, i.e., accommodate new optimizations and revisions to existing optimizations
- Support codes written in different languages or in multiple languages
- Load debugging information on demand because of the large amount of debugging information

4. THE COMPILER-DEBUGGER INTERFACE (CDI)

The CDI consists of three components:

- Compiler extensions to generate requisite debugging information
- Data files containing debugging information
- Access methods within the debugger to load debugging information

The last item will not be addressed in this paper. However, it should be mentioned that the debugging information and its external representation were designed so the data files could be loaded incrementally and the internal data structures easily built on the fly.

Currently the CDI supports all levels of optimization performed by the CONVEX FORTRAN and C compilers [CONV90, CONV91], namely, local and global scalar optimizations, vectorization, and parallelization. Table 1 lists a representative set of optimizations for each level.

Level	Optimization
Scalar	Redundant-assignment elimination, assignment substitution, common subexpression elimination, redundant-use elimination, constant propagation and folding, algebraic and trigonometric simplification, dead-code elimination, hoisting and sinking scalar and array references, copy propagation, code motion, strength reduction, global register allocation, instruction scheduling
Vector	Strip mining, loop distribution, loop interchange, conditional induction variables, loop unrolling, if-do interchange
Parallel	parallel strip mining, independent tasks (by directive), dynamic selection

Table 1: Optimizations by Level

4.1 Debugging Information

Table 2 lists the components of the debugging information.

The suffixed data files (.ns, .vt, etc.) are kept in a hidden directory. For data files generated by the front-end, there is one for each *primary source file*, i.e., file submitted to the compiler for compilation. For data files generated by the back-end, there is one for each object file generated by the compiler. Multiple object files can be generated by the CONVEX Ada and Application Compiler.

The **Name Space Table** for a single source file identifies the declaration of top-level symbols in the program, thereby allowing .tsi files to be selectively loaded upon demand.

The **Type/Scope Environment Table** contains the information needed to resolve the definition of a program identifier at debug time. This information consists of attributes determined by a compiler front end, such as lexical scope, type definition, and kind. The kind is used in name resolution (e.g., when identical C identifiers are used both as a variable and typedef within the same scope). This table contains many of the same identifier attributes typically found in a debugger symbol table. However, it

Component	Purpose	Data File	Compiler Generation
Source File Map	Relates an object file to source file(s)	executable	back-end
Section Table	Delineates the bounds of object module components in the executable's address space	executable	back-end
Name Space	Lists external identifiers in the program	.ns	front-end
Type/Scope Environment	Defines attributes of program data types; disambiguates identifiers and other lexical program symbols	.tsi	front-end
Source Unit Table	Contains the abstracted tree of source code elements that reflects the syntax of a program	.sut	front-end
Source Range Table	Correlates source units with ranges of instructions in the executable	.srt	back-end
Variable Table	Lists the attributes of program variables	.vt	back-end
Location Range Table	Correlates the location of a variable with ranges of instructions in the executable	.lrt	back-end
Expression Table	Maps compiler-synthesized variables back to user-defined variables	.xpt	back-end

Table 2: Debugging Information

does not include the allocated location of a variable identifier, since a variable can exist in many different locations or be replaced by another variable due to compiler optimizations. To determine the runtime value of a variable requires using this table in conjunction with the Variable Table, Location Range Table, and the Expression Table.

The **Source Unit Table** provides a tree of source units that reflects the syntax of the program, and is used in highlighting program text. An entry for a source unit in the table consists of:

- Index — A unique integer that identifies the source unit.
- Kind — The granularity of the source unit (see Table 3 and Figure 1 below which illustrates each).
- Text section — Start and end character positions of the source unit.
- Scope — The lexical scope in which the source unit occurs.
- Parent — Parent's source unit index.

Granularity	Purpose
Expression	Any valid combination of constants, operators, and operands valid in the current source language
Statement	Any valid statement in the current source language
Block	Statements that constitute the body of a routine, loop or conditional construct
Loop	An iterative construct (e.g., FOR, DO)
Routine	A main routine, subroutine, or function

Table 3: Source Unit Granularities

Multiple source unit granularities have the additional advantage of permitting a more robust stepping mechanism (e.g., commands such as *finish loop*, *next expression*) and allowing the user to think in terms of language constructs instead of source line numbers in a file.

The **Source Range Table** is used to map between executable source units and corresponding instructions in the executable image. An entry in the Source Range Table consists of a source unit index, and a start and end instruction address in the executable image. There may be multiple address ranges for a source unit due to optimization (e.g., instruction scheduling which interleaves code for an expression). Given an instruction address, the table is used to determine which source units are active. This mapping is used, for example, to determine which source units to highlight at debugger eventpoints. Given a source unit, the table is used to determine the source unit's address ranges. This mapping is used for stepping and the setting/unsetting of breakpoints, eventpoints and tracepoints.

The **Variable Table** enumerates all user-defined and compiler-synthesized variables in a program, along with their attributes. An entry in the Variable Table contains the following components:

- Home location — The storage class and offset for a variable whose lifetime extends across the entire program. Possible home locations in global memory are absolute, base-offset (for FORTRAN common block variables), and object module relative (for static variables in C).
- Scope entry — A pointer to the scope entry for the variable in the name space (i.e., .tsi data file) which contains the variable's name.
- Additional flags, e.g., a row-major array, a Cray pointer, etc.

The **Location Range Table** is used to track the ephemeral variable-to-location bindings. An entry in the Location Range Table consists of a variable index in the Variable Table, a start and end instruction address in the executable image over which the value of the variable resides in a particular machine location, and the machine location. Possible machine locations are registers or stack frame relative (for local and argument variables). There may be multiple overlapping entries for a variable due to optimization. Given a program address and variable, the table is used to determine which location, if any, is associated with a variable. This mapping is used to find the value of a variable. If no ephemeral location is bound to the variable, the home location applies. If there is no home location, the variable is said to be *unavailable*; this can occur, for example, due to constant propagation and redundant assignment elimination. Given a program address and a data location, the table is used to determine which variables reside in the location. This mapping is used when examining the registers or stack frames to determine the associated variable(s).

The **Expression Table** tracks compiler-synthesized variables back to the user-defined variables in the source code. Within the optimized code, the uses of many variables are replaced with more efficient uses of other variables. A common example occurs with loop strength reduction, where the loop induction variable is transformed from an array index to a pointer for the current element in the array. For example:

```
INTEGER*4 A(100)
DO I = 1, 100
  A(I) = 0
ENDDO
```

Here, a loop induction variable, `?foo`, is synthesized that is a pointer into the array `A`.

```
?foo = loc(A) + 4*(I-1)
```

All uses of `A(I)` within the loop are replaced with references to `?foo`. The Expression Table maintains the linear function that expresses the direct relationship between a synthesized variable and the respective user-defined variables, and the reason for the synthesization.

4.2 Generation of Debugging Information

CDI debugging information is gathered and generated in a series of stages that spans all phases of the compiler. The compiler phases are: a front-end (syntax and semantic analysis), a middle phase (machine independent optimizations), and a back-end (code generation, machine-dependent optimizations, assembly). There is a separate front-end for FORTRAN and C; the other phases are common. Debugging information is communicated from one phase to another by annotating compiler nodes and entries in the compiler's symbol table.

Table 2 indicates the phase in which each component of the debugging information is generated. The .ns, .tsi, and .sut data files are emitted at the end of the front-end phase. The lexical analyzer and parser determine the starting and ending source positions of selected syntactic units and annotate the parse tree with this information. During semantic analysis, the source positions are used to construct the source units which are then associated with compiler nodes. Also constructed is the type and scope information.

During the middle phase and back-end, source units are tracked through each optimization. Expressions are determined at the point where the synthesized variable is introduced during the compilation. The symbol table entry for that variable is annotated with the expression. At the end of code generation, but before instruction assembly, all variable attributes have been resolved and the instruction order completely fixed. The .vt and .xpt files are formed by walking the symbol table. Compiler nodes are annotated with labels representing program points of interest to the debugger and with assembler directives for propagating .srt, .vt, and .lrt debugging information during assembly. After the instructions are assembled and address labels resolved, the .srt, .vt, and .lrt data files are generated along with the object module.

5. EXAMPLE

The FORTRAN example in Figure 1 demonstrates how highlighting can convey the execution behavior of optimized code. In particular, it demonstrates that repetitive stepping can convey a precise understanding of how the code was optimized. The pictures were extracted from an X

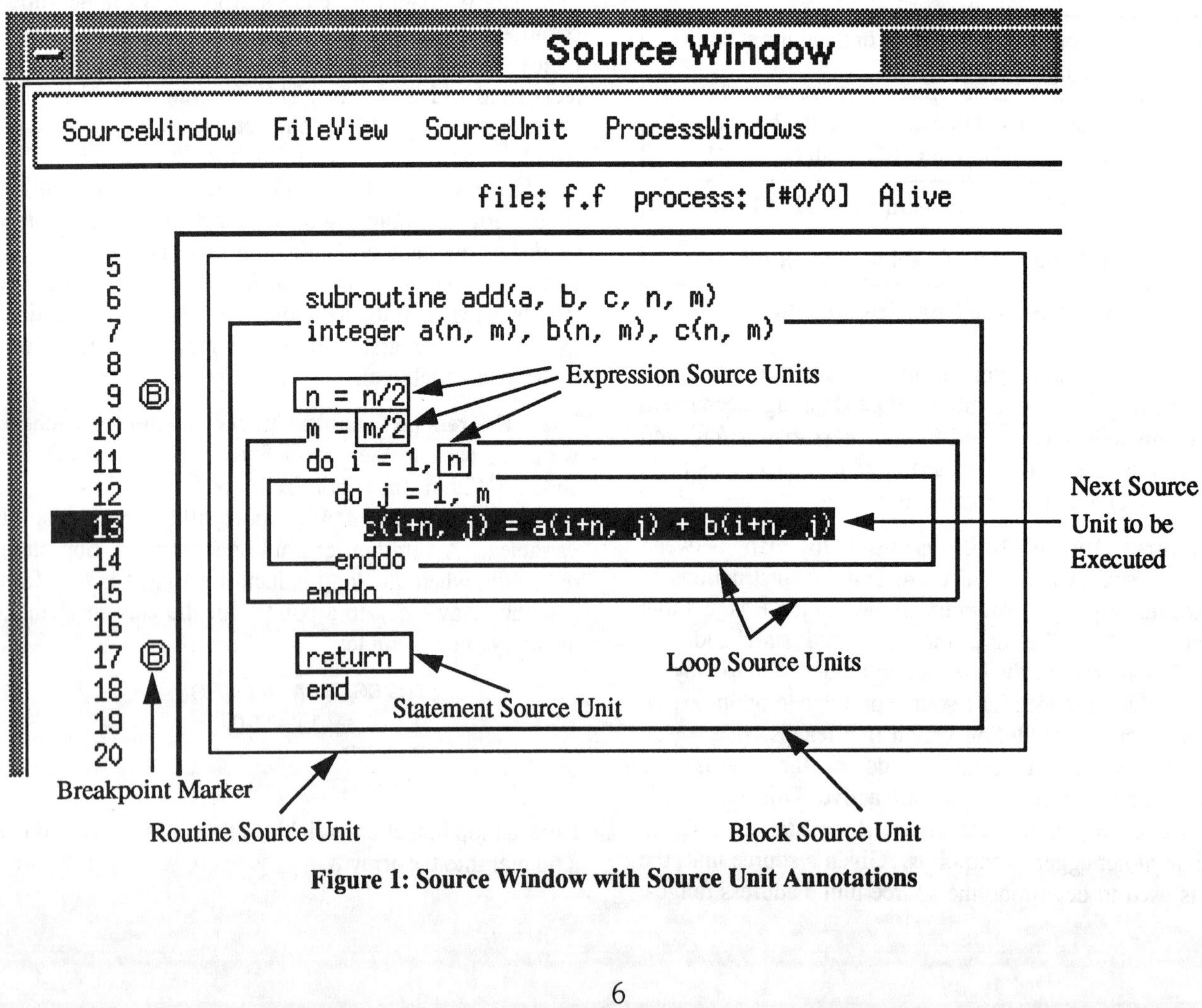

Figure 1: Source Window with Source Unit Annotations

```
_add_:               sub.w     #16,a0            Entry Point
_add_+(0x4):         ld.w      @12(ap),s6
_add_+(0x8):         ld.w      @12(ap),s0        Use of parameter N
_add_+(0xc):         ld.w      @16(ap),s1        Use of parameter M
_add_+(0x10):        le.w      #0,s0             Test N, if less than 0, add 1
_add_+(0x14):        brs.t     _add_+(0x1a)
_add_+(0x16):        add.w     #1,s0
_add_+(0x1a):        le.w      #0,s1             Test M, if less than 0, add 1
_add_+(0x1e):        brs.t     _add_+(0x24)
_add_+(0x20):        add.w     #1,s1
_add_+(0x24):        cvtw.l    s0,s0             Convert N and M to longwords
_add_+(0x26):        cvtw.l    s1,s1
_add_+(0x28):        shf       #-1,s0            Divide both N and M by 2
_add_+(0x2c):        shf       #-1,s1
_add_+(0x30):        st.w      s0,@12(ap)        Store N
_add_+(0x34):        lt.w      #0,s0
_add_+(0x38):        st.w      s1,@16(ap)        Store M
_add_+(0x3c):        brs.f     _add_+(0xe8)      Branch if N < 0 to routine exit
_add_+(0x3e):        ld.w      @12(ap),a5        Use of N in loop
_add_+(0x42):        ld.w      @16(ap),s4        Use of M in loop
_add_+(0x46):        mov       a5,a1             Set up induction variables for loop
_add_+(0x48):        shf       #2,a1
_add_+(0x4a):        ld.w      #1,s5             Load addresses of A and C
_add_+(0x4e):        ld.w      0(ap),a2
_add_+(0x52):        ld.w      8(ap),a3
_add_+(0x56):        shf.w     #2,s6
_add_+(0x5a):        add.w     a1,a2
_add_+(0x5c):        mov       a5,s2
_add_+(0x5e):        ld.w      4(ap),a5          Load address of B
_add_+(0x62):        add.w     a1,a3
_add_+(0x64):        st.w      a2,-12(fp)
_add_+(0x68):        add.w     a1,a5
_add_+(0x6a):        st.w      a3,-4(fp)         Store loop induction values
_add_+(0x6e):        st.w      s6,-16(fp)
_add_+(0x72):        sub.w     s4,s5
_add_+(0x74):        st.w      a5,-8(fp)
_add_+(0x78):        neg.w     s4,s4
_add_+(0x7a):        le.w      #0,s4             Top test of outer loop
_add_+(0x7e):        brs.t     _add_+(0xba)
```

Figure 2: Assembly Code for FORTRAN Example

window that displays the source code [BuCh91]. Slightly restricted functionality is also available on character-oriented terminals (CRTs).

The current point of execution is communicated to the user by highlighting, in reverse video, the innermost source unit(s) to be executed *next*. The FORTRAN code was compiled at optimization level -O2 (which contains all local and global scalar optimizations and vectorization, but excludes parallelization, loop unrolling, and dynamic selection). Examples of each kind of source unit are illustrated. To aid in following the example at the source level, Figure 2 gives the corresponding machine instructions, annotated with appropriate comments, that lead up to the physical loop. Examining the assembly code is unnecessary in practice. However, when there is a source and assembly window, corresponding code is highlighted in both. For the assembly window, only the first instruction of the source unit will be highlighted.

The example illustrates the following optimizations: instruction scheduling, strength reduction, vectorization, code motion, redundant use elimination, and assignment substitution. Also illustrated are synthesized variables and mapping of their values back to the respective user-defined induction variables. Step granularity is an expression source unit.

Upon entry to the routine, prolog code is executed that sets up the runtime environment and then execution stops on the first source unit (`_add_+(0x8)`):

`n = N/2`

Stepping once stops on the second source unit to be

executed (`_add_+(0xc)`).

```
m = n/2
```

This highlighting sequence is caused by instruction scheduling. To utilize the instruction pipeline most efficiently, uses of variables in memory are usually executed first within a basic block. The next step by expression stops at `_add_+(0x10)` and results in

```
n = n/2
m = m/2
do i = 1, n
```

Both n/2 and n are highlighted because of assignment substitution which eliminated the assignment to n. Stepping by expression once more stops at `_add_+(0x1a)` and results in

```
m = m/2
```

The use of m within the inner loop is not highlighted because assignment substitution was not performed on the assignment to m. Several more steps results in the assignment to the parameters n and m, respectively.

```
n = n/2
m = m/2
```

```
n = n/2
m = m/2
```

The next step stops at `_add_+(0x3e)` and results in

```
c(i+n, j) = a(i+n, j) + b(i+n, j)
```

All uses of n are highlighted because of code motion and redundant use elimination. Changing the step granularity from expression to block and stepping once results in entering the body of the outermost loop, i.e, the i loop.

```
do j = 1, m
   c(i+n, j) = a(i+n, j) + b(i+n, j)
enddo
```

Requesting the values for both i and j at this point results in the response:

```
I = (INTEGER*4) 1
J = Value is not available.
```

The reason for this is that the uses of i and j have been replaced, using loop strength reduction, with new compiler synthesized induction variables whose uses are more efficient. The values of i and j are only determinable when the synthesized variables are alive. In this case, j doesn't have a value because the j loop hasn't been entered yet, i.e., the synthesized variables for j are alive only within the body of the loop. (Liveness is tracked by the global register allocator.) By stepping one more block, only line 13 is highlighted and j now has its initial value of 1:

```
I = (INTEGER*4) 1
J = (INTEGER*4) 1
```

Stepping by loop followed by a step by block results in:

```
I = (INTEGER*4) 129
J = (INTEGER*4) 1
```

The compiler optimization summary would show that the i loop was vectorized and the i and j loop interchanged. The i loop is divided into two nested loops, i.e., an inner loop vectorized with a size of 128 and an outer strip-mine loop that iterates n/128 times. The vectorized loop of i has been interchanged with the j loop. Thus, i is 129 since the stride of the strip-mined outer loop is 128.

In order to determine the values of both i and j, a set of linear equations is solved. For example, i has the following set of linear equations associated with it (obtained by invoking the command `info expression i`):

```
used to create 11 synthesized variable(s):
  1. <OSTR>   ?i0 = (1+(N/2))+(I-1)
  2. <TRIP>   ?i1 = (-1*(N/2))+(I-1)
  3. <TRIP>   ?i2 = (N/2)+((I-1)*-1)
  4. <ISTR>   ?i8 = ?i0+((I-1)%128)
  5. <INDV>   ?ia = ((N*2)+loc(C))+((?i0-(1+(N/2)))*4)
  6. <INDV>   ?ib = (loc(B)+(N*2))+((?i0-(1+(N/2)))*4)
  7. <INDV>   ?ic = ((N*2)+loc(A))+((?i0-(1+(N/2)))*4)
  8. <INDV>   ?id = ?i2
  9. <INDV>  ?i12 = ?ia+((4*N)*?i6)
 10. <INDV>  ?i13 = ?ib+((4*N)*?i6)
 11. <INDV>  ?i14 = ?ic+((4*N)*?i6)
```

The abbreviations in angular brackets to the left of the equations identify the reason for the synthesization. (OSTR stands for outer strip, TRIP for trip count, ISTR for inner strip, and INDV for induction variable.) The variables prefixed with a question mark are the compiler synthesized variables. For example, ?i14, ?i13, and ?i12 are pointers into the arrays a, b, and c, respectively. Using these variables as pointers caused the address calculations within the body of the two loops to be eliminated.

This example makes the following points:

- Traceability to the current logical source unit, and thus, point of execution is possible. This can be done even when the machine code for the source units have been merged together or interweaved. It does not imply that any source code before or after a source unit has been executed.
- Successive stepping by expression provides a sequence of highlighting patterns from which the user can infer

Optimization	Highlighting Behavior	Example

Redundant Assignment Elimination	The eliminated code is never highlighted. The optimization can be verified using the `info line` command; there will be no address ranges for the eliminated code.	`N = K + 1 ...`
		`N = K * J`
		`DO I = 1, N`

Assignment Substitution	Both the expression being assigned and the subsequent uses of the assigned variable are highlighted.	`N = K + 1 ...` `DO I =  1, N`
Common Subexpression Elimination	The common subexpressions are highlighted.	`A = X + 1 ...` `B = C * (X + 1)`
Redundant Use Elimination	Multiple references to a variable between assignments within a basic block are highlighted.	`A = X + X / 3`
Algebraic/Trig Simplification	The code for the expression simplified is not highlighted. The optimization can be verified using the `info line` command; there will be no address ranges for the simplified source unit.	1. `A = X * 1` 2. `A = X * 1`
Dead Code Elimination	The eliminated code is never highlighted. The optimization can be verified using the `info line` command; there will be no address ranges for the dead code.	

Code Motion; Hoisting and Sinking References	The reference to a variable or a syntactic element within the loop is highlighted before the body of the loop is entered and highlighted.	`DO I = 1, 10`
		`A[I] = 2 * N`
		`ENDDO`

Copy Propagation	References to equivalent variables are highlighted.	`A = 7.23 * 1.14` `B = A; C = B`
Instruction Scheduling	Expressions in a basic block are highlighted in execution order which is different than indicated by the source code.	1. `A = X * 3 - Y` 2. `A = X * 3 - Y` 3. `A = X * 3 - Y` 4. `A = X * 3 - Y`
Strength Reduction	Noticeable when viewing both a source window and assembly window; both the current expression and current instruction are highlighted.	`J = I * 2` `shf #1,I`
Global Register Allocation	Not noticeable unless examining liveness ranges via the `info variable` command.	
Strip Mining	The loop induction variable is incremented by the strip mine length, whose default is 128.	
Loop Distribution	The body of the loop will be highlighted depending on how its parts were distributed and how the distributed loops were optimized.	
Loop Interchange	The inner loop is highlighted before the outer loop.	
Conditional Induction Variables	The value of a conditional induction variable is incremented by a conditional amount, and when displayed its value is derived from the compiler synthesized variable.	
Loop Unrolling	For complete unrolling, the loop induction variable is completely removed. For partial unrolling, it is incremented by multiples of 4.	

If-Do Interchange	The expression within the IF statement is highlighted before entering the loop body. The behavior of the loop differs based upon the result of the IF expression.	`DO I = 1, N`
		`IF X .LE. Y ...`
		`ENDDO`

Parallel Strip	A new source window is instantiated in the second iteration of the loop.	
Dynamic Selection	Different highlighting behavior occurs, depending on whether the scalar, vectorized, or parallelized version of the loop is selected. Selection is based on the value of runtime variables.	

Table 4: Current Highlighting Patterns

possible optimizations. However, the deductions are dependent upon the user's expertise in understanding the effects of each optimization. Possible effects may be the nonsequential execution of code or the unexpected change in a variable's value.

- Full source level debugging capabilities can be achieved when examining user variables in optimized loops. That is, the value of a user defined loop induction variable can still be calculated even if all references to that variable have been optimized away.

Table 4 describes the current highlighting pattern for each optimization mentioned in Table 1. When appropriate, an example is given. For illustration purposes, the portion of the example that would be highlighted is expressed in boldface font. If it takes several steps to see the pattern, the steps are numbered.

6. PERFORMANCE MEASUREMENTS

A number of representative FORTRAN and C programs were compiled to compare differences between the use of UNIX stabs (symbol table structures) and CDI data files. The two performance measurements of interest are the increase in compilation time to generate symbolic debugger information and the size of the information. The codes used were two typical C system programs and two typical FORTRAN application programs. The programs ranged in size from 10K to 150K lines. The measurements were made on an unloaded C240 system.

To compare compilation times and debugging information sizes, all programs were compiled multiple times at various optimization levels. First, each program was compiled three times at optimization level -no (minimal optimization[1]), generating stabs, CDI data files, and neither, respectively. Then they were compiled twice at optimization level -O1 (scalar optimizations) and twice at optimization level -O3 (all optimizations at the lower levels plus vectorization and parallelization of loops), generating CDI data files or no information, respectively. (NOTE: stabs are not generated at high optimization levels because they would be distorted due to the optimizations and cause problems while using a conventional debugger.)

The average increase in compilation time to generate debugger information over not generating the information was:

at -no using stabs	4%
at -no using CDI	33%
at -O1 using CDI	36%
at -O3 using CDI	29%

1. Optimizations always performed are instruction scheduling, span-dependent instructions, register allocation, and tree-height reduction. See [CONV90] or [CONV91] for a detailed description.

Thus, on the average, compilation time increased 33% when generating the CDI information instead of stabs.

The average increase in the size of the debugger information over not generating the information was:

at -no using stabs	2.19
at -no using CDI	3.66
at -O1 using CDI	3.91
at -O3 using CDI	3.96

Thus, on the average, the size of the debugger information increased approximately by a factor of 1.65 when generating the CDI instead of stabs.

Even though compilation takes longer and debugger information is larger when using the CDI, it is worthwhile because the CDI permits additional debugging functionality unattainable by a conventional debugger using stabs. In particular, the CDI permits optimized code to be debugged, and one has finer control of the debugging process, for example, one can step by one of five syntactic units instead of just by statement.

7. FUTURE ENHANCEMENTS

The new approach to debugging optimized code is implemented in the new CONVEX visual debugger, CXdb V1.1, and supported by the FORTRAN and C compilers. Plans are to support the CONVEX Application Compiler, Ada compiler, and C++ compiler. All of these compiler products require CDI support for inlined routines. (C++ inlines routines as text, Ada as parse trees, and the Application Compiler as intermediate language dags.)

The use of highlighting as a means of visually conveying the effects of optimization has just begun to be explored. Much work is needed to complete and enhance this approach, for example, the use of hierarchical highlighting to convey the effects of loop optimizations, and stippling to explicitly identify dead code. Other possibilities to be explored are the use of multiple fonts (e.g., italic to identify loop invariant code, common subexpressions, or variables being watched), the use of different highlighting styles (e.g., different shades of gray or color to convey code fragments already executed versus those yet to be, and boxing with dotted, dashed, or various thickness lines).

Currently, the user is required to infer the optimizations performed. We plan to investigate better means of conveying this information, for example, by annotating source/assembly code with icons to indicate the optimizations performed (e.g., a tilted → to indicate vectorization or || for parallelization). Clicking on the icon would display details of the optimization, such as that provided by the compiler's optimization summary report.

CDI debugging information represents an increased investment in compilation time and space requirements. Means to reduce compilation time and space requirements using additional compression techniques will be investigated.

8. CONCLUSIONS

Although the CDI debugging information represents an increased investment in compilation time and space requirements over the use of stabs, we think the increases are reasonable and acceptable considering the beneficial gains in debugger functionality.

We have also demonstrated the approach is effective and viable by illustrating four problems it solves:

- Current execution state is mapped back to the original source even though there are 1-to-many and many-to-1 mappings that arise from optimization, in particular, optimizations involving movement of code.
- The liveness of variables are tracked so correct values are displayed regardless of whether the value is in memory and/or a register.
- The values of compiler-synthesized variables are mapped back to the value of the user-defined induction variable.
- The behavior of an optimized program is conveyed via visual feedback. Even though limited highlighting capabilities are currently provided, the technique proved effective.

ACKNOWLEDGEMENTS

We would like to acknowledge our colleagues who participated in the definition and development of **CXdb**, in particular, Larry Streepy, Russ Buyse, Mark Chiarelli, David Lingle, Jeff Woods, Mike Garzione, Ken Harward, Ray Cetrone, Lloyd Tharel, Tim Powell, Rich Bleikamp, and Bill Torkelson.

REFERENCES

[Bean 83] Beander, B., ``VAX DEBUG: An interactive, Symbolic, Multilingual Debugger", *ACM Proceedings of the Software Engineering Symposium on High-Level Debugging*, SIGPLAN Notices **8**,4 (August 1983) 173-179.

[BuCh 91] Buyse, R. and Chiarelli, M., ``A User Interface Strategy for CXdb", Xhibition 91 Conference Proceedings (June 1991) 9-15.

[CoMe 88] Coutant, D.S., Meloy, S. and Ruscetta, M., ``DOC: A Practical Approach to Source-Level Debugging of Globally Optimized Code", *ACM Proceedings on Programming Language Design and Implementation*, SIGPLAN Notices 23,7 (July 1988) 125-134.

[Conv 90] CONVEX FORTRAN Optimization Guide, 2nd edition, CONVEX Computer Corporation (1990).

[Conv 91] CONVEX C Optimization Guide, 2nd edition, CONVEX Computer Corporation (1991).

[Henn 82] Hennessy, J., ``Symbolic Debugging of Optimized Code", *ACM Transactions on Programming Languages and Systems*, **3**,3 (July 1982) 323-344.

[WaSr 85] Wall, D., Srivastava, A. and Templin, F., ``A Note on Hennessy's "Symbolic Debugging of Optimized Code"", *ACM Transactions on Programming Languages and Systems*, **7**,1 (January 1985) 176-181.

[Zell 83] Zellweger, P.T., ``An Interactive High-Level Debugger for Control-Flow Optimized Programs", *ACM Proceedings of the Software Engineering Symposium on High-Level Debugging*, SIGPLAN Notices, **18**,8 (August 1983) 159-171.

[Zell 84] Zellweger, P.T., ``Interactive Source-Level Debugging of Optimized Programs", PhD Thesis, University of California, Berkeley, CA (1983); also Report CSL-84-5, Xerox PARC, Palo Alto, CA (May 1984).

[ZuJo 90] Zurawski, L.W. and Johnson, R.E., ``Debugging Optimized Code with Expected Behavior", University of Illinois at Urbana-Champaign (unpublished paper) (August 1990).

Dynascope:
A Tool for Program Directing

Rok Sosič
Department of Computer Science
University of Utah
Salt Lake City, UT 84112

Abstract

This paper introduces program *directing*, a new way of program interaction. Directing enables one program, the *director*, to monitor and to control another program, the *executor*. One important application of program directing is human interaction with complex computer simulations.

The Dynascope programming environment is designed specifically to support directing in traditional, compiled languages. It provides a framework and building blocks for easy construction of sophisticated directors. Directors are regular programs that perform the directing of executors through Dynascope primitives. Dynascope is built around the concept of the *execution stream* which provides a complete description of the executor's computational behavior. The source code of executors requires no changes in order to be subjected to directing.

This paper gives an overview of the Dynascope system. Sample applications are presented: debugging register allocation, animation of procedure calls, and a complex artificial life simulation. The performance of Dynascope is illustrated by real time measurements.

1 Introduction

Although programmers confront increasingly more complex programs, the tools they use to deal with the dynamics of program execution are usually very primitive. This paper presents *directing*, a new approach to program interaction.

ACM SIGPLAN '92 PLDI-6/92/CA
© 1992 ACM 0-89791-476-7/92/0006/0012...$1.50

Program *directing* involves two processes, an *executor* and a *director*. The executor executes the basic program and the director directs the executor. Directing consists of *monitoring* and *controlling*. Monitoring is the analyzing of the executor's computational behavior. This behavior is captured in the *execution stream* emitted dynamically by the executor. The director controls the executor by changing its data values as well as its program.

Monitoring is a well known concept. One approach to monitoring involves special hardware monitors [15, 16]. These enable monitoring in real time, but usually they are not a standard part of computer equipment and are not integrated into programming environments. Therefore, general programming tools cannot rely on the availability of hardware monitors.

Software approaches to monitoring include event generation and processing [1, 3, 6, 8, 12, 13, 14, 17, 18]. An executor, written in a high level language, produces events that are related to concepts in that high-level language. Examples of such events include function calls or changes in variable values. Events are processed by event handlers included in the program itself [10], by a postprocessing program after the execution, or by a monitoring program during the execution. If event handlers are a part of the executor itself it will be impossible to perform dynamic creation or change in the event processing part of the executor. If events are processed after the execution by a postprocessing program, then the program will lack the means to control the executor. Monitoring programs are usually special purpose programs, tailored mainly for debugging or program visualization [2, 14]. Since events seen by these monitoring programs are specialized, they capture only some aspects of program execution. Furthermore, events are usually predefined at compile time.

Directors are a class of systems called *reactive systems* [7]. A reactive system monitors the environment and reacts to it. Recent work on reactive systems is described in [4, 11]. A reactive system uses sensors to monitor the environment and actuators to respond.

The set of sensors and actuators used by a reactive system is specified at compile time.

In Dynascope, the execution stream provides events that are a complete description of the executor's behavior. Since events in the execution stream give the complete behavior, no modifications to the executor's code are needed to support event generation. The execution stream is the basis for dynamically adaptive sensors and high-level events that are capable of capturing any level of detail about the executor's behavior. The Dynascope programming environment implements the execution stream to facilitate the directing of programs written in traditional, compiled languages. It provides a framework for a variety of applications, such as debugging, program visualization and reactive systems.

This paper starts with a description of Dynascope. The basic concept underlying Dynascope, namely the *execution stream*, is discussed. An overview of the implementation is given, describing the main parts of Dynascope: a C compiler, an interpreter, and directing routines. Sample applications of Dynascope are presented. An analysis demonstrates real time performance of Dynascope.

2 A Description of Dynascope

2.1 An Overview

Dynascope supports directing of vanilla C programs. The structure of Dynascope is shown in Figure 1.

A C program, representing the executor, can be compiled to the code for a hypothetical processor, *hypothetical code*, or to the code for the host processor, *host code*. The hypothetical processor is a generic RISC type processor with 32 32-bit registers and a simple load/store architecture [9]. The host processor is a computer that runs Dynascope. The compiled executor is executed under the guidance of an *interpreter*. Hypothetical parts of code are interpreted by the interpreter, and the host code is executed directly by the host processor.

The interpreter provides a framework for directing. This framework includes the communication with a director and the maintenance of internal tables in support of directing. The director, a regular C program separated from the executor, communicates with the interpreter and the executor through the library of *directing routines*. Directing is supported on hypothetical code, but not on host code. In dealing with the executor, the programmer of the director can choose between the directing capabilities of hypothetical code or the execution speed of host code.

Directing requires bidirectional communication between the interpreter and the director. From the interpreter to the director there flows a stream of events describing the execution, called the *execution stream*. The execution stream is emitted automatically for any executor. In the opposite direction, there is a flow of directing *commands*. Since a complete execution stream contains a large number of events, the interpreter provides an event *filter*. This filter is set up by the director and removes from the execution stream those events not interesting to the director.

2.2 The Execution Stream

The execution stream is a central concept of Dynascope. It provides the description of the executor's computational behavior. Normally, this behavior is implicit in the program execution and is not available to an external process. The execution stream makes the behavior explicit to a director.

To provide complete information on execution, events in the execution stream are very fine grained. An event is emitted for each instruction executed from the hypothetical code. In the current implementation of Dynascope, an event includes information on the program counter, the instruction executed and the result. By combining together instructions and results in one event, the execution stream merges the information on control flow and data flow.

Events at the level of machine instructions have many advantages. They are *complete*, *bounded in size*, *uniform*, and *language independent*. Events are complete in the sense that each change in the process is represented by an event; there are no hidden parts in the execution. Since each machine instruction changes only a limited part of the process state, event size can be fixed in advance with uniform event content. In contrast, high level language constructs like loops or procedure calls can change arbitrarily large parts of the state. Machine instructions are common to all compiled languages, which makes events language independent. Disadvantages of using instruction level events are the large number of events and machine dependence. A large number of events, however, can be significantly reduced by an event filter. Since Dynascope provides directing of a hypothetical processor, it can be easily ported to other computer platforms.

The structure of an event in the execution stream is shown in Figure 2. `evtime` is zero at the start of the execution. It is incremented for each executed hypothetical instruction. `evpc` is the program counter, the address of the last executed instruction. `evinst` contains the last executed instruction. `evaddr` is the address of result and `evres` is the value of result. Since instructions in the hypothetical processor have the property

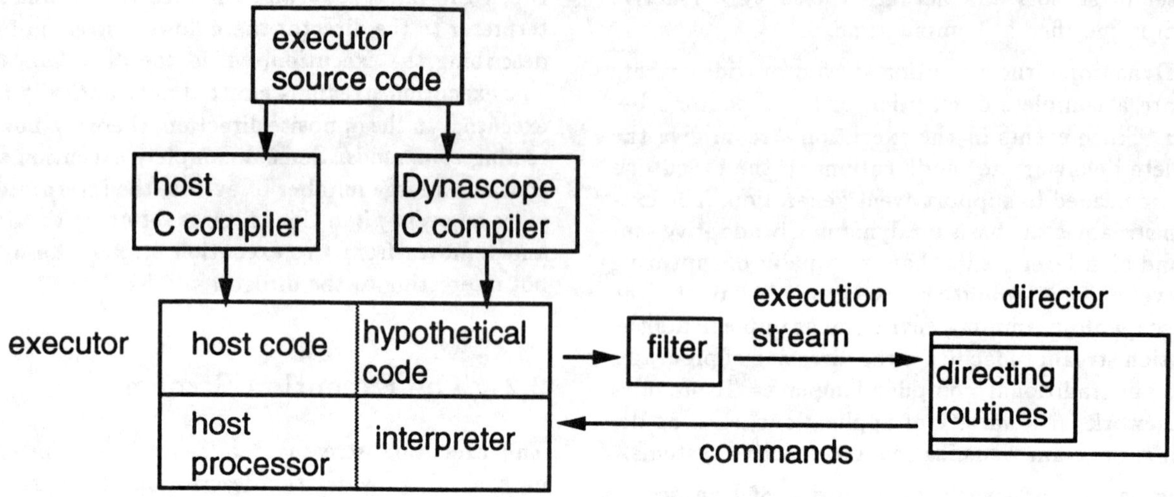

Figure 1: The Dynascope Programming Environment

```
struct event {
            /* instruction counter */
   Word evtime;
            /* program counter */
   Word evpc;
            /* instruction */
   Word evinst;
            /* result address */
   Word evaddr;
            /* result value */
   Word evres;
            /* evaluated conditions */
   Word evcond;
};
```

Figure 2: Event Data Structure

that they change at most one word in the address space of executor, one word is enough to describe the result of an instruction. The filter reports its status in **evcond**.

2.3 The C Compiler

The compiler translates ANSI C programs to hypothetical code. The compiler is based on the **lcc** compiler [5]. The **lcc** compiler provides a very simple interface between a processor-independent front end and a processor-specific back end. A new back end has been written for the Dynascope hypothetical processor.

2.4 Interpreter

The interpreter represents the main part of Dynascope. The basic purpose of the interpreter is to emulate the hypothetical processor. The interpreter has the following features in support of directing:

- it emits the execution stream,
- it communicates with directing routines,
- it combines hypothetical and host code,
- it supports dynamic loading and linking of hypothetical and host code,
- it supports the filtering of the execution stream, and
- it maintains symbol tables.

An event is automatically emitted into the execution stream for every interpreted instruction of the hypothetical processor. Any function in the executor source code can be compiled to hypothetical code or to host code. The interpreter supports function calls from hypothetical code to host code and vice versa. Furthermore, under the control of the director, functions compiled to hypothetical code or host code can be dynamically loaded and linked to the executor. These functions can change the behavior of some already existing functions or they can be new. Besides the time for loading and linking, dynamically linked code does not impose any execution time overhead over regularly linked code.

Hypothetical code runs on the interpreter at a slower speed with complete support for directing constructs.

Host code runs at full host speed, but directing constructs are not supported. Any call to host code is represented as one event with limited execution information. The interpreter has no influence on the execution of host code. It has to wait until the control is returned back to hypothetical code. Operating system calls and standard library routines are always executed in host code.

Two different approaches to filters have been implemented, an interpretative and a compiled approach. An interpretative filter consists of predefined tables, capable of evaluating multiple Boolean expressions on event values. The director loads these tables to determine a specific filtering operation. In a compiled approach, the director supplies the filtering function which is then dynamically loaded in the interpreter. A compiled filter can thus execute an arbitrary function.

2.5 Directing Routines

A library of directing routines is used by the director to communicate with the interpreter and the executor. Since the director is a regular computer program, its code can be arbitrarily complex and optimized for a particular executor. The director can dynamically attach or detach from an executor and its execution stream. Based on the content of the execution stream, the director can send commands back to the interpreter. The separation of the directing part from the execution part enables the development of general purpose directors that can be used for any executor. Examples of possible uses include: consistency tests for internal data structures, control flow directing, and statistics of heap allocation.

Two basic directing routines are:

- `dsopen`,
- `dsclose`.

Routine `dsopen` creates the connection between the interpreter and the director and `dsclose` breaks this connection.

Several directing routines are related to the execution stream:

- `dsconnect`,
- `dsdisconnect`,
- `dsgetevent`,
- `dsrunsync`,
- `dsrunasync`.

When the interpreter is executing and there is a connection between the interpreter and the director, the director connects to the execution stream with the `dsconnect` command. Routine `dsdisconnect` is used by the director to disconnect from the execution stream. After `dsdisconnect` is issued, no further events are emitted by the interpreter. Routine `dsgetevent` returns next event from the execution stream. Routine `dsrunsync` continues execution of the executor in synchronous mode. In this mode, the interpreter waits for the response from the director after each emitted event. Routine `dsrunasync` is the same as `dsrunsync`, except that the executor continues in asynchronous mode. Events are continuously sent in the execution stream without a response from the director. Synchronous mode is commonly used when the director is waiting for a certain condition in the executor. An application of asynchronous mode is tracing.

The filter is controlled by routines:

- `dsldfilter`,
- `dsrmfilter`.

Both have an object file name as a parameter. When the director calls `dsldfilter`, the named object file is loaded in the interpreter and routines from that file are designated as filter routines. Routine `dsrmfilter` removes the file from the interpreter.

Dynamic loading and linking is controlled by routines:

- `dsldfile`,
- `dsrmfile`,
- `dslink`.

Routines `dsldfile` and `dsrmfile` have an object file name as a parameter. The object file can contain host code or hypothetical code. Routine `dsldfile` loads the file in the interpreter, `dsrmfile` removes it. Routine `dslink` has two parameters, a file name and a symbol name. When `dslink` is called, the value of the symbol from the named file is used as the value of that symbol in all object files loaded in the interpreter.

Other directing routines provide for reading the symbol table, reading a part of the state of the executor, and changing a part of the state of the executor.

Besides a check for undefined symbols, the interpreter provides no other safety mechanisms. It is the responsibility of the director to maintain the integrity of the executor's program code. The semantic equivalence of a function in hypothetical code and in host code is provided at the level of C source code.

2.6 An Implementation

The Dynascope programming environment runs on a NeXT computer under the Mach operating system. Dynascope is written entirely in C and is thus portable. The communication between the executor and the director is performed through sockets, a standard interprocess communication feature in BSD Unix and Mach. If necessary, an equivalent interprocess communication method could be used instead. Since the executor and the director are two separate programs, they can execute on different computers. This feature is currently not supported, although it would be easy to add to the system.

3 Applications

3.1 Register Allocation

Dynascope has been applied in its own development. An example is the debugging of register allocation routines, one of the most difficult parts of a compiler to debug.

During early stages in the development of Dynascope, there was an error in the register allocation of the Dynascope C compiler. A register with an uninitialized value was used. The error occurred during a recursive function call several million instructions into the program execution. The conditions for the error were very hard to reproduce. Instead of painfully debugging by hand, a simple director was written. The director analyzes the execution stream and reports the use of an uninitialized register. The core of the director is a recursive procedure *Check_Register_Allocation* that instantiates itself for each new function call in the executing program. A skeleton of this procedure is shown in Figure 3. To simplify the presentation, it is assumed that no register values are kept over procedure calls. Using this director, the error in the register allocation was quickly found.

Since the director to check register allocation calls itself recursively, it can match the dynamic behavior of the executor. To provide a similar capability in traditional debuggers, the debugging environment would need to support coroutines which are normally not available.

3.2 An Animation of Function Calls

During the development of complex programs, we often want to see the dynamic sequence of function calls as they are executed. This feature is easily implemented in Dynascope. The director first reads the symbol table from the interpreter. This provides function names and their corresponding addresses. Then a filter is set up that passes only events describing function calls and function returns (see Figure 4). After the filter is set up, the executor continues its execution. The director dynamically reads the execution stream and displays the chain of active functions. Function addresses are provided by information in the events.

In Dynascope, a program can be animated without modifications to its program, since the sequence of function calls and function returns is captured in the execution stream. Previous approaches to program animation require that the executor's code is annotated by event emitting code. The approach in Dynascope is more flexible. It is simple to dynamically change or switch off the filter, whereas the modification of annotations in the executor's program can be a complex process.

3.3 An Artificial Life Simulation

The full power of Dynascope has been indispensable in assisting a research project in the artificial life area. Artificial life involves computer simulations of life–like phenomena and are a good representative of complex scientific simulations. Three properties of an artificial life simulation make human interaction with the simulation hard: extremely unpredictable behavior, large size, and long running time. Traditional approaches, such as print statements of selected variables or a regular output of the entire simulation are an incomplete solution. The selection of interesting aspects of a simulation to be displayed is made impossible by its unpredictable behavior. Besides, the set of interesting aspects changes dynamically during the simulation. The output of the entire simulation at regular intervals is a problem, since the amount of data produced soon becomes prohibitively large due to the large size and long running time of the program.

The problems of interaction with artificial life simulations were solved by using Dynascope. A simulation runs continuously as an executor with only a very rudimentary output. The bulk of interaction is provided by directors. These are dynamically constructed by a human user depending on the simulation behavior. The directors dynamically connect to the execution stream and interact with the simulation at different time intervals. A sample set of directors is shown in Figure 5. *Periodic analysis* is a background director that periodically obtains a copy of the entire simulation and prepares a summary of interesting statistics. The process itself or its period can be changed anytime. *Analysis on demand* is a user driven director similar to periodic analysis. It is used by the user to supplement the periodic analysis at the time of particularly fast changes or to perform additional analysis. *Change of parame-*

```
Check_Register_Allocation () {
   Mark_All_Registers;
   do {
      event = Read_Next_Event();
      if (event->evinst == CALL) {
         Record_Register_Values;
         Check_Register_Allocation();
         Mark_Registers_Whose_Values_Differ_From_Recorded_Values;
      };
      if (event->evinst_Modifies_Register_i) Unmark_Register_i;
      if (event->evinst_Reads_Register_i && Register_i_Is_Marked) Error();
   } while (event->evinst != RETURN);
};
```

Figure 3: Director to Check Register Allocation

```
Filter (event) {
   if (event->evinst == CALL  ||  event->evinst == RETURN)
      Send_To_Execution_Stream(event);
};
```

Figure 4: A Filter to Report Function Calls and Returns

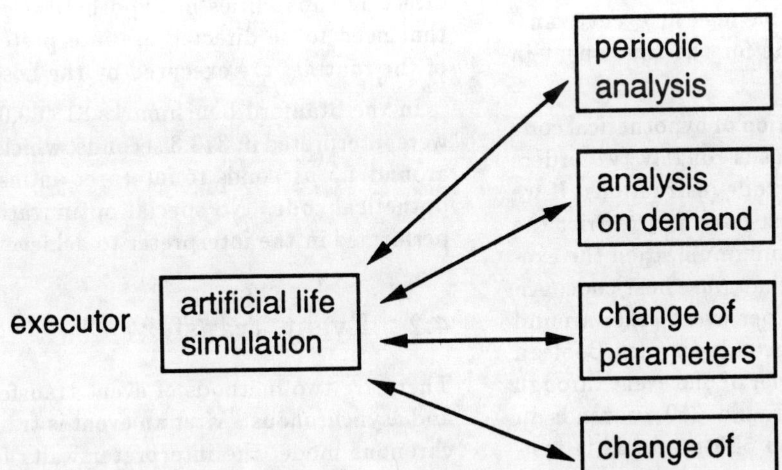

Figure 5: An Artificial Life Simulation

ters is a director that controls global parameters of the simulation. In an artificial life simulation, examples of such parameters could include the rate of growth of artificial organisms, the availability of food and so on. Since the director is a regular computer program, these parameters can be related to the simulation in a very complex way. *Change of code* is the most powerful director. It is used by the user to dynamically implant new parts of code in the simulation or to modify old code. The main usage of this director is to add new behaviors to artificial organisms.

Directors were successfully applied to simulations that ran uninterrupted for weeks. Without Dynascope, it would be impossible to steer simulations on the fly or to obtain an equal amount of information about the simulation's behavior.

4 Performance Measurements

This section reports the performance of Dynascope on a NeXT computer with a 25 Mhz M68040 processor, using the standard C compiler supplied by NeXT. The performance depends on three time parameters: the execution of an instruction of hypothetical code, an evaluation of the filter, and a transfer of an event. An overview of Dynascope performance follows below with details presented later.

The time to transmit an event from the executor to the director is significantly higher than the time to interpret an instruction. Results show that compiled filters represent a fairly modest overhead. The construction of filters with low passing rates can thus significantly speed up the directing, especially since the passing rate of a filter does not considerably change the transfer time per event. Savings in event transfer time more than compensate for the time spent in evaluating filters.

The execution of one instruction of hypothetical code takes around 4.5 μseconds. This is roughly two orders of magnitude slower than host code instructions. If we mix hypothetical code with host code and restrict the hypothetical code to the bare minimum, then the execution takes only 15 % longer than pure host code. An evaluation of a compiled filter per event takes around 1 μsecond plus around 0.25 μseconds for each Boolean expression in the filter. A transfer of one event through the execution stream takes around 350 μseconds in asynchronous mode and around 550 μseconds in synchronous mode.

Buffering of events can speed up event transfer. Although it is not implemented in the latest version, an earlier implementation of Dynascope supported an event buffer. There was no significant performance degradation when a few hundred events were buffered together. The transfer time for one unbuffered event and the transfer time for more than hundred buffered events are practically the same. Buffering can thus bring the event transfer time to within the range of the instruction execution time. If an application requires the transfer of a large number of events in asynchronous mode, as in tracing, then the buffering of events considerably improves performance.

4.1 The Speed of Interpretation

Two programs were used in execution speed measurements: the Stanford benchmarks and an artificial life simulation. The Stanford benchmarks are a set of small programs without any system or library calls. The artificial life simulation uses a lot of calls to memory management routines.

Each program was executed using three different types of code: hypothetical, host, and mixed. Using hypothetical code, the entire program was interpreted. Host code was executed as a regular compiled C program on the host. In mixed code, the top level function was in hypothetical code, while the rest of the functions were in host code. Mixed code combines fast execution with the ability to use directing, since host code can be replaced by hypothetical code if necessary. To support this replacement, at least a part of executed code must be hypothetical. Results are shown in Table 1. It can be observed that the interpretation of hypothetical code is around 50 to 100 times slower than the execution of the same program on the host. Using a mixed code approach, the overhead of hypothetical code is reduced to only 10 % to 20 %. Mixed code thus represents a good balance between the speed of host code and the directing capabilities of hypothetical code. Functions that need to be directed are interpreted, and the rest of the routines are executed by the host.

In the Stanford benchmarks 81,400,000 instructions were interpreted in 373.3 seconds, which means it takes around 4.5 μseconds to interpret an instruction in hypothetical code. No special optimization efforts were performed in the interpreter to achieve this speed.

4.2 Event Transfer

There are two methods of event transfer, synchronous and asynchronous. After an event is transferred in synchronous mode, the interpreter waits for a command from the director. In asynchronous mode, the interpreter continues with the execution and does not wait for a response from the director.

To measure event transfer rate under different conditions, execution time was obtained for varying rates

Table 1: Execution Time

Type of Code	Hypothetical	Host	Mixed
Stanford benchmarks			
Time in Seconds	373.3	3.4	3.8
Ratio to Host Code	110	1	1.12
Artificial Life			
Time in Seconds	13938.9	259.6	309.4
Ratio to Host Code	54	1	1.19

Table 2: Event Transfer Time with Different Filter Pass Rates (in Seconds)

Filter Pass Rate in %	0 %	0.01 %	0.1 %	1 %	10 %	100 %
Nr. of Events Transferred	0	8140	81389	813876	8138743	81387414
Asynchronous Mode						
User Time	612.5	613.0	617.5	680.7	860.2	3153.4
System Time	1.6	4.3	27.0	245.4	2609.1	18047.6
Total Execution Time	614.1	617.3	644.5	926.1	3469.3	21201.0
Transfer Time (1000 Events)		0.39	0.37	0.38	0.35	0.25
Synchronous Mode						
User Time	612.5	614.1	620.9	706.6	1165.7	4243.5
System Time	1.6	5.1	35.8	320.3	3191.4	33885.7
Total Execution Time	614.1	619.2	656.7	1026.9	4357.1	38129.2
Transfer Time (1000 Events)		0.63	0.52	0.51	0.46	0.46

Table 3: Execution Time in the Filter Performance Measurement

Number of Boolean Expressions	no filter	0	1	2	4	8
Interpreted Filter (Seconds)	373.3	526.8	665.0	794.0	1078.9	1741.3
One Boolean Expression (10^{-6} Seconds)			1.70	1.64	1.70	1.87
Compiled Filter (Seconds)	373.3	451.6	468.7	488.8	529.5	618.0
One Boolean Expression (10^{-6} Seconds)			0.21	0.23	0.24	0.27

of filtering using the Stanford benchmarks. Table 2 presents the results. *Filter Pass Rate* shows the percentage of events that passed through the filter in the execution stream. Rows *User Time*, *System Time*, and *Total Execution Time* show corresponding execution times. Row *Transfer Time* shows the time spent in the interpreter to transfer one thousand events to the director. To get the event transfer time from the measured time, we need to subtract the time in the column with zero events from the total time in the corresponding column and divide by the number of events. Transfer time of an asynchronous event takes from 250 to 390 μseconds, while that of a synchronous event takes from 460 to 630 μseconds. The filter pass rate has only a limited influence on the event transfer time.

4.3 Filter Performance

Filter overhead is another important parameter. Two implementations of the filter have been measured: interpreted and compiled. The complexity of the filter varied from an empty filter with no Boolean expressions to a filter with eight Boolean expressions. Each Boolean expression involved one Boolean operation and one comparison. The performance of filters was measured on the Stanford benchmarks (see Table 3). *Number of Boolean Expressions* denotes the complexity of the filter. Row *Interpreted Filter* shows execution time for an interpreted filter. Row *Compiled Filter* shows execution time for a compiled filter. The overhead of an empty filter is the difference between the filter with zero Boolean expressions and no filter. Taking into account that around 81,400,000 instructions were executed, the filter overhead per one instruction is around 1 μsecond for the compiled filter and around 1.9 μsecond for the interpreted filter. Row *One Boolean Expression* shows the contribution of one Boolean expression to the execution time of one hypothetical instruction. This time is calculated as a difference to the column with no Boolean expressions, divided by the number of Boolean expressions, divided by the number of instructions executed. The time overhead of one Boolean expression per one instruction is from 0.21 μseconds to 0.27 μseconds for the compiled filter and from 1.64 μseconds to 1.87 μseconds for the interpreted filter. The overhead of a filter increases approximately linearly with increasing filter complexity.

5 Conclusion

Program directing is a new approach to program interaction. It enables the manipulation of processes from "outside".

The execution stream is the central concept in program directing. The stream provides low-level events which describe the complete computational behavior of a process. By analyzing the stream, any execution detail can be obtained. The execution stream is emitted automatically without changes to the program's code.

The practicality of directing is demonstrated by its implementation in the Dynascope system. Dynascope has already been successfully used in practical applications. Directing capabilities of Dynascope are indispensable in interaction with large, long running, complex computer programs.

6 Acknowledgements

I gratefully acknowledge the guidance, encouragement, and support of Robert R. Johnson. I thank David Hanson and Christopher Fraser for their **lcc** compiler and for their explanation of the compiler's internals. Comments from Venkatesh Akella, Armin Liebchen, Cliff Miller and Gita Mani significantly improved the presentation in the paper.

References

[1] R. M. Balzer. EXDAMS - EXtendable Debugging and Monitoring System. In *AFIPS Conference Proceeedings, Vol. 34*, pages 567–586. SJCC, 1969.

[2] M. Brown. *Algorithm Animation.* ACM Distinguished Dissertation. MIT Press, 1988.

[3] J. Cohen and N. Carpenter. A language for inquiring about the run-time behaviour of programs. *Software–Practice and Experience*, 7(4):445–460, jul/aug 1977.

[4] R. Cooper and K. Marzullo. Consistent detection of global predicates. In *Proceedings of the ACM/ONR Workshop on Parallel and Distributed Debugging*, pages 167–174. ACM, 1991.

[5] C. W. Fraser and D. R. Hanson. A retargetable compiler for ANSI C. *SIGPLAN Notices*, 26(10):29–43, October 1991.

[6] D. R. Hanson. Event association in SNOBOL4 for program debugging. *Software–Practice and Experience*, 8(2):115–129, March/April 1978.

[7] D. Harel and A. Pnueli. On the development of reactive systems. In K. R. Apt, editor, *Logics and Models of Concurrent Systems, vol. 13 of NATO ASI Series F*, pages 477–498. Springer–Verlag, New York, 1985.

[8] J. Heering and P. Klint. Towards monolingual programming environments. *ACM Transactions on Programming Languages and Systems*, 7(2):183–213, April 1985.

[9] J. L. Hennessy and D. A. Patterson. *Computer Architecture: A Quantitative Approach.* Morgan Kaufmann Publishers, 1990.

[10] A. Kishon, P. Hudak, and C. Consel. Monitoring semantics: A formal framework for specifying, implementing, and reasoning about execution monitors. *ACM SIGPLAN '91 Conference on Programming Language Design and Implementation, Sigplan Notices*, 26(6):338–352, June 1991.

[11] K. Marzullo, R. Cooper, M. D. Wood, and K. P. Birman. Tools for distributed application environment. *IEEE Computer*, 42(8):42–51, August 1991.

[12] C. E. McDowell and D. P. Helmbold. Debugging concurrent programs. *ACM Computing Surveys*, 21(4):593–622, December 1989.

[13] M. L. Model. Monitoring system behavior in a complex computational environment. Technical Report CSL-79-1, Xerox PARC, 1979.

[14] T. G. Moher. PROVIDE: A process visualization and debugging environment. *IEEE Transactions on Software Engineering*, 14(6):849–857, June 1988.

[15] B. Plattner. Real-time execution monitoring. *IEEE Transactions on Software Engineering*, 10(6):756–764, November 1984.

[16] B. Plattner and J. Nievergelt. Monitoring program execution: A survey. *IEEE Computer*, 14(11):76–93, November 1981.

[17] R. Snodgrass. A relational approach to monitoring complex systems. *ACM Transactions on Computer Systems*, 6(2):157–196, May 1988.

[18] A. P. Tolmach and A. W. Appel. Debugging standard ML without reverse engineering. In *Proc. ACM Lisp and Functional Programming Conference '90*, Nice, June 1990. ACM.

A Retargetable Debugger

Norman Ramsey and David R. Hanson
Department of Computer Science, Princeton University
Princeton, NJ 08544
nr@princeton.edu drh@princeton.edu

Abstract

We are developing techniques for building retargetable debuggers. Our prototype, ldb, debugs C programs compiled for the MIPS R3000, Motorola 68020, SPARC, and VAX architectures. It can use a network to connect to faulty processes and can do cross-architecture debugging. ldb's total code size is about 16,000 lines, but it needs only 250–550 lines of machine-dependent code for each target.

ldb owes its retargetability to three techniques: getting help from the compiler, using a machine-independent embedded interpreter, and choosing abstractions that minimize and isolate machine-dependent code. ldb reuses existing compiler function by having the compiler emit PostScript code that ldb later interprets; PostScript works well in this unusual context.

1 Introduction

Retargeting some programming environment components, such as compilers and editors, is now common, thanks to well developed retargeting techniques. For example, compiler writers use machine-independent intermediate representations and code-generator generators. We are developing techniques for building retargetable, multiple-target debuggers. This paper describes the design and implementation of ldb, a prototype retargetable debugger. ldb is a source-level debugger like gdb or dbx [15, 22]. It can be used with C programs compiled with lcc [11], a retargetable compiler that generates code for the MIPS R3000, Motorola 68020, SPARC, and VAX architectures. Users can set and remove breakpoints, start and stop programs, evaluate expressions, and make assignments to variables.

ldb's contribution lies in implementing these operations in a retargetable way. It does so by using three techniques: getting help from the compiler, using a machine-independent embedded interpreter, and choosing abstractions that minimize and isolate machine-dependent code.

ACM SIGPLAN '92 PLDI-6/92/CA
© 1992 ACM 0-89791-476-7/92/0006/0022...$1.50

ldb is an experiment in coupling between compiler and debugger; they are separate tools, but ldb depends on and uses existing compiler function as much as possible. The division of labor between ldb and lcc shows that making modest demands on the compiler can simplify the debugger substantially. lcc's assistance in generating machine-independent symbol tables, in implementing breakpoints, and in evaluating expressions are examples.

ldb is connected to the compiler by PostScript programs, which its embedded PostScript interpreter evaluates as necessary. This approach provides a uniform mechanism for representing symbol tables, shields the debugger from irrelevant information, and supports machine-independent expression evaluation.

ldb's design embodies a set of engineering choices that collaborate to minimize and isolate machine-dependent code. For example, it controls target processes with a small "debug nub" that is loaded with the target program. It exchanges messages with this nub using a machine-independent protocol, and it establishes a connection to a nub by connecting to an existing process over the network, by forking the target process as a child, or by being forked by a faulty process asking to be debugged.

The bulk of ldb, including its embedded PostScript interpreter, is written in Modula-3 [18]. The nub is written in C and assembly language, and much of the symbol table and expression evaluation support is written in PostScript. ldb's machine-dependent code depends only on which architecture the target program and its nub run on, not on which architecture ldb runs on. As a result, cross-architecture debugging with ldb is identical to single-architecture debugging, and ldb can change architectures dynamically.

2 PostScript Symbol Tables

Production versions of lcc generate machine-dependent, symbol-table "stabs" for dbx and gdb. We changed this code to generate *machine-independent* symbol tables represented by PostScript programs that build PostScript objects, such as dictionaries. Symbol tables contain code as well as data, e.g., procedures that ldb can interpret to print structured data, so ldb need not know the layout of runtime data structures.

Embedded in ldb is an interpreter for a dialect of PostScript. This dialect omits font and imaging types and operators, but adds new types and operators for debugging. For example, `ldb`'s PostScript dialect supports "abstract memories," which, as described in Sec. 4.1, are a machine-independent representation of target registers and memory.

A *symbol-table entry* is a PostScript dictionary describing a source-language identifier: a variable, procedure, type, or constant. The symbol-table entry for `i`, on line 6 of the sample C program shown in Fig. 1, is associated with the name `S10`:

```
/S10 <<
  /name (i)
  /type << /decl (int %s) /printer {INT} ... >>
  /sourcefile (fib.c) /sourcey 6 /sourcex 8
  /kind (variable)
  /where 30 Regset0 Absolute
  /uplink S8
>> def
```

Brackets (`<<...>>`) surround dictionaries; within each dictionary, names preceded by slashes are associated with the values that follow. `name`, `type`, `sourcefile`, `sourcey`, `sourcex`, `kind`, and `uplink` appear in all symbol-table entries; `where` appears only in entries for variables and procedures. The value associated with `where` represents `i`'s location (register 30) and is computed when the symbol table is interpreted.

A source-level type dictionary, associated with `type`, must contain at least two values: a string used to declare variables of the type and a PostScript procedure used to print values of the type. The procedure's arguments are abstract memory, location, and type dictionary; the machine-independent procedure `INT` ignores the dictionary, fetches a 32-bit integer from the abstract memory, and prints it. The ellipsis in the type dictionary shown above stands for information not used by `ldb` proper, but used by PostScript code that supports expression evaluation.

In entries for local symbols, `uplink` is associated with the entry for the preceding symbol in the current or enclosing scope; `i`'s `uplink` value is the symbol-table entry for `a` (Fig. 1, line 2), which is associated with `S8`. The `uplink` values link symbol-table entries in a tree that handles nested scopes; using a tree avoids complications that can arise with the flattened tables emitted by typical assemblers and loaders [6].

Fig. 2 shows the tree for `fib`. The symbol-table entry for a procedure associates `formals` with the entry for the procedure's last parameter and `loci` with a PostScript array of *stopping points*. Each element of this array contains a source location, an object location, and a symbol-table entry; the symbol and its ancestors are visible from that stopping point. For example, the 9th element of `fib`'s stopping-point array contains the entry for the symbol `j`. This point corresponds to the expression `j<n` in line 11 of Fig. 1, from which `j`, `a`, `n`, and `fib` are visible.

A context for name resolution is determined by a particular stopping point in a particular procedure, normally the place where control has stopped. `ldb` resolves names by walking up the tree of entries for local symbols, beginning with the symbol-table entry contained in the stopping point. When it reaches the root, it searches two PostScript dictionaries; one contains entries for symbols local to this

```
1  void fib(int n) ^0{
2    static int a[20];
3
4    if (^1n > 20) ^2n = 20;
5    ^3a[0] = a[1] = 1;
6    { int i;
7      for (^4i=2; ^5i<n; ^7i++)
8        ^6a[i] = a[i-1] + a[i-2];
9    }
10   { int j;
11     for (^8j=0; ^9j<n; ^11j++)
12       ^10printf("%d ", a[j]);
13   }
14   ^12printf("\n");
15 ^13}
```

Figure 1: Example program.
Superscripts show stopping points.

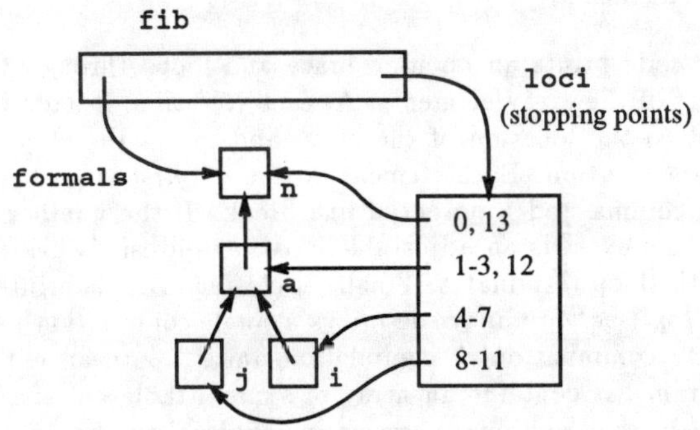

Figure 2: The tree structure of `fib`'s symbol table.

compilation unit (C `statics`) and the other contains entries for global symbols (C `externs`). The first is associated with `statics` in the current procedure's symbol-table entry; the second is associated with `externs` in the "top-level dictionary" for the program.

`a`'s symbol table entry is associated with `S8`:

```
/S8 <<
  /name (a)
  /type <</decl (int %s[20]) /printer {ARRAY} ...>>
  /sourcefile (fib.c) /sourcey 2 /sourcex 13
  /kind (variable)
  /uplink S7
  /where {(_stanchor__V2935334b_e288a) 8 LazyData}
>> def
```

`uplink` is associated with `n`'s symbol-table entry, named `S7`. `a` is `static`, so its location is not determined until link time. The value associated with `where` is a PostScript procedure that is interpreted at debug time; it computes `a`'s location by calling `LazyData`. `LazyData` gets the location of the generated *anchor* symbol, `_stanchor__V2935334b_e288a`, from `ldb`'s linker interface (see Sec. 3) and fetches the address of `a` from the 8th word following that location. This anchor-symbol technique is also used to compute the object-code locations of stopping points.

ldb prints values using the procedure associated with /printer in the value's type dictionary. The machine-independent PostScript procedure ARRAY prints C arrays. Like INT, its arguments are an abstract memory, a location, and a type dictionary. From the type dictionary, it fetches the type of an element, the element size, and the size of the whole array. This information, which may be machine-dependent, is placed in the type dictionary by the compiler. It is elided in the example above because it is used only by PostScript code like the ARRAY procedure, not by ldb proper.

The part of ARRAY that prints a's value is

```
({) Put 0 Begin
0 &elemsize &arraysize 1 sub
{ dup 0 ne { (, ) Put 0 Break } if
  dup &limit ge { (...) Put pop exit } if
  &machine &loc 3 -1 roll Shifted &elemtype print
} for
(}) Put End
```

This code prints an opening brace and loops through the offsets of the array elements. At each iteration, it adds the offset to the location of the array and prints the element at that location. Each element except the first is preceded by a comma and a potential line break. If the number of elements exceeds an adjustable limit, an ellipsis is printed and the loop terminates. Finally, a closing brace is printed.

A *top-level dictionary* describes a single compilation unit or any combination of compilation units, up to an entire program. It contains an array of symbol-table entries for procedures, a dictionary associating external symbol names with their symbol-table entries, a dictionary associating file names with arrays of symbol-table entries for the procedures defined in the files, and an array of the names of all anchor symbols used. The anchor-symbol names are compared with the anchor-symbol names in the loader table (see Sec. 3) to ensure that the top-level dictionary matches the object code. A top-level dictionary also contains the name of the architecture for which the program was compiled, which ldb uses at debug time to find its machine-dependent code and data.

Assuming that S1 and S6 represent the symbol-table entries for procedures main and fib, the top-level dictionary for fib.c is

```
<<
  /procs [ S1 S6 ]
  /externs <<
    /main S1
    /fib  S6
  >>
  /sourcemap <<
    /fib.c [ S1 S6 ]
  >>
  /anchors [ /_stanchor__V2935334b_e288a ]
  /architecture (sparc)
>>
```

The structure of top-level dictionaries is determined by the operations ldb needs to perform. When given a program counter, ldb must find the symbol-table entry of the corresponding procedure. ldb uses the procs array to build a table mapping procedure addresses to symbol-table entries. (Mapping from program counters to procedure addresses is done by the linker interface described in Sec. 3.) ldb uses the externs dictionary to resolve names of global symbols. ldb uses the sourcemap dictionary to build a map from source locations to stopping points, making it possible to set breakpoints by source location. Because of the C preprocessor, a single source location may correspond to more than one stopping point.

3 Division of Labor

ldb gets link-time information by cooperating with lcc's compiler driver. After linking a program, the driver uses the UNIX program nm to generate PostScript that, when interpreted, builds a *loader table*, which is a PostScript dictionary. The loader table contains the program's top-level dictionary, a dictionary associating the names of anchor symbols with their addresses, and an array of (address, name) pairs for each procedure in the program. ldb's linker interface hides machine dependencies and provides access to this table as a Modula-3 object. fib's loader table is

```
<<
  /symtab << top-level dictionary >>
  /anchormap <<
    /_stanchor__V2935334b_e288a 16#000023d8
    ...
  >>
  /proctable [
    16#00002270 (_fib)
    16#00002374 (_main)
    ...
  ]
>>
```

The loader table supports debugger operations that need information not available until link time. ldb needs the locations of variables and procedures; Sec. 2's anchor-symbol technique reduces the problem to finding the locations of the anchor symbols, which are stored in the anchormap dictionary. The proctable enables ldb to find the address of the procedure containing a given program counter, which is the first step in mapping a program counter to the symbol-table entry of the corresponding procedure.

To plant breakpoints, users specify source locations or procedure names; ldb computes the locations of the corresponding instructions. ldb plants a breakpoint at an instruction I by overwriting I with a trap instruction. To resume execution, it interprets I out of line, then continues with the next instruction. For now, ldb can set breakpoints only at no-op instructions, which can be skipped instead of interpreted. The implementation is machine-independent, but it manipulates machine-dependent data: the bit patterns used for break and no-op, the type used to fetch and store instructions, and the amount to advance the program counter after "interpreting" the no-op. This interim scheme relies on compiler support: lcc already places labels at stopping points, so putting no-ops there requires no extra effort. The no-ops increase the number of instructions by 16–19%, depending on the target.

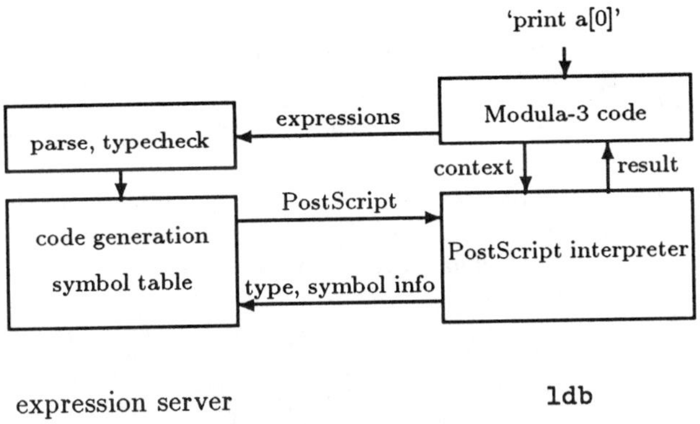

Figure 3: Communication paths between ldb and an expression server

The possibility of stopping the program before any top-level expression reduces the benefit of instruction scheduling because the scheduler may rearrange instructions only within such expressions, not within basic blocks. lcc does not do instruction scheduling, but the MIPS assembler does. When lcc compiles for debugging, the MIPS code size increases by 13%, because there are load delay slots that the assembler is unable to fill using the more restricted scheduling. This penalty is independent of the cost of the explicitly inserted no-ops.

Assignment and expression evaluation use an "expression server," with which ldb communicates via pipes, as shown in Fig. 3. To evaluate an expression, ldb sends it to the server, which is a variant of the compiler. The server attempts to parse and type-check the expression and to produce an intermediate-code tree. When it fails to find an identifier a in its symbol table, it does not print an error message and stop; its symbol-table code has been modified to send "/a ExpressionServer.lookup" back to ldb. The PostScript procedure ExpressionServer.lookup, when interpreted by ldb, finds the PostScript dictionary representing a's symbol-table entry and sends information from that dictionary back to the expression server. The server's modified symbol-table code uses that information to reconstruct a's symbol-table entry on the fly, and it returns the newly created entry to the parser just as if the entry had always been present. The expression server discards new symbol-table entries after the evaluation of each expression, but it saves type information until the user switches to a different target program.

The server's intermediate-code tree is not passed to the usual compiler back end; instead it is rewritten as a PostScript procedure. This PostScript procedure is sent to ldb, followed by "ExpressionServer.result", which tells ldb that the procedure is on the stack and that it can stop listening to the expression server. ldb then takes the procedure from the stack and interprets it, which has the effect of evaluating the expression.

Rewriting intermediate code into PostScript takes little effort, and doing so instead of interpreting intermediate code directly should make it easier to support different languages, compilers, and intermediate codes. One interpreter supports code in symbol-table entries and expression evaluation.

The expression-server architecture has two benefits: reuse of the compiler and simplicity in the debugger. The changes that make the compiler front end act as a server affect only the input, lexical analysis, symbol, and type modules. The debugger treats each expression as a string; it sends the string to the expression server, then interprets PostScript code until the expression server tells it to stop. The operation of interpreting until told to stop is implemented by applying "cvx stopped" to the open pipe from the server.

Reusing the compiler has a limitation: the debugger cannot provide an extended language for debugging. Such facilities could be provided by implementing an extended language as an expression server.

Because it puts the expression server in a separate address space, ldb can reuse a range of compiler implementations. The compiler and debugger need not be written in the same language, need not support the same data types, and need not agree on how to manage storage or share input and output. The cost of this flexibility is that the compiler writer must devise PostScript procedures that take symbol-table data and send it to the expression server over a byte stream. The lcc expression server receives sequences of C tokens that represent type and symbol data. If the lcc front end could easily have shared an address space with ldb, ldb could have made procedure calls to expression-server code instead of sending messages between processes.

4 Design for Retargetability

Three aspects of ldb's design contribute most to its retargetability: abstract memories, the debug nub, and the use of Modula-3 subtyping.

ldb is written in Modula-3 and uses Modula-3 interfaces and subtypes to minimize and isolate machine dependencies. Each target architecture requires Modula-3 objects that contain machine-dependent data, methods, or both. When possible, machine-dependent function is specified by Modula-3 objects containing machine-dependent data but no code.

Machine-independent classes[1] define the important abstractions in ldb; machine-dependent code is isolated in machine-dependent subtypes of such classes. (A similar technique has been used in implementations of I/O streams [18, p. 143].) One such class is ldb's stack-frame abstraction. The machine-independent class includes the value of the program counter, the symbol-table entry of the corresponding procedure, and several machine-independent methods, which perform such tasks as computing scopes for name resolution. Machine-dependent instances of the class supply only two methods: one that walks down the stack and one that restores registers from the stack.

4.1 Abstract Memories

Abstract memories represent the registers and memory of a target process. An abstract memory is a collection of *spaces*, denoted by lower-case letters, e.g., d for data space, r for

[1] A *class* is a Modula-3 type that has no exact instances; all instances have types that are proper subtypes of the class.

registers, etc. Locations within a space are determined by an integer offset. `ldb` provides several "addressing modes" to refer to locations, including an immediate mode. Given a memory and location, `ldb` can fetch and store three sizes of integers (8, 16, and 32 bits) and three sizes of floating-point values (32, 64, and 80 bits).

`ldb` assumes that every machine has code and data spaces. Other spaces can be added to the abstract memory model as necessary for a particular machine. On the MIPS, for example, we add `r` for general-purpose registers, `f` for floating-point registers, and `x` for "extra registers." The extra registers are the program counter and the virtual frame pointer.[2] The code and data spaces may refer to the same locations or different locations depending on the target architecture.

Abstract memory is another Modula-3 class; `ldb` combines several different instances to represent the state of memory and registers during a particular procedure activation. The instances form a directed acyclic graph, shown in Fig. 4. The *wire* is an abstract memory that holds a connection to the nub; it forwards fetch and store requests to the nub, which executes them and returns the results. The nub, located in the target process, can respond to requests only for locations in the code and data spaces. Registers are saved either on the stack or in a *context*, which is an area in memory that holds the state of a stopped program. The *alias* memory translates requests for locations in register spaces into requests for locations in the code or data spaces (or for immediate locations).

The *register* memory solves a problem that occurs when fetching the least significant byte from a register. The alias memory records the location in memory of the whole register, but the location of the byte depends on the target's byte order. The register memory transforms fetches and stores into full-word operations on the underlying memory, making byte order irrelevant. For example, if `ldb` fetches a character from a 32-bit register, the register memory fetchs the whole register, but returns only the least significant 8 bits. Register memories enable `ldb` to execute the same code whether debugging a little-endian or a big-endian MIPS, for example.

The *joined* memory combines memories that serve different spaces, routing fetch and store requests to the appropriate underlying memory. The joined memory is the instance presented to the rest of the debugger as representing the abstract memory for a stack frame.

`ldb` uses abstract memories to print the values of variables. If a breakpoint is planted at stopping point 7 of `fib` (line 7 of Fig. 1), `ldb` can access `i`, `a`, `n`, and `fib` when it stops there. For example, it prints `i` by executing the PostScript procedures shown in Sec. 2, which generate fetch requests that travel through Fig. 4's abstract memories. `i` is located at offset 30 of space `r` (register 30), so the joined memory fetches `i` from the register memory. The request is for a full word, so the register memory fetches the word from the alias memory, which notes that register 30 is an alias for a location in the data space 92 bytes after the beginning of the context and asks the wire to fetch the word at that location. The wire sends a message to the nub, which

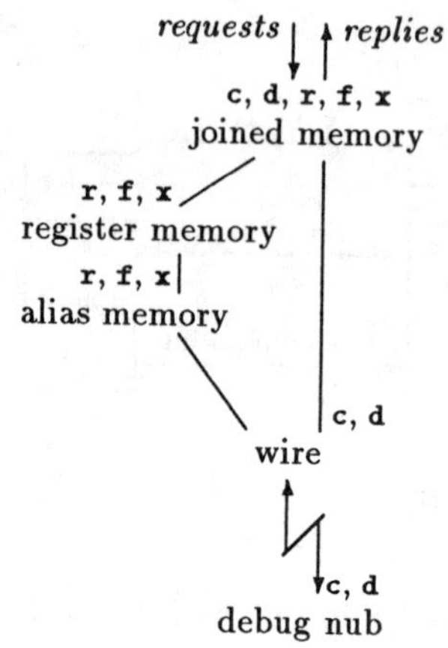

Figure 4: Abstract memory for a frame.

fetches `i` using the target's byte order and sends the value back to the debugger in little-endian order, where it gets returned up the dag of abstract memories and put on the PostScript operand stack, whence it is printed. Printing the value of `a` is similar, but its elements are located in the data space, so the fetch requests are routed from the joined memory directly to the wire, which sends them to the nub.

In the abstract memory dag, machine-independent code manipulates machine-dependent data: the aliases recorded in the alias memory. Fetches that use the immediate addressing mode return immediate values; all other fetches and all stores are eventually done on target memory by the nub. Only the data is machine-dependent, so it doesn't matter what architecture the code runs on; except for floating-point data, cross-debugging is free.

`ldb` creates abstract memories using machine-dependent stack-walking procedures. On the MIPS, for example, `MipsFrame.New` takes the context from the nub and creates a machine-dependent instance of the stack-frame abstraction, a representation of the topmost frame on the target call stack. The stack frame includes an abstract memory, which is a joined memory that is part of a dag like the one shown in Fig. 4. Since the general-purpose and floating-point registers are saved in the context, those locations are made aliases for the appropriate locations in the target. The extra registers (program counter and virtual frame pointer) are aliases for immediate locations, not for locations in target memory. `MipsFrame.New` uses the program counter to find the procedure's dictionary, then computes the virtual frame pointer by adding the size of procedure's frame to the stack pointer. The machine-dependent frame size is stored in the dictionary by the MIPS implementation of `ldb`'s linker interface (see Sec. 4.3).

The stack-frame object created by `MipsFrame.New` has two machine-dependent methods. When a user walks the stack, one of these methods finds the calling frame, and the other constructs a new abstract memory for that frame. The aliases in the new alias memory usually stand for locations on the stack, not in the context, but when callee-save registers are not modified by the called procedure, the aliases from the called frame are reused.

[2] The MIPS has no actual frame pointer, but `lcc` uses the virtual frame pointer to address local variables. The other targets have other idiosyncrasies of similar complexity.

4.2 The Debug Nub

The nub executes in user space; at program startup it installs a signal handler that gets control when the target process faults or encounters a breakpoint. When such an event occurs, the nub uses a socket to notify `ldb` of the signal, passing a signal number, an associated code, and a context that holds the values the registers had when the signal arrived. It then services `ldb`'s fetch and store requests until told to continue execution, to terminate, or to break the connection. Normally, when a connection is broken, even by a debugger crash, the nub preserves the state of the target program and waits for a new connection from another instance of `ldb`. The nub may be told to continue execution instead. The little-endian communication protocol between `ldb` and the nub has been used on all combinations of host and target byte orders and has been validated [13].

The nub supports several connection mechanisms, including debugging over the network. Since the nub is always loaded with the target program, it can catch unexpected faults and wait for a connection from `ldb`; the target program need not be a child of the debugger.

The nub isolates dependencies on the host operating system. Using sockets and signal handlers makes it easier to retarget the nub; these mechanisms are more uniform on different UNIX implementations than are mechanisms that support debugging more directly, such as system facilities permitting one process to control another.

The principle guiding the design of the nub has been to keep it as small as possible. The nub is loaded with every program, so the cost for programs that are never debugged should be small. The smaller the nub is, the simpler it is, and the easier to retarget. It is easier to make a simple nub reliable, and the nub must preserve the state of the target program even if the debugger crashes.

In user space, the debug nub is vulnerable; if a faulty program destroys the nub's data structures it becomes impossible to debug that program. Moving the nub into the operating-system kernel would solve this problem; it could also reduce the number of context switches needed to perform a nub operation. The smaller and simpler the nub is, the more reasonable it is to consider putting it in the kernel. Finally, the nub *interface* should be small as well. A small interface will be easier to implement in a variety of environments, e.g., PCR [24] or the Topaz TeleDebug server [21].

4.3 Retargeting `ldb`

The debugger proper, the PostScript, and the nub all have machine-dependent parts, and each must be retargeted for a new machine. This section lists all such parts.

Machine-dependent Modula-3 code plants breakpoints, communicates with the nub, gets machine-dependent data bound at link time, and walks the call stack. `ldb`'s interim breakpoint implementation requires four items of machine-dependent data (see Sec. 3). The code that communicates with the nub is machine-independent, but it uses three machine-dependent procedures or objects: a procedure that distinguishes breakpoint faults from other faults, an object used to fetch and store the program counter located in a context, and a procedure that takes a context and creates the top frame on the call stack (see Sec. 4.1). Likewise, the code that fetches and stores fields of a context is machine-independent, but is parameterized by a machine-dependent description of those fields.

The VAX, SPARC, and 68020 share a single, machine-independent implementation of the linker interface. The MIPS cannot use this implementation because it has no frame pointer. To be able to walk past a MIPS stack frame, `ldb` needs to know its size. That information is available, even for procedures without debugging symbols, in the MIPS runtime procedure table [17]. The MIPS implementation of `ldb`'s linker interface uses the runtime procedure table to find the addresses and frame sizes of procedures, as well as other machine-dependent data.

The top-of-stack procedure, for example, `MipsFrame.New` of Sec. 4.1, hides the rest of the machine-dependent stack-walking code, i.e., the machine-dependent methods of the stack-frame object. The implementations for all four targets are similar.

`ldb` uses machine-dependent PostScript to address local variables and to enumerate a target's registers.

Most of the nub is machine-independent, but it has a few machine dependencies. The target architecture determines the type of the signal handler and whether, as on the MIPS and SPARC, the `struct sigcontext` can serve as a context or, as on the VAX and 68020, another representation must be used [8]. On a big-endian MIPS, nub code for doubleword fetches and stores of saved floating-point registers must swap the words.[3] Each machine has a different one-line "pause" procedure, which stops the target program before it calls `main`. The VAX and 68020 require assembly code to save and restore registers, and the 68020 requires assembly code to fetch and store 80-bit floating-point values.

To give the nub initial control, the system-dependent startup code must be modified to call the nub instead of `main`. It is most easily modified by editing the object code.

The following table lists the number of lines of machine-dependent Modula-3, ANSI C, and PostScript code that collaborate to implement the machine-dependent parts of `ldb` on each of its targets. The amount of machine-independent code is listed in the rightmost column.

	MIPS	68020	SPARC	VAX	shared
Debugger (M3)	476	187	206	199	12193
PostScript	15	18	18	13	1203
Nub (C, asm)	34	73	5	72	632

A few numbers stand out. The MIPS requires an extra 250 lines of Modula-3 code in the linker interface because the machine has no frame pointer. There is very little SPARC-dependent code in the nub because the operating system provides most of the registers and there is no other machine-dependent dirt. The nub sizes for the 68020 and VAX are large because of the assembly language used on those machines.

The effort required to retarget `ldb` is minimal. The authors' ports to the 68020 and VAX architectures each took

[3] On a big-endian MIPS, doubleword floating-point values are stored with the most significant word first, except that when the kernel saves floating-point registers in a `struct sigcontext`, it stores the least significant word first.

less than a week of one programmer's time. A colleague independently retargeted the Modula-3 code for the SPARC; he spent about two weeks working half-time.

5 Why PostScript?

The language embedded in the debugger should be easy for people to read and for tools to manipulate, so bytecode and machine code are inappropriate. Designing a new language is best avoided, so we considered PostScript, Scheme, FORTH, and Tcl [20]. The latter two offer too few data types. Although most of the benefits of using PostScript would also be obtained with Scheme, there are a number of reasons to prefer PostScript.

Both the compiler and the expression server have to generate code for the debugger, and PostScript was designed to be generated by other programs [2, p. 2]. Our experience confirms that it is easy to generate PostScript; for example, the expression server code that rewrites `lcc`'s intermediate representation into PostScript is only 124 lines of C, even though the intermediate representation has 112 operators.

PostScript dictionaries provide a convenient notation for symbol-table entries. Dictionaries are easily extended with machine-dependent data by adding entries; we have done so for two targets. For example, the compiler adds register-save masks when compiling procedures for the 68020. Most of `ldb` ignores these masks, but they are used by the machine-dependent stack-walking code.

Every PostScript object has an attribute that tells explicitly whether the object is literal or executable; the distinction need not be inferred from context. Because attempts to execute a literal object put that object on the stack, procedures that are interpreted at most once can be replaced with their results. We use this technique when fetching addresses relative to anchor symbols (see Sec. 2).

We can defer not only the interpretation but also the lexical analysis of PostScript code by quoting it with parentheses; the scanner reads the resulting string quickly. This deferral technique reduces by 40% the time required to read a large symbol table.

PostScript names are bound dynamically, and the "dictionary stack" used to resolve names is both distinct from the call stack and explicitly controlled by the PostScript program. When `ldb` changes architectures, it rebinds machine-dependent names by placing a dictionary on the dictionary stack; we supply one such dictionary for each target architecture.

As noted in Sec. 2, `ldb`'s PostScript implementation has extra types and operators to support debugging, and it omits types and operators that support fonts and graphics. The debugging support includes abstract memory and location types and operators. It includes an interface to a prettyprinter supplied with Modula-3; the prettyprinter procedures are called by the PostScript code that prints structured data. We made several other changes that make PostScript work better when embedded in a Modula-3 program. Strings are immutable, for compatibility with Modula-3 `TEXT`s. There are no save and restore operators; memory is reclaimed by the Modula-3 garbage collector. There are no substrings or subarrays. Interpreter errors raise Modula-3 exceptions. Files are readers or writers.

6 Related Work

Implementation strategies for debuggers vary. In some experimental systems, the compiler and debugger are tightly coupled. DEC SRC's Vulcan debugger executes in the same address space as the compiler, sharing its annotated abstract syntax trees. The DICE debugger cooperates with an incremental compiler as part of an integrated environment [12]. Most debuggers, like VAX DEBUG [4] and `dbx` [15], are separate tools which communicate with the compiler only through symbol-table information. This information is placed in the object file in a machine-dependent format. `ldb` is like these debuggers, but it uses PostScript as a machine-independent, language-independent, symbol-table format.

Most debuggers must re-implement some facilities for every language that they support [4]. Debuggers must recognize expressions and assignments, must be able to print values, including structured data, and must apply the language's scope rules to resolve names. `ldb`'s expression-server architecture and its use of PostScript reduce this kind of re-implementation effort. `ldb` has a fixed name resolution algorithm, but its implementation of printing values and its interaction with the expression server are independent of C. The name resolution algorithm could handle nested procedures, but not overloading.

`gdb` 4.0 [22] supports 20 different target machines and many different versions of UNIX, but of its more than 150,000 lines, over 47,000 are noted in the documentation as machine-dependent. This figure does not include over 10,000 lines that deal with machine-dependent object code formats like `a.out` and COFF. The long delay between the availability of MIPS machines and the availability of `gdb` for them also suggests that substantial effort is needed to retarget `gdb`.

Like parts of the Cedar programming environment [23], `ldb` defines a client interface so that it can be used by other programs, e.g., user interfaces. If `gdb` and `dbx` defined client interfaces, it would simplify the implementation of better user interfaces (e.g., `dbxtool` [1]) and of higher-level debugging tools (e.g., Dalek [19]). Event-action debugging techniques [3, 5, 19] seem well suited for implementation above `ldb`. `ldb` can debug on multiple architectures simultaneously, so it can process events from pieces of client-server applications that execute on different hardware.

`ldb`'s abstract memory model is low-level, close to the hardware. By contrast, the Cedar debugger manipulates an *abstract machine*, whose abstractions are those of the Cedar programming language [23, §6.4]. The abstract machine's interface to Cedar data is used by clients other than the debugger, including a user interface tool that lets users manipulate fields (including procedures) of records chosen dynamically. A similar abstraction could be built on top of `ldb`'s PostScript symbol tables and abstract memories, but it, like the expression server, would need detailed knowledge of the contents of the symbol tables; it would not be isolated from the details of C.

`ldb`'s nub interface is derived from the Topaz TeleDebug protocol, TTD [21], with some simplifications. `ldb` uses code outside the nub to connect to a target process. `ldb`'s nub does not support multiple threads or multiple processors. `ldb` and TTD use different data models; `ldb`'s model makes it easier to write code that is independent of target byte order, but TTD's model makes it easier to cache copies of target memory in the debugger process. The important simplification in `ldb` is that the protocol and nub do not mention breakpoints or single-stepping; breakpoints are implemented entirely in `ldb` using fetches and stores without assuming the ability to single-step. Other remote debuggers use more complex interfaces [16].

One way to resume execution after a breakpoint is to return the overwritten instruction to memory, execute it by single-stepping the target machine, and replant the breakpoint [7]. Single-stepping can be avoided by using a memory-patching implementation [9]; in that case, the overwritten instruction can be interpreted or transformed so that it can be correctly executed out of line [14].

7 Discussion

Work is divided between `ldb` and `lcc` to facilitate `ldb`'s retargeting, even at the cost of sacrificing other features. Having `lcc` insert no-ops at stopping points makes it possible to specify a breakpoint implementation in four lines, but makes target programs bigger and slower. Inserting relocatable addresses into locations known relative to anchor symbols simplifies the debugger's interface to the linker (`ldb` never needs the value of a private or static symbol), but makes target programs bigger. Using `nm` to extract information from the linked program makes `ldb` independent of linker formats.[4] Using PostScript for symbol tables makes the compiler interface machine-independent, but is incompatible with existing compilers, linkers, and debuggers. Having `lcc` emit PostScript procedures that `ldb` interprets to print values makes `ldb` independent of C's type structure and of the details of the runtime layout of data structures; the compiler writer determines both how values are represented in memory and how they are printed by the debugger.

The use of `nm` and the anchor-symbol technique could be avoided if `lcc` used a linker that recorded information about the locations of global and private symbols. This information should be in a machine-independent format and should make it possible to distinguish identically named private symbols from different compilation units. It is unnecessary to have the linker "relocate" the information in the PostScript symbol tables. For external symbols, `nm` is a good compromise; its output is mostly machine-independent and is easily transformed into PostScript.

`lcc` generates PostScript symbol tables using the same internal interface that is used by the production versions to generate machine-dependent symbol-table "stabs" for `dbx` and `gdb`. The implementation is somewhat more complex; about 1000 lines of C to generate PostScript versus about 300 for stabs. The additional cost is reasonable considering that the PostScript contains more information; it must be enough to enable the expression server to reconstruct the compiler's symbol-table and type information at debug time.

[4] `ldb`'s MIPS linker interface gets machine-dependent data from the runtime procedure table located in the target address space [17], not from the object file.

`ldb`'s PostScript symbol tables can be manipulated by PostScript programs. For example, we wrote PostScript code that reads the top-level dictionary for the nub and constructs a Modula-3 description of one of the nub's machine-dependent data structures.

`ldb` takes about 6 seconds to start up on a one-line "hello world" program, and about 9 seconds to start up on a 13,000-line version of `lcc`. The costs of initializing the Modula-3 runtime system and of interpreting PostScript increase the startup time of `ldb`. The following table shows the elapsed time required to execute the initial phases of `ldb`, `dbx`, and `gdb`. All programs were executed on a lightly loaded DECstation 5000/200 with 16M of main memory. Times shown are the average of seven measurements made with a stopwatch; errors are a few percent.

Modula-3 initialization	1.9 sec
Read initial PostScript	1.6
Read symbol table for `hello.c` (1 line)	2.2
Read symbol table for `lcc` (13,000 lines)	5.5
Connect to `hello.c` (one machine)	1.8
Connect to `lcc` (one machine)	5.1
Connect to `lcc` (two MIPS machines)	6.2
Connect to `lcc` (host MIPS, target SPARC)	5.0
`dbx`: start and read `a.out` for `lcc`	1.5
`gdb`: start and read `a.out` for `lcc`	1.1

All PostScript symbol tables include symbol-table information for the nub. The extra time required to debug a MIPS target is spent fetching information from the runtime procedure table in the target address space.

PostScript symbol-table information is about 9 times larger than `dbx` stabs for the same program. The `dbx` information is in a binary format, so it may be fairer to compare the PostScript after compression by the UNIX program `compress`, in which case the ratio is about 2.

`ldb` originally used an abstract memory model based on C primitive types; for example, it distinguished signed from unsigned integers. The current abstract memory model (Sec. 4.1) uses three sizes of integers and three sizes of floating-point values. These values and types correspond closely to the values and types manipulated in `lcc`'s intermediate representation [10]. The change simplified both `ldb` and the PostScript symbol tables, and it enables the expression server to share more code with the compiler front end.

Floating point complicates cross-debugging. Different precision in `ldb`'s machine and the target machine is the most obvious problem, but even if both machines use IEEE floating point, each floating-point unit can hold a different state — rounding mode, for example. One possible solution to these problems is to extend the nub and its protocol to do all floating-point operations in the target. Even then, the floating-point state may be correct only for the topmost procedure activation. Other debuggers can suffer from these problems, too, unless the operating system or compiler tracks floating-point state changes.

`ldb` can connect to multiple targets simultaneously, so it must not leave target-specific state in global variables. It stores such state in *target objects*. Dependence on such state is surprisingly pervasive; many procedures require a target object for reasons not immediately obvious. One might expect, for example, that values of variables could be printed without access to a target object, but to print the function name associated with a C function pointer requires the loader table, which is accessed from the target object. A second problem with the target object is that several parts of the debugger must know whether the debugger is connected to a target process and whether that process is running or stopped. These parts include the user interface, the breakpoint implementation, the debugger end of the nub protocol, and the implementation of the client interface.

Both problems are exacerbated by the use of the anchor-symbol technique, because every computation of a location might fetch data from the target address space. This operation not only requires the target object, it requires that it be connected to a stopped process. Fortunately, the fetches from the target address space have little impact on performance because such fetches are performed only on demand and at most once per symbol-table entry.

7.1 Future Work

The expression server is not yet complete; in particular, `ldb` cannot evaluate expressions that include procedure calls into the target process. We expect to use the existing nub protocol when adding procedure-call support. `ldb`'s interface with the expression server is defined precisely by the relevant code, but our experience suggests that we can formulate a more abstract interface analogous to `lcc`'s code generation interface [10].

The PostScript approach may extend gracefully to languages with more semantic complexity, like C++ and Modula-3. If `dbx` "stabs" are extended to describe a richer language, `dbx` itself must also be extended [15], but `ldb`'s capabilities can be extended by changing only the PostScript symbol tables; `ldb` itself need not change. `ldb` may well suit language implementations that compile to C, because the first compiler can emit PostScript code that manipulates the symbols emitted by the C compiler, producing one set of symbols that combines the results of two compilations.

PostScript invites further exploitation; for example, it might help debug optimized code. If an optimizer performs strength reduction and replaces the use of `i` in `a[i]` with an induction variable *p*, the compiler can emit Postscript that recovers `i` from *p*.

The similarity of the stack-walking procedures on the four targets suggests that formal descriptions of stack-frame layout and calling conventions might be devised and used to generate all or part of the stack-walking code. Such descriptions might also be useful for providing a compiler back end with information about register usage or calling conventions.

`ldb`'s model of breakpoints should be replaced with one based on instruction-level single-stepping. Single-stepping lends itself to simpler machine-dependent implementation than does interpretation, and it would eliminate the no-ops emitted by `lcc`. Implementing breakpoints entirely in the debugger keeps the nub simple, but runs the risk of losing important state in a debugger crash, and of being unable to resume debugging with a new debugger. We can solve this problem by enriching the protocol with a special store operation used only for planting breakpoints and by making the nub capable of reporting to a new debugger the instructions overwritten by such stores, in case the connection to the original debugger is lost.

`ldb` needs facilities like source-level single stepping. Implementing such facilities on top of breakpoints is complex, because the event that is expected may not be the one that occurs; a fault may occur when a breakpoint is expected. One solution is to make the debugger internals event-driven [15]. Exporting the mechanisms used to make the debugger event-driven would simplify the implementation of event-driven clients. Event-driven debugging subsumes conditional breakpoints as a special case.

Sec. 4.2 describes the potential reliability and performance benefits of moving the nub into the kernel. Reimplementing the nub interface on top of operating-system support for debugging might have similar benefits, but at some cost in retargetability. Using operating-system facilities has an additional advantage: they may provide access to instruction single-stepping, breakpoints, threads, signals, or exceptions. `ldb` could be designed to take advantage of these kinds of extensions to the nub protocol when they are available, but should continue to function correctly when they are not available.

8 Acknowledgements

Mike Spreitzer helped clarify retargeting issues by independently writing Modula-3 code for the SPARC. Anne Rogers insisted that we write more about ideas and less about code. John Ellis's thorough reading of an earlier draft uncovered many important omissions.

This work was supported by a Fannie and John Hertz Fellowship, an AT&T Bell Laboratories Fellowship, and a summer research internship at Xerox PARC.

References

[1] E. Adams and S. S. Muchnick. Dbxtool: A window-based symbolic debugger for Sun workstations. *Software—Practice & Experience*, 16(7):653–669, July 1986.

[2] Adobe Systems Incorporated. *PostScript Language Reference Manual.* Addison-Wesley, 1985.

[3] P. C. Bates and J. C. Wileden. High-level debugging of distributed systems: The behavioral abstraction approach. *Journal of Systems and Software*, 3(4):255–264, Dec. 1983.

[4] B. Beander. VAX DEBUG: An interactive, symbolic, multilingual debugger. *Proceedings of the ACM SIGSOFT/SIGPLAN Software Engineering Symposium on High-Level Debugging,* in *SIGPLAN Notices*, 18(8):173–179, August 1983.

[5] B. Bruegge. *Adaptability and Portability of Symbolic Debuggers.* PhD thesis, Carnegie Mellon University, September 1985.

[6] T. A. Cargill. Pi: A case study in object-oriented programming. *Proceedings of OOPSLA'86, SIGPLAN Notices*, 21(11):350–360, Nov. 1986.

[7] D. Caswell and D. Black. Implementing a Mach debugger for multithreaded applications. In *Proceedings of the Winter USENIX Conference*, pages 25–39, Washington, DC, Jan. 1990.

[8] G. V. Cormack. A micro-kernel for concurrency in C. *Software—Practice & Experience*, 18(5):485–491, May 1988.

[9] Digital Equipment Corporation, Maynard, MA. *DDT—Dynamic Debugging Technique*, 1975.

[10] C. W. Fraser and D. R. Hanson. A code generation interface for ANSI C. *Software—Practice & Experience*, 21(9):963–988, Sept. 1991.

[11] C. W. Fraser and D. R. Hanson. A retargetable compiler for ANSI C. *SIGPLAN Notices*, 26(10):29–43, Oct. 1991.

[12] P. Fritzson. Symbolic debugging through incremental compilation in an integrated environment. *Journal of Systems and Software*, 3(4):285–294, Dec. 1983.

[13] G. J. Holzmann. *Design and Validation of Computer Protocols*. Prentice Hall, Englewood Cliffs, NJ, 1991.

[14] P. B. Kessler. Fast breakpoints: Design and implementation. *Proceedings of the ACM SIGPLAN '90 Conference on Programming Language Design and Implementation*, in *SIGPLAN Notices*, 25(6):78–84, June 1990.

[15] M. A. Linton. The evolution of Dbx. In *Proceedings of the Summer USENIX Conference*, pages 211–220, June 1990.

[16] P. Maybee. pdb: A network oriented symbolic debugger. In *Proceedings of the Winter USENIX Conference*, pages 41–52, Jan. 1990.

[17] MIPS Computer Systems, Inc. *MIPS Assembly Language Programmer's Guide*, May 1989.

[18] G. Nelson, editor. *Systems Programming with Modula-3*. Prentice Hall, Englewood Cliffs, NJ, 1991.

[19] R. A. Olsson, R. H. Crawford, and W. W. Ho. A dataflow approach to event-based debugging. *Software—Practice & Experience*, 21(2):209–229, Feb. 1991.

[20] J. K. Ousterhout. Tcl: An embeddable command language. In *Proceedings of the Winter USENIX Conference*, pages 133–146, Jan. 1990.

[21] D. D. Redell. Experience with Topaz TeleDebugging. *Proceedings of the ACM SIGPLAN/SIGOPS Workshop on Parallel and Distributed Debugging*, in *SIGPLAN Notices*, 24(1):35–44, January 1989.

[22] R. M. Stallman and R. H. Pesch. Using GDB: A guide to the GNU source-level debugger, GDB version 4.0. Technical report, Free Software Foundation, Cambridge, MA, 1991.

[23] D. C. Swinehart, P. T. Zellweger, R. J. Beach, and R. B. Hagmann. A structural view of the Cedar programming environment. *ACM Trans. Prog. Lang. Syst.*, 8(4):419–490, Oct. 1986.

[24] M. Weiser, A. Demers, and C. Hauser. The portable common runtime approach to interoperability. *Proceedings of the 12th SOSP*, in *Operating Systems Review*, 23(5):114–122, Dec. 1989.

In a multipass program, the earlier passes must transmit information to the later passes. This information is often transmitted most efficiently in a somewhat machine-like language, as a set of instructions for the later pass; the later pass is then nothing but a special purpose interpretive routine, and the earlier pass is a special purpose "compiler." This philosophy of multipass operation may be characterized as telling *the later pass what to do, whenever possible, rather than simply presenting it with a lot of facts and asking it to* figure *out what to do.*

— D. E. Knuth, *The Art of Computer Programming*, vol. 1, 2nd ed., p. 198. Addison-Wesley, 1973.

Debugging Optimized Code with Dynamic Deoptimization

Urs Hölzle
Computer Systems Laboratory
CIS 57
Stanford University
Stanford, CA 94305
urs@cs.stanford.edu

Craig Chambers
Dept. of Computer Science and Engineering
Sieg Hall, FR-35
University of Washington
Seattle, WA 98195
chambers@cs.washington.edu

David Ungar
Sun Microsystems Laboratories
MTV29-116
2500 Garcia St.
Mountain View, CA 94043
ungar@eng.sun.com

Abstract: SELF's debugging system provides complete source-level debugging (*expected behavior*) with globally optimized code. It shields the debugger from optimizations performed by the compiler by dynamically *deoptimizing* code on demand. Deoptimization only affects the procedure activations that are actively being debugged; all other code runs at full speed. Deoptimization requires the compiler to supply debugging information at discrete *interrupt points*; the compiler can still perform extensive optimizations between interrupt points without affecting debuggability. At the same time, the inability to interrupt between interrupt points is invisible to the user. Our debugging system also handles *programming changes* during debugging. Again, the system provides expected behavior: it is possible to change a running program and immediately observe the effects of the change. Dynamic deoptimization transforms old compiled code (which may contain inlined copies of the old version of the changed procedure) into new versions reflecting the current source-level state. To the best of our knowledge, SELF is the first practical system providing full expected behavior with globally optimized code.

1. Introduction

SELF is a pure object-oriented language designed for rapid prototyping, increasing programmer productivity by maximizing expressiveness and malleability [US87]. SELF's pure message-based model of computation requires extensive optimization to achieve good performance [CU91, HCU91]. Without aggressive procedure integration (inlining), for example, performance would be abysmal [Cha92]. But an interactive programming environment also demands rapid turnaround time and complete source-level debugging. To make SELF practical, the system must provide interpreter semantics at compiled-code speed, combining *expected behavior* [Zel84] with global optimization.

This work has been supported in part by the Swiss National Science Foundation (Nationalfonds), an IBM graduate student fellowship, NSF Presidential Young Investigator Award # CCR-8657631, and by Sun, IBM, Apple, Cray, Tandem, TI, and DEC.

ACM SIGPLAN '92 PLDI-6/92/CA
© 1992 ACM 0-89791-476-7/92/0006/0032...$1.50

Most existing systems do not support the debugging of optimized code. Programs can either be optimized for full speed, or they can be compiled without optimizations for full source-level debugging. Recently, techniques have been developed that strive to make it possible to debug optimized code [Hen82, Zel84, CMR88]. However, none of these systems is able to provide full source-level debugging. For example, it generally is not possible to obtain the values of all source-level variables, to single-step through the program, or to change the value of a variable. Optimization is given priority over debugging, and consequently these systems provide only restricted forms of debugging.

To the best of our knowledge, SELF is the first practical system providing full expected behavior with globally optimized code. Compared to previous techniques, our use of *dynamic deoptimization* and *interrupt points* permits us to place fewer restrictions on the kind of optimizations that can be performed while still preserving expected behavior.

The remainder of this paper is organized as follows. Section 2 discusses the optimizations performed by the SELF compiler and how they affect debugging. Section 3 describes how optimized code can be deoptimized, and section 4 explains how running programs can be changed. Section 5 discusses the implementation of common debugging operations. Section 6 discusses the benefits and limitations of our approach, and section 7 examines its run-time and space cost. Section 8 relates this paper to previous work, and section 9 contains our conclusions.

2. Optimization and debugging

This section briefly outlines the optimizations that the SELF compiler performs and discusses some of the problems they cause for the debugger.

2.1 Optimizations performed by the SELF compiler

SELF uses dynamic compilation [DS84, CUL89]: instead of compiling whole programs prior to execution, code is generated incrementally at run-time and kept in a cache. Whenever a source method is invoked which hasn't already been compiled, a new compiled method is created and cached. (In the SELF system, source code is accessible at all times so that methods can be (re-)compiled at any time.)

In addition to standard optimizations such as global constant propagation, constant folding, and global register allocation, our compiler relies extensively on three optimizations which are important for pure object-oriented languages: inlining, customization, and splitting [CUL89, CU90, CU91]. *Inlining* reduces the call overhead and enables optimizations which span source method boundaries. *Customization* creates multiple compiled copies of source methods, each copy specialized for a particular receiver type. Customization allows many dynamically-dispatched calls to be statically bound and subsequently inlined. *Splitting* creates multiple compiled copies of a source-level expression and optimizes each copy for a particular set of types.

Additionally, the compiler performs dead code elimination, strength reduction, and global common subexpression elimination of arithmetic expressions, loads, and stores. Redundant computations are eliminated only if they cannot cause observable side effects such as arithmetic overflow. The compiler sometimes unrolls loops to avoid repeating type tests in every iteration of the loop, which frequently has the effect of hoisting invariant code out of loops. Low-level optimizations such as delay slot filling are also performed; more extensive instruction scheduling could easily be supported but has not been implemented. Induction variable elimination could be supported by extending the structure of our debugging information.

Since it must always provide full source-level debugging, the SELF compiler does not perform certain optimizations. In general, dead stores cannot be eliminated, and the registers of dead variables cannot be reused without spilling the variable to memory first. Both optimizations can be performed, however, if there is no interrupt point within the variable's scope (see section 3.4). Finally, the SELF compiler does not perform tail recursion elimination or tail call elimination because they cannot be supported transparently: in general, it is not possible to reconstruct the stack frames eliminated by these optimizations. Instead, iteration is supported through a primitive which restarts execution of the current scope. (The SELF language does not pre-define common control structures such as `if` and `while`; such control structures are user-defined).

2.2 Problems caused by optimization

The code transformations performed by global optimization make it hard to debug optimized code at the source level. Because optimizations delete, change, or rearrange parts of the original program, they become visible to the user who tries to debug the optimized program. This sections presents some of the problems that must be solved to provide source-level debugging of optimized code.

2.2.1 Displaying the stack

Optimizations such as inlining, register allocation, constant propagation, and copy propagation create methods whose activation records have no direct correspondence to the source-level activations. For example, a single physical stack frame may contain several source-level activations because message sends have been inlined. Variables may be in different locations at different times, and some variables may not have run-time locations at all.

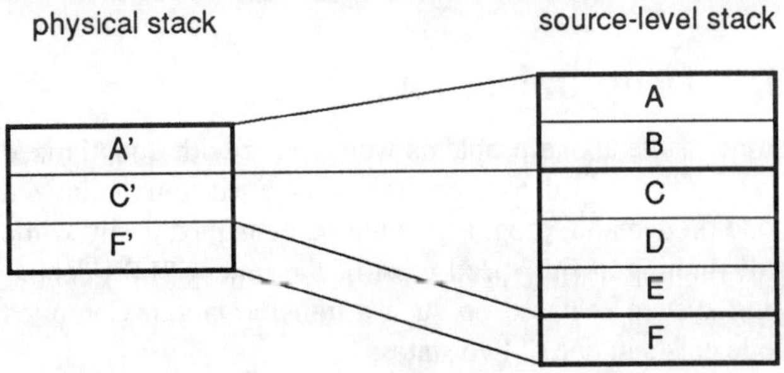

Figure 1. Displaying the stack

The example in Figure 1 shows the effects of inlining. The physical stack contains three activations A', C', and F'. In contrast, the source-level-stack contains additional activations which were inlined by the compiler. For example, the activation B was inlined into A', and so B does not appear in the physical stack trace.

2.2.2 Single-stepping

To single-step, the debugger has to find and execute the machine instructions belonging to the next source operation. Optimizations such as code motion or instruction scheduling make this a hard problem: the instructions for one statement may be interspersed with those of neighboring statements, and statements may have been reordered to execute out of source-level order. In contrast, single-stepping is simple with unoptimized code since the code for a statement is contiguous.

2.2.3 Changing the value of a variable

Consider the following code fragment:

```
i := 3;                        i := 3;
j := 4;     optimization       j := 4;
k := i + j;  ---------->       k := 7;
```

Since the expression `i + j` is a compile-time constant, the compiler has eliminated its computation from the generated code. But what if the program is suspended just before the assignment to `k` and the programmer changes `j` to be 10? Execution of the optimized code cannot be resumed since it would produce an unexpected value for `k`. With unoptimized code, of course, there would be no problem since the addition would still be performed by the compiled code.

2.2.4 Changing a procedure

A similar problem arises when an inlined procedure is changed during debugging. Suppose that the program is suspended just before executing the inlined copy of function `f` when the programmer changes `f` because she has found a bug. Obviously, execution cannot simply continue since `f`'s old definition is hard-wired into its caller. On the other hand, it would be easy to provide expected behavior with unoptimized code: `f`'s definition could simply be replaced, and the subsequent call to `f` would execute the correct code.

3. Deoptimization

None of the above problems would exist with unoptimized code. If optimized code could be converted to unoptimized code on demand, programs could be debugged easily while still running at full speed most of the time. SELF's debugging system is based on such a transformation. Compiled code exists in one of two states:

- *Optimized code*, which can be suspended only at relatively widely-spaced interrupt points; at every interrupt point, the source-level state can be reconstructed, and
- *Unoptimized code*, which can be suspended at any arbitrary source-level operation and thus supports all debugging operations (such as single-stepping).

Section 3.1 explains the data structures used to recover the source-level state from the optimized program state. Sections 3.2 and 3.3 describe how optimized code can be transformed into unoptimized code on demand, and section 3.4 discusses how interrupt points lessen the impact of debugging on optimization.

3.1 Recovering the unoptimized state

To display a source-level stack trace and to perform deoptimization, the system needs to reconstruct the source-level state from the optimized machine-level state. To support this reconstruction, the SELF compiler generates *scope descriptors* [CUL89] for each scope contained in a compiled method, i.e., for the initial source method and all methods inlined within it. A scope descriptor specifies the scope's place in the virtual call tree of the physical stack frame and records the locations or values of its arguments and locals (see Figure 2). The compiler also describes the location or value of each subexpression within the compiled method. This information is needed to reconstruct the stack of evaluated expressions that are waiting to be consumed by later message sends.

To find the correct scope for a given physical program counter, the debugger needs to know the *virtual program counter* (source position), i.e., the pair of a scope description and a source position within that scope. Therefore, the debugging information generated with each compiled method also includes a mapping between physical and virtual program counters.

With the help of this information, the debugger can hide the effects of inlining, splitting, register allocation, constant propagation, and constant folding from the user. For example, if the compiler eliminates a variable because its value is a compile-time constant, the variable's descriptor would contain that constant. A straightforward extension of the descriptor structure could be used to handle variables whose values can be computed from other values (such as eliminated induction variables).

```
struct ScopeDesc {
    oop method;                        // pointer to the method object
    ScopeDesc* caller;                 // scope into which this scope was inlined (if any)
    int posWithinCaller;               // source position within caller
    ScopeDesc* enclosingScope;         // lexically enclosing scope (if any)
    NameDesc args[];                   // descriptors for receiver and arguments
    NameDesc locals[];                 // descriptors for locals
    NameDesc expressionStack[];        // descriptors for all subexpressions
};

struct NameDesc {
    enum { const, loc } tag;           // compile-time constant or run-time value
    union {
        oop value;                     // constant value
        Location location;             // run-time location
    };
};
```

Figure 2. Pseudo-code declarations for scope data structures

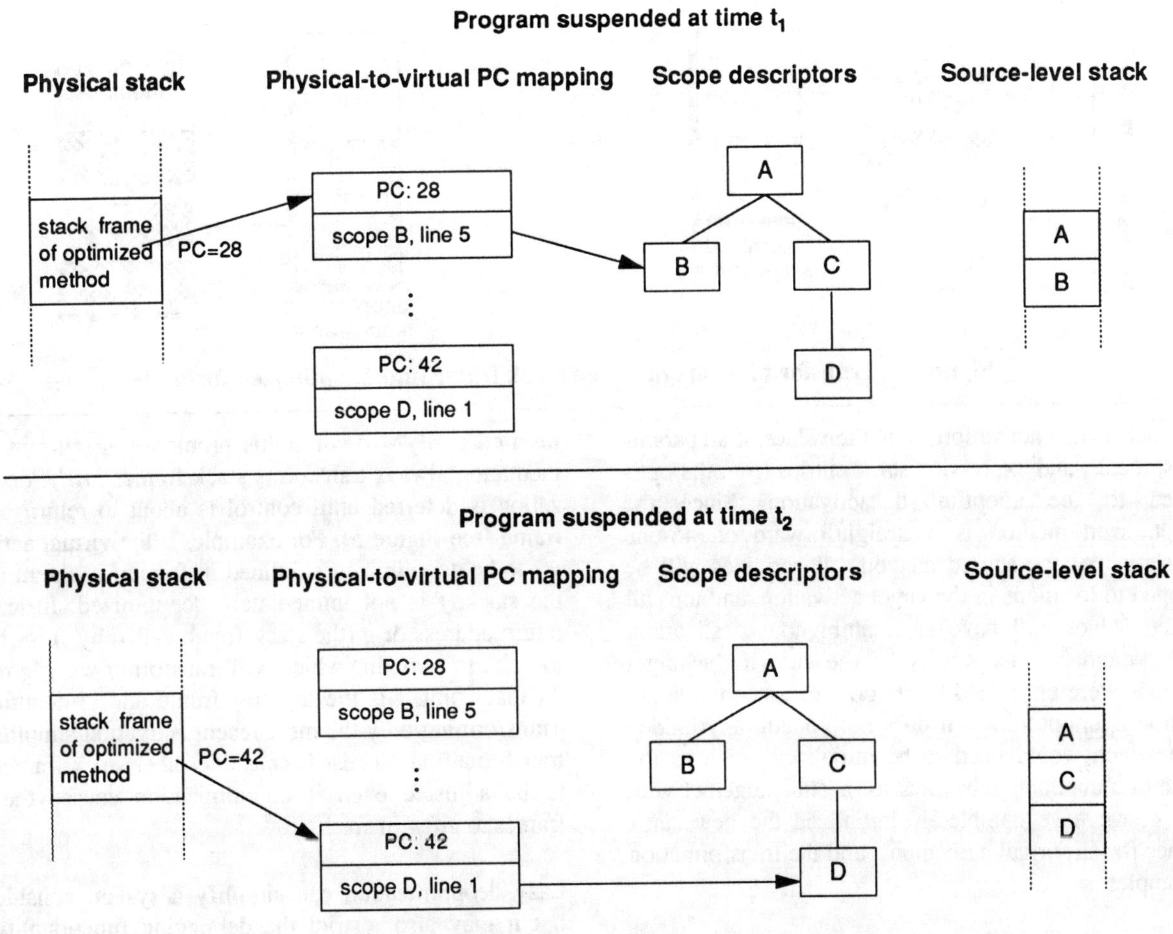

Figure 3. Recovering the source-level state

Figure 3 shows a method suspended at two different times. When the method is suspended at time t_1, the physical PC is 28 and the corresponding source position is line 5 of method B. A stack trace would therefore display B being called by A, hiding the fact that B has been inlined into A by the compiler. Similarly, at time t_2 the source-level view would show D being called by C being called by A, displaying three virtual stack frames instead of the single physical stack frame. To display a complete stack trace, this process is simply repeated for each physical stack frame

3.2 The transformation function

Our approach transforms an optimized method into one or more equivalent unoptimized methods. For the moment, we assume that only the topmost stack activation needs to be transformed so that stack frames can easily be removed or added; section 3.3 explains how to remove this restriction. The deoptimizing transformation can then be performed as follows:

1. Save the contents of the physical activation (stack frame) which is to be transformed, and remove it from the run-time stack.
2. Using the mechanisms described in the previous section, determine the source-level (*virtual*) activations contained in the physical activation, the values of their locals, and their virtual PC.
3. For each virtual activation, create a new compiled method and a corresponding physical activation. To simplify the transformation function and subsequent debugging activities, the new methods (the *target* methods) are completely unoptimized: every message send corresponds to a call, and no optimizations such as constant folding or common subexpression elimination are performed.
4. For each virtual activation, find the new physical PC in the corresponding compiled method. Since the target method is unoptimized, there will be exactly one physical PC for the given virtual PC. (This would not necessarily be the case if the target methods were optimized.) Initialize the stack frames created in the previous step by filling in the return PC and other fields needed by the run-time system, such as the frame pointer.

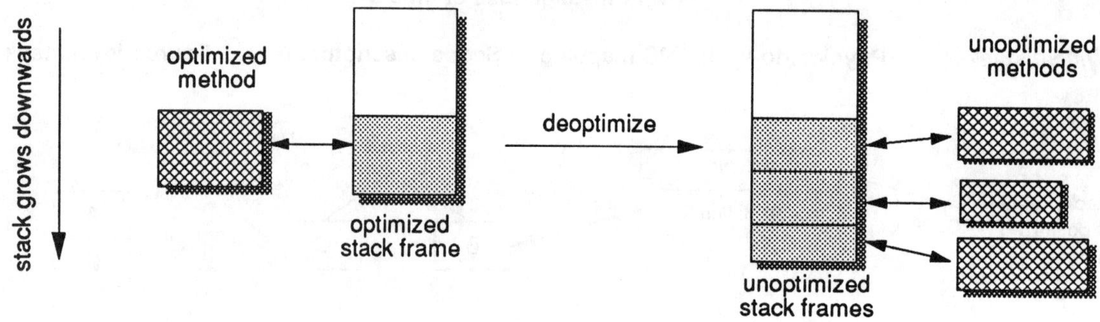

Figure 4. Transforming an optimized stack frame into unoptimized form

5. For each virtual activation, copy the values of all parameters, locals, and expression stack entries from the optimized to the unoptimized activation. Since the unoptimized method is a straightforward one-to-one translation of the source method, all variables will be mapped to locations in the target activation, and thus all copied values will have an unambiguous destination. (This would not necessarily be the case if the target methods were optimized.) Furthermore, since the target method is unoptimized, it does not contain any hidden state which would need to be initialized (such as the value of a common subexpression). Thus, together with step 4, we have completely initialized the new stack frames for all virtual activations, and the transformation is complete.

Figure 4 illustrates the process. The transformation expands an optimized stack frame containing three virtual activations into a sequence of three unoptimized stack frames, thus creating a one-to-one correspondence between virtual and physical frames.

Only those parts of the program which are actively being debugged (e.g., by stepping through them) need to be transformed. These parts will be the only parts of the program running unoptimized code; all other parts can run at full speed. No transformations are necessary just to inspect the program state, as described in section 3.1.

3.3 Lazy deoptimization

But how can a stack frame be deoptimized when it is in the *middle* of the stack, where new stack frames cannot be inserted easily? To solve this problem, our current implementation always transforms stack frames *lazily*: deoptimization is deferred until control is about to return into the frame (see Figure 5). For example, if the virtual activation vf_2 to be deoptimized is inlined in frame *f* in the middle of the stack, *f* is not immediately deoptimized. Instead, the return address of *g* (the stack frame called by *f*) is changed to point to a routine which will transform *f* when *g* returns. At that point, *f* is the topmost frame and is deoptimized. Transforming only the most recent activation simplifies the transformation process because no other stack frames need to be adjusted even if deoptimization causes the stack frames to grow in size.

Lazy deoptimization can simplify a system considerably, but it may also restrict the debugging functionality. Our system currently does not allow the contents of local variables to be changed during debugging because a variable might not have a run-time location. In order to create a run-time location for the variable, it might be necessary to transform an activation in the middle of the stack, which our system currently cannot do. However, this is not a fundamental problem; for example, the transformed stack frames could be heap-allocated as described in [DS84]. An even simpler solution would be to always allocate stack locations for eliminated variables. These locations would be unused during normal program execution but would spring into life when the programmer manually changes the value of an eliminated variable. Since the compiled code depended on the old (supposedly constant) value, it would be invalidated as if the programmer had changed the method's source code (see section 4).

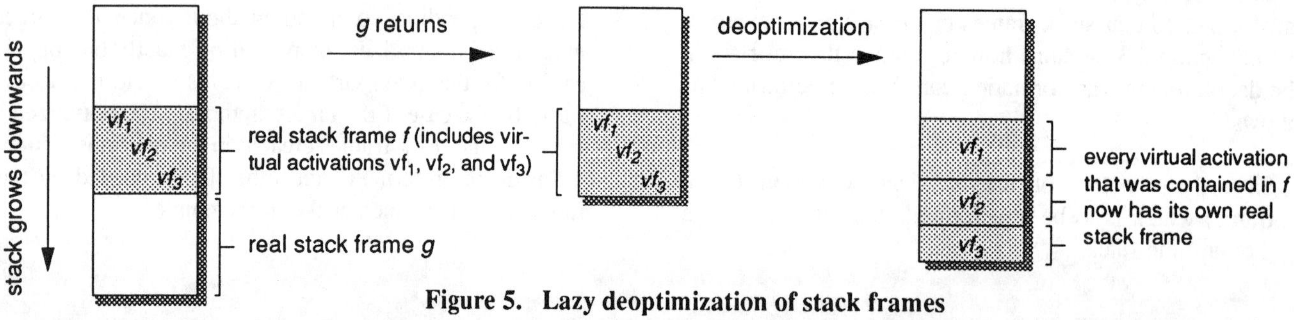

Figure 5. Lazy deoptimization of stack frames

3.4 Interrupt points

If optimized programs could be interrupted at any instruction boundary, debugging optimized code would be hard, since the source-level state would have to be recoverable at every single point in the program. To ease the restrictions that this would impose on optimization, an optimized SELF program can be interrupted only at certain *interrupt points*† where its state is guaranteed to be consistent. Notification of any asynchronous event occurring between two interrupt points is delayed until the next interrupt point is reached. Currently, the SELF system defines two kinds of interrupt points: method prologues (including some process control primitives) and the end of loop bodies ("backward branches"). This definition implies that the maximum interrupt latency is bounded by the length of the longest code sequence containing neither a call nor a loop end, typically only a few dozen instructions. Because the latency is so short, the use of interrupt points is not noticed by the programmer. (If only sends were interrupt points, loops without calls could not be interrupted.)

Interrupt points need to cover all possible points where a program could be suspended; that is, they also need to handle synchronous events such as arithmetic overflow. In our system, all possible run-time errors are interrupt points because all SELF primitives are safe: if the requested operation cannot be performed, the primitive calls a user-defined error handler which usually invokes the debugger.

Once an optimized program is suspended, the current activation can be deoptimized if necessary to carry out debugging requests. In an unoptimized method, every source point is an interrupt point, and the program can therefore stop at any point.

Since the debugger can be invoked only at interrupt points, debugging information need be generated only for those points. This reduces the space used by the debugging information, but more importantly it allows extensive optimizations between interrupt points. Essentially, the compiler may perform any optimization whose effects either do not reach an interrupt point or can be undone at that point. For example, the compiler can reuse a dead variable's register as long as there are no subsequent interrupt points within the variable's scope. The more widely-spaced interrupt points are, the fewer restrictions source-level debugging imposes on optimization.

Interrupt points also lessen the impact of garbage collection on compiler optimization. Garbage collections can only occur at interrupt points, and so the compiler can generate code between interrupt points that temporarily violates the invariants needed by the garbage collector [Cha87].

† Interrupt points have been used in other systems before; see section 8 for a discussion of the Deutsch-Schiffman Smalltalk-80 system.

4. Updating active methods

During debugging, a programmer might not only change the value of a variable but also the definition of a method. To invalidate the compiled code affected by such a change, the SELF system maintains *dependency links* between compiled code and the objects representing source code methods [CUL89]. For example, if a compiled method contains inlined copies of a method that was changed, the compiled method is discarded.

However, if a compiled method containing an inlined copy of a changed method is active (i.e., has at least one activation), it cannot simply be discarded. Instead, the compiled method must be replaced by a new compiled method before execution can continue. Fortunately, deoptimization can be used for this purpose. After the active compiled method has been deoptimized, it will no longer contain any inlined methods. When its execution continues, all subsequent calls to the changed method will correctly invoke the new definition.

If the changed method itself is currently active, updating its activation is hard. Fortunately, in SELF we don't have to solve this problem because in SELF's language model, activations are created by cloning the method object. Once created, the clone is independent from its original, so changes to the original do not affect the clone.

Lazy transformation elegantly solves the problem of invalidated compiled methods in the middle of the stack: we simply wait until the invalid method is on top of the stack, then transform it. Lazy transformation is very desirable in an interactive system since it spreads out the repair effort over time, avoiding distracting pauses. Furthermore, it handles sequences of changes well, for example when reading in a file containing new definitions for a group of related objects. With eager transformation, every new definition would cause all affected compiled methods to be recompiled, and many methods would be recompiled several times since they are likely to be affected by several of the changes. With lazy transformation, these compiled methods will be invalidated repeatedly (which is no problem since invalidation is very cheap) but only transformed once.

In conclusion, with our debugging mechanisms it is almost trivial to support changing running programs. Our current implementation consists of less than a hundred lines of C++ code on top of the previously described debugging functionality and the code maintaining the dependencies.

5. Common debugging operations

This section describes the debugging operations implemented in the SELF system and outlines possible implementations of additional operations. With deoptimization, it is relatively easy to implement common debugging operations such as *single-step* and *finish* because these operations are simple to perform in unoptimized code, and deoptimization can supply unoptimized code for every program piece on demand. In contrast, neither *single-step* nor *finish* could generally be provided by previous systems for debugging optimized code [Zel84, CMR88].

5.1 Single-step

Because every source point has an interrupt point associated with it in a deoptimized method, the implementation of single-stepping becomes trivial. The system deoptimizes the current activation and restarts the process with the interrupt flag already set. The process will relinquish control upon reaching the next interrupt point, i.e. after executing a single step.

5.2 Finish

The *finish* operation continues program execution until the selected activation returns. It is implemented by changing the return address of the selected activation's stack frame to a special routine that will suspend execution when the activation returns. Thus, the program is not slowed down during the *finish* operation because it can run optimized code.

If the selected activation does not have its own physical stack frame (because it was inlined into another method), its stack frame is deoptimized using lazy deoptimization. In this case, the program can still run optimized code most of the time; only at the very end (when lazy deoptimization is performed) does it run unoptimized code.

5.3 Next

The *next* operation (also called "step over") executes the next source operation without stepping into calls. That is, the program will stop after the next source operation has completed. *Next* can be synthesized by performing a *single-step*, possibly followed by a *finish* (if the operation was a call). Consequently, *next* is implemented by a few lines of SELF code in our system.

5.4 Breakpoints and watchpoints

SELF currently supports breakpoints through source transformation: the programmer inserts a breakpoint by simply inserting a send of `halt` into the source method (`halt` explicitly invokes the debugger). To implement breakpoints without explicit changes by the programmer, the debugger could perform this source transformation transparently.

Watchpoints ("stop when the value of this variable changes") are also easy to provide because SELF is a pure object-oriented language, and all accesses are performed through message sends (at least conceptually; the compiler will usually optimize away such sends). To monitor all accesses to an object's instance variable `x`, we can rename the variable to `private_x` and install two new methods `x` and `x:` which monitor accesses and assignments, respectively, and return or change `private_x`. The dependency system will invalidate all code that inlined the old definition of `x` or `x:` (i.e., that directly accessed or changed `x`).

6. Discussion

In this section, we discuss some of the strengths and weaknesses of our approach and assess its generality.

6.1 Benefits

Our debugging technique has several important advantages. First, it is simple: the current implementation of the transformation process consists of less than 400 lines of C++ code on top of the code implementing the debugging information described in section 3.1. Second, it allows a loose coupling between debugger and compiler—neither has to know very much about the other. Third, it places no additional restrictions beyond those described in section 2 on the kind of optimizations which can be performed by the compiler. Thus, many common optimizations such as inlining, loop unrolling, common subexpression elimination, and instruction scheduling can be used without affecting debuggability. Finally, our method is well suited for an interactive system since it is incremental: usually, at most one stack frame needs to be converted as a result of a user command.

6.2 Current limitations

Using unoptimized code during debugging introduces a potential performance problem when the user decides to continue execution. Execution should proceed at full speed, but some of the stack frames may be unoptimized. However, this problem usually is not severe: only a few frames are running unoptimized code, and the unoptimized code will be discarded as soon as these frames return. All other parts of the system can run at full speed.

Methods containing loops could still pose a problem since they could remain on the stack in unoptimized form indefinitely. However, we currently are working to solve the more general problem of *adaptive compilation* [HCU91]. With adaptive compilation, methods are created in unoptimized form first to minimize compile pauses. Later, the frequently-used parts are automatically recompiled with optimization. Therefore, a system with adaptive compilation would automatically reoptimize any unoptimized loops created by debugging. The current SELF system already contains a primitive form of adaptive compilation.

6.3 Generality

The debugging approach presented here is not specific to SELF and could be exploited in other languages as well. Our system appears to require run-time compilation for deoptimization, but systems without run-time compilation could include an unoptimized copy of every procedure in an executable or dynamically link these in as needed.

For pointer-safe languages like Lisp, Smalltalk, or a pointer-safe subset of C++, our approach seems directly applicable. In pointer-unsafe languages† like C which allow pointer errors, interrupt points might be more closely spaced. The debugger could potentially be invoked at every load or store where the compiler could not prove that no address fault would occur. But even if interrupt points caused by unsafe loads or stores were indeed very frequent, our approach would still allow at least as many optimizations as other approaches for source-level debugging.

Pointers into the stack require special care during deoptimization if the locations of such pointers are unknown. In this case, the address of a stack variable potentially referenced by a pointer may not be changed. However, this problem could probably be solved at the expense of some stack space by requiring the layout of optimized and unoptimized stack frames to be identical.

6.4 Implementation status

The first implementation of the debugging system was completed in the spring of 1991 (recovering the source-level state of optimized programs was implemented in 1989). Today's system implements all functions described in section 5 and is in daily use at several research institutions. A source-level debugger (written in SELF by Lars Bak) is also part of the system. The SELF implementation is available free of charge via ftp from self.stanford.edu.

7. Cost

Providing full source-level debugging in the presence of an optimizing compiler does not come for free. In this section, we examine the impact of our techniques on responsiveness, run-time performance, and memory usage.

† In a way, true source-level debugging of unsafe languages is something of an oxymoron: since programs can overwrite arbitrary memory regions, they can always produce behavior which cannot be explained at the language (source) level. For example, if an integer is erroneously stored into the location of a floating-point variable, the resulting behavior cannot be explained without referring to the particular integer and floating-point representations used by the system.

7.1 Impact on responsiveness

Neither the deoptimization process nor the use of interrupt points are perceptible to users. The compiler typically creates the unoptimized methods in about one millisecond on a SPARCStation 1, and thus the pauses introduced by dynamic deoptimization are negligible. Interrupt points increase the latency for user and system interrupts by only a few microseconds because an interrupt point is usually reached within a few dozen instructions after the run-time system has set the interrupt flag. In summary, providing full source-level debugging in the SELF system has not reduced its responsiveness.

7.2 Impact on run-time performance

Ideally, the performance impact of full source-level debugging could be measured by completely disabling it and re-measuring the system. However, this is not possible because source-level debugging was a fundamental design goal of the SELF system. Disabling debugging support would require a major redesign of the compiler and run-time system if any better performance is to be achieved. Furthermore, the garbage collector already imposes some constraints on the optimizer, such as the requirement that live registers may not contain derived pointers (pointers into the middle of objects). In many cases, the optimizations inhibited by garbage collection are very similar to those inhibited by debugging requirements, such as dead store elimination and some forms of common subexpression elimination [Cha87]. Thus, it would be difficult to separate the impact of garbage collection on optimization from the impact of full source-level debugging.

However, we have measured some effects of source-level debugging in the SELF system. To determine the impact of debugger-visible names, the compiler was changed to release registers allocated to dead variables even if they were visible at an interrupt point. The performance improvement with the changed compiler was insignificant (less than 2%) for a wide range of programs [Cha92]. That is, the extension of variable lifetimes needed to support debugging seems to incur virtually no cost in our system. (One reason for this might be that SELF methods are typically very short, so that few variables are unused in significant portions of their scope.)

The system currently detects interrupts by testing a special register; each test takes two cycles on a SPARC. This polling slows down typical programs by about 4%; some numerical programs with very tight loops are slowed down by up to 13% [Cha92]. With a more complicated run-time system using conditional traps, the overhead could be reduced to one cycle per check, and loop unrolling could further reduce the problem for tight loops. Alternatively, we could switch to a non-polling system where the interrupt handler would patch the code of the currently executing procedure to cause a process switch at the next interrupt point.

While we could not measure the full performance impact of our debugging scheme, inspection of the generated code indicated no obvious debugging-related inefficiencies. In fact, the current SELF system has attained excellent performance, executing a set of benchmarks four to six times faster than ParcPlace Smalltalk-80[†] and about half the speed of optimized C [CU91].

7.3 Memory usage

The debugging and dependency information for compiled methods is kept in virtual memory in the current SELF system. Table 1 shows the memory usage of the various parts of compiled methods relative to the space used by the machine instructions. For example, the physical-to-virtual PC mapping is about 17% the size of the actual machine code. The column labelled "adaptive" represents the default configuration where only often-used methods are optimized, while the "optimized only" column represents a system which always optimizes. The data were obtained from two interactive sessions using the prototype SELF user interface (written in SELF). Both runs represent more than 7 Mbytes of compiler-generated data.

The space consumption can be split into three main groups. The first group contains the method headers and the machine instructions; together, these represent all the information needed to actually execute programs. The second group contains the dependency links needed to invalidate compiled code after programming changes (see section 4). The third group contains all debugging-related information: the scope descriptors and the PC mapping (see section 3.1), relocation information for the garbage collector (to update object pointers contained in the debugging information), and the various objects representing the methods, message name strings, and object literals corresponding to the compiled code. This includes all information needed to recompile methods but not the source code itself.[‡]

[†] Smalltalk-80 is a trademark of ParcPlace Systems.

The space consumed by debugging information varies with the degree of optimization. Optimized methods show a higher relative space overhead than unoptimized methods because the debugging information for an inlined method is typically larger than the inline-expanded code. Therefore, the debugging information grows faster with more aggressive inlining than the compiled code.

The total space overhead for debugging is reasonable. In the standard system, debugging information uses slightly more space (122%) than the instructions themselves; in the system that optimizes everything, the overhead is 233%. In other words, adding the debugging information increases space usage (excluding the dependencies) by a factor of between 2.2 and 3.3.

In order to be conservative, we have left out the space used by the method headers even though they would also be needed in a system without debugging. (The headers contain the lookup key and various control information.) If we include the headers, debugging increases space usage by a factor of between 1.8 and 2.6.

The cost of supporting changes to running programs is smaller. The dependency information occupies between 0.9 and 1.6 times the size of the instructions. Furthermore, the

[‡] This grouping is a slight simplification. For example, the compiler occasionally generates instructions just to support debugging. Also, a small portion of the relocation information can be attributed to the code rather than the debugging information. However, these simplifications do not significantly distort the numbers presented here.

<table>
<tr><th colspan="2">Category</th><th>adaptive (default)</th><th>optimized only</th></tr>
<tr><td>Machine instructions</td><td rowspan="2">actual machine instructions and control information</td><td>1.00</td><td>1.00</td></tr>
<tr><td>Method headers</td><td>0.56</td><td>0.43</td></tr>
<tr><td>Dependency links</td><td>to invalidate code after programming changes</td><td>0.92</td><td>1.69</td></tr>
<tr><td>Scope descriptors</td><td rowspan="4">to recreate the source-level state of optimized code and to recompile methods</td><td>0.42</td><td>1.09</td></tr>
<tr><td>Physical-to-virtual PC mapping</td><td>0.17</td><td>0.17</td></tr>
<tr><td>Relocation information for GC</td><td>0.24</td><td>0.39</td></tr>
<tr><td>Method objects, strings, etc.</td><td>0.39</td><td>0.69</td></tr>
</table>

Table 1: Space cost of debugging information (relative to instructions)

current representation of the dependencies contains significant redundancies. An alternate implementation could probably reduce the space usage significantly [Cha92].

As a rough comparison, when compiling the SELF virtual machine, a standard commercial C++ 2.1 compiler generated 55 Mbytes of debugging information on top of an executable of 2.4 Mbytes, incurring an overhead of a factor of 24. Apparently, the compiler produced multiple copies of identical debugging information, one copy per object file, and the linker included them all in the executable file. Using the GNU C++ compiler and GNU-specific pragmas, we were able to reduce the space overhead of debugging information to 11.2 Mbytes, for a factor of 5.7.[†] While this comparison should be taken with a grain of salt, it indicates that despite the increased functionality, the space overhead of debugging in our system is probably comparable to other systems.

During the design and implementation of our current data structures, simplicity was considered more important than space efficiency, and we did not optimize our representation much. For example, our method headers and scope representations use 32-bit words in many places where 16 or even 8 bits would suffice. A reorganization of these data structures could therefore result in significant savings. Other techniques such as generating the debugging information on demand by re-executing the optimizing compilation could save even more space at the expense of longer pauses during debugging interactions.

Furthermore, little of the debugging information needs to remain in main memory at all times, and much of it can be paged out. Ultimately, only the machine instructions need be in main memory for working, debugged programs, thus keeping real memory costs down to a fraction of the total virtual memory costs.

8. Related work

The Smalltalk-80 system described by Deutsch and Schiffman [DS84] pioneered the use of dynamic compilation and interrupt points. To hide the effects of compilation to native code, compiled methods included a mapping from compiled code to source position. Activations normally were created on the stack for run-time efficiency but were converted on demand to the full-fledged activation objects required by the language definition, and converted back when needed for execution. As in our system, interrupts were delayed until the next call or backward branch. Since the compiler performed no global optimizations, the system could provide expected behavior without deoptimization.

Zurawski and Johnson [ZJ91] describe a model for a debugger (developed concurrently with this work) which closely resembles ours, using "inspection points" and dynamic deoptimization to provide expected behavior for optimized code. However, the system does not use lazy conversion. Furthermore, their definition of inspection points allows asynchronous events such as user interrupts to be delayed arbitrarily. Some of their ideas were implemented for the Typed Smalltalk compiler [JGZ88], but the system apparently could only run very small programs and was not used in practice, unlike our system which is in daily use.

Most of the other work on debugging optimized code places the priority on optimization; the goal was to get as much debugging as possible while preserving code efficiency [CMR88, SW78]. Hennessy [Hen82] addresses the problem of recovering the values of variables in the presence of selected local and global code reordering optimizations. His algorithms can usually detect when a variable has an incorrect value (in terms of the source program) and can sometimes reconstruct the source-level value. In contrast, we are not willing to accept any debugging failures and therefore do not perform optimizations which would create such situations at an interrupt point.

Zellweger [Zel83, Zel84] describes an interactive source-level debugger for Cedar which handles two optimizations, procedure inlining and cross-jumping, to provide expected behavior in most cases. While her techniques can always recover the source-level values of variables, they cannot hide certain code location problems; for example, single-stepping through optimized code would be difficult. Since our system uses unoptimized code in these situations, we are able to circumvent these problems.

LOIPE [Fei83] uses transparent incremental recompilation for debugging purposes. For example, when the user sets a breakpoint in some procedure, this procedure is converted to unoptimized form to make debugging easier. However, LOIPE cannot perform such transformations on active procedures. Thus, if the program is suspended in an optimized procedure, it is generally not possible to set a breakpoint in this procedure or to continue execution by single-stepping. To mitigate this problem, users were able to specify the amount of optimization to be performed (possibly impacting debuggability) and the amount of debugging transparency needed (possibly affecting code quality). As far as we know, most of the support for optimized code in LOIPE was not actually implemented.

[†] GNU C++ allows the source-level debugging of optimized code but offers only restricted functionality. Many optimizations are not transparent to the programmer. The compiler version used for the measurements was GCC 1.94.7; version 2.0 generates a significantly larger executable.

Tolmach and Appel [TA90] describe a debugger for ML where the compiler always performs optimizations, but where the program is automatically annotated with debugging statements before compilation. To debug an optimized program, the programmer has to manually recompile and re-execute the program. Like unoptimized programs, annotated programs run significantly slower than fully optimized programs.

9. Conclusions

Global optimization need not impair source-level debugging. The SELF system increases programmer productivity by providing full source-level debugging of globally optimized code. To the best of our knowledge, SELF is the first system to do so; other systems either compromise on debugging functionality or severely restrict the kinds of optimizations that can be performed. In SELF, the compiler can perform optimizations such as constant folding, common subexpression elimination, dead code elimination, procedure integration, code motion, and instruction scheduling without affecting debuggability.

Two techniques make this possible: *lazy deoptimization* and *interrupt points*. The optimizations performed by the compiler are hidden from the debugger by deoptimizing code whenever necessary. Deoptimization supports single-stepping, running a method to completion, replacing an inlined method, and other operations, but only affects the procedure activations which are actively being debugged; all other code runs at full speed. Debugging information is only needed at relatively widely-spaced interrupt points, so that the compiler can perform extensive optimizations between interrupt points without affecting debuggability. Our debugging techniques is not specific to SELF and could be applied to other programming languages as well.

Acknowledgments: We wish to thank Ole Agesen, Lars Bak, Bay-Wei Chang, Peter Deutsch, David Keppel, and John Maloney for their valuable comments on earlier drafts of this paper.

References

[Cha87] David Chase. *Garbage Collection and Other Optimizations*. Ph.D. dissertation, Computer Science Department, Rice University, 1987.

[Cha92] Craig Chambers. *The Design and Implementation of the SELF Compiler, an Optimizing Compiler for Object-Oriented Programming Languages*. Ph.D. dissertation, Computer Science Department, Stanford University. March 1992.

[CMR88] Deborah S. Coutant, Sue Meloy, and Michelle Ruscetta. DOC: A Practical Approach to Source-Level Debugging of Globally Optimized Code. In *Proceedings of the SIGPLAN '88 Conference on Programming Language Design and Implementation*, pp. 125-134.

[CUL89] Craig Chambers, David Ungar, and Elgin Lee. An Efficient Implementation of SELF, a Dynamically-Typed Object-Oriented Language Based on Prototypes. In *OOPSLA '89 Conference Proceedings*, pp. 49-70, New Orleans, LA, October, 1989. Published as *SIGPLAN Notices 24(10)*, October, 1989. Also published in *Lisp and Symbolic Computation 4(3)*, Kluwer Academic Publishers, June, 1991.

[CU90] Craig Chambers and David Ungar. Iterative Type Analysis and Extended Message Splitting: Optimizing Dynamically-Typed Object-Oriented Programs. In *Proceedings of the SIGPLAN '90 Conference on Programming Language Design and Implementation*, pp. 150-164, White Plains, NY, June, 1990. Published as *SIGPLAN Notices 25(6)*, June, 1990. Also published in *Lisp and Symbolic Computation 4(3)*, Kluwer Academic Publishers, June, 1991.

[CU91] Craig Chambers and David Ungar. Making Pure Object-Oriented Languages Practical. In *OOPSLA '91 Conference Proceedings*, pp. 1-15, Phoenix, AZ, October, 1991. Published as *SIGPLAN Notices 26(11)*, November, 1991.

[DS84] L. Peter Deutsch and Allan M. Schiffman. Efficient Implementation of the Smalltalk-80 System. In *Conference Record of the Eleventh Annual ACM Symposium on Principles of Programming Languages*, pp. 297-302, Salt Lake City, UT, January, 1984.

[Fei83] Peter H. Feiler. *A Language-Oriented Interactive Programming Environment Based on Compilation Technology*. Ph.D. dissertation, Carnegie-Mellon University, 1983.

[HCU91] Urs Hölzle, Craig Chambers, and David Ungar. Optimizing Dynamically-Typed Object-Oriented Programming Languages with Polymorphic Inline Caches. In *ECOOP '91 Conference Proceedings*, pp. 21-38, Geneva, Switzerland, July, 1991. Published as Springer Verlag LNCS 512, 1991.

[Hen82] John L. Hennessy. Symbolic Debugging of Optimized Code. *ACM Transactions of Programming Languages and Systems 4(3)*, July 1982.

[JGZ88] Ralph E. Johnson, Justin O. Graver, and Lawrence W. Zurawski. TS: An Optimizing Compiler for Smalltalk. In *OOPSLA '88 Conference Proceedings*, pp. 18-26, San Diego, CA, October, 1988. Published as *SIGPLAN Notices 23(11)*, November, 1988.

[SW78] H. Schlaeppi and H. Warren. Design of the FDS Interactive Debugging System. IBM Research Report RC7214, IBM Yorktown Heights, July 1978.

[TA90] Andrew P. Tolmach and Andrew W. Appel. Debugging Standard ML Without Reverse Engineering. In *Proceedings of the 1990 ACM Conference on Lisp and Functional Programming*, Nice, France, June 1990, pp. 1-12.

[US87] David Ungar and Randall B. Smith. SELF: The Power of Simplicity. In *OOPSLA '87 Conference Proceedings*, pp. 227-241, Orlando, FL, October, 1987. Published as *SIGPLAN Notices 22(12)*, December, 1987. Also published in *Lisp and Symbolic Computation 4(3)*, Kluwer Academic Publishers, June, 1991.

[Zel83] Polle T. Zellweger. *An Interactive High-Level Debugger for Control-Flow Optimized Programs*. Xerox PARC Technical Report CSL-83-1, January 1983.

[Zel84] Polle T. Zellweger. *Interactive Source-Level Debugging of Optimized Programs*. Ph.D. dissertation, Computer Science Department, University of California, Berkeley, 1984. Also published as Xerox PARC Technical Report CSL-84-5, May 1984.

[ZJ91] Lawrence W. Zurawski and Ralph E. Johnson. *Debugging Optimized Code With Expected Behavior*. Unpublished manuscript, 1991.

The Design and Implementation of HoME

Kazuhiro Ogata, Satoshi Kurihara, Mikio Inari and Norihisa Doi

Department of Computer Science
Graduate School of Science and Technology
Keio University
3-14-1 Hiyoshi, Kohoku-ku, Yokohama 223 Japan
+81-45-561-2739
{ogata, kurihara, inari, doi}@doi.cs.keio.ac.jp

Abstract

HoME is a version of Smalltalk which can be efficiently executed on a multiprocessor and can be executed in parallel by combining a Smalltalk process with a Mach thread and executing the process on the thread. HoME is nearly the same as ordinary Smalltalk except that multiple processes may execute in parallel. Thus, almost all applications running on ordinary Smalltalk can be executed on HoME without changes in their code.

HoME was designed and implemented based on the following fundamental policies: (1) theoretically, an infinite number of processes can become active; (2) the moment a process is scheduled, it becomes active; (3) no process switching occurs; (4) HoME is equivalent to ordinary Smalltalk except for the previous three policies.

The performance of the current implementation of HoME running on OMRON LUNA-88K, which had four processors, was measured by benchmarks which execute in parallel with multiple processes. In all benchmarks, the results showed that HoME's performance is much better than HPS on the same workstation.

1 Introduction

Smalltalk [8] is not only an object-oriented programming language, but also a graphical, interactive programming environment. The concept of object-oriented programming is very useful in developing software. It is well known that developing software in the Smalltalk environment can increase its productivity. In ParcPlace Smalltalk-80[1] Version 2.5 and Release 4, which are both generally called HPS, the CPU directly executes the machine-code by translating byte-code into machine-code (n-code) during execution [6], resulting in high performance.

Although processor technology, including processing speed, has been making steady advances, it seems difficult to make a far reaching improvement in the speed of a single processor due to physical limitations. Such a far reaching improvement has been attempted by connecting multiple processors and load balancing, that is, making a workstation into a multiprocessor. Multiprocessor workstations have already appeared in the marketplace. Operating systems in which multiprocessor workstations can be efficiently used have been developed. Typical multiprocessor operating systems are Mach [18] developed at CMU, and the V distributed operating system [4] developed at Stanford university.

In this paper, the design and implementation of a version of Smalltalk, called HoME (HPS on Mach Environment) [13], which can be efficiently executed on a multiprocessor are described. The multiprocessor used is the shared-memory multiprocessor OMRON LUNA-88K. Mach is used as the underlying operating system and the HPS of Smalltalk-80 Version 2.5 is used as the base Smalltalk. It is necessary to introduce concurrency into Smalltalk so that Smalltalk can be efficiently executed on a multiprocessor. The class Process is provided as the framework of concurrent programming in Smalltalk. An instance of the class Process, or a process, is the basic unit of execution in Smalltalk. The concept *light-weight process* denotes multiple threads of control within a single ordinary process. In Mach, light-weight processes are called threads and the Mach kernel adopts threads as units of scheduling. Units of concurrent execution are threads and multiple threads may execute in parallel on a multiprocessor. Since a Smalltalk process closely resembles a light-weight process, it can be combined with a Mach thread, and concurrent execution is realized by having the thread exe-

[1] Smalltalk-80 is a trademark of ParcPlace Systems.

ACM SIGPLAN '92 PLDI-6/92/CA
© 1992 ACM 0-89791-476-7/92/0006/0044...$1.50

cute the process.

HoME is nearly the same as ordinary Smalltalk except that multiple processes may execute in parallel. Thus, almost all applications running on ordinary Smalltalk can be executed on HoME without changes in their code.

Section 2 briefly describes concurrent programming in Smalltalk. In section 3, four fundamental design policies for HoME are given and their meanings are stated. In section 4, the implementation details are explained: namely, synchronization between threads, management of regions for n-code, garbage collection, modified and newly added methods and so on. Section 5 shows performance measurements of the current implementation of HoME running on OMRON LUNA-88K and compares them with those of HPS on the same workstation. Section 6 discusses work related to this research and compare HoME with other concurrent Smalltalk. Concurrent programming in HoME is discussed in section 7. Section 8 states the future work and lastly the conclusions are stated.

2 Concurrent Programming in Smalltalk

The classes Process and Semaphore can be used to program concurrency in Smalltalk [7]. In this section these classes are explained and a simple program is illustrated.

2.1 Class Process

In Smalltalk, the class which represents independent threads of control is Process. Processes are created by sending a *fork*, *forkAt:*, *newProcess* or *newProcessWith:* message to a block expression (which is enclosed by '[' and ']'). A process created by *fork* or *forkAt:* is placed in a scheduled state, while one created by *newProcess* or *newProcessWith:* is placed in a suspended state. A suspended process is scheduled by sending it a *resume* message.

There is only one process which can actually execute at a given time, and it is said to be active. *Processor*, which is the only instance of the class ProcessorScheduler, is used to select one of the scheduled processes and make it active. An FCFS (First-Come-First-Serve) ready queue with priorities is used for selecting an active process. More precisely, a multi-queue scheduling algorithm which uses an FCFS ready queue for each priority is adopted. That is, the higher the priority of a process, and the longer it has waited for a processor, the sooner it becomes active. Once a process becomes active, it stays active unless a process with higher priority is scheduled or it yields the processor itself. When a process with higher priority than an active process is scheduled, the newly scheduled process preempts the processor.

2.2 Class Semaphore

The class Semaphore is used for synchronizing multiple processes. A semaphore is created by sending a *new* or *forMutualExclusion* message to the class Semaphore. A semaphore created by *new* has 0 as its semaphore value, and one created by *forMutualExclusion* has 1. The P-operation is performed by sending a *wait* message to a semaphore and the V-operation is done by sending a *signal* message. Since a semaphore is a counting semaphore whose value is a non-negative integer, when a V-operation is performed before a P-operation, the semaphore value is recorded.

When a *wait* message is sent to a semaphore, if the semaphore value is positive, the value is simply decremented. If the value is zero, a process executing the *wait* method, the active process, is appended to the tail of the semaphore queue and an appropriate process among the scheduled processes is made active. When a *signal* message is sent to a semaphore, if the semaphore queue is empty, the semaphore value is simply incremented. If the queue contains one or more processes, the process with the highest priority and the longest waiting time in the queue is dequeued and is scheduled.

2.3 Example

A program which creates two processes, where one prints the string "DOG" 20 times and the other prints the string "CAT" 20 times, is as follows:

```
| lock |
lock ← Semaphore forMutualExclusion.
[20 timesRepeat: [
     lock wait.
     Transcript show: ' DOG '.
     lock signal. ]] fork.
[20 timesRepeat: [
     lock wait.
     Transcript show: ' CAT '.
     lock signal. ]] fork
```

3 Design Policy

HoME was designed and implemented based on the following fundamental policies:

1. Theoretically, an infinite number of processes can become active.
2. The moment a process is scheduled, it becomes active.
3. No process switching occurs.

4. HoME is equivalent to ordinary Smalltalk except for the three policies described above.

The first policy implies that a great number of processes can run in parallel, and there is no limit to the number of processes. Only one process can actually execute at one time in ordinary Smalltalk, while the number of processes actually executing at one time is unlimited in HoME.

In ordinary Smalltalk, when a suspended process is sent a *resume* message, it may not start executing immediately. The process is usually placed in a scheduled state. The scheduled and active states are different states in ordinary Smalltalk. On the other hand, in HoME, the scheduled and active states denote the same state. As soon as a suspended process is sent a *resume* message, it can start executing independently and concurrently with other running processes. From the first and second policies, no concept of priority of processes exists. All processes, such as those for managing inputs from a keyboard and a mouse, for monitoring real time, for monitoring a region for objects in the virtual machine (object memory), and those that users create by sending a *fork*, *forkAt:*, *newProcess* or *newProcessWith:* message to block expressions, are treated equally.

The execution of a process will not be stopped as the result of scheduling a new process. In short, process switching does not occur. Once a process is scheduled, it cannot yield the processor until it terminates.

HoME is equivalent to ordinary Smalltalk except that multiple processes can actually execute concurrently. A process starts immediately executing when scheduled, and process switching does not occur. That is, almost all applications developed on ordinary Smalltalk can be executed on HoME without changes in their code, and if the application can be executed in parallel with multiple processes, it can be done more quickly than on ordinary Smalltalk.

Concurrent execution in HoME is realized by having a Mach thread execute a Smalltalk process. As Mach threads can be thought of as processors and theoretically an infinite number of threads can be created and execute in parallel, an infinite number of processors can be thought to exist in HoME. Since an infinite number of processes can run simultaneously, the moment a process is scheduled, it can start executing and there is no need for process switching.

4 Implementation

This section describes the techniques used in the implementation of HoME.

4.1 Spinlocking

As OMRON LUNA-88K is a shared-memory multiprocessor workstation, and the regions to be protected – critical sections – are relatively small, synchronization between threads is done by using busy-waiting spinlocking. OMRON LUNA-88K uses an MC88100 RISC microprocessor as its CPU. In MC88100, there is an indivisible exchange instruction (xmem) for implementing spinlocking [11]. Various queue-based spinlocking methods [1][9] were implemented on OMRON LUNA-88K, but none showed good performance. It has been reported that simply by introducing delay, the simple *test & set* spinlocking could improve in performance [1]. In multiprocessors where the coherency of the cache is guaranteed, the cached value can be tested. Rather than executing the *test & set* instruction each time, it can be executed only when the test of the cached value succeeds. This type of spinlocking is called a *test, test & set* spinlocking. MC88100 adopts the snoop cache for maintaining the coherency of the cache. In LUNA-88K, the *test, test & set* spinlocking showed better performance than the simple *test & set* spinlocking. Therefore, we used the *test, test & set* spinlocking with delay, which resulted in better performance than the *test & set* with delay.

4.2 Region for N-code

High performance is achieved in HPS by dynamically translating byte-code into machine-code (n-code) and having the CPU directly execute the machine-code. The region in which n-code is stored is allocated on heap as with object memory. As the size of the region is finite, if there is no space for storing newly translated n-code, an operation similar to garbage collection must be performed to make space. Since access to n-code occurs frequently, a cache is used to access n-code at high speed.

In HoME, because a region and a cache for n-code are given to each process, it is not necessary to synchronize threads executing processes when they access these resources. In other words, when n-code is written into a region, or a cache is read or written, it is not necessary to synchronize the threads. A thread executing a process can scavenge the region for n-code independently and concurrently with other processes when there is no space in the region to allocate n-code. The other processes can continue their private work independently and concurrently with the scavenging of the region.

If a region for n-code containing no n-code is given to a newly created process, this causes a decline in performance. This is because the high performance of HPS greatly depends on the reusability of a translated n-code. So, in HoME, when a process terminates, the region and the cache for n-code used by it are appended to the head of a list for unused regions without doing anything. The next time a new process is created, the region and the cache for n-code which are at the head of the list are removed and given to it. Since a new process can reuse an n-code which was translated by older processes, the overhead due to translation becomes low and the overall performance is improved.

4.3 Object Allocation

There is only one object memory, which is the region for allocating objects, and it is global to the system. In HPS, the automatic storage management uses Generation Scavenging, which is a stop-and-copy scheme. The allocation of an object using this scheme is quite fast – it amounts to little more than incrementing a pointer. So, object allocation is serialized by using spinlocking.

4.4 Garbage Collection

In HPS, two garbage collectors, the Generation Scavenging collector and the mark and sweep collector, are used. Garbage collection is ordinarily done only within the new space by using Generation Scavenging. When the old space becomes full, an overall garbage collection is done on the object memory by using the mark and sweep collector.

Since processes execute only sequentially in HPS, when a process starts collecting garbage, it does not need to be concerned about the other processes. In HoME, however, since multiple processes may be running simultaneously, garbage collection cannot be done in the same way. There is a special thread for executing Generation Scavenging, and it is different from the threads executing Smalltalk processes. This thread is usually suspended. When Generation Scavenging must be carried out, it starts by resuming the thread. The thread does the following:

1. When Generation Scavenging starts, all processes must be suspended, so it is necessary to suspend threads executing processes. Execution of a process, however, cannot be stopped at any given time because the instance variable *suspendedContext* of the process must contain a context which is the activation record used when the process starts executing again. Thus, the Generation Scavenging thread notifies all processes currently executing to suspend. Each process has a private flag in the virtual machine layer, and it is notified to suspend for Generation Scavenging by setting a bit in the flag. Processes can know if there is a need to suspend for Generation Scavenging by checking the flag periodically. It is possible to decide if a process is currently running by checking whether or not the thread executing the process is currently running. All threads executing the notified processes are registered in the array *suspendThreads.*

2. The Generation Scavenging thread checks whether there is a running process. If a process is still running and the thread executing the process is not registered in *suspendThreads,* the Generation Scavenging thread notifies the process to suspend and registers the thread executing it in *suspendThreads.* If the thread executing the process has already been registered in *suspendThreads,* the Generation Scavenging thread does nothing. The Generation Scavenging thread does so repeatedly until all processes are suspended.

3. After all processes are suspended, Generation Scavenging actually starts.

4. When Generation Scavenging is finished, only processes corresponding to the threads registered in *suspendThreads* and suspended for Generation Scavenging resume their processing. Not all processes notified to suspend for Generation Scavenging actually suspend because of it. This is because after a process is notified, it may suspend by executing the *suspend* method of the class Process or the *wait* method of the class Semaphore. The Generation Scavenging thread is suspended until the next scavenging.

Mark and sweep is done when the old space becomes full during Generation Scavenging or when users execute the *garbageCollect* method of the class SystemDictionary. There is no problem with the former because all processes are suspended. When the *garbageCollect* method is executed, the thread corresponding to the process executing the method plays a role similar to the Generation Scavenging thread described above. The thread has the same function as the Generation Scavenging thread except that it does not suspend the process corresponding to itself.

4.5 Stack

In Smalltalk, an activation record (context in Smalltalk terminology) is created whenever a message is sent. Most of the contexts are never referred to as objects during their lifetime, however, resulting in most of the contexts being allocated as frames on activation stacks in HPS. Contexts allocated on stacks are called "volatile contexts." When contexts are treated as objects, they are allocated in the object memory and are called "stable contexts." Contexts which are allocated on stacks, but have a header as an object, are called "hybrid contexts." Volatile contexts are converted to hybrid contexts when they are referred to as objects, for example, when a message is sent.

In HoME, each process manages stacks for allocating contexts suitable for execution (i.e., volatile contexts). A different stack for executing functions written in C, such as those for primitive methods, translating bytecode into n-code and so on, is also given to each process.

4.6 Input from Keyboard and Mouse

Input from a keyboard or a mouse is treated by using a UNIX[2] signal. Input from a keyboard or a mouse causes the SIGIO signal, so a signal handling routine is used. When SIGIO occurs, usually it is necessary to redraw windows, such as when moving and resizing a window or outputing characters from a keyboard.

If a thread executing a process is interrupted and redraws a window, the execution of the process is temporarily stopped. Therefore in HoME there is a special thread for treating signals so that an interrupted thread does not have to handle the interruption. So, all the signal handling routine has to do is to notify the thread of the SIGIO signal. The Mach system call msg_send() is used for notifying the thread of signals, and the system call msg_receive() for receiving the notification. This thread can handle signals other than SIGIO, for instance SIGALRM. The thread sends the *signal* message to the semaphore where the process handling input is queued when SIGIO occurs, and where the process monitoring real time is queued when SIGALRM occurs.

4.7 Request to Window Server

The X11 window system is used for the visual interface. The current version of the X11 window system cannot support concurrency with multiple threads. When multiple threads make requests to a window server simultaneously, since these requests are not processed atomically and the response of the window server for the requests are interleaved, a consistent result is not achieved. Thus, requests to a window server are serialized by using spinlocking.

4.8 Process Structure in the Virtual Machine Layer

The process structure in the virtual machine layer is defined by using C's structure. The structure contains the id number of the thread executing the process, pointers to the region and cache for n-code, a field for managing stacks that allocate volatile contexts, a pointer to the stack for executing C functions, and so on. The structure does not contain an object pointer to the process because the pointer may change whenever Generation Scavenging is performed. The process structure in the virtual machine layer can correspond to the process in the virtual image layer by using the id number of the thread executing the process. This is realized by adding a new instance variable containing the id number of the thread to the class Process. The structures are registered in the global hash table *HoMEPtable*.

[2]UNIX is a trademark of AT & T Bell Laboratories.

4.9 Method

The modified methods are as follows: the instance methods *resume* and *suspend* in the class Process, the instance methods *wait* and *signal* in the class Semaphore, and the instance methods *activeProcess* and *yield* in the class ProcessorScheduler. A new instance method *kill* is added to the class ProcessorScheduler and is used in the instance method *newProcess* in the class BlockClosure.

1. Process>>resume — When a *resume* message is sent to a process, and a thread and other resources (region and cache for n-code et al.) are not allocated to the process, then the resources (a process structure in the virtual machine layer) are allocated to it, the structure is registered in the *HoMEPTable*, and the process starts executing by executing the thread. If the resources are already allocated to the process, the process is resumed by resuming the thread. The existence of an allocated resource is determined by checking whether or not the structure corresponding to the process is already registered in the *HoMEPTable*.

2. Process>>suspend — When a *suspend* message is sent to a process, if the process receiving the message is the same process that actually carries out the *suspend* method, then the process is suspended by suspending the thread corresponding to it at that time. If the process receiving the message is different from the process actually executing the *suspend* method, the process executing the *suspend* method does not immediately suspend the thread corresponding to the process receiving the message. A thread corresponding to a process cannot be suspended at any given time because the instance variable *suspendedContext* of the process must contain the context being executed when the process is suspended. So, the process executing the *suspend* method notifies the process receiving the message to suspend. The notification is carried out in the same way as in Generation Scavenging. That is, a process is notified to suspend by setting a bit in its private flag. A process checks the flag periodically, and if the suspend bit is set, it suspends by suspending the thread corresponding to it.

3. Semaphore>>wait — When a *wait* message is sent to a semaphore, if the instance variable *excessSig-*

nals of the semaphore is positive, then *excessSignals* is decremented. If *excessSignals* is zero, the process executing the *wait* method is appended to the tail of the semaphore queue and the corresponding thread is suspended.

4. Semaphore>>signal — When a *signal* message is sent to a semaphore, if the semaphore queue is empty, then *excessSignals* is incremented. If the queue contains one or more processes, the head of the queue is dequeued and resumed by resuming the corresponding thread.

5. ProcessorScheduler>>activeProcess — When an *activeProcess* message is sent to Processor, which is the only instance of the class ProcessorScheduler, in ordinary Smalltalk the value of the instance variable *activeProcess* is returned. Only one active process can exist at one time, and the instance variable *activeProcess* points to the active process. In HoME, the *activeProcess* method has been modified to return the process which executes it. So, this method is implemented as a primitive method, unlike ordinary Smalltalk.

6. ProcessorScheduler>>yield — In ordinary Smalltalk, the *yield* method is used so that the active process can give the other processes a chance to execute. In HoME, as all processes can run simultaneously, this method has been modified so as to do nothing.

7. ProcessorScheduler>>kill — This method has been added so that resources allocated to a process can be released. When a process executes this method, it releases its resources, that is, removes the structure in the virtual machine layer from the *HoMEPTable* and appends it to the head of the list for unused resources, and terminates itself by suspending the thread executing the process.

8. BlockClosure>>newProcess — In ordinary Smalltalk this method uses the *terminateActive* method in the class ProcessorScheduler for terminating an active process. In HoME, however, the *kill* method is used instead of the *terminateActive* method.

4.10 Modification in VI

A new instance variable *thread* is added to the class Process so that a process in the virtual image layer can correspond to the process structure in the virtual machine layer. The instance variable *thread* of a process contains the id number of the thread executing it. A hash table for registering scheduled processes (running processes) is represented by a newly added instance variable *hoMEProcessList* in the class ProcessorScheduler. In order to point to the next process in the *hoMEProcessList*, a new instance variable *nextProcess* is added to the class Process.

When the *activeProcess* message is sent to the Processor, the process executing the *activeProcess* method is returned. The following are carried out in the *activeProcess* method:

1. Get the id number of the thread executing the *activeProcess* method by using the Mach system call thread_self().

2. Find the process corresponding to the id number in the instance variable *hoMEProcessList* of the Processor, and return it.

The *wait* and *signal* method in the class Semaphore are critical sections since multiple processes may run simultaneously. If the methods are protected by a global lock variable, processes may wait even when there is no need to be mutually excluded. For example, suppose there are two different semaphores sem1 and sem2, and two different processes send the *wait* or *signal* messages to sem1 and sem2 respectively. One process must wait until the other process finishes executing the *wait* or *signal* method though there is no need for mutual exclusion. So, a private lock variable *semLock* is added to the class Semaphore as an instance variable to protect the semaphore itself. This can remove any unnecessary waiting.

The instance variables *activeProcess* and *quiescentProcessLists* in the class ProcessorScheduler are not used in HoME.

4.11 Snapshot and Booting

The snapshot is done in the same way as when the *garbageCollect* method in the class SystemDictionary is executed. That is, when the snapshot is taken, all processes excluding the process executing the snapshot are suspended. In ordinary Smalltalk, all scheduled processes are enqueued, according to their priority, to the ready queue in the instance variable *quiescentProcessLists* of the Processor, and an active process which is the process executing the snapshot is pointed to by the instance variable *activeProcess* of the Processor. So, when Smalltalk is booted, only the process pointed to by the *activeProcess* starts executing. In HoME, the *quiescentProcessLists* and the *activeProcess* are not used, and all scheduled (running) processes are registered in the instance variable *hoMEProcessList* in the Processor. So, when HoME is booted, all processes which are registered in the *hoMEProcessList* must start executing. Since a thread that executes a process may change after booting, the instance variable *thread* of all processes existing in object memory must be initialized.

5 Performance

This section describes the results of the performance of HoME currently running on OMRON LUNA-88K. The results of the performance of HPS on the same workstation are shown and compared with the results of HoME. The OMRON LUNA-88K which was used for the measurement carries four MC88100 RISC microprocessors and has a main memory of 64 megabytes. The size of the creation space and the region for n-code were both 1 megabyte in HPS and HoME.

5.1 Benchmark

The benchmarks used for the measurement of HoME's performance are the computation of factorial, Quicksort, Boyer theorem-proving, Multi Lisp interpreter, and fuzzy information retrieval system.

The algorithm for the computation of factorial was *odd-even divide & conquer factorial* [2]. Suppose a function f is defined as follow:

$$f(n,m) = \textbf{if } m \geq n \textbf{ then } n \\ \textbf{else } f(n,2m) * f(n-m,2m)$$

The factorial of n ($n!$) can be then computed by $n! = f(n,1)$. When computing factorial in parallel, a new process is forked in the topmost recursive call and it computes a subproduct. For example, when the factorial of n is computed in parallel by four processes, the four processes compute $f(n,4)$, $f(n-2,4)$, $f(n-1,4)$ and $f(n-3,4)$ respectively and the four subproducts are multiplied.

Quicksort is an algorithm which sorts by dividing a sorting partition into two subpartitions where one contains numbers less than a particular number and the other contains those not less than it. So, quick sort can also be done in parallel like the computation of factorial described above. The divided subpartitions may not be balanced very well depending on the dividing number and sorting may not be efficiently done in parallel by multiple processes. Thus, for balancing subpartitions the middle number of the first 10% of a sorting partition is found by *find*, and it is divided into two subpartitions by using that number.

Boyer theorem-proving is a modified version of the one which is used in [15] as MS's benchmark. In MS, a newly scheduled process does not start executing immediately when the number of running processes is the same as the number of replicated interpreters. In HoME, however, as a newly scheduled process starts executing immediately independently of other processes, HoME cannot efficiently execute the Boyer benchmark used in [15]. So, in HoME, the following decision was adopted: when a subproblem is to be processed, if the number of running processes is less than a certain number, a new process is forked and the subproblem is executed by it concurrently with other subproblems; if not, the subproblem is executed sequentially within the process in which it occurs.

The Multi Lisp interpreter is a Lisp interpreter which can evaluate Lisp expressions in parallel with multiple processes. The number of simultaneously running processes can be specified when evaluating Lisp expressions.

Fuzzy information retrieval is a modified version of the proposed method in [12]. In [12], fuzzy information retrieval is designed based on object-oriented concurrent languages, and the units of concurrent execution are objects. In HoME, fuzzy information retrieval is redesigned so that processes are units of concurrent execution and the number of running processes simultaneously is limited as in the Boyer benchmark.

5.2 Result

Table 1 shows the execution time for the benchmarks. Labels in table 1 are as follows:

Fact Computation of the factorial of 2000.

Sort Sort of a sequence of 100,000 real numbers by Quicksort.

Boyer Boyer theorem-proving benchmark used in [15].

Lisp Evaluation of the Fibonacci number 17 by Multi Lisp interpreter.

FIR Retrieval of documents by fuzzy information retrieval system where the depth of inference is 14.

The execution time was measured for the five benchmarks described above with a single process in HPS, and with 1, 2, 4, 8, 16, 32 and 64 processes in parallel in HoME. Executing with a single process means executing sequentially.

5.3 Evaluation

Table 2 shows the normalized execution time for benchmarks based on HPS. In the simple benchmarks **Fact** and **Sort**, overhead from introducing concurrency in HoME is not found. In the more complex benchmarks **Boyer**, **Lisp** and **FIR**, however, overhead is found – 8% to 30%. In every benchmark, the results of executing concurrently with multiple processes in HoME are better than HPS. In the complex benchmarks, however, when the number of processes is excessive, HoME is slower than HPS. In **Boyer**, the result of executing with 64 processes in HoME is five times slower than HPS. Since the amount of the work which a single process executes in **Boyer** is much smaller than in the other benchmarks, the overhead for creating processes

Number of Processes	1 HPS	1 HoME	2 HoME	4 HoME	8 HoME	16 HoME	32 HoME	64 HoME
Fact	36.50	36.52	24.35	22.16	22.10	22.12	22.15	22.22
Sort	52.08	52.10	31.10	21.41	21.18	20.58	20.87	21.20
Boyer	5.00	5.87	5.50	3.66	4.47	9.21	15.54	25.67
Lisp	72.05	77.83	59.11	52.26	64.06	76.92	78.92	82.93
FIR	276.63	359.17	230.41	186.88	179.36	219.61	291.62	336.89

Table 1: Execution time (in seconds) for benchmarks

Number of processes	1 HPS	1 HoME	2 HoME	4 HoME	8 HoME	16 HoME	32 HoME	64 HoME
Fact	1.00	1.00	0.67	0.61	0.61	0.61	0.61	0.61
Sort	1.00	1.00	0.60	0.41	0.41	0.40	0.40	0.41
Boyer	1.00	1.17	1.10	0.73	0.89	1.84	3.11	5.13
Lisp	1.00	1.08	0.82	0.73	0.89	1.07	1.10	1.15
FIR	1.00	1.30	0.83	0.68	0.65	0.79	1.05	1.22

Table 2: Normalized benchmark time based on HPS

becomes relatively large when the number of processes executing concurrently becomes large. The workstation OMRON LUNA-88K used in these evaluations had four CPUs. In **Fact**, **Sort** and **FIR**, a better result was achieved with more than four processes on four CPUs.

HoME's performance is much better than HPS if applications can be executed in parallel with multiple processes.

5.4 Generation Scavenging

In HoME, when Generation Scavenging starts, all running processes are suspended and Generation Scavenging is executed. The execution time for an application in a state where Generation Scavenging does not occur is compared with one in a normal state (where Generation Scavenging occurs) so that the rate of Generation Scavenging in executing the application can be examined. In order for Generation Scavenging not to occur, the size of creation space must be large. The size of creation space was enlarged from 1 to 30 megabytes so that Generation Scavenging would not occur during the execution of benchmarks.

The benchmarks used in the examination are as follows:

Lisp2 Evaluation of the Fibonacci number of 12 by Multi Lisp interpreter.

FIR2 Retrieval of documents by the fuzzy information retrieval system, where the depth of inference is 9.

Table 3 and 4 show the execution times for 30 megabytes of creation space size (no GS (in seconds)), the execution time for 1 megabyte of creation space size (with GS (in seconds)), the time exhausted for Generation Scavenging (GS time (in seconds)) and the rate of Generation Scavenging (GS rate) for **Lisp2** and **FIR2** respectively.

In both **Lisp2** and **FIR2**, the rate of Generation Scavenging shows the same tendency. When the benchmarks are executed sequentially (with a single process), the rate in which Generation Scavenging occurs in HoME is approximately the same as HPS. The rate of executing with a couple of processes is a little greater than executing with a single process in HoME, but the rates are little different. When executing more than four processes, the rate exhausted by Generation Scavenging is much larger than when executing with a single process. However, the rate of Generation Scavenging does not become very large when the number of processes becomes large. The rates exhausted by Generation Scavenging with 4, 8, 16, 32 and 64 processes are approximately same in both **Lisp2** and **FIR2**. The average is 16.99%. The difference between the rate of a single process (the average of **Lisp2** and **FIR2** with a single process in HoME: 3.41) and multiple processes is 13.58%, which is the rate of the overhead exhausted by suspending all running processes for Generation Scavenging. This means that suspending all running processes is not a big load when starting Generation Scavenging when a great number of processes are running.

Number of processes	1 HPS	1 HoME	2 HoME	4 HoME	8 HoME	16 HoME	32 HoME	64 HoME
No GS	6.21	6.92	4.91	4.33	4.37	5.54	5.84	6.78
With GS	6.38	7.10	5.06	4.97	5.33	6.89	7.03	8.21
GS time	0.17	0.18	0.15	0.64	0.96	1.35	1.19	1.43
GS rate(%)	2.66	2.54	2.96	12.88	18.01	19.59	16.93	17.42

Table 3: Rate of GS's overhead for **Lisp2**

Number of processes	1 HPS	1 HoME	2 HoME	4 HoME	8 HoME	16 HoME	32 HoME	64 HoME
No GS	6.39	7.40	4.83	3.59	3.57	3.78	4.30	6.25
With GS	6.65	7.73	5.09	4.31	4.38	4.49	5.21	7.49
GS time	0.26	0.33	0.26	0.72	0.81	0.71	0.91	1.24
GS rate(%)	3.91	4.27	5.11	16.71	18.49	15.81	17.47	16.56

Table 4: Rate of GS's overhead for **FIR2**

6 Related Work

Examples of Smalltalk which have introduced concurrency are MultiprocessorSmalltalk (MS) [14][15] and ConcurrentSmalltalk (CST) [21].

MS is an example of Smalltalk where processes (units of execution) execute in parallel like HoME, and it is a system which implements Berkeley Smalltalk [19] on the FireFly multiprocessor [17] with the V distributed operating system [4]. Berkeley Smalltalk is a type which unlike HPS interprets byte-code. In MS, concurrent execution is realized by replicating the interpreter and having the same number of interpreters as the number of physical processors. The ready queue for processes is not replicated. There is only one ready queue in MS. Each interpreter gets the next process to be executed from the queue, and interprets the byte-code corresponding to the process.

The Smalltalk used in HoME is a type which dynamically translates byte-code into machine-code during execution, and the CPU directly executes the code. In MS, concurrent execution is realized by replicating the interpreter. It is realized by executing a Smalltalk process on a Mach thread in HoME. The number of processes running simultaneously is dependent on the number of replicated interpreters in MS, in contrast with the number in HoME being unlimited. Table 5 shows a comparison of HoME with MS.

In MS, the interpreter is replicated up to the number of physical processors for efficiency of processing speed. This method does not seem to be suitable for all applications which are executed in parallel. For example, when **Fact**, **Sort** and **FIR** are executed in parallel by HoME on a multiprocessor, these are finished more quickly using more than 4 processes, than with 4 processes, without changing the number of physical processors.

In CST, concurrent execution is realized by providing concurrent constructs and atomic objects. Objects in CST unify the concepts of ordinary objects and processes, and are called concurrent objects. Synchronization between concurrent objects is done by atomic objects. Atomic objects execute only one message at a time. That is, when an atomic object is sent messages by more than one object simultaneously, the atomic object handles these messages one by one. Concurrent execution units in HoME are processes, in contrast with being objects in CST. CST is thus an object-oriented concurrent language [22]. HoME is just an object-oriented language in which processes can be executed in parallel. CST is implemented on a uniprocessor, not a multiprocessor.

Examples of Smalltalk which can be used on a distributed environment are [3] [5] [16]. These systems allow objects on different machines to be connected by a network for sending and responding to messages. We did not design HoME on the premise that HoME can be executed on a distributed environment.

7 Concurrent Programming in HoME

Section 2 discussed concurrent programming in Smalltalk and illustrated it with a simple example. When the program in 2.3 is executed in ordinary Smalltalk, the two processes do not run simultaneously. The process created second waits until the process created first terminates; in short, first DOG is printed 20 times and then CAT is printed 20 times. The *yield*

	MS	HoME
Base Smalltalk	a type which interprets byte-code	a type which dynamically translates byte-code into machine-code
Concurrent execution	replicating interpreters as the same number of CPU	executing a Smalltalk process with a Mach thread
Number of processes running simultaneously	the number of replicated interpreters	no limit of the number of running processes

Table 5: Comparison of MS with HoME

method in the class ProcessorScheduler needs to be used so that the processor is alternately allocated to multiple processes. When problems which include concurrency are programmed in Smalltalk, in addition to modeling units of concurrent execution in the problems as processes, it is necessary to consider where the *yield* method is to be used, but this is not the essence of the problem.

In HoME, since all processes can execute independently and concurrently with other processes, there is no need for such considerations. That is, the problem can be programmed simply by considering its essence. When the program in 2.3 is executed in HoME, because the two processes can run simultaneously, the strings DOG and CAT are printed in random order on the Transcript.

In ordinary Smalltalk, when writing concurrent programs, even if an object is shared by multiple processes, there are cases where it does not have to be protected with semaphores. For example, in program 2.3, Transcript is shared by two processes, but it does not have to be protected in ordinary Smalltalk. However, in HoME, since all processes execute in parallel, objects which are shared by multiple processes must be protected with semaphores.

8 Future Work

Class BitBlt has the role of drawing windows on a display in Smalltalk. Window display management in Smalltalk is very simple, as BitBlt just draws the whole window when the window is to be drawn or redrawn on a display. When multiple processes can execute concurrently as in HoME, multiple processes should be able to draw and redraw multiple windows simultaneously. In the window display management of Smalltalk, however, since BitBlt would draw and redraw all these windows simultaneously, this cannot be done consistently[3]. So, the window system must be redesigned or newly designed on the premise that multiple processes execute simultaneously. For example, a window display management method based on rectangles could be introduced into the window system in HoME. Also, the window control manager in Smalltalk is not designed on the premise that multiple processes access it simultaneously. So, the synchronization of multiple processes must be done when they access the resources of the window control manager, such as a list of controllers.

As the debugger in Smalltalk is not designed and implemented for supporting concurrent programming, a debugger based on parallel debugging techniques [10] or a newly designed debugger should be implemented for debugging concurrent programs easily.

In the present implementation of HoME, each process has a region for n-code, and an object memory is shared with all processes. We have nearly completed the design of sharing a region for n-code with all processes and Generation Scavenging when each process is given a new space. We plan to incorporate them into HoME in the near future.

9 Conclusion

The design and implementation of a version of Smalltalk (HoME) which can be efficiently executed on a multiprocessor were described. HoME can be executed in parallel by having processes as execution units. This is done by mapping a Smalltalk process onto a Mach thread and having the thread execute the process so that HoME can be executed efficiently on a multiprocessor. In all benchmarks measured, if an application is processed concurrently with multiple processes, HoME can finish the application more quickly than HPS.

From the implementation of HoME, the following can be concluded:

- The overhead for suspending all running processes for Generation Scavenging is acceptable.
- Some applications can be executed more efficiently with processes numbering more than the number of physical processors rather than processes whose number is the same as physical processors.

[3] In ParcPlace Smalltalk-80 Release 4, since a window in Smalltalk is represented as a window of X11, this may not happen.

- Since Smalltalk is designed and implemented on the premise that Smalltalk executes sequentially on uniprocessors, some systems in Smalltalk must be redesigned and newly designed when introducing concurrency into Smalltalk. Examples are the window system and the debugger.

10 Acknowledgments

The authors would like to thank OMRON Corporation for supporting this research. Kazuki Yasumatsu, Fusayuki Minamoto, and Mineharu Yokoyama of Fuji Xerox Co., Ltd. made useful suggestions.

References

[1] Thomas E. Anderson, The Performance of Spin Lock Alternatives for Shared-Memory Multiprocessors, IEEE Tran. on Parallel and Distributed Systems, Vol. 1, No. 1, 6-16, 1990.

[2] Hans Boehm, Odd-even divide & conquer factorial, Personal communication, March 1992.

[3] John K. Bennett, The Design and Implementation of Distributed Smalltalk, Proc. of OOPSLA'87, 318-330, 1987.

[4] David R. Cheriton, The V kernel: a software base for distributed systems, IEEE Software, 1 (2), April 1984.

[5] Dominique Decouchant, Design of a Distributed Object Manager for the Smalltalk-80 System, Proc. of OOPSLA'86, 444-452, 1986.

[6] Peter Deutch and Allan Schiffman, Efficient Implementation of the Smalltalk-80 System, Proc. of 11th ACM POPL, 297-302, 1984.

[7] Norihisa Doi and Kiyoshi Segawa, On the concurrent programming in Smalltalk-80, Advances in Software Science and Technology, Vol. 1, Academic Press, 187-207, 1989.

[8] Adele Goldberg and David Robson, *Smalltalk-80: The Language and its Implementation*, Addision-Wesley, 1983.

[9] John M. Mellor-Crummey and Michael L. Scott, Algorithms for Scalable Synchronization on Shared-Memory Multiprocessors, ACM Tran. on Computer Systems, Vol. 9, No. 1, 21-65, 1991.

[10] Charles E. McDowell and David P. Helmbold, Debugging Concurrent Programs, ACM Computing Surveys, Vol. 21, No. 4, 593-622, 1989

[11] Motorola, *MC88100 RISC MICROPROCESSOR USER'S MANUAL SECOND EDITION*, Prentice Hall, 1990.

[12] Kazuhiro Ogata and Norihisa Doi, Knowledge Representation and Inference –An Approach from Object-Oriented Computing and Fuzzy Theory–, Proc. of PRICAI'90, 729-734, 1990.

[13] Kazuhiro Ogata, Satoshi Kurihara, Mikio Inari and Norihisa Doi, HoME: Smalltalk on Mach Environment, Proc. of TOOLS Pacific'91, 153-161, 1991.

[14] Joseph Pallas and David Ungar, Multiprocessor Smalltalk: A Case Study of a Multiprocessor-Based Programming Environment, Proc. of SIGPLAN'88, 268-277, 1988.

[15] Joseph Pallas, *Multiprocessor Smalltalk: Implementation, Performance, and Analysis*, PhD thesis, Stanford Univ., 1989.

[16] Marcel Schelvis and Eddy Bledoeg, The Implementation of a Distributed Smalltalk, Proc. of ECOOP'88, 212-232, 1988.

[17] Charles P. Thacker and Lawrence C. Stewart, Firefly: a multiprocessor workstation, Proc. of APSLOS II, Computer Society Press of the IEEE, 164-172, October 1987.

[18] Avadis Tevanian, Jr. and Richard F. Rashid, MACH: A Basis for Future UNIX Development, CMU-CS-87-139, 1987.

[19] David M. Ungar and David A. Patterson, Berkeley Smalltalk: Who knows where the time goes?, In *Smalltalk-80: Bits of History, Words of Advice*, Glen Krasner (Ed), Addison-Wesley, 189-206, 1983.

[20] David Ungar, Generation Scavenging: a nondisruptive high performance storage reclamation algorithm, Software Engineering Symposium on Practical Software Development Environments, 157-167, 1984.

[21] Yasuhiko Yokote and Mario Tokoro, The Design and Implementation of ConcurrentSmalltalk, Proc. of OOPSLA'86, 331-340, 1986

[22] Akinori Yonezawa and Mario Tokoro, *Object-Oriented Concurrent Programming*, The MIT Press, 1987.

A Customizable Substrate for Concurrent Languages

Suresh Jagannathan Jim Philbin
NEC Research Institute
4 Independence Way
Princeton, NJ 08540
{suresh | philbin}>@research.nj.nec.com

Abstract

We describe an approach to implementing a wide-range of concurrency paradigms in high-level (symbolic) programming languages. The focus of our discussion is STING, a dialect of Scheme, that supports lightweight threads of control and virtual processors as first-class objects. Given the significant degree to which the behavior of these objects may be customized, we can easily express a variety of concurrency paradigms and linguistic structures within a common framework without loss of efficiency.

Unlike parallel systems that rely on operating system services for managing concurrency, STING implements concurrency management entirely in terms of Scheme objects and procedures. It, therefore, permits users to optimize the runtime behavior of their applications without requiring knowledge of the underlying runtime system.

This paper concentrates on (a) the implications of the design for building asynchronous concurrency structures, (b) organizing large-scale concurrent computations, and (c) implementing robust programming environments for symbolic computing.

1 Introduction

The growing interest in parallel computing has led to the creation of a number of parallel programming languages that define explicit high-level program and data structures for expressing concurrency. Parallel languages targeted for non-numerical application domains typically support (in varying degrees of efficiency) concurrency structures that realize dynamic lightweight process creation[13, 15] high-level synchronization primitives[28, 29], distributed data structures[6], and speculative concurrency[8, 25]. In effect, all these parallel languages may be viewed as consisting of two sublanguages – a coordination language responsible for managing and synchronizing the activities of a collection of processes, and a computation language responsible for manipulating data objects local to a given process.

ACM SIGPLAN '92 PLDI-6/92/CA

In this paper, we describe the implementation of a coordination substrate that permits the expression of a wide range of concurrency structures within the context of a symbolic computation language. Our intention is to define a general-purpose coordination model on top of which a number of specialized coordination languages can be efficiently implemented. We use Scheme[27] as our computation base. We emphasize, however, that the design of the substrate could be incorporated into any high-level symbolic programming language.

One obvious way of implementing a high-level parallel language is to build a dedicated (user-level) virtual machine. The virtual machine serves primarily as a substrate that implements the high-level concurrency primitives found in the coordination sublanguage. Given a coordination language L supporting concurrency primitive P, the role of L's virtual machine (L_P) is to handle all implementation aspects related to P; this often requires that the machine manage process scheduling, storage management, synchronization, etc. Because L_P is tailored only towards efficient implementation of P, however, it is often unsuitable for implementing significantly different concurrency primitives. Thus, to build a dialect of L with concurrency primitive P' usually requires either building a new virtual machine or expressing the semantics of P' using P. Both approaches have their obvious drawbacks: the first is costly to implement given the complexity of implementing a new virtual machine; the second is inefficient given the high-level semantics of P and L_P's restricted functionality.

Rather than building a dedicated virtual machine for implementing concurrency, a language implementation may use low-level operating system services[5, 30]. Process creation and scheduling is implemented by creating a heavy- or lightweight OS-managed thread of control; synchronization is handled using low-level OS-managed structures. These implementations tend to be more portable and extensible than systems built around a dedicated runtime system, but they necessarily sacrifice efficiency[2] since every (low-level) kernel call requires a context switch between the application and the operating system. Moreover, generic OS facilities perform little or no optimization at either compile time or runtime since they are usually insensitive to the semantics of the concurrency operators of interest.

The dialect of Scheme described here (called STING) includes a coordination language (implemented via a dedicated virtual machine) for expressing asynchronous lightweight concurrency that combines the best of both approaches. In contrast to other parallel Scheme systems[12, 13, 19] and parallel dialects of similar high-level languages[10, 28], the basic concurrency objects in STING (threads and virtual processors) are streamlined data structures with no complex synchronization or value transmission semantics. Unlike parallel systems that rely on OS services for managing concurrency, STING implements all concurrency management issues in terms of Scheme objects and procedures, permitting users to optimize the runtime behavior of their applications without requiring knowledge of underlying OS services. We argue that STING supports the features essential to creating and managing various forms of asynchronous parallelism within a conceptually unified, very general framework.

Our results show that it is possible to build an efficient substrate upon which various parallel dialects of high-level symbolic languages can be built. STING is not intended merely to be a vehicle that implements stand-alone short-lived programs, however. We envision this system as providing a framework for building a rich programming environment for parallel symbolic computing. In this regard, the system provides support for thread preemption, per-thread asynchronous garbage collection, exception handling across thread boundaries, and application dependent scheduling policies. In addition, it contains the necessary functionality to handle persistent long-lived objects, multiple address spaces and other features commonly associated with advanced programming environments.

This paper concentrates on the implications of the STING design for building asynchronous concurrency structures, organizing large-scale concurrent computations, and implementing robust programming environments. A detailed description of its implementation is given in [18]. The paper is structured as follows. In the next section, we give an overview of STING focusing primarily on the structure of the coordination model. Section 3 describes the thread and virtual processor abstractions. Section 4 describes the dynamics of thread execution and synchronization in the context of implementating of several well-known concurrency paradigms (*e.g.*, result-parallel (fine-grained) parallelism[3], master-slave computations[11], speculative concurrency, and barrier synchronization). We argue that despite obvious syntactic and methodological differences, these paradigms all impose common requirements on the underlying runtime system: they require throttling of dynamically generated processes, cheap synchronization, efficient storage management, and the ability to treat processes as *bona fide* data objects. Section 5 presents some performance figures, and comparison to related work is given in Section 6.

2 The Context

Four features of the STING design, when taken as a whole, distinguish the system from many other symbolic parallel languages:

1. *The Concurrency Abstraction:* Concurrency is expressed in STING is via a lightweight thread of control. A thread is a non-strict first-class data structure that superficially resembles the object created by a MultiLisp *future*[13], for example. We elaborate upon the differences in the following section.

2. *The Processor and Policy Abstractions:* Threads execute on a virtual processor (VP) that represents an abstraction of a physical computing device. There may be many more virtual processors than the actual physical processors available. Like threads, virtual processors are also first-class objects. A VP is closed over a policy manager that determines the scheduling and migration regime for the threads that it executes. Different VPs can be closed over different policy managers without incurring any performance penalty.

   A collection of virtual processors can be combined to form a virtual machine. A virtual machine is closed over an address space managed by its virtual processors. Multiple virtual machines can execute on a single physical machine consisting of a set of physical processors. Virtual machines are also denotable Scheme objects and may be manipulated as such.

3. *Storage Model:* A thread allocates data on a stack and heap that it manages exclusively. Thus, threads garbage collect their state independently of one another; no global synchronization is necessary in order for a thread to initiate a garbage collection. Data may be referenced across threads. Inter-area reference information maintained by areas is used to garbage collect objects across thread boundaries[4, 26]. Storage is managed via a generational scavenging collector[21, 32]; long-lived or persistent data allocated by a thread thread is accessible to other threads in the same virtual machine.

   The design is sensitive to storage locality concerns; for example, storage for running threads are cached on VPs and are recycled for immediate reuse when a thread terminates. Moreover, multiple threads may share the same dynamic context whenever data dependencies warrant.

4. *The Program Model:* STING permits exceptions to be handled across threads, supports non-blocking I/O, permits the scheduling of virtual processors on physical processors to be customizable in the same way that the scheduling of threads on a virtual processor is customizable, and provides an infra-structure for implementing multiple address spaces and long-lived shared persistent objects.

3 Threads and Virtual Processors

The computation sublanguage of STING is Scheme[27], a higher-order lexically scoped dialect of Lisp. The compiler used is a modified version of Orbit[20].

The main components in the coordination sublanguage of STING are lightweight threads of control and virtual processors. Threads are simple data structures that encapsulate local storage (*e.g.*, registers, stack and heap organized into areas), code, and relevant state information (*e.g.*, status, priorities, preemption bits, locks, etc.). They define a separate locus of control. The code associated with a thread is executed for effect, not value; thus, threads do not adhere to any particular synchronization protocol. The system imposes no constraints on the code encapsulated by a thread: any valid Scheme expression can be treated as a distinct process.

Each virtual processor (VP) is closed over a (1) a thread controller that implements a state transition function on threads, and (2) a policy manager that implements both a thread scheduling and thread migration policy. A VP is also closed over a set of registers and interrupt handlers. Most of the dedicated registers found in the VP are managed by Orbit; these include a register containing the return address of the current procedure, registers to hold the arguments to a procedure, and registers that refer to the top-of-stack and top-of-heap. Another register points to the currently executing thread. Besides various handlers and a policy manager, a VP also retains the identity of its virtual machine, and the physical processor on which it is executing.

Virtual processors are multiplexed on physical processors in the same way that threads are multiplexed on virtual processors; associated with each physical processor is a policy manager that dictates the scheduling of the virtual processors which execute on it.

3.1 Threads

Threads are first-class objects in STING. Thus, they may be passed as arguments to procedures, returned as results, and stored in data structures. Threads can outlive the objects that create them. A thread is closed over a thunk, a nullary procedure, that is applied when the thread executes. The value of the application is stored in the thread on completion.

The static component of a thread also contains state information on the thread's status. A thread can be either *delayed, scheduled, evaluating, stolen* or *determined.* A *delayed* thread will never be run unless the value of the thread is explicitly demanded. A *scheduled* thread is a thread scheduled to evaluate on some virtual processor but which has not yet started executing. An *evaluating* thread is a thread that has started running. A thread remains in this state until the application of its thunk yields a result. At this point, the thread's state is set to *determined.* Stolen threads are discussed in Section 4.1.

In addition to state information and the code to be evaluated, a thread also holds references to

1. other threads waiting for it to complete,
2. references to the thunk's dynamic and exception environment, and
3. genealogy information indicating the thread's parent, siblings, and children.

Dynamic and exception environments are used to implement fluid bindings and inter-process exceptions. Genealogy information serves as a useful debugging and profiling tool that allows applications to monitor the dynamic unfolding of a process tree.

Evaluating threads are associated with a dynamic context called a *thread control block* (TCB). Besides encapsulating thread storage (stacks and heaps), the TCB contains information about the current state of the active thread (*e.g.*, is the thread currently running on some VP, is it blocked, suspended, terminated, etc?), requested state transitions on this thread made by other threads, the current quantum for the thread, and the virtual processor on which the thread is running. TCBs hold some other information for implementing speculative and barrier synchronization that we discuss in Section 4.3.

The implementation of threads requires no alteration to the implementation of other primitive operations in the language. The synchronization semantics of a thread is a more general (albeit lower-level) form of the synchronization facility available via *e.g.*, MultiLisp's **"touch"**, Linda's tuple-space[7], or CML's **"sync"**[28]. The application completely control the condition under which blocked threads may be resumed. However, there is explicit system support for dataflow (*i.e.*, future-touch), nondeterministic choice, and constraint-based or barrier synchronization.

Users manipulate threads via a set of procedures (listed below) defined by a thread controller (TC) that implements synchronous state transitions on thread state. The TC is written entirely in Scheme with the exception of a few primitive operations to save and restore registers. The thread controller allocates no storage; thus, a TC call never triggers garbage collection. Besides these operations, a thread can enter the controller because of preemption.

`(fork-thread` *expr vp*`)` creates a thread to evaluate *expr*, and schedules it to run on *vp*.

`(create-thread` *expr*`)` creates a *delayed* thread that when demanded evaluates *expr*.

`(thread-run` *thread vp*`)` inserts a delayed, blocked or suspended *thread* into the ready queue of the policy manager for *vp*.

`(thread-wait` *thread*`)` causes the thread executing this operation to block until *thread*'s state becomes *determined.*

`(thread-value` *thread*`)` returns the value of the application associated with *thread.*

`(thread-block` *thread* `.` *blocker*`)` requests *thread* to block; *blocker* is the condition on which the thread is blocking.

`(thread-suspend` *thread* `.` *quantum*`)` requests *thread* to suspend execution. If the *quantum* argument is provided, the thread is resumed when the period specified has elapsed; otherwise, the thread is suspended indefinitely until it is explicitly resumed using `thread-run`.

`(thread-terminate` *thread* `.` *values*`)` requests *thread* to terminate with *values* as its result.[1]

[1] As in some other Scheme dialects, expressions can yield multiple values.

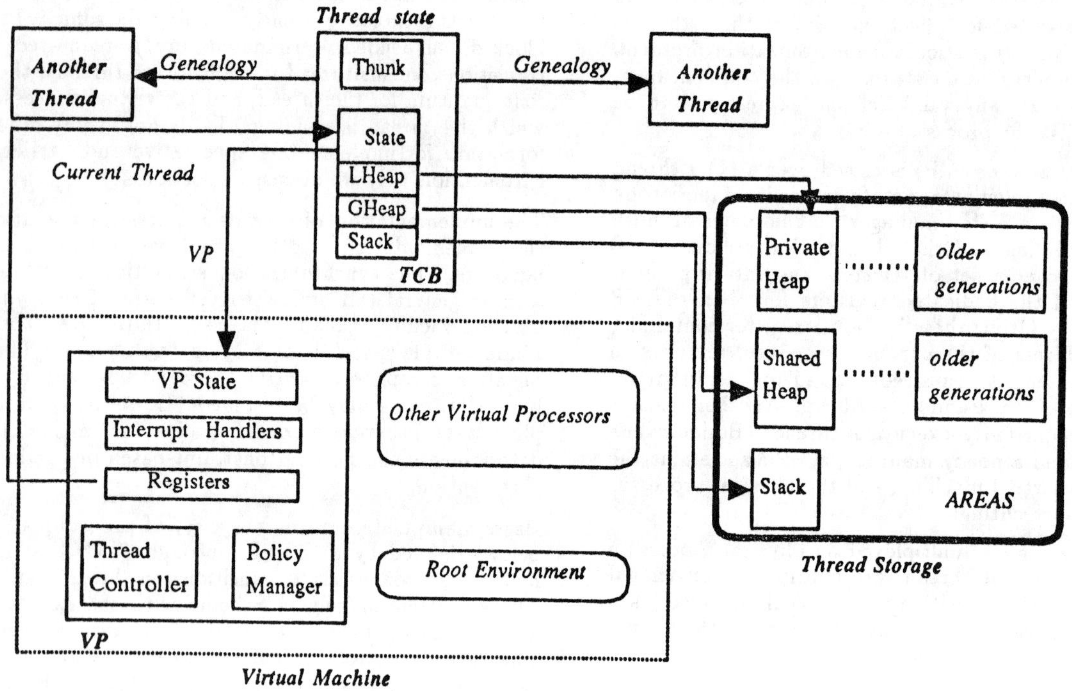

Figure 1: Threads and Virtual Processors

(yield-processor) causes the current thread to relinquish control of its VP. The thread is inserted into a suitable ready queue.

(current-thread) returns the thread executing this operation.

3.1.1 A Simple Example

To illustrate how users might program with threads, consider the program shown in Fig. 2 that defines a Sieve of Erasthosenes prime finder implementation.

Note that the definition makes no reference to any particular concurrency paradigm; such issues are abstracted by its op argument.

This implementation relies on a user-defined synchronizing stream abstraction that provides a blocking operation on stream access (hd) and an atomic operation for appending to the end of a stream (attach).

We can define various implementations of a prime number finder that exhibit different degrees of asynchronous behavior. For example,

```
(let ((filter-list (list)))
  (sieve (lambda (thunk)
           (set filter-list
                (cons (create-thread (thunk))
                      filter-list)))
         n))
```

```
(define (filter op n input)
  (let loop ((x (hd input))
             (output  (make-stream))
             (last? true))
    (cond ((zero? (mod x n))
           (loop (rest input)
                 output
                 last?))
          (last?
            (op (lambda ()
                  (filter op n output)))
            (loop (rest input)
                  (attach x output)
                  false))
          (else (loop (rest input)
                      (attach x output)
                      last?)))))

(define (sieve op n)
  (let ((input (make-integer-stream n)))
    (op (lambda ()
          (filter op 2 input)))))
```

Figure 2: An abstraction of a concurrent prime finder.

defines an implementation in which filters are generated lazily; once a demanded, a filter repeatedly removes elements off its input stream, and generates potential primes onto its output stream. To initiate a new filter scheduled on a VP using a round-robin thread placement discipline, we might write:

```
(thread-run
  (car filter-list)
  (mod (1+ (vm.vp-vector (current-vp).vm))
       n))
```

(Current-vp) returns the vp on which the expression is evaluated; ((current-vp).vm defines the virtual machine of which the current VP is a part. A virtual machine's public state includes a vector containing its virtual processors.

By slightly rewriting the above call to sieve, we can express a more lazy implementation:

```
(let ((filter-list (list)))
  (sieve (lambda (thunk)
           (set filter-list
                (cons (create-thread
                        (block
                          (map thread-unblock
                               filter-list)
                          (thunk)))
                      filter-list))
           (map thread-block filter-list))
         n))
```

In this definition, a filter that encounters a potential prime p, creates a lazy thread object L and requests all other filters in the chain to block. When L's value is demanded, it unblocks all the elements in the chain, and proceeds to filter all multiples of p on its input stream. This implementation throttles the extension of the sieve and the consumption of input based on demand.

We can also define an eager version of the sieve as follows:

```
(sieve
  (lambda (thunk)
    (fork-thread (thunk)))
  n)
```

Evaluating this application schedules a new thread responsible for filtering all multiples of a prime.

This simple exercise highlights some interesting points about the system. First, STING treats thread operations as ordinary procedures, and manipulates the objects referenced by them just as any other Scheme object; if two filters attached via a common stream are terminated, the storage occupied by the stream may be reclaimed. STING imposes no *a priori* synchronization protocol on thread access – application programs are expected to build abstractions that regulate the coordination of threads.

The threads created by `filter` maybe terminated in one of two ways. The top-level call to `sieve` may be structured so that it has an explicit handle on these threads; the `filter-list` data structure used to create a lazy sieve is such an example. One can then evaluate:

```
(map thread-terminate filter-list)
```

to terminate all threads found in the sieve. STING also provides *thread groups* as a means of gaining control over a related collection of threads[19]. A thread group is closed over debugging and thread operations that may be applied *en masse* to all of its members. Every thread has a thread group identifier that associates it with a given group. Thread groups provide operations analogous to ordinary thread operations (*e.g.*, termination, suspension, etc.) as well as operations for debugging and monitoring (*e.g.*, resetting, listing all threads in a given group, listing all groups, profiling genealogy information, etc..) Thus, when the thread T under which the call to `sieve` is terminated, users can request all of T's children (which are defined to be part of T's group to be terminated) thus:

```
(kill-group (thread.group T))
```

Second, lazy threads are distinguished from scheduled ones. A lazy thread defines a thread object closed over a thunk and dynamic state (but which is unknown to any virtual processor). A scheduled thread is also a lightweight data structure, but is known to some VP and will eventually be assigned a TCB. Applications can choose the degree of laziness (or eagerness) desired. Only the thread controller can initiate a thread transition to *evaluating* – the interface does not permit applications to insist that any specific thread immediately run on some virtual processor. All default policy managers implement a fair scheduling policy, but STING imposes no constraints on user-defined policy managers in this regard.

Third, threads can request state changes to other threads; the change itself takes place only when the target thread next makes a TC call (either synchronously or because of preemption). Requested state changes to a thread T made by another T' are recorded as part of T's next state in its TCB. State changes are recorded only if they do not violate the state transition semantics (*e.g.*, *evaluating* threads cannot be subsequently *scheduled*; *terminated threads* cannot become subsequently *blocked*, etc.), and the requesting thread has appropriate authority.

Only threads can actually effect a change to their own state. This invariant implies that a TCB can perform a state transition without acquiring locks.

3.2 Virtual Processors

Virtual processors (and by extension, virtual machines) are first-class objects in STING. According first-class status to VPs has several important implications that distinguish STING from other high-level thread systems[9, 10] or other asynchronous parallel languages. First, one can organize parallel computations by explicitly mapping processes onto specific virtual processors. For example, a process P known to communicate closely with Q should execute on a VP topologically near V. Such considerations can be expressed in STING since VPs can be directly enumerated. Systolic style programs for example can be expressed by using self-relative addressing off the current VP (*e.g.*, `left-VP`, `right-VP`, `up-VP`, etc.). The system provides a number of default addressing modes for many common topologies (*e.g.*, hypercubes, meshes, systolic arrays, etc.). Furthermore, since VPs can be mapped onto specific physical processors, the ability to manipulate virtual processors as first-class data values gives STING programmers a great deal of flexibility in expressing different parallel algorithms that are defined in terms of specific processor topologies[16].

More significantly, since VPs can be closed over different virtual policy managers, different groups of threads created by an application may be subject to different scheduling regimes. Virtual machines or VPs can be tailored to handle different scheduling protocols or policies. We discuss the implications of customizable schedulers in the following section.

3.3 The Policy Manager

The STING thread controller defines a thread state transition procedure, but does not define *a priori* scheduling or migration policies. These policies can be application dependent. Although several default policies are provided as part of the overall STING runtime environment, users are free to write their own. In fact, each virtual processor is closed over its own policy manager; thus, different VPs in a given virtual machine may implement different policies. The PM handles thread scheduling, processor/thread mapping, and thread migration.

The ability to partition an application into distinct scheduling groups is important for long-lived parallel (or interactive) programs. Threads executing I/O bound procedures have different scheduling requirements than those executing compute bound routines; applications with real-time constraints should be implemented using different scheduling protocols than those that require only a simple FIFO scheduling policy.

Tree-structured parallel programs may realize best runtime performance using a LIFO-based scheduler; applications running master/slave or worker farm algorithms may do better using a round-robin preemptive scheduler for fairness. Since all of these applications may be components of a larger program structure or environment, the flexibility afforded by having them evaluate with different policy managers is significant. Distinct applications can exist as independent executing threads evaluating on the same virtual machine. Moreover, each distinct scheduler is realized by a policy manager with different performance characteristics and implementation concerns.

Our design seeks to provide a flexible framework able to incorporate and experiment with different scheduling regimes transparently without requiring modification to the thread controller itself. To this end, all PMs provide the same interface although no constraints are imposed on the implementations themselves. The interface shown below provides operations for choosing a new thread to run, enqueuing an evaluating thread, setting thread priorities, and migrating threads. These procedures are expected to be used exclusively by the TC; in general, user applications need not be aware of the policy/thread manager interface.

`(pm-get-next-thread` *vp*`)` returns the next ready TCB or thread to run on *vp*. If a TCB is returned, its associated thread is *evaluating*; if a thread is returned, its state is not *evaluating*, and a new TCB must be allocated for it.

`(pm-enqueue-thread` *obj vp state*`)` enqueues *obj* which may be either a thread or a TCB into the ready queue of the policy manager associated with *vp*. The state argument indicates the state in which the the call to the procedure is made: *delayed*, *kernel-block*, *user-block*, or *suspended*.

`(pm-priority` *priority*`)` and `(pm-quantum` *quantum*`)` use their *priority* and *quantum* arguments as hints to establish a new priority and quantum for the currently executing thread.

`(pm-allocate-vp)` returns a new virtual processor on the current virtual machine.

`(pm-vp-idle` *vp*`)` is called by the thread manager if there are no evaluating threads on *vp*. This procedure can migrate a thread from another virtual processor, do bookkeeping information, or call the physical processor to have the processor switch itself to another VP.

Besides determining a scheduling order for evaluating threads, the PM implements two basic load-balancing decisions: (1) it may choose a VP on which a newly created thread should be run, and (2) it determines which threads on its VP can be migrated, and which threads it will choose for migration from other VPs.

The first decision point is important to handle initial load-balancing; the second is important to support dynamic load-balancing protocols. Determining the initial placement of a newly evaluating thread is often based on priorities different from those used to determine the migration of currently evaluating threads. The PM interface preserves this distinction.

Scheduling policies can be classified along several important dimensions:

Locality: Is there a single global queue of threads in this system, or does each PM maintain its own local queues?

Granularity: Are threads distinguished based on their current state or are all threads viewed as equals by the PM? For example, an application might choose an implementation in which all threads occupy a single queue regardless of their current state. Alternatively, it might choose to classify threads into different queues based on whether they are evaluating, scheduled, previously suspended etc.

Structure: Are the queues implemented as FIFO's, LIFO's, round-robin, priority, or realtime structures (among others)?

Serialization: What kind of locking structure does an application impose on various policy manager queues?

Choosing different alternatives in this classification scheme leads to different performance characteristics. For example, if we adopt a granularity structure that distinguishes evaluating threads (*i.e.*, threads with TCBs) from scheduled ones, and we impose the constraint that only scheduled threads can be migrated, then no locks are required to access the evaluating thread queue; this queue is local to the VP on which it was created. Queues holding scheduled and suspended threads however must be locked because they are targets for migration by PMs on other VPs. This kind of scheduling regimen is useful if dynamic load-balancing is not an issue. Thus, when there exist many long-lived non-blocking threads (of roughly equal duration), most VPs will be busy most of the time executing threads on their own local ready queue. Eliminating locks on this queue in such applications is therefore beneficial. On the other hand, applications that generate threads of varying duration may exhibit better performance when used with a policy manager that permits migration of both scheduled and evaluating threads even if there is an added cost associated with locking the runnable ready queue.

Global queues imply contention among policy managers whenever they need to execute a new thread, but such an implementation is useful in implementing many kinds of parallel algorithms. For example, in master/slave (or worker-farm) programs, the master initially creates a pool of threads; these threads are long-lived structures that do not spawn any new threads themselves. Once running on a VP, they rarely block. Thus, a PM executing such a thread has no need to support the overhead of maintaining a local thread queue. Local queues are useful, however, in implementing result-parallel programs in which the process structure takes the form of a tree or graph; these queues can be used in such applications to load balance threads fairly among a set of virtual processors.

4 The Dynamics of Thread Execution and Synchronization

Obvious differences exist in program methodology, syntax, etc. among the numerous proposals for incorporating concurrency structures into high-level symbolic programming languages. STING supports the functionality required by the semantics of many of these proposals: (a) threads may be dynamically instantiated and require runtime scheduling, (a) communication among threads takes place via concurrent data structures that may be shared by many readers and writers, (c) communicating threads execute within a single address space, and (d) threads synchronize either by waiting for values generated by other processes, or by waiting at explicit barrier points.

4.1 Support for Result (Fine-Grained) Parallelism

In a result parallel program, each concurrently executing process contributes to the value of a complex data structure (*e.g.*, an array or list). Process communication is via this result structure. Expressions that attempt to access a component of the result whose contributing process is still evaluating block until the process completes.

```
(define (primes limit)
  (let loop ((i 3)
             (primes (future (list 2))))
    (cond ((> i limit)
           (touch primes))
          (else
           (loop
             (+ i 2)
             (future
               (filter i primes)))))))

(define (filter n primes)
  (let loop ((j 3))
    (cond ((> (* j j) n)
           (cons n (touch primes)))
          ((zero? (mod n j)) primes)
          (else (loop (+ j 2))))))
```

Figure 3: An implementation of primes using futures. A future must be explicitly touched to access its value in this implementation.

Futures[13] are a good example of an operation well-suited for implementing result parallel algorithms. The object created by the MultiLisp or Mul-T expression, `(future` *E*`)`, creates a thread responsible for computing *E*; the object returned is known as a future. When *E* finishes, yielding *v* as its result, the future is said to be *determined.* An expression that *touches* a future either blocks if *E* is still being computed or yields *v* if the future is determined. Threads are a natural representation for futures.

To motivate the implementation of result parallelism in STING, Figure 3 is an implementation of a parallel prime number finder using futures.

In this program, a future is created for each odd element between 2 and `limit`. A number is added onto a current prime list if `filter` determines it to be a prime number. In a naive implementation, each instantiation of a future will entail the creation of a new thread; thus, the number of threads allocated in executing this program (under this implementation) is proportional to `limit`. This behavior is undesirable because a future computing the primality of i has an implicit dependence with the future created to compute the primality of $i-2$ and so on. Poor processor and storage utilization will results given the data dependencies found in this program. This is because many of the lightweight processes that are created will either:

1. need to block when they request the value of other yet-unevaluated futures or,
2. in the case of processes computing small primes, do a small amount of computation relative to the cost incurred in creating them.

Because the dynamic state of a thread consists of large objects (*e.g.*, stacks and heaps), cache and page locality is compromised if process blocking occurs frequently or if process granularity is too small.

The semantics of touch and future dictate that a future F which touches another future G must block on G if G is not yet determined. Assume T_F and T_G are the thread representation of F and G, respectively. The runtime dynamics of the touch operation on G can entail accessing T_G either when T_G is (a) delayed or scheduled, (b) evaluating, or (c) determined. In the latter case, no synchronization between these threads is necessary. Case (b) requires T_F to block until T_G completes. STING performs an important optimization for case (a), however, which we discuss below.

4.1.1 Thread Stealing

T_F can evaluate the closure encapsulated within T_G (call it E) using its own stack and heap, rather than blocking a forcing a context switch if T_G is delayed or scheduled. In effect, this implementation treats E as an ordinary procedure, and the touch of G as a simple procedure call; we say that T_F *steals* T_G in this case. The correctness of this optimization lies in the observation that that T_F would necessarily block otherwise; by applying E using T_F's dynamic context, the VP on which T_F executes does not incur the overhead of executing a context switch. In addition, no TCB need be allocated for T_G since T_F's TCB is used instead.

The optimization may only lead to observably different results if used in instances where the calling thread need not necessarily block. For example, suppose T_G was an element of a speculative call by T_F. Furthermore, assume T_G diverges, but another speculative thread (call it T_H) does not. In the absence of stealing, both T_G and T_H would spawn separate thread contexts. T_H returns a value to T_F. In the presence of stealing, however, T_F will also loop because T_G does. Users can parameterize thread state to inform the TC if a thread can steal or not; STING provides interface procedures for this purpose.

Like load-based inlining[33] or lazy task creation[24], stealing throttles process creation. Unlike these other techniques, however, stealing also improves locality. Locality is increased because a stolen thread is run using the TCB of a currently evaluating thread; consequently, the stack and heap of this TCB remains in the virtual machine's working set.

Because of stealing, STING reduces the overhead of context switching, and increases process granularity for programs in which processes (a) exhibit strong data dependencies among one another, and (b) block only when they require data from other processes. Of course, for the operation to be most effective, appropriate scheduling policies must be adopted. For example, a preemptible FIFO scheduler in the prime number code would not take full advantage of stealing since processes computing small primes would be run before processes that compute large ones. Stealing operations will be minimal in this case: processes exhibit few data dependencies with processes instantiated earlier, and threads computing small primes must necessarily be determined before threads computing large primes can proceed. On the other hand, a LIFO scheduling policy will cause processes computing large primes (*i.e.*, primes close to `limit`) to be run first. Stealing will occur much more frequently here since processes will demand the results of

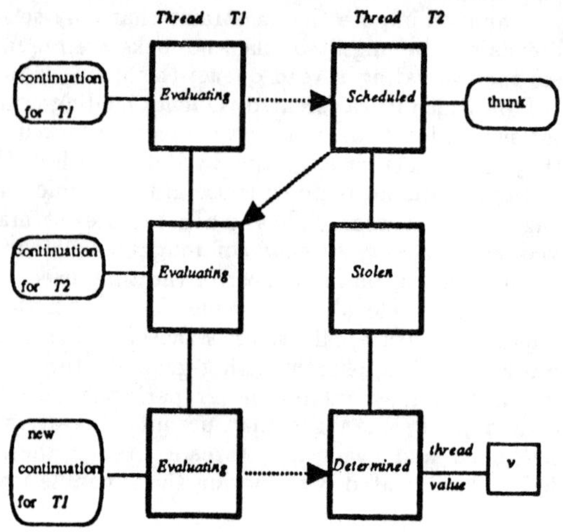

Figure 4: Dynamics of thread stealing. Dashed lines indicate dataflow constraints, solid lines specify thread transitions.

other processes computing smaller primes which have not yet run; the process call graph will, therefore, unfold more effectively.

4.2 Master-Slave Programs: Blocking and Synchronization

The master-slave paradigm is a popular parallel program structuring technique. In this approach, the collection of processes generated is bounded *a priori*; a master process generates a number of worker processes and collates their results. Process communication typically occurs via shared concurrent data structures or variables. Master-slave programs often are more efficient than result parallel ones on stock multiprocessor platforms because workers rarely need to communicate with one another except to publish their results, and process granularity can be better tailored for performance.

We have used STING to build an optimizing implementation of first-class *tuple-spaces* in Scheme. A tuple-space is an object that serves as an abstraction of a synchronizing content-addressable memory[6]; tuple-spaces are a natural implementation choice for many master/slave-based algorithms.

The semantics of tuple-spaces in our system differ significantly from their definition in C.Linda, for example. Besides the added modularity brought about by denotable tuple-space objects, our system also treats tuples as objects, and tuple operations as binding expressions, not statements. We have built a customized type inference procedure to specialize the representation of tuple-spaces whenever possible[17]. In our current implementation, tuple-spaces can be specialized as synchronized vectors, queues, sets, shared variables, semaphores, or bags; the operations permitted on tuple-spaces remains invariant over their representation. In addition, applications can specify an inheritance hierarchy among tuple-spaces if so desired.

Processes can read, remove or deposit new tuples into a tuple-space. The tuple argument in a read or remove operation is called a *template* and may contain variables prefixed with a "?". Such variables are referred to as *formals* and acquire a binding-value as a consequence of the match operation. The bindings acquired by these formals are used in the evaluation of a subordinate expression: thus, we can write:

```
(get TS [?x]
     (put TS [(+ x 1)]))
```

to remove atomically a singleton tuple from `TS`, increment it by one, and deposit it back into `TS`.

Our implementation, in the general case, uses two hash-tables (call them H_R and H_P) as the representation structures for a fully associative tuple-space. Processes that attempt to read or remove a tuple first hash on their non-formal tuple elements in H_P. If at least one match exists, the proper bindings for the formals are established, the retrieved tuple is marked as deleted in the case of a remove operation, and the executing process proceeds. When a match does not exist, the process hashes on its non-formal tuple elements in H_R, deposits a structure that indicates its identity. and blocks.

A depositing process is defined symmetrically – any processes waiting for its tuple in H_R are unblocked and rescheduled. Otherwise, the tuple is deposited into H_P using its fields as hash keys. The implementation minimizes synchronization overhead by associating a mutex with every hash bin rather than having a global mutex on the entire hash table. This permits multiple producers and consumers of a tuple-space to concurrently access its hash tables.

The implementation also takes advantage of stealing to permit the construction of fine-grained parallel programs that synchronize on tuple-spaces. We use threads as *bona fide* elements in a tuple. Consider a process P that executes the following expression:

(rd TS [x1 x2] *E*)

where `x1` and `x2` are non-formals. Assume furthermore that a tuple in `TS` is deposited as a consequence of the operation:

(spawn TS [E_1 E_2])

This operation schedules two threads (call them T_{E_1} and T_{E_2}) responsible for computing E_1 and E_2. If both T_{E_1} and T_{E_2} complete, the resulting (passive) tuple contains two determined threads; the matching procedure applies `thread-value` when it encounters a thread in a tuple; this operation retrieve the thread's value.

If T_{E_1} is still scheduled at the time P executes, however, P is free to steal it, and then determine if its result matches `x1`. If a match does not exist, P may proceed to search for another tuple, leaving T_{E_2} still in a scheduled state. Another process may subsequently examine this same tuple and steal T_{E_2} if warranted. Similarly, if T_{E_1}'s result matches `x1`, P is then free to steal T_{E_2}. If either T_{E_1} or T_{E_2} are already evaluating, P may choose to either block on one (or both) thread(s), or examine other potentially matching tuples in `TS`. The semantics of tuple-spaces impose no constraints on the implementation in this regard.

STING's combination of first-class threads and stealing allows us to write quasi-demand driven fine-grained (result) parallel programs using shared data structures. In this sense, the thread system attempts to minimizes any significant distinction between structure-based (*e.g.,* tuple-space) and dataflow style (*e.g.,* future/touch) synchronization.

4.2.1 Mutexes

Operations on tuple-spaces or similar high-level synchronization structures make use of mutex operations, `mutex-acquire` and `mutex-release`.

Mutexes are created by the mutex operation, (`make-mutex` *active passive*). `Mutex-acquire` attempts to acquire a mutex. If the mutex is locked, the executing thread actively spins for the period specified by *active*; active spinning causes the thread to retain control of its virtual processor during the period that it is blocked waiting for the mutex to be released. When the active spin count becomes zero, the thread relinquishes control of its VP, and inserts itself into an appropriate ready queue. When next run, it attempts to re-acquire the mutex, yielding its processor if unsucessful. This operation is repeated *passive* number of times. If the passive spin count is exhausted, and the mutex has not yet been acquired, the executing thread blocks on the mutex. When the mutex is ultimately released, (via `mutex-release`) all threads blocked on this mutex are restored onto some ready queue.

Using mutex primitives, macros, and Scheme's support for exception handling, one can easily build a "safe" version of a mutex acquire operation, (`with-mutex` *mutex body*). This operation ensures that *mutex* is released if *body* raises an exception during its evaluation that causes control to exit the current dynamic environment.

4.2.2 Preemption and Interrupts

A preemptive round-robin or FIFO scheduling policy is best suited for master-slave applications in which the master performs relatively little processing after the initial set of spawned workers complete. A round-robin policy allocates a specified quantum for each worker in the worker pool. Support for preemption is important because workers rarely block; in its absence, long-running workers might occupy all available VPs at the expense of other enqueued ready threads.

Preemption is sometimes best disabled in master/slave programs that make significant use of barrier synchronization. In these applications, the master generates a new set of worker processes after all previously created workers complete. If the time to execute a particular set of workers is small relative to the total time needed to complete the application, enabling preemption may degrade performance[31]. Threads can disable an initial preemption by setting a flag in their TCB; if preemption takes place when this quantum flag is false, another bit in the TCB state is set indicating that a subsequent preemption should not be ignored. Users can encapsulated time critical code using the the syntactic form, `(without-preemption` *body*`)` that evaluates *body* with preemption disabled. The `without-preemption` form is in fact a specialized version of a more general construct, `without-interrupts`, that disables all interrupts during the evaluation of its body.

4.3 Speculative Parallelism and Barrier Synchronization

Speculative parallelism is an important programming technique that often cannot be effectively utilized because of runtime overheads incurred in its implementation. The two features most often associated with systems that support a speculative programming model are the ability to favor certain (more promising) tasks over others, and the means to abort, reclaim (and possibly undo) unnecessary computation.

STING permits programmers to write speculative applications by:

1. allowing users to explicitly program thread priorities,
2. permitting a thread to wait on the completion of other threads, and
3. allowing threads to terminate other threads.

Promising tasks can execute before unlikely one because priorities are programmable. A task α that completes first in a set of tasks can awaken any thread blocked on its completetion; this functionality permits STING to support a simple form of OR-parallelism[8]. α can terminate all other tasks in its task set once it has been determined that their results are unnecessary. Speculative computation using STING, however, will not be able to undo non-local side-effects induced by useless tasks; the system does not provide a primitive backtracking mechanism[2].

Consider the implementation of a `wait-for-one` construct. This operator evaluates its list of arguments concurrently, returning the value yielded by the first of its arguments to complete. Thus, if a_i yields v in the expression:

`(wait-for-one` $a_1\ a_2\ \ldots\ a_i\ \ldots\ a_n$`)`

the expression returns v, and, if desired by the programmer, terminates the evaluation of all the remaining a_j, $j \neq i$.

The specification of a `wait-for-all` construct that implements an AND-parallel operation is similar; it also evaluates its arguments concurrently, but returns true only when all its arguments complete. Thus, the expression:

`(wait-for-all` $a_1\ a_2\ \ldots\ a_i\ \ldots\ a_n$`)`

acts as a barrier synchronization point since the thread executing this expression is blocked until all the a_i complete. The implementation of this operation is very similar to the implementation of the speculative wait-for-one operation.

[2] Sting does not support first-class continuations across thread boundaries.

```
(define (block-on-group count group)
  (let loop ((i count)
             (threads group))
    (cond
      ((zero? i))
      ((null? group)
       (set-TCB.wait-count (current-TCB) i)
       (thread-block (current-thread)))
      (else
        (let ((thread (car threads)))
          (mutex-acquire thread.mutex)
          (cond
            ((determined? thread)
             (mutex-release thread.mutex)
             (loop (1- i) (cdr threads)))
            (else
              (let ((tb (make-tb)))
                (set-tb.tcb tb
                            (current-tcb))
                (set-tb.thread tb thread)
                (set-tb.next tb
                        (thread.waiters thread))
                (set-thread.waiters thread tb))
                (mutex-release mutex))
                (loop (1- i)
                       (cdr threads)))))))))
```

Figure 5: Definition of `block-on-group`.

The TC implements these operations using a common procedure, `block-on-group`. Threads and TCBs are defined to support this functionality. For example, associated with a TCB structure is information on the number of threads in the group that must complete before the TCB's associated thread can resume.

`Block-on-group` takes a list of threads and a count. These threads correspond to the arguments of the `wait-for-one` and `wait-for-all` operations shown above; the count argument represents the number of threads that must complete before the current thread (*i.e.*, the thread executing this procedure) is allowed to resume. If the count is one, we get an implementation of `wait-for-one`; if the count is equal to n, we get an implementation of `wait-for-all`.

The relationship between a thread T_g in the group and the current thread (T_w) that is to wait on T is maintained in a data structure (called a thread barrier (TB)) that contains references to:

1. T_w's TCB.
2. the TB of another waiter blocked on T_g (if one exists).
3. T_g – this is used only for debugging purposes.

We give a definition for `block-on-group` in Fig. 5.

The call:

`(block-on-group` $m\ T_1\ T_2\ \ldots\ T_n$`)`

causes the current thread (call it T) to block on the completion of m of the T_i, $m \leq n$. Each of these T_i have a reference to T in their chain of waiters. The procedure checks if a thread in the thread group has already been determined; in the case, the `wait-count` is decremented, but no thread barrier is constructed. Otherwise, a TB is constructed as well. When all threads in group have been examined, the procedure sets the current thread's `wait-count` field to the extant count, and issues a `thread-block` operation.

Applications use `Block-on-group` in conjunction with a `wakeup-waiters` procedure that is invoked by the a_i when they complete. `Wakeup-waiters` examines the list of waiters chained from the `waiters` slot in its thread argument. A waiter whose `wait-count` becomes zero is enqueued on the ready queue of some VP. The TC invokes `wakeup-waiters` whenever a thread T completes (*i.e.*, whenever it terminates or abnormally exits). All threads waiting on T's completion are thus rescheduled.

Given these two procedures `wait-for-one` can be defined simply:

```
(define (wait-for-one block-group)
  (block-on-group 1 block-group)
  (map thread-terminate block-group))
```

If T executes `wait-for-one`, it blocks on all the threads in its `block-group` argument. When T is resumed, it is placed on a queue of ready threads in the policy manager of some available virtual processor. The `map` procedure executed upon T's resumption terminates all threads in its group.

STING's `wait-for-all` procedure can omit this operation since all threads in its `block-group` are guaranteed to have completed before the thread executing this operation is resumed.

5 Performance

STING is currently implemented on an 8 processor Silicon Graphics MIPS R3000 shared-memory (cache-coherent) multiprocessor. The physical machine configuration maps physical processors to lightweight Unix threads; each node in the machine runs one such thread. We ran the benchmarks shown below using a virtual machine in which each physical processor implements a single virtual processor.

Fig. 6 gives baseline figures for various thread operations; these timings were derived using a single LIFO queue.

The "Thread Creation" timing is the cost to create a thread not placed in the genealogy tree, and which has no dynamic state. "Thread Fork and Value" measures the cost to create a thread that evaluates the null procedure and returns. "Scheduling a Thread" is the cost of inserting a thread into the ready queue of the current VP. A "Synchronous Context Switch" is the cost to make a `yield-processor` call in which the calling thread is resumed immediately. The cost for "Stealing" does not include the time to schedule the thread being stolen. "Thread Block and Resume" is the cost to block and resume a null thread. "Tuple Space" is the cost to create a tuple-space, insert and then remove a singleton tuple. The speculative synchronization timings reflects the cost to compute two null threads speculatively; the barrier synchronization is the cost to build a barrier synchronization point on two threads both computing the null procedure. We present detailed benchmarks of several application programs in a companion paper[18].

Case	*Timings(in μseconds)*
Thread Creation	8.9
Thread Fork and Value	44.9
Scheduling a Thread	18.9
Synchronous Context Switch	3.77
Stealing	7.7
Thread Block and Resume	27.9
Tuple-Space	170
Speculative Fork (2 threads)	68.9
Barrier Synchronization (2 threads)	144.8

Figure 6: Baseline timings.

6 Related Work and Conclusions

Insofar as STING is a programming system that permits the creation and management of lightweight threads of control, it shares several common traits with thread package systems developed for other high-level languages[9, 10, 23]. These systems also view threads as a manifest datatype, support preemption in varying degrees, and in certain restricted cases, permit programmers to specify a specialized scheduling regimen. The thread abstraction defines the coordination sublanguage in these systems.

There are some important differences however that clearly distinguish STING from these other systems. First, the scheduling and migration protocol STING uses is *completely* customizable; different applications can run different schedulers without modifying the thread manager or the virtual processor abstraction; such customization can be applied to the organization of the virtual machine itself. Second, STING's support for data locality, storage optimization, and process throttling via stealing is absent in other systems. Moreover, all thread operations are implemented directly within the STING virtual machine: there is no context switch to a lower level kernel that must be performed in order to execute a thread operation. STING is built on abstract machine intended to support long-lived applications, persistent objects, and multiple address spaces. Thread packages provide none of this functionality since (by definition) they do not define a complete program environment.

STING also differs from programming languages that provide high-level abstractions (*e.g.*, continuations[34, 14] to model concurrency. Because we designed STING as a systems programming language, it provides low-level concurrency abstractions – application libraries can directly create thread objects, and can define their own scheduling and thread migration strategies. High-level concurrency constructs are realizable using threads, but the system does not prohibit users from directly using thread operations in the ways described above if efficiency considerations warrant. In particular, the same application may define concurrency abstractions with different semantics and efficiency concerns within the same runtime environment.

In certain respects, STING resembles other advanced multi-threaded operating system environments[1, 22]: for example, it supports non-blocking I/O calls with call-back, user control over interrupts, and local address space management as user-level operations. It cleanly separates user-level and kernel-level concerns: physical processors handle (privileged) system operations and operations across virtual machines; virtual processors implement all user-level thread and local address-space functionality. However, because STING is an extended dialect of Scheme, it provides the functionality and expressivity of a high-level programming language (*e.g.*, first-class procedures, general exception handling, and rich data abstractions) that typical operating system environments do not offer.

STING is a platform for building asynchronous programming primitives and experimenting with new parallel programming paradigms. In addition, the design also allows different concurrency models to be evaluated competitively. Scheme offers an especially rich environment in which to undertake such experiments because of its well-defined semantics, its overall simplicity, and its efficiency. However, the STING design itself is language independent; we believe it could be incorporated fairly easily into any high-level programming language.

STING does not merely provide hooks for each concurrency paradigm and primitive we considered interesting. We focussed instead on basic structures and functionality common to a broad range of parallel programming structures; thus, the implementation of blocking is easily used to support speculative computation, the "stealing" optimization used to throttle the execution of threads is well-suited for implementing futures and tuple-space synchronization, and, finally, customizable policy managers make it possible to build fair and efficient schedulers for a variety of other paradigms.

References

[1] Thomas Anderson, Edward Lazowska, and Henry Levy. The Performance Implications of Thread Management Alternatives for Shared Memory MultiProcessors. *IEEE Transactions on Computers*, 38(12):1631–1644, December 1989.

[2] Thomas E. Anderson, Brian N. Bershad, Edward D. Lazowska, and Henry M. Levy. Scheduler activations: effective kernel support for the user-level management of parallelism. In *Proceedings of 13th ACM Symposium on Operating Systems Principles*, pages 95–109. Association for Computing Machinery SIGOPS, October 1991.

[3] Arvind, Rishiyur Nikhil, and Keshav Pingali. I-Structures: Data Structures for Parallel Computing. *Transactions on Programming Languages and Systems*, 11(4):598–632, October 1989.

[4] Peter Bishop. *Computer Systems with a Very Large Address Space and Garbage Collection.* PhD thesis, MIT Laboratory for Computer Science, 1977.

[5] David Black. Scheduling Support for Concurrency and Parallelism in the Mach Operating System. *IEEE Computer*, 23(5):35–43, May 1990.

[6] Nick Carriero and David Gelernter. How to Write Parallel Programs: A Guide to the Perplexed. *ACM Computing Surveys*, 21(3), September 1989.

[7] Nick Carriero and David Gelernter. Linda in Context. *Communications of the ACM*, 32(4):444 – 458, April 1989.

[8] K.L Clark and S. Gregory. PARLOG: Parallel Programming in Logic. *ACM Transactions on Programming Languages and Systems*, 8(1):1–49, 1986.

[9] Eric Cooper and Richard Draves. C Threads. Technical Report CMU-CS-88-154, Carnegie-Mellon University, June.

[10] Eric Cooper and J.Gregory Morrisett. Adding Threads to Standard ML. Technical Report CMU-CS-90-186, Carnegie-Mellon University, 1990.

[11] J. Dongarra, D. Sorenson, and P. Brewer. Tools and Methodology for Programming Parallel Processors. In *Aspects of Computation on Asynchronous Processors*, pages 125–138. North-Holland, 1988.

[12] R. Gabriel and J. McCarthy. Queue-Based Multi-Processing Lisp. In *Proceedings of the 1984 Conf. on Lisp and Functional Programming*, pages 25–44, August 1984.

[13] Robert Halstead. Multilisp: A Language for Concurrent Symbolic Computation. *Transactions on Programming Languages and Systems*, 7(4):501–538, October 1985.

[14] Robert Hieb and R. Kent Dybvig. Continuations and Concurrency. In *Second ACM SIGPLAN Symposium on Principles and Practice of Parallel Programming*, pages 128–137, March 1990.

[15] Waldemar Horwat, Andrew Chien, and William Dally. Experience with CST: Programming and Implementation. In *ACM SIGPLAN '89 Conference on Programming Language Design and Implementation*, pages 101–109, June 1989.

[16] Paul Hudak. Para-Functional Programming. *IEEE Computer*, 19(8):60–70, August 1986.

[17] Suresh Jagannathan. Optimizing Analysis for First-Class Tuple-Spaces. In *Third Workshop on Parallel Languages and Compilers.* MIT Press, August 1990.

[18] Suresh Jagannathan and James Philbin. A Foundation for an Efficient Multi-Threaded Scheme System. In *Proceedings of the 1992 Conf. on Lisp and Functional Programming*, June 1992.

[19] David Kranz, Robert Halstead, and Eric Mohr. Mul-T: A High Performance Parallel Lisp. In *Proceedings of the ACM Symposium on Programming Language Design and Implementation*, pages 81–91, June 1989.

[20] David Kranz, Richard Kelsey, Jonathan Rees, Paul Hudak, James Philbin, and Norman Adams. ORBIT: An Optimizing Compiler for Scheme. *ACM SIGPLAN Notices*, 21(7):219–233, July 1986.

[21] Henry Lieberman and Carl Hewitt. A Real-Time Garbage Collector Based on the Lifetime of Objects. *Communications of the ACM*, 26(6):419–429, June 1973.

[22] Brian D. Marsh, Michael L. Scott, Thomas J. LeBlanc, and Evangelos P. Markatos. First-class user-level threads. In *Proceedings of 13th ACM Symposium on Operating Systems Principles*, pages 110–21. Association for Computing Machinery SIGOPS, October 1991.

[23] Sun Microsystems. *Lightweight Processes*, 1990. In SunOS Programming Utilities and Libraries.

[24] Rick Mohr, David Kranz, and Robert Halstead. Lazy Task Creation: A Technique for Increasing the Granularity of Parallel Programs. In *Proceedings of the 1990 ACM Conference on Lisp and Functional Programming*, June 1990.

[25] Randy Osborne. Speculative Computation in MultiLisp. In *Proceedings of the 1990 ACM Conference on Lisp and Functional Programming*, pages 198–208, 1990.

[26] James Philbin. *STING: An Operating System Kernel for Highly Parallel Computing.* PhD thesis, Dept. of Computer Science, Yale University, 1992. Forthcoming.

[27] Jonathan Rees and William Clinger, editors. The Revised^3 Report on the Algorithmic Language Scheme. *ACM Sigplan Notices*, 21(12), 1986.

[28] John Reppy. CML: A Higher-Order Concurrent Language. In *Proceedings of the SIGPLAN'91 Conference on Programming Language Design and Implementation*, pages 293–306, June 1991.

[29] Vijay Saraswat and Martin Rinard. Concurrent Constraint Programming. In *Proceedings of the 17th ACM Symposium on Principles of Programming Languages*, pages 232–246, 1990.

[30] A. Tevanian, R. Rashid, D. Golub, D. Black, E. Cooper, and M. Young. Mach Treads and the UNIX Kernel: The Battle for Control. In *1987 USENIX Summer Conference*, pages 185–197, 1987.

[31] A. Tucker and A. Gupta. Process Control and Scheduling Issues for Multiprogrammed Shared-Memory Machines. In *Proceedings of the 12th Annual ACM Symposium on Operating Systems Principles*, pages 114–122, 1989.

[32] David Ungar. Generation Scavenging: A Non-Disruptive High Performance Storage Reclamation Algorithm. In *Proceedings of the ACM SIGSOFT/SIGPLAN Software Engineering Symposium on Practical Software Development Environments*, pages 157–167, 1984.

[33] M. Vandevoorde and E. Roberts. WorkCrews: An Abstraction for Controlling Parallelism. *International Journal of Parallel Programming*, 17(4):347–366, August 1988.

[34] Mitch Wand. Continuation-Based MultiProcessing. In *Proceedings of the 1980 ACM Lisp and Functional Programming Conference*, pages 19–28, 1980.

A Concurrent Compiler for Modula-2+

David B. Wortman,
Michael D. Junkin*
Computer Systems Research Institute
University of Toronto
6 Kings College Road
Toronto, Ontario, Canada M5S 1A4

wortman@csri.toronto.edu

Abstract

In this paper we describe a collection of techniques for the design and implementation of concurrent compilers. We begin by describing a technique for dividing a source program into many *streams* so that each stream can be compiled concurrently. We discuss several compiler design issues unique to concurrent compilers including source program partitioning, symbol table management, compiler task scheduling and information flow constraints. The application of our techniques is illustrated by a complete design for a concurrent Modula-2+ compiler. After describing the structure of this compiler we present an experimental evaluation of the compiler's performance that demonstrates that significant improvements in compilation time can be achieved through the use of concurrency.

1 Introduction

The Concurrent Compiler Development (CCD) Project at the University of Toronto was a long term effort to explore issues in the design and implementation of concurrent compilers for modern programming languages. We developed techniques for structuring compilers to achieve significant compilation time speedups through concurrent processing. Although we describe a particular prototype concurrent compiler in this paper, the techniques we have developed are applicable to compilers for a broad range of languages.

To provide a realistic environment for developing and evaluating our ideas we built a prototype concurrent compiler [JW90] for the Modula-2+ superset of Modula-2 [Rov86]. Modula-2+ was chosen as the target language partly for reasons of expediency (i.e. availability of an existing compiler that served as a starting point) , but primarily because Modula-2+ is a large modern programming language that presented many challenges to the language implementor. We felt that if we could produce an efficient compiler for Modula-2+ then it would be easy to handle languages that are easier to compile concurrently such as Pascal and C. During the CCD project we implemented seven major variations of our concurrent compiler design to test various implementation strategies. The compiler described in this paper is the "best of 7" compiler that represents the culmination of our efforts.

Our paper in the 1988 PLDI conference [SWJ+88] discussed the narrow issues of semantic analysis and symbol table management in concurrent compilers. A longer discussion of this topic has been published elsewhere [SW91]. This paper describes the design and evaluation of a complete concurrent compiler for the Modula-2+ superset of Modula-2. A more detailed discussion of our prototype compilers has been published as a technical report [JW90].

The research described in this paper differs from previous work in the area in a number of ways:

- It describes a complete, implemented, concurrent com-

*Current address: IBM Canada Ltd., Toronto Laboratory, 844 Don Mills Rd., North York, Ontario, Canada M3C 1V7

ACM SIGPLAN '92 PLDI-6/92/CA
© 1992 ACM 0-89791-476-7/92/0006/0068...$1.50

piler. In their comprehensive bibliography on Concurrent Compilation [SB90] the authors identified only three implemented modern compilers for shared memory multiprocessors [Van87],[Sch79] and ours. The remaining work that they cite are theoretical studies, paper designs or concern only one phase of compilation (e.g. parallel parsing).

- It goes much further than previous efforts in restructuring compilers to take advantage of concurrent hardware. We have taken a very aggressive approach to partitioning compilation into separately executable tasks and to splitting the source program into separately compilable sub-units. For example, Vandevoorde [Van87] split his compiler into a scanning phase and an "everything else" phase. He did not address the Doesn't Know Yet problem discussed in Section 2.2.

- The symbol table search mechanism (Skeptical Handling) presented in Section 2.2 is a new approach to dealing with the problem of incomplete symbol tables that arises in concurrent compilers. It supersedes our previous work [JW90, SW91].

- The discussion of information flows that constrain concurrent processing in Section 2.4 is a new approach to analyzing the performance of concurrent compilers.

- By careful design and optimization of the entire compiler, we have been able to achieve much better parallel speedups than previous efforts. We have also been able to demonstrate that compilers built using our techniques perform better as the size of the program being compiled increases. The closest comparable effort is Vandevoorde's parallel C compiler[Van87]. On a 5 processor Firefly he was able to achieve a speedup of 2.5 .. 3.3 on large programs and 1.0 .. 2.0 on smaller ones. In the limiting case of a "best" source program we have been able to demonstrate almost linear parallel speedup (see Figure. 4).

Early in the CCD project we decided to concentrate our efforts on compilers for modern block-structured procedural programming languages. Considering a broader class of languages would have diluted our resources. We concentrated on the design of compilers for shared memory multiprocessor systems with modest numbers (i.e. tens not hundreds) of processors. We restricted ourselves to languages in which reserved words were used to determine the lexical structure of programs. This restriction allows us to partition programs for concurrent processing during lexical analysis. Languages which use keywords rather than reserved words to determine program structure usually can't be partitioned for concurrent processing until after syntax analysis thereby reducing the potential for achieving faster compilation through concurrency.

The concurrent compilers that we have designed operate by splitting the source program into separately compilable *streams* that correspond to scopes of declaration in the program. Each stream is then processed through conventional parsing, semantic analysis and code generation phases. At the end of compilation the code generated for all of the streams is merged together to produce the compiler output. The structure of the compiler is discussed in more detail in Section 3. We begin with a discussion of the major design issues that lead to this structure.

2 Compiler Design Issues

During the CCD project we identified four design issues that had a dominant effect on the performance of our concurrent compilers:

1. *Early* splitting of the source program into separately compilable streams and *late* merging of separately compiled object code into a a complete object module.

2. Management of the compiler symbol table and the Doesn't Know Yet Problem.

3. Management and scheduling of the compiler tasks for each stream.

4. Inter-scope flows of information that constrain concurrent processing.

There are many other small design details that must be handled well to achieve maximum compiler performance, but doing well on these four issues is essential.

2.1 Source Splitting and Merging

Opportunities for concurrent processing are increased by splitting the program being compiled into independently compilable streams as early in the compilation as possible. In compiling a Modula-2+ module, separately compilable streams arise from three sources:

- The body of the module being compiled.
- Procedures contained in the module body.
- Interfaces (definition modules) that are directly or indirectly imported by the module.

The requirement that reserved words determine source program structure means that these streams can be identified by a simple finite state recognizer that processes the sequence of tokens produced during or just after lexical analysis. A small amount of token stream lookahead may be necessary to resolve lexical tokens that have multiple interpretations (e.g., PROCEDURE in Modula-2). In our concurrent compiler design the procedure is the smallest program unit that is compiled concurrently. It is a straightforward exercise to generate code for each procedure separately and to merge this code using simple concatenation. Most previous efforts to build concurrent compilers performed splitting during parsing and thereby limited opportunities for parallel processing of the source program. Many paper designs for concurrent compilers proposed splitting the source program being compiled at arbitrary points without adequate consideration for the difficulties that arbitrary splitting would cause for symbol table management and code generation.

2.2 Symbol Table Management and the Doesn't Know Yet Problem

Management of the compiler's symbol table is a critical issue in achieving good performance and correct semantic analysis in a concurrent compiler. The compilation of parts of a program concurrently introduces new problems in symbol table management that do not exist in conventional sequential compilers [SWJ+88, SW91].

In our compiler the units of compilation correspond directly to major scopes of declaration. The main reason for this design decision was to allow the compiler symbol table to be organized on a scope basis [SGR79]. This has the desirable effect of minimizing inter-stream dependencies and making the detection of incomplete tables easier. We use a separate symbol table for each scope of declaration (definition module, main module, procedure). These symbol tables are linked together to provided the correct scope ancestry path for resolving names.

A problem unique to our style of concurrent compilers is the Doesn't Know Yet (DKY) problem [SWJ+88, Ses88, SW91]. In a sequential compiler, a search of the symbol table for a given identifier either succeeds indicating that the identifier is known or fails, indicating unequivocally that the identifier is not known to the compiler (assuming a suitable scheme for handling allowable forward references). In a concurrent compiler there is a third possible result from a search of the symbol table. The identifier may not be found because the symbol table being searched is incomplete[1]. The table that was being searched may be being constructed concurrently by some other compiler task. A concurrent compiler must recognize when this Doesn't Know Yet condition arises and deal with it in a way that doesn't violate the semantics of the language being compiled. Symbol table search must correctly locate declared symbols and never fail to detect an undeclared symbol.

We experimented with a number of strategies for dealing with the DKY problem [Ses88, JW90]. The differences between these strategies are in the amount of delay incurred when a DKY occurs, the amount of concurrent processing that can be achieved, and the effort required to implement the strategy. The list of strategies presented below is roughly ordered by decreasing DKY delay, increasing concurrent processing potential and increasing implementation effort. The major DKY strategies that we investigated are:

- *Avoidance*: delay the start of semantic analysis for a scope until the declaration analysis of its parent scope is complete. This order guarantees that symbol table searches originating in the scope will never encounter an incomplete symbol table in an outer scope.
- *Pessimistic Handling*: symbol table search blocks and

[1] We assume that creation of symbol table entries is atomic with respect to symbol table search so that the possibility of symbol table search finding an incomplete symbol table entry does not arise.

waits for table completion when it encounters an incomplete symbol table in some outer scope.

- *Skeptical Handling*: symbol table search blocks and waits for table completion when it fails to find the identifier it is searching for in an incomplete symbol table in some outer scope.

- *Optimistic Handling*: symbol table search blocks and waits for completion of a symbol table *entry* or the completion of a symbol table (whichever comes first) when it fails to find the identifier it is searching for in an incomplete symbol table in some outer scope.

When a symbol table search blocks, the embedded scheduler in our compiler (See Section 2.3) is notified. It attempts to find another task to run. It will preferentially try to run the task which will resolve the DKY blockage. In our performance testing, the choice of a method for dealing with the DKY problem caused a variation of about 10% in overall compiler performance. The Skeptical Handling algorithm described in Figure 6 is our recommendation for the best compromise between compiler performance and ease of implementation. This algorithm incurs the cost of a duplicate search for identifiers that are found after a DKY blockage, but it gains performance by searching incomplete tables before incurring a DKY blockage. The performance of the Skeptical Handling algorithm is analyzed in Section 4.3.

Another symbol table issue is the handling of builtin names, i.e., identifiers that are automatically provided by the compiler. These names are typically builtin input/output routines or mathematical routines like *sin* and *sqrt*. In a conventional compiler the typical way to implement builtin names is to create a global scope that is logically the parent scope of the module being compiled. The symbol table for this global scope is preinitialized by the compiler to contain all builtin names. With this organization, the normal scope-chaining symbol table search will automatically find the builtin names if they have not been redeclared in the program. This mechanism is not suitable for a concurrent compiler because it causes the first reference to a builtin name to potentially incur DKY waits on all scopes out to the global scope. In particular, the scope corresponding to the module body can be quite large so an unnecessary DKY wait on this scope can cause a significant delay. We took advantage of the fact that builtin names could not be redefined in Modula-2+ and treated builtin names as if they were declared local to each scope. This approach did not require any replication of symbol table entries, instead it was done by a simple modification of the symbol table search mechanism.

2.3 Compiler Task Scheduling

In our compiler structure, we exploit parallelism on two levels. First, as already mentioned, the compilation is split into streams which are processed in parallel. There is one stream for the main module, one for each procedure stream defined therein and one stream for each definition module imported directly or indirectly by the module. Second, we exploit parallelism within the processing of a stream by partitioning the stream into a number of *tasks*, which correspond to the traditional phases of compilation. The number and type of the tasks a particular stream is partitioned into depends not only on the type of the stream but also on the version of the compiler. There are between 2 and 5 tasks per stream (see Figure 5). The task types of the skeptical handling compiler are described in section 3. The task types were chosen to partition the compilation as quickly as possible, in an effort to get all the compiler's worker threads busy. The early tasks are large in number but, in general, small, while the later ones, such as the statement analyzer/code generator tasks, are large but fewer in number. However, there is no need to partition these later tasks further (although there may be parallelism that can be exploited) because there are almost always enough of these tasks to ensure that all processors are fully utilized.

2.3.1 Tasks

The task is the atomic unit of parallelism in our compilers. The execution of a given task is constrained by the rate the tasks on which it depends for information are progressing (See sections 2.2 and 2.4). These constraints are embodied by *events*, the concurrency mechanism used. An event is simply something that either has or has not occurred. A task waits on an event if and only if it hasn't occurred. Events are discussed further in section 2.3.3 below.

A task communicates with the tasks on which it depends, and which depend on it, as a producer/consumer pair on a particular data structure. Each such data structure has associated with it one or more events, signaled by the producer when the events occur. The signaling of such an event indicates that a particular portion of a shared data structure is complete and ready to be used. As an example, the Splitter task and the Lexor task of a main module stream communicate via a lexical token queue. The elements in this queue are blocks of tokens. Each block is associated with one event. When the Lexor fills a token block, the block's event is signaled, indicating to the Splitter that it now may begin to read the tokens of that block.

2.3.2 The Supervisors Approach

The number of tasks in a compilation ranges from a dozen or so in a very small compilation to a few hundred in a large compilation. We concur with the results of Vandevoorde and Roberts [VR88] that the best performance on the type of multiprocessors we are considering results from carefully limiting the amount of concurrent activity in the system so as not to overwhelm machine resources. If an attempt was made to execute all of these tasks concurrently saturation of the operating system and the virtual memory would make concurrent compilation effective only for small source modules. Instead, we initiate one compiler process (Worker) for each real hardware processor. These workers are managed by a *supervisor* which oversees the assignment of tasks to workers. This approach, called "Supervisors", is an extension of WorkCrews [VR88] that handles blockable tasks.

At compiler initialization time, the tasks of the main module stream are created by the compiler initialization thread, and then a number of worker threads corresponding to the number of hardware processors are created. The initialization thread then blocks, waiting for the workers to perform the compilation. The workers begin by searching the supervisor's task queuing structure for tasks to perform. One begins the main module stream's Lexor task, and the compilation begins.

2.3.3 Events

Events are classified into three categories. First, *avoided* events are those events that must occur before the task(s) that will wait on them can begin. They are called this because we avoid waiting on the event by simply not assigning the task to a worker until the event has occurred. The rationale is that the amount of work a task could do before being forced to wait on such an event is so little so as to be outweighed by the scheduling cost when the wait occurs.

The second type of event is the *handled* event. We allow tasks that may wait on handled events to begin, hoping that the amount of work they can do before being forced to wait on such an event outweighs the scheduling cost should the wait occur. If the wait does occur, the worker performing the task searches for other tasks to execute, showing preference to those tasks whose execution will lead toward the event occurring.

Lastly, *barrier* events are a special kind of handled event for which the worker executing the waiting task is not rescheduled. The worker simply waits for the event to occur. Barrier events are only used in the token streams. We know it is safe to simply wait because token consumers (the Splitter task and the parser tasks of definition module streams) are only started once their corresponding Lexor tasks have begun, and Lexor tasks never block. Thus, the possibility of deadlock is avoided. Our measurements show that the delays due to workers waiting on barrier events are quite small in typical compilations.

The tasks and events of the different major versions of our compilers vary primarily in how DKY events are treated. In the Avoidance compiler, there is one DKY event per symbol table, and it is an avoided event. This means that the tasks of a stream that depend on another stream's symbol table are not begun until that symbol table is complete. In the Pessimistic Handling compiler, there is again one DKY event per symbol table, but each is a handled event. Here, tasks are allowed to begin regardless of the completion status of the symbol tables on which they (may) depend, but must block as soon as they try to look up a symbol in an incomplete symbol table. These events are signaled when their corresponding symbol table is completed. A refinement of this strategy is presented in a Skeptical Handling compiler, where a searching task is allowed to look into an incomplete symbol table and will block only if the symbol is not found. As before, the blocked task is signaled when the symbol table is completed, and it attempts again to find the symbol in the now complete table.

The Optimistic Handling compiler implements a different scheme. Here, there is one DKY event per symbol. In this method, when a task looks up a symbol, it waits on the symbol's DKY event (should it be in the process of being defined), or creates an empty symbol with the name being searched for (if it isn't in the table) and waits on that symbol's event. If the symbol is really in that scope, the task is signaled and allowed to proceed. Otherwise, when the table is completed, it is traversed and all unsignaled events (corresponding to symbols that are being looked up in the table but are not defined in the scope) are signaled, allowing blocked tasks to continue searching. While this method allows the maximum parallelism to be exploited, and indeed has the best self-relative speedup, the overhead of maintaining so many events outweighs the advantages of the technique.

2.3.4 Worker Scheduling

The role of the Supervisor is to assign tasks to workers in such a manner as to minimize compilation time. This is accomplished in two ways. First, free workers are assigned tasks in an intelligent manner, attempting to select the tasks whose execution will benefit the most tasks. Second, handled events are implemented in such a way that allows workers whose tasks are blocked on handled events perform other tasks.

Task assignment is optimized in two ways. First, avoided events prevent a task that will have to wait almost immediately from being selected for execution. Also, the Supervisor implements the list of tasks waiting to be executed as a priority queue. In the Skeptical Handling compiler, the queues are searched for new work in the following way:

1. Lexor tasks
2. Splitter task
3. Importer tasks
4. Definition Module Parser/Declarations Analyzer tasks
5. Module Parser/Declarations Analyzer task
6. Procedure Parser/Declarations Analyzer tasks
7. Long Procedure Statement Analyzer/Code Generator tasks
8. Short Procedure Statement Analyzer/Code Generator tasks

Code is generated for long procedures before short ones to avoid a long sequential tail at the end of the compilation, as one worker struggles to generate code for one long procedure after finishing a number of short ones and all the other workers are finished.

When a task waits on a handled event, its associated worker does not simply block but instead is assigned another task that it is eligible to execute. This task is always the one that signals the event on which the worker is waiting, unless that task has been started by another worker.

This leads to an interesting problem. A task that is begun by a particular worker must be completed by that worker, even if it blocks during execution. This is required by the underlying implementation of threads. Thus, the set of tasks a blocked worker is eligible to execute consists of only those tasks that do not block on any event not yet signaled by some task in the set of tasks being executed the worker (who are all currently blocked), otherwise deadlock may occur.

2.4 Inter–scope Information Flows

The implementation of block structured programming languages requires that information in the compilers symbol table be shared among different scopes. By processing scopes concurrently we introduce constraints on this sharing that do not exist in a sequential compiler. Delays waiting for this shared information can constitute a major impediment to concurrent processing.

An example of an information flow constraint arises in the processing of procedure headings in Modula-2+. A procedure heading contains the procedure's name, the name and specification for each of the procedure's formal parameters. The information in the procedure header needs to be shared between the parent scope in which the procedure is declared where it is used to validate and generate code for calls on the procedure and the child scope (the body of the procedure) where it is used to validate and generate code for access to the procedure parameters. In sequential compilers the sharing of this information occurs automatically given the usual order of program processing and symbol table construction. The information that is shared consists of the compiler symbol table entry for the procedure and the entries for its parameters.

We investigated three alternatives for implementing this particular case of sharing in our concurrent compiler:

1. Process the procedure heading in the parent scope and copy the symbol table entries generated by this processing into the symbol table for the child scope.

2. Process the procedure heading in the child scope and copy the symbol table entries produced into the parent scope.

3. Process the parameter heading separately in the parent and child scopes taking care to guarantee that identical symbol table entries are produced in both scopes.

In the first alternative, processing of the child scope should be delayed until the procedure header has been processed in the parent scope. This synchronization is in effect a DKY blockage from the child scope to its parameter definitions in the parent scope. Since this DKY is inevitable and since very little work can be done on a procedure stream until the procedure's parameters have been processed, we found it more efficient to change this particular instance of a handled DKY event into an avoided event by delaying processing the child scope until the parent scope had completely processed the procedure heading[2]. The second alternative is very difficult to implement without introducing the possibility of a parent/child deadlock. The third alternative eliminates the information sharing between parent and child scopes. It is the cleanest solution, however in our evaluation it was about 3% slower than the first alternative due to redundant effort.

[2]Procedures with no parameters could be started earlier as a special case, but we found them to be so infrequent that the extra effort was not justified

3 Compiler Structure

The unit of compilation is a Modula-2+ module (M) that is physically represented as a definition module file (M.def) and an implementation module file (M.mod)[3]. The file M.def contains declarations for the interface between M and its clients. The file M.mod contains declarations for constants, variables, types and procedures that are the implementation of M.

The task structure of our concurrent compiler is shown in Figure 5 The three columns in the figure show the compiler tasks that are applied to the streams for definition modules, implementation modules[4] and procedures respectively. The tasks in the left column are applied to each definition module that is imported directly or indirectly by the module. The tasks in the right column are applied to each procedure in the module. We have used an unorthodox task division in the middle and back part of the compiler as a part of our strategy for dealing with DKYs. One compiler task performs syntax analysis on the entire stream and semantic analysis on declarations as would be done in a traditional sequential compiler. A parse tree is built for statements, but semantic analysis of statements is deferred to a subsequent task that performs semantic analysis on statements and then generates code for the statements. The symbol table for the declarations is marked complete before the statment parse tree is built. Building the statement parse tree is sufficiently fast that the added complexity of parsing statments separately was not considered. The rationale behind this division is that fast processing of the declaration parts of streams will assist in resolving DKY blockages by causing symbol tables to be completed earlier in the compilation. By the time the statement analysis and code generation tasks are ready to run there is usually many more parallel tasks available to run than there are processors on which to run them, so we incur no loss in processing efficiency by combining statement semantic analysis with code generation in a single task.

The compilation of module M begins with the lexical analysis of the file M.mod. The compiler optimistically anticipates the existence of a file M.def and tries to start

[3]We ignore the relatively rare self contained program module

[4]the import task for the implementation module is shown in the left column for convenience.

processing this file as soon as possible. The token stream produced by the lexical analysis phase is directed to the splitter and import tasks. The import task searches the token stream for IMPORT declarations and starts a new stream for each imported definition module that it discovers. It starts a lexical analysis, importer, syntax and semantic analysis sequence for each new definition module stream. The token stream produced by the lexical analysis of each imported definition module is also fed into its import task to detect indirectly imported interfaces. A "once-only" table is used to guarantee that each definition module referenced in a compilation is processed exactly once.

The splitter task searches for the reserved word PROCEDURE in the token stream of M.mod. It creates a new stream for each procedure it detects and diverts the lexical tokens for the procedure to that stream. It then starts a syntax analysis, semantic analysis, code generation sequence for that stream. The main module body which has now been striped of all embedded streams is processed through syntax analysis, semantic analysis and code generation. At the end of compilation, a merge task concatenates the output of separate code generation streams to form the complete compiler result. Because the unit of merging is the code for an entire procedure, this concatenation can be done in any order and concurrently with other compiler activity.

4 Compiler Performance

We have conducted numerous experiments to evaluate the performance of our prototype concurrent compilers. In this section we summarize the results of those experiments.

4.1 Test Environment

The concurrent compiler was written in Modula-2+. The compiler runs on DEC Firefly prototype workstations [TSS88] under the Topaz operating system [MS87]. The Firefly used to obtain the results presented here was configured with 64 Mb of main memory and eight CVax processors. The compiler performance results presented in this section should be view in the context of the known performance limitations of the Firefly hardware. At high levels of concurrent activity, memory bus saturation effects and fixed processor priorities for access to memory degrade the performance of all processors [TSS88]. Topaz provides a lightweight threads mechanism within a single address space. This mechanism was used extensively within the compiler.

The suite of 37 programs used to evaluate our compiler were taken from a very large library of Modula-2+ software that was made available to us by the DEC Systems Research Center. The programs in the test suite represent the efforts of a large number of authors and include a variety of programming styles. The programs in the test suite were chosen at the start of the CCD project to be a representative sample of the load that might be seen by a typical compiler. The programs in the test suite range from very small to very large. The gross characteristics of the test suite are given in Table 1. In this table *Imported Interfaces* are the number if definition modules imported directly or indirectly by the module being compiled. *Import Nesting Depth* is the maximum length of the import nesting chain for each module. More details on the test suite are available in [SW91, JW90].

Attribute	Minimum	Median	Maximum
Module size (bytes)	2,371	13,180	336,312
Seq. Compile Time (sec)	2.30	10.27	107.85
Imported Interfaces	4	17	133
Import Nesting Depth	1	5	12
Number of Procedures	2	16	221
Number of Streams	15	37	315

Table 1: Description of Test Suite

4.2 Speedup Results

To evaluate the improvement in compilation time that we were able to achieve through concurrent processing, we evaluated our concurrent compiler against a traditional sequential compiler for Modula-2+ and against itself. All test runs were made on an otherwise idle Firefly workstation. The results presented are the average of 10 runs. The run-to-run variation in our timing results was very small, on the order of 1%. Running on one processor, the concurrent compiler was 4.3% slower than the sequential compiler. This is due to the extra processing that was introduced to achieve concurrency which is wasted on a single processor. Figure 1 shows the self-relative speedup of our compiler as it was run on 1 through 8 processors[5]. To test the limits of our technique, we mechanically generated a synthetic module (Synth.mod) that would have the best possible speedup for our technique. This module has been constructed so that it generates ample parallel work for the compiler and never incurs a DKY blockage. The speedup results for the synthetic module are shown in Figure 2. For comparison we have included a reference line for linear speedup and results for the human-authored module that had the best overall speedup in the test suite.

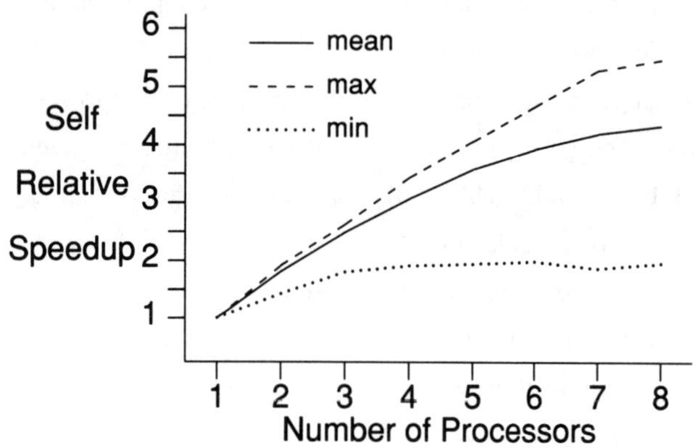

Figure 1: Test Suite Self Relative Speedup

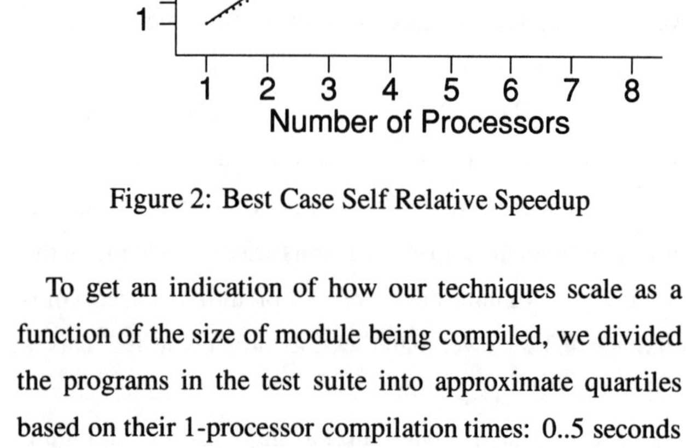

Figure 2: Best Case Self Relative Speedup

To get an indication of how our techniques scale as a function of the size of module being compiled, we divided the programs in the test suite into approximate quartiles based on their 1-processor compilation times: 0..5 seconds (10 programs), 5..10 seconds (8 programs), 10..30 seconds (10 programs) and 30..109 seconds (9 programs). Figure 3 shows the self-relative speedup data plotted separately for the programs in each quartile. From these plots we can see that the speedup obtainable through concurrent processing is limited for small programs, but increases as the size of program being compiled increases. For programs with a sequential compile time of less than 10 seconds, a speedup of 2.5 is obtained with 4 processors and there is no real advantage in using more processors. It is evident from the first two compilations in Figure 6 that small modules don't generate enough parallel work to fully utilize the multiprocessor. For larger programs (sequential compile time greater than 10 seconds), the speedup continues to increase although at a decreasing rate as more processors are used. We attribute this to the greater amount of parallel work available in these programs. As a graphical illustration of our compilers operation, we present the WatchTool snapshots in Figure 4. This figure shows processor activity (vertical axis) as a function of time (horizontal axis) as a program from each of the quartiles was compiled on an eight processor Firefly. There is a ten second delay between compilations. For comparison purposes, the rightmost peak in this figure is a compilation of the synthetic module that was described above.

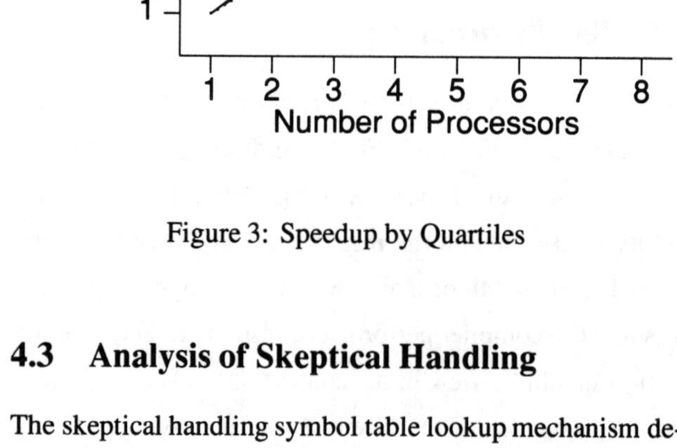

Figure 3: Speedup by Quartiles

4.3 Analysis of Skeptical Handling

The skeptical handling symbol table lookup mechanism described in Section 2.2 is an attempt to gain performance by

[5] Table 3 contains the data used to generate Figures 3,4 and 5

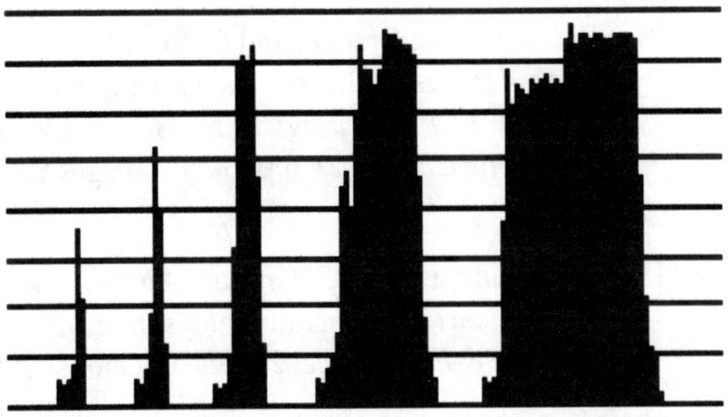

Figure 4: WatchTool Snapshot

searching incomplete symbol tables. To measure the effectiveness of this strategy, we gathered performance data for this mechanism for one compilation of our test suite. The lookup mechanism is applied in two circumstances: search for a simple identifier occurring in a procedure or the main module, and search for a qualified identifier (i.e. an identifier explicitly associated with an imported definition module). The statistics for identifier search are given in Table 2. The "Found when" column indicates the conditions under which the identifier was found. "Search" indicates that the identifier was found during an outward search through the scope parentage chain. "After DKY" indicates that the identifier was found in a scope that was completed after a DKY blockage. The "scope" column indicates the scope in which the identifier was found. "Self" is the scope of the stream that initiated the search, "other" is some other explicitly designated initial search scope, "outer" is a scope that was accessed chaining outward through the scope parentage chain, "WITH" is the scope of a WITH statement and "Builtin" is the scope containing all identifiers predefined by the compiler. The "completeness column" indicates that state of the scope at the start of the search. The last two columns given the number and percentage of lookups that succeeded for the particular combination of Found, scope and completeness. The interesting cases in this table are the searches that found an identifier in an incomplete table. This is the case where Skeptical Handling has an edge over more conservative strategies. The higher frequency of search success in incomplete tables and DKY blockages in the case of qualified names can be attributed to to the higher usage of qualified names in declarations. The majority of simple identifier references arise from the statements in the bodies of procedures. By the time these are processed there is a high probability that the symbol tables for outer scopes and definition modules have been completed. This table also shows that blockage due to the DKY condition is relatively rare. The low frequency of DKY blockages is one reason why the choice of a DKY strategy has only a small effect on overall compiler performance.

4.4 An Activity View of Concurrent Compilation

In the early part of a compilation the dominant activity is the lexical, syntax and semantic analysis of definition modules. The definition modules imported directly and indirectly by the main module form a tree. The need to resolve DKY blockages quickly and the task scheduling strategy used by our scheduler typically causes this tree to be processed in a bottom up order. At this point, the streams corresponding to the procedures in the main module have been identified by the splitter but processing of these streams is deferred until the corresponding procedure headings have been processed in the main module stream. Once processing of the main module stream reaches the procedure headers, a large amount of parallel work becomes available as processing of many procedure streams can be initiated. From this point on a high level of concurrent processing is possible through to the end of the compilation.

Figure 7 illustrates the compiler activities in a typical concurrent compilation. The horizontal axis is time, the vertical axis is processor number for an eight processor Firefly. The bars in this figure indicate different kinds of compiler activity. The dark gray bars at the left side are lexical analysis tasks. The light gray bars in the middle are parser/declaration semantic analysis tasks. The darker gray bars on the right side of the figure represent statement analysis/code generation tasks. The light gray bar for processor 7 is the splitter task. At the scale of this figure, the importer and merge tasks are too small to be easily visible. The activity lull in the center of this figure is caused by delays waiting for DKYs to be resolved and by the delay involved in waiting for procedure headers to be processed in the main module body as described in Section 2.4.

5 Conclusions

This paper has described the design and evaluation of a concurrent compiler for Module-2+. The compiler is designed to maximize opportunities for concurrent processing of source programs. We have demonstrated experimentally that the compiler achieves good compilation time speedups for a representative set of test programs and very good speedups for larger programs. The techniques we developed should be applicable to the design of concurrent compilers for a wide variety of programming languages.

Acknowledgements

The research described in this paper has been generously supported by the Digital Equipment Corporation Systems Research Center and by the Ontario University Research Incentive Fund. Ven Seshadri [Ses88] made many useful contributions to the design of the DKY processing strategies.

References

[JW90] M.D. Junkin and D.B. Wortman. The implementation of a concurrent compiler. Technical Report CSRI-235, Computer Systems Research Institute, University of Toronto, 1990.

[MS87] P. R. McJones and G. F. Swart. Evolving the UNIX system interface to support multithreaded programs. Technical Report 21, Digital Equipment Corporation Systems Research Center, 1987.

[Rov86] P. Rovner. On extending modula-2 for building large, integrated systems. *IEEE Software*, 3(6):46–57, Nov. 1986.

[SB90] D.B. Skillicorn and D.T. Barnard. A survey of parallel compilation. Technical report, Dept. of Computing and Information Science, Queens University, 1990.

[Sch79] R.M. Schell. *Methods for Constructing Parallel Compilers for use in a Multiprocessor Environment.* PhD thesis, University of Illinois, 1979.

[Ses88] V. Seshadri. Concurrent semantic analysis. Master's thesis, Dept. of Electrical Engineering, University of Toronto, 1988. reprinted as Computer Systems Research Institute Technical Report CSRI-216.

[SGR79] W.N. Joy S.L. Graham and O. Roubine. Hashed symbol tables for languages with explicit scope control. In *Proceedings of the SIGPLAN Symposium on Compiler Construction*, pages 50–57, 1979.

[SW91] V. Seshadri and D.B. Wortman. An investigation into concurrent semantic analysis. *Software – Practice & Experience*, 21(12), December 1991.

[SWJ+88] V. Seshadri, D. B. Wortman, M. D. Junkin, S. Weber, C. P. Yu, and I. Small. Semantic analysis in a concurrent compiler. In *Proceedings of the SIGPLAN '88 Conference on Programming Language Design and Implementation*, pages 233–240, 1988.

[TSS88] C. P. Thacker, L. C. Stewart, and E. H. Satterthwaite. Firefly: A multiprocessor workstation. *IEEE Transactions on Computers*, 37(8):909–920, August 1988.

[Van87] M. T. Vandevoorde. Parallel compilation on a tightly-coupled multiprocessor. Master's thesis, Dept. of Computer Science, Massachusetts Institute of Technology, 1987.

[VR88] M.T. Vandevoorde and E. Roberts. Workcrews: An abstraction for controlling parallelism. *International Journal of Parallel Programming*, 17(4), 1988.

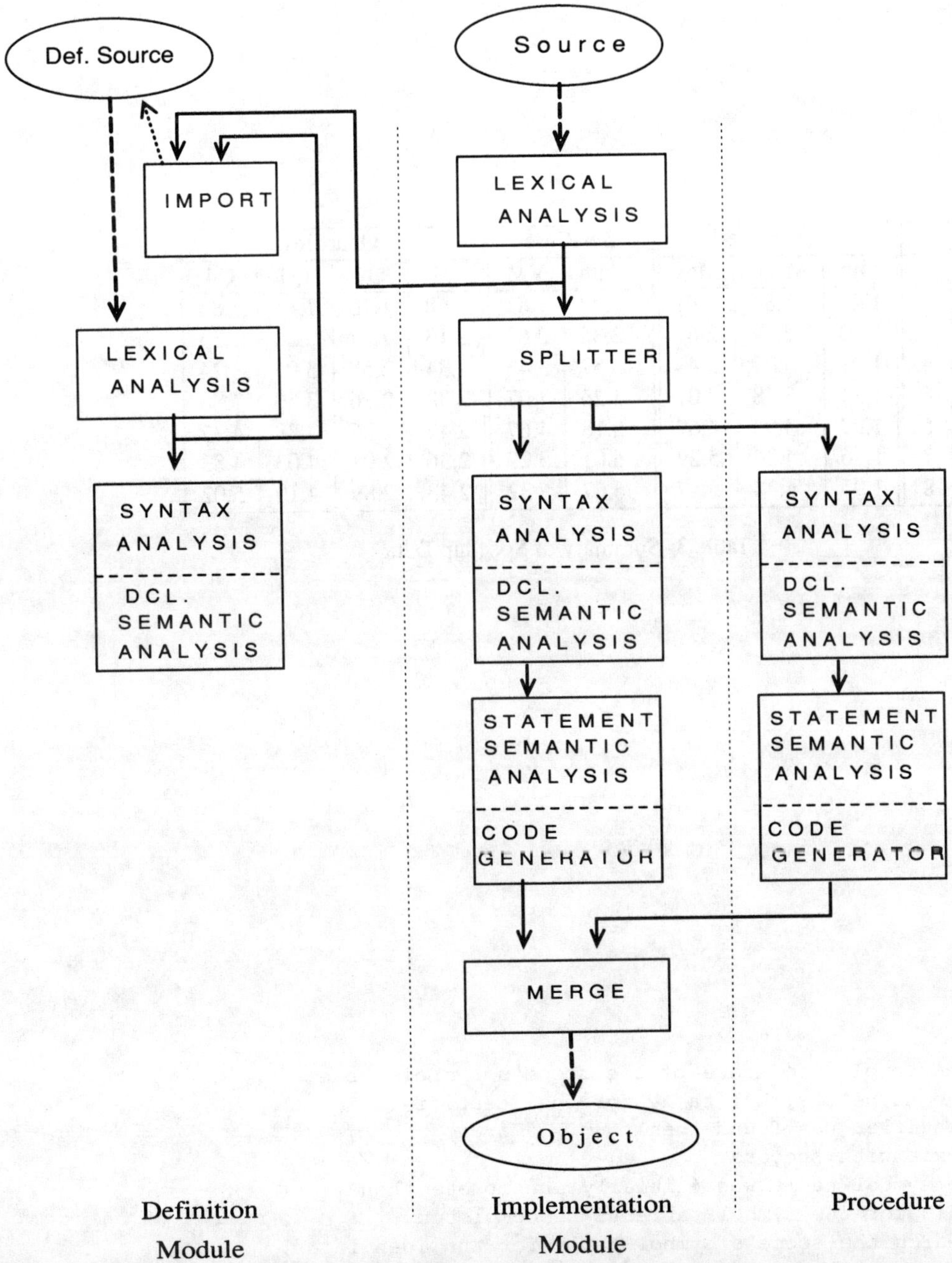

Figure 5: Compiler Task Structure

Simple Identifier					Qualified Identifier			
Found when	scope	completeness	number	%	Found when	completeness	number	%
First try	self	complete	52,544	57.87				
First try	other	complete	5,457	6.01				
Search	outer	incomplete	3,228	3.55	First try	incomplete	505	4.00
Search	outer	complete	12,879	14.18	First try	complete	11,775	93.30
After DKY	outer	complete	69	0.08	After DKY	complete	341	2.70
First Try	WITH	complete	2,699	2.97				
First Try	Builtin	complete	13,744	15.14				
Never			184	0.20				

Table 2: Identifier Lookup Statistics

N	Test Suite			BestCase		Quartiles			
	Min	Mean	Max	Synth	VM	Q1	Q2	Q3	Q4
2	1.42	1.81	1.91	1.99	1.81	1.68	1.70	1.81	1.84
3	1.80	2.49	2.62	2.85	2.62	2.13	2.27	2.50	2.55
4	1.91	3.07	3.43	3.57	3.43	2.34	2.57	3.05	3.24
5	1.94	3.58	4.07	4.26	4.07	2.38	2.76	3.56	3.88
6	1.99	3.93	4.67	5.18	4.67	2.42	2.85	3.88	4.37
7	1.86	4.20	5.29	6.01	5.29	2.36	2.91	4.03	4.83
8	1.95	4.34	5.47	6.67	5.32	2.43	2.89	4.19	5.02

Table 3: Summary of Speedup Data

```
Record the completion state of the scope's symbol table
Search the scope's symbol table for the identifier.
   If identifier was found then
        exit with success.
   If the symbol table was initially incomplete then
       Wait for the symbol table to be completed.
       Search the scope's symbol table for the identifier.
       If identifier was found then
           exit with success.
If current scope is outermost scope then
    exit with failure
else
    Continue search in next outermost scope
```

Figure 6: Skeptical Handling Symbol Table Lookup

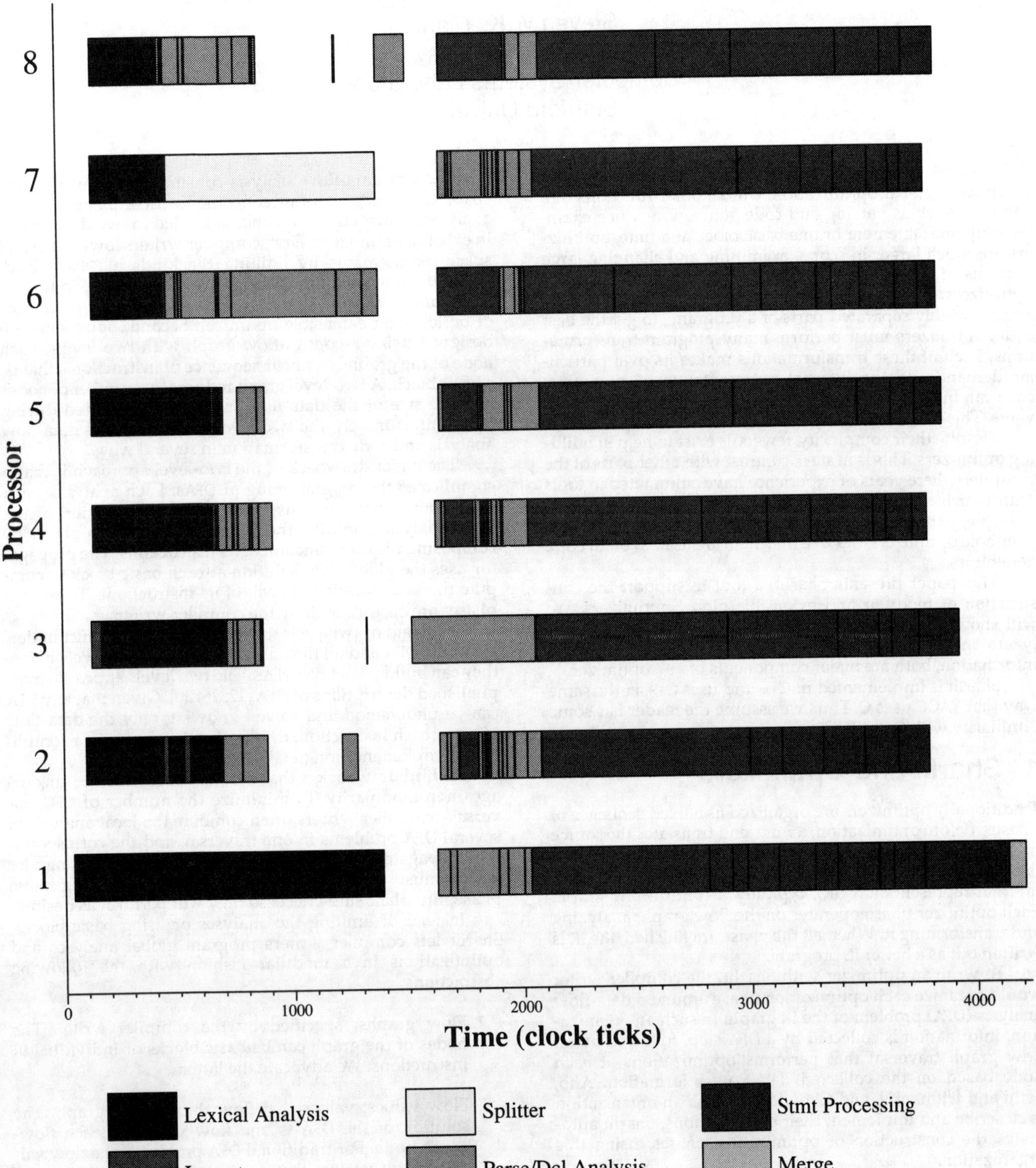

Figure 7: Concurrent Compiler Processor Activity

Sharlit—A tool for building optimizers

Steven W.K. Tjiang
John L. Hennessy
Computer Systems Laboratory
Stanford University

A complex and time-consuming function of a modern compiler is global optimization. Unlike other functions of a compiler such as parsing and code generation which examine only one statement or one basic block at a time, optimizers are much larger in scope, examining and changing large portions of a program all at once. The larger scope means optimizers must derive and use complex relationships among widely separated parts of a program. To get the best code, optimizers must perform many program transformations. Each of these transformations makes its own particular demands on the internal representation of programs; each can interact with and depend on the others in different ways. This makes optimizers large and complex.

Despite their complexity, few tools exist to help in building optimizers. This is in stark contrast with other parts of the compiler where years of experience have culminated in tools with which these other parts can be constructed easily. For example, parser generators are used to build front-ends, and peephole optimizers and tree matchers are used to build code generators.

This paper presents Sharlit, a tool to support the construction of modular and extensible global optimizers. We will show how Sharlit helps in constructing data-flow analyzers and the transformations that use data-flow analysis information, both are major components of any optimizer.

Sharlit is implemented in C++ and uses C++ in the same way that YACC uses C. Thus we assume the reader has some familiarity with C++ [9].

1 Sharlit and Optimizers

Traditionally optimizers are organized as a fixed sequence of phases. Before optimization, a front-end translates the source program into an intermediate language. The optimizer reads the IL program one procedure at a time, converting it into an internal representation (IR), typically a control-flow graph. Each optimizer phase operates on the flow graph, analyzing and transforming it. When all the phase are finished, the IR is written out as a better IL program.

To write an optimizer with Sharlit, the compiler writer would organize each optimization phase around a data-flow analysis (DFA) problem of the IR graph. In such an organization, information is collected by a DFA step, followed by an flow graph traversal that performs optimizations at each node based on the collected data-flow information. Aho, Sethi and Ullman[1], and Chow[4] use such an organization to describe and implement their optimizations. Sharlit automates the construction of optimization phases, using this organization.

ACM SIGPLAN '92 PLDI-6/92/CA
© 1992 ACM 0-89791-476-7/92/0006/0082...$1.50

Because data-flow analysis consumes a lot of time and space, compiler writers are concerned with implementing the analyzers efficiently. This concern has led to two deficiencies in existing optimizers. First, compiler writers lower time and space requirements by limiting the kinds of DFA solved. Unfortunately, such limits also restrict the kinds of code optimizations that can be done, a restriction contrary to our goal of building an extensible optimizer. Second, optimizers are designed using a control-flow graph with two levels. Each node of the graph is a linear sequence of instructions, that is, a basic block. A two-level graph reduces the number of nodes and the size of the data-flow information required during DFA. Unfortunately, the two-level graph obscures data-flow analysis and code transformation in several ways.

The major drawback of the two-level approach is that it complicates the programming of DFAs. Each analyzer must have both a local analysis phase and a propagation phase. Local analysis computes the flow function of a basic block by composing the flow function of its instructions. The propagator uses the global DFA solution at each basic block to compute the local solution at each of its instructions. These two phases are custom built by the compiler writer.

A second drawback is that compiler writers must understand the DFA and all the data structures at two levels before they can build prototype DFAS. The two levels appear in most published descriptions of DFAs [2, 16, 30]. Given that any DFA can be understood and solved knowing only the data-flow effect of each instruction, the two-level structure is a complicating implementation detail.

A third drawback is that the two-level structure encourages non-modularity. To minimize the number of CFG traversals, compiler writers often combine the local analysis of several DFA problems in one traversal, and the corresponding propagators in another traversal. Hence, the compiler writer must shoulder the burden of orchestrating these phases and their side-effects so they will perform as desired.

Instead of limiting the analyses or using basic blocks, Sharlit lets compiler writers program global analyses and optimizations in a modular fashion with the following abstractions:

1. Flow graphs: specified by the compiler writer. The nodes of the graph can be basic blocks or individual IR instructions. We advocate the latter.

2. Flow values: values that flow through the graph. The solution of the DFA is one flow value for each flow-graph node. For traditional DFA problems, the flow values are bit vectors that represent, for example, sets of expressions.

3. Flow functions: functions that represent the effect of flow graph nodes and paths on the flow values; these are specified as input to Sharlit.

4. Action routines: routines that use the DFA solution to perform program optimizations.

5. Path simplification rules: rules that show how to combine flow functions into other flow functions. There are four kinds of rules: **create, absorb, join,** and **star.**

With these abstractions, the compiler writers can pose their DFA problems as if each node of the CFG is an instruction.

Using Sharlit, the compiler writer can implement a wide range of program analysis, from the traditional bit-vector based DFAs to ones using sophisticated symbolic analysis. Sharlit generates efficient data-flow analyzers that use path simplification rules to simplify the graph.

Path simplification allows a compiler writer to use the simple *one-instruction-one-node* graph in Sharlit and still obtain efficient solvers for the DFA problems.

1.1 Path simplification

Path simplification is based on a version of Tarjan's fast path algorithm [11]. Tarjan's algorithm finds a *path expression* representing all paths from the source to every node in a graph. Path expressions are regular expressions built from node labels and the operators: ·, +, and *. For example, in Figure 1, the path expression from the exit of the source node to the exit of node D is $A((B+C)DA)^*(B+C)D$. Sharlit uses path expressions in data-flow analysis by interpreting the node labels as flow functions, path concatenation(·) as function composition, path addition(+) as taking the *meet* of functions, and the Kleene-star (*) as finding the fixed point of a function. The compiler writer tells Sharlit how to perform these operations with path simplification rules.

Path simplification is versatile: the rules can describe a wide range of DFA solvers, from simple iterative ones, to solvers using local analysis, to sophisticated solvers that use interval analysis. When confronted with irreducible graphs or incomplete sets of rules, path simplification degrades gracefully—it is still able to simplify significant portions of the graph.

2 Writing DFAs with Sharlit

This section provides an overview of Sharlit and path simplification, and shows how one can use Sharlit to write DFAs. We demonstrate Sharlit with three examples, all solving the *available expression problem* (AVP)[1]. An expression is available at a node n if every path from the source to n has evaluated the expression and the value of the expression remains the same if reevaluated at n. Determining available expressions is important in code motion [4].

These three examples show Sharlit's ability to apply a variety of solution techniques and solve versions of AVP using progressively more sophisticated and potentially faster solution techniques.

To underscore the extensibility of Sharlit-generated analyzers, we build each example from the previous one by adding new flow functions and new path simplification rules. The first example is a prototype solver that uses iteration. In this first example, each IR instruction is a node in the flow graph, making the prototype inefficient. By adding some simplification rules, we extend the prototype to do local analysis, reducing the work needed during iteration. By adding yet more rules—meet and the star rules—we enhance the solver to use interval analysis.

2.1 Preliminaries

Figure 2 shows how an internal phase of an optimizer is created using Sharlit. Each automatically generated data-flow

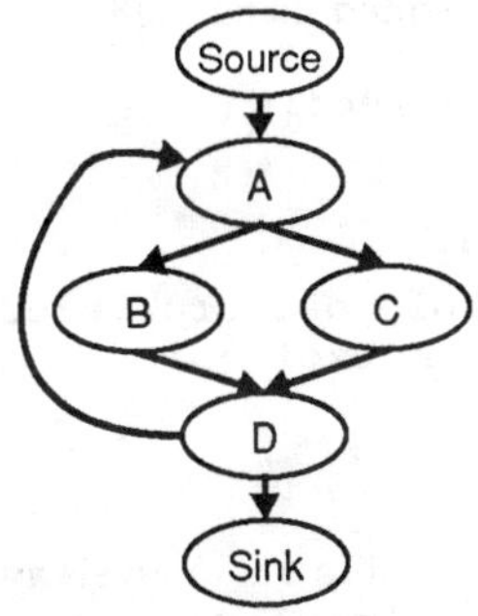

Figure 1. A small graph.

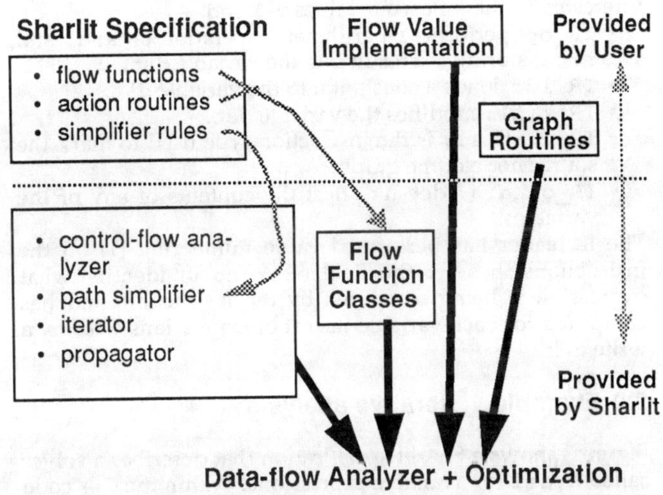

Figure 2. Structure of a Sharlit-based optimizer phase.

analyzer consists of four major components: control-flow analyzer, path simplifier, iterator, and propagator. The control-flow analyzer discovers the loop structure of the control-flow graph and summarizes the structure (control-flow analysis is done once for several DFAs) [8, 10]. The path simplifier, generated from the rules in the description, uses the control-flow information to eliminate nodes from the flow graph, creating a reduced graph that is easier to solve. The iterator makes one or more phases over the reduced graph, calling flow functions until a solution (consisting of flow values) to the data-flow problem is found. The propagator computes the solution at nodes eliminated by the path simplifier. In the process, the propagator calls user-supplied action routines for each node, routines that use the solution to perform program optimizations.

All the components are compiled and linked (black arrows) into an internal phase of the optimizer. The flow value is implemented as a C++ class by the compiler writer. The compiler writer can implement the flow graph in any way, but must provide graph routines that let the generated data-flow analyzer *view* the flow graph as a doubly-linked directed graph with edges stored as adjancy vectors.

In our examples, the IR is quad based and each IR

instruction is implemented using the following structure:

```
class IR_instruction {
    ...
public:
    int kind;
    IR_variable dst,src1,src2;
    Expression expr_no;
    ...
};
```

Only those fields relevant to our analysis are shown.

The IR has several types of instructions, distinguishable by the value of the field `kind`. Since expressions are built recursively from arithmetic operations and variables, we are interested in the following values of `kind`:

- `IR_op`: performs an arithmetic operation on `src1` and `src2`, storing the result into the variable `dst`.
- `IR_ldc`: loads a constant into the variable `dst`.
- `IR_kill`: modifies the variable `dst`.
- `IR_initial`: is the instruction type used to mark the source node of the graph.
- `IR_others`: doesn't affect the contents of any of the variables.

The IL reader has performed value numbering [1] on the instructions, has set the field `expr_no` to identify what expression is being computed by the instruction, and has computed for each variable the set of expressions *killed* by a write to it.

2.2 Example 1: iterative analysis

Figure 3 shows a Sharlit specification that describes a solver called `Avail` for available expressions. Within the C++ code of Sharlit specifications, special variables begin with an underscore and are capitalized.

1. *Flow graph nodes and Flow values:*

   Part A describes flow graph nodes and flow values. Sharlit incorporates this information as fields and functions of the data-flow analyzer. The brace-enclosed C++ declaration following the keyword **solver** declares variables to be use by other parts of the specification. In this case, there is only one field, an array of kill sets that can be accessed as `_P->kill_sets` in the flow functions. The **node_base** and **value_base** tell Sharlit the class name of the flow graph node and flow value.

   Part A also describes three functions that are called as the DFA problem is being solved. The **new_value** function returns a new flow value initialized to the universal set containing all expressions. The **copy_value** function copies a source flow value pointed to by `_SRC` to a destination pointed to by `_DST`. At the same time, **copy_value** returns a boolean value (1 or 0) indicating whether the copy will change the value of the destination `*_DST`. The **meet** function combines several flow values, stored in the array `_SRCS`, into one value which will be stored into the destination `*_DST`. For available expressions, **meet** takes the intersection of the values stored in `_SRCS`.

2. *Flow functions:*

   Part B describes the flow functions. The incoming flow value is pointed to by the variable `_V`. The C++ code following the keyword **flow** computes an output flow value, leaving a pointer to it in `_V`. In available expressions, and many other DFAs, the code can modify the incoming value directly into the outgoing value. For large, complex values, modification-in-place avoids unnecessary copies.

   There is a flow function corresponding to each instruction type discussed above.

- `AV_expression` corresponds to `IR_ldc` and `IR_op` instructions. This function inserts `expr_no`, the expression number being generated by the current node `_N`, into the incoming flow value, then removes from it the killed expressions, those whose value may change when the variable `_N->dst` is modified.
- `AV_kill` corresponds to the instruction `IR_kill`. This function removes all the killed expressions from the flow value.

```
Avail: =
solver: {
    Expr_set *kill_sets[];
};
node_base = IR_instruction;
value_base = Expr_set;
new_value: {
    Expr_set *v=new Expr_set(etable);
    v->mk_universal();
    return v;
};
copy_value: {                                          A
    if(*_SRC == *_DST)
        return 0;
    *_DST = *_SRC;
    return 1;
};
meet: {
    int i;
    _DST->mk_universal();
    for(i=0;i<_NSRCS;i++)
        *_DST &= *_SRCS[i];
};
AV_expression: flow {
    *_V += _N->expr_no;
    *_V-=_P->kill_sets[_N->dst];
};
AV_initial: flow{                                      B
    _V->mk_empty();
};
AV_kill:flow {
    *_V-=_P->kill_sets[_N->dst];
};
AV_identity: flow {};
flow_map: {
    switch(*_N->kind){
    case IR_op:
    case IR_ldc:
        return new AV_expression;
    case IR_kill:
        return new AV_kill;                            C
    case IR_initial:
        return new AV_initial;
    case IR_others:
        return AV_identity;
    }
};
end;
```

Figure 3. Iterative solver for available expression.

- `AV_initial` corresponds to the initial node `IR_initial`. This function initializes its output value to the empty set.
- `AV_identity` corresponds to the `IR_others` instruction. This function uses its incoming flow value as its outgoing value.

We must provide the above mapping between instructions and flow functions. Part C is a flow map function called from control-flow analysis to establish the correspondence between flow functions and instructions.

Figure 4 shows the iteration procedure that Sharlit uses to solve DFA problems. The procedure takes as its input a list of nodes ordered in the depth-first order [6], computed during control-flow analysis. The ordering is used because it is easy to compute and it has fast convergence for bit-vector problems [6].

The iterator uses the following information about the DFA problem:

- flow(u) is the flow function of the node u. The compiler writer provides this node to flow function mapping.
- ancestor(u) and new_flow(u) are computed during path simplification. Since this example has no rules, the condition ancestor$(u_i) \neq u_i$ is always false. Thus, for now, we can ignore the first if statement in the loop.
- $O(u)$ is the flow value (data-flow information) on exit of node u. Not every node will have one of these.
- has_meet(u) indicates whether a meet operation is necessary to compute the input flow value of u.

In the one-instruction-one-node flow graph, if Sharlit kept a copy of data-flow information—a flow variable—at every node, the data-flow analyzers would use a prohibitive amount of storage. The last two fields are important for eliminating flow variables.

2.3 Eliminating flow variables I

When there are no simplification rules, the iterate procedure in Figure 4 will call the flow function of every node in the graph as it iterates. However, not every node needs a flow variable.

In a Sharlit specification, a compiler writer cannot write code that references flow variables directly. In particular, flow functions can only modify the variable _V. At the beginning of a flow function, _V contains the input flow value of the node u with which the flow function is associated. The flow function modifies _V directly to arrive at the output flow value of u.

Denying direct access to flow variables frees Sharlit to chose how flow variables are stored. Sharlit allocates flow variables at three kinds of nodes. We show two of the three below. The third kind will be discussed later in Section 2.7.

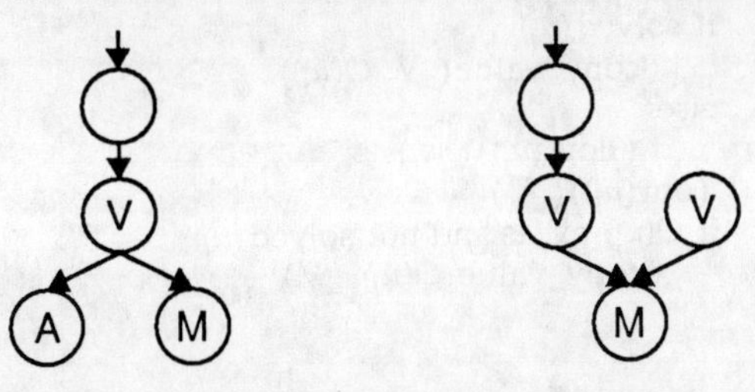

Nodes labelled V need flow variables and nodes labelled M need a meet operation or a copy operation to compute their input flow values. In the graph on the left, the node V needs an output flow variable because one of its successors, the node M, does not follow it in the depth-first order. Although _V as computed by V can be used directly as input to node A, V's flow value needs to be stored until node M is referenced during iteration. In the graph on the right, the nodes labelled V need variables because node M may not follow them directly in the depth-first order.

In general, a node u requires a flow variable $O(u)$ when u has more than one successor, or when u is the predecessor of a node that requires a meet operation to compute its input flow value.

Similarly, has_meet(w) is true for a node w—indicating that w requires a meet operation to compute its input flow value—when w is the successor of a node which has more than one successor, or when w has more than one predecessor. In the left graph above, M needs a meet operation to copy the flow variable of its predecessor. In the right graph, M needs a meet operation to combine the flow variables of its predecessors.

Sharlit's approach does not rely on basic blocks as traditional DFA does to reduce the amount of data-flow information stored in the flow graph. Traditional DFAs would have a flow variable at the input and output of each node or basic block. Instead, Sharlit needs only to keep an output flow variable at the end of a linear sequence of instructions. Consider two nodes u and w within such a linear sequence. Then u's unique successor is w and w's unique predecessor is u. After calling the flow function for u, _V contains the output flow value, which is equal to the input flow value of w. Hence, _V can be passed directly to the flow function of w as its input. Since no other nodes need the value of $O(u)$, it can be eliminated.

```
iterate(L)
{
    Let L = [u1, u2, ..., un] be a df-order of the CFG.
    Let O(u) be the output flow variable associated with u
    _V ← new_value()
    c ← true
    (flow(u1))(_V)
    copy_value(O(u1), _V)
    while c is true {
        c ← false
        for i=2 to s {
            if ancestor(ui) ≠ ui {
                copy_value(_V, O(ancestor(ui)))
                (new_flow(ui))(_V)
            } else if has_meet(ui) {
                Let {w1, w2, ..., wa} be predecessors of ui
                meet(_V, [O(w1), O(w2), ..., O(wa)])
                (flow(ui))(_V)
            } else
                (flow(ui))(_V)
            if O(ui) exists {
                c ← c| copy_value(O(ui), _V)
            }
        }
    }
    solved(ui) ← true for i = 1, 2, ..., s
}
```

Figure 4. The iterator—solution by iteration.

2.4 Example 2: local analysis

Even though the Sharlit example in Figure 3 saves space by

eliminating many flow variables, it must still visit every IR instruction on every iteration, using a lot of time. Our second version of AVP shows how we can reduce the number of nodes visited by adding path simplification to Figure 3.

Many optimizers reduce the number of variables and nodes by using a flow graph where the nodes are basic blocks. These optimizers have two additional data-flow analysis steps. *Local analysis* composes the effects of the instruction sequence into one flow function for the basic block. *Propagation* computes the data-flow solution at each instruction from the solution for the basic block. These steps are usually written in an *ad hoc* fashion.

By adding path simplification rules to a Sharlit specification, a compiler writer can get the same effect as local analysis from an efficiency viewpoint. In the following example, we show how rules can shrink the flow graph so that it contains only those nodes that form the boundaries of *extended basic block*.

To add local analysis to Figure 3, we add the code in Figure 5. Part A declares a path function `AV_bb` that represents the data-flow effect of a sequence of instructions. In the flow function `AV_bb`, two local variables, `defs` and `kills`, are used in computing the effect of a path:

$$Out = (In - \text{kills}) \cup \text{defs}.$$

The simplification rules compute `defs` and `kills` as a path is being built.

Two kinds of rules—create and absorb rules—follow the definition of `AV_bb`; our third example will show more kinds. Create rules generate identity flow functions for the empty basic block or empty path. Absorb rules grow this empty path by *absorbing* the flow function that immediate follows

```
....
AV_bb: local{
    Expr_set defs;
    Expr_set kills;
}                                            A
path {
    _V -= kills;
    _V += defs;
};
....
simplifier
(:AV_bb) create = {};
(b:AV_bb) absorb (l:AV_identity) = {};
(b:AV_bb) absorb (l:AV_expression,N) = {
    Expr_set*kill_set=&_P->kills_set[N->dst];
    b->kills += *kill_set;
    b->defs.add(N->expr_no);
    b->defs -= *kill_set;
};
(b:AV_bb) absorb (l:AV_kill,N) = {
    Expr_set*kill_set=&_P->kills_set[N->dst];
    b->kills += *kill_set;
    b->defs -= *kill_set;
};
(b:AV_bb) absorb (l:AV_bb) = {
    b->defs -= l->kills;
    b->defs += l->defs;
    b->kills += l->kills;
};
```

Figure 5.The sharlit specification for available expressions augmented with local analysis.

the path.

We summarize what the path simplifier (Section 2.7) does for extended basic blocks in Figure 6. By applying a series of **create** and **absorb** rules, the simplifier computes instances of the flow function `AV_bb` that relates the flow value leaving node A to the value leaving the leaves. Thus the nodes B and C are no longer necessary and are eliminated for consideration by the iterator.

For example, say the flow functions at node C and F are both of type `AV_expression`. To find the path function from the exit of A to the exit of F, the path simplifier uses the create rule to create a new path function. That path function *absorbs* the `AV_expression` function of C, using the rule

```
(b:AV_bb) absorb (l:AV_expression,N)
```

When the code part of this rule executes, the variable `b` points to the path function `AV_bb`; the variable `l` to `AV_expression`; and the variable `N` to the node C. The code updates the path function so that it represents the data-flow effect of the original path function composed with the flow function of C. Another application of the above rule will compose the above path with the flow function of node F.

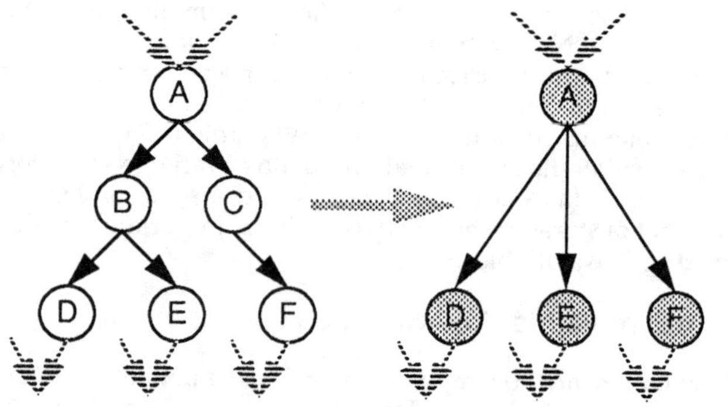

Figure 6. Simplifying extended basic blocks.

propagate(L)
{
  Let $L = [u_1, u_2, \ldots, u_n]$ be a df-order of the CFG.
  _V ← new_value( )
  for i = 2 to s do {
    if has_meet(u_i) {
      Let $\{v_1, v_2, \ldots, v_a\}$ be predecessors of u_i
      meet(_V, $[O(v_1), O(v_2), \ldots, O(v_a)]$)
    }
    (in(u_i))(_V)
    if solved(u_i)
      copy_value(_V, $O(u_i)$)
    else
      (flow(u_i))(_V)
    (out(u_i))(_V)
    if $O(u_i)$ exists and not solved(u_i)
      copy_value($O(u_i)$, _V)
  }
}

Figure 7. Propagation—computing solutions on the whole flow graph using the solutions from the reduced graph.

2.5 Propagation

Path simplification builds a smaller list that consists only the nodes at the boundaries of extended basic blocks, such as nodes A, D, E and F in Figure 6. It sets the *ancestor* of the leaves to the node that heads their corresponding block. For nodes D, E and F, that node is A. It computes for each leaf u a new flow function new_flow(u) representing the data-flow effect from ancestor(u) to u. The reduced list is given to **iterate**. The test for ancestor in **iterate** now has a purpose—to call new_flow(u) instead of flow(u).

Once iteration has found a solution to the smaller list, the routine **propagate** in Figure 7 is called to compute the flow values of nodes in the larger flow graph.

As **propagate** computes the flow values, it calls in(u) and out(u), action routines that can use the flow values at the input and output of u to perform optimizations. The compiler writer specify these action routines together with a flow function, as shown in Figure 8.

2.6 Example 3: Interval analysis

The advantage of iteration, with or without local analysis, is that it works on all graphs, even irreducible graphs. But for reducible graphs, we can avoid iteration, potentially speeding up DFA and allowing us to solve those DFAs which may not converge with iteration.

The example of Section 2.4 uses path simplification to perform local analysis, building a reduced graph with fewer nodes. We can use path simplification to perform interval analysis, building a reduced graph in which there are no loop back-edges. For an reducible flow graph, Sharlit can remove all back-edges, and the DFA problem can be solved by making one pass of the reduced graph, followed by a propagation step.

To remove a back-edge, path simplification summarizes the data-flow effect of a loop and *replaces* the loop with a tree consisting of some of the nodes of the loop. The flow functions of the nodes are replaced. This replacement occurs with the innermost loop, proceeds outwards, and ends with the entire graph.

For example, in graph of Figure 9(1), a tree replaces the innermost loop, whose header is the node D. The result in Figure 9(2) has the single tree node highlighted. The node E is eliminated[1], just as the local analysis of Section 2.4 would. The flow function of F is replaced by a new flow function f which is equal to EF. The graph Figure 9(3) shows the resulting graph after processing the loop headed by A. Here, the new flow functions are d=D(fD)* and g=(BC+df)G. Replacing A's loop eliminated the back-edge entering into D—it's data-flow effect has been summarized into the flow function f. Finally, in Figure 9(4), the outermost interval headed by Source is replaced and that removes the back-edge entering A.

In the example, all the back-edges were removed and the DFA problem can be solved by making one iteration over the much smaller, acyclic graph of Figure 9(4), followed by a propagation step that computes the solution at all the other nodes from the solution at A and D.

To add interval analysis to Figure 5, we add two types of rules—**join** rules and a **star** rule—shown in Figure 10. These rules tell Sharlit how to take the meet of two alternative paths that share the same end-points; and how to take the Kleene-star of a path. The last rule is necessary for removing back-edges.

2.7 Eliminating flow variables II

After path simplification in the examples of Section 2.4 and

```
name: local {
      local variables
}
flow {
      ....
}
in {
      code that uses flow value at entry of node
}
out {
      code that uses flow value at exit of node
};
```

Figure 8. Flow function declaration with in and out functions.

1. The nodes are actually only marked and eliminated in a later step, but we show eliminate them eliminated here to simplify the explanation.

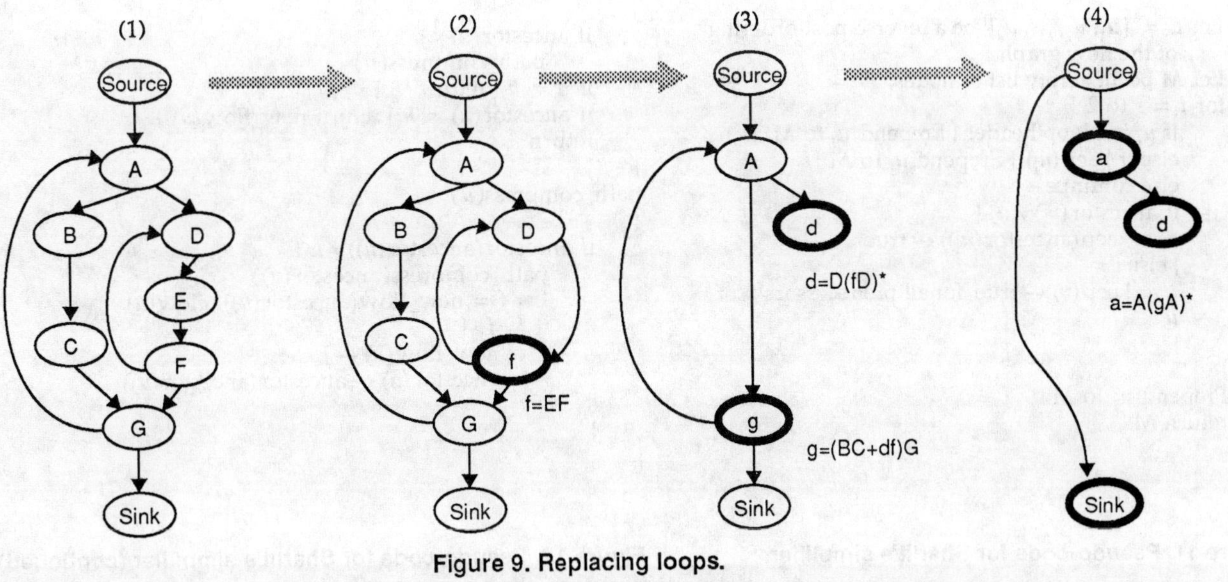

Figure 9. Replacing loops.

```
(b1: AV_bb) join (b2: AV_bb) = {
  Expression_set sum1, sum2;
  sum1.universal(_P->etable);
  sum2.universal(_P->etable);
  sum1 -= b2->defs;
  sum1 *= b2->kills;
  sum2 -= b1->defs;
  sum2 *= b2->kills;
  sum2 += b1->kills;
  b1->kills = sum1;
  b1->kills *= sum2;
  b1->defs *= b2->defs;
};
(b:AV_bb) star = {
  b->kills -= b->defs;
  b->defs.clear();
};
```

Figure 10. Enhancing solver to use interval analysis.

```
cfa(G) /* Control-flow analysis */
{
    Let G be the control-flow graph.
    Perform a depth-first traversal to discover the loop
        structure of G.
    The output are two lists: L which is a df-ordering of
        the G, and a list of lists [L_1, ..., L_K]. Each list is
        a df-ordering of the nodes within a loop body.
        The lists are mutually exclusive—all pairwise
        intersections are empty. The lists satisfies the
        condition
        depth(L_1) ≥ depth(L_2) ≥ ... ≥ depth(L_K).
    Also computes for each node u the loop_head(u),
        the node which heads the loop in which u
        belongs.
}
simplify(L, [L_1, ..., L_K])
{
    Let L and [L_1, ..., L_K] be the result of control-flow
        analysis.
    for i=1 to K
        simplify_loop(L_i)
    return reduce(L)
}
reduce(L)
{
    Let L = [u_1, u_2, ..., u_s] be a reverse post-ordering
        of the flow graph
    Let M be an empty list of nodes.
    for i = s to 2 {
        if u_i is a loop header { Prepend u_i to M. }
        else if keep(u_i) { Prepend u_i to M }
        else continue
        if ancestor(u_i) ≠ u_i {
            keep(ancestor(u_i)) ← true
        } else {
            keep(v) ← true for all predecessors v of
        u_i.
        }
    }
    Prepend u_1 to M
    return M
}
```

Figure 11. Pseudo-code for Sharlit's simplifier.

```
simplify_loop(L)
{
    let L= [u_1, u_2, ..., u_l] a df-order of a loop.
    for i=1 to l {
        Let f = flow(u)
    /* Classify predecessors */
        Let V = {v_1, v_2, ..., v_a} be predecessors such that
            u_i = loop_head(v_j) and v_j → u_i is a back-edge for
            j = 1, 2, ..., a.
        Let {w_1, w_2, ..., w_b} be the other predecessors of u_i
    /* Compute the path expression through back-edges */
        if V ≠ ∅ {
            q_j ← eval(v_j, u_i) for j = 1, 2, ..., a
            q ← ((q_1 + q_2 + ... + q_a) f) /* form path expression */
        } else
            q ← f_Id /* the identity flow function */
    /* Compute the path expression from a dominator to u */
        Call eval(w_j) for j = 1, 2, ..., b
    /* Find common ancestor */
        if ancestor(w_1) = ancestor(w_2) = ... = ancestor(w_b) {
            Let a = ancestor(w_j)
            Let p_j = new_flow(w_j) for j = 1, 2, ..., b
            p ← (p_1 + p_2 + ... + p_b) f /* form path expression */
        } else if we can't find a then
            p ← f_⊥
    /* Compute new_flow */
        p ← pq*
        if p ≠ f_⊥ {
            ancestor(u_i) ← a
            new_flow(u_i) ← p
        } else {
            keep(u_i) = true
            keep(v_j) = true for j = 1, 2, ..., a
        }
    }
}
eval(u)
{
    if ancestor(u) ≠ u {
        path_compress(u)
        return new_flow(u)
    }else
        return f_Id
}
eval(u,h)
{
    if ancestor(u) ≠ u
        path_compress(u)
    if u = h { return f_Id }
    if ancestor(u) = h { return new_flow(u) }
    return f_⊥
}
path_compress(u)
{
    if ancestor(ancestor(u)) ≠ u {
        path_compress(ancestor(u))
        Let f = new_flow(ancestor(u)) · flow(u)
        if f ≠ f_⊥ {
            new_flow(u) ← f
            ancestor(u) ← ancestor(ancestor(u))
        }
    }
}
```

Figure 12. Pseudo-code for Sharlit's simplifier (continued).

Section 2.6, Sharlit needs to store variables at the nodes that are ancestors to others. This is necessary because **iterate** the flow values at the exit of an ancestor may be required as input to many other nodes.

3 The Path Simplifier

Sharlit's simplifier is shown in Figure 11 and Figure 12, and is based on Tarjan's algorithm for the single-source path problem. The algorithm computes for each node a path expression representing all the paths from the source to that node. Sharlit's path simplifier uses this path expression computation to guide the composition, meet and taking the Kleene-star of flow functions. In this section, we discuss the four key ideas behind the operation of the simplifier. We explain the simplifier in the context of computing path expressions; Section 3.1 will show how that computation corresponds to calls of the rules provided in a Sharlit specification.

First, changing the graph directly to replace loops is expensive. Instead a tree edge (a, u) is represented by setting ancestor(u) to a. In Figure 9(2) for example, ancestor(E) and ancestor(F) are both D. Also, the new flow functions computed when replacing the loop are stored in new_flow(u). Notice that ancestor only allows traversals up the tree from the leaves upward, not from the root downwards.

Second, the simplifier builds the ancestor tree by visiting each loop in depth-first order, and visits loops from the innermost to the outermost. This ensures that when it comes time to compute the path expression for a node u, the simplifier has already computed the path expressions for the predecessors of u within the loop. For example, in Figure 9, the visit order is [E, F] for the loop headed by D, [B,C,D,G] for the loop headed by A, and [A,Sink] for the outermost interval headed by Source.

Third, tree nodes—those nodes u whose ancestor is not u—have their path expressions computed on demand. In Figure 9(2) for example, the path expression between A and f is computed during calls to eval when the simplifier is visiting G. A chronology of the order in which path expressions are computed follows:

- path expression E for the path from D to E.
- EF for path from D to F.
- B for path from A to B.
- BC for path from A to C.
- When visiting D, the simplifier calls eval(F, D) which returns f=EF. Hence, the path expression computed for D is d=D(fD)*.
- When visiting G, the simplifier calls eval(F) which yields df, the path expression from A to F. Hence the path expression for G is g=(BC+df)G.
- A(gA)* for the path from Source to A, with a call of eval(G, A).
- Finally A(gA)*gSink for the node Sink, with a call of eval(G).

Fourth, when forming path expression the simplifier can fail because it is unable to find a sequence of simplification rules that can simplify the path expression into a single flow function. When that occurs, the result of the path expression formation is $f_{\perp}$. When that occurs for a node u, its ancestor remains u, and u becomes eligible to become ancestors of other nodes (See Section 3.2).

3.1 Path simplification rules

Path simplification builds path expressions and in the process computes flow functions using composition, join, and taking the Kleene-star of other flow functions. These operations are directed by the compiler writer with path simplification rules.

An obvious way to tell the analyzer how to combine flow functions is to use the *times table* approach. For example, when the analyzer needs to compose two flow functions, it would index a special table with the two flow functions to find what actions are necessary to do the composition. Although tables are simple, specifying them directly is tedious: A complete specification of the composition table for M flow functions would require M^2 entries. Instead Sharlit can generate a complete table using only $M+1$ rules and a new kind of flow function: a path function.

During iteration (the solution of the DFA problem), a path function behaves just like any other flow function, except that it represents the data-flow effect of a path computed by the path simplifier. During path simplification, a path function is treated differently for efficiency reasons—they are modified directly or reused.

Below we show the five kinds of rules and describe how they work conceptually. Each rule has a code part that when executed computes a new path function by modifying the path function specified in the left-hand side of the rule.

1. p create: Create a new path p whose data-flow effect is the identity. This rule is used in the situations depicted in Figure 13. The analyzer inserts identify flow functions with the intention of extending that path (see below). This insertion does not change the data-flow problem—the solution is the same as the solution without the insertion of p.

2. p create f: Create a new path p whose data-flow effect is the same as the flow function f (see Figure 14). Again this replacement will not change the solution of the data-flow problem. This replacement is used by the analyzer to create paths in the graph that begins with nodes with flow function f.

3. p absorbs f: Extend a path p so that it has the same data-flow effect as the old p composed with f, that is modify p so that it represents the data-flow effect $p \cdot f$ (Figure 15).

4. p star: Replace the path p with a path that represents the data-flow effect of p^*. This rule, together with other rules, is used to remove back-edges (See Figure 16).

5. p_1 join p_2: Replace the path p_1 with a path that represents the data-flow effect of the path $p_1 + p_2$ (Figure 17).

Relating this back to Figure 11, we can see that the path computation steps are application of these rules. So computing a path expression, such as $q \leftarrow ((q_1 + q_2 + \ldots + q_a) f)$ means applying a sequence of path simplification rules.

3.2 Incomplete path simplification

Sharlit's path simplification differs from Tarjan's algorithm in how it handles irreducibilities and incomplete rule sets. For both situations, path simplification can still reduce significant parts of the graph, although it may not be able to remove all back-edges. Tarjan's algorithm works only on reducible

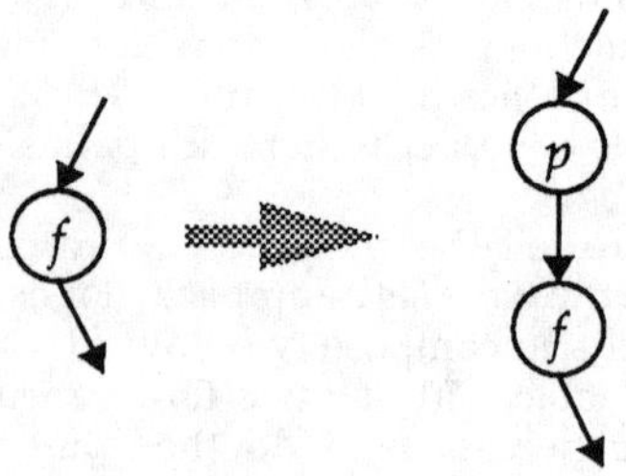

Figure 13. Applying the "p create" rule.

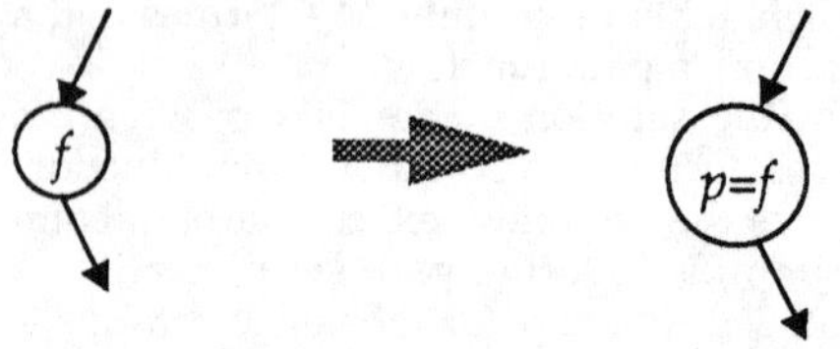

Figure 14. Applying the "p create f" rule

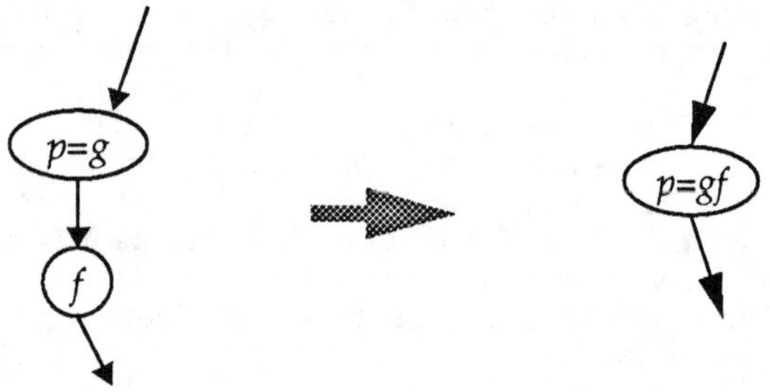

Figure 15. Applying the "p absorb f" rule

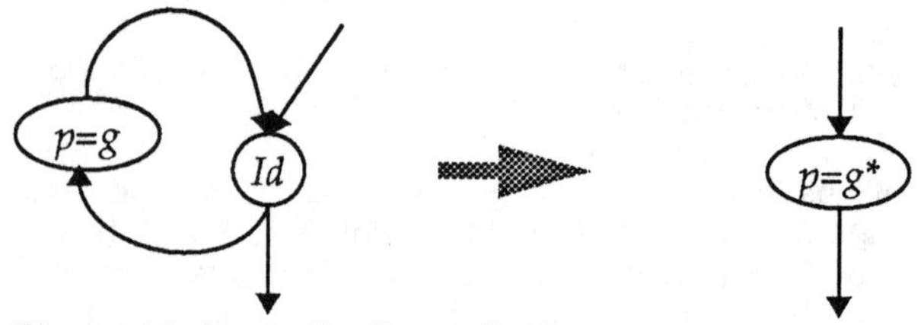

Figure 16. Apply the "p star" rule
The node labelled *Id* is an identity node. They are not actually present in the graph but are present for expository reasons only.

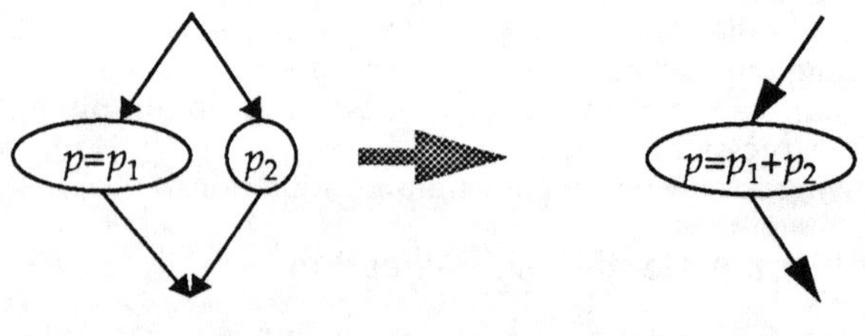

Figure 17. Applying the "p_1 join p_2" rule
This rule only applies when the two paths share common endpoints. This condition is enforce in the path simplifier because the ancestors of the nodes must be the same

flow graphs.

We can characterize **simplify** by saying that it tries to find a flow function from a dominator of u whose path to u can be simplified into one flow function. Simplification can fail to find such a flow function when the simplification rules are incomplete—they cannot simplify some combination of flow functions—or when the graph is irreducible. When there are no meet rules but the rules are otherwise complete, this farthest dominator will be the entry node of the extended basic block. For irreducible graphs, **simplify** fails because a common ancestor cannot be found (see Figure 11). Even then, the simplifier can still succeed on the reducible parts of the graph.

The simplifier degrades gracefully, reverting to local analysis where it can, or even to just partial local analysis (only parts of extended basic blocks are simplified) when the rules are extremely incomplete. This gradual degradation makes it easy to test and develop DFA incrementally.

3.3 Using rules in path computation

The procedures **simplify**, **eval**, and **path_compress** build path expressions abstractly using operators ·, +, and *. We show how Sharlit turns this process of computing path expressions into invocations of rules. We define three functions corresponding to the path operators:

1. compose(f, g):
   a) If $f = f_\perp$ or $g = f_\perp$ then return $f_\perp$ to indicate failure.
   b) If $f = f_{Id}$ then create a new path function representing g, that is, with the same data-flow effect as g. This creation can occur by either applying the rules—p create g; or the sequence—p create f followed by p absorb g. If exactly one of these possibilities are possible by the rules given in the specification, then return p; otherwise return
   c) If $f = p$ for some path function p. Then apply p absorb g if possible; otherwise go to the next case.
   d) Otherwise, return compose(compose(f_{Id},f),g) but only if the rule sequence to do it exists.

2. join(p_1, p_2, ..., p_a):
   a) If $a = 1$ return p_1.
   b) Make a copy of the first path by doing $p \leftarrow$ compose(f_{Id}, p_1), then apply p join p_2, ..., p join p_a. Return p if successful, otherwise return f_{Id}.

3. star(p):
   a) Invoke the rule p join, if the rule is present in the specification, otherwise return $f_\perp$

With these functions, we can interpret the path computation $(p_1 + p_2 + \ldots + p_a)f$ as compose(join(p_1, p_2, ..., p_a), f), and pq as compose(p, star(q)).

The above functions are generated as table lookups. For example, compose would index into a composition table to determine what action to take. Because rule sets are small, Sharlit generates these tables by exhaustive search of the rule sequences.

3.4 Absorb rules save space

Path functions computed by the analyzers can potentially take a lot of storage. For example, the path function AV_bb in Figure 5 has two sets of expressions.Thus, just as we must be careful about which flow variables to retain, we must be care-

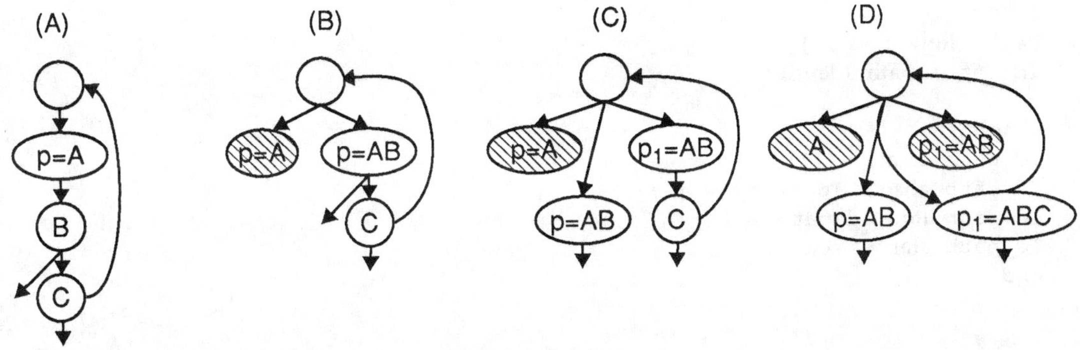

Figure 18. Reusing flow functions in sequences of node

ful about which path functions to retain. The traditional way of dealing with this problem in traditional optimizers is to group instructions into basic block. Therefore only one path function is required for each basic block.

In Sharlit, the primary mechanism to save space is absorb rules coupled with reference counting of flow functions. To see how absorption saves on space, see Figure 18. Assume that we have the rules: *p* create, *p* absorb *p*, *p* absorb A, *p* absorb B, and *p* absorb C. In Figure 18(A) we apply the rules *p* create, followed by *p* absorb *A* to compute the path function corresponding to the path expression A. In (B), we apply *p* absorb *B* giving the path expression AB. We can reuse *p* because we know that the node A won't need a path function because it will be eliminated by **reduce**. However, in Figure 18(B) this cannot be done because the node B (now corresponding to path expression AB) cannot be reused because its other successor will need it. Hence, the path expression AB must be copied, as shown in Figure 18(C). Absorption continues in Figure 18(D) and reuses the copy of AB.

To decide when to reuse a path function, we keep a reference count—a count of the successors—for each path function. When composing a path function *p* with its successor, and *p*'s count is one, we can use it directly in an absorb rule; if its count is not one, then it must be copied, its count decremented, and its copy is used directly in absorption. When we add a successor to a path function (as when path simplification connect nodes to their ancestors), its count must be incremented.

There are two exceptions to the reference counting. Path functions associated with loop headers are treated as though they have infinite reference counts. This is necessary to ensure that they are never eliminated because they are never eliminated by **reduce**. Identity flow functions are treats similarly. But because identity flow functions have no local variables they can be allocated statically and copies do not take up more space.

4 Sparse Data-flow Evaluation Graphs

Besides being able to do local analysis and interval analysis, path simplification can also build sparse data-flow evaluation graph (SDFEG) [4] for reducible flow graphs to solve sparse data-flow problems efficiently. In the context of reaching definitions problem, a SDFEG corresponds to a SSA graph for one variable. But unlike SSA, SDFEGs can be applied to other data-flow problems.

To compute an SDFEG, it is necessary to find paths which consists solely of identity flow functions, and to prune away all those flow-graph nodes which are connected to nodes in the SDFEG nodes through identity paths. Sharlit can identify such paths with the path simplification rules in Figure 19. In that specification the keywords **identity** tells Sharlit the flow function or path function is the identity flow function. Figure 20 compares an SDFEG computed using Sharlit and that of Choi's.

Sharlit's SDFEG differs in that we use nodes to represent some of the edges in the Choi's SDFEG—We indicate those nodes with dashed circles. These nodes are required because the only way Sharlit can modify a node *u*'s edges in the graph is to replace all of *u*'s edges with one edge from *u*'s ancestor to *u*. Therefore, at the node F, the only way to connect F to its SDFEG predecessor is indirectly, as ancestors of C and E.

The key point that makes SDFEG efficient is it can eliminate so many more flow variables than our current scheme. The current version of Sharlit's simplifier is capable of finding the paths composed of identity flow function. However, the current version of **propagate** and **reduce** needs to be modified in order for us to eliminate the flow variables at the ends of these identity paths. We continue to work on integrating SDFEG into Sharlit.

5 Conclusion

We have found Sharlit to be a useful tool. Its facilities are ideal for describing DFAs, from simple iterative ones, to ones that use symbolic analysis (recurrence detection) to ones that use interval analysis. Because of its extensibility, it is ideal for prototyping optimizations and to experiment with different internal representations.

We have used Sharlit to build an optimizer as part of the Stanford SUIF compiler project [12]. Our results (Figure 21) show that this optimizer can optimize large, real programs—such as the PERFECT club [3]—as effectively as commercial compilers. Our optimizer uses Sharlit to implement all its internal phases:

1. Value numbering.
2. Reaching definitions.
3. Elimination of partial redundancy[7]: Global common subexpression elimination, strength reduction, backward code motion out of loops.
4. Global register allocation.
5. Constant propagation and copy propagation.

```
...
Defs: flow { ... }
Id_path: path Identity;
...
simplifier
Id_path create = {};
Id_path absorb Identity = {};
Id_path join Id_path = {};
Id_path star = {}
end
```

Figure 19. Rules for doing SDFEG.

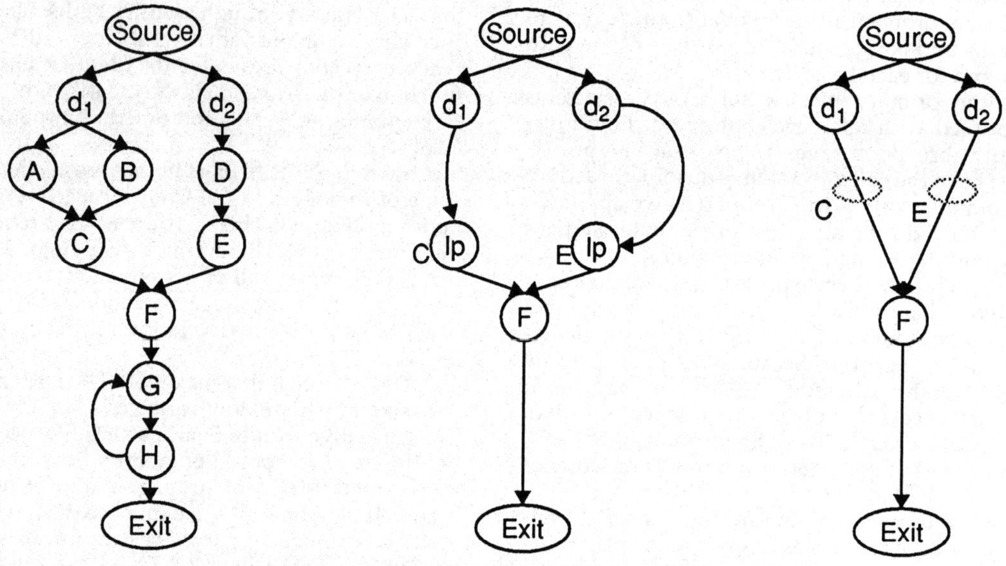

Figure 20. Example of Sharlit's version SDFEG. Ip represents an Identity path.

	SUIF -O	MIPS -O2	SUIF/MIPS
LG	97	106	0.82
LW	1437	1405	1.02
NA	421	377	1.12
SD	88	105	0.84
SR	1270	1253	1.01
TF	243	232	1.05
TI	259	244	1.06

Figure 21. PERFECT club execution results in seconds from runs on a Decstation 5000 with version 1.31 of the Mips compiler.

6. Liveness analysis and Dead code elimination.

7. Recurrence detection[2].

Our experiences suggest that Sharlit is a good and practical. Constructing the optimizer using Sharlit has required much less effort and has resulted in a compiler that is simpler, easier to extend, and more versatile.

6 Acknowledgments

This research has been supported by DARPA under contract N00039-91-C-0138. We would like to thank Rob French, Monica Lam, Bob Wilson, and Michael Wolf for their helpful comments.

7 References

1. A.V. Aho, R. Sethi, J.D. Ullman, *Compilers, Principles, Techniques, and Tools.* Addison-Wesley, 1986.
2. Z. Ammarguellat and W. L. Harrison III, Automatic recognition of induction variables and recurrence relations by abstract interpretation. In *Proceedings of the ACM SIGPLAN '90 Conference on Programming Language Design and Implementation.*
3. M. Berry et al, The PERFECT Club Benchmarks: effective performance evaluation of supercomputers. Technical Report UIUCSRD Rep. No. 827, University of Illinois Urbana-Champaign, 1989.
4. J. Choi, R. Cytron, and J. Ferrante, Automatic construction of sparse data flow evaluation graphs, In *POPL 1991.*
5. F. Chow, *A Portable Machine-Independent Global Optimizer,* PhD thesis, Stanford University, 1983
6. M.S. Hecht and J.D. Ullman. A simple algorithm for global data-flow analysis programs, In *SIAM J. Computing.* (4):519-532.
7. E. Morel and C. Renvoise, Global optimization by suppression of partial redundancies, In *Communications of the ACM.* (22):96-103
8. M. Sharir. "Structural analysis: a new approach to flow analysis in optimizing compilers". *Computer Languages 5* (1980), 141-153.
9. B. Stroustrup, *The C++ Programming Language,* Addison-Wesley, Reading, Mass.
10. R. E. Tarjan. "Testing flow graph reducibility". *J. of Comput. and Syst. Sci.* (9 1974), 355-365.
11. R.E. Tarjan, Fast algorithms for solving Path problems. *Journal of the ACM,* 3(28):591-642, July 1981.
12 S. Tjiang, M. E. Wolf, M. S. Lam, K. L. Pieper, and J. L. Hennessy, Integrating scalar optimization and parallelization, In *4th Workshop on Languages and Compilers for Parallel Computing,* Aug 1991.
13 J. D. Ullman. "Fast algorithms for the elimination of common subexpressions". *Acta Inf. 2,* 3 (July 1973), 191-213.

Prototyping Fortran-90 Compilers for Massively Parallel Machines

*Marina Chen & James Cowie**
Department of Computer Science, Yale University
chen-marina@cs.yale.edu cowie-james@cs.yale.edu

Abstract

Massively parallel architectures, and the languages used to program them, are among both the most difficult and the most rapidly-changing subjects for compilation. This has created a demand for new compiler prototyping technologies that allow novel styl. of compilation and optimization to be tested in a reasonable amount of time.

*Using formal specification techniques, we have produced a data-parallel Fortran-90 subset compiler for Thinking Machines' Connection Machine/2 and Connection Machine/5. The prototype produces code from initial Fortran-90 benchmarks demonstrating sustained performance superior to hand-coded *Lisp and competitive with Thinking Machines' CM Fortran compiler. This paper presents some new specification techniques necessary to construct competitive, easily retargetable prototype compilers.*

1 Introduction

Existing compilers for massively parallel machines have generally been constructed using traditional methods, combining generation from specification for a few subsets of the problem (typically the syntactic analysis) with hand-coded solutions for most others. One such compiler is Thinking Machines' CM Fortran [1], which targets the Connection Machine/2, a massively parallel, SIMD supercomputer. CMF was awarded a 1990 Gordon Bell Prize honorable mention for compiled code performance.

*Support for this work is provided by the Defense Advanced Research Project Agency, monitored by the Army Directorate of Contracting, under contract DABT 63-91-C-0031.

ACM SIGPLAN '92 PLDI-6/92/CA
© 1992 ACM 0-89791-476-7/92/0006/0094...$1.50

While CMF and similar compilers unarguably achieve production quality, they are difficult and expensive to construct, maintain, and extend as a result of their target-specific, highly-tuned, hand-coded nature. By contrast, traditional systems for generating compilers from denotational semantics drew on the flexibility and power of formal specification to build and maintain systems that were truly machine-independent. They remain unacceptable for production use, however, due to the generally poor performance of the code they produce, and their size and speed.

The MESS system [5] introduced "separable semantic specification" as an alternative to denotational semantics approaches. MESS used a two-level semantic specification to separate high-level language properties from model detail. This enforced separation helped alleviate the performance problems associated with compilers generated from formal descriptions. Such systems, however, were still limited in practice to sequential-execution, uniprocessor implementations of simple imperative languages. MESS-generated compilers had no systematic framework for program transformation, focusing instead on simple two-pass translation. They lacked the necessary semantic features to express parallelism, and thus did not attempt to model or target parallel systems.

Other research has shown the importance of a unified intermediate representation in constructing optimizing compilers. The SUIF language of Tjiang, Wolf, *et al.* [7] successfully preserves high-level information for low-level transformations, and begins to show how multiple levels of optimization concerns must be coordinated, but was not used in the context of formal compiler specification. Pingali *et al* use abstract interpretation techniques in their intermediate representation [6], and use a true imperative store and explicit formulation of loops. They are primarily concerned, however, with dataflow analysis, and do not have an abstraction that unifies data and control parallelism, nor a treatment of back-end concerns.

In this paper we propose a methodology for compiler design that brings together lessons learned from previous compilers for massively parallel machines with techniques from formal specification. Like the MESS system, our prototype compilers define a semantic algebra as their intermediate format, and use production rule sets to define the translation process from the user's syntactic forms to constructs of this algebra. Adding a framework for intermediate program transformation, support for multilayered target systems, and a shape abstraction for data parallel computation, we then show how to model massively parallel machines in a working compiler specification.

Finally, we present initial results from our prototype Fortran-90-Y compiler for the CM/2 and CM/5. After eight months of development, the prototype implementation generates code for multiple platforms exhibiting sustained performance superior to that of hand-coded *Lisp and competitive with Thinking Machines' CM Fortran compiler. Furthermore, the prototype's space and time requirements are comparable to those of native language tools for the CM. We argue that competitive performance, coupled with rapid prototyping and target flexibility, have become persuasive arguments for developing compilers for massively parallel machines using formal specification techniques.

2 Problem Overview

To clarify our motivations, we introduce brief overviews of the data-parallel features of Fortran 90 and the slicewise programming model for the Connection Machine/2. We then break down the problems to be solved in a prototype compiler for that machine, and describe the overall prototyping and optimization strategies that need to be developed as a result.

2.1 Source Language: Data Parallelism in Fortran 90

The Fortran 90 language [2] contains many extensions to the old Fortran 77 standard that are of interest for data parallelism. Specifically, the ability to refer to and compute directly with whole arrays and arbitrary subsections give the programmer the ability to express program parallelism that would previously have been stated only implicitly or through the use of source-level annotation. The wide selection of intrinsic procedures for examining, reshaping, or performing reductions over Fortran 90 arrays serve to replace many common transformations that programmers were previously forced to approximate with serial syntax.

For example, the Fortran 77 code

```
      INTEGER K(128,64), L(128)
      DO 10 I=1,128
        L(I) = 6
        DO 20 J=1,64
          K(I,J) = 2 * K(I,J) + 5
20        CONTINUE
10      CONTINUE
```

could be replaced by the Fortran 90 assignments

```
      L = 6
      K = 2*K+5
```

Similarly, the loop

```
      DO 30 I=32,64
        L(I) = L(I+64)
        DO 40 J=1,64
          K(I,J) = K(I,J)**2
40        CONTINUE
30      CONTINUE
```

can be rewritten in Fortran 90 as

```
      L(32:64) = L(96:128)
      K(32:64,:) = K(32:64,:)**2
```

To some extent, then, our compiler has high-level parallelism pre-packaged for it by the user's choice of Fortran-90 constructs. We can therefore concentrate on matching the source's parallelism to that of the target, and avoid the tangle of extracting parallelism from serial code.

2.2 Machine Model: Slicewise CM/2 Programming

The Connection Machine Model CM/2 in slicewise mode [1] consists of up to 2,048 Slicewise Processing Elements (*nodes* or *PEs*), each consisting of 32 bit-serial processors coupled with one Weitek WTL3164 64-bit floating-point ALU. The PEs are connected by a 11-dimensional boolean hypercube with two wires along each dimension. The bit-serial nature of the processor set is hidden from the programmer, who sees a conventional bit-parallel, word-serial interface to memory and to the Weitek FPU.

The programming language designed by the CM Fortran group for this PE abstraction is PEAC (Processing Element Assembly Code). PEAC allows the Weitek chip to be programmed as a four-wide vector processor; it also allows accesses to CM memory to be overlapped with arithmetic operations, and supports the Weitek chained multiply-add instruction.

Each slicewise processor synchronously executes instructions issued from the CM sequencer. Each instruction processes a vector of four 32- or 64-bit elements – "slices" through local memory. PEAC code is only

[1] as opposed to the more traditional fieldwise, or Paris mode.

used to express purely elemental program segments; that is, under the normal programming model, there can be only pointwise dependencies between data that are aligned to the same geometry and used in the same PEAC routine. When an instruction sequence is applied serially to each of the (potentially very many) elements local to each processor memory, the result is a *virtual subgrid loop* parameterized by a set of strided data pointers and a subgrid loop count.

For computations that are not purely elemental, but have some degree of locality or regularity, the CM runtime system provides a large set of special-purpose uniform communication primitives, efficiently implemented in microcode. When dependencies in user code exceed the restrictions of both the elemental and the special-purpose uniform styles, however, general router communications result, at significant performance expense.

For example, the Fortran 90 code fragment

```
real, array(n,n) :: I
I(:,:) = 6.0
```

might be compiled as a single PEAC node routine storing the 32-bit scalar value `6.0` to each local element serially, in batches of four. On the other hand, the Fortran 90 assignment

```
I(:,2:n) = I(:,1:n-1)
```

might be implemented by the CM runtime system call `CMRT_cshift`, and the negative-strided array section assignment

```
I(:,n:1:-2) = I(:,1:n:2)
```

would be implemented via the router as general point-to-point communication from `I` to `I`.

2.3 Main Compiler Issues

Clearly, the main tension in CM code arises between communication and computation. Specifically, given a section of user code, an effective compiler must perform decompositions and transformations to minimize interprocessor communication. Simultaneously, the code generation process should maximize in-processor performance through efficient vectorization. There are, therefore, multiple levels of program optimization to consider.

The relatively high cost of data movement forces the compiler to address the high-level challenges of data layout and communication. Simultaneously, those codes that are naturally computation-dominated, easily vectorized due to elemental locality, will benefit most from treatment of processor-level concerns.

These two optimization levels are not entirely orthogonal. High-level compilation strategies for reducing interprocessor communication, which typically group computations with similar layout, minimize conversion between rival layouts, and aggressively unroll serial loops, all help to maximize the PEAC elemental codeblock size as well. This in turn allows more efficient low-level coding.

Node processor complexity, which continues to track advances in microprocessor technology, will continue to increase this pressure for multilevel optimization. As the CM/1 bit-serial processor gave way conceptually to the Weitek-augmented abstraction of the CM/2, so too the CM/2 PE will eventually be replaced by the CM/5's SPARC node, augmented with optional vector hardware. For massively parallel architectures in general, increases in node sophistication will dramatically increase the need for compilers that can orchestrate strategies for cooperative optimization at many levels of target abstraction, from high- to low-level.

These, then, are the primary concerns that a realistic prototype compiler must satisfy:

- Because the project is primarily a prototyping system, intended to serve as a testbed for research into optimization strategies, minimizing development time is critical, as is support for staged development. Formal specification techniques help support "attack strategies" for extremely rapid compiler development.

- The problem therefore requires a framework for compilation that will help apply minimal effort to compiler scaffolding (front end data, serial code, and bookkeeping concerns) while optimizing the compiler's critical paths — selecting appropriate forms of communication, efficient register allocation and effective vectorization of the node code.

- The final goal is to produce compiled object code whose performance is competitive with traditional compilation techniques for massively parallel architectures, and, in many cases, with equivalent hand-coded solutions, for a fraction of the total development cost. Simultaneously, generated compilers must run in reasonable space and time on available workstations, generally within an order of magnitude of hand-coded equivalents, if they are to be considered "realistic" for production use.

3 Theoretical Basis

In the Fortran-90-Y compiler we use formal specification techniques to address the dual challenges of performance and development time, using an abstract semantic algebra with special operators for describing se-

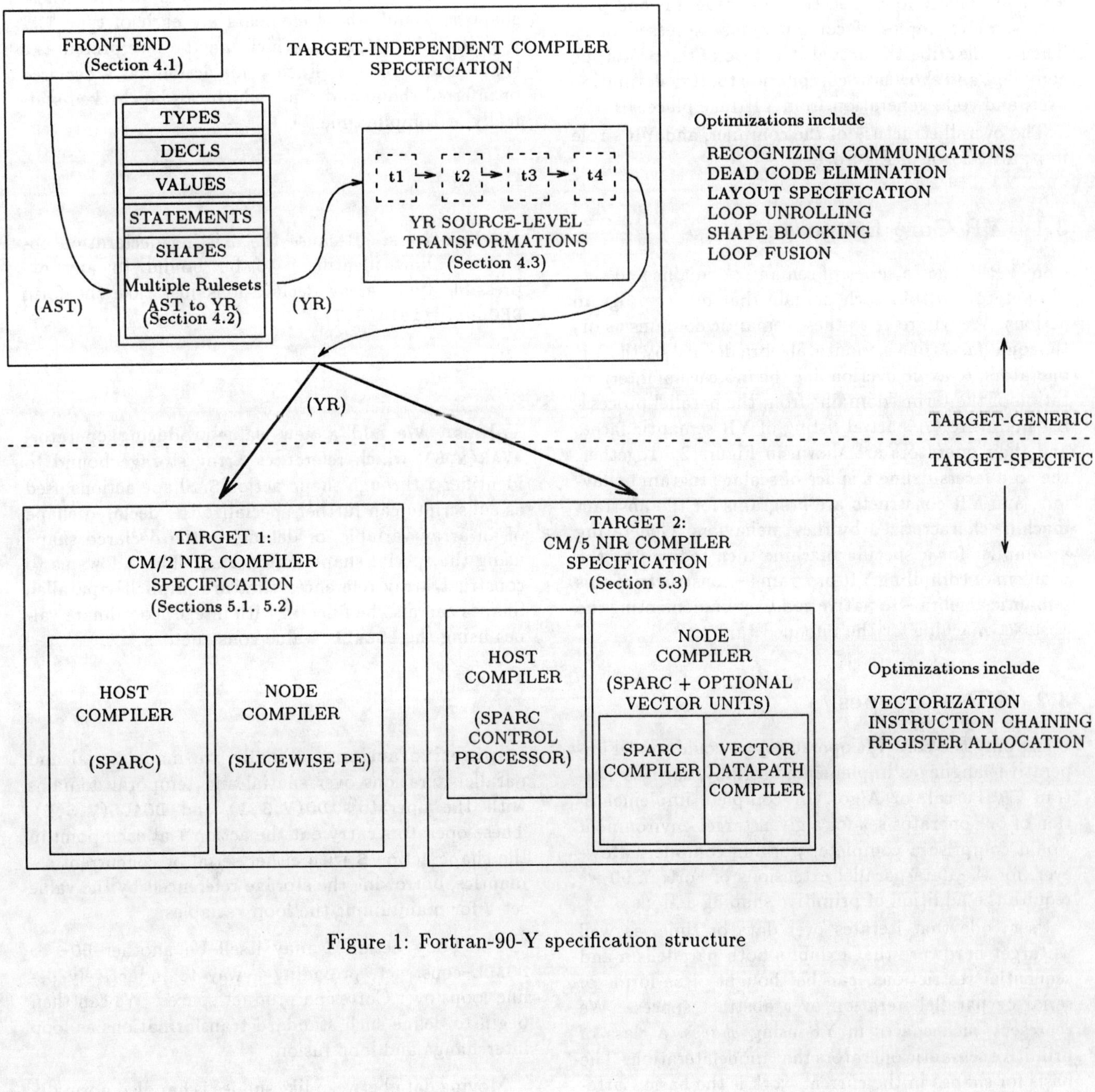

Figure 1: Fortran-90-Y specification structure

rial and parallel iteration to formulate an appropriate machine model.

These operators are collected in the central notation of the Fortran-90-Y compiler specification, *Yale Intermediate Representation* (YR). YR serves as the basis for target-independent program transformation, as well as for specific compilation to the SPARC control processor, the CM/2 slicewise node processor, the CM/5 SPARC node processor, and the CM/2 and CM/5 as a whole. The following sections describe YR and provide some examples of computations expressed in it. Then we describe the actual structure of the prototype compiler, and show how compilation to, transformation over, and code generation from YR take place.

The overall structure of the compiler, and YR's role in it, are shown in Figure 1.

3.1 YR Core Language

Core YR defines a series of semantic domains and sets of operators within each domain that model program actions. We will refer to these semantic domains as orthogonal *facets* of a semantic algebra defined by the YR operators, to avoid overloading the more usual interpretation of the term "domain" from the parallel processing literature. A partial listing of YR semantic facets and their operators are shown in Figure 2. Together, the core facets define a space of scalar program behaviors, and YR constructs are programs for the abstract machine characterized by these behaviors. Generating a compiler for a specific machine then reduces to the problem of compiling YR programs – constructs of this semantic algebra – to native code, by implementing the abstract machine for the intended target.

3.2 YR + Shapes

Using only the core YR operators, we could model imperative languages implemented serially, such as Fortran 77, Pascal, or Algol. A complete implementation of our operator set for a given target environment would comprise a complete, working compiler. However, for the data-parallel extensions of Fortran 90 we require the addition of primitive shaping actions.

User code that iterates over data or time, as well as target hardware that exhibits both parallelism and sequential restrictions, can be thought of as forms of serial or parallel iteration over abstract spaces. We represent such spaces in YR using *shapes*, a class of primitive semantic operators that model iteration. The basis for shapes in the current work is the basic Cartesian product space, although future work may include tree, hypercube, or butterfly domains as shape primitives, as suggested by previous research into domains and data fields [4].

To integrate these shape operators into scalar YR, bridge actions are added to each of the other semantic facets. The additional operators are marked with asterisks in figure 2.

Types. To model array types, we add the type operator `dfield:S*T`, which defines a new type whose shape is `S` and whose elements are each of type `T`. `T` may itself be a `dfield`, which may be interpreted as a shape cross-product. Each value action has a declared or inferred shape and type, which can be checked statically at compile time.

Declarations. Because the existing declaration operators allow identifiers to be bound to any expressible type, array declarations just take the form `DECL(i,dfield(S,T))`.

Values. We add a new value-producing operator, `AVAR(i,S)`, which references array storage bound to identifier `i` through shape action `S`. Shape actions used as subscripts can further specialize the declared shape of an array variable, or default to the declared shape using the special shape action `all`. This allows us to construct array references that are implicitly parallel. Shapes can also be filled in with integer coordinate values using the `LOCALLY` value-constructor.

Imperative actions. Finally, we model serial and parallel iterations over spatial and temporal domains with the operators `DO(V,S,I)` and `DOALL(V,S,I)`. These operators carry out the action `I` at each point in the shape action `S` with either serial or concurrent semantics, borrowing the storage referenced by the value set `V` for maintaining the loop variables.

The body action `I` may itself be another `DO`- or `DOALL`-construct, providing a way to inductively define loops over Cartesian product spaces. We can then begin to define such standard transformations as loop interchange and loop fusion.

Moving data between like shapes is handled normally as part of the general data motion operator `MOVE`, where the left- and right-hand types are `dfields` with matching shapes and elemental types, and the storage phase of the movement is executed under an optional mask.

TYPE FACET (T)	operator signature	interpretation * – Shape augmentation to core YR
integer_32	T	32-bit integer
logical_32	T	32-bit logical
float_32	T	single-precision floating point
float_64	T	double-precision floating point
dfield	S*T->T	* a field of elements of the given type
DECLARATION FACET (D)		
DECL	id * T -> D	simple declaration
DECLSET	D list -> D	multiple declarations
INITIALIZED	id * T * V -> D	declaration plus initial value
VALUE FACET (V)		
COMPUTE	op*V*V -> V	arithmetic computation
SVAR	id -> V	scalar variable
SCALAR	T*s_rep -> V	scalar constant
FUNCALL	id*(T*V)list -> V	function call
AVAR	id*S -> V	* array variable
LOCALLY	S*int -> V	* coord array constructor
IMPERATIVE FACET (I)		
PROGRAM	I->I	top-level program action
SEQUENTIALLY	I list ->I	sequential composition
CONCURRENTLY	I list ->I	concurrent composition
MOVE	(V*V)list -> I	data movement
MMOVE	(V*(V*V))list -> I	move under mask
IFTHENELSE	(V*I*I) -> I	classical if-then-else
WHILE	(V*I) -> I	classical while-construct
REF_OUT	V->I	passes call-by-reference parameter
COPY_OUT	V->I	passes call-by-value parameter
WITH	D*I -> I	execute in extended environment
SKIP	I	defines (SEQUENTIALLY nil)
DO	V list*S*I -> I	* execute over the given shape
DOALL	V list*S*I -> I	* ..in parallel
SHAPE FACET (S)		
point	int -> S	* single point
gen_interval	S*S*int -> S	* strided interval
interval	S*S -> S	* stride-1 interval
prod_dom	S list -> S	* shape cross-product
dyn	V -> S	* dynamically determined shape
all	S	* select all elements

Figure 2: Partial Listing of YR Domains and Operators

The Fortran 90 code mentioned earlier,

```
INTEGER K(128,64), L(128)
L = 6
K = 2*K+5
```

might be expressed in full YR as

```
WITH (DECLSET
  [DECL('k',dfield
   {shape=prod_dom
     [interval(point 1,point 128),
      interval(point 1,point 64)],
    element=integer_32}),

   DECL('l',dfield
   {shape=interval(point 1,point 64),
    element=integer_32})],
 SEQUENTIALLY
 [ ...
   MOVE [(SCALAR(integer_32,'6'),
               AVAR('l',all))],

   MOVE [(COMPUTE(bin Plus,
               [COMPUTE(bin Mul,
                 [SCALAR(integer_32,'2'),
                  AVAR('k',all)]),
                SCALAR(integer_32,'5')]),
               AVAR('k', all))],
... ]);
```

The program consists of a declaration section, wrapped around two data movements composed sequentially. The first assigns the scalar integer value 6 to all elements of array `l` in parallel; the second computes the function `2k+6` for all points in `k` simultaneously, and moves the result back into corresponding elements of `k`. Note that the `all` operator is used for the array variable subscript to specialize different shapes, with the meaning specified by context. `All` thus allows us to express elemental parallelism in data movement decoupled from the specific shape associated with the array variables.

4 Fortran-90-Y: Target-Independent Phase

The target-independent phases of the prototype compiler include modules for syntactic analysis, initial translation to YR and static semantic analysis, and YR source-to-source optimization. Each phase is specified as a set of Standard ML modules.

4.1 Syntactic Analysis

Syntactic analysis is performed by a front end system whose target is a generic AST format. The implementation of syntactic analysis by way of formal specification is well understood, and we elide further details here. The current front end in the Fortran-90-Y prototype, for example, is a custom subset lexer/parser in the form of a ruleset guiding the accumulation of lexical tokens into simple tree form, and the recognition and tagging of a number of multistatement constructs.

4.2 Static Semantic Analysis

Following syntactic analysis, the resultant AST is matched against a set of production rules that guide the construction of a valid YR program and perform static semantic checking. These rules are grouped according to the semantic facet within which their resultant program action is classified. The current prototype includes nine rule sets that govern the transformation of ASTs into YR program fragments according to their parent semantic facets: right and left-hand side expressions (valuations), types and shapes, simple and block-structured statements (imperatives), and variable and constant declarations.

The rule sets are mutually recursive, and call each other to fill in the missing parts of parameterized actions. For example, the `DO` operator for serial iteration is parameterized by a list of value-resources that may be borrowed to serve as loop variables, a shape over which the looping occurs, and a body instruction, possibly including the loop variables, to execute at each iteration. The production rule that creates a `DO`-statement is just one clause of the rule set `AST_to_Stmt`. One pseudocode form of the rule to produce a YR `DO`-statement from an AST encoding a simple lower-bound, upper-bound loop with unit stride is

```
AST_to_Stmt(env,
  [[do /loopvar/=/lb/,/ub/ /body/]]) =>

  let val bodyaction = AST_to_Stmt(body,env)
      and lvaraction = AST_to_LHS(env,loopvar)
      and lb_shape   = AST_to_Shape(env,lb)
      and ub_shape   = AST_to_Shape(env,ub)

  in DO([lvaraction],
          interval(lb_shape,ub_shape),
          bodyaction)
  end
```

If the user's program contains such a simple `DO`-loop, the AST fragment that encodes the loop will be matched against each rule in the ruleset `AST_to_Stmt` sequentially. It will trigger this particular clause, which will in turn extract the syntactic subtrees containing the loop bounds (point shapes), the loop index variable, and the statement that forms the loop body. The rulesets **AST_to_[Stmt, LHS, and Shape]** are used recursively to construct their semantic values. These values are then combined under the **DO**-operator into a single entity, which is returned as the YR compilation of the original AST.

Similarly, the **LHS**-rule that translates unqualified identifiers to assignable variable actions is

```
AST_to_LHS(env,[[/vname/]]) =>

(case typeof(env,vname) of
     dfield{...} => AVAR(vname,all)
   | other       => SVAR vname)
```

Note that if the type associated with the variable name in the static environment **env** is an array type (**dfield**), the rule assumes that the whole-array reference is intended, and produces the correct YR encoding for an array variable used as a left-hand side.

Finally, the rule that handles simple assignment is just

```
AST_to_Stmt(env,[[/somelhs/=/somerhs/]]) =>

let val lhs' = AST_to_LHS(env,somelhs)
    and rhs' = AST_to_RHS(env,somerhs)
in
 if types_agree(env,lhs',rhs')
 andalso shapes_agree(env,lhs',rhs')

 then MOVE[(rhs',lhs')]
 else
   raise AST_to_Stmt_Error
    ("Mismatch in assign")
end
```

Here, the functions **types_agree** and **shapes_agree** look up or derive the type and shape of the supplied YR valuation actions and trivially check them for agreement before allowing the compilation to proceed. [2]

The final result from this phase should be a single imperative action that describes the entire user computation, and has been statically type- and shape-checked. No attempts at program optimization have been made. The YR action can then be passed through a series of optimizing transformations, or directly to a target-specific YR compiler for code generation.

4.3 YR Transformations

The current Fortran-90-Y optimization stage performs a chain of source-to-source transformations over YR code. This framework supports program transformation within each semantic facet, propagating the effects of transformations through the program by way of YR's bridging operators, where facets meet. The object is to produce programs in which computations over like shapes are blocked as much as possible, forming computation phases punctuated by communication.

These shape-based program transformations allow us to express standard compilation techniques such as various loop transformations, as well as specific goals such as exploiting communication patterns that are well-supported by the target.

Each is implemented as a single Standard ML functor, defining a transformation function whose type is **YR.statement -> YR.statement**. Each has a set of input assertions that must be satisfied, or the transformation fails, displaying a warning of assertion failure and passing the input program through unmodified. Like the static semantic phase, each transformation function is defined as a rule set partitioned along semantic facets. Generally, each transform is triggered by a particular context or YR construct, and so can be defined in just a few hundred lines of SML code.

The selection and ordering of these optimization modules are currently statically determined at the time the compiler is built to satisfy whatever input assertions the back end YR compilers may have, and to precondition code for good performance.

4.3.1 Constant propagation

The constant propagation module performs simple value tracking to simplify expressions in crucial contexts. This is primarily useful in statically resolving otherwise compile-time indeterminate subscript ranges, and thus can greatly extend the potential for later optimization. For example, if the user codes

```
B(2:np1) = A(2:np1) + B(1:n)
```

and variable **np1** is clearly only used to store the value **n+1** for some parameter **n**, then rewriting the array expressions to include that information will resolve a dynamic shape checking dilemma at compile time.

Simple value tracking is accomplished by passing over the input YR program with an environment that stores, for each variable, either a current constant valuation, an uninitialized marker, or an unknown status. This simple tracking does not cross the boundaries of basic blocks.

4.3.2 DOALL reduction

Unlike the Fortran 90 standard, but like most compilers that implement a subset of Fortran 90 features, the

[2]Nontrivial shapes, including arrays and intervals with runtime-determinate bounds, also exist in YR in the form of the **dyn** operator for dynamic shapes. Certain shape checking operations may therefore be postponed until runtime.

Fortran-90-Y prototype implements a FORALL statement, though the YR operator is named DOALL. Perhaps its most significant use is to allow pointwise computations in which the local array coordinates participate.

The subset of FORALL expressions that involve only local array elements and coordinates are detected and reduced by this transformation module to whole-array expressions that use the YR value-constructor LOCALLY. For example, the Fortran 90 statement

```
      forall (i=1:m, j=1:m)
c       A(i,j) = i*B(i,j)+j
```

where A and B were defined over the common shape S equal to (1:m)*(1:m), would emerge from the static semantic phase as the YR fragment

```
DOALL([SVAR i, SVAR j], DOMAIN "S",
 MOVE

  [COMPUTE(bin Add,
    [COMPUTE(bin Mul,
      [AVAR("B",prod_dom
          [dyn(SVAR "i"),dyn(SVAR "j")]),
       SVAR "i"]),
     SVAR "j"]),

  AVAR("A",prod_dom
   [dyn(SVAR "i"),dyn(SVAR "j")])])
```

Although the individual shapes can be inferred, the exact subscript values remain unspecified, leaving complicated source and target expressions for the MOVE. The problematic subscript expressions each exactly match the list of variables that the DOALL borrows to store loop indices, triggering the DOALL reduction module. This transformation introduces parallel YR temporaries of the same shape and distribution as A and B using the YR LOCALLY operator, and reduces this YR fragment to the simpler pointwise computation

```
MOVE

[COMPUTE(bin Add,
  [COMPUTE(bin Mul,
    [AVAR("B",all),
     LOCALLY(S,dimension 1)]),
  LOCALLY(S,dimension 2)]),

 AVAR("A",all)]
```

4.3.3 Communication introduction

Expressions that involve mixed communication and computation must be broken into separate pieces executed serially, often with temporary storage to hold intermediate results. This module passes over the input YR program, using a rule set to detect such expressions and perform the necessary splitting transformations. For example, if the module sees YR code expressing

```
  A = B + CSHIFT(B,DIM=2,SHIFT=2)
```

such as

```
MOVE

[COMPUTE(bin Add,
   [AVAR("B",all),
    PRIM("cshift",
       AVAR("B",all), ...)]),

  AVAR("A",all)]
```

it converts this to multiple moves with a local declaration

```
WITH(DECL("t0",dfield{shape=S,...}),
SEQUENTIALLY

[MOVE
 [PRIM("cshift",
       AVAR("B",all), ...),

    AVAR("t0",all)],

MOVE
  [COMPUTE(bin Add,
     [AVAR("B",all),AVAR("t0",all)]),

    AVAR("A",all)]])
```

that computes the CSHIFT into locally scoped storage t0 of the appropriate shape before performing the addition and (presumably) releasing the local storage. Later transformation phases may choose to bring some outside computations within the scope of the generated temporary storage, increasing the length of the elemental code block at the expense of keeping some allocated heap space longer than necessary.

4.3.4 Parallel loop fusion

Finally, the loop fusion module passes over the YR program, looking for successive MOVE statements with purely elemental computation and like shape. Those it finds it groups together within a single MOVE set. In the CM/2 YR implementation, this results in these assignments being compiled into a single PEAC node routine, potentially resulting in increased vectorization. This is equivalent to fusing sequences of parallel loops, since in a synchronous context

```
SEQUENTIALLY[DOALL(V,S,I1),DOALL(V,S,I2)]
```

is exactly equivalent to

```
DOALL(V,S,SEQUENTIALLY[I1,I2])
```

5 Fortran-90-Y: Target-Specific Phase

5.1 CM2/YR Compiler

The problem of compiling a valid YR program into code for the CM/2 is broken down into a hierarchy of YR compilers for different levels of target abstraction. The top-level abstraction (CM2/YR) models the CM/2 host and nodes together as a single machine, and then partitions input YR programs into YR subprograms for each half.

The source YR program will have been restructured by the optimization phase to consist of blocked computation and communication phases. The CM2/YR compiler passes over this series of blocks, cutting out and compiling a list of the elemental computation phases. Then it patches the remaining program skeleton with the appropriate YR calling code. Each extracted computation phase is passed to the CM/2 node YR compiler to be turned into a node procedure. The remainder is transformed into native frontend code by the CM/2 front end compiler.

5.2 CM2/Host and CM2/Node YR Compilers

The CM2/Host YR compiler translates the YR remainder progam into SPARC assembly code plus CM runtime system library calls. DO- and MOVE-constructs over serial shapes become explicit front-end iteration. References to front-end data, along with CM data used in a front-end context all become front-end code. Declarative YR constructs become memory allocations, with their home determined by usage. Certain primitive function calls that represent communication intrinsics are replaced by calls to their CM runtime library implementations. For each computation block being executed remotely, the compiler inserts calling code to push PEAC procedure arguments over the IFIFO to the node processors. The Node/YR compiler then passes over the chain of extracted loopnests, transforming each straightforwardly into a single PEAC node routine. An illustration of the code partitioning process can be seen in Figure 3.

The host and node compilers in the current CM/2 implementation represent the point where true specification ends. They compile YR fragments to native code directly, using hand-coded algorithms to achieve competitive performance. The formalism of YR is still

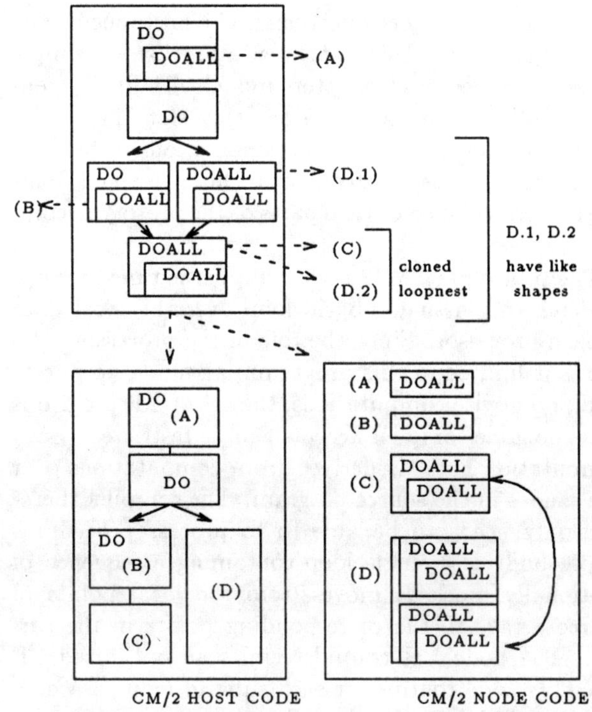

Figure 3: Decomposition to Host and Node Code

present, however, insofar as these implementations are organized internally at the top level as production rule sets. The CM2/Host compiler, for example, defines functions `compile_[i, v, d]action` that compile YR fragments from the imperative, valuation, and declarative semantic facets, respectively, to SPARC assembly code. The CM2/Node compiler performs a similar function, translating a narrow set of pointwise parallel loop constructs into optimized slicewise PE assembly code. Pushing the level of specification down into the FE and PE compilers is an ongoing process, guided by this facetwise organization.

Recall that earlier compiler stages defined the translation of AST fragments to YR fragments, and synthesized a single YR imperative program from them. The backend rulesets perform componentwise decomposition, rather than synthesis, of the constructed YR imperative, producing an equivalent program in the target language.

Having these separate compilers for the host and nodes allows effort to be expended intelligently to bring the prototype up to speed. In codes that contain a high degree of data parallelism, the node processor and runtime libraries' speeds are the limiting factor for performance. The SPARC front end can easily keep up, feeding PEAC code and data through the sequencer and calling the runtime system. As problem size increases, front end time comprises a negligible fraction of the overall execution profile. This allows SPARC front-end performance questions to be postponed. The current front-end YR implementation uses a simple memory-to-memory load/store model with little attention to effective register use or delay slot filling. Allowing the host and node implementations to be fully separated gives us the freedom to filter out and focus on the performance-critical parts of the prototype compiler instead.

The prototype CM/2 node compiler is tuned for optimizing the virtual subgrid loop over the local data in each processor. Since the role of the processing elements is limited in this programming model to purely local, pointwise computations, the set of YR programs that the node compiler accepts can be restricted. Each computation burst is derived from computations over like shapes in the source program. The compiler therefore only needs to be able to to process procedures whose body is a single loop containing a sequence of (optionally masked) moves from the local points of source arrays to the corresponding points in the target. The node YR compiler emits an optimized PE assembly code routine for each subgrid loop passed to it by the CM/YR code partitioner.

After the host and node compilers have reduced their YR source programs to SPARC assembly code and PEAC, their output is then compiled and linked normally, and can be executed on any CM/2 equipped with Weitek 64-bit FPUs.

5.3 CM5/YR Compiler

The initial CM/5 YR compiler retains the majority of its structure and, therefore, its specification from the CM/2 version. To use the CM/5 in SIMD mode to run codes written for the CM/2, the Fortran-90-Y prototype shares all code in common up to and including the CM/2 whole-machine YR compiler, which splits a single program into host and node code.

The CM/5 host compiler required less than 200 lines of additional code to handle both machines' front end requirements. A CM/5 node compiler that translates old node YR to regular C programs similarly allows CM/2 node code to compile transparently to the new machine. As a result, the total additional time required to construct this preliminary CM/5 prototype compiler was less than two weeks.

Compiling to a CM/5 augmented with optional vector hardware at each node will present more target levels due to the increased node complexity. In the new model a single YR program will be split three ways rather than two; one part will go to the control processor, as before; a second part will be executed on the SPARC node processor, and a third part will carry out floating point vector operations on the CM/5 vector datapaths. This structure is represented in the second back-end diagram of Figure 1. Most importantly, the new system will still be able to take advantage of the machine-independent block-lengthening YR transformations defined in the common compiler modules.

5.4 Other Computation Models

There are, in practice, no reasons why the compiler should adhere to a single, restrictive programming model at the expense of flexibility. For example, many codes would benefit from the ability to occasionally break the CM/2's virtual processor runtime model, restricted to pointwise locality and subgrid looping. A more flexible model would allow the compiler to pipeline communication and computation, or perform general neighborhood computations directly, using the full register set to store intermediate results and performing physical communications as required.

Likewise, a more flexible compiler will be able to take advantage of the MIMD features available in the CM/5 and other machines. Implementing new programming models only requires the specification of new host and node YR compilers, and adjustments to the top-level compiler to make use of them. The YR source transformation stage would also benefit from extra modules to provide services from the runtime system previously taken for granted, such as explicit data layout.

6 Experimental Results

The basic specification methods were tested in the Fortran-90-Y compiler prototype, which we regard as "realistic" by the following standards:

Development time. The current work began in July 1991, with initial research into the slicewise CM programming model, the Fortran-90 language, and the CM Fortran compiler. Implementation of the prototype compiler actually began in mid-August. The CM/2 compiler began generating code for simple test programs by late October, and was compiling benchmark code by November. We gained access to a working CM/5 in February, and began compiling simple codes to it as well shortly thereafter.

Direction of Effort. By modeling the CM with a unified phase (CM/YR), we recognized that the machine taken as a whole is still a useful abstract target for compilation. But by dividing the labor of compilation between the host and node compilers, imposing restrictions on the constructs each accepts, and optimizing the compiler's critical path first, we were able to develop a competitive system for multiple target machines, and an interesting subset of the source language, in less than eight months.

Compiler Performance. The time and space requirements for building and using generated compilers have been traditional obstacles to their acceptance for production use. By constrast, on a moderately loaded Sun 4/390 with 32 MB of physical memory, the current prototype CM/2 compiler can be generated from specification source code in about ten minutes. During actual development, rebuilds generally take much less time – on the order of two or three minutes – due to specification modularity and Standard ML's separate compilation facilities. The resultant CM/2 compiler image is just over one megabyte in size; this compares favorably with other language tools available for the Connection Machine. Object files produced by the generated prototype system are, on average, close in size to those produced by CM Fortran. Compilation rates are generally within twenty percent of CMF as well.[3]

Object Code Performance. The initial benchmark was an updated Fortran-90 version of a dusty deck code to implement a meteorological model, the "shallow-water equations," or SWE. It has good locality, consisting of a series of circular shifts interspersed with blocks of local computation, and so represents an ideal problem for a SIMD, data-parallel machine like the CM/2.

A hand-coded *Lisp version of SWE running under fieldwise mode peaked at 1.89 gigaflops. The slicewise CM Fortran compiler (v1.1) reached an extrapolated 2.77 gigaflops. The prototype Fortran-90-Y compiler, after the first eight months of development, produced code that attained a competitive sustained rate of 2.71 gigaflops. The initial CM/5 prototype, using untuned C program stubs for expressing node code, still attains roughly 85% of the gigaflop rate of CM Fortran on the CM/5.

7 Conclusions

In this paper we have presented a brief overview of an approach to parallelizing compiler design incorporating concepts from both formal specification and traditional high-performance computing. The original motivation of this work was to demonstrate that developing scalable, portable, competitive compilers from specification for massively parallel computing environments was feasible, in terms of reasonable development time and competitive performance.

The achievements of the current Fortran-90-Y prototype implementation suggest that these methodologies are on their way to being generally applicable to the real-world challenge of developing compilers for complex parallel targets at reasonable cost.

[3] Exclusive of linking time; as linking can comprise two-thirds or more of overall compile time, practical compilation rates are thus almost identical.

8 Acknowledgements

The authors thank Young-Il Choo for his advice regarding earlier versions of YR, and Yu Hu for his many comments and technical advice. Also, thanks to Woody Lichtenstein, Bob Millstein, and Gary Sabot of Thinking Machines for their help with CM Fortran, CM/RT, and the slicewise programming model. Finally, special appreciation is due Lennart Johnsson, also of Thinking Machines, for his help in formulating the problems to be addressed and information on all aspects of the CM.

References

[1] *CM Fortran Reference Manual*, 1991.

[2] *Fortran 90 Standard*, 1991.

[3] M. Bromley, S. Heller, T. McNerney, and G. Steele Jr. Fortran at ten gigaflops: The connection machine convolution compiler. *ACM SIGPLAN '91 Conference on Programming Language Design and Engineering*, 26(6):145–156, 1991.

[4] Marina Chen, Young-il Choo, and Jingke Li. Theory and pragmatics of generating efficient parallel code. In *Parallel Functional Languages and Compilers*, chapter 7. ACM Press and Addison-Wesley, 1991.

[5] Peter Lee. *Realistic Compiler Generation*. MIT Press, 1988.

[6] K. Pingali, M. Beck, R. Johnson, M. Moudgill, and P. Stodghill. Dependence flow graphs: An algebraic approach to program dependencies. In *Eighteenth Annual ACM Symposium on Principles of Programming Languages*, pages 67–78, 1991.

[7] S. Tjiang, M. Wolf, M. Lam, K. Piper, and J. Hennessy. Integrating scalar optimizations and parallelism. In *Fourth Workshop on Languages and Compilers for Parallel Computing*, pages c1–c16, 1991.

Compiling Dataflow Analysis of Logic Programs

Jichang Tan I-Peng Lin

Department of Computer Science and Information Engineering
National Taiwan University
Taipei, 10764
Taiwan
jctan@csman.csie.ntu.edu.tw

Abstract

Abstract interpretation is a technique extensively used for global dataflow analyses of logic programs. Existing implementations of abstract interpretation are slow due to interpretive or transforming overhead and the inefficiency in manipulation of global information. Since abstract interpretation mimics standard interpretation, it is a promising alternative to compile abstract interpretation into the framework of the WAM (Warren Abstract Machine) for better performance. In this paper, we show how this approach can be effectively implemented in a low-cost manner. To evaluate the possible benefits of this approach, a prototype dataflow analyzer has been implemented for inference of mode, type and variable aliasing information of logic programs. For a subset of benchmark programs in [15], it significantly improves the performance by a factor of over 150 on the average.

1 Introduction

Like many conventional languages, the performance of the logic programming language Prolog has been significantly improved through compilation [21]. In particular, the WAM (Warren Abstract Machine) [22] is a virtual machine that has emerged as the de facto standard for the compilation and implementation of Prolog. The benefits of the WAM basically rest on local optimizations through a simple intra-procedural (clause-level) program analysis. However, substantial optimizations [12, 13, 15, 18, 23] all depend on inter-procedural information such as *mode* (the input and output direction of procedure arguments), *type* (the possible bindings of data-structures for program variables), and *variable aliasing* (the co-references of logical variables). The dataflow information is not only important to enable more performance improvement of Prolog, it also paves the way for efficient implementation of different classes of logic programs which support Independent And-Parallelism [23, 13], concurrent processes [2], or constraint satisfaction [10].

Instead of inferring various information about a program through different analysis procedures, a technique called *abstract interpretation* can be used for global dataflow analyses of a programming language based on a unified model [4]. The idea is to execute a program to be analyzed over a finite *abstract domain* rather than the possibly infinite *concrete domain* over which the language is defined. This includes the definition of a mapping from elements and operators of the standard (i.e., concrete) domain to those of the abstract domain. Abstract interpretation is then carried out by a *fixpoint* execution of the abstracted program. The result of the execution gives information about the original program over the specified abstract domain. For abstract interpretation of logic programs, there are two major issues. First, the unification procedure and variable substitutions have to be redefined over the abstract domain. For soundness of the dataflow analysis, there are certain criteria to be met in their definitions. Second, termination and completeness of the control scheme must be ensured. This means a different interpretation strategy is required instead of the top-down depth-first method used by ordinary Prolog systems. Due to general interests and applications, both issues have been extensively studied [1, 2, 3], [5]-[16], [20].

To the best of our knowledge, all global dataflow analyzers for logic programs have been implemented on top of Prolog. The implementation can be based on a meta-circular interpreter [6, 17] or a program transformer [5, 23]. The *meta-interpreting approach* directly interprets programs by using the redefined control scheme and unification procedure over an abstract domain. Instead of direct interpretation, the *transforming approach*

ACM SIGPLAN '92 PLDI-6/92/CA
© 1992 ACM 0-89791-476-7/92/0006/0106...$1.50

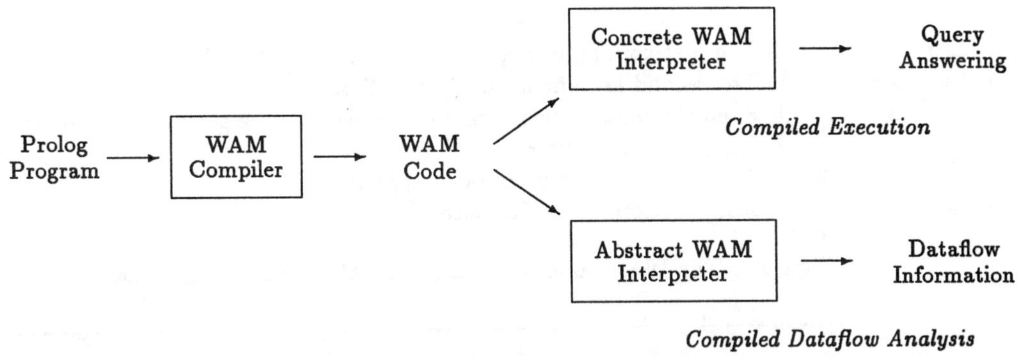

Figure 1: Compiled Execution and Compiled Dataflow Analysis

proach first partially evaluates the programs over the abstract domain, and then runs transformed programs to do the abstract interpretation. For efficiency, a different control scheme can be incorporated [11, 12, 15]. However, both approaches are slow due to the interpretive or transforming overhead and the inefficiency in manipulation of global dataflow information. Since abstract interpretation mimics standard interpretation, it should be a promising alternative to compile abstract interpretation into a similar framework like the WAM for better performance.

Rather than reinventing a new virtual machine and a dedicated compiler for it, it is much cheaper to *reuse* the framework of the WAM and current compilers to the maximal extent. This idea turns out to be quite successful because there is almost no design in the WAM which is restricted to execution over the concrete domain. For a typical abstract domain such as the one considered in this paper, the instruction set of the WAM can be easily reinterpreted according to the redefined control scheme and unification procedure. The outline of this approach is illustrated in Figure 1. We will use the term *abstract WAM* for the rest of this paper to refer to this reinterpretation of the WAM for dataflow analysis, and the term *concrete* or *standard WAM* for the original framework of Prolog compilation. To evaluate the possible benefits of this approach, we have implemented a prototype dataflow analyzer for the inference of mode, type and variable aliasing information of logic programs. For a subset of benchmark programs in [15], it significantly improves the performance by a factor of over 150 on the average.

The most obvious source of performance improvements is the removal of the overhead of interpretation and transformation incurred in other approaches. As a comparison, the technique of compilation improved the performance of Prolog by a factor of about 30 in Warren's original work [21]. Of course, the WAM code does not come for free. However, it appears that a translation to unification primitives like those of the WAM before dataflow analyses is indispensable for other approaches as well [15, 17]. Another important source of performance improvements is the efficiency in manipulation of global dataflow information. The handling of global information is required in abstract interpretation while it is discouraged by existing implementations of Prolog. Therefore, concerns for its efficiency of implementation have been explicitly addressed in the work of [23, 15, 17]. For our approach, it does not pose any problem because we use a conventional language like C for the implementation.

2 Preliminaries

2.1 Warren Abstract Machine

The basic idea of optimization is to generate specialized code for different cases of source programs. This works for Prolog as well as other conventional languages. Consider executing the head of a clause with two arguments in a Prolog program:

$$p(a, [f(V)|L]) \leftarrow ...$$

If it is directly carried out by an interpreter, a *general* unification procedure will be used for both arguments 'a' and '$[f(V)|L]$' when this predicate is invoked. Since the interpreter cannot take advantage of knowledge of the source program, the information has to be generated at run-time. Due to the abstract semantics of logic programs, this overhead can be considerably expensive. If the head is compiled into the framework of the WAM, a sequence of unification primitives will be generated as the one given in Figure 2. We can see that there are specialized unification subroutines, i.e., the WAM instructions, defined for each type of term. For example, the instructions `get_const`, `get_list`, and `get_struct` are defined for constants, lists, and structures that appear in the head of a clause. For a complex

```
get_const  a, A1      % The first coming-in argument must unify with 'a'.
get_list   A2         % The second argument has to be a list.
unify_var  X3         % Keep the first subterm (car) of the list using a temporary register.
unify_var  L          % Unify its next subterm (cdr) with L.
get_struct f/1, X3    % The car of the list must be an f/1 term.
unify_var  V          % And its subterm unifies with V.
```

Figure 2: The WAM code instructions for the head of the clause

term such as $[f(V)|L]$, the generated instructions will proceed in a ***breadth-first*** order. For example, the two `unify_var` instructions after the `get_list` instruction correspond to the unification of the first level subterms, and the third `unify_var` instruction which is after the `get_struct` instruction corresponds to the unification of the second level subterm. Through this sequence of primitive unification subroutines, much of the overhead in the general unification procedure is eliminated.

Based on similar ideas, the instruction set of the WAM can be defined. According to Warren [22], they are classified into *get*, *put*, *unify*, *procedural*, and *indexing* instructions. The *put* instructions are specialized *get* instructions which are dedicated to term construction in the body of a clause. The *procedural* instructions are responsible for the control transfer and environment allocation associated with procedure calling. The *indexing* instructions, the last group of instructions, control the access to different clauses of a predicate procedure. For other relevant details of the WAM, appropriate descriptions will be given in the following sections.

2.2 The Control Scheme for Abstract Interpretation

Due to the requirement of *compile-time* completeness and termination, researchers have proposed several control schemes for abstract interpretation of logic programs [1, 3, 8, 9, 16, 20]. In this paper, we only consider the *extension table-based* method [8] (a variant of *OLDT Resolution* [16]) because it is simple and can be easily incorporated into the compilation approach presented.

The basic idea of the extension table-based method is to employ a *dynamic programming technique* to program interpretation in which intermediate results are saved and later reused to avoid redundant work and to prevent the execution from diving into an infinite loop. The table is simply a memo structure containing a set of pairs of "calling pattern" (the description of the call) and its "success patterns" (the description of the successful return) which have been found so far. Instead of repeated computation, the extension table is consulted first whenever we try to interpret a calling pattern. If any such solutions are found, they are returned directly; if the call has been made earlier but no solution has been recorded, this call is considered failed. To ensure *completeness*, the interpretation has to execute in multiple iterations such that another iteration will be initiated whenever a new success pattern is found in one iteration. When the interpretation terminates, the table will provide approximate run-time information for each predicate in the program to be analyzed.

The outline of an extension table-based abstract interpretation can be described as follows. The interpretation starts from a given top-level calling pattern. Globally, it executes in the standard top-down depth-first order. When a clause is successfully executed, the extension table is updated with the success pattern. However, the control is then transferred to the next clause of the predicate procedure by an *artificial failure* such that all clauses will be explored. If there are multiple success patterns found for a calling pattern, they may be summarized into a single pattern by taking the *least upper bound* based on the abstract domain used. By keeping at most one success pattern for a calling pattern, it also simplifies the control flow of the interpretation since any invocation of a predicate always results in a deterministic return. Through iterative deepening, the interpretation will eventually terminate for a finite abstract domain when *least fixpoint* of the dataflow analysis is reached.

There are a few analyzers [5, 17, 23] which are based on this control scheme. However, the extension table is expensive to implement in Prolog because it is an inherently global data structure.

3 An Abstract Domain for Global Dataflow Analysis

To infer run-time information about a logic program, we classify all run-time terms into interesting subsets that form a complete lattice ordered by set inclusion. Each subset is represented by an ***abstract type*** in the abstract domain. An instance of an abstract type is referred to as an ***abstract term*** of that type. The abstract domain is briefly defined as follows.

- any represents the set of all terms, the top element ($\top$) of the abstract domain.
- nv represents all non-variable terms.
- ground (or g, for short) represents the set of ground terms.
- const represents the set of constant terms. It is the union of two subsets which are represented by atom and integer.
- struct($f/n, \alpha_1, .., \alpha_n$) represents the set of structure terms which principal functor is f/n and each argument is of type α_i ($1 \le i \le n$) in the abstract domain. For sake of clarity, the set of terms will be written as $f(\alpha_1, .., \alpha_n)$ when there is no ambiguity.
- α-list represents the set of lists with a type parameter α. It is a precise type for the union of constant '[]' (the empty list) and [α|α-list] (the structure terms struct('.'/2,α, α-list)) while [$\cdot$|$\cdot$] in general remains to be an ordinary structure term. For example, glist stands for the set of terms [], [g], [g, g], and so forth. Due to the extensive application of lists in logic programs, list-awareness is usually very useful.
- var represents the set of all variables.
- empty represents the set of non-existing term, the bottom element ($\perp$) of the abstract domain.

To make the abstract domain finite, we impose a ***term-depth restriction*** for complex abstract terms in the analysis. Given an artificial limit k, the subterms with depth k or greater in a complex term will be simplified to other simple elements in the abstract domain. Consequently the precision of the analysis for general recursive datatypes is traded for a guarantee of analysis termination.

The abstract domain presented here is actually a slightly simplified version of the one used by Taylor's analyzer [17]. The dataflow analysis based on this abstract domain implements an inference of mode, type, and variable aliasing information in logic programs. This domain is considerably more complex than the one used by the Aquarius analyzer [15] whose run-time performance will be compared to that of our analyzer in Section 6.

4 Compiling Abstract Unifications

4.1 Representation and Manipulation of Abstract Terms

Since each abstract term represents a set of terms in the concrete domain, ***abstract unifications*** can be characterized by ***set unification*** as follows. Let T_1 and T_2 be two sets of terms. Set unification of T_1 and T_2 can be defined as:

$$\text{s\_unify}(T_1, T_2) \;=\; \{t \mid t = \textit{unify}(t_1, t_2) : t_1 \in T_1 \wedge t_2 \in T_2\}$$

Abstract substitution can also be formalized as a set of concrete substitutions:

$$\{X/T\} \;=\; \{X/t \mid t \in T\}$$

where X is a variable occurred in T_1 or T_2, and T is a set of terms. More theoretical details can be found in [1, 6]. Here are some examples for the abstract domain considered:

- s_unify(any,ground) = ground.
- s_unify(any, $f(X, Y)$) = f(any, any) with an abstract substitution {X/any, Y/any}.
- s_unify(glist,[***Head***| ***Tail***]) = [g|glist] with an abstract substitution {***Head***/g, ***Tail***/glist}.

By these examples, we can see that the instances of most abstract types, such as any or list, are similar to logical variables in that they become ***more specific*** through unifications. It is therefore natural to represent these abstract terms like variables such that each of them is encoded in a single word before unification, and can be instantiated to another type of term or a complex structure later. They will also be subscripted hereafter to stand for different instances. Finally, the definition of abstract substitution should be extended to include substitutions for these abstract terms in addition to that for variables. Instances of atom, integer and specific structure terms such as f(atom), however, remain unchanged through unifications because there is no smaller (i.e., more specific) element other than '$\perp$' in the abstract domain considered.

Based on the definitions, consider the abstract interpretation of the head of the example clause in Section 2:

$$p(a, [f(V)|L]) \leftarrow ...$$

```
                           % call p(atom, glist1);
get_const  a, A1           %                              { (1) Succeeds for a ≈ atom.          }
get_list   A2              % glist1 ← [g1|glist2];        { (2.1) Get a [·|·] instance of glist. }
unify_var  X3              % X3 ← g1;                     {        The car of glist1             }
unify_var  L               % L ← glist2;                  {        The cdr of glist1             }
get_struct f/1, X3         % X3↑ ← f(g2);                 { (2.2) Get an f(·) instance of g.     }
unify_var  V               % V ← g2;                      {        The argument of f/1           }
```

Figure 3: The WAM Code Reinterpreted

over the abstract domain given a calling pattern $p(\text{atom}, \text{glist}_1)$. In breadth-first order, the abstract unification for this particular head can be decomposed into a sequence of three simple s_unify's:

(1) s_unify(atom,atom) = atom with an empty substitution { }.

(2.1) $\text{s\_unify}(\text{glist}_1, [\cdot|L]) = [g_1|\text{glist}_2]$ with a substitution $\{\text{glist}_1/[g_1|\text{glist}_2], L/\text{glist}_2\}$.

(2.2) $\text{s\_unify}(g_1, f(V)) = f(g_2)$ with a substitution $\{g_1/f(g_2), V/g_2\}$.

Composing the substitutions, the head of the clause succeeds with an abstract substitution:

$$\{\text{glist}_1/[f(g_2)|\text{glist}_2], L/\text{glist}_2, V/g_2\}.$$

4.2 Reinterpretation of the Instruction Set

To continue the refinement, the three s_unify's can be mapped into the sequence of WAM code instructions described in Section 2 as given in Figure 3. By this example, it is not difficult to define an appropriate reinterpretation of these WAM instructions over the abstract domain. For example, the algorithm to reinterpret **get_list** is outlined in Figure 4 where the following primitive operations about abstract terms are required.

- *Primary Approximation.* Function $AbsType(T)$ is defined to approximate a term T, either concrete or abstract, to an abstract type regardless of its subterms. For example, $AbsType(a)$ = atom, $AbsType(\text{glist})$ = glist, $AbsType(f(V)) = f(\top)$ or simply denoted by struct($f/1$).
- *Approximate Unifiability.* Ignoring the subterms, two terms T_1 and T_2 are unifiable, denoted by $T_1 \approx T_2$, if $\text{s\_unify}(AbsType(T_1), AbsType(T_2)) \neq \emptyset$. For example, $a \approx$ atom, glist $\approx [\cdot|\cdot]$, and g $\approx f(\cdot)$ have been used for the instructions **get_const**, **get_list**, and **get_struct** $f/1$, respectively, in abstract interpretation of the call $p(\text{atom}, \text{glist}_1)$.
- *Complex-Term Instantiation* (ComplexTermInst). If an abstract term is approximately unifiable with a complex term, the generation of the unification result will be necessary for subsequent subterm unifications. For example, the term $[g_1|\text{glist}_2]$ and $f(g_2)$ are complex-term instantiations of glist_1 and g_2, generated by the instructions **get_list** and **get_struct** $f/1$, respectively.

If we represent each run-time object by a tag and a value encoded in a computer word as in the standard WAM [22], the primary approximation function *AbsType* simply returns the tag of a simple object. For predefined abstract types (e.g. any or g), tabulation is sufficient to implement approximate unifiability and complex-term instantiation. For inferred data-types, such as glist, a type-description database will be necessary.

The instructions **get_struct** and **get_const** shown in the example can be reinterpreted in a similar way, while the interpretation of instruction **unify_var** over the concrete domain can be completely reused over this abstract domain.

5 Compiling the Control Scheme

Consider a simple predicate procedure p and its WAM code as follows.

```
p(X) ← q, r(X).        % clause p.1
p(a).                  % clause p.2

p.1:  get args of p(X)
      call q
      put args of r(X)
      execute r(X)
```

```
get_list Ai ≡
begin
    deref(Ai);                                  { Same as standard WAM interpretation }
    if concrete(Ai) then                        { True for atom, integer, struct, list, and var }
        concrete WAM code definition
    elsif Ai ≈ struct('.'/2) then               { True for ground, nv, any and list }
        Ai↑← tag(list,H); Trail(Ai);            { Generate a [·|·] instance of Ai on Heap }
        S ← ComplexTermInst(Ai, H);             { Set S pointer to the con-cell for subsequent }
        H ← H + 2; Mode ← Read;                 { subterm unifications and proceed in read mode }
    else fail
    fi
end
```

Figure 4: The Outline of the Reinterpreted get_list Instruction

```
p.2:  get args of p(a)
      proceed
```

The instruction proceed corresponds to a successful *return* of a clause, instruction call corresponds to a predicate *procedure invocation*, and instruction execute is equivalent to a call immediately followed by a proceed (the last-call optimization). If we apply the extension table-based interpretation scheme described in Section 2 to the source program, the result is a set of transformed programs:

$p'(X) \leftarrow abstract(X, X_\alpha),$
$\quad$ if $explored(p(X_\alpha))$ then $lookupET(p(X_\alpha))$
$\quad$ else $assert(explored(p(X_\alpha))), p(X_\alpha)$
$\quad$ fi .

$p(X) \leftarrow q', r'(X), updateET(p(X)), fail.$
$p(a) \leftarrow updateET(p(\text{atom})), fail.$
$p(Lub) \leftarrow lookupET(p(Lub)).$

where the predicate *explored*(P) is true if a calling pattern P has been explored in current iteration. The predicate *lookupET*(P) and *updateET*(P) are used to look up and update the extension table entry for P respectively. Every invocation of predicate p in the source program is replaced by an invocation of an artificially-introduced predicate p' such that the calculation of the calling pattern (through *abstract*) and the consulting of the extension table will be performed before exploration of p's clauses. The transformed predicate p is a deterministic procedure of the original code such that it updates the extension table for p and then fails to the next clause if a clause of p has been completely executed. When all clauses have been explored, the summarized success pattern, if any, will be returned.

This control scheme can be incorporated into the abstract WAM as follows. Instruction call should be reinterpreted to execute like the artificially-introduced predicate by calculating calling patterns, consulting the extension table, or exploring the clauses. Instruction proceed should be reinterpreted as the part of code "*updateET, fail*" in the end of each transformed clause and "*lookupET*" when the original clauses are exhausted. Instruction execute can simply be reverted to a call followed by a proceed. The reinterpretation technique can be better explained by the annotated WAM code sequence in Figure 5.

In this discussion, we have intentionally omitted some relevant WAM instructions, including some *procedural* instructions and all *indexing* instructions. Their reinterpretation is almost identical to that of a standard WAM with few exceptions. For instance, creation and reclamation of backtracking points would better be incorporated into instructions call and proceed rather than instructions try and trust. By such reinterpretation, the WAM code compiler and the code it generates can be reused without any modification.

6 Implementation and Performance Evaluation

To evaluate the benefits of the proposed approach, we have implemented a prototype analyzer. It is written in C and ported to several platforms. The input WAM code programs are generated by the PLM Prolog compiler[1] for a subset of benchmark programs [16]. The analyzer is about 2500 lines of code, including lots of comments, debugging and conditional compilation statements. In comparison to the size of other analyzers reported (from 1200 lines [16] to over 3000 lines [18]

[1] The original code was from Peter Van Roy [15] and modified by Herve' Touati for the Aquarius Project at UC Berkeley, 1989.

```
p.1:  get args of p(X)
      call q              % If explored(q) then ... else ... call q fi .
      put args of r(X)
      call r(X)           % ... if explored(r(X_α)) then ... else ... call r(X_α) fi .
      proceed             % ⇒ updateET(p(X)), fail.
p.2:  get args of p(a)
      proceed             % ⇒ updateET(p(atom)), fail.
                          % last clause of p ⇒ lookupET(p(Lub)).
```

Figure 5: The Reinterpretation of the Control Instructions

of Prolog code), the implementation cost of this analyzer is relatively low considering the precision of the analysis.

Important implementation features of the analyzer are briefly described as follows. For term abstraction before a predicate invocation, the constant for term-depth restriction is set to 4, which is also used by Taylor's analyzer [17]. Like the analyzer reported in [23], this analyzer tries to keep complete aliasing information of variables (and also other abstract terms). The extension table is implemented as a linear list of (calling-pattern, success-pattern) pairs. Multiple calling patterns are maintained for a predicate while the success patterns for each of the calling patterns are "lubbed" (least-upper-bound is taken) together. This implementation of the extension table is equivalent to the *assert* database technique described in [23, 17]. However, it is obviously more straightforward and efficient to be implemented in C. It is worth mentioning that the three-stack scheme used by the standard WAM (i.e., the *Heap*, the *Stack*, and the *Trail*) and most other design considerations remain effective for reinterpretation over the abstract domain considered. Nevertheless, it is possible to ignore some of the optimization techniques designed for the concrete domain. In particular, the *environment trimming* technique which strives for a quick stack reclamation appears to be overkill in this abstract WAM.

The analysis time is measured on a Sun 3/60 to compare with the performance of the Aquarius analyzer [15] which is the only publicly available source for both benchmark programs and analyzer efficiency. The Aquarius analyzer's times are running under Quintus Prolog version 2.0. The run-time performance of the analyzer is typical among the analyzers reported (including [23] and [17]). Table 1 gives the results of the measurements of analysis time of our analyzer (*Ours*), the speed-up factors (*Speed-Up Factor*), and the average of speed-up factors. A rough profile of the benchmarks is given by the number of argument places (*Args*) and predicates (*Preds*) in each source program. Additional information includes the static code size (*Size*) and the number of (abstract) WAM code executed (*Exec*) at analysis-time. Neither the times of our analyzer nor those of the Aquarius analyzer (*Aquarius*) include any preprocessing time. Since we use WAM codes generated from the PLM compiler, the compilation times are also included in the table (*PLM*). However, the PLM compiler is not especially fast by doing many optimizations which do not appear justified as far as our analyzer is concerned.

The result of the improvements in analysis time performance is significant and encouraging. The speed-up factors range from 14 (zebra) to 575 (tak), and have an (arithmetic) average of 152. The fluctuation of the speed-up factors is mainly due to the different abstract domains and interpretation algorithms used. If the same abstract domain is used, our conservative estimation is that the speedup would be over 100 for all benchmarks. As a prototype, the implementation was meant to be simple. We believe that there is plenty of room left for more improvements in performance based on better algorithms for abstract interpretation such as those described in [3, 20]. For a reference, the measurements of analysis time on several other platforms are given in Appendix A. This information should be useful for those who do not have access to a Sun 3/60.

7 Conclusions

Theoretically, the time complexities of most interesting dataflow analyses have been shown to be exponential in the worst case [7]. In particular, the precise dataflow analysis considered in this paper is an example. In the average case, however, it appears that the analysis time is proportional to the number of arguments in the program and the precision of the abstract domain used. This is shown in the measurement results presented in this paper and also the results given in [15, 23, 17]. For a practical system, it becomes a design tradeoff between time and precision of the analysis. More precise

Benchmarks	*Args*	*Preds*	*Aquarius* (in sec)	*PLM* (in sec)	*WAM code* *Size*	*Exec*	*Ours* (in msec)	*Speed-Up Factor*
log10	3	2	2.9	4.5	179	749	38.6	75
ops8	3	2	3.0	4.5	180	400	23.3	129
times10	3	2	3.0	4.5	186	971	48.4	62
divide10	3	2	2.9	4.6	186	1043	50.7	57
tak	4	2	2.3	1.2	53	110	4.0	575
nreverse	5	3	2.2	1.6	99	479	26.7	82
qsort	7	3	3.4	2.5	164	763	44.0	77
query	7	5	4.2	4.3	264	626	25.8	163
zebra	9	5	3.5	7.5	271	1262	257.9	14
serialise	16	7	4.2	3.6	205	912	53.4	79
queens_8	16	7	6.0	3.1	117	324	16.5	364
average								152

Table 1: The Efficiency of Dataflow Analyzers

dataflow analysis can be used if the analyzer is more efficient.

The compilation approach of dataflow analysis presented in this paper integrates two important ideas: the efficient compilation framework of the WAM, and the similarity between abstract and concrete interpretations. It is more efficient than other implementation approaches for abstract interpretation such as meta-interpretation or program transformation because the interpretive or transforming overhead incurred is removed. Moreover, the manipulation of global dataflow information is straightforward and efficient with this approach. Most of all, the approach can be incorporated into an existing compilation-based system in a low-cost manner. Our experience in implementing an abstract WAM and its excellent improvement in analysis-time performance have demonstrated the significance of the approach. It is probable that this approach can also be effectively applied to different classes of dataflow analyses of logic programs or even to different classes of logic programming languages other than Prolog.

Acknowledgements

Martha Kosa, Jin-Kun Lin, and Ting-Wei Hou helped to proof-read this paper. Jieh Hsiang and Jin-Kun Lin always help to provid necessary information promptly. The theoretical work by Saumya K. Debray, David S. Warren, and Suzanne W. Dietrich helps us to do this work in a very simple way. We thank Peter Van Roy for his helpful comments and the results from the Aquarius project. The first author was supported in part by the NSC Taiwan.

References

[1] M. Bruynooghe and G. Jenssens, "An Instance of Abstract Interpretation Integrating Type and Mode Inferencing," In *Proc. of 5th Int'l Logic Programming Conf.*, 1988.

[2] C. Codognet, P. Codognet, and M.-M. Corsini, "Abstract Interpretation for Constraint Logic Languages," In *Proc. of North American Conf. on Logic Programming*, 1990.

[3] B. Le Charlier, K. Musumbu and P. Van Hentenryck, "A Generic Abstract Interpretation Algorithm and its Complexity Analysis," In *Proc. of 8th Int'l Conf. on Logic Programming*, Paris, 1991.

[4] P. Cousot and R. Cousot, "Abstract Interpretation: a Unified Lattice Model for Static Analysis of Programs by Constructions of Fixed Points," In *Conf. Rec. of 4th POPL*, pp. 78-88, 1977.

[5] S. K. Debray and D. S. Warren, "Automatic Mode Inference for Prolog Programs," In *Proc. of 3rd Symp. on Logic Programming*, Salt Lake, 1986.

[6] S. K. Debray, "Efficient Data Flow Analysis of Logic Programs," In *Proc. of the 14th Symp. of Principles of Programming Languages*, San Diego, 1988.

[7] S. K. Debray, "The Mythical Free Lunch (Notes on the Complexity/Precision Tradeoff in Dataflow Analysis of Logic Programs)," In *Proc. of Int'l Logic Programming Symp.* 1991.

[8] S. W. Dietrich, "Extension tables: memo relations in logic programming," In *Proc. of 4th IEEE*

Benchmarks	*Aquarius 3/60*	*Ours 3/60*	*Mac IIx TC 4.0*	*μVax 3100*	*Vax 8530*	*DecS 3100*	*SS1+*	*DecS 5000*	*SS2*
log10	1	75	37	49	86	284	363	500	630
ops8	1	129	63	59	139	469	612	833	1034
times10	1	62	30	37	71	231	294	400	500
divide10	1	57	28	34	65	215	266	372	453
tak	1	575	288	383	639	2091	3286	3833	5750
nreverse	1	82	41	56	108	297	333	595	579
qsort	1	77	38	45	95	281	318	548	540
query	1	163	84	60	183	618	894	1167	1556
zebra	1	14	5.7	9.4	16	55	63	95	107
serialise	1	79	39	47	94	296	375	538	656
queens_8	1	364	182	200	448	1364	1935	2500	3333
average	1	152	76	89	177	564	794	1035	1376
Index	.007	1	.50	.58	1.2	3.7	5.21	6.8	9.0

Table 2: The Speed Ratios on Various Platforms

Int'l Symp. on Logic Programming, San Francisco, 1987.

[9] K. Marriott and H. Søndergaard, "Bottom-Up Abstract Interpretation of Logic Programs," In *Proc. of 5th Int'l Conf. on Logic Programming*, 1988.

[10] K. Marriott and H. Søndergaard, "Analysis of Constraint Logic Programs," In *Proc. of North American Conf. on Logic Programming*, 1990.

[11] C. S. Mellish, The Automatic Generation of Mode Declarations for Prolog Programs, DAI Research Paper No. 163, 1981.

[12] C. S. Mellish, "Some Global Optimizations for a Prolog Compiler," In *Jour. of Logic Programming*, 1985:1:43-66.

[13] K. Muthukumar and M. Hermenegildo, "Determination of Variable Dependence Information Through Abstract Interpretation," In *Proc. of North America Conf. on Logic Programming*, 1989.

[14] R. A. O'Keefe, "Finite Fixed-Point Problems," In *Proc. of 4th Int'l Conf. on Logic Programming*, 1987.

[15] P. Van Roy, "A Prolog Compiler for the PLM", Report No. UCB/CSD 84/203, UC Berkeley, November 1984.

[16] P. Van Roy and A. M. Despain, "The Benefits of Global Dataflow Analysis for an Optimizing Prolog Compiler," In *Proc. of North American Conf. on Logic Programming*, 1990.

[17] H. Tamaki and T. Sato, "OLD Resolution with Resolution," In *Proc. 3rd Int'l Logic Programming Conf.*, London, 1986. LNCS 255.

[18] A. Taylor, "Removal of Dereferencing and Trailing in Prolog Compilation," In *Proc. of 6th Int'l Conf. on Logic Programming*, Lisbon, June 1989.

[19] A. Taylor, "LIPS on a MIPS: Results form a Prolog Compiler for a RISC," *Proc. of 7th Int'l Conf. on Logic Programming*, Jerusalem, 1990.

[20] A. Wærn, "An Implementation Technique for the Abstract Interpretation of Prolog," In *Proc. of 5th Int'l Conf. on Logic Programming*, 1988.

[21] D. H. D. Warren, Applied Logic - its Use and Implementation as a Programming Tool, Ph. D. Thesis, Univ. Edinburgh, Scotland, 1977.

[22] D. H. D. Warren, An Abstract Prolog Instruction Set, Tech. Note 309, SRI, October, 1983.

[23] R. Warren, M. Hermenegildo and S. K. Debray, "On the Practicality of Global Flow Analysis of Logic Programs," In *Proc. of 5th Int'l Conf. on Logic Programming*, 1988.

A Performance Evaluation on Various Platforms

Table 2 is supplied to compare the speed ratios for the Aquarius analyzer [16] running on a Sun 3/60 workstation (*Aquarius*) and our implementation on eight different platforms:

- Sun 3/60/SunOS 4.1.1 (*Ours 3/60*).
- Apple Macintosh IIx with THINK C 4.0 (*Mac IIx, TC 4.0*).
- DEC microVax 3100/VMS 5.4 (*μVax 3100*).
- DEC Vax 8530/Ultrix-32 v3.0 (*Vax 8530*).
- DECstation 3100/Ultrix 4.2 (*DecS 3100*).
- Sun Sparc station 1+/SunOS 4.1.1 (*SS1+*).
- DECstation 5000/200/Ultrix 4.2 (*DecS 5000*).
- Sun Sparc Station 2/SunOS 4.1.1 (*SS2*).

For simplicity, the figures of the analysis time on each platform have been omitted. They can be recalculated based on the figures given in Table 1. All timings of our analyzer have been measured with a resolution of 0.1 mSec, and represent the average execution times over 100 to 1000 iterations. For Unix-based versions, the "cc -O" option on the C compiler is used. The average speed-indexes of the analyzer/platform configurations are given in the last row (*Index*) of the table.

Escape Analysis on Lists*

Young Gil Park†and Benjamin Goldberg
Department of Computer Science
Courant Institute of Mathematical Sciences
New York University
251 Mercer Street, New York, N.Y. 10012

Abstract

Higher order functional programs constantly allocate objects dynamically. These objects are typically cons cells, closures, and records and are generally allocated in the heap and reclaimed later by some garbage collection process. This paper describes a compile time analysis, called escape analysis, for determining the lifetime of dynamically created objects in higher order functional programs, and describes optimizations that can be performed, based on the analysis, to improve storage allocation and reclamation of such objects. In particular, our analysis can be applied to programs manipulating lists, in which case optimizations can be performed to allow cons cells in spines of lists to be either reclaimed immediately or reused without incurring any garbage collection overhead. In a previous paper on escape analysis [10], we had left open the problem of performing escape analysis on lists.

Escape analysis simply determines when the argument (or some part of the argument) to a function call is returned by that call. This simple piece of information turns out to be sufficiently powerful to allow stack allocation of objects, compile-time garbage collection, reduction of run-time storage reclamation overhead, and other optimizations that are possible when the lifetimes of objects can be computed statically.

Our approach is to define a high-level non-standard semantics that, in many ways, is similar to the standard semantics and captures the escape behavior caused by the constructs in a functional language. The advantage of our analysis lies in its conceptual simplicity and portability (i.e. no assumption is made about an underlying abstract machine).

*This research was funded in part by the National Science Foundation (CCR-8909634) and by DARPA/ONR (N00014-90-1110).

†Present address: School of Computer Science, University of Windsor, 401 Sunset Ave, Windsor, Ontario, Canada N9B 3P4, Email: ypark@cs.uwindsor.ca

ACM SIGPLAN '92 PLDI-6/92/CA
© 1992 ACM 0-89791-476-7/92/0006/0116...$1.50

1 Introduction

Higher order functional programs constantly allocate objects dynamically. These objects are typically cons cells, closures, and records and are generally allocated in the heap and reclaimed later by some garbage collection process. Garbage collection overhead can be reduced by performing compile time analyses that allow the following optimizations to be performed:

- *Stack allocation*: Objects that would otherwise be allocated in the heap and then reclaimed using garbage collection are allocated in an activation record on the stack and automatically (and cheaply) reclaimed when the activation record is popped off the stack.

- *In-place Reuse*: When objects (such as cons cells) are no longer needed, they can be reused directly by the program without invoking the garbage collector. A typical example of this is when a function constructs a new list by destructively modifying the cons cells that were contained in an argument to that function.

- *Block Allocation/Reclamation*: A number of objects (such as the cons cells of a list) are allocated together in a contiguous block of memory. Eventually, the whole block is put on the free list, rather than the individual objects. This allows reclamation of larger segments of memory,

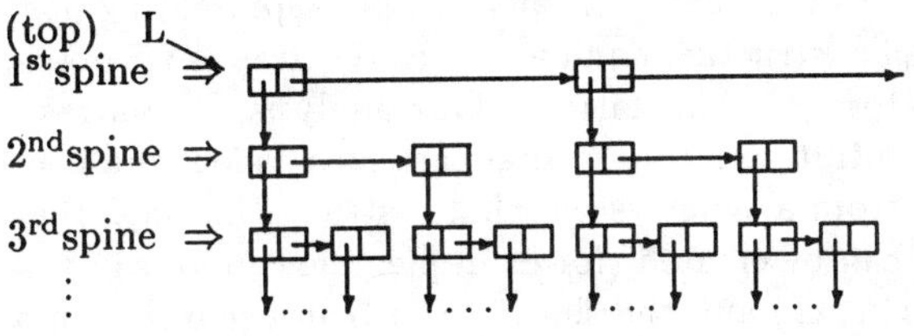

Figure 1: Spines of a List

and reduces run-time overhead by avoiding the traversal of the individual objects (in a mark-sweep collection, for instance).

In this paper, we present a compile time analysis that provides sufficient information to perform all of these optimizations on higher order functional programs. The analysis is called *escape analysis.* In a previous paper [10] we described an escape analysis for non-list objects, such as closures, and left open the problem of performing the analysis in the presence of lists. This paper solves that problem. Escape analysis answers a simple question: Given a function application, does a parameter (or some part of a parameter) get returned in the result of the application? If so, the parameter is said to *escape* from the application. If the escaping parameter is a list, we would particularly like to know which spines of the parameter escape. The spines of a list are a way of describing substructures of a list and are defined as follows:

Definition 1 (Spines of a list) *Given a list L and some $i \geq 1$, the top i^{th} spine of L is defined as the set of cons cells accessible by a sequence of operations consisting of* `car` *and* `cdr` *where the number of occurrences of* `car` *is $(i-1)$. Similarly, given a list L with d spines and some $j \geq 1$, the bottom j^{th} spine of L is defined as the* top *$(d-j+1)$ spine of L.*

In Figure 1 we illustrate what we mean by the spines of a list. Naturally, an empty list (`nil`) and any non-list objects have no (or zero) spine.

We have chosen to analyze the escape properties of lists in terms of their spines for two reasons:

- It is an approximation to the run-time behavior that allows a compile-time analysis.
- It reflects the programming style commonly used for strongly typed languages, such as ML, in which lists are homogeneous (all elements have the same type) and functions (such as `append`, `map`, etc.) often operate over complete spines of lists.

The first point reflects our inability to determine precisely, without actually running the program, which individual cells of a list might escape. To form a terminating compile-time escape analysis, one must choose an approximation of program behavior. The second point reflects our belief that the spines are a good choice of approximation, since the cells of each spine of a list tend to be treated identically. Many functions, such as `append`, `reduce`, `map`, `length`, etc., operate on all cells of a spine. Many other functions have the form:

```
f L = if predicate(car L) then ....
      else f (cdr L)
```

or

```
f L x = if x = n then ...
        else f (cdr L) (arith-op x)
```

In general, it is impossible to determine at compile time when the recursion will bottom out. One simply has to assume that all cells in the spine of the list `L` will be visited.

Consider, for example, the following program:

```
let map f l = if (l=nil) then nil
                else cons (f (car l))
                          (map f (cdr l)) ;
    pair x = [car x, car (cdr x)] ;
in map pair [[1,2],[3,4],[5,6]]
```

An escape analysis would allow us to determine the following properties of the program at compile time:

1. The top spine of `pair`'s parameter does not escape from `pair`, only some elements do.
2. The top spine of `map`'s parameter `l` does not escape from `map`, and the elements of `l` escape from `map` to the extent they escape from the unknown function `f`.
3. In the call `(map pair [[1,2],[3,4],[5,6]])`, the top two spines of the second argument of `map` do not escape.

This means that (at least) the following optimizations could be performed:

- *Stack Allocation:* The spine of the list `[[1,2],[3,4],[5,6]]` and the spine of each element of the list could be allocated in the activation record for `map`. Thus, when `map` returns, the cons cells of those spines would disappear. It seems strange to allocate a list in a stack, but there is really no reason not to (as long as we keep in mind the safety considerations outlined in [6]).

- *In-place Reuse*: If the parameter `l` of `map` is unshared (sharing information can also be obtained from escape information), we can recycle the cells of the spine of `l` within `map` to be used in the spine of the result (since `l`'s spine does not escape). The call to `cons` inside `map` can reuse the first cell in the spine of `l` for the result. `Pair` can reuse the spine of `x` in its result.

- *Block Allocation/Reclamation*: If neither of the above optimizations are used, then the top two spines of the list `[[1,2],[3,4],[5,6]]` can be allocated in some block in the heap. When `map` finishes, that whole block can be placed on the free list, freeing all the cons cells without traversing the list.

This paper describes an escape analysis on lists in higher-order, polymorphically-typed functional programs, and describes optimizations and another analysis (sharing analysis) that can be performed based on this analysis to improve storage allocation and reclamation of such objects. Our approach for lists could be applied to other data structures such as tuples, trees, etc.

2 Related Work

There has been a number of papers describing analyses for optimizing storage of lists and other structures. Most of these analyses have been first-order (i.e. not accounting for higher order functions) or have analyzed first-order languages. Brooks, Gabriel, and Steele [3] describe an escape analysis for numbers, but do not extend it for arbitrary objects. Ruggieri and Murtagh [18] describe a lifetime analysis for a language with side-effects and complex data structures, but, again, it is first order. Jones and Le Metayer [13] describe an algorithm, based on forward and backward analysis, for detecting sharing of objects in first order functional languages, and describe a method for reusing of cells based on the sharing analysis. We use only forward analysis providing, perhaps, a simpler conceptual framework for higher-order languages. Inoue, Seki, and Yagi [12] describe an analysis for functional languages to detect, and reclaim, run-time garbage cells based on formal language theory and grammars. The paper focuses only on the explicit reclamation of cons cells and it is unclear that this approach could be extended for higher-order languages. Besides being higher order, the escape analysis described here is a more general lifetime analysis that can be applied to objects other than lists, and other optimizations are supported. Chase, Wegman, and Zadeck [7] describe an first-order analysis for LISP that constructs graphs representing possible list structures and analyzes the graphs for possible storage optimizations. Our analysis, in contrast, concentrates on typed languages such as ML and benefits from a type system that restricts the ways that lists can be created (for example, one cannot say `f = cons(x,x)`) and the sharing that can occur within a list. Orbit, an optimizing compiler for Scheme, uses a simple first-order escape analysis to stack allocate closures [15]. Other analyses for optimizing storage allocation were proposed in [14, 5].

Deutsch [8] presents a lifetime and sharing analysis for higher order languages. While the goals of the paper seem to be similar to ours, the approach is very different. The analysis consists of defining a low-level operational model for a higher order functional language, translating a program into a sequence of operations in this model, and then performing an analysis to determine the lifetimes of dynamically created objects. The approach is also one of collecting interpretation, in that it analyzes a whole program to infer properties of program points. Our approach is to define a high-level non-standard semantics that in many ways is similar to the standard semantics and captures the precise escape behavior caused by the constructs in a functional language. We then define an abstraction of these semantics which provides less precise information but which allows the analysis to be performed at compile time. The advantage of our analysis lies in its conceptual simplicity and lower computational cost (compared to a collecting interpretation).

Baker [2] describes an interesting approach to higher-order escape analysis of functional languages based on the type inference (unification) technique. The analysis sketched there provides escape information on lists only, and might be extended to give information comparable to what our analysis gives. Our analysis, based on abstract interpretation, provides escapement about other objects (closures) as well as lists. We also describe how to use escape information for various optimizations.

The notion of spines of a list is used in [17] as a way of modeling the location of dynamically created references in a list structure.

3 Escape Semantics

3.1 The Language - nml

We define a simple, strict, monomorphically-typed, higher-order functional language. For lack of a better name, we will call this language **nml**, for **n**ot **m**uch of a language. The syntax of **nml** is defined as follows:

$c \in Con$	Constants (including primitives) $= \{\ldots, -1, 0, 1, \ldots, \texttt{true}, \texttt{false}, \texttt{+}, \texttt{-}, \texttt{=}, \texttt{nil}, \texttt{cons}, \texttt{car}, \texttt{cdr}\}$
$x \in Id$	Identifiers
$e \in Exp$	Expressions, defined by $e ::= c \mid x \mid e_1 e_2 \mid \texttt{lambda}(x).e \mid \texttt{if}\ e_1\ \texttt{then}\ e_2\ \texttt{else}\ e3 \mid \texttt{letrec}\ x_1 = e_1; \ldots x_n = e_n\ \texttt{in}\ e$
$pr \in Pgm$	Programs, defined by $pr ::= \texttt{letrec}\ x_1 = e_1; \ldots x_n = e_n\ \texttt{in}\ e$

For convenience, we omit type declarations. Our analysis assumes that monomorphic type inference (perhaps requiring declarations) has already been performed. Subsequently, we will relax the monomorphic typing restriction and show that our analysis works for a polymorphic version of **nml**. Also for convenience, we will allow function definitions of the form $f\ x_1 \ldots x_n\ =\ e$ and assume that this is just syntactic sugar for $f\ = \texttt{lambda}(x_1)\ldots\texttt{lambda}(x_n).e$.

3.2 An Exact Escape Semantics

We first define a non-standard semantics of **nml**, called the *escape semantics*, such that the meaning of an expression is exact information about what escapes in the result of the expression. Since **nml** is a higher order language, the result of an expression may be a function. Such a function, represented by a closure, has two important characteristics with respect to the escape semantics:

1. The closure is an object itself. We may be interested in whether the closure escapes or not, or we may be interested in another object that is captured (bound) within the closure. Thus, the value of an expression returning a function must indicate whether an interesting object has escaped.

2. A function value may be applied to arguments (which may themselves escape from the application). Therefore, in our non-standard semantics, the escape value of a function must include its behavior as a function.

Thus, the value of an expression in our non-standard escape semantics is an element of a non-standard escape domain and must have two components. First, it must contain information about what is contained within the result of the expression. Second it must contain a function over the values in the escape domain. This approach (a two component value) was used by Hudak and Young for performing higher order strictness analysis [11].

We perform escape analysis on each argument of a function call separately. Thus, at any time we are only interested in whether or not a single object escapes. Other objects may escape in the result of a function call, but are ignored by our analysis. An object is *interesting* if it is the one whose escape behavior we are trying to determine. If a function has n parameters, then we perform escape analysis n times, each time treating a different parameter as interesting. Thus, our escape semantics is defined in terms of interesting objects; The value of an expression in our escape semantics will indicate if some portion of, or all of, an interesting object is contained in the result.

Given an expression, we want its corresponding value in the escape semantic domain to tell us how many spines (if any) of an interesting object are returned by that expression. Values in our semantic domain D_e have two components; The first component is an element of the *basic escape domain* B_e, which is a domain of pairs ordered as follows:

$$\langle 0,0\rangle \sqsubseteq \langle 1,0\rangle \sqsubseteq \langle 1,1\rangle \sqsubseteq \ldots \sqsubseteq \langle 1,d-1\rangle \sqsubseteq \langle 1,d\rangle$$

where d is some integer constant, i.e. for $a = \langle a_1, a_2\rangle \in B_e$ and $b = \langle b_1, b_2\rangle \in B_e$, $a \sqsubseteq b$ iff $a_1 \leq b_1$ and $a_2 \leq b_2$. The constant d is fixed for each program on which our escape analysis is performed. Each expression in the program returns a value whose first component has the following meaning:

- $\langle 1, i\rangle$: The bottom i spines of an interesting object *is* contained in the value of the expression. (If an interesting object is not a list then i will always be 0, which means that an indivisible interesting object is contained in the value of the expression.)

- $\langle 0, 0\rangle$: *No* part of any interesting object is contained in the value of the expression.

The second component is a function in $(D_e \rightarrow D_e)$.

The escape semantic domains are defined as follows (in the style of [4]):

$$\begin{array}{lcl} D_e^{int} & = & B_e \times \{err\} \\ D_e^{bool} & = & B_e \times \{err\} \\ D_e^{\tau_1 \rightarrow \tau_2} & = & B_e \times (D_e^{\tau_1} \rightarrow D_e^{\tau_2}) \\ D_e^{\tau\ list} & = & (B_e \times \{err\}) + (D_e^{\tau} \times D_e^{\tau\ list}) \end{array}$$

where err is a function (weaker than all others) that can never be applied.

$$\begin{array}{lcll} D_e & = & \sum_{\tau} D_e^{\tau} & \text{escape semantic domain} \\ Env_e & = & Id \rightarrow D_e & \text{escape environment} \end{array}$$

Given an $x \in D_e$ we use the notation $x_{(1)}$ and $x_{(2)}$ to refer to the first and second elements of x, respectively. The two components of the first element of x are referred to as $x_{(1)(1)}$ and $x_{(1)(2)}$, respectively (i.e., x has the form $\langle\langle x_{(1)(1)}, x_{(1)(2)}\rangle, x_{(2)}\rangle$.

The escape semantic functions are:

$$\begin{array}{lcl} C & : & Con \to D_e \\ E & : & Exp \to Env_e \to D_e \\ P & : & Pgm \to D_e \end{array}$$

The semantic function C for constants is defined as follows:

$$\begin{array}{l} C[\![c]\!] = \langle\langle 0,0\rangle, err\rangle, \text{ where} \\ \quad c \in \{\ldots, \mathtt{0}, \mathtt{1}, \ldots, \mathtt{true}, \mathtt{false}, \mathtt{nil}\} \\ C[\![c]\!] = \langle\langle 0,0\rangle, \lambda x.\langle x_{(1)}, \lambda y.\langle\langle 0,0\rangle, err\rangle\rangle\rangle, \\ \quad \text{where } c \in \{+,-,=\} \\ C[\![\mathtt{cons}]\!] = \langle\langle 0,0\rangle, \lambda x.\langle x_{(1)}, \lambda y.\ \text{pair}(x,y)\rangle\rangle \\ C[\![\mathtt{car}]\!] = \langle\langle 0,0\rangle, \lambda x.\ \text{fst}(x)\rangle \\ C[\![\mathtt{cdr}]\!] = \langle\langle 0,0\rangle, \lambda x.\ \text{snd}(x)\rangle \\ \quad \text{where pair}(x,y)=\langle x,y\rangle,\ \text{fst}(x)=x_{(1)}, \\ \quad\quad \text{and snd}(x)=x_{(2)}. \end{array}$$

The escape semantic function E for expressions and P for programs are defined as follows:

$$\begin{array}{l} E[\![c]\!]env_e = C[\![c]\!] \\ E[\![x]\!]env_e = env_e[\![x]\!] \\ E[\![\mathtt{if}\ e_1\ \mathtt{then}\ e_2\ \mathtt{else}\ e_3]\!]env_e = \\ \quad \text{if } \mathbf{oracle}(e_1) \text{ then } E[\![e_2]\!]env_e \text{ else } E[\![e_3]\!]env_e \end{array}$$

In order to return the actual escape value of each expression, we must be able to determine which branch of the conditional primitive `if-then-else` would be evaluated at run-time. Here, for convenience, we instead resort to an *oracle* to choose the appropriate branch of the `if`. This can be otherwise be accomplished by having the escape semantics directly compute the standard meaning as well as escape meaning of expressions.

$$\begin{array}{l} E[\![e_1 e_2]\!]env_e = (E[\![e_1]\!]env_e)_{(2)}\ (E[\![e_2]\!]env_e) \\ E[\![\mathtt{lambda}(x).e]\!]env_e = \\ \quad \langle V, \lambda y.E[\![e]\!]env_e[x \mapsto y]\rangle \\ \quad \text{where} \\ \quad V = \langle 0,0\rangle \sqcup (\bigsqcup_{z \in F^{non\_list}} (env_e[\![z]\!])_{(1)}) \\ \quad\quad \sqcup (\bigsqcup_{z \in F^{list}} (\bigsqcup_{p \ \mathbf{in}\ (env_e[\![z]\!])} p_{(1)})) \end{array}$$

Here, p **in** $(env_e[\![z]\!])$ denotes that p is an escape pair in $env_e[\![z]\!]$, F^{non_list} is the set of non-list type free identifiers in $\mathtt{lambda}(x).e$, and F^{list} is the set of list type free identifiers in $\mathtt{lambda}(x).e$). The escape value of a lambda expression reflects whether an interesting object is contained in the resulting closure as a free identifier as well as its functional behavior when it is applied. Note that free identifiers are treated separately according to whether they are of a list type or a non-list type.

$$\begin{array}{l} E[\![\mathtt{letrec}\ x_1 = e_1; \ldots x_n = e_n;\ \mathtt{in}\ e]\!]env_e = \\ \quad E[\![e]\!]env'_e \\ \quad \text{where} \\ \quad env'_e = env_e[x_1 \mapsto E[\![e_1]\!]env'_e, \\ \quad\quad \ldots, x_n \mapsto E[\![e_n]\!]env'_e] \\ P[\![pr]\!] = E[\![pr]\!]nullenv_e \end{array}$$

$nullenv_e$ is a escape environment that maps every identifier to the least element of its escape semantic domain.

3.3 Correctness

One naturally wonders what the relationship between the standard semantics and our non-standard escape semantics is. This is especially important if one wants to prove that the information provided by escape analysis is correct. However, it should be noticed that our escape analysis strives to gain information about the run-time behavior of a certain implementation that uses a stack and a heap and uses aliasing, rather than copying, of aggregate objects. Therefore, it is an operational semantics (perhaps couched in denotational semantic terms) of which our escape semantics can be considered an abstraction. Although we do not have space in this paper to provide the operational definition of our abstract machine, we can give such a definition and prove correctness properties of our analysis with respect to that definition. To be complete, of course, we would have to prove that the abstract machine implements the standard semantic definition of the language.

3.4 Abstraction of the Escape Semantics

The escape semantics presented in the last section specifies exact escape information about functions. But, it is not suitable as a basis for compile time analysis because conditionals cannot be evaluated at compile time and the subdomain of escape values for lists is infinite.

In this section, we present a safe and computable but less complete abstraction of the exact escape semantics that allows an approximation of the exact escape behavior to be found at compile time. We modify the meanings of elements in the basic escape domain B_e. We represent lists as finite objects by combining the escape values of all the elements into a single value. We also modify the escape semantic functions for constants and expressions to approximate the escape behavior of expressions by assuming that both branches of a conditional could be taken.

The interpretation of elements of the basic escape domain B_e is modified as follows:

- $\langle 1, i\rangle$: The bottom i spines of an interesting object *may be* contained in the value of the expression. (If an interesting object is not a list then i will always be 0.)
- $\langle 0, 0\rangle$: *No* part of any interesting object is contained in the value of the expression.

The escape semantic subdomain $D_e^{\tau\ list}$ for lists of type τ *list* is modified as follows:

$$D_e^{\tau\ list} = D_e^{\tau}$$

The escape semantic function C for constants associated with lists is modified as follows:

$$\begin{aligned}
&C[\![\texttt{nil}^{\tau\ \texttt{list}}]\!] = \bot_\tau \\
&\quad (\bot_\tau \text{ is the bottom element in } D_e^\tau) \\
&C[\![\texttt{cons}]\!] = \langle\langle 0,0\rangle, \lambda x.\langle x_{(1)}, \lambda y.x \sqcup y\rangle\rangle \\
&C[\![\texttt{car}^{\texttt{s}}]\!] = \langle\langle 0,0\rangle, \lambda x.\mathrm{sub}^{\mathrm{s}}(x)\rangle \\
&\quad \text{where } \mathrm{sub}^{\mathrm{s}}(z) = \text{if } (z_{(1)(2)} = \mathrm{s}) \\
&\qquad\quad \text{then } \langle z_{(1)(1)}, z_{(1)(2)} - 1, z_{(2)}\rangle \\
&\qquad\quad \text{else } z \\
&C[\![\texttt{cdr}]\!] = \langle\langle 0,0\rangle, \lambda x.x\rangle
\end{aligned}$$

The typed constant function $\texttt{car}^{\texttt{S}}$ is applied to a list that has s spines. The value of s may be arbitrary large, but fixed at compile-time. For each **car** in a program, s can be statically determined by type checking or inference because our language is statically typed. If that list contains the bottom n spines of an interesting object then the first component of the list's escape value will be $\langle 1, n\rangle$. There are two possible results when $\texttt{car}^{\texttt{S}}$ is applied:

- If $\mathrm{s} = n$, then the nth spine (from the bottom) of the interesting object is part of the top spine of the list. Thus, taking the car of the list returns an object containing at most $n-1$ spines of the interesting object. Thus the result should have the value $\langle 1, n-1\rangle$.
- If $\mathrm{s} > n$, then the nth spine (from the bottom) of the interesting object is not part of the top spine of the list. Thus, applying car to the list returns a list that could contain the n spines of the interesting object.

Notice that s cannot be less than n, since a list with s spines cannot contain a list with more than s spines.

The escape semantic function E for expressions of **if-then-else** and **lambda(x).e** is modified as follows:

$$\begin{aligned}
&E[\![\texttt{if } e_1 \texttt{ then } e_2 \texttt{ else } e_3]\!]env_e = \\
&\quad (E[\![e_2]\!]env_e)_{(2)} \sqcup (E[\![e_3]\!]env_e)
\end{aligned}$$

The abstraction for the conditional expression **if** no longer makes an appeal to the *oracle*, but rather takes the least upper bound of the escape values of both branches.

$$\begin{aligned}
&E[\![\texttt{lambda}(x).e]\!]env_e = \\
&\quad \langle V, \lambda y.E[\![e]\!]env_e[x \mapsto y]\rangle \\
&\quad \text{where} \\
&\quad V = \langle 0,0\rangle \sqcup (\bigsqcup_{z \in F} (env_e[\![z]\!])_{(1)})
\end{aligned}$$

Here, F is the set of all free identifiers in $\texttt{lambda}(x).e$. Notice that this abstract definition is considerably simpler than the exact escape semantic function.

3.5 Safety and Termination

The safety of interpretation under the abstract escape semantics with respect to the exact escape semantics means that whenever an object escapes under the exact escape semantics it escapes in the abstract escape semantics. This can be proved by showing that, using the principle of abstract interpretation, the abstract escape semantics is a safe abstraction of the exact escape semantics [16].

The termination of interpretation under the abstract escape semantics can be proved as follows: Since **nml** functions are recursive, their values in the escape domain may be computed by the usual fixpoint iteration. The body of the functional corresponding to a recursive function is composed of the monotonic least upper bound operator and other monotonic operators. Thus each functional is monotonic and its fixpoint can be found in finite time if the domain is finite. For each type τ, we defined a finite domain D_e^τ. When computing the fixpoint of a functional of type $\tau \to \tau$, we need only iterate over values in the finite domain D_e^τ. Thus, the fixpoint iteration terminates.

4 Escape Test on Lists

We use the abstract escape semantics to infer escape properties of programs. Below we show how it is used to determine both the global and local escape properties of programs. Global escape analysis is performed on a function definition, and thus gives general information about the escape properties of that function in any possible application. Local escape analysis determines the escape behavior of a particular function call, and yields more specific results.

4.1 Global Escape Test

In global escape analysis, we find escape information about a function **f** in an **nml** program that holds true for every possible application of **f**. To do so, we apply the abstract escape semantic value of **f** to arguments that cause the greatest escapement possible.

Definition 2 (Worst-case escape function) *For each non-list type τ, we define the function W^τ that corresponds to an* **nml** *function from which every argument escapes:* $W^\tau = \lambda x_1.\langle x_{1(1)}, \lambda x_2.\langle x_{1(1)} \sqcup x_{2(1)}, \ldots, \lambda x_m.\langle \bigsqcup_{i=1}^{m} x_{i(1)}, err\rangle \ldots\rangle\rangle$ *for* $m \geq 1$ *and* $W^\tau = err$ *for* $m = 0$*, where m is the number of arguments that a function of type τ can take before returning a primitive value. For each list type τ list, $W^{\tau\ list}$ is defined to be W^τ.*

Given a function f of n arguments, the position i of an interesting parameter, and the abstract escape semantic environment env_e mapping f to an element of the abstract escape semantic domain D_e, the global escape test function $G(f, i, env_e)$ determines how much of the ith parameter of f could possibly escape f globally. It is defined as follows:

$$G(f, i, env_e) = (E[\![f\ x_1\ \ldots\ x_n]\!]\ env_e[x_i \mapsto y_i])_{(1)}$$

where $y_i = \langle\langle 1, s_i\rangle, W^{\tau_i}\rangle$, s_i is the number of spines of the ith parameter of f (if it is a list type, otherwise s_i is 0), τ_i is the type of the ith parameter of f, and for all $j \leq n$ and $j \neq i$, $y_j = \langle\langle 0, 0\rangle, W^{\tau_j}\rangle$, τ_j is the type of the jth parameter of f. Note that the whole i^{th} argument with s_i spines is interesting, and any other argument is not interesting. Then, from the result of the global escape test function, we can conclude as follows:

- If $G(f, i, env_e) = \langle 0, 0\rangle$ then we conclude that none of the ith argument escapes f in any possible application of f to n arguments.
- If $G(f, i, env_e) = \langle 1, k\rangle$ then we conclude that, if $s_i \geq 1$ then, the top $(s_i - k)$ spines of the ith argument *do not* escape f in any possible application of f to n arguments, but the bottom k spines of the ith argument *could* escape f in some application of f to n arguments. (If $s_i = 0$ then the ith argument, which is not a list type, *could* escape in some application of f to n arguments.)

4.2 Local Escape Test

Generally, we would like to know if an argument escapes from a *particular call* to a function f. This depends on the values of the arguments of that call. Given a function of n arguments in an application $f\ e_1\ \ldots\ e_n$, the position i of an interesting parameter, and the abstract escape semantic environment env_e mapping f and the free identifiers within e_1 through e_n to elements of the abstract escape semantic domain D_e, the local escape test function $L(f, i, e_1, \ldots, e_n, env_e)$ determines how much of the ith parameter of f could escape f in the evaluation of $f\ e_1\ \ldots\ e_n$. It is defined as follows:

$$L(f, i, e_1, \ldots, e_n, env_e) = (E[\![f\ x_1\ \ldots\ x_n]\!]\ env_e[x_i \mapsto z_i])_{(1)}$$

where $z_i = \langle\langle 1, s_i\rangle, (E[\![e_i]\!]\ env_e)_{(2)}\rangle$, s_i is the number of spines of e_i (if it is a list type, otherwise s_i is 0), and for all $j \leq n$ and $j \neq i$, $z_j = \langle\langle 0, 0\rangle, (E[\![e_j]\!]\ env_e)_{(2)}\rangle$. Similarly, we can determine local escape information from the result of the local escape test function.

4.3 Complexity

The abstract interpretation framework for the escape analysis uses a finite abstract domain of size $(d + 2) \geq 2$. In the case of first-order functions, the order of time complexity is exponential in the number of arguments to the function being analyzed. In the case of higher-order functions, the complexity is much worse than exponential, and depends on the types of its arguments. The time complexity of the escape analysis is comparable to that of strictness analysis for higher-order functional languages with non-flat domains (lists) [19].

5 Polymorphic Invariance of Escape Analysis

Up to this point, we have assumed that **nml** is a monomorphically-typed language. It remains to be shown that escape analysis works on polymorphically-typed **nml** as well. We concentrate on parametric polymorphism. To show this, we prove that escape analysis exhibits the property of polymorphic invariance [1]. This means that given a polymorphic function, escape analysis will return the same result on any two monotyped instances of that function. Actually, escape analysis is *polymorphically invariant* when it is stated the following way (essentially the converse of the way it was stated previously): *Given a function application, how many spines of an argument are not returned in the result of the application.* This is important because it is the portions of an argument that do not escape from the application that can be stack allocated or reused (if unshared).

Theorem 1 (Polymorphic Invariance) *Let f be a polymorphic function of arity n, and let f' and f'' be any two monomorphic instances of f. Assume that env'_e and env''_e are escape semantic environments that map f' and f'' to elements of D_e, respectively. Then, for $1 \leq i \leq n$,*
$G(f', i, env'_e) = \langle 0, 0 \rangle \Longleftrightarrow G(f'', i, env''_e) = \langle 0, 0 \rangle$ *and*
$G(f', i, env'_e) = \langle 1, k' \rangle \Longleftrightarrow G(f'', i, env''_e) = \langle 1, k'' \rangle$
such that $s'_i - k' = s''_i - k''$ where s'_i and s''_i are the number of spines of the ith parameter of f' and f'', respectively.

Proof : This is shown by structural and fixpoint induction on the expression e (the body of f) [16]. □

Polymorphic invariance indicates that to analyze a function definition in a polymorphic language, we need only perform the analysis on the simplest monotyped instance of that function. The result is then applicable to all possible instances of that function.

6 Application of Escape Analysis

As mentioned in the introduction, escape information can be used in a number of other analyses and optimizations [16]. Due to space limitations, we will only sketch them.

Several papers [8, 9] have been published on sharing analysis of objects in higher order functional languages (and many papers for first-order languages). It turns out that for strict languages (in which the evaluation order is obvious), sharing analysis of lists becomes easy in the presence of escape information.

Theorem 2 (Sharing Information) *Let f be a function which takes n arguments such that d_i is the number of spines of the ith parameter of f for $i = 1 \ldots n$, and let f return a list with d_f spines. If esc_i is the number of escaping spines of the ith parameter of f, for $i = 1 \ldots n$ (statically inferred by escape analysis), then*

1. *all cons cells in the top $(d_f - max\{min\{esc_1, (d_1 - u_1)\}, \ldots, min\{esc_n, (d_n - u_n)\}\})$ spines of the result of $(f\ e_1 \ldots e_n)$ are unshared when u_i is the number of unshared spines of e_i for $1 \leq i \leq n$.*

2. *all cons cells in the top $(d_f - max\{esc_1, \ldots, esc_n\})$ spines of the result of $(f\ e_1 \ldots e_n)$ are unshared for any set of arguments $e_1, \ldots . e_n$.*

Proof : 1. The number of spines of e_i that are shared is $(d_i - u_i)$. The number of shared spines of e_i that could escape f is $min\{esc_i, (d_i - u_i)\}$. In the result of $(f\ e_1 \ldots e_n)$, the bottom $max\{min\{esc_i, (d_i - u_i)\}\}$ spines will be shared. Thus, all cells in the top $(d_f - max\{min\{esc_1, (d_1 - u_1)\}, \ldots, min\{esc_n, (d_n - u_n)\}\})$ spines of the result are not shared.
2. Since we consider any set of arguments $e_1, \ldots . e_n$, and we have no sharing information of e_i, we assume that $u_i = 0$ as the worst-case. Then, $min\{esc_i, (d_i - 0)\} = esc_i$ because $esc_i \leq d_i$. Thus, all cells at top $(d_f - max\{esc_1, \ldots, esc_n\})$ spines of the result are not shared. □

Both escape information and sharing information that are determined by escape analysis can be used for the in-place reuse optimization. Consider an expression of the form of $(f\ e_1 \ldots\ e_i\ \ldots e_n)$ where f is a function with n parameters, the ith parameter of f is a list type with d_i spines, and there occurs some `cons` in the body of f. Let all cons cells at the top u_i spines of the result of e_i be unshared. Using the *global* escape information of parameters of f, the in-place reuse of cons cells can be performed as follows:

- If the bottom esc_i spines of the ith parameter of f escapes f globally then the expression can safely be transformed into $(f'\ e_1 \ldots\ e_i\ \ldots e_n)$ where f' is a new version of f which directly reuses cons cells in the top $s = min\{u_i, (d_i - esc_i)\}$, spines of the ith argument of f for new cons cells needed in the body of f.

- Let f be defined as $f\ x_1\ \ldots\ x_n$ = ... (`cons` $e_1\ e_2$) .... If there is no further use of the ith parameter x_i of f after the evaluation of the subexpression (`cons` $e_1\ e_2$) then a new version f' of f which uses the in-place reuse optimization can be defined as follows:
$f'\ x_1 \ldots x_n$ = ... (`DCONS` $x_i\ e_1\ e_2$) ... where `DCONS` is a destructive version of `cons` defined by `DCONS` $a\ b\ c$ = $\{p := a;$ `car`$(a) := b;$ `cdr`$(a) := c; return(p)\}$

7 Conclusions

We have presented an analysis that answers a simple question, but in doing so, subsumes a number of other program analyses for storage optimization described in the literature. It works on higher order functional languages in the presence of lists, is relatively simple and (hopefully) easy to understand, and makes no assumptions about an underlying abstract machine. It remains to be seen if it is useful in practice due to the computational complexity of finding fixpoints of higher order functions. However, the fact that the analysis is polymorphically invariant allows one to analyze only the simplest instance of each polymorphic function, and we hope that in practice this makes the analysis useful at compile-time.

References

[1] S. Abramsky. Strictness analysis and polymorphic invariance. In *Workshop on Programs as Data Objects*, LNCS 217, Springer-Verlag, pp. 1-24, 1986.

[2] H. Baker. Unifying and conquer (garbage, updating, aliasing ...) in functional languages. In *Proceedings of the ACM Conference on Lisp and Functional Programming*, pp. 218-226, 1990.

[3] R.A. Brooks, R.P. Gabriel and G.L. Steele. An optimizing compiler for lexically scoped LISP. In *Proceedings of the SIGPLAN Symposium on Compiler Construction*, pp. 261-275, 1982.

[4] G.L. Burn, C.L. Hankin, and S. Abramsky. Strictness analysis for higher order functions. *Science of Computer Programming*, 7:249-278, 1986.

[5] D.R. Chase. *Garbage Collection and Other Optimizations.* Ph.D. Thesis, Rice University, 1987.

[6] D.R. Chase. Safety considerations for storage allocation optimizations. In *Proceedings of the SIGPLAN Conference on Programming Language Design and Implementation*, pp. 1-9, 1988.

[7] D.R. Chase, M. Wegman, F. K. Zadeck. Analysis of pointers and structures. In *Proceedings of the SIGPLAN Conference on Programming Language Design and Implementation*, pp. 296-310, 1990.

[8] A. Deutsch. On determining lifetime and aliasing of dynamically allocated data in higher-order functional specifications. In *Proceedings of the ACM Symposium on Principles of Programming Languages*, pp. 157- 168, 1990.

[9] B. Goldberg. Detecting sharing of partial applications in functional programs. In *Proceedings of the Conference on Functional Programming and Computer Architecture*, LNCS 274, Springer-Verlag, pp. 408-425, 1987.

[10] B. Goldberg and Y.G. Park. Higher order escape analysis: Optimizing stack allocation in higher order functional program implementations. In *Proceedings of the European Symposium on Programming*, LNCS 432, Springer-Verlag, pp. 152-160, 1990.

[11] P. Hudak and J. Young. Higher-order strictness analysis for the untyped lambda calculus. In *Proceedings of the ACM Symposium on Principles of Programming Languages*, pp. 107-118, 1986.

[12] K. Inoue, H. Seki, and H. Yagi. Analysis of functional programs to detect run-time garbage cells. *ACM Transactions on Programming Languages*, 10(4):555-578, October 1988.

[13] S.B. Jones and D. Le Metayer. Compile-time garbage collection by sharing analysis. In *Proceedings of the Conference on Functional Programming Languages and Computer Architecture*, pp. 54-74, 1989.

[14] N. Jones and S. Muchnick. Binding time optimization in programming languages: An approach to the design of an ideal language. In *Proceedings of the ACM Symposium on Principles of Programming Languages*, pp. 77-94, 1976.

[15] D. Kranz. *ORBIT: An Optimizing Compiler for Scheme.* Ph.D. Thesis, Yale University, May 1988.

[16] Y.G. Park. *Semantic Analyses for Storage Management Optimizations in Functional Language Implementations.* Ph.D. Thesis, New York University, 1991.

[17] Y.G. Park and B. Goldberg. Reference escape analysis: Optimizing reference counting based on the lifetime of references. In *Proceedings of the ACM Symposium on Partial Evaluation and Semantics Based Program Manipulation*, pp. 178-189, 1991.

[18] C. Ruggieri and T.P. Murtagh. Lifetime analysis of dynamically allocated objects. In *Proceedings of the ACM Symposium on Principles of Programming Languages*, pp. 285-293, 1988.

[19] P. Wadler. Strictness analysis on non-flat domains (by abstract interpretation over finite domains). In *Abstract Interpretation of Declarative Languages,* S. Abstramsky and C.L. Hankin, editors, pp. 266-275, Ellis Horwood, 1987.

A Examples

Consider the following partition sort (often mistakenly called quicksort) program:

```
letrec PS x = if (x=nil) then nil
                  else letrec y = SPLIT (car x) (cdr x) nil nil;
                      in APPEND(PS (car y))
                                  (cons (car x) (PS (car (cdr y))));

              SPLIT p x l h = if (x=nil) then (cons l (cons h nil))
                                  elseif (car x)<p then
                                              SPLIT p (cdr x) (cons (car x) l) h
                                  else SPLIT p (cdr x) l (cons (car x) h);

              APPEND x y = if (x=nil) then y
                              else cons (car x) (APPEND(cdr x) y);
in PS [5,2,7,1,3,4]
```

We assume that the type of each function is given by PS : *int list* → *int list*, SPLIT : *int* → *int list* → *int list* → *int list* → *int list list*, and APPEND : *int list* → *int list* → *int list* and that each car in the program is annotated as $\texttt{car}^{\texttt{s}}$ which denotes the car takes as its argument a list with s spines.

A.1 Escape Analysis

The definitions of the escape semantic values *append*, *split*, and *ps* of APPEND, SPLIT, and PS (shown uncurried for convenience) are:

$$\begin{aligned}
append\ x\ y &= y \sqcup (\mathrm{sub}^1(x) \sqcup append\ x\ y) \\
split\ p\ x\ l\ h &= l \sqcup h \sqcup (split\ p\ x\ (\mathrm{sub}^1(x) \sqcup l)\ h) \sqcup (split\ p\ x\ \ (\mathrm{sub}^1(x) \sqcup h)) \\
ps\ x &= append\ (ps\ \mathrm{sub}^2(split\ \mathrm{sub}^1(x)\ x\ \langle\langle 0,0\rangle err\rangle\ \langle\langle 0,0\rangle err\rangle)) \\
&\quad (\mathrm{sub}^1(x) \sqcup (ps\ \mathrm{sub}^2(split\ \mathrm{sub}^1(x)\ x\ \langle\langle 0,0\rangle err\rangle\ \langle\langle 0,0\rangle err\rangle)))
\end{aligned}$$

The meaning of each function in the escape semantic domain is found by fixpoint iteration. Here is the fixpoint iteration for APPEND:

$$\begin{aligned}
append^{(0)}\ x\ y &= \bot_{int\ list} \\
append^{(1)}\ x\ y &= y \sqcup (\mathrm{sub}^1(x) \sqcup append^{(0)}\ x\ y) \\
&= y \sqcup \mathrm{sub}^1(x) \\
append^{(2)}\ x\ y &= y \sqcup (\mathrm{sub}^1(x) \sqcup append^{(1)}\ x\ y) \\
&= y \sqcup (\mathrm{sub}^1(x) \sqcup (y \sqcup \mathrm{sub}^1(x))) \\
&= y \sqcup \mathrm{sub}^1(x)
\end{aligned}$$

and for SPLIT:

$$\begin{aligned}
split^{(0)}\ p\ x\ l\ h &= \bot_{(int\ list)\ list} \\
split^{(1)}\ p\ x\ l\ h &= l \sqcup h \sqcup \bot_{(int\ list)\ list} \sqcup \bot_{(int\ list)\ list} \\
&= l \sqcup h \\
split^{(2)}\ p\ x\ l\ h &= l \sqcup h \sqcup (split^{(1)}\ p\ x\ (\mathrm{sub}^1(x) \sqcup l)\ h) \sqcup (split^{(1)}\ p\ x\ \ (\mathrm{sub}^1(x) \sqcup h)) \\
&= l \sqcup h \sqcup ((\mathrm{sub}^1(x) \sqcup l) \sqcup h) \sqcup ((\mathrm{sub}^1(x) \sqcup h)) \\
&= l \sqcup h \sqcup \mathrm{sub}^1(x) \\
split^{(3)}\ p\ x\ l\ h &= l \sqcup h \sqcup (split^{(2)}\ p\ x\ (\mathrm{sub}^1(x) \sqcup l)\ h) \sqcup (split^{(2)}\ p\ x\ \ (\mathrm{sub}^1(x) \sqcup h)) \\
&= l \sqcup h \sqcup ((\mathrm{sub}^1(x) \sqcup l) \sqcup h) \sqcup (l \sqcup (\mathrm{sub}^1(x) \sqcup h) \sqcup \mathrm{sub}^1(x)) \\
&= l \sqcup h \sqcup \mathrm{sub}^1(x)
\end{aligned}$$

and for PS (using the values computed for APPEND and SPLIT):

$$
\begin{aligned}
ps^{(0)}\ x &= \bot_{int\ list} \\
ps^{(1)}\ x &= append(ps^{(0)}\ \mathrm{sub}^2(\mathrm{sub}^1(x)))\ (\mathrm{sub}^1(x) \sqcup (ps^{(0)}\ \mathrm{sub}^2(\mathrm{sub}^1(x))) \\
&= append\ \bot_{int\ list}\ (\mathrm{sub}^1(\mathrm{sub}^1(x)) \sqcup \bot_{int\ list}) \\
&= \mathrm{sub}^1(x) \\
ps^{(2)}\ x &= append(ps^{(1)}\ \mathrm{sub}^2(\mathrm{sub}^1(x)))\ (\mathrm{sub}^1(x) \sqcup (ps^{(1)}\ \mathrm{sub}^2(\mathrm{sub}^1(x))) \\
&= append\ \mathrm{sub}^1(\mathrm{sub}^2(\mathrm{sub}^1(x)))\ (\mathrm{sub}^1(x) \sqcup \mathrm{sub}^1(\mathrm{sub}^2(\mathrm{sub}^1(x))) \\
&= \mathrm{sub}^1(x)
\end{aligned}
$$

Let $env_e = [\mathtt{APPEND} \mapsto append, \mathtt{SPLIT} \mapsto split, \mathtt{PS} \mapsto ps]$. Then,

$$
\begin{aligned}
G(\mathtt{APPEND}, 1, env_e) &= (E_e[\![\mathtt{APPEND\ x\ y}]\!]env_e[\mathtt{x} \mapsto \langle\langle 1,1\rangle, err\rangle, \mathtt{y} \mapsto \langle\langle 0,0\rangle, err\rangle])_{(1)} \\
&= (\langle\langle 0,0\rangle, err\rangle \sqcup \mathrm{sub}^1(\langle\langle 1,1\rangle, err\rangle))_{(1)} \\
&= \langle 1,0\rangle \\
G(\mathtt{APPEND}, 2, env_e) &= (E_e[\![\mathtt{APPEND\ x\ y}]\!]env_e[\mathtt{x} \mapsto \langle\langle 0,0\rangle, err\rangle, \mathtt{y} \mapsto \langle\langle 1,1\rangle, err\rangle].)_{(1)} \\
&= (\langle\langle 1,1\rangle, err\rangle \sqcup \mathrm{sub}^1(\langle\langle 0,0\rangle, err\rangle))_{(1)} \\
&= \langle 1,1\rangle
\end{aligned}
$$

Thus, we conclude that APPEND returns all of its second argument y, and all but the top spine of the first argument x.

$$
\begin{aligned}
G(\mathtt{SPLIT}, 1, env_e) &= (E_e[\![\mathtt{SPLIT\ p\ x\ l\ h}]\!]env_e[\mathtt{p} \mapsto \langle\langle 1,0\rangle, err\rangle, \mathtt{x}, \mathtt{l}, \mathtt{h} \mapsto \langle\langle 0,0\rangle, err\rangle])_{(1)} \\
&= (\langle\langle 0,0\rangle, err\rangle \sqcup \langle\langle 0,0\rangle, err\rangle \sqcup \mathrm{sub}^1(\langle\langle 0,0\rangle, err\rangle))_{(1)} \\
&= \langle 0,0\rangle \\
G(\mathtt{SPLIT}, 2, env_e) &= (E_e[\![\mathtt{SPLIT\ p\ x\ l\ h}]\!]env_e[\mathtt{x} \mapsto \langle\langle 1,1\rangle, err\rangle, \mathtt{p}, \mathtt{l}, \mathtt{h} \mapsto \langle\langle 0,0\rangle, err\rangle].)_{(1)} \\
&= (\langle\langle 0,0\rangle, err\rangle \sqcup \langle\langle 0,0\rangle, err\rangle \sqcup \mathrm{sub}^1(\langle\langle 1,1\rangle, err\rangle))_{(1)} \\
&= \langle 1,0\rangle \\
G(\mathtt{SPLIT}, 3, env_e) &= (E_e[\![\mathtt{SPLIT\ p\ x\ l\ h}]\!]env_e[\mathtt{l} \mapsto \langle\langle 1,1\rangle, err\rangle, \mathtt{p}, \mathtt{x}, \mathtt{h} \mapsto \langle\langle 0,0\rangle, err\rangle].)_{(1)} \\
&= (\langle\langle 1,1\rangle, err\rangle \sqcup \langle\langle 0,0\rangle, err\rangle \sqcup \mathrm{sub}^1(\langle\langle 0,0\rangle, err\rangle))_{(1)} \\
&= \langle 1,1\rangle \\
G(\mathtt{SPLIT}, 4, env_e) &= (E_e[\![\mathtt{SPLIT\ p\ x\ l\ h}]\!]env_e[\mathtt{h} \mapsto \langle\langle 1,1\rangle, err\rangle, \mathtt{p}, \mathtt{x}, \mathtt{l} \mapsto \langle\langle 0,0\rangle, err\rangle].)_{(1)} \\
&= (\langle\langle 0,0\rangle, err\rangle \sqcup \langle\langle 1,1\rangle, err\rangle \sqcup \mathrm{sub}^1(\langle\langle 0,0\rangle, err\rangle))_{(1)} \\
&= \langle 1,1\rangle
\end{aligned}
$$

From above, we conclude that SPLIT returns all of its third and fourth arguments l and h, none of the first argument p, and all but the top spine of the second argument x.

$$
\begin{aligned}
G(\mathtt{PS}, 1, env_e) &= (E_e[\![\mathtt{PS\ x}]\!]\ env_e[\mathtt{x} \mapsto \langle\langle 1,1\rangle, err\rangle])_{(1)} \\
&= (\mathrm{sub}^1(\langle\langle 1,1\rangle, err\rangle))_{(1)} \\
&= \langle 1,0\rangle
\end{aligned}
$$

So, we conclude that PS returns all but the top spine of its argument x.

A.2 Sharing Information from Escape Analysis

PS takes a list with one spine as its argument, and returns a list with one spine. From the global escape analysis, we know that no spine of the argument escapes PS globally. SPLIT takes four arguments p, x, l and h where p is an integer, and x, l and h are lists with one spine, respectively, and returns a list with two spines. From the global escape analysis, we know that none of the first parameter p, all but the top spine of the second parameter x, and all of the third and fourth parameters l and h escape SPLIT globally. Thus, we can determine the following sharing properties (among others) of the program:

- For the expression (PS e) where e is any list with one spine, the top spine of the result list of (PS e) is *not* shared.
- For the expression of (SPLIT e_1 e_2 e_3 e_4) where each e_i is any possible expression, the top spine of the result list of (SPLIT e_1 e_2 e_3 e_4) is *not* shared.

A.3 Optimizations based on Escape Analysis

A.3.1 Stack Allocation

Our escape analysis has determined that the spine of the original list [5,2,7,1,3,4] does not escape from PS. Thus the spine of that list can be allocated in PS activation record. All the cells of the spine will disappear when PS's activation is removed from the stack.

A.3.2 In-place Reuse

From the global escape analysis, we know that APPEND returns all of its second argument y, and all but the top spine of the first argument x. We also know that, for any expression (PS *e*) where *e* is a list with one spine, the top spine of the result of (PS *e*) is *unshared*. Thus, the definition of PS can be transformed into PS' as follows:

```
PS' x = if (x=nil) then nil
        else letrec y = SPLIT (car x) (cdr x) nil nil;
             in APPEND' (PS' (car y))
                  (cons (car x) (PS' (car (cdr y))));
```

where APPEND' is a version of APPEND in which cons cells in the top spine of its first argument x are directly reused. It is defined by

```
APPEND' x y = if (x=nil) then y
              else DCONS x (car x) (APPEND' (cdr x) y);
```

Furthermore, if we know that the top spine of the argument of PS is unshared, then the definition of PS can be transformed into PS'' in which cons cells in the top spine of its argument x are reused as follows:

```
PS'' x = if (x=nil) then nil
         else letrec y = SPLIT (car x) (cdr x) nil nil;
           in APPEND' (PS'' (car y))
              (DCONS x (car x) (PS'' (car (cdr y))));
```

Consider, as another example, a naive reverse function REV:

```
REV l = if (l=nil) then nil
        else APPEND (REV (cdr l)) (cons (car l) nil);
```

From our analysis, REV can be transformed into REV' which reuses cons cells in the top spine of its argument l, if unshared, as follows:

```
REV' l = if (l=nil) then nil
         else APPEND' (REV' (cdr l)) (DCONS l (car l) nil);
```

A.3.3 Block Allocation/Reclamation

Suppose we are given a program identical to the partition sort program, except that the result expression was

```
PS (create_list i)
```

where create_list is some recursive function creating a list and i is some variable. The list that create_list returns cannot be allocated in PS's activation record because the activation record doesn't exist when the list is created. An optimization that can be performed is as follows: create_list should allocate the spine of the list in some block of memory. The spine of the list does not escape from PS, so when PS is finished, the whole block of memory can be put back on the free list. This block of memory is the "local heap" described by Ruggieri and Murtagh [18].

An Abstract Machine for CLP($\mathcal{R}$)

JOXAN JAFFAR* SPIRO MICHAYLOV†
PETER J. STUCKEY‡ ROLAND H.C. YAP*§

Abstract

An abstract machine is described for the CLP($\mathcal{R}$) programming language. It is intended as a first step towards enabling CLP($\mathcal{R}$) programs to be executed with efficiency approaching that of conventional languages. The core Constraint Logic Arithmetic Machine (CLAM) extends the Warren Abstract Machine (WAM) for compiling Prolog with facilities for handling rea' arithmetic constraints. The full CLAM includes facilities for taking advantage of information obtained from global program analysis.

1 Introduction

The CLP($\mathcal{R}$) language is an instance of the Constraint Logic Programming scheme (CLP) [3], a class of rule based constraint languages. CLP($\mathcal{R}$) embodies constraints over the domain of uninterpreted functors over real arithmetic terms. Appendix A contains an introduction to CLP($\mathcal{R}$). In this paper we present the design of the Constraint Logic Arithmetic Machine (CLAM) for the efficient execution of CLP($\mathcal{R}$) programs.

*IBM T.J. Watson Research Center, P.O. Box 704, Yorktown Heights, NY 10598, USA.

†School of Computer Science, Carnegie Mellon University, Pittsburgh, PA 15213, USA.

‡Dept. of Computer Science, Univ. of Melbourne, Parkville, Victoria 3052, Australia.

§On leave from Dept. of Computer Science, Monash University, Clayton, Victoria 3168, Australia.

ACM SIGPLAN '92 PLDI-6/92/CA

Abstract machines have been used for implementing programming languages for many reasons. Portability is one: only an implementation of the abstract machine needs to be made available on each platform. Another is simply convenience: it is easier to write a native code compiler if the task is first reduced to compiling for an abstract machine that is semantically closer to the source language. The best abstract machines sit at just the right point on the spectrum between the conceptual clarity of the high-level source language and the details of the target machine. In doing so they can often be used to express programs in exactly the right form for tackling the efficiency issues of a source language. For example, the Warren Abstract Machine (WAM) [10] revolutionized the execution of PROLOG, since translating programs to the WAM exposed many opportunities for optimization that were not apparent at the source level. An example from further afield is the technique of optimizing functional programs by first converting them to Continuation Passing Style (CPS) [4]. CPS conversion has lead to highly optimizing compilers for Scheme and Standard ML. The benefit from designing an appropriate abstract machine for a given source language can be so great that even executing the abstract instruction code by interpretation can lead to surprisingly efficient implementations of a language. For example, many commercial PROLOG systems compile to WAM-like code. Certainly more efficiency can be obtained from native code compilation, but the step that made PROLOG usable was that of compiling to the WAM.

While the WAM made PROLOG practical, global analysis shows the potential of making another major leap. For example, Taylor [8] and Van Roy [9] used fairly efficient analyzers to generate high quality native code. Based on certain examples, they showed that the code quality was comparable to that obtained from a C compiler. In the case of CLP($\mathcal{R}$), the opportunities for obtaining valuable information from global analysis [7] are even greater than in PROLOG [1].

In what follows we describe the core CLAM, which includes a comprehensive set of basic instructions. The full CLAM is described next, the focus being on special instructions to take advantage of information obtained from analysis. The subsequent discussion of empirics compares the efficiency of interpretive code, core CLAM code, and optimized CLAM code.

2 CLP($\mathcal{R}$) Implementation Issues

The central implementation issue in CLP($\mathcal{R}$) is based on an observation about programming methodology: while the expressive power of the language comes from its considerable generality, much of the execution of typical programs involves solving simple constraints. These are often just PROLOG-like unifications, arithmetic tests, simple evaluations and assignments. This suggests that the generality of the language should not be allowed to compromise the efficiency of the more basic features. In particular, PROLOG programs should run as efficiently as in a PROLOG system. Furthermore, it is desired that simple arithmetic should be performed efficiently — without resorting to a general constraint solving mechanism. Another major implementation issue is incrementality. Throughout a computation, constraints are being added to or removed from a typically large set of collected constraints. For efficiency reasons this process should be performed without constantly having to resolve all of the collected constraints.

The original CLP($\mathcal{R}$) interpreter [5] satisfied these criteria in the sense that it executed PROLOG programs at least as efficiently as other PROLOG interpreters, and handled simple constraints directly without using the constraint solver. The interpreter was divided into a PROLOG-like inference engine, an interface, and a constraint solver. The inference engine, which was based on structure sharing, was responsible for search, control and unification. The job of the interface was to directly execute arithmetic tests, assignments and simple evaluations where possible. Otherwise it broke up complex constraints into a simpler form to be passed to the constraint solver. The constraint solver itself was partitioned into an equation solver based on Gaussian elimination, an inequality solver which used a highly modified incremental simplex algorithm, and a nonlinear handler which managed the delay and wakeup of nonlinear constraints.

Clearly the desirable features of the interpreter should be retained in a compiler-based system. Thus the objectives of the core CLAM are as follows.

- It should be based on the WAM, because of the latter's suitability for PROLOG.
- It should provide a set of instructions directly "interfacing" to the constraint solver. These being used to replace the functions of the interface in the interpreter.
- The granularity of instructions should be "right" in the sense that constraints can be broken up in a way corresponding to the structure of the constraint solver.

Another objective of the full CLAM is to effectively make use of the kind of information that can be obtained from a global analyzer.

- A special datatype of mutable arithmetic variables should be available. These assume fixed but changeable values, as opposed to normal (logical) variables.
- Simple evaluation of expressions based on mutable variables, and assignment to such variables, should be supported. Mixed constraints, obtaining some coefficients and constants from the mutable variables, should be supported.
- Optimizations based on variables that will no longer be used, and constraints that will become redundant, should be expressible.

As is typical in PROLOG, we assume that optimizing compilation is performed on a program in the context of a *calling pattern* which defines the set of allowed queries. Thus, for one program, different code may be obtained for each different pattern. While the specific nature of such patterns need not concern us here, they typically describe which arguments of a predicate are ground[1], and what their types are.

Next we describe the CLAM, and as we shall see, the extension from the WAM to the CLAM has two essential aspects. One is the *generalization* to arithmetic constraints, and the other is *specialization* for low-level optimizations.

3 Core CLAM

Presented here is a set of basic instructions which are sufficient to execute CLP($\mathcal{R}$) programs in general. In order to understand the design of the instructions, it

[1] A variable is ground if it has one fixed value.

is necessary to discuss some key aspects of the constraint solver. Mainly, we will describe basic instructions which organize constraints for the solver. Some specialized versions of these instructions are also described. We conclude with a short discussion of runtime structures.

3.1 Constraints

A *linear parametric form* is $c_0 + c_1 V_1 + \cdots + c_n V_n$, where $n \geq 1$, each c_i is a real number and each V_i is a distinct *solver variable*. A linear equation, say $V = c_0 + c_1 W_1 + \cdots + c_n W_n$ equates a solver variable and a parametric form. The variables W_i are known as *parameters* and V is a non-parameter. Linear inequalities are stored in the form $lpf \geq 0$ or $lpf > 0$ where lpf is a linear parametric form. The solver ensures that every solver variable appearing in an equation either is a parameter, or appears as a non-parameter in at most one equation. It also ensures that every variable in the inequalities is parametric if it appears in an equation.

The basic instructions of the core CLAM build and manipulate parametric forms:

- `initpf`[2] `c0`
  initializes a parametric form with constant `c0`.
- `addpf_va{lr}`[3] `ci, Vi`
  adds the term `ci * Vi` to the parametric form[4]. The two versions of the instruction (`var` or `val`) correspond to whether V_i is a local variable appearing for the first time (a *new variable*). If so, we need to create storage for the variable, and we may also simplify constraint solving. The variable V_i may be a parameter, in which case c_i is added to the coefficient of V_i in the parametric form, or already have a parametric representation lpf, in which case $c_i * lpf$ is added.
- `solve_eq0`
  signifies the end of the construction of the linear form. The equation $c_0 + c_1 V_1 + \cdots + c_n V_n = 0$ is solved by the equation solver.
- `solve_ge0` and `solve_gt0`
  Similar to the above, but forming an inequality or strict inequality instead of an equation.

For example, consider the constraint $5 + X - Y = 0$, where X is a new variable. It could be compiled as shown in Figure 1. We also indicate how the instructions are executed in the case where Y is non-parametric, say $Y = Z + 3.14$ is in the solver.

Recall that a constructed parametric form contains only parametric and new variables. The process of solving an equation built using such a parametric form roughly amounts to (a) finding a parameter V in the form to become non-parametric, (b) writing the equation into the normalized form $V = lpf$, (c) substituting out V using lpf in all other constraints, and finally (d) adding the new constraint $V = lpf$ to the solver.

Suppose there is a new variable in the equation to be compiled. Then it will always appear in the parametric form at runtime hence it can be chosen in step (a). Since this choice is made at compile time, much of the work of step (b) can also be compiled away. Step (c) is not needed since the variable is new. Hence all we need is a new instruction for step (d), one for which the solver always returns *true*. A similar simplification can be made for the compilation of inequalities which contain a new variable. The new instructions:

- `solve_no_fail_eq V`
- `solve_no_fail_ge V`
- `solve_no_fail_gt V`

For example, the above constraint $5 + X - Y = 0$, where X is new, can be better compiled into the instructions in Figure 2.

Finally, there are a number of simple enhancements we can make to the instruction set to cater for commonly occurring cases. The cases where the constant is zero or the coefficient is 1 or -1 occur in the majority of instances, so special instructions can be expected both to keep down the code size and cut down on decode time. This can be done using

- `initpf_0`
  start a new linear form with constant 0.
- `addpf_va{lr}_{+-} Vi`
  add a term consisting of a variable with coefficient ± 1.

Nonlinear constraints are separated out at compile time so that they appear in one of a few particular forms: $X = Y \times Z$, $X = pow(Y, Z)$, $X = abs(Y)$, $X = sin(Y)$, $X = cos(Y)$. CLP($\mathcal{R}$) delays the satisfiability of nonlinear constraints until they become linear. To detect when a nonlinear constraint becomes linear, the nonlinear constraint handler associates with each constraint a number of *wakeup degrees* representing the information currently known about the variables appearing in the constraint. As variables become ground, a partic-

[2] The "pf" stands for parametric form.
[3] This brace notation indicates `addpf_val` or `addpf_var`
[4] V_i is either a register or a local variable in the stack; the distinction is not important for this paper.

`initpf`	`5`	*lpf*: 5
`addpf_var`	`1, X`	*lpf*: $5 + 1 * X$
`addpf_val`	`-1, Y`	*lpf*: $1.86 + 1 * X - 1 * Z$
`solve_eq0`		*solve*: $1.86 + 1 * X - 1 * Z = 0$

Figure 1: Core CLAM code for the constraint $5 + X - Y = 0$

`initpf`	`-5`	*lpf*: -5
`addpf_val`	`1, Y`	*lpf*: $-1.86 + 1 * Z$
`solve_no_fail_eq`	`X`	*add*: $X = -1.86 + 1 * Z$

Figure 2: Optimized CLAM code for the constraint $5 + X - Y = 0$

ular instance of a nonlinear constraint passes from one degree to another until it reaches a point where it can be awoken. For a full description see [6].

Instructions are provided for creating a nonlinear constraint in any one of its degrees, so for example there are five instructions for *pow* corresponding to the various wakeup degrees:

- `pow_vvv` `Vi, Vj, Vk` for $V_i = pow(V_j, V_k)$ with variables V_i, V_j, V_k
- `pow_cvv` `Vj, Vk` for $c = pow(V_j, V_k)$
- `pow_vcv` `Vi, c, Vk` for $V_i = pow(c, V_k)$
- `pow_vvc` `Vi, Vj, c` for $V_i = pow(V_j, c)$
- `pow_cvc` `c0, Vj, c2` for $c_0 = pow(V_j, c_2)$

For example, $X = pow(3, Y)$ is compiled into the instruction `pow_vcv X, 3, Y`. The remaining forms of a *pow* constraint, e.g. $8 = pow(2, X)$, are equivalent to linear equations and hence the exponentiation is evaluated at compile time, and replaced with a linear equation, e.g. $X = 3$. There is also a class of variants of these instructions, such as `pow_Vcv`, which allow a variable (the one indicated by `V`) to be initialized. The other nonlinears are handled similarly.

3.2 Data Structures

Some of the data structures needed to support the CLAM are a routine extension of those for the WAM — the usual register, stack, heap and trail organization. The main new structures pertain to the solver. Their description is beyond the scope of this paper; see [5]. All that is needed here is that variables involved in arithmetic constraints have a *solver identifier*, which is used to refer to that variable's location in the solver data structures.

The routine modifications to the basic WAM architecture are:

- *Solver identifiers*
  Arithmetic variables need to be represented differently from PROLOG variables. In addition to the usual WAM cell data types, one more is required. Cells of this type contain a solver identifier. Note that the basic unification algorithm needs to be augmented to deal with this new type.

- *Tagged trail*
  In the WAM, the trail merely consists of a stack of addresses to be reset on backtracking. For CLP($\mathcal{R}$), the trail is also used to store changes to constraints. Hence a tagged value trail is required.

- *Choice points*
  Choice points are expanded slightly so as to save the high water mark for solver identifiers and inequalities.

- *Linear form accumulator*
  A linear constraint is built up using one instruction for the constant term, and one for each linear component. During this process, the partially constructed constraint is represented in an accumulator. One of the `solve` instructions then passes the constraint to the solver.

4 CLAM

Above we described the core CLAM and associated runtime structures. Here we present specialized as well as new instructions which implement some key optimization steps in arithmetic constraint solving. Specific kinds of global analysis are required in order to utilize these instructions. A compiler for the core CLAM, in contrast, requires no global analysis.

4.1 Modes

One of the principle mechanisms for enhancing efficiency is to avoid invoking the fully general solver in cases where the constraints are simple. For example when they are equivalent to tests or assignments. Given some fixed calling pattern for a predicate, including information about which variables are ground or unconstrained at call time, we can determine which constraints can be executed as tests or assignments.

Consider the following simple program, whose structure is typical of recursive definitions in CLP($\mathcal{R}$):

```
sum(0, 0).
sum(N, X) :-
        N >= 1, N' = N - 1,
        X' = X - N, sum(N', X').
```

and consider executing the query `sum(7, X)`. The first constraint encountered, $N \geq 1$, can be implemented simply as a test since the value of N is known. The second constraint, $N' = N - 1$, can be implemented simply as an evaluation and assignment to N' because N' is a new variable and the value of N is known. These observations continue to hold when executing the resulting subgoal `sum(6, X')` and for each subsequent subgoal. Hence for any query `sum(c, X)`, where c is a number, the constraint $N \geq 1$ is *always* a test, and $N' = N - 1$ is always an evaluation/assignment.

To take advantage of such constraints, a new data type, *fp_val*, is provided to represent arithmetic variables whose value is known to be ground. (In CLP($\mathcal{R}$) fp_vals are in fact stored in adjacent pairs of registers, or in adjacent stack locations.) The new instructions using fp_vals are given in Figure 3.

For example, the constraints $N \geq 1, N' = N - 1$ can be compiled into

```
        subcf     N, 1, Tmp
        jgef      Tmp, cont
        fail
cont:   mvf       Tmp, N'
```

Even when compilation into the above special instructions is not possible, some simplifications can be made. For example, consider the constraint $V = I * R + V_0$ where the values of I and V_0 will be known when the constraint is encountered. Since I will be known, it is clear at compile time that the constraint will be linear and hence there is no need to separate out the multiplication. Furthermore, the constraint becomes a linear equation on two variables since V_0 is also known.

We add new instructions for creating parametric forms using fp_val variables:

- `initpf_fp FPi`
  begin a parametric form obtaining constant from an fp_val.
- `addpf_fp_va{rl} FPi, Vi`
  add a linear component obtaining the coefficient from an fp_val.

The constraint $V = I * R + V_0$ can be compiled to

```
initpf_fp        V0
addpf_fp_val     I, R
addpf_val_-      V
solve_eq0
```

We finally remark that the instructions for nonlinears are also augmented to make use of variables stored in fp_vals.

4.2 Redundancy

An obvious way to enhance efficiency is to minimize the number of constraints in the solver. Toward this aim we want to eliminate redundant constraints, and an obvious starting point is to eliminate newly encountered constraints which are redundant. Unfortunately such constraints are rare. What is more common however is that new constraints make some *earlier* collected constraints redundant. We concentrate on linear constraints in this subsection since detecting redundancy involving nonlinear constraints is intractable.

We now discuss two forms of redundancy: one associated with variables and the other with constraints.

Redundancy of Variables

We say that a variable is redundant at a certain point in the computation if it will never appear again. The elimination of these variables from the solver produces a more compact representation of the constraints on the variables of interest. Eliminating these variables not only saves space, but also reduces solver activity associated with these variables when adding new constraints. Every variable becomes redundant eventually; thus to gain the most compact representation we may project the constraints onto the remaining variables. (For example, if the only variables of interest are S and T, the constraints $T = T_1, T_1 = T_2 + T_3 - T_4, T_4 - T_3 = 1, T_2 = S+2$ can be better represented by $T = S+1$.) However, projection can be expensive, especially when inequalities are involved. It is only worthwhile in certain cases, one of which is identified below. We note that identifying redundant variables could be achieved at runtime

• `litf`	`c, FPi`	load a numeric constant into an fp_val;
• `getf`	`Vi, FPj`	convert a solver variable to an fp_val;
• `putf`	`FPi, Vj`	convert an fp_val to a solver variable;
• `stf`	`FPi, S`	put an fp_val on the stack frame (offset S);
• `ldf`	`S, FPi`	read an fp_val from stack frame (offset S);
• `mvf`	`FPi, FPj`	copy one fp_val to another;
• `addf`	`FPi, FPj, FPk`	add fp_vals; similarly for `mulf`, `subf`, `divf`;
• `addcf`	`FPi, c, FPk`	add a constant to an fp_val; similarly for `mulcf`, `subcf`, `divcf`;
• `jeqf`	`FPi, L`	jump to label `L` if `FPi` is zero;
• `jgtf`	`FPi, L`	jump to label `L` if `FPi` is positive.
• `jgef`	`FPi, L`	jump to label `L` if `FPi` is nonnegative.

Figure 3: Full CLAM instructions using fp_vals

as part of general garbage collection. However, greater benefit can be obtained by utilizing CLAM instructions to remove these variables in a timely fashion.

Consider the `sum()` program above. After compiling away the simple constraints as described above, the following sequence of constraints, among others, arise from executing the goal `sum(7, X)` :

(1)	X'	$=$	$X - 7$
(2)	X''	$=$	$(X-7)-6$
(3)	X'''	$=$	$((X-7)-6)-5$
...	...		

Upon encountering the second equation $X'' = X' - 6$ and simplifying into (2), note that the variable X' will never occur in future. Hence equation (1) can be deleted. Similarly upon encountering the third equation $X''' = X'' - 5$ and simplifying into (3), the variable X'' is redundant and so (2) can be removed. In short, only one equation involving X need be stored at any point in the computation. We hence add the following instructions to the CLAM:

- `addpf_va{lr}e` `ci, Vi`
- `addpf_va{lr}e_{+-}` `Vi`
- `addpf_fp_va{lr}e` `FPi, Vi`

As before, these augment the current parametric form with an entry involving V_i, but now they indicate that the variable V_i is redundant and can be eliminated (hence the "e"). Returning to the example above, a possible sequence of

```
(1)   init_pf              -7
      addpf_val_+          X
      solve_no_fail_eq0    X'
(2)   init_pf              -6
      addpf_vale_+         X'
      solve_no_fail_eq0    X''
(3)   init_pf              -5
      addpf_vale_+         X''
      solve_no_fail_eq0    X'''
...
```

Notice that a different set of instructions is required for the first equation from that required for the remaining equations. Hence the first iteration needs to be unrolled to produce the most efficient code.

We conclude this subsection with a brief discussion about implementation. Eliminating a variable X from the constraint solver is quite simple: if X is a non-parametric variable, then we just remove the linear form associated with X (as in the above example). If, however, X is a parameter, then to eliminate X we must (i) find an equation containing X, (ii) rewrite the equation with X as the subject, (iii) substitute out X everywhere else using this equation, and finally, (iv) remove the equation. Thus when X is a parameter, there is a trade-off between having one less equation and performing the work toward this aim (because this work is essentially equivalent to adding one new equation). For example, removing an equation is not worthwhile if execution immediately backtracks after its removal.

The following illustrates a typical execution sequence. Suppose the solver contained $X = Y + 1, T = U + Y + 1$ and a new constraint $Y + X - T = 0$ is encountered. Suppose further that it is known that Y does not appear henceforth and so can be eliminated. A straightforward implementation would (a) write the new constraint into parametric form $U - Y = 0$, (b) substitute out U everywhere by Y, (c) add the new constraint $U = Y$, and finally (d) using the information that Y is redundant, process the three resulting equations $X = Y + 1, T = 2*Y + 1, U = Y$ in order to eliminate Y in the manner described above. A much better implementation will (a) write the new constraint into parametric form $U - Y = 0$, and (b) substitute out Y everywhere by U (instead of vice versa).

program	Quintus 3.0b	CLP($\mathcal{R}$) interpreter	CLP($\mathcal{R}$) compiler
nrev	0.66	1.91	0.79
dnf	0.61	1.89	0.78
zebra	1.33	2.58	1.57

Figure 4: *Prolog benchmarks*

Redundancy of Constraints

Of concern here are constraints which become redundant as a result of new constraints. One class of this redundancy that is easy to detect is *future redundancy* defined in [7], where a constraint added now will be made redundant in the future, but it does not effect execution in between these points.

Consider the `sum()` program once again, and executing the goal `sum(N, X)` using the second rule. We obtain the subgoal

```
N >= 1, N' = N - 1, sum(N', X')
```

and note that we have omitted writing the constraint involving X. Continuing the execution we have two choices: choosing the first rule we obtain the new constraint $N' = 0$, and choosing the second rule we obtain the constraint $N' \geq 1$ (among others). In each case the original constraint $N \geq 1$ is made redundant. The main point of this example is that the constraint $N \geq 1$ in the second rule should be implemented simply as a test[5], and not added to the constraint store. We hence add the new instructions

- `solve_no_add_eq0`
- `solve_no_add_ge0`
- `solve_no_add_gt0`

that behave like the `solve` class of instructions, but which do not add the new constraint. In general this task involves significantly less work than the usual constraint satisfiability check and addition since we do not have to detect implicit equalities and may avoid substitutions.

We finally remark that, in our experiments, implementing future redundancy has lead to the most substantial efficiency gains compared to the other optimizations discussed here. The main reason is that inequalities are prone to redundancy, and the cost of maintaining inequalities in general is already relatively high. Equations in contrast are maintained in a form that is essentially free of this kind of redundancy.

[5]In general, these tests are not just simple evaluations.

4.3 Optimizing Compilation

The kinds of program analysis required to utilize the specialized CLAM instructions include those familiar from PROLOG — most prominently, detecting special cases of unification and deterministic predicates. Algorithms for such analysis have become familiar; see [1, 2] for example. The extension to constraints involves no more than a straightforward extension to these algorithms.

Detecting redundant variables and future redundant constraints can in fact be done without dataflow analysis. One simple method involves unfolding the predicate definition (and typically once is enough), and then, in the case of detecting redundant variables, simply inspecting where variables occur last in the unfolded definitions. For detecting a future redundant constraint, the essential step is determining whether the constraints in an unfolded predicate definition imply the constraint being analyzed. Some further discussions appear in [7].

While we do not have a fully engineered analyzer, our experimental analyzer indicates that many CLP($\mathcal{R}$) programs can be analyzed quite effectively.

5 Some Empirics

Throughout this section, all timings (in seconds) were obtained on an IBM RS 6000/530 workstation running AIX Version 3.0. The C compiler used throughout was the standard AIX C compiler with '–O' level optimization. The systems tested are

- The CLP($\mathcal{R}$) interpreter, written entirely in C, whose inference engine uses standard PROLOG structure sharing techniques.
- The CLP($\mathcal{R}$) compiler system, executing core CLAM code. The CLAM code is interpreted, using an emulator written in C.
- An emulator, as above, for the full CLAM, executing handwritten code.
- Quintus PROLOG version 3.0b, a widely-used commercial system.

```
mortgage(P, T, I, R, B) :-
    T > 1,
    T1 = T - 1,
    P >= 0,
    P1 = P * I - R,
    mortgage(P1, T1, I, R, B).
mortgage(P, T, I, R, B) :-
    T = 1,
    B = P * I - R.
```

Figure 5: *Program for reasoning about mortgage repayments*

Q_1 : $mortgage(100000,\ 360,\ 1.01,\ 1025,\ B)$
Q_2 : $mortgage(P,\ 360,\ 1.01,\ 1025,\ 12625.9)$
Q_3 : $R > 0 \wedge B \geq 0 \wedge mortgage(P,\ 360,\ 1.01,\ R,\ B)$
Q_4 : $0 \leq B \wedge B \leq 1030 \wedge mortgage(100000,\ T,\ 1.01,\ 1030,\ B)$

Figure 6: *Four queries for the mortgage program*

```
double mg1(p, t, i, r)
double p, t, i, r;
{
  if (t == 1.0) return (p*i - r);
  else if (t > 1.0 && p >= 0.0)
    return mg1(p*i - r, t - 1.0, i, r);
  else exit(1);
}
```

```
double mg2(t, i, r, b)
double t, i, r, b;
{
double p;
  if (t == 1.0) return ((b + r)/i);
  else if (t > 1.0) {
    p = (mg2(t - 1.0, i, r, b) + r)/i;
    if (p >= 0.0) return p; else exit(1);
  } else exit(1);
}
```

Figure 7: *C functions for Q_1 and Q_2*

query	CLP($\mathcal{R}$) *interpreter*	CLP($\mathcal{R}$) *core CLAM*	CLP($\mathcal{R}$) *full CLAM but no redundancy*	CLP($\mathcal{R}$) *full CLAM*	*C program*
Q_1	0.10	0.05	0.0042	0.0042	0.0010
Q_2	2.08	1.78	0.0054	0.0054	0.0016
Q_3	2.35	1.84	1.05	0.0700	n/a
Q_4	4.20	2.05	1.78	0.0640	n/a

Figure 8: *Timings for Mortgage program*

- Two C programs, for comparison with a CLP($\mathcal{R}$) program compiled into CLAM code.

In Figure 4 we compare CLP($\mathcal{R}$) with Quintus. The programs chosen are a naive reverse benchmark (six times on a 150 element list, built using a normal functor rather than the list constructor), a program for converting boolean formulae into disjunctive normal form, and a program which solves a standard logic puzzle by combinatorial search. The programs in themselves are not interesting, and hence the code is omitted. The important point is that they test major aspects of a PROLOG inference engine. The purpose of this comparison is first to indicate the relative speeds of the inference engines of the two CLP($\mathcal{R}$) systems, and more importantly, to give evidence that the CLAM can be implemented without significantly compromising PROLOG execution speed.

The main part of this section deals with the constraint aspects of the CLAM. We use the program in Figure 5 in four different ways, as shown in Figure 6, so as to utilize different constraint solving instructions[6]. Appendix C contains the core CLAM code for the mortgage program, and also the (full) CLAM code obtained for this program given the calling patterns of the first and third queries. The code for the second (fourth) query is similar to that for the first (third).

Given the calling pattern associated with the first query, the program can be compiled as though it were a simple recursive definition. Similarly for the second query, though a different recursive definition is obtained. Figure 7 contains C functions which implement these two definitions. The third query essentially propagates constraints, and hence it cannot be compiled so simply. Similarly for the fourth query which essentially carries out a search.

In Figure 8, timings are tabulated for the interpreter, core CLAM and full CLAM. To separate the effects of the mode-based optimizations from those of the redundancy-based optimizations, Figure 8 also contains timings for full CLAM code that does not take advantage of redundancy. The first two timing columns illustrate the benefit of compilation over interpretation. For the next two columns, the program is specialized w.r.t. the modes corresponding to the four queries.

While we have not presented results for a comprehensive set of benchmarks, the mortgage program is somewhat typical in structure for recursive definitions. It was chosen because the four different classes of queries require most of the main components of the constraint solver. Similar tests on a number of other programs, not presented here for space reasons, yielded similarly favorable results.

[6] Similar measurements were carried out in [7] for this program and queries. Their focus was evaluating specific analyses; here it is the efficiency of specific CLAM code.

6 Conclusion

We have described an abstract machine for the efficient execution of compiled CLP($\mathcal{R}$) programs. In addition to providing a basis for executing CLP($\mathcal{R}$) programs with an efficiency comparable to that of commercial Prolog compilers, it is suitable for taking advantage of global optimization techniques that are currently on the leading edge of logic programming implementation techniques.

References

[1] S. K. Debray, "Static Inference of Modes and Data Dependencies in Logic Programs", *ACM Transactions on Programming Languages and Systems* **11** (3), 1989, pp 418–450.

[2] S. K. Debray and D.S. Warren, "Functional Computations in Logic Programs", *ACM Transactions on Programming Languages and Systems* **11** (3), 1989, pp 451–481.

[3] J. Jaffar and J-L. Lassez, "Constraint Logic Programming", *Proceedings* 14th *ACM Symposium on Principles of Programming Languages*, January 1987, pp 111–119.

[4] D. Kranz, R. Kelsey, J. Rees, P. Hudak, J. Philbin, and N. Adams, "ORBIT: an optimizing compiler for Scheme", *SIGPLAN'86 Symposium on Compiler Construction*, June 1986, pp 219–233.

[5] J. Jaffar, S. Michaylov, P.J. Stuckey and R.H.C. Yap", "The CLP($\mathcal{R}$) Language and System", *ACM Transactions on Programming Languages and Systems*, to appear, July 1992.

[6] J. Jaffar, S. Michaylov and R.H.C. Yap, "A Methodology for Managing Hard Constraints in CLP Systems", *Proceedings ACM-SIGPLAN Conference on Programming Language Design and Implementation*, June 1991, pp 306–316.

[7] N. Jørgensen, K. Marriott and S. Michaylov, "Some Global Compile-time Optimizations for CLP($\mathcal{R}$)", *Proceedings 1991 International Logic Programming Symposium*", October 1991, pp 420–434.

[8] A. Taylor, "LIPS on a MIPS: Results from a Prolog Compiler for a RISC", *Proceedings 7th International Conference on Logic Programming,* June 1990, pp 174–185 [Also Ph.D. thesis, CS, Univ. of Sydney, 1991].

[9] P. van Roy and A.M. Despain, "The Benefits of Global Dataflow Analysis for an Optimizing Prolog Compiler", *Proceedings 1990 North American Conference on Logic Programming,* October 1990, pp 501–515 [Also Ph.D. thesis by Van Roy, CS/EE, UC Berkeley, 1990].

[10] D.H.D. Warren, "An Abstract PROLOG Instruction Set", Technical note 309, AI Center, SRI International, Menlo Park, October 1983.

Appendix

A An Overview of CLP($\mathcal{R}$)

Real constants and real variables are both *arithmetic terms.* If t, t_1 and t_2 are arithmetic terms, then so are (t_1+t_2), (t_1-t_2), (t_1*t_2), (t_1/t_2), $abs(t)$, $sin(t)$, $cos(t)$ and $pow(t_1,t_2)$. Uninterpreted constants and functors are like those in PROLOG. Uninterpreted constants and arithmetic terms are *terms*, and so is any variable. If f is an n-ary uninterpreted functor, $n \geq 0$, and $t_1, ..., t_n$ are terms, then $f(t_1, ..., t_n)$ is a term. If t_1 and t_2 are arithmetic terms, then $t_1 = t_2$, $t_1 < t_2$ and $t_1 \leq t_2$ are all arithmetic *constraints.* If at least one of t_1 and t_2 is not an arithmetic term, then only the expression $t_1 = t_2$ is a constraint.

An *atom* is of the form $p(t_1, t_2, \ldots, t_n)$ where p is a predicate symbol distinct from $=$, $<$, and $\leq$, and $t_1, ..., t_n$ are terms. A CLP($\mathcal{R}$) program is defined to be a finite collection of *rules*: $A_0 :- \alpha_1, \alpha_2, \ldots, \alpha_k$ where each α_i, $0 \leq i \leq k$, is either a constraint or an atom. A CLP($\mathcal{R}$) *goal* is of the form $?\!-\ C \mid \alpha_1, \alpha_2, \ldots, \alpha_k$ where C is a conjunction of constraints and each α_i, $1 \leq i \leq k$, is either a constraint or an atom.

A *derivation step* for the above CLP($\mathcal{R}$) goal selects the first atom or constraints α_1. If α_1 is a constraint c, then if $c \wedge C$ is satisfiable the new goal is $?\!-\ C \wedge c \mid \alpha_2, \ldots, \alpha_k$. If the constraints are unsatisfiable then execution "backtracks" to a point where an alternate choice of matching rule is available and proceeds using this rule. If α_1 is an atom $p(s_1, \ldots, s_n)$ and a rule in the program of the form $p(t_1, \ldots, t_n) :- \beta_1, \beta_2, \ldots, \beta_l$. The resulting new goal is of the form
$?\!-\ C \mid s_1 = t_1, \ldots, s_n = t_n, \beta_1, \ldots, \beta_l, \alpha_1, \ldots, \alpha_k$.

Ideally the constraint solver would detect whenever the constraints are unsatisfiable. In practice, because of the intractability of detecting unsatisfiability of nonlinear constraints, our implementation of CLP($\mathcal{R}$) only detects the satisfiability/unsatisfiability of all the non-arithmetic and linear arithmetic constraints in the goal, including nonlinear constraints that are effectively linear in the context of the non-arithmetic and linear constraints.

A *derivation sequence* is a possibly infinite sequence of goals, starting with an initial goal, wherein there is a derivation step to each goal from the preceding goal. A derivation sequence is *successful* if it is finite and its last goal contains only constraints. The constraints in the last goal of successful derivation sequences are called *answer constraints.*

Consider the program in Figure 5. and the goal `?- | mg(P, 2, 1.1, MP, B)`. Execution proceeds by first matching with the first rule to obtain the new goal

```
?- | 2 > 1, T1 = 2 - 1, P >= 0,
    P1 = P*1.1 - MP,
    mortgage(P1, T1, 1.1, MP, B).
```

After four steps in which all the constraints are satisfiable, we obtain (ignoring trivial constraints)

```
?- P >= 0, P1 = P*1.1 - MP |
    mortgage(P1, 1, 1.1, MP, B).
```

The next derivation step matches the first rule again,

```
?- P >= 0, P1 = P*1.1 - MP | 1 > 1,
    T1' = 1 - 1, P1 >= 0, P1' = P1*1.1 - MP,
    mortgage(P1', T1', 1.1, MP, B).
```

In the next step, the constraint is unsatisfiable (`1 > 1`) and hence execution backtracks and the next matching rule is attempted, resulting in

```
?- P >= 0, P1 = P*1.1 - MP | 1 = 1,
    B = P1*1.1 - MP.
```

After two more steps the constraints have been added to the solver and found to be satisfiable. Now as only satisfiable constraints remain, the derivation is successful. The answer constraint after simplification is

```
P = 0.826446*B + 1.73554*MP, P ≥ 0.
```

B Summary of main CLAM instructions

Instruction	Operands	Description
`litf`	`c, FPi`	load numeric constant into fp_val
`getf`	`Vi, FPj`	convert solver variable to fp_val
`putf`	`FPi, Vj`	convert fp_val to solver variable
`stf`	`FPi, S`	put fp_val on stack frame (offset S)
`ldf`	`S, FPi`	read fp_val from stack frame (offset S)
`mvf`	`FPi, FPj`	copy one fp_val to another
`addf`	`FPi, FPj, FPk`	add fp_vals; similarly for `mulf`, `subf`, `divf`
`addcf`	`FPi, c, FPk`	add a constant to an fp_val; similarly for `mulcf`, `subcf`, `divcf`, `subfc`, `divfc`
`jeqf`	`FPi, L`	jump to label `L` if `FPi` is zero
`jgtf`	`FPi, L`	jump to label `L` if `FPi` is positive
`jgef`	`FPi, L`	jump to label `L` if `FPi` is nonnegative
`initpf`	`c0`	initialize accumulator *lpf* with constant `c0`
`initpf_0`		initialize accumulator *lpf* with constant 0
`initpf_fp`	`FPi`	initialize *lpf* with constant from fp_val
`addpf_va{lr}`	`ci, Vi`	add `ci * Vi` to *lpf* in accumulator
`addpf_va{lr}_{+-}`	`Vi`	add linear component, with 1 or -1 coefficient
`addpf_fp_va{rl}`	`FPi, Vi`	add linear component, with coefficient from fp_val
`addpf_va{lr}e`	`ci, Vi`	like `addpf_va{lr}`, eliminating V_i if possible
`addpf_va{lr}e_{+-}`	`Vi`	like `addpf_va{lr}_{+-}` , eliminating V_i if possible
`addpf_fp_va{lr}e`	`FPi, Vi`	like `addpf_fp_va{lr}` , eliminating V_i if possible
`solve_eq0`		invoke equation solver on $lpf = 0$
`solve_ge0`		invoke inequality solver on $lpf \geq 0$
`solve_gt0`		invoke inequality solver on $lpf > 0$
`solve_no_fail_eq`	`V`	simply add $V = lpf$ to solver
`solve_no_fail_ge`	`V`	simply add $V \geq lpf$ to solver
`solve_no_fail_gt`	`V`	simply add $V > lpf$ to solver
`solve_no_add_eq0`		check $lpf = 0$, do not add to solver
`solve_no_add_ge0`		check $lpf \geq 0$, do not add to solver
`solve_no_add_gt0`		check $lpf > 0$, do not add to solver
`pow_vvv`	`Vi, Vj, Vk`	for $V_i = pow(V_j, V_k)$ where V_i, V_j, V_k are variables
`pow_cvv`	`Vj, Vk`	for $c = pow(V_j, V_k)$
`pow_vcv`	`Vi, c, Vk`	for $V_i = pow(c, V_k)$
`pow_vvc`	`Vi, Vj, c`	for $V_i = pow(V_j, c)$
`pow_cvc`	`c0, Vj, c2`	for $c_0 = pow(V_j, c_2)$
		similar groups of instructions for *cos*, *sin*, *abs* and multiplication

C Example CLAM Code

General Program

```
mg    try            mg1, 5
      trust          mg2
mg1   initpf         -1
      addpf_val_+    T
      solve_gt0
      initpf         1
      addpf_val_-    T
      addpf_var_+    Tmp1
      solve_eq0
      initpf_0
      addpf_val_+    P
      solve_ge0
      mult_Vvv       Tmp3, P, I
      initpf_0
      addpf_val_+    R
      addpf_val_-    Tmp3
      addpf_var_+    Tmp2
      solve_eq0
      getvar         P, Tmp2
      getvar         T, Tmp1
      jump           mg
mg2   gettnum        1, T
      mult_Vvv       Tmp1, P, I
      initpf_0
      addpf_val_+    R
      addpf_val_-    Tmp1
      addpf_val_+    B
      solve_eq0
      proceed
```

Specialized for Q_1

```
mg    subcf          T, 1, Tmp
      jgtf           Tmp, mg1
      jeqf           Tmp, mg2
      fail
mg1   mvf            Tmp, T
      jgef           P, cont
      fail
cont  mulf           P, I, Tmp
      subf           Tmp, R, P
      jump           mg
mg2   mulf           P, I, Tmp
      subf           Tmp, R, B
      proceed
```

Specialized for Q_3

```
mg    subcf                T, 1, Tmp
      jgtf                 Tmp, mg1
      jeqf                 Tmp, mg2
      fail
mg1   subcf                T, 1, T
      jgtf                 T, cont1
      fail
cont1 initpf_0
      addpf_val_+          P
      solve_no_add_ge0
      initpf_0
      addpf_fp_val         I, P
      addpf_val_-          R
      solve_no_fail_eq     Tmp3
      getvar               P, Tmp3
      jump                 mg
mg2   subcf                T, 1, Tmp4
      jeqf                 Tmp4, cont2
      fail
cont2 subfc                0, I, Tmp2
      initpf_0
      addpf_val_+          R
      addpf_fp_val         Tmp2, P
      addpf_val_+          B
      solve_eq0
      proceed
```

Eliminating False Data Dependences using the Omega Test *

William Pugh
Dept. of Computer Science
Univ. of Maryland, College Park, MD 20742
pugh@cs.umd.edu, (301)-405-2705

David Wonnacott
Dept. of Computer Science
Univ. of Maryland, College Park, MD 20742
davew@cs.umd.edu, (301)-405-2726

Abstract

Array data dependence analysis methods currently in use generate false dependences that can prevent useful program transformations. These false dependences arise because the questions asked are conservative approximations to the questions we really should be asking. Unfortunately, the questions we really should be asking go beyond integer programming and require decision procedures for a subclass of Presburger formulas. In this paper, we describe how to extend the Omega test so that it can answer these queries and allow us to eliminate these false data dependences. We have implemented the techniques described here and believe they are suitable for use in production compilers.

1 Introduction

Recent studies [HKK+91, CP91] suggest that array data dependence analysis methods currently in use generate false dependences that can prevent useful program transformations. For the most part, these false dependences are *not* generated by the conservative nature of algorithms such as Banerjee's inequalities [SLY89, KPK90]. These false dependences arise because the *questions* we ask of dependence analysis algorithms are conservative approximations to the questions we really should be asking (methods currently in use are unable to address the more complicated questions we should be asking).

*This work is supported by NSF grant CCR-9157384 and a Packard Fellowship.

ACM SIGPLAN '92 PLDI-6/92/CA
© 1992 ACM 0-89791-476-7/92/0006/0140...$1.50

For example, there is a flow dependence from an array access $A(\mathbf{i})$ to an array access $B(\mathbf{j})$ iff

- A is executed with iteration vector $\mathbf{i}$,
- B is executed with iteration vector $\mathbf{j}$,
- $A(\mathbf{i})$ writes to the same location as is read by $B(\mathbf{j})$,
- $A(\mathbf{i})$ is executed before $B(\mathbf{j})$, and
- there is no write to the location read by $B(\mathbf{j})$ between the execution of $A(\mathbf{i})$ and $B(\mathbf{j})$.

However, most array data dependence algorithms ignore the last criterion (either explicitly or implicitly). While ignoring this criterion does not change the total order imposed by the dependences, it does cause flow dependences to become contaminated with output dependences (storage dependences). There are techniques (such as privatization, renaming, and array expansion) that can eliminate storage-related dependences. However, these methods cannot be applied if they appear to affect the flow dependences of a program. Also, flow dependences represent more than ordering constraints: they also represent the flow of information. In order to make effective use of caches or distributed memories, a compiler must have accurate information about the flow of information in a program.

Similarly, many dependence testing algorithms do not handle assertions about relationships among non-induction variables or array references that appear in subscripts or loop bounds. To be useful, a system must not only be able to incorporate assertions about these relationships, but also be able to generate a useful dialog with the user about which relationships hold.

Unfortunately, the questions we really should be asking go beyond integer programming and require decision procedures for a subclass of Presburger formulas.

Presburger formulas are those that can be built up from integer constants, integer variables, addition, $>$, $=$, $\neg$, $\wedge$, $\vee$, $\Rightarrow$, $\forall$ and $\exists$. We can use these primitives to allow us to also handle subtraction, multiplication by integer constants, and the other arithmetic relations ($\geq$, $<$, $\leq$). Presburger formulas are decidable, but the only known decision procedures that handle the full class take at least doubly-exponential worst-cast time.

Our original work on the Omega test [Pug91] described efficient ways to answer the usual questions asked for dependence analysis. In this paper, we show how the Omega test can be extended so that it can be used to answer questions in a subclass of Presburger arithmetic. We then show how to phrase within that subclass the questions we need to ask. We also describe experiences with an implementation of the methods described here that convince us that these techniques are suitable for use in production compilers.

2 Notation

The notation in Table 1 is adapted from [ZC91]. Below, we briefly discuss dependence distance, direction and restraint vectors.

2.1 Dependence Distance

A data dependence has a dependence distance in each loop, which is is the difference between the values of the loop variables for some pair of iterations involved in the dependence.[1] The dependence distance vector for a dependence is a vector of the dependence distances for the loops common to both statements involved in the dependence.

Often, a dependence distance is not constant, and the dependence distance in one loop can be coupled to the dependence distance in another loop. For example a dependence might have dependence distances $\{(\Delta i, \Delta j) \mid 0 \leq \Delta i \leq 5 \wedge 1 \leq \Delta i + \Delta j \leq 10\}$. Since dependences represent a constraint from one statement execution to a later statement execution, dependence distances must be lexicographically positive[2], with a zero dependence distance in all loops possible only if the dependence is syntactically forward.

2.1.1 Direction vectors

A direction vector summarizes, for each loop, the possible signs of the dependence distance in that loop. For example a dependence with dependence distances $(\Delta i, \Delta j)$ such that $0 \leq \Delta i \leq 5 \wedge 0 \leq \Delta j \leq 10$ would be represented by the direction vectors $\{(0+, 0+)\}$. We also can give a specific distance or range of distances in a direction vector (e.g., $\{(0+, 1)\}$ or $\{(0:1, 1)\}$).

It is not always possible to summarize accurately the possible signs of the dependence distance with a single direction vector. The signs of the dependence distances $\{(\Delta i, \Delta j) \mid \Delta i = \Delta j\}$ can be accurately represented by the direction vectors $\{(+,+), (0,0), (-,-)\}$. After filtering for lexicographically forward directions, this dependence is represented by $\{(+,+), (0,0)\}$. If these two are compressed into a single direction vector $(0+, 0+)$, it falsely suggests the signs $(0,+)$ and $(+,0)$ are possible.

Given a set of constraints that describe the possible forward and backward dependence distances, we analyze the constraints to produce a set of partially compressed direction vectors (as described in [Pug91]). These direction vectors are filtered to produce a set of forward direction vectors.

2.1.2 Restraint vectors

While checking for dependence killing, covering and refinement (Section 4), we deal with dependences as integer programming problems. We need to force the dependence directions to be lexicographically positive (e.g., force $\Delta i > 0 \vee \Delta i = 0 \wedge \Delta j \geq 0$). Unfortunately, this is not a conjunction of linear constraints. However, we can often find a conjunction of linear constraints that will force the dependence distance to be lexicographically forward. For example, we can force the dependence distances $\Delta i = \Delta j$ to be lexicographically positive by adding the constraint $\Delta i \geq 0$.

We represent constraints that force the dependence directions to be lexicographically positive in the same form as direction vectors (specifying the possible signs for each dependence distance). However, these "restraint" vectors only have to filter out lexicographically negative directions which are legal solutions to the integer programming problem that describes all forward and backward dependence distances. We can use the set of direction vectors as a set of restraint vectors, but using restraint vectors usually requires that fewer constraints be added to the problem.

Our algorithms in Sections 4 and 5 are unable to deal directly with dependences that cannot be represented

[1] There is some disagreement within the research community as to whether dependence distance reflects the difference in the values of the loop variables ([ZC91]), or the difference in the loop trip counts ([Wol89]). This disagreement is usually submerged by the fact that many researchers only discuss normalized loops with an increment of 1. One problem with using the difference in loop trip counts is that it is not always well defined. For example, in the following code segment, the dependence distance is $(1, -2)$ if the difference in the loop variables is used; however, the dependence distance doesn't seem to be defined if loop trip counts are used and the loop is not normalized:

```
for i := 0 to 10
    for j := i to 10 by 3
        A[i,j] := A[i-1,j+2]
```

The problem with using the difference in the values of loop variables as dependence distance is that negative steps complicate our discussion of forward dependence distances (usually described as lexicographically positive distances) and the description of the conditions under which loop interchange and circulation are allowed. In this paper, we use the difference in the loop variables as the dependence distance, and ignore the side issue of complicating the definition of forward dependence distances.

[2] Assuming loop increments are positive, see footnote 1 for details.

$A, B, \ldots$	Refers to a specific array reference in a program
$\mathbf{i}, \mathbf{j}, \mathbf{k}, \ldots$	An iteration vector that represents a specific set of values of the loop variables for a loop nest.
$[A]$	The set of iteration vectors for which A is executed
$A(\mathbf{i})$	The instance of array reference A when the loop variables have the values specified by $\mathbf{i}$
$A(\mathbf{i}) \stackrel{sub}{=} A'(\mathbf{i}')$	The references A and A' refer to the same array and the subscripts of $A(\mathbf{i})$ and $A'(\mathbf{i}')$ are equal.
$A(\mathbf{i}) \ll A'(\mathbf{i}')$	Execution of $A(\mathbf{i})$ occurs previous to $A'(\mathbf{i}')$
$A(\mathbf{i}) \ll_D A'(\mathbf{i}')$	The dependence distance from $A(\mathbf{i})$ to $A'(\mathbf{i}')$ is described by the direction/distance vector D
`Sym`	The set of symbolic constants (e.g., loop-invariant scalar variables)

Figure 1: Notation used in this paper

by a single restraint vector. Therefore, such dependences are split into several dependences, one for each restraint vector.

3 Extending the Omega test

The Omega test [Pug91] is an integer programming algorithm based on Fourier-Motzkin variable elimination. The basic operation supported by the Omega test is projection. Intuitively, the projection of a set of constraints is the shadow of a set of constraints. More formally, given a set of linear equalities and inequalities on a set of variables V, projecting the constraints onto the variables $\widehat{V}$ (where $\widehat{V} \subset V$) produces a set of constraints on variables $\widehat{V}$ that has the same integer solutions for $\widehat{V}$ as the original problem. For example, projecting $\{0 \leq a \leq 5; b < a \leq 5b\}$ onto a gives $\{2 \leq a \leq 5\}$. We use the notation $\pi_{x_1,\ldots,x_n}(S)$ to represent the projection of the problem S onto the set of variables $x_1, \ldots, x_n$ and the notation $\pi_{\neg x}(S)$ to represent the projection of the problem S onto all variables other than x.

The Omega test determines if a set of constraints has integer solutions by using projection to eliminate variables until the constraints involve a single variable, at which point is it easy to check for integer solutions.

There are many other applications of projection. For example, if we define a set of constraints for an array pair that includes variables for the possible dependence distances, we can project that set of constraints onto the variables for the dependence distance. The projected system can be efficiently used to determine the dependence directions and distances.

Because the Omega test checks for integer solutions, not real solutions, it is sometimes unable to produce a single set of constraints when computing $\pi_x(S)$. Instead, the Omega test is forced to produce a set of problems $S_0, S_1, \ldots, S_p$ and a problem T such that $\pi_x(S) = \bigcup_{i=0}^{p} S_i \subseteq T$. This is called *splintering*, and we call S_0 the Dark Shadow of $\pi_x(S)$ and call T the Real Shadow of $\pi_x(S)$ (the Real Shadow may include solutions for x that only have real but not integer solutions for the variables that have been eliminated).

In practice, projection rarely splinters and when it does, S_0 contains almost all of the points of $\pi_x(S)$, T doesn't contain many more points than $\pi_x(S)$, and p is small. If we are checking to see if S has solutions, we first check if $S_0 \neq \emptyset$ or $T = \emptyset$. Only if both tests fail are we required to examine $S_1, S_2, \ldots, S_p$. Also, when checking for integer solutions, we choose which variable to eliminate to avoid splintering when possible.

Although integer programming is an NP-Complete problem, the Omega test is efficient in practice [Pug91].

3.1 How the Omega test works

Fourier-Motzkin variable elimination [DE73] eliminates a variable from a linear programming problem. Intuitively, Fourier-Motzkin variable elimination finds the $n-1$ dimensional shadow cast by an n dimensional object.

Consider two constraints on z: a lower bound $\beta \leq bz$ and an upper bound $az \leq \alpha$ (where a and b are positive integers). We can combine these constraints to get $a\beta \leq abz \leq b\alpha$. The shadow of this pair of constraints is $a\beta \leq b\alpha$. Fourier-Motzkin variable elimination calculates the shadow of a set of constraints by combining all constraints that do not involve the variable being eliminated with the result from each combination of a lower and upper bound on the variable being eliminated. The real shadow is a conservative approximation to the integer shadow of the set of constraints.

In [Pug91], we extended Fourier-Motzkin variable elimination to be an integer programming method. Even if $a\beta \leq b\alpha$, there may be no integer solution to z such that $a\beta \leq abz \leq b\alpha$. However, if $a\beta + (a-1)(b-1) \leq b\alpha$, we know that an integer solution to z must exist. This is the dark shadow of this pair of constraints (described in [Pug91]). The dark shadow is a pessimistic approximation to the integer shadow of the set of constraints. Note that if $a = 1$ or $b = 1$, the dark shadow and the real shadow are identical, and therefore also identical to the integer shadow.

There are cases when the real shadow contains integer points but the dark shadow does not. In this case, determining the existence of integer solutions to the original set of constraints requires the use of special case techniques, described in [Pug91], that are almost never needed in practice.

3.2 Determining the validity of Presburger formulas

Assume that p and q are propositions that can each be represented as a conjunction of linear equalities and inequalities. We can determine the truthfulness of the following predicates:

Is p a tautology? Trivial to check when p is a conjunction.

Is p satisfiable? We can check this using techniques described in Section 3.1 and in [Pug91].

Is $p \Rightarrow q$ a tautology? This could not be efficiently answered using the techniques described in [Pug91], but can be efficiently answered in practice using techniques described in Section 3.3.

The projection transformation offered by the Omega test allows us to handle embeded existential qualifiers: $\pi_{\neg x}(p) = (\exists x \text{ s.t. } p)$. We can combine these abilities, as well as any standard transformation of predicate calculus, to determine the validity of certain Presburger formulas. We have not attempted to formally capture the subclass of Presburger formulas we can answer efficiently. The following are examples of some Presburger formulas we can answer efficiently:

$\forall x, \exists y$ s.t. p: True iff $\pi_{\neg y}(p)$ is a tautology.

$\forall x, (\exists y \text{ s.t. } p) \Rightarrow (\exists z \text{ s.t. } q)$: True iff $\pi_{\neg y}(p) \Rightarrow \pi_{\neg z}(q)$ is a tautology. We can easily determine this if $\pi_{\neg z}(q)$ does not splinter.

$\forall x, \neg p \vee q \vee \neg r$: True iff $p \wedge r \Rightarrow q$ is a tautology.

where p, q and r are conjunctions of linear equalities and inequalities

3.3 Computing Gists and Checking when $p \Rightarrow q$ is a tautology

Intuitively, we define (gist p given q) as the new information contained in p, given that we already know q. More formally, (gist p given q) is a conjunction containing a minimal subset of the constraints of p such that ((gist p given q) $\wedge q) = (p \wedge q)$). Note that (gist p given q) $=$ True $\equiv q = (p \wedge q) \equiv (q \Rightarrow p)$.

When computing (gist p given q), we first convert any equalities in p into a matched pair of inequalities (e.g., convert $x = 1$ into $1 \leq x \leq 1$). The following is a naive method for computing gists. The algorithm treats a conjunction as a list of individual constraints:

$$
\begin{aligned}
&\text{gist } [\,]\ q = [\,] \\
&\text{gist } (e : p)\ q = e : (\text{gist } p\ (e : q)), \\
&\qquad\qquad \text{if } (\neg e) \wedge p \wedge q \text{ is satisfiable} \\
&\text{gist } (e : p)\ q = \text{gist } p\ q, \text{ otherwise}
\end{aligned}
$$

This algorithm requires many satisfiability tests, each of which takes a non-trivial amount of time. We handle this problem by checking for a number of special cases (listed in order of increasing difficulty to check):

- For each equation e in p, we check to see if e is implied by any single constraint in p or q. If so, e is redundant and not in the gist.
- We check to see if there is any variable that has an upper bound in p but not in q. If so, we know that at least one of the upper bounds from p must be in the gist. A similar check is made for lower bounds.
- If there does not exist some constraint e' in p or q such that the inner product of the normals of e and e' is positive, then e must be in the gist.
- For each equation e in p, we check to see if e is implied by any two constraints in p and/or q (other than e).

These fast checks often completely determine a gist. When they do not, they usually greatly simplify the problem before we utilize the naive algorithm.

3.3.1 Checking implications

As noted earlier, we determine if $q \Rightarrow p$ is a tautology by checking if (gist p given q) $=$ True. When performing subset tests using the above algorithms, we short-circuit the computation of the gist as soon as we are sure that the gist is not "True".

3.3.2 Combining Projection and Gist computation

If is often the case that we need to compute problems of the form gist $\pi_{\neg y}(p)$ given $\pi_{\neg z}(q)$. We could perform this computation by performing the projections independently, and then computing the gists. However, if z is free in p and y is free in q, there is a more efficient solution. We can combine p and q into a single set of constraints, tagging the equations from p red and the equations from q black. We then project away the variables y and z and eliminate any obviously redundant red equations as we go. Once we have projected away y and z, we then compute the gist of the red equations with respect to the black equations.

3.4 Related Work

Several authors have explored methods for using integer programming methods to decide subclasses of Presburger formulas [Ble75, Sho77, JM87]. Previous approaches have not had any way to compute projections (and thereby handle embeded existential quantifiers) nor have they had special efficient methods for checking when an implication is a tautology. We have not yet looked at wider applications of our work or done any direct comparison of our implementation against implementations of other approaches. We believe our approach and implementation will compare favorably with previous ones.

```
a(n) := ...
for L1 := n to n+10 do
  a(L1) := ...

for L1 := n to n+20 do
  ... := a(L1)
```

Example 1: Killed flow dep

```
a(m) := ...
for L1 := 1 to 100
  a(L1) := ...
  for L2 := 1 to n do
    a(L2) := ...
    a(L2-1) := ...
  for L2 := 2 to n-1 do
    ... := a(L2)
```

Example 2: Covering and Killed dep

```
for L1 := 1 to n do
  for L2 := 2 to m do
    a(L2) := a(L2-1)
```

Unrefined flow dependence: (0+,1)
Refined flow dependence: (0,1)

Example 3: Refinement

```
for L1 := 1 to n do
  for L2 := n+2-L1 to m do
    a(L2) := a(L2-1)
```

Unrefined flow dependence: (0+,1)
Refined flow dependence: (0,1)

Example 4: Trapezoidal Refinement

```
for L1 := 1 to n do
  for L2 := L1 to m do
    a(L2) := a(L2-1)
```

Unrefined flow dependence: (0+,1)
Refined flow dependence: (0:1,1)

Example 5: Partial Refinement

```
for L1 := 1 to n do
  for L2 := 2 to m do
    a(L1-L2) := a(L1-L2)
```

Unrefined flow dependence: $(\alpha, \alpha), \alpha \geq 1$
Refined flow dependence: (1,1)

Example 6: Coupled Refinement

4 Handling array kills

In this section, we discuss the elimination of false dependences in which an intervening write eliminates an apparent dependency. These techniques are most useful when applied to flow dependences. However, we can also apply them to output and anti-dependences.

There are four kinds of analysis we perform:

Killing A dependence from a read or write A to a read or write C is killed by the dependence from a write B to C iff all array elements accessed by A are overwritten by B before C can access them.

Covering A write A covers a read or write B iff it writes to all the elements of the array that will be accessed by B. In this case, any dependence to B from an access that precedes A is killed by the dependence from A.

Terminating A dependence from a read or write A to a write B terminates A if B overwrites all elements that were accessed in A. In this case, any dependences from A to a read or write after B is killed by the dependence from A to B.

Refinement It may be possible to refine the dependence distances for a dependence from a write A to a read or write B to a subset D of these dependence distances. This is possible iff any dependence with a distance not in D is killed by a dependence in D.

We first compute all output dependences (output dependences give us fast checks for when to test for killing and refinement). Then, for each array read reference B, we start computing flow/anti dependences to/from B. For each apparent flow dependence from a write A, we attempt to refine the dependence distance, and then check if it is covering. If it is covering, we can rule out a flow dependence from any write that occurs completely before A. If there appear to be multiple flow dependences to B, we check them pairwise for killing.

4.1 Killing dependences

A dependence from a read or write A to a read or write C is killed by the dependence from a write B to C iff all elements accessed by A are overwritten by B before C can access them. This is the case if:

$$\begin{aligned}&\forall\, \mathbf{i}, \mathbf{k}, \mathtt{Sym},\ \mathbf{i} \in [A] \wedge \mathbf{k} \in [C] \\ &\qquad \wedge A(\mathbf{i}) \ll C(\mathbf{k}) \wedge A(\mathbf{i}) \overset{sub}{=} C(\mathbf{k}) \Rightarrow \\ &\quad \exists \mathbf{j} \text{ s.t. } \mathbf{j} \in [B] \wedge A(\mathbf{i}) \ll B(\mathbf{j}) \ll C(\mathbf{k}) \\ &\qquad \wedge B(\mathbf{j}) \overset{sub}{=} C(\mathbf{k})\end{aligned}$$

In Example 1, the write to `a(L1)` kills the flow from the write of `a(n)` to the read of `a(L1)`:

$$\begin{aligned}&\mathbf{i} \in [A] \wedge \mathbf{k} \in [C] \wedge A(\mathbf{i}) \ll C(\mathbf{k}) \wedge A(\mathbf{i}) \overset{sub}{=} C(\mathbf{k}) \\ &\quad \equiv \mathbf{k}_1 = \mathbf{n}\end{aligned}$$

$$\begin{aligned}&\exists \mathbf{j} \text{ s.t. } \mathbf{j} \in [B] \wedge A(\mathbf{i}) \ll B(\mathbf{j}) \ll C(\mathbf{k}) \wedge B(\mathbf{j}) \overset{sub}{=} C(\mathbf{k}) \\ &\quad \equiv \mathbf{n} \leq \mathbf{k}_1 \leq \mathbf{n} + 10\end{aligned}$$

$$\mathbf{k}_1 = \mathbf{n} \Rightarrow \mathbf{n} \leq \mathbf{k}_1 \leq \mathbf{n} + 10$$

If the first write were to `a(m)`, we would not be able to verify the kill:

$$\begin{aligned}&\mathbf{i} \in [A] \wedge \mathbf{k} \in [C] \wedge A(\mathbf{i}) \ll C(\mathbf{k}) \wedge A(\mathbf{i}) \overset{sub}{=} C(\mathbf{k}) \\ &\quad \equiv \mathbf{n} \leq \mathbf{k}_1 \leq \mathbf{n} + 20 \wedge \mathbf{k}_1 = \mathtt{m}\end{aligned}$$

$$\begin{aligned}&\exists \mathbf{j} \text{ s.t. } \mathbf{j} \in [B] \wedge A(\mathbf{i}) \ll B(\mathbf{j}) \ll C(\mathbf{k}) \wedge B(\mathbf{j}) \overset{sub}{=} C(\mathbf{k}) \\ &\quad \equiv \mathbf{n} \leq \mathbf{k}_1 \leq \mathbf{n} + 10\end{aligned}$$

$$\mathbf{n} \leq \mathbf{k}_1 \leq \mathbf{n} + 20 \wedge \mathbf{k}_1 = \mathtt{m} \not\Rightarrow \mathbf{n} \leq \mathbf{k}_1 \leq \mathbf{n} + 10$$

If $\mathtt{n} \le \mathtt{m} \le \mathtt{n}+10$ had been asserted by the user, we would be able to verify the kill.

4.2 Covering dependences

A dependence from a write A to a read or write B is a covering dependence iff every location accessed by B is previously written to by A. If the dependence from A to B is a covering dependence, we need not examine any dependences to B from any accesses that would precede the writes of A (since the dependence from A would kill such a dependence).

A dependence from a write A covers B iff:

$$\begin{aligned}&\forall\, \mathtt{j}, \mathtt{Sym},\ \mathtt{j} \in [B]\\ &\quad \Rightarrow \exists \mathtt{i} \text{ s.t. } \mathtt{i} \in [A] \wedge A(\mathtt{i}) \ll B(\mathtt{j}) \wedge A(\mathtt{i}) \overset{sub}{=} B(\mathtt{j})\end{aligned}$$

In Example 2, the read of `a(L2)` is covered by the write to `a(L2-1)`:

$$\begin{aligned}&\mathtt{j} \in [B]\\ &\quad \equiv 1 \le \mathtt{j}_1 \le 100 \wedge 2 \le \mathtt{j}_2 \le \mathtt{n}-1\end{aligned}$$

$$\begin{aligned}&\exists \mathtt{i} \text{ s.t. } \mathtt{i} \in [A] \wedge A(\mathtt{i}) \ll B(\mathtt{j}) \wedge A(\mathtt{i}) \overset{sub}{=} B(\mathtt{j})\\ &\quad \equiv 1 \le \mathtt{j}_1 \le 100 \wedge 0 \le \mathtt{j}_2 \le \mathtt{n}-1\end{aligned}$$

$$\begin{aligned}&1 \le \mathtt{j}_1 \le 100 \wedge 2 \le \mathtt{j}_2 \le \mathtt{n}-1\\ &\quad \Rightarrow 1 \le \mathtt{j}_1 \le 100 \wedge 0 \le \mathtt{j}_2 \le \mathtt{n}-1\end{aligned}$$

Since we have determined that this dependence is a covering dependence, there is no need to check for dependencies with writes that must precede `a(L2-1)` (such as the write to `a(m)`). However, for writes that may be executed after some executions of the cover (such as the write to`a(L2)`), we must check separately for a kill. In general, we may have to determine which loop carries the cover to know which write accesses must precede it. The cover in this example is loop independent, so we know that all executions of the write `a(L1)` must precede the cover. Note that we only find out that the cover is loop independent when we refine its dependence vector from (0+) to (0). For this reason, we perform refinement before coverage analysis.

4.3 Terminating dependences

A dependence from a read or write A to a write B is a terminating dependence iff every location accessed by A is subsequently overwritten by B. If the dependence from A to B is a terminating dependence, we need not examine any dependences from A to any accesses that would follow the writes of B.

A dependence from A to a write B terminates A iff:

$$\begin{aligned}&\forall\, \mathtt{i}, \mathtt{Sym},\ \mathtt{i} \in [A] \Rightarrow\\ &\quad \exists \mathtt{j} \text{ s.t. } \mathtt{j} \in [B] \wedge A(\mathtt{i}) \ll B(\mathtt{j}) \wedge A(\mathtt{i}) \overset{sub}{=} B(\mathtt{j})\end{aligned}$$

4.4 Refining dependence distances/directions

If all iterations of a read or write B that receive a dependence from a write A also receive a dependence from a more recent iteration of A within distance D, the dependence distances can be refined to D:

$$\begin{aligned}&\forall\, \mathtt{i}, \mathtt{k}, \mathtt{Sym},\ \mathtt{i} \in [A] \wedge \mathtt{k} \in [B]\\ &\qquad \wedge A(\mathtt{i}) \ll B(\mathtt{k}) \wedge A(\mathtt{i}) \overset{sub}{=} B(\mathtt{k})\\ &\quad \Rightarrow A(\mathtt{i}) \ll_D B(\mathtt{k})\\ &\qquad \vee \exists \mathtt{j} \text{ s.t. } \mathtt{j} \in [A]\\ &\qquad\qquad \wedge A(\mathtt{i}) \ll A(\mathtt{j}) \ll_D B(\mathtt{k})\\ &\qquad\qquad \wedge A(\mathtt{j}) \overset{sub}{=} B(\mathtt{k})\end{aligned}$$

When we attempt to refine dependence vectors, we do so in a way that ensures that the refined dependence contains the most recent executions of A, or in other words:

$$\begin{aligned}&A(\mathtt{i}) \ll B(\mathtt{k}) \wedge A(\mathtt{i}) \not\ll_D B(\mathtt{k}) \wedge A(\mathtt{j}) \ll_D B(\mathtt{k})\\ &\quad \Rightarrow A(\mathtt{i}) \ll A(\mathtt{j})\end{aligned}$$

In this case, we can simplify the condition under which we can perform refinement to:

$$\begin{aligned}&\forall\, \mathtt{i}, \mathtt{k}, \mathtt{Sym},\ \mathtt{i} \in [A] \wedge \mathtt{k} \in [B]\\ &\qquad \wedge A(\mathtt{i}) \ll B(\mathtt{k}) \wedge A(\mathtt{i}) \overset{sub}{=} B(\mathtt{k})\\ &\quad \Rightarrow \exists \mathtt{j} \text{ s.t. } \mathtt{j} \in [A] \wedge A(\mathtt{j}) \ll_D B(\mathtt{k})\\ &\qquad \wedge A(\mathtt{j}) \overset{sub}{=} B(\mathtt{k})\end{aligned}$$

which can be further transformed to

$$\begin{aligned}&\forall\, \mathtt{k}, \mathtt{Sym},\\ &\quad (\exists \mathtt{i} \text{ s.t. } i \in [A] \wedge \mathtt{k} \in [B] \wedge A(\mathtt{i}) \ll B(\mathtt{k}) \wedge A(\mathtt{i}) \overset{sub}{=} B(\mathtt{k}))\\ &\quad \Rightarrow (\exists \mathtt{j} \text{ s.t. } \mathtt{j} \in [A] \wedge A(\mathtt{j}) \ll_D B(\mathtt{k}) \wedge A(\mathtt{j}) \overset{sub}{=} B(\mathtt{k}))\end{aligned}$$

Example 3 shows a loop with a flow dependence that can be refined from (0+,1) to (0,1):

$$\begin{aligned}&\exists \mathtt{i} \text{ s.t. } \mathtt{k} \in [B] \wedge i \in [A] \wedge A(\mathtt{i}) \ll B(\mathtt{k}) \wedge A(\mathtt{i}) \overset{sub}{=} B(\mathtt{k})\\ &\quad \equiv 1 \le \mathtt{k}_1 \le \mathtt{n} \wedge 3 \le \mathtt{k}_2 \le \mathtt{m}\end{aligned}$$

$$\begin{aligned}&\exists \mathtt{j} \text{ s.t. } \mathtt{j} \in [A] \wedge A(\mathtt{j}) \ll_D B(\mathtt{k}) \wedge A(\mathtt{j}) \overset{sub}{=} B(\mathtt{k})\\ &\quad \equiv 1 \le \mathtt{k}_1 \le \mathtt{n} \wedge 3 \le \mathtt{k}_2 \le \mathtt{m}\end{aligned}$$

$$\begin{aligned}&1 \le \mathtt{k}_1 \le \mathtt{n} \wedge 3 \le \mathtt{k}_2 \le \mathtt{m}\\ &\quad \Rightarrow 1 \le \mathtt{k}_1 \le \mathtt{n} \wedge 3 \le \mathtt{k}_2 \le \mathtt{m}\end{aligned}$$

Example 4 is similar to Example 3, but includes a triangular loop. Example 5 is similar to Example 4, but here the distance can only be refined to (0:1,1) because iterations such that $1 < \mathtt{L1} = \mathtt{L2}$ receive a flow from iteration $(\mathtt{L1}-1, \mathtt{L2}-1)$. Example 6 shows a case where the dependence distances are coupled. Neither of the two approaches similar to ours ([Bra88, Ros90]) would handle Examples 4, 5 or 6.

The above methods allow us to check to see if any specific D is a correct refinement of a direction/distance vector. We generate the D's by attempting to fix the dependence distance, starting with the outermost loop. For each loop, we attempt to set the dependence distance to be the minimum possible distance in that loop (which is easily extracted from the set of constraints describing the possible (unrefined) dependence distances). If we succeed, we move on to the next loop. If we fail, we stop refining that dependence (attempts to further refine the dependence distance for inner loops would not satisfy $A(\mathbf{i}) \ll B(\mathbf{k}) \wedge A(\mathbf{i}) \not\ll_D B(\mathbf{k}) \wedge A(\mathbf{j}) \ll_D B(\mathbf{k}) \Rightarrow A(\mathbf{i}) \ll A(\mathbf{j})$).

This method for generating D's to test will not automatically find the partial refinement in Example 5.

4.5 Quick tests for when to check for the above

We can often avoid performing the general tests described above by doing some quick tests for special cases. For example, for the dependence from B to C to kill the dependence between A and C, there must be an output dependence between A and B, and it must be possible for the dependence distance from A to C to equal the total distance from A to B and B to C. Similarly, for there to be any possibility of refining the dependence distance in that loop from A to C, A must have a self-output dependence with a non-zero distance in a loop in order.

If a dependence from A to B does not include the distance 0 in some loop l, it can not cover the execution of B the first time through l, so we do not test it for coverage. Note that A may actually cover B if B is not executed the first time through l - we would fail to detect this cover, and be forced to kill the covered dependencies with the A to B dependence later.

Finally, if we are trying to kill a dependence from A to C with a covering dependence from B to C, and the dependence from B is always closer than the dependence from A, then we know the dependence from A to C is killed without having to perform the general test.

4.6 Related Work

In analyzing false array flow data dependences (caused by output dependences), there are two basic approaches:

- Extend scalar dataflow methods by recording which array sections are killed and/or defined [GS90, Ros90].

- Extend the pair-wise methods typically used for array data dependence to recognize array kills [Bra88, Rib90].

Both approaches have merits. Our work is an example of the second approach, and we believe it corrects several limitations and flaws in previous work on that approach.

Brandes [Bra88] describes methods factoring out transitive dependences to determine "direct" dependences, and his work is similar to our computations for refinement, killing and covering. However, his methods do not apply if the dependence distances are coupled or the loop is non-rectangular.

Ribas describes [Rib90] techniques to refine dependence distances. However, Ribas only discusses perfectly nested loops, and there are some problems with his Theorem 1:

> Given two references $M_v x + m$ and $U_{v,r} y + u$, the refined dependence distance from x to y is constant iff $M_v = U_{v,r}$.

In our Example 5, we have $M_v = U_{v,r}$ (using Ribas's terminology), but the dependence distance is not constant. The error is that (6) in [Rib90] should include $(y - \delta^i_{v,r}(y)) \in Int(A, b)$ and (7) in [Rib90] should include $(x + \delta^i_{v,r}(x)) \in Int(A, b)$. Ribas's Theorem holds only for iterations not near the beginning or end of any loop.

Ribas uses a slightly different definition of "constant dependence distance" than we do. His definition states that a dependence from A to B has constant distance d iff for all iteration vectors $\mathbf{i} \in [A]$ and $\mathbf{j} \in [B]$, there is a flow dependence from $A(\mathbf{i})$ to $B(\mathbf{j})$ iff $\mathbf{j} - \mathbf{i} = d$. The definition we use is that a dependence from A to B has constant distance d iff for all iteration vectors $\mathbf{i} \in [A]$ and $\mathbf{j} \in [B]$, a flow dependence from $A(\mathbf{i})$ to $B(\mathbf{j})$ implies $\mathbf{j} - \mathbf{i} = d$. While Ribas's definition is useful in the context of deriving VLSI designs, our definition is more appropriate for standard compiler optimizations.

Rosene [Ros90] extended standard scalar data flow analysis techniques by using Data Access Descriptors [BK89] to keep track of an approximation of the set of array elements that are defined, modified and/or killed by each statement. Rosene only determines which levels carry a dependence, and doesn't calculate the dependence distance or direction. Thus, his approach would be unable to handle our Example 6. His use of Data Access Descriptors means that his techniques are approximate in situations in which our methods are exact. It should be possible to modify his tests to use integer programming constraints to define sets of array elements, but that would involve significant work beyond that described in [Ros90] (the Omega test could be used to represent array regions, but the Omega test cannot directly form the union of two sets of constraints). Rosene's techniques have not been fully implemented.

Thomas Gross and Peter Steenkiste describe [GS90] methods similar to that of Rosene. Gross and Steenkiste's work is not as thorough as that of Rosene's.

```
      SUBROUTINE CHOLSKY (IDA, NMAT, M, N, A, NRHS, IDB, B)
C
C     CHOLESKY DECOMPOSITION/SUBSTITUTION SUBROUTINE.
C
C     11/28/84  D H BAILEY  MODIFIED FOR NAS KERNEL TEST
C     1/28/92  W W PUGH   PERFORMED FORWARD SUB. AND
C                  NORMALIZED LOOP THAT HAD STEP OF -1
C
      REAL A(0:IDA, -M:0, 0:N), B(0:NRHS, 0:IDB, 0:N), EPSS(0:256)
      DATA EPS/1E-13/
C
C     CHOLESKY DECOMPOSITION
C
      DO 1 J = 0, N
C
C     OFF DIAGONAL ELEMENTS
C
        DO 2 I = MAX(-M,-J), -1
          DO 3 JJ = MAX(-M,-J) - I, -1
            DO 3 L = 0, NMAT
3             A(L,I,J) = A(L,I,J) - A(L,JJ,I+J) * A(L,I+JJ,J)
          DO 2 L = 0, NMAT
2           A(L,I,J) = A(L,I,J) * A(L,0,I+J)
C
C     STORE INVERSE OF DIAGONAL ELEMENTS
C
        DO 4 L = 0, NMAT
4         EPSS(L) = EPS * A(L,0,J)
        DO 5 JJ = MAX(-M,-J), -1
          DO 5 L = 0, NMAT
5           A(L,0,J) = A(L,0,J) - A(L,JJ,J) ** 2
        DO 1 L = 0, NMAT
1         A(L,0,J) = 1. / SQRT ( ABS (EPSS(L) + A(L,0,J)) )
C
C     SOLUTION
C
      DO 6 I = 0, NRHS
        DO 7 K = 0, N
          DO 8 L = 0, NMAT
8           B(I,L,K) = B(I,L,K) * A(L,0,K)
          DO 7 JJ = 1, MIN (M, N-K)
            DO 7 L = 0, NMAT
7             B(I,L,K+JJ) = B(I,L,K+JJ) - A(L,-JJ,K+JJ) * B(I,L,K)
C
        DO 6 K = 0, N
          DO 9 L = 0, NMAT
9           B(I,L,N-K) = B(I,L,N-K) * A(L,0,N-K)
          DO 6 JJ = 1, MIN (M, N-K)
            DO 6 L = 0, NMAT
6             B(I,L,N-K-JJ) = B(I,L,N-K-JJ) - A(L,-JJ,N-K) * B(I,L,N-K)
C
      RETURN
      END
```

Figure 2: Source code for CHOLSKY, one of the original NASA NAS benchmark kernals

However, they have implemented their approach, and obtained some experience with it.

4.7 Experimental Results

We have implemented the extensions to the Omega test described in Section 3, and have added tests from section 4 to an augmented version of Wolfe's **tiny** tool [Wol91]. Our efforts to date have focused on testing flow dependences, so our changes have no effect on the output or anti dependences computed, and we do not test for terminating or covering output dependences.

We have performed an analysis of the time taken by the Omega test to analyze dependencies. These timing figures were measured on on Sun Sparc IPX, and are inclusive: they include the time required to scan the loop bounds and subscriptions, the time required to build and analyze the array pair, and the cost of overhead routines such as malloc and free. We ran our tests on the program CHOLSKY from the original NASA NAS benchmark kernals, the source files that were originally distributed all the **tiny** source files distributed with **tiny**, (which include Cholesky decomposition, LU decomposition, several versions of wavefront algorithms, and several more contrived examples), as well as several of our own test programs. Unfortunately, FORTRAN

FROM	TO	dir/dist	status
3: A(L,I,J)	3: A(L,I,J)	(0,0,1,0)	[r]
3: A(L,I,J)	2: A(L,I,J)	(0,0)	
2: A(L,I,J)	3: A(L,I+JJ,J)	(0,+)	
2: A(L,I,J)	3: A(L,JJ,I+J)	(+,*)	
2: A(L,I,J)	5: A(L,JJ,J)	(0)	[C]
2: A(L,I,J)	7: A(L,-JJ,K+JJ)		[C]
2: A(L,I,J)	6: A(L,-JJ,N-K)		[C]
4: EPSS(L)	1: EPSS(L)	(0)	[Cr]
5: A(L,0,J)	5: A(L,0,J)	(0,1,0)	[r]
5: A(L,0,J)	1: A(L,0,J)	(0)	
1: A(L,0,J)	2: A(L,0,I+J)	(+)	
1: A(L,0,J)	8: A(L,0,K)		[C]
1: A(L,0,J)	9: A(L,0,N-K)		[C]
8: B(I,L,K)	7: B(I,L,K)	(0,0)	[C]
8: B(I,L,K)	9: B(I,L,N-K)	(0)	[C]
8: B(I,L,K)	6: B(I,L,N-K-JJ)	(0)	[C]
7: B(I,L,K+JJ)	8: B(I,L,K)	(0,1)	[r]
7: B(I,L,K+JJ)	7: B(I,L,K+JJ)	(0,1,-1,0)	[r]
9: B(I,L,N-K)	6: B(I,L,N-K)	(0,0)	[C]
6: B(I,L,N-K-JJ)	9: B(I,L,N-K)	(0,1)	[r]
6: B(I,L,N-K-JJ)	6: B(I,L,N-K-JJ)	(0,1,-1,0)	[r]

Figure 3: Live flow dependencies for CHOLSKY

FROM	TO	dir/dist	status
3: A(L,I,J)	3: A(L,I+JJ,J)	(0,+,*,0)	[k]
3: A(L,I,J)	3: A(L,JJ,I+J)	(+,*,*,0)	[k]
3: A(L,I,J)	5: A(L,JJ,J)	(0)	[k]
3: A(L,I,J)	7: A(L,-JJ,K+JJ)		[k]
3: A(L,I,J)	6: A(L,-JJ,N-K)		[k]
5: A(L,0,J)	2: A(L,0,I+J)	(+)	[k]
5: A(L,0,J)	8: A(L,0,K)		[k]
5: A(L,0,J)	9: A(L,0,N-K)		[k]
8: B(I,L,K)	6: B(I,L,N-K)	(0)	[c]
7: B(I,L,K+JJ)	7: B(I,L,K)	(0,1,*,0)	[kr]
7: B(I,L,K+JJ)	9: B(I,L,N-K)	(0)	[k]
7: B(I,L,K+JJ)	6: B(I,L,N-K)	(0)	[c]
7: B(I,L,K+JJ)	6: B(I,L,N-K-JJ)	(0)	[k]
6: B(I,L,N-K-JJ)	6: B(I,L,N-K)	(0,1,*,0)	[kr]

Figure 4: Dead flow dependencies for CHOLSKY

programs must be translated by hand to restricted language before tiny can analyze them, and so we have been unable to to try our analysis methods on large benchmarks. However, we feel the data presented here gives a good feel for the range of analysis times, even if it cannot be used to predicate an average analysis time.

4.7.1 Effects on flow dependences

We have found that, in many cases, the techniques described here significantly simplify the set of flow dependences. Figure 2 shows our version of the NAS kernel test that performs the Cholesky decomposition of a set of banded matrices. We have modified the original test by forward-substituting the expression $MAX(-M, -J)$, which was originally computed at the top of the J loop, and by normalizing the second K loop (which had a negative step).

Figure 3 lists all of the flow dependencies that are the Omega test has determined are live (i.e., not dead). The dependences in Figure 3 that have been refined are marked with the suffix $[r]$. Those that cover their read have been marked with $[C]$ (note that this tag does not affect the dependence itself, but shows that it can be used to eliminate other dependences).

The flow dependences in Figure 4 are dead: because of an intermediate write, no actual data flows from the source to the destination. These dependencies have been eliminated by being either covered (marked with $[c]$) or killed ($[k]$). Almost all other dependence analysis algorithms would report these as true flow dependencies.

4.7.2 Efficiency

Figure 6 shows timing results for 417 write/read access pairs in CHOLSKY and a variety of other test programs. The graph on the left compares the time needed to perform an extended analysis of an array pair that includes checking for refinement and coverage against the cost of standard analysis (no checks for refinement or covering). Both times were obtained using the Omega test to perform the analysis. The solid lines show $y = x$, $y = 2x$, and $y = 4x$. In 264 cases, the extended capabilities of the Omega test were not needed (i.e., we could determine that refinement and coverage were not possible without needing to consult the Omega test). The 81 $\star$'s show the cases in which we performed the general test for either covering or refinement on one flow dependence vector. These generally took 2 or 3 times the amount of time needed to generate the dependence. The 72 $\diamond$'s show the cases in which we performed the general test for covering or refinement and in which we were forced to split the dependence into several dependence vectors.

The graph on the right of Figure 6 contains one point for each pair of dependences to the same read access (that is, one point for each possible kill). It compares the time needed to test for a kill (horizontal axis) to the time needed to generate and perform coverage and refinement testing of the dependence being killed (vertical axis). The solid line shows $y = x$. Note that one point on the left graph may correspond to zero, one, or many points on the right. The 284 points with kill time below 0.3 msecs correspond to cases in which we did not have to consult the Omega test to perform a kill test; there were 54 cases in which the Omega test was consulted, leading to kill test times of longer than 0.3 msecs.

In Figure 7, we show the time required to perform standard and extended analysis of each array pair (extended analysis includes checks for refinement, covering and killing). The timing results were sorted according to the times required for extended analysis.

5 Symbolic dependence analysis

A data dependence may only exist if certain variables take on particular values. In Example 7, there is a flow dependence iff $2\mathtt{x} \leq \mathtt{n} \wedge 1 \leq \mathtt{y} \leq \mathtt{m} \wedge (\mathtt{x} > 0 \vee \mathtt{x} = 0 \wedge \mathtt{y} < \mathtt{m})$. We can determine the set of constraints under which a dependence exists by setting up the integer programming problem describing when there is a dependence, and projecting the problem onto the set of loop-invariant scalar variables. If we are interested in the set of constraints under which a flow dependence exists, we first determine a set of restraint vectors (Section 2.1.2) for the flow dependence, assuming nothing about the symbolic variables. We then add the restraint vectors to the integer programming problem before projecting onto the symbolic variables.

Alternatively, we can add any user assertions about the relations between variables to any integer programming problem involving those variables.

What if we have some information about relations between variables, but not enough to rule out a dependence? We use our ability to compute gists (Section 3.3) to determine the appropriate concise queries to make of the user, given what we already know. We consider the analysis of Example 7, in the circumstance that that the user has asserted that all array references are in bounds, $50 \leq \mathtt{n} \leq 100$ and no additional information is available about n. There are two apparent restraint vectors for this dependence: $(+, *)$ and $(0, +)$.

For the first restraint vector (which corresponds to a dependence carried by the outer loop), we define p as the things that are known plus the fact that there the outer loop has multiple iterations (which must be true in order for a dependence carried by that loop to be interesting). We define q to be the additional things we known when there actually is a dependence. The constraints that define p and q for this example are shown in Figure 5. The conditions on variables (other than n) under which this dependence actually exists,

```
real A[1:n,1:m], C[1:n,1:m]
...
for L1 := x to n do
  for L2 := 1 to m do
    A[L1,L2] := A[L1-x,y] + C[L1,L2];
```

Example 7

```
int Q[1:n]
...
for L1 := 1 to n do
  A[Q[L1]] := A[Q[L1+1]-1] + C[L1];
```

Example 8

```
for b := 1 to maxB
  for i := B[b] to B[b+1]-1
    for j := B[b] to B[b+1]-1
      A[i,j] := ...
```

Example 9

```
for i := 1 to n do
  for j := 1 to n do
    A[i*j] := ...
```

Example 10

```
for i := 1 to n do
  k := i*(i-1)/2+i
  for j := i to n do
    a[k] := a[k] + bb[i,j]
    k := k+j
```

Example 11

$$p = \left\{ \begin{array}{ll} \left(\begin{array}{l} x \le i_1 < j_1 \le n \\ 1 \le i_2, j_2 \le m \end{array} \right) & \text{loop bounds and restraint vector} \\ \left(\begin{array}{l} 1 \le i_1, j_1 - x \le n \\ 1 \le i_2, y \le m \end{array} \right) & \text{array references in bounds} \\ 50 \le n \le 100 & \text{user assertion} \end{array} \right\}$$
$$q = \left\{ \left(\begin{array}{l} i_1 = j_1 - x \\ i_2 = y \end{array} \right) \quad \text{dependence exists} \right\}$$

Figure 5: Set-up of equations for symbolic analysis of outer loop carried dependence Example 7

given that we know p, are given by (gist $\pi_{x,y,m}(p \wedge q)$ given $\pi_{x,y,m}(p)) = \{1 \le x \le 50\}$. For the restraint vector $(0, +)$, we similarly compute that it exists only if $\{x = 0 \wedge y < m\}$. We can then ask the user whether or not this condition must always hold.

What about expressions other than scalar loop-invariant variables (such as `i*j` or `P[i]`) that appear in a subscript or loop bound? In this case, we add a different symbolic variable for each appearance of the expression. If the expression is parameterized by a set of other symbolic variables, we also introduce additional symbolic variables for those parameters. We can now use the methods described above to ask the user queries about the relations between these symbolic variables.

In Example 8, we first check for an output dependence, assuming nothing about Q. This leads to an output dependence with direction/restraint vector $(+)$. We next take the set of constraints for determining if there is a dependence and, constraints that enforce the restraint vector $(+)$, and add variables for the index array subscripts (s_1 and s_2) and the index array values (Q_{s_1} and Q_{s_2}). Given that all array references are in bounds and the dependence has a restraint vector $(+)$, we set-up p and q as:

$$p = \left\{ \begin{array}{l} 1 \le i_1 < j_1 \le n \\ 1 \le Q_s, Q_{s'}, s, s' \le n \\ s = i_1 \wedge s' = j_1 \end{array} \right\}$$
$$q = \{ \ Q_s = Q_{s'} \ \}$$

We then determine that:

$$(\text{gist } \pi_{s,s',Q_s,Q_{s'},n}(p \wedge q) \text{ given } \pi_{s,s',Q_s,Q_{s'},n}(p)) \equiv Q_s = Q_{s'}$$

This would prompt us to ask the user the following:

```
Is it the case that for all a & b such that
1 <= a < b <= n, the following never happens?

        Q[a] = Q[b]
```

If the user answers yes, we rule out an output dependence and add $\forall a \& b$ s.t. $1 \le a < b \le n, Q[a] \ne Q[b]$ as an assertion.

Checking for a flow dependence would produce the query:

```
Is it the case that for all a & b such that
1 <= a < b-1 <= n-1, the following never happens?

        Q[a] = Q[b]-1
```

Instead of answering such a question directly, the user may choose to tell us more specifically what properties the array has. For example, the user might tell us that the array is strictly increasing, or is a permutation array. This has the advantage of being more natural to the user, and possibly supplying more information than a yes/no answer would.

By applying these techniques, we can handle a wide range of situations. These techniques apply directly to situations where array values appear in loop bounds (such as Example 9). We handle non-linear terms (such as `i*j` in Example 10) as an array indexed by all the non-constant variables. In other words, a term `i*j` would be treated as an array $Q[i, j]$, with the actual term substituted whenever conducting a dialogue with the user. By adding additional algorithms that perform non-linear induction variable recognition and recognize summations and by knowning appropriate linear constraints on summations, these techniques allow us to handle Example 11 (from program `s141` of [LCD91]), which could not be handled by any compiler tested by [LCD91].

5.1 Related Work

Methods for incorporating assertions about invariant scalar variables into dependence analysis algorithms and producing queries to ask the user have been part of the compiler folklore for some time (see [HP91] for a recent discussion). However, previous work has not addressed how to ask concise questions given that some information is already known.

Kathryn McKinley [McK90] describes how to handle index arrays in dependence analysis. Her work enumerates many typical cases and discusses how each can be handled. It is not a general purpose method and cannot handle cases such as array values in loop bounds or complicated subscripts of index arrays. Special purpose methods may prove useful from an efficiency viewpoint for dealing with typical, common cases. Our goal here is to describe as general a method as possible to fall back on.

6 Availability

An implementation of the Omega test is freely available for anonymous ftp from **ftp.cs.umd.edu** in the directory pub/omega. The directory contains a standalone implementation of the Omega test, papers describing the Omega test, and an implementation of Michael Wolfe's `tiny` tool [Wol91] augmented to use the Omega test as described in this paper.

7 Conclusions

We have shown how the Omega test can be extended and utilized to answer a wide range of questions that previous analysis methods could not address. The primary questions we considered are

- array kills,
- handling assertions and generating a dialog about the values of scalar variables, and
- handling assertions and generating a dialog about array values and non-linear expressions.

While previous methods could handle special cases of the problems considered here, our work describes much more general methods.

Previous approaches to these problems have not been widely implemented. By taking advantage of the power of the Omega test, we have been able to add these advanced data dependence analysis capabilities with relatively modest implementation investment. We hope that our approach will lead to a more widespread incorporation of these capabilities in compilers and interactive analysis tools.

8 Acknowledgements

Thanks to Udayan Borkar and Wayne Kelly for their help in obtaining the experimental results and their comments on the paper.

Also, special thanks to Michael Wolfe for making his `tiny` program freely available.

References

[BK89] Vasanth Balasundaram and Ken Kennedy. A technique for summarizing data access and its use in parallelism enhancing transformations. In *ACM SIGPLAN'89 Conference on Programming Language Design and Implementation*, 1989.

[Ble75] W.W̃. Bledsoe. A new method for proving certain presburger formulas. In *Advance Papers, 4th Int. Joint Conference on Artif. Intell.*, Tibilisi, Georgia, U.S.S.R, 1975.

[Bra88] Thomas Brandes. The importance of direct dependences for automatic parallelism. In *Proc of 1988 International Conference on Supercomputing*, July 1988.

[CP91] D. Y. Cheng and D. M. Pase. An evaluation of automatic and interactive parallel programming tools. In *Supercomputing '91*, November 1991.

[DE73] G.B. Dantzig and B.C. Eaves. Fourier-Motzkin elimination and its dual. *Journal of Combinatorial Theory (A)*, 14:288–297, 1973.

[GS90] Thomas Gross and Peter Steenkiste. Structured dataflow analysis for arrays and its use in an optimizing compiler. *Software – Practice and Experience*, 20:133–155, February 1990.

[HKK+91] M. W. Hall, T. Karvey, K. Kennedy, N. McIntosh, K.S. McKinley, J. D. Oldham, M. Paleczny, and G. Roth. Experiences from the parascope editor workshop. Technical Report RICE COMP TR91-173, Dept. of Computer Science, Rice University, September 1991.

[HP91] Mohammand Reza Haghighat and Costantine D. Polychronopoulos. Symbolic dependence analysis for high-performance parallelizing compilers. In *Advances in Languages and Compilers for Parallel Processing*. The MIT Press, 1991.

[JM87] Farnam Jahanian and Aloysius Ka-Lau Mok. A graph-theoretic approach for timing analysis and its implementation. *IEEE Transactions on Computers*, 1987.

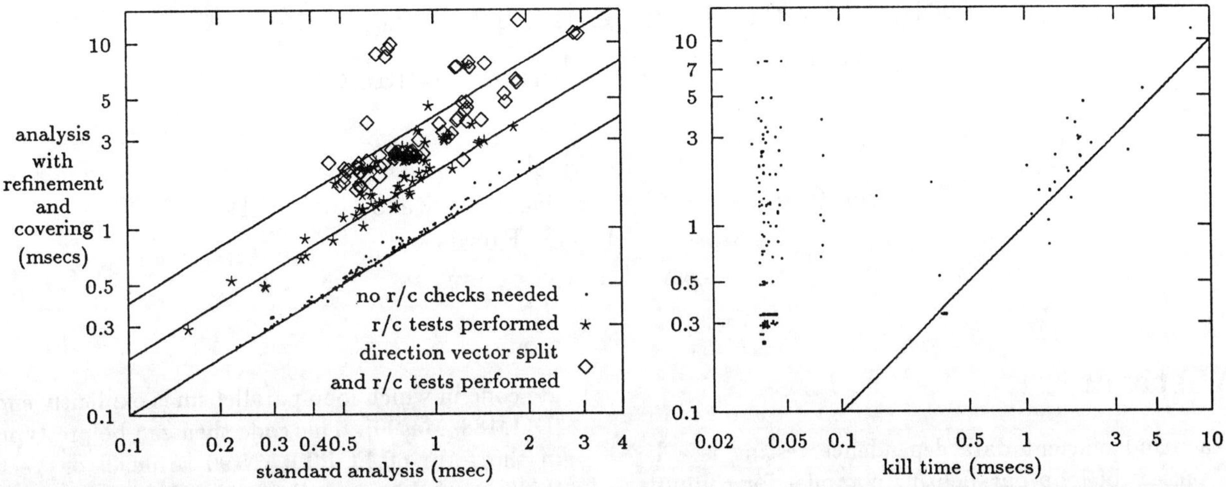

Figure 6: Relative times of standard analysis, analysis time including computing refinement and covering infomation, and time to compute killing information

[KPK90] David Klappholz, Kleanthis Psarris, and Xiangyun Kong. On the perfect accuracy of an approximate subscript analysis test. In *Supercomputing '90*, November 1990.

[LCD91] David Levine, David Callahan, and Jack Dongarra. A comparative study of automatic vectorizing compilers. Technical Report MCS-P218-0391, Argonne National Laboratory, April 1991.

[McK90] Kathryn S. McKinley. Dependence analysis of arrays subscripted by index arrays. Technical Report RICE COMP TR91-162, Dept. of Computer Science, Rice University, December 1990.

[Pug91] William Pugh. The omega test: a fast and practical integer programming algorithm for dependence analysis. In *Supercomputing '91*, Nov 1991. To appear in Communications of the ACM.

[Rib90] Hudson Ribas. Obtaining dependence vectors for nested-loop computations. In *Proc of 1990 International Conference on Parallel Processing*, August 1990.

[Ros90] Carl Rosene. *Incremental Dependence Analysis.* PhD thesis, Dept. of Computer Science, Rice University, March 1990.

[Sho77] Robert E. Shostak. On the sup-inf method for proving presburger formulas. *Journal of the ACM*, 24(4):529–543, October 1977.

[SLY89] Z. Shen, Z. Li, and P. Yew. An emperical student of array subscripts and data dependences. In *Proc of 1989 International Conference on Parallel Processing*, August 1989.

[Wol89] Michael Wolfe. *Optimizing Supercompilers for Supercomputers.* Pitman Publishing, London, 1989.

[Wol91] Michael Wolfe. The tiny loop restructuring research tool. In *Proc of 1991 International Conference on Parallel Processing*, 1991.

[ZC01] Hans Zima and Barbara Chapman. *Supercompilers for Parallel and Vector Computers.* ACM Press, 1991.

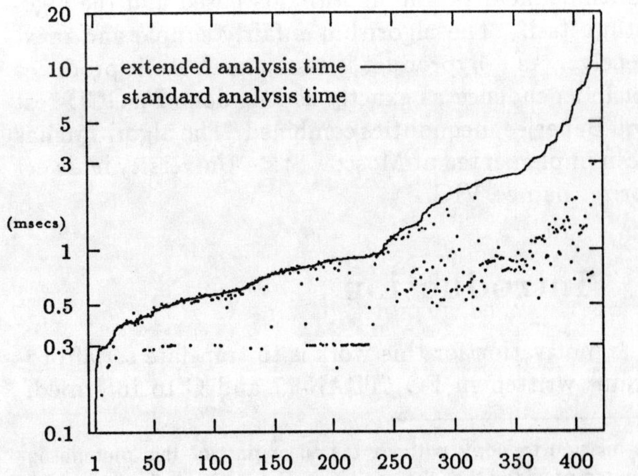

Figure 7: Graph of analysis time per array pair, with and without extended analysis, sorted in order of extended analysis time

Delinearization: an Efficient Way to Break Multiloop Dependence Equations

Vadim Maslov
Research Computing Center, Moscow State University
Moscow 119899, Russia
maslov@vadik.srcc.msu.su

Abstract

Exact and efficient data dependence testing is a key to success of loop-parallelizing compiler for computationally intensive programs. A number of algorithms has been created to test array references contained in parameter loops for dependence but most of them are unable to answer the following question correctly: Are references $C(i_1 + 10j_1)$ and $C(i_2 + 10j_2 + 5)$, $0 \le i_1, i_2 \le 4$, $0 \le j_1, j_2 \le 9$ independent? The technique introduced in this paper recognizes that i_1, i_2 and j_1, j_2 make different order contributions to the subscript index, and breaks dependence equation $i_1 + 10j_1 = i_2 + 10j_2 + 5$ into two equations $i_1 = i_2 + 5$ and $10j_1 = 10j_2$ which then can be solved independently. Since resulting equations contain less variables it is less expensive to solve them. We call this technique *delinearization* because it is reverse of the *linearization* much discussed in the literature.

In the introduction we demonstrate that linearized references are used not infrequently in scientific FORTRAN and C codes. Then we present a theorem on which delinearization algorithm is based and the algorithm itself. The algorithm is fairly simple and inexpensive. As a byproduct it tests equations it produces for independence as exactly as it is done by GCD-test and Banerjee inequalities combined. The algorithm has been implemented at Moscow State University in a vectorizer named VIC.

1 Introduction

The motivation for this work is to translate serial programs written in FORTRAN-77 and C to intermediate code in which loop parallelism is explicitly encoded [DMM88, Mas90]. This code then can be prettyprinted in the form of FORTRAN-90 [Ame90] or Vector C [Li86] or used by compiler backend to generate code for vector/parallel computers. Currently the translation is done automatically as in [ABC+87, AK87, KKP+81, Kus89, AGS91] though possibility of user participation in translation process as in [KMT90, IJT90] is considered.

To decide whether loop iterations can be run in parallel or not the translator should know whether data are transferred between iterations or not.

For example, the iterations of a loop in the fragment

```
    REAL D(0:9)
    DO 1 i = 0, 8
1     D(i+1)=D(i)*Q
```

can not be run in parallel because every iteration uses memory location written on previous iteration (the first iteration uses memory location computed before the loop). Parallelizing compiler achieves this conclusion by finding out that assignment statement data-depends on itself. Data dependence exists because there exist integer $i_1, i_2 \in [0, 8]$ such that $i_1 + 1 = i_2$ and therefore $D(i_1 + 1)$ and $D(i_2)$ may use the same memory locations.

Quite the opposite, references to D in the fragment

```
    REAL D(0:9)
    DO 1 i = 0, 4
1     D(i)=D(i+5)*Q
```

are independent because for all integer $i_1, i_2 \in [0, 4]$ we have $i_1 \ne i_2 + 5$. Therefore in this case iterations of the loop can be run in parallel.

Finding out whether two references are dependent or not is in general case equivalent to integer programming. As is stated in [MHL91], best algorithms known to solve this problem have complexity that depends on the value of loop bounds or the complexity is $O(n^{O(n)})$ where n is the number of loop variables. Even for simple cases these algorithms are too expensive.

ACM SIGPLAN '92 PLDI-6/92/CA

Existing techniques vs linearized multiloop references. A number of dependence testing algorithms have been created that sacrifice accuracy for efficiency [KKP+81, AK87, WB87, MHL91, GKT91]. However, even for the best algorithms this sacrifice is significant. Below we show that most existing algorithms are unable to detect independence for a pair of linearized 2-loop references.

References to C in the program

```
      REAL C(0:99)
      DO 1 i = 0, 4
        DO 1 j = 0, 9
1         C(i+10*j)=C(i+10*j+5)
```

are independent because the constrained equation

$$\begin{cases} i_1 + 10j_1 = i_2 + 10j_2 + 5 \\ i_1, i_2 \in [0,4] \\ j_1, j_2 \in [0,9] \end{cases} \quad (1)$$

has no integer solutions. However, this equation has real solutions. For example, $i_1 = i_2 = 2$, $j_1 = 4.5$, $j_2 = 4$ satisfy the equation.

The existing techniques capable of handling multi-loop dependence equations return 'dependent' if there are real solutions. Therefore they can not prove independence for this equation. The following techniques belong to this category: Banerjee inequalities [AK87, WB87], λ-test [LYZ89], Fourier-Motzkin elimination [MHL91, DE73]. It should be noted, however, that normalization (tightening) of constraints proposed in [Pug91] being applied to this problem together with Fourier-Motzkin elimination returns 'independent'. Nevertheless, it is better to avoid Fourier-Motzkin elimination because of its high cost [Tri85].

The integer-exact techniques in this case are also ineffective because the equation containing four variables, each with different coefficients, is too complicated for these techniques. We found the following techniques inadequate to disprove this dependence: Single Variable Per Constraint Test [MHL91, Ban88], Acyclic Test [MHL91], Simple Loop Residue Test [MHL91], Shostak algorithm [Sho81, BC86], GCD-test [AK87, Ban88].

Our approach. Our approach is to break dependence equation (1) into two equations:

$$\begin{cases} 10j_1 - 10j_2 = 0 \\ j_1, j_2 \in [0,9] \end{cases}$$

and

$$\begin{cases} i_1 - i_2 - 5 = 0 \\ i_1, i_2 \in [0,4] \end{cases}$$

which then can be solved independently of each other by existing techniques.

Let us prove that such a break can be done. To do it we make the following substitutions: $A = 10j_1 - 10j_2$, $B = i_1 - i_2 - 5$. Taking in account loop bounds gives us $|B| < 10$, $|A| = 0$ or $|A| \geq 10$. Therefore $A + B = 0$ can hold only if $A = 0$ and $B = 0$ hold.

We call our approach *delinearization* because it is reverse of *linearization*. For FORTRAN programs, linearization is replacement of a reference $A(i_1, ..., i_n)$ to an n-dimensional array $A(0 : H_1, ..., 0 : H_n)$ with a reference $A(i_1 + \sum_{k=2}^{n} i_k \prod_{l=1}^{k-1}(H_l+1))$ to a 1-dimensional array $A(0 : (\prod_{l=1}^{n}(H_l + 1)) - 1)$. Array linearization is done by most compilers to map multidimensional arrays to 1-dimensional memory.

Replacement of the above program fragment with

```
      REAL C(0:9,0:9)
      DO 1 i = 0, 4
        DO 1 j = 0, 9
1         C(i,j)=C(i+5,j)
```

is delinearization in the literal sense of the word — two dimensions are introduced instead of one. We interpret delinearization more subtly — as breaking single dependence equation into smaller independently solved equations.

For the cases when delinearized dependence equations show dependence we still have an advantage compared to existing techniques because we can calculate direction and distance vectors more exactly. In [MHL91] authors say that they can not discover that distance vector is (2,0) for the following fragment:

```
      DO 10 i = 1, 8
        DO 10 j = 1, 10
10        A(10*i+j)=A(10*(i+2)+j)+7
```

Using delinearization we are able to prove that distance vector is (2,0).

One may think that linearized references are very exotic and not worth of special consideration. This is not so. Next we discuss where and how often linearized references are used.

Array references linearized by hand. First of all, linearized references can be used in programs 'as is'.

To find out how often linearized references are used in practice we analyzed 8 FORTRAN programs from RiCEPS benchmark suite [Por89]. We discovered that array references linearized by hand are used in 6 out of 8 programs. Number of outermost loop nests that contain linearized references for each examined program is given in Figure 1.

We also found that large programs use linearization to arrange *run-time dimensioning.* The largest programs examined, BOAST and CCM, use linearized references for this purpose. The amount of linearization

Program	Type	Lines	Loop nests containing linearized references
BOAST	Reservoir Simulation	7000	> 28
CCM	Atmospheric	24000	> 24
LINPACKD	Linear Algebra	400	0
QCD	Quantum Chromodynamics	2000	2
SIMPLE	Fluid Flow	1000	0
SPHOT	Particle Transport	1000	2
TRACK	Trajectory Plot	4000	5
WANAL1	Wave Equation	2000	4

Figure 1: Number of loop nests containing linearized references for RiCEPS

in these programs is so great that it may be impossible to analyze them with acceptable precision without applying delinearization.

Linearized references do not always appear explicitly. For example, in the the following fragment, derived from a loop nest in BOAST, we have an induction variable controlled by 3 loops.

```
      IB = -1
      DO 1 I=0,II-1
        DO 1 J=0,JJ-1
          DO 1 K=0,KK-1
            IB=IB+1
            C(J)=C(J)+1
1           B(IB)=B(IB)+Q
```

Existing techniques treat it as controlled by only innermost loop. We can parallelize the last assignment statement with respect to all 3 loops if we recognize that all loops control IB, replace IB with K+J*KK+I*KK*JJ:

```
      DO 1 I=0,II-1
        DO 1 J=0,JJ-1
          DO 1 K=0,KK-1
            C(J)=C(J)+1
1           B(K+J*KK+I*KK*JJ)=
 #          B(K+J*KK+I*KK*JJ)+Q
```

and delinearize references to B.

Another way is to convert these 3 loops to one loop with variable IB and II*JJ*KK iterations. It doesn't work in general, because the loop nest can contain statements referencing not only IB but I, J, K too. In our example next to last assignment statement references J. Should such a conversion be done these references will become non-linear. This alternative method also doesn't work for imperfectly nested loops.

Array aliasing. In FORTRAN-77 array aliasing is caused by EQUIVALENCE, COMMON statements and by association of dummy and actual parameters of procedure call. FORTRAN ANSI standard [Ame78] states that in time of association (aliasing) participating arrays are considered to be linearized. This requirement allows programmers to associate arrays of different *form* and encourages compilers to linearize array references in order to handle all possible cases.

In the program fragment

```
      REAL A(0:9,0:9)
      REAL B(0:4,0:19)
      EQUIVALENCE (A,B)
      DO 1 i = 0, 4
        DO 1 j = 0, 9
1         A(i,j)=B(i,2*j+1)
```

arrays A and B are associated by EQUIVALENCE statement. Since arrays have different form all the references to them must be linearized:

```
      REAL C(0:99)
      DO 1 i = 0, 4
        DO 1 j = 0, 9
1         C(i+10*j)=C(i+10*j+5)
```

Applying delinearization we prove independence.

If we have references of different form to the same array, we need not linearize all dimensions. It even can be harmful. In the program fragment

```
      REAL A(0:9,0:9,0:9,0:9)
      REAL B(0:4,0:19,0:9,0:9)
      EQUIVALENCE (A,B)
      DO 1 i = 0, 4
        DO 1 j = 0, 9
          DO 1 k = 0, 9
            DO 1 l = 0, 9
1             A(i,j,k,IFUN(10))=
 #            B(i,2*j+1,k,l)
```

linearization of i and j subscripts is necessary to make precise dependence testing for aliased subarrays possible. Adding to this group subscript k is possible because delinearization will separate it back but it only wastes time. Linearization of subscript l make analysis impossible because IFUN(10) ranges over unknown values and will spoil the whole index. So it is wise to linearize (and then delinearize) i and j subscripts and leave k and l subscripts as they are:

```
      REAL C(0:99,0:9,0:9)
      DO 1 i = 0, 4
        DO 1 j = 0, 9
          DO 1 k = 0, 9
            DO 1 l = 0, 9
1             C(i+10*j,k,IFUN(10))=
     #        C(i+10*j+5,k,l)
```

C array references. Considering C programs, we find several obvious cases when hand-linearization is likely to be used. First, since only constant array boundaries are allowed in C one must linearize by hand references to dynamically-allocated (by `malloc`) multidimensional arrays — run-time dimensioning again. Second, to make analysis in the presence of pointers possible translator should treat pointer which is used to traverse some array as index in the *linearized* version of that array.

Consider the following C program fragment:

```
float d[100];
float *i,*j;
for(j=d; j<=d+90; j+=10)
  for(i=j; i<j+5; i++)
    *i=*(i+5);
```

It uses pointers i and j to traverse array d. Since the program doesn't use these pointers for any other purpose they can be replaced with integer index variables:

```
float d[100];
int i,j;
for(j=0; j<10; j++)
  for(i=0; i<5; i++)
    d[j*10+i]=d[j*10+i+5];
```

The references to d then can be delinearized and finally we have

```
float d[10][10];
int i,j;
for(j=0; j<10; j++)
  for(i=0; i<5; i++)
    d[j][i]=d[j][i+5];
```

which clearly demonstrates independence.

In fact it is possible to state that to perform precise dependence testing for C programs compiler has to assume that *all array references are linearized.* On one hand, ANSI C standard requires value of subscript expression to fit into corresponding subscript boundaries. On the other hand, subscript-out-of-range check is not performed by most C compilers and this requirement is unknown to majority of users. So we have to linearize all the references in order to analyze correctly working programs which may be not standard conforming.

2 Background

In this section we give formal definition of dependence taken from [BC86, AK87, WB87]. Let us consider two FORTRAN-77 loop nests with $n_0 > 0$ common outermost loops (Figure 2).

```
DO x_1 = 0, X_1
  ...
  DO x_n0 = 0, X_n0
    DO x_n0+1 = 0, X_n0+1
    ...
      DO x_n1 = 0, X_n1
S1      A(f_1(x_1,...,x_n1),...,f_l(x_1,...,x_n1)) = ...
      ENDDO
    ...
    ENDDO
    DO y_n0+1 = 0, Y_n0+1
    ...
      DO y_n2 = 0, Y_n2
S2      ... = A(g_1(y_1,...,y_n2),...,g_l(y_1,...,y_n2))
      ENDDO
    ...
    ENDDO
  ENDDO
  ...
ENDDO
```

Figure 2: Loop nests for dependence definition

Statements S_1 and S_2 are wrapped in n_1 and n_2 loops respectively. Since n_0 outermost loops are common, $\forall i \in [1, n_0]$ $X_i = Y_i$. Each DO-loop is assumed to be normalized to run from 0 to its upper bound by 1. If source loops are not normalized they can be easily converted to the normalized form.

We assume that loop upper bounds $X_1, ..., X_{n_1}$ and $Y_1, ..., Y_{n_2}$ are integer constants. If in practice we encounter a loop bound $X_i = F(x_1, ..., x_{i-1})$ we replace it with $\max_{x_1,...,x_{i-1}} F(x_1, ..., x_{i-1})$ [1]. If a loop bound is an expression in variables of unknown value (for example, values supplied from the program input) we have to perform symbolic calculations in the delinearization algorithm (see Section 4).

For simplicity, we assume that all statements of the nest other than DO and ENDDO are assignment statements. It is so because in this paper we consider only data dependences and not control dependences.

A is array with l dimensions.

[1]Replacing iteration space by its rectangular extension is a trade-off necessary to make delinearization cost-effective. Delinearization will proceed much better if we calculate the exact max and min for subscript functions in the exact iteration space (which in case of X_i being linear function of $x_1, ..., x_{i-1}$ is a polyhedron). But exact calculations will make delinearization too slow.

Definition of dependence. Under such assumptions we say that there is a *dependence* between statements S_1 and S_2 if and only if there exist integer numbers $\alpha_1 \in [0, X_1]$, ..., $\alpha_{n_1} \in [0, X_{n_1}]$, $\beta_1 \in [0, Y_1]$, ..., $\beta_{n_2} \in [0, Y_{n_2}]$ such that:

$$\forall i \in [1, l] \quad f_i(\alpha_1, ..., \alpha_{n_1}) = g_i(\beta_1, ..., \beta_{n_2}) \qquad (2)$$

If there are no dependences between two references then these references are called *independent.*

On an intuitive level, the existence of dependence between S_1 and S_2 means that there exist instances of S_1 and S_2 that use the same memory locations.

Direction and distance vectors. The vector $d = (d_1, ..., d_{n_0})$ such that $\forall i \in [1, n_0]$

$$d_i = \begin{cases} < & \text{if } \alpha_i < \beta_i \\ = & \text{if } \alpha_i = \beta_i \\ > & \text{if } \alpha_i > \beta_i \end{cases}$$

is called the *direction vector* of the dependence [Wol82].

Since there may exist more than one set of integer numbers α_i, β_i that satisfy the system of dependence equations (2), there may exist more than one dependence between S_1 and S_2. Dependences which have the same direction vector are counted as one dependence. Dependences that have different direction vectors can be summarized. For example, two dependences with direction vectors $(=,<)$ and $(=,=)$ can be represented by one dependence with direction vector $(=,\leq)$. Similarly, $(>)$ plus $(=)$ is $(\geq)$, $(>)$ plus $(<)$ is $(\neq)$, $(<)$ plus $(=)$ plus $(>)$ is $(*)$. However not all direction vectors should be summarized. For example, $(<,=)$ and $(=,<)$ dependences should not be replaced with a $(\leq,\leq)$ dependence because this dependence have decompositions that are not present in the original pair of dependences — for example, $(\leq,\leq)$ can be decomposed to $(=,=)$ and $(<,<)$.

Distance vectors [Mur71, Lam74] are more exact version of direction vectors. The vector $D = (\alpha_1 - \beta_1, ..., \alpha_{n_0} - \beta_{n_0})$ is a distance vector for the above defined dependence. In general case all dependences existing between two references may have different distance vectors. If a number of distinct distance vectors depends on the size of iteration space then it is said that there is no 'good' distance vector.

Distance-direction vectors. If some element of distance vector is not constant we can replace it with the corresponding element of direction vector thus constructing *distance-direction vector.* Such a vector carries all the information that is carried by direction and distance vector combined. For example, in the program

```
   DO i=0,5
     DO j=0,8
1      A(i,j)=A(2i,j+1)
```

direction vector of the only dependence is $(\leq,>)$ and distance vector is $(?,-1)$. Combining these two vectors gives us distance-direction vector $(\leq,-1)$.

Non-direction vector constraints. Several techniques were invented to provide dependence information which is more precise than distance and direction vectors. Let us mention some of them.

Wolf and Lam in [WL91] proposed generalization of distance and direction vectors in which each element of their vector is a *range* of integers.

Lu and Chen in [LC90] treat set of distance vectors of dependences that hold between a pair of array references (they call them *dependence vectors*) as a space of vectors, not packing this space into single representing vector.

Voevodin in [Voe91] proposed to draw dependence arcs in parametrized acyclic graph depicting computational history of affine program fragment (called the *algorithm graph*) rather than in conventional static statement graph, thus replacing direction and distance vectors with exact description of set of solutions.

These techniques are flexible and exact. However they are expensive enough, so it is unclear whether they can be used in production compilers.

Dependence classification. Dependences that we obtain using the definition (2) are further classified as *true, anti, output, input* [BC86, AK87, WB87]. Since this classification is done after establishing the existence of dependence and calculating direction and/or distance vector and delinearization is done before it we don't discuss this classification here.

Linear subscript functions. Proving automatically that two references are independent is impractical unless subscript functions f_i and g_i are restricted to some class. Following a majority of researchers we restrict f_i and g_i to a class of linear functions of loop variables. That is

$$f_i(x_1, \ldots, x_{n_1}) = a_0 + \sum_{k=1}^{n_1} a_{ik} x_k \qquad (3)$$

$$g_i(y_1, \ldots, y_{n_2}) = b_0 + \sum_{k=1}^{n_2} b_{ik} y_k \qquad (4)$$

where a_{ik} and b_{ik} are integer constants. More general case when a_{ik} and b_{ik} are integer loop-invariant expressions is discussed in the Section 4.

Example. Figure 3 contains FORTRAN-77 program adapted from [AK87] and table that lists pairs of dependent references, dependence direction and distance-direction vectors for this program.

```
      REAL X(200), Y(200), B(100)
      REAL A(100,100), C(100,100)
      DO 30 i=1,100
S1       X(i) = Y(i) + 10
         DO 20 j=1,99
S2          B(j) = A(j,20)
            DO 10 k=1,100
S3             A(j+1,k) = B(j) + C(j,k)
   10       CONTINUE
S4          Y(i+j) = A(j+1,20)
   20    CONTINUE
   30 CONTINUE
```

Pair of references	Direction vector	Distance–direction vector
S_2:B S_2:B	(*,=)	(*,0)
S_2:B S_3:B	(*,=)	(*,0)
S_3:A S_3:A	(*,=,=)	(*,0,0)
S_3:A S_2:A	(*,<)	(*,+1)
S_3:A S_4:A	(*,=)	(*,0)
S_4:Y S_1:Y	(<)	(<)

Figure 3: Program and its dependences

3 Delinearization

Let us consider one of the dependence equations from the system of equations (2):

$$f(x_1, \ldots, x_{n_1}) = g(y_1, \ldots, y_{n_2})$$

Taking in account (3), (4) and loop bounds we transform this equation to

$$\begin{cases} c_0 + c_1 z_1 + \cdots + c_n z_n = 0 \\ z_1 \in [0, Z_1], \ \ldots, \ z_n \in [0, Z_n] \end{cases} \quad (5)$$

where $n = n_1 + n_2$, z_i are integer numbers, and

$$c_0 = a_0 - b_0,$$
$$c_k = a_k, \ z_k = x_k, \ Z_k = X_k, \qquad 1 \le k \le n_1$$
$$c_k = -b_{k-n_1}, \ z_k = y_{k-n_1}, \ Z_k = Y_{k-n_1}, \quad n_1 < k \le n$$

Theorem. The set of solutions for the constrained equation (5) coincides [2] with the *cartesian product* of the set of solutions of constrained equation

$$\begin{cases} d_0 + c_1 z_1 + \cdots + c_m z_m = 0 \\ z_1 \in [0, Z_1], \ \ldots, \ z_m \in [0, Z_m] \end{cases} \quad (6)$$

and the set of solutions of constrained equation

$$\begin{cases} D_0 + c_{m+1} z_{m+1} + \cdots + c_n z_n = 0 \\ z_{m+1} \in [0, Z_{m+1}], \ \ldots, \ z_n \in [0, Z_n] \end{cases} \quad (7)$$

[2] Two sets coincide iff both sets are empty or both sets have identical elements.

if there exist integer numbers m, d_0, D_0 such that $m \in [1, n]$,

$$\gcd(D_0, c_{m+1}, \ldots, c_n) > \max(|d_0 + \textstyle\sum_{k=1}^{m} c_k^- Z_k|, \ |d_0 + \sum_{k=1}^{m} c_k^+ Z_k|) \quad (8)$$

and

$$c_0 = d_0 + D_0. \quad (9)$$

By $|x|$ we denote absolute value of x. By $\gcd(x, y, \ldots, z)$ we denote greatest common divisor of $x, y, \ldots, z$. Functions c^+ and c^- are defined by the following:

$$c^+ = \begin{cases} c & \text{if } c \ge 0 \\ 0 & \text{if } c < 0 \end{cases} \qquad c^- = \begin{cases} 0 & \text{if } c \ge 0 \\ c & \text{if } c < 0 \end{cases}$$

This theorem gives us solid base for performing delinearization correctly. On an intuitive level the theorem means that if variables taking part in the equation can be divided in two groups such that minimal change of the left hand part of (5) caused by one group is greater than its maximal change produced by another group then these groups are separable and can be analyzed independently.

Proof. It is quite obvious that for all B, C, v, G the statements $B \le v \le C$ and $\max(|B|, |C|) < G$ imply $-G < v < G$ or $|v| < G$. Let us make the following substitutions in this statement:

$$B = d_0 + \sum_{k=1}^{m} c_k^- Z_k,$$
$$C = d_0 + \sum_{k=1}^{m} c_k^+ Z_k,$$
$$v = d_0 + \sum_{k=1}^{m} c_k z_k,$$
$$G = \gcd(D_0, c_{m+1}, \ldots, c_n).$$

It is easy to prove that

$$\forall z_1 \in [0, Z_1], \ \ldots, \ z_m \in [0, Z_m] \quad B \le v \le C$$

(to do it we can use the proof of Banerjee inequalities from [AK87]). Combining this with the theorem condition we have:

$$\forall z_1 \in [0, Z_1], \ \ldots, \ z_m \in [0, Z_m] \quad |d_0 + \sum_{k=1}^{m} c_k z_k| < G. \quad (10)$$

Let us consider

$$M = |\frac{D_0}{G} + \frac{c_{m+1}}{G} z_{m+1} + \cdots + \frac{c_n}{G} z_n|.$$

M is integer because $D_0, c_{m+1}, \ldots, c_n$ are all divisible by G according to definition of G. If $M \ne 0$, then $G \le$

GM. Combining this with (10) gives us $M \neq 0 \Rightarrow$

$$|d_0 + \sum_{k=1}^{m} c_k z_k| < G|\frac{D_0}{G} + \sum_{k=m+1}^{n} \frac{c_{k+1}}{G} z_{k+1}|$$

or

$$D_0 + \textstyle\sum_{k=m+1}^{n} c_k z_k \neq 0 \Rightarrow$$
$$|d_0 + \textstyle\sum_{k=1}^{m} c_k z_k| < |D_0 + \sum_{k=m+1}^{n} c_k z_k|. \quad (11)$$

Now it is relatively easy to prove the theorem.

If one of equations (6), (7) has solutions and another equation has no solutions then by adding these equations we prove that equation (5) has no solutions. If both equations (6), (7) have no integer solutions then

$$\sigma_1 = d_0 + \sum_{k=1}^{m} c_k z_k \neq 0$$

and

$$\sigma_2 = D_0 + \sum_{k=m+1}^{n} c_k z_k \neq 0.$$

Combining this with (11) gives us $|\sigma_1| < |\sigma_2|$ and, therefore, $\sigma_1 + \sigma_2 \neq 0$. Taking in account (9) we conclude that equation (5) has no integer solutions. On the other hand, if left hand part of (5) is nonzero for any $z_1, ..., z_n$ then $\sigma_1 + \sigma_2 \neq 0$. Therefore either $\sigma_1 \neq 0$ or $\sigma_2 \neq 0$. That means that cartesian product of sets of solutions of equations (6) and (7) is empty.

If both equations (6) and (7) have solutions then by adding them we prove that equation (5) has solutions. On the other hand, if equation (5) has integer solutions then $\sigma_1 + \sigma_2 = 0$ and according to (11), either $\sigma_2 = 0$ or $|\sigma_1| < |\sigma_2|$. It is possible only if $\sigma_1 = 0$ and $\sigma_2 = 0$. □

Algorithm. Figure 4 is an overview of the delinearization algorithm. This algorithm breaks original dependence equation into smaller equations for individual dimensions using the above theorem.

The goal set for the algorithm is to produce as many dimensions (and equations) as possible. The number of produced dimensions is limited by the number of variables in the source equation because each resulting dimension must contain at least one variable and no variable can appear in more than one dimension.

The idea of the algorithm is based on the following observation: the condition (8) of the theorem implies that any of $c_1, ..., c_m$ are less than any of $c_{m+1}, ..., c_n$. It means that dimensions produced by the algorithm are ordered according to absolute value of coefficients standing before these dimensions' variables. So the algorithm begins with ordering coefficients of the source equation by their absolute value. Then scanning ordered coefficients from smaller ones to bigger ones the algorithm tries to establish that the barrier between already processed variables and variables that are still not processed is the barrier between dimensions.

The algorithm applies the theorem correctly. The line 'IF max(|*cmin*|, |*cmax*|) $< g_k$ THEN' is a place where the condition of the theorem is checked. Indeed, on iteration k of the loop right before that line we have:

$$smin = \sum_{l=kBeg}^{k-1} c_{I_l}^{-} Z_{I_l}, \quad smax = \sum_{l=kBeg}^{k-1} c_{I_l}^{+} Z_{I_l},$$

$$d_0 = r = c_0 \bmod g_k, \quad D_0 = c_0 - r,$$

$$G = g_k = \gcd_{l=k}^{n}(c_{I_l}).$$

Since $D_0 = c_0 - (c_0 \bmod g_k)$, D_0 is divisible by g_k and therefore $\gcd(g_k, D_0) = g_k$. Taking in account these substitutions and making index substitution $I_{kBeg} \mapsto 1$, $I_{kBeg+1} \mapsto 2$, ..., $I_{k-1} \mapsto m$, $I_k \mapsto m+1$, $I_{k+1} \mapsto m+2$, ..., $I_n \mapsto n$ gives us exactly the condition (8).

If the condition of the theorem is satisfied we single out the equation $r + \sum_{l=kBeg}^{k-1} c_{I_l} z_{I_l} = 0$. If *cmin* and *cmax* for this equation are consistent the existing techniques are applied to the equation to compute the set of dependences it produces. Then *smin*, *smax*, *kBeg*, c_0 are tuned to cast away this equation.

What does the algorithm produce? The algorithm produces the set of dependences that hold between two references denoting each dependence with direction vectors. Some dependences can be summed up without loss of precision (see the paragraph 'Distance-direction vectors'). If precision is not important and time/storage are in great demand one can keep only one summary direction vector instead of several distinct vectors. On the other hand if one wishes more precision being ready to sacrifice some storage, one can keep distance-direction vectors instead of direction vectors.

Performing GCD and Banerjee tests 'on the fly'. Besides separating dimensions the algorithm 'on the fly' performs test for independence which has the same sharpness as combined GCD and $(*, *, ..., *)$ Banerjee tests performed on separated dimensions. Let us prove it.

Variables *cmin* and *cmax* represent minimum and maximum values for left hand expression of equation (6). If for some subscript (which was just separated from the other subscripts) $cmin > 0$ or $cmax < 0$ then $c_0 + \sum_{l=kBeg}^{k-1} c_l z_l \neq 0$ for all z_l. This proves independence for the separated dimension in the same way as it is done in Banerjee inequalities.

On the first step of DO loop in the algorithm we have $cmin = cmax = r = c_0 \bmod g_{k_0}$. Since $c_0 \bmod g_{k_0} < g_{k_0}$ we execute IF statement body. The first statement of the IF body (also IF) is reduced to 'IF $r > 0$ or $r < 0$ THEN RETURN ∅'. That means that dependence is

INPUT: dependence equation (5), that is, integers $c_0,\ c_1, ..., c_n,\ Z_1, ..., Z_n$.
OUTPUT: set of dependence direction vectors (if this set is empty then there is no dependence).

$\quad$ Order c_k, that is, compute I_k such that $\forall k \in [1, n-1]\ \ |c_{I_{k+1}}| \geq |c_{I_k}|$;
$\quad$ Let k_0 be minimal number such that $c_{I_{k_0}} \neq 0$;
$\quad$ Compute $g_k:\ \ \forall k \in [k_0, n]\ \ g_k = \gcd(c_{I_k}, c_{I_{k+1}}, ..., c_{I_n});\ \ g_{n+1} = \infty$;
$\quad$ $DirVecs = \{(*, ..., *)\};\ \ kBeg = k_0;\ \ smin = smax = 0$;
$\quad$ DO $k = k_0, n+1, 1$
$\quad\quad$ $r = c_0 \bmod g_k;\ \ cmin = smin + r;\ \ cmax = smax + r$;
$\quad\quad$ IF $\max(|cmin|, |cmax|) < g_k$ THEN
$\quad\quad\quad$ IF $cmin > 0$ or $cmax < 0$ THEN RETURN $\emptyset$ (independent);
$\quad\quad\quad$ Compute set of direction vectors $NV = (nv_1, ..., nv_l)$ for dependence equation
$\quad\quad\quad\quad$ $r + \sum_{l=kBeg}^{k-1} c_{I_l} z_{I_l} = 0$ using existing techniques [WB87, GKT91, MHL91];
$\quad\quad\quad$ $DirVecs = \{dv \cap nv \mid dv \in DirVecs,\ nv \in NV,\ dv \cap nv \neq \emptyset\}$;
$\quad\quad\quad$ $smin = smax = 0;\ \ kBeg = k;\ \ c_0 = c_0 - r$;
$\quad\quad$ ENDIF
$\quad\quad$ $smin = smin + c_{I_k}^{-} Z_{I_k};\ \ smax = smax + c_{I_k}^{+} Z_{I_k}$;
$\quad$ ENDDO
$\quad$ RETURN $DirVecs$;

Figure 4: Dependence testing algorithm based on delinearization

possible only if $r = 0$, that is only if c_0 is divisible by g_{k_0}. Condition that we extracted from the algorithm is classic GCD-test. So we have proved that GCD-test is equivalent to Banerjee test performed in the least significant dimension.

Example. Let us apply the algorithm to the following dependence equation:

$$\begin{cases} 100k_1 - 100k_2 + 10j_1 - 10i_2 + i_1 - j_2 - 110 = 0 \\ i_1, i_2, k_1, k_2 \in [0, 8],\ \ j_1, j_2 \in [0, 9] \end{cases}$$

Values that algorithm variables have on each iteration right before applying the theorem and separated equations are present at Figure 5.

Efficiency. The algorithm has linear time complexity $O(n)$ where n is the number of variables in the source equation. Sorting of c_k takes more than linear time, but since n is usually small ($n \leq 6$), this time is negligible.

The time needed to perform the algorithm is significantly less than the time needed to solve linearized equation because there are fewer participating variables. The precision gains of delinearization are therefore almost free.

4 Symbolics handling

To analyze real life programs we have to allow $c_0, c_1, ..., c_n,\ Z_1, ..., Z_n$ from equation (5) to be not only integer constants but *loop invariant integer expressions* too. Extending class of analyzable indexes in such a way we can still apply the theorem and the algorithm but computations in them have to be performed symbolically.

Let us consider an example of symbolic delinearization. We try our algorithm on the FORTRAN program

```
      REAL A(0:N*N*N-1)
      DO 1 i = 0, N-2
        DO 1 j = 0, N-1
          DO 1 k = 0, N-2
1           A(N*N*k+N*j+i)=A(N*N*k+j+N*i+N*N+N)
```

which is to be delinearized to the following program:

```
      REAL A(0:N-1,0:N-1,0:N-1)
      DO 1 i = 0, N-2
        DO 1 j = 0, N-1
          DO 1 k = 0, N-2
1           A(i,j,k)=A(j,i+1,k+1)
```

According to the algorithm we must delinearize the difference between index expressions thus breaking dependence equation into system of 3 equations. Here for the sake of simplicity we demonstrate delinearization for `A(j,i+1,k+1)` reference only.

Since $N^3 - 1$ is upper bound of array `A`, $N^3 > 1$ and therefore $N > 1$. Knowing this we can do ordering of coefficients. The results are: $c_0 = N^2 + N$, $c_1 = 1$, $c_2 = N$, $c_3 = N^2$, $g_1 = 1$, $g_2 = N$, $g_3 = N^2$.

On the 1st iteration we have: $smin = smax = 0$, $r = (N^2 + N) \bmod 1 = 0$. Since $0 < 1$ first iteration of the algorithm produces $0 = 0$ dependence equation which doesn't change summary set dependence vectors.

On the 2nd iteration we have: $smin = 0$, $smax = N - 1$, $r = (N^2 + N) \bmod N = 0$. Since $N - 1 < N$ is true inequality for any N the barrier can be drawn

k	c_k	$smin$	$smax$	c_0	r	g_k	Separated equation
1	-1	0	0	-110	0	1	
2	1	-9	0	-110	0	1	
3	-10	-9	8	-110	0	10	$i_1 - j_2 = 0$
4	10	-80	0	-110	-10	10	
5	-100	-80	90	-110	-10	100	$10j_1 - 10i_2 - 10 = 0$
6	100	-800	0	-100	0	100	
7		-800	800	-100	-100	∞	$100k_1 - 100k_2 - 100 = 0$

Figure 5: Example of the delinearization algorithm work

between j and i dimensions. c_0 remains the same after the iteration.

On the 3rd iteration we have: $smin = 0$, $smax = N(N-2)$, $r = (N^2+N) \bmod N^2 = N$, $\max(N, N(N-2)+N) = N(N-2)+N = N^2+N$. Since inequality $N^2 + N < N^2$ is also true for any $N > 1$ we draw barrier between i and k dimensions. After the iteration $c_0 = N^2$.

On the 4th iteration we have: $smin = 0$, $smax = N^2(N-2)$, $r = N^2 \bmod \infty = N^2$, $\max(...) < \infty$. Since any number is less than infinity we always separate the last dimension. After the last iteration $c_0 = 0$ always.

This example demonstrates that operations used in the algorithm are simple enough to be computed symbolically. It should be also noted that for precise handling of symbolics translator has to be able to keep and process predicates.

5 Conclusion

We presented dependence testing method that under certain conditions breaks multiloop dependence equations into smaller equations. Since each resulting equation contains less variables than source equation it has better chances to be solved exactly. Equations that we break originate from linearized references which are used rather often in the real programs. Delinearization algorithm is inexpensive and it proves independence of references 'on the fly' with the same precision as GCD and Banerjee tests applied to each dimension. The method makes computation of direction and distance vectors by other techniques more precise and less time-consuming.

6 Acknowledgements

The author is grateful to Lev Korolyov and Igor Mashechkin from the Computational Mathematics and Cybernetics department of Moscow State University and to Vladimir Repin and Paul Ruban from the Research Computing Center of MSU for their guidance and advice. Thanks to everyone who helped me to write this paper. Special thanks to Paul Havlak from Rice University for his thorough reading of this paper and numerous helpful suggestions.

References

[ABC+87] F. Allen, M. Burke, P. Charles, R. Cytron, and J. Ferrante. An overview of the PTRAN analysis system for multiprocessing. In *Proceedings of the First International Conference on Supercomputing*. Springer-Verlag, Athens, Greece, 1987.

[AGS91] V. M. Andreyev, I. S. Golosov, and S. V. Sprogis. Fortran for MKP (in Russian). *Programmirovaniye (Programming)*, September 1991.

[AK87] J. R. Allen and K. Kennedy. Automatic translation of Fortran programs to vector form. *ACM Transactions on Programming Languages and Systems*, 9(4):491–542, October 1987.

[Ame78] American National Standards Institute X3J3 Comittee. *FORTRAN-77*, 1978.

[Ame90] American National Standards Institute X3J3 Comittee. *FORTRAN-90*, 1990.

[Ban88] U. Banerjee. *Dependence Analysis for Supercomputing*. Kluwer Academic Publishers, Boston, 1988.

[BC86] M. Burke and R. Cytron. Interprocedural dependence analysis and parallelization. In *Proc. of the SIGPLAN '86 Symposium on Compiler Construction*, July 1986.

[DE73] G. Dantzig and B.C. Eaves. Fourier-Motzkin elimination and its dual. *Journal of Combinatorial Theory*, A(14):288–297, July 1973.

[DMM88] T. I. Daniyarhodzhayev, V. Yu. Maslov, and I. V. Mashechkin. Multilanguage programming system intermediate language (in Russian). In *Arhitektura EVM i Chislenniye Metodi (Computer Architecture and Numerical Methods)*. Computational Mathematics Division, USSR Academy of Sciences, 1988.

[GKT91] G. Goff, K. Kennedy, and C. Tseng. Practical dependence testing. In *ACM SIGPLAN '91 Conference on Programming Languages Design and Implementation*, 1991.

[IJT90] F. Irigoin, P. Jouvelot, and R. Triolet. Overview of the PIPS project. In *Proceedings of the International Workshop on Compilers for Parallel Computers*, Paris, France, November 1990.

[KKP+81] D. J. Kuck, R. H. Kuhn, D. A. Padua, B. Leasure, and M. Wolfe. Dependence graphs and compiler optimizations. *Conference Record of the Eighth ACM Symposium on Principles of Programming Languages*, January 1981.

[KMT90] K. Kennedy, K. S. McKinley, and C. Tseng. Interactive parallel programming using the ParaScope Editor. Technical Report TR90-137, Dept. of Computer Science, Rice University, October 1990.

[Kus89] E. S. Kusikov. The algorithm for parallelizing iterative loops (in Russian). *Programmirovaniye (Programming)*, March 1989.

[Lam74] L. Lamport. The parallel execution of DO loops. *Communications of the ACM*, 17(2):83–93, February 1974.

[LC90] L.-C. Lu and M. Chen. New loop transformation techniques for massive parallelism. Technical Report YALEU/DCS/TR-833, Department of Computer Science, Yale University, October 1990.

[Li86] Kuo-Cheng Li. A note on the Vector C language. *SIGPLAN Notices*, 21(1), 1986.

[LYZ89] Z. Li, P. Yew, and C. Zhu. Data dependence analysis on multi-dimensional array references. In *International Conference on Supercomputing*, Crete, Greece, June 1989.

[Mas90] Vadim Yu. Maslov. Program vectorization in cross-translator system (in Russian). In *Smeshanniye Vichisleniya i Preobrazovaniya Program (Mixed Calculations and Program Transformations)*, Novosibirsk, USSR, 1990. Siberian Division of USSR Academy of Sciences.

[MHL91] Dror E. Maydan, John L. Hennesy, and Monica S. Lam. Efficient and exact data dependence analysis. In *ACM SIGPLAN '91 Conference on Programming Languages Design and Implementation*, June 1991.

[Mur71] Y. Muraoka. *Parallelism Exposure and Exploitation in Programs*. PhD thesis, Dept. of Computer Science, University of Illinois at Urbana-Champaign, February 1971.

[Por89] A. K. Porterfield. *Software Methods for Improvement of Cache Performance on Supercomputer Applications*. PhD thesis, Rice University, May 1989.

[Pug91] William Pugh. The Omega Test: a fast and practical integer programming algorithm for dependence analysis. In *Supercomputing '91*, October 1991.

[Sho81] R. Shostak. Deciding linear inequalities by computing loop residues. *ACM Journal*, 28(4):769–779, 1981.

[Tri85] R. Triolet. Interprocedural analysis for program restructuring with Parafrase. Technical Report CSRD Rpt. No. 538, Dept. of Computer Science, University of Illinois at Urbana-Champaign, December 1985.

[Voe91] V. V. Voevodin. *Mathematical Foundations of Parallel Computations (in Russian)*. Moscow University Publishing House, Moscow, 1991.

[WB87] M. Wolfe and U. Banerjee. Data dependence and its application to parallel processing. *International Journal of Parallel Programming*, 16(2):137–178, 1987.

[WL91] Michael E. Wolf and Monica S. Lam. A data locality optimizing algorithm. In *ACM SIGPLAN '91 Conference on Programming Languages Design and Implementation*, June 1991.

[Wol82] M. J. Wolfe. *Optimizing Supercompilers for Supercomputers*. PhD thesis, University of Illinois, October 1982.

Beyond Induction Variables

Michael Wolfe *
Oregon Graduate Institute of Science and Technology

Abstract

Induction variable detection is usually closely tied to the strength reduction optimization. This paper studies induction variable analysis from a different perspective, that of finding induction variables for data dependence analysis. While classical induction variable analysis techniques have been used successfully up to now, we have found a simple algorithm based on the the Static Single Assignment form of a program that finds all linear induction variables in a loop. Moreover, this algorithm is easily extended to find induction variables in multiple nested loops, to find nonlinear induction variables, and to classify other integer scalar assignments in loops, such as monotonic, periodic and wrap-around variables. Some of these other variables are now classified using ad hoc pattern recognition, while others are not analyzed by current compilers. Giving a unified approach improves the speed of compilers and allows a more general classification scheme. We also show how to use these variables in data dependence testing.

1 Introduction

In classical compiler analysis, induction variable recognition is inextricably linked to the *strength reduction* transformation; in fact, the two terms are sometimes used interchangeably. The most common candidates for strength reduction (and therefore the most important induction variable candidates) are array address calculations in inner loops.

*Supported in part by NSF Grant CCR-8906909 and by DARPA Grant MDA972-88-J-1004.

ACM SIGPLAN '92 PLDI-6/92/CA

Nowadays, many compilers now include advanced loop transformations (such as *loop distribution* and *loop interchanging*). These transformations have been proven to be useful (and are commercially used) for a wide variety of systems, ranging from high performance vector multiprocessor supercomputers down to uniprocessor workstations, where the transformations improve the cache utilization. These transformations require analysis of array subscripts to determine the data dependence relations in loops. Current methods to test and characterize data dependence relations for subscripted array references require the subscript expressions to be a linear combination of induction variables in the enclosing loops.

The long history of research into data dependence testing has found that many variables used in subscript expressions are not induction variables, but can be characterized as one of several special cases. Current compilers classify these variables using ad hoc pattern recognition algorithms. Many compilers do not include these recognition algorithms at all, ignoring potential optimization opportunities.

This paper gives a simple algorithm for finding linear induction expressions in nested loops. The strength of the algorithm is that it is fast and that it will also characterize other scalar integer variables in the loops, such as

- wrap-around variables,
- flip-flop variables,
- families of periodic variables,
- non-linear induction variables (polynomial and geometric), and
- monotonically increasing or decreasing variables.

Finally, we look at how to apply dependence tests for these new cases. Our algorithm is based on the Static Single Assignment form of the program.

2 Induction Variables and Static Single Assignment

An *induction variable* is typically defined in compiler texts as a variable whose value is systematically incremented or decremented by a constant value in a loop [ASU86, FL88]. This is sometimes broken into *basic induction variables, i.e.* variables which appear only in statements of the form:

```
       i = i0
L1:    loop
          :
          i = i + k
          :
       endloop
```

where k is a constant or loop invariant, and other induction variables, which are linear combinations of known induction variables. Many programming languages include a loop construct with an index variable that is defined to be an induction variable. One of the early improvements in induction variable analysis was to extend the definition of basic induction variables to the maximal set of variables which are assigned by simple expressions of the form:

```
i = j ± k
```

where j and k are invariants or induction variables (note j may be zero) [CK77, ACK81]. This allows mutually-defined induction variables, such as:

```
       j = n
L2:    loop
          :
          i = j + c
          :
          j = i + k
          :
       endloop
```

where c and k are invariants in the loop.

With each induction variable a compiler associates its initial value and its increment, or step. We represent this by a tuple $\langle l, i, s\rangle$, where l is the name of the loop, i is the initial value (represented symbolically if it cannot be determined) and s is the step. The examples here will number the loops; thus in the first example, i is a basic induction variable which can be described as $\langle L1, i0 + k, k\rangle$.

In nested loops, an induction variable in the inner loop may have an initial value or step that varies in the outer loop; they may even be induction variables in the outer loop:

```
       i = 0
L3:    loop
          i = i + 1
          j = i
L4:       loop
             j = j + i
          endloop
       endloop
```

Here, i is an induction variable $\langle L3, 1, 1\rangle$, while j is an induction variable $\langle L4, i+i, i\rangle$; even though the step of j varies in the outer loop, it is still a linear induction variable in the inner loop.

We define a *multiloop induction variable* as an induction variable in an inner loop with a step that is invariant in the outer loop, and an initial value that is an induction variable in the outer loop:

```
       i = 0
L5:    loop
          i = i + 2
          j = i
L6:       loop
             j = j + 1
          endloop
       endloop
```

Here, i=$\langle L5, 2, 2\rangle$, while j=$\langle L6, i + 1, 1\rangle$. We will represent such multiloop induction variables with nested tuples, so that j=$\langle L6, \langle L5, 3, 2\rangle, 1\rangle$.

2.1 The Static Single Assignment Form

Since the algorithm presented here is based on the Static Single Assignment (SSA) form, we briefly cover the main ideas behind SSA and show a quick example; readers familiar with Static Single Assignment can skip to the next section. The SSA form of a program can be considered as a sparse representation of *use-def chains.* The algorithms to convert a sequential program into SSA form are based upon the *Control Flow Graph* (CFG), which is a graph $G = \langle V, E, \mathit{Entry}, \mathit{Exit}\rangle$, where V is a set of nodes representing basic blocks in the program, E is a set of edges representing sequential control flow in the program and *Entry* and *Exit* are distinguished nodes representing the unique entry point into the program and the unique exit from the program respectively.

After a program has been converted into its SSA form, it has two key properties:

1. Every use of any variable in the program has exactly one *reaching definition*, and
2. at confluence points in the CFG, merge functions called ϕ-functions are introduced. A ϕ-function for a variable merges the values of the variable from distinct incoming control flow paths, and it has one argument for each control flow predecessor.

```
        (a)                    (b)

        j = n                  j1 = n1
L7:     loop            L7':   loop
                                 i2 = φ(i1,i3)
                                 j2 = φ(j1,j3)
          i = j + c              i3 = j2 + c1
          j = i + k              j3 = i3 + k1
        endloop                endloop
```

$$j_2 = \langle L7', n_1, c_1 + k_1 \rangle$$
$$i_3 = \langle L7', n_1 + c_1, c_1 + k_1 \rangle$$
$$j_3 = \langle L7', n_1 + c_1 + k_1, c_1 + k_1 \rangle$$

Figure 1: Example loop with SSA form.

The two key algorithms used to convert a program into SSA form are the *placement* of ϕ-functions to satisfy the second property, and the *renaming* of variables to satisfy the first property. Intuitively, a ϕ-function for variable `X` is placed at the first CFG vertex v where two distinct definitions of `X` reach; the ϕ-function itself counts as a new definition of `X`, and so the algorithm iterates. Once ϕ-functions are inserted, each variable generation is renamed to a unique name (here represented by subscripted names), and each use of a variable is replaced by the unique reaching SSA definition; ϕ-function arguments are renamed to the SSA name that reaches the corresponding control flow edge. The reader is encouraged to read the SSA paper [CFR+91] for more details on these algorithms, and [AWZ88, RWZ88, WZ91] for details on applications of the SSA form. An example of a loop with its SSA form is given in Figure 1; the SSA names that correspond to induction variables are shown.

3 The SSA Graph

As with previous related work, we assume the program is represented by a CFG, as explained earlier. Moreover, we assume that each basic block is represented by a linked list of tuples of the form

$$\langle op, left, right, ssalink \rangle$$

where *op* is the operation code, *left* and *right* are the two operands, and *ssalink* is used only for loads (and indexed stores, which are not discussed here) to indicate the single reaching SSA name for this variable. The operators available include those given in the table in Figure 2. Load and store operations have additional arguments describing the variable for which they apply.

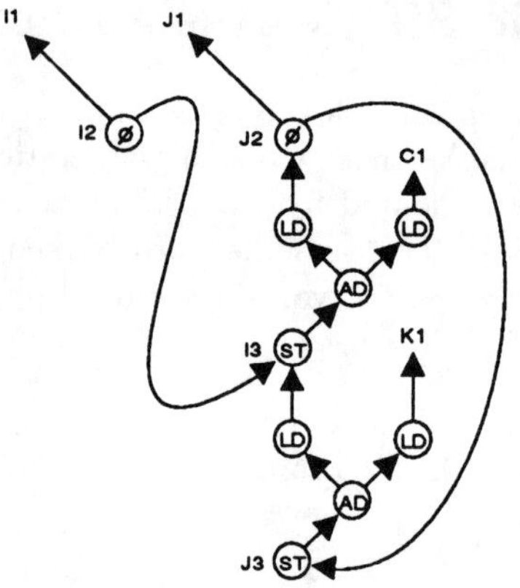

AD	addition
SB	subtraction
MP	multiplication
DV	division
EX	exponentiation
NG	negate
PH	ϕ-function
LD	load
ST	store
LT	literal

Figure 2: SSA graph for example program.

Indexed loads and stores are denoted by the presence of subscripts; since we are concerned only with scalars here, we will not elaborate.

The algorithm to analyze the program uses a graphical abstraction called the SSA graph. When analyzing a loop, the vertices in SSA graph are the tuples representing operations within that loop. The edges go from each tuple to the *left* and *right* operands as well as (for loads) to the *ssalink*. The SSA graph for the loop in Figure 1 is given in Figure 2. Note that the edges go from the operators to the *source* operands. Edges from the `LD` vertices correspond to the *ssalink* field.

3.1 Basic Linear Induction Variables

Our algorithm to find the induction variables is based on Tarjan's well-known algorithm to find strongly connected regions (SCRs) in directed graphs [Tar72]. The primary observation is that each basic linear induction variable will belong to a nontrivial SCR in the SSA graph. Each such SCR in the SSA graph must include a loop-header ϕ-function, since all values cycling around the loop must pass through a ϕ-function. The advantage to using Tarjan's algorithm is that when it identifies an SCR in the graph, it will have visited all the successors of the SCR; because of the way the edges are directed in our graph, when an SCR is identified, all the source operands reaching the SCR will already have been visited and identified. Our modifications to Tarjan's algorithm are to classify each SCR as an induction variable (or something else) at the time the SCR is identified; this information will then be immediately available for other SCRs which use the value of any operator in this SCR.

A simple method to identify an SCR in the SSA graph as a family of basic linear induction variables is to require that it satisfy the following simple constraints:

- The SCR contains only one ϕ-function (at the header of the loop).
- The SCR contains only addition and subtraction operators, and the right operand of the subtraction is not part of the SCR (no `i=n-i` assignments).
- The other operand of each addition or subtraction is loop invariant.
- Any loads and stores are to unsubscripted variables (*i.e.* load/store addresses are loop invariant).

There is one strongly connected region in the graph in Figure 2 which satisfies all these constraints, thus we know that it defines a family of basic linear induction variables. The *step* for all variables in the family is computed as the cumulative effect of all the increment and decrements in the SCR. The first member of the family is the left hand side of the ϕ-function; the initial value of this linear induction variable is the "other" argument to the ϕ-function, the reaching SSA name from outside the loop. Thus we can describe the linear induction variable j_2 as $\langle L7', j_1, c_1 + k_1\rangle$. The other members of the family differ only by a constant in the initial value. Often the initial value coming in from outside the loop can be evaluated and substituted, using an algorithm such as constant propagation [WZ91].

Actually, the rules for basic linear induction variables can be relaxed a bit. As long as the variable is incremented by the same amount on each path through the loop, the compiler can classify it as an induction variable. An example is shown in Figure 3. The only operators in the strongly connected region in the SSA graph are addition and ϕ-functions and the only values added are loop invariants. Starting with the loop-header ϕ-function, the compiler can determine the offset of each SSA variable from the value of the first ϕ-function for that iteration. As long as each ϕ-function within the loop (e.g., at `endif` statements) has the same offset for all arguments, the SCR defines a family of basic linear induction variables.

```
        (a)                        (b)

        i = 1                      i1 = 1
L8:     loop               L8':    loop
                                     i2 = φ(i1,i5)
          if exp then                if exp then
            i = i+2                    i3 = i2+2
          else                       else
            i = i+2                    i4 = i2+2
          endif                      endif
                                     i5 = φ(i3,i4)
        endloop                    endloop
```

$$i_2 = \langle L8, 1, 2\rangle$$
$$i_3 = \langle L8, 3, 2\rangle$$
$$i_4 = \langle L8, 3, 2\rangle$$
$$i_5 = \langle L8, 3, 2\rangle$$

Figure 3: Example loop with SSA form.

4 Beyond Induction Variables

4.1 Wrap-Around Variables

After examining many user programs to find how to improve their compilers, vendors and researchers found some particular patterns that appeared often enough to warrant special recognition and handling in a compiler. One of these is called a *wrap-around variable* [PW86], such as `im1` below:

```
       im1 = n
L9:    for i = 1 to n loop
           A(i) = A(im1) + ...
           im1 = i
       endloop
```

In all iterations but the first, the value of `im1` is equal to `i-1`; in the first iteration, however, `im1` has some other value, usually the index of the last element of the array `A`. Typically, `im1` is used to wrap the array `A` around a cylinder, hence the name. The standard compiler trick, once a wrap-around variable is found, is to peel off the first iteration of the loop and replace the wrap-around variable with the appropriate induction variable. Typically, wrap-around variables are found with a separate pattern matching analysis of the loops, following induction variable analysis.

In the SSA graph, a wrap-around variable is possible when a loop-header ϕ-function appears in a strongly connected region by itself. If the SSA name carried around the loop is an induction variable of some type, then the loop-header value is a first-order wrap-around value; that is, in all but the first iteration, its value

```
      i = 1                  i1 = 1
L10: loop              L10':loop
                             k2 = φ(k1,k3)
                             j2 = φ(j1,j3)
                             i2 = φ(i1,i3)
        k = j                k3 = j2
        j = i                j3 = i2
        i = i + 1            i3 = i2 + 1
      endloop              endloop
```

Figure 4: Wrap-around variable in SSA form.

will be an induction variable in the loop. This is the case with j_2 in Figure 4; as we will see in the next section, this will then define k_3 as a first-order wrap around variable. Wrap-around variables can be cascaded; any loop-header ϕ-function with one argument corresponding to a n-th order wrap-around variable is itself an $(n+1)$-th order wrap-around variable. Thus, k_2 is a second-order wrap-around variable. In general, any of the other known classes of variables described below could also be "wrapped around" the loop, meaning that the variable will have that property only after some fixed number of iterations around the loop. A wrap-around variable would then be identified by its order and the class of the variable that is wrapped around the loop.

If the initial value for the wrap-around variable fits the induction sequence, it may be more precisely identified as an induction variable. For instance, if the initial value of j_1 in loop L10 above had been 0, then j_2 could have been identified as the induction variable $\langle L10, 0, 1\rangle$.

4.2 Flip-Flop and Periodic Variables

A method used in some relaxation codes is the generation of "new" values for a matrix from the "old" values; one common way to program this is to add a dimension to the matrix with size 2, then to use `A(1,*,*)` as the "old" values and generate the new values into `A(2,*,*)`. For the next iteration of the relaxation, the program flips the definition of "old" and "new". Two programming constructs are typically used to implement this. The first switches the values of the two variables:

```
     j = 1
     jold = 2
L11: for iter = 1 to n loop
        ··· relaxation code ···
        jtemp = jold
        jold = j
        j = jtemp
     endloop
```

```
L13: loop        L13':loop
                      t2 = φ(t1,t3)
                      j2 = φ(j1,j3)
                      k2 = φ(k1,k3)
                      l2 = φ(l1,l3)
        t = j         t3 = j2
        j = k         j3 = k2
        k = l         k3 = l2
        l = t         l3 = t3
     endloop        endloop
```

Figure 5: Example periodic variable in SSA form.

Another method takes advantage of the equality `jold=3-j` to compute the new values of `jold` and `j`:

```
     j = 1
     jold = 2
L12: for iter = 1 to n loop
        ··· relaxation code ···
        j = 3-j
        jold = 3-jold
     endloop
```

Methods have been proposed to recognize the latter form of flip-flop variable, but are not typically implemented in commercial products. In either case, it is extremely important and useful for the compiler to realize that for any fixed value of `iter`, `j` and `jold` have different values, though it may not know what those values are.

A generalization of flip-flop variables is a tuple of variables whose values are rotated around the tuple, as around a ring; see Figure 5. Here, we see the tuple $\langle$j, k, l$\rangle$ which comprises a set of *periodic variables* with period 3. Again, it is useful to know that for any given iteration, no two of these variables will have the same value (assuming the initial values of these variables are distinct). Flip-flop variables as shown in loop L11 are then immediately recognized as periodic variables with period 2.

In the SSA graph, when a strongly connected region contains more than one loop-header ϕ-function and has no arithmetic and no other ϕ-functions, then it corresponds to a family of periodic variables. The *period* is equal to the number of loop-header ϕ-functions in the SCR. In the example in Figure 5, this number is three; note that t_2 does not appear in the strongly connected region with the other variables. It is important to note that the compiler will need to determine that the initial values for the periodic variables are distinct in order to take advantage of the periodicity for data dependence testing; these initial values are easily found from the "other" arguments to the loop-header ϕ-functions in the SCR.

4.3 Non-Linear Induction Variables

The classical definition of an induction variable is that it follows a linear sequence of values. With little additional effort, we can also find polynomial and geometric series. In the program below the various induction variables are given in the table on the right:

```
          j = 1
          k = 1
          l = 1
     L14: for i = 1 to n loop
            j = j + i
            k = k + j + 1
            l = l * 2 + 1
          endloop
```

variable	sequence	closed form
i	$1,2,3,4,\ldots$	$i = \langle L14,1,1\rangle$
j	$2,4,7,11,\ldots$	$(h^2+3h+4)/2$
k	$4,9,17,29,\ldots$	$(h^3+6h^2+23h+24)/6$
l	$3,7,15,31,\ldots$	$2^{h+2}-1$

where h is a basic loop counter that starts at zero ($h = \langle L14,0,1\rangle$). Incrementing a variable by a polynomial induction variable produces an induction variable of the next higher order. In general, finding the closed form for polynomial and geometric induction variables is simplified since (a) the nonzero coefficients can always be identified by the compiler, and (b) the coefficients will always be rational. We use simple matrix inversion with rational arithmetic to find the coefficients, as shown below. Finding polynomial induction variables for strength reduction may not be so interesting, since the operation is already only addition. From the point of view of data dependence, there are currently few dependence testing algorithms that can take advantage of this additional knowledge. We will revisit this point briefly in a later section. It is interesting to note that the second form of flip-flop variable described above can be recognized as a geometric induction variable with base -1; in loop L12 at iteration i, the value assigned to variable j is $-1^i + 3 \times \sum_{k=0}^{i-1} -1^k$.

In the SSA graph, when Tarjan's algorithm has found a strongly connected region that fails one of the conditions of a linear induction variable, the SCR can be analyzed to see if it is an identifiable non-linear induction variable. In all cases analyzed here, the SCR must include a single ϕ-function at the loop header. The key is to classify the cumulative effect of all the operations in the SCR on the value reaching the loop-header ϕ-function relative to the value of that ϕ-function in the previous iteration.

- If the effect is to increment the loop-header value by a linear induction variable, the SCR is a family of polynomial induction variables of second order.
- If the effect is to increment the value by a polynomial induction variable of order n, this SCR is a family of polynomial induction variables of order $n+1$.
- If the cumulative effect is to multiply the loop-header value by a known integer, the SCR corresponds to a family of geometric induction variables.
- If the cumulative effect is to subtract the loop-header value from a loop invariant, the SCR corresponds to a flip-flop variable, equivalent to a periodic variable of period two.

This could be taken to extreme, such as recognizing that multiplying by a linear induction variable generates a factorial sequence. A polynomial induction variable can be represented in the compiler by extending the linear induction variable tuple to include the coefficients of each power of the basic loop counter; thus we write $\langle l, i, s_1, s_2, \ldots, s_m\rangle$ represents an induction variable for loop l whose value on the first iteration is i, and whose value on iteration h is $i + \sum_{k=1}^{m} s_k h^k$, or letting $s_0 = i$, $\sum_{k=0}^{m} s_k h^k$. A compiler can find the coefficients s_k by matrix inversion. The number of unknowns (the values of s_k) is equal to $m+1$, where m is the order of the polynomial; since m can be determined by the compiler, the number of unknowns is fixed. By inverting the matrix of elements

$$a_{ij} = i^j,\ 0 \le i \le m,\ 0 \le j \le m$$

and multiplying the inverse by the computed (perhaps symbolic) first k values of the induction variable, the coefficients can be found. Since the entries of the matrix a_{ij} are all integer, the inverse will have only rational entries. For instance, in loop L14 above, since k is a third-order polynomial induction variable, the corresponding matrix is:

$$A = \begin{bmatrix} 1 & 0 & 0 & 0 \\ 1 & 1 & 1 & 1 \\ 1 & 2 & 4 & 8 \\ 1 & 3 & 9 & 27 \end{bmatrix}$$

The inverse of this matrix is:

$$A^{-1} = \frac{1}{6}\begin{bmatrix} 6 & 0 & 0 & 0 \\ -11 & 18 & -9 & 2 \\ 6 & -15 & 12 & -3 \\ -1 & 3 & -3 & 1 \end{bmatrix}$$

which, when multiplied by the computed first four values of k gives the coefficients of the closed form of the induction variable:

$$A^{-1}\left[\, 4 \;\; 9 \;\; 17 \;\; 29 \,\right]^T = \left[\, 4 \;\; \tfrac{23}{6} \;\; 1 \;\; \tfrac{1}{6} \,\right]^T$$

A geometric induction variable has both geometric and polynomial terms; we represent this by the polynomial coefficients followed by the coefficients of each exponential term. We write

$$\langle\langle l, s_0, s_1, \ldots, s_m\rangle, g_p, g_{p+1}, \ldots, g_q\rangle$$

to represent the induction variable for loop l with initial value s_0, and whose value on iteration h is

$$\sum_{k=0}^{m} s_k h^k + \sum_{k=p}^{q} g_k k^h$$

A matrix inversion technique to find the coefficients also applies. A basic geometric induction variable will have only a single exponential term (though it may have any number of polynomial terms); if the geometric base is g, the matrix to be inverted is:

$$a_{ij} = \begin{cases} i^j, & 0 \le i \le m+1,\ 0 \le j \le m \\ g^i, & 0 \le i \le m+1,\ j = m+1 \end{cases}$$

Suppose we had an assignment in loop L14 above of the form `m=3*m+2*i+1` (with initial value `m=0`); the geometric base of this induction variable is 3, while the polynomial part would seem to have a quadratic term (since a linear induction variable is being added). Thus, the matrix to be inverted is:

$$\begin{bmatrix} 1 & 0 & 0 & 1 \\ 1 & 1 & 1 & 3 \\ 1 & 2 & 4 & 9 \\ 1 & 3 & 9 & 27 \end{bmatrix}$$

The inverted matrix, multiplied by the first four computed values, is:

$$\frac{1}{8}\begin{bmatrix} 9 & -3 & 3 & -1 \\ -12 & 16 & -4 & 0 \\ 6 & -14 & 10 & -2 \\ -1 & 3 & -3 & 1 \end{bmatrix}\begin{bmatrix} 3 \\ 14 \\ 49 \\ 156 \end{bmatrix} = \begin{bmatrix} -3 \\ -1 \\ 0 \\ 6 \end{bmatrix}$$

Thus, `m` can be described by $m = 6 \times 3^h - h - 3$ (note there is no quadratic term after all).

4.4 Monotonic Variables

Variables that are conditionally incremented or decremented can not generally be recognized as induction variables. However, they often do exhibit useful properties. A common pattern is to increment a variable conditionally, for instance, to pack certain values from one vector to another:

```
     k = 0
L15: for i = 1 to n loop
          if A(i) > 0 then
               k = k + 1
               B(k) = A(i)
          endif
     endloop
```

```
L16: loop                    L16':loop
                                   k2 = φ(k1,k5)
        if exp then                if exp then
           k = k+1                    k3 = k2+1
        else                       else
           k = k+2                    k4 = k2+2
        endif                      endif
     endloop                       k5 = φ(k3,k4)
                                endloop
```

Figure 6: Example monotonic variable in SSA form.

Some compilers recognize this whole pattern as a pack operation, as might be converted into the Fortran-90 PACK intrinsic function. Our approach is to realize that within the range of the conditional, **k** will never have the same value for two different iterations of the loop. Moreover, even outside the range of the conditional, the compiler can determine that the value of **k** will never decrease for subsequent iterations; we say that **k** is *monotonically increasing.*

Sometimes our approach can discover stronger relations. If the variable is incremented for each iteration, even though it is not always incremented by the same value, we can say that the variable is *monotonically strictly increasing,* as in Figure 6. Even though we have no way to determine a closed form for **k** here, we will see that this information can be used effectively in dependence analysis.

In the SSA graph, a monotonic variable appears as a strongly connected region that contains ϕ-functions other than at the loop-header, perhaps at an **endif**, as in Figure 6. Since the arguments to the ϕ-function at the **endif** assigning k_5 have have different offsets from the loop-entry value k_2, namely $k_2 + 1$ and $k_2 + 2$, the SCR does not correspond to a family of induction variables. Nonetheless, it is easy to realize that regardless of the path through the loop, the value of **k** is always monotonically increasing. Regardless of the operations in the SCR, if the compiler can determine that the values being merged at a ϕ-function are always larger than the loop-header value, it can classify all variables in the SCR as monotonic. Multiply operations can also be allowed, such as `2*i+1` as long as the initial value of `i` is known. If the value of a monotonic variable is *always* changed in the loop, then it can be called *strictly monotonic.* We will see how this distinction is used in dependence testing.

5 Other Concerns

5.1 Non-Basic Induction Variables

Basic induction variables (linear and nonlinear) and monotonic and periodic variables arise from nontrivial strongly connected regions (cycles) in the SSA graph. Variables which are functions of these variables must also be classified. To reiterate, one of the advantages of using Tarjan's algorithm is that when it comes time to classify a non-basic variable, all its arguments will have been already visited and classified. The result of each type of operation depends on how its operands have been classified.

The rules for classifying some operators are simple. For a load instruction, if the address is not invariant (such as indexed arrays, or computed pointer dereferencing) the type is unknown; if the address is invariant, and the *ssalink* of the load comes from outside the loop, the load is classified as invariant; otherwise, the load takes the classification of the *ssalink*. A store always takes the classification of the value being stored. A literal is always invariant.

The classification of arithmetic operators can be much more complex. The simple cases, adding or multiplying an invariant to an induction variable, etc., are easily handled. A generalized induction variable added to another induction variable will always be an induction variable, but multiplication may not be. For instance, multiplying $(2^i + 1)$ by $(3^i - 5)$ results in the geometric induction variable $(6^i + 3^i - 5 \times 2^i - 5)$, but multiplying $(2^i + i)$ by $(3^i - 2i)$ results in the expression $(6^i + i3^i - i2^{i+1} - 2i^2)$, which does not match the form of a generalized induction variable; it may, however, be classified as monotonic. In general the compiler needs an algebra of types and operators; space prevents a complete table of the algebra here, but the reader can come up with obvious examples (adding wrap around variables to get another wrap around variable, adding a monotonic variable to an induction variable to get another monotonic variable, etc.).

5.2 Trip Counts

The trip count of a loop can often be determined by finding the sequence of values used for the exit condition. If there is a single loop exit and the condition is an integer comparison, the compiler can convert the comparison into the form:

    if(left ≤ right) exit the loop

using the table below. If the loop conditional expression is as given on the left and the true branch exits the loop, it can be converted to the expression in the middle column (where we use rules of integer arithmetic to convert $\leq$ to $<$); if the false branch exits the loop, then the condition must first be negated, so we get the expression in the right column below:

condition	exit	stay in
$a < b$	$a \leq b - 1$	$b \leq a$
$a \leq b$	$a \leq b$	$b \leq a - 1$
$a > b$	$b \leq a - 1$	$a \leq b$
$a \geq b$	$b \leq a$	$a \leq b - 1$

The compiler can treat the comparison as a subtraction, and try to classify it as a linear induction sequence $\langle L, i, s\rangle$. The trip count of the loop (that is, the number of times the loop exit condition chooses to stay in the loop) can be computed as

$$tripcount = \begin{cases} 0 & \text{if } i \leq 0 \\ \lceil i/(-s) \rceil & \text{if } i > 0 \text{ and } s < 0 \\ \infty & \text{if } i > 0 \text{ and } s \geq 0 \end{cases}$$

If the trip count can be found, the loop is called a *countable* loop. This is necessary below for handling multi-level induction variables. When a loop has multiple exits, the compiler may not be able to determine the exact number of iterations, but it may be able to find a maximum trip count; this information is useful for dependence testing, to place bounds on the solution space.

Note that some code in the loop above the exit test may have been executed even if the trip count is zero; in general, if the trip count is tc, some code above the exit test will have been executed $tc + 1$ times while code below the exit test can have only been executed tc times. In single exit loops (where this is important), any unconditional code in the loop that is not *dominated* by the exit test will be executed one more iteration than unconditional code below the exit.

5.3 Nested Induction Variables

When dealing with nested loops, induction variable recognition proceeds from the inner loops outward. While processing any loop, any SSA links to code outside the loop are treated as loop invariant (for the purposes of Tarjan's algorithm and induction variable classification); these links may be chased down to find constant values. When an inner loop is classified as a countable loop, the cumulative effect of the execution of the loop on all induction variables in the loop can be expressed in closed form. Given a trip count tc, an induction variable $\langle L, i, s\rangle$ will end up with the value $i + tc \times s$, if all the increments are below the exit condition. By our definition of trip count, however, some induction variable increments may have been above the loop exit; the correct general formula is $i + tc \times s + s_{early}$, where s_{early} is the cumulative effect of any increment statements that can happen before the loop exits.

When the inner loop is processed, the compiler can construct an exit value for the induction variables, as

```
        k1 = 0
L17: loop
          k2 = φ(k1,k5)
          i1 = 1
L18:      loop
               k3 = φ(k2,k4)
               i2 = φ(i1,i3)
               k4 = k3 + 2
               if i2 > 100 exit
               i3 = i2 + 1
          endloop
          k5 = k4 + 2
     endloop
```

Figure 7: Nested induction variables.

```
        k1 = 0
L17':loop
          k2 = φ(k1,k5)
          i1 = 1
L18':     loop
               k3 = φ(k2,k4)
               i2 = φ(i1,i3)
               k4 = k3 + 2
               if i2 > 100 exit
               i3 = i2 + 1
          endloop
          k6 = k2 + 101*2
          i4 = i1 + 100*1
          k5 = k6 + 2
     endloop
```

Figure 8: After processing inner loop induction variables.

shown in Figures 7 and 8. This value can be assigned to a new variable, and all references outside this inner loop to the exit value are changed to refer to the new variable. In this example, the induction variables for the inner loop are:

$$\begin{aligned} k_3 &= \langle L18, k_2, 2\rangle \\ k_4 &= \langle L18, k_2+2, 2\rangle \\ i_2 &= \langle L18, 1, 1\rangle \\ i_3 &= \langle L18, 2, 1\rangle \end{aligned}$$

where i_1 is resolved to its constant value. The exit condition is converted to $100 \leq i_2 - 1$, which is treated as the induction expression $100-(i_2-1)$ or $\langle L18, 100, -1\rangle$; thus the trip count is 100. To compute the exit value of the induction variables **k** and **i**, the compiler notices that the k_4 statement preceeds the exit condition, so its increment value must be counted one extra time, and the k_6 and i_4 statements are added.

Now the induction variables for the outer loop can be found; if there are any remaining SSA links to variables in inner loops, these must correspond to non-induction variables or induction variables for which the exit value is unknown; in either case, the value can be treated as an unknown without tracing further. In this example, the outer loop has the induction variables:

$$\begin{aligned} k_2 &= \langle L17, 0, 204\rangle \\ k_6 &= \langle L17, 202, 204\rangle \\ k_5 &= \langle L17, 204, 204\rangle \end{aligned}$$

When the outer loops have all been processed, an outer-to-inner loop traversal can replace any outer loop induction variable expressions in inner loop induction variable initial values, if desired, changing k_3 and k_4 to:

```
      j1 = 0
L19: for i = 1 to n loop
        j2 = φ(j1,j4)
        j3 = j2 + 1
L20:    for k = 1 to i loop
           j4 = φ(j3,j5)
           j5 = j4 + 1
        endloop
     endloop
```

Figure 9: Generalized induction variable from triangular inner loop.

$$\begin{aligned} k_3 &= \langle L18, \langle L17, 0, 204\rangle, 2\rangle \\ k_4 &= \langle L18, \langle L17, 2, 204\rangle, 2\rangle \end{aligned}$$

It is interesting to note that the case of generalized induction variables found to be so difficult in [EHLP92] is simple in this framework. Their given example has a doubly nested loop where the inner loop is *triangular*, that is, its upper limit depends on the outer loop index variable, as in Figure 9. Our method will process the inner loop, recognizing j_4 and j_5 as linear induction variables in that loop, with the trip count of that loop equal to a variable computed in the outer loop. The exit value of **j** will be computed as $j_6 = j_3 + i \times 1$, and j_4 will be replaced by j_6 in the assignment to j_2. When processing the outer loop, **i** will be recognized as a linear induction variable, while j_2, j_3 and j_6 will be recognized as a family of quadratic induction variables:

```
        k1 = 0
L15':for i = 1 to n loop
        k2 = φ(k1,k4)
        F(k2) = A(i)
        if A(i) > 0 then
            C(k2) = D(i)
            k3 = k2 + 1
            B(k3) = A(i)
            E(i) = B(k3)
        endif
        k4 = φ(k3,k2)
        G(i) = F(k4)
     endloop
```

Figure 10: Mixed monotonic and strictly monotonic variable

$$j_2 = \langle L19, 0, \frac{3}{2}, \frac{1}{2} \rangle$$

$$j_3 = \langle L19, 1, \frac{3}{2}, \frac{1}{2} \rangle$$

$$j_6 = \langle L19, 2, \frac{5}{2}, \frac{1}{2} \rangle$$

When the value for j_3 is substituted into the induction representations for the inner loop, we get:

$$j_4 = \langle L20, \langle L19, 1, \frac{3}{2}, \frac{1}{2} \rangle, 1 \rangle$$

$$j_5 = \langle L20, \langle L19, 2, \frac{3}{2}, \frac{1}{2} \rangle, 1 \rangle$$

5.4 Loop Exit and Conditional Gates

When processing nested induction variables, our algorithm inserted a new assignment to a new SSA name (*e.g.* k_6 in Figure 8). Proper engineering can make this a low-cost insertion, but it would have been nice if there had already been an SSA name to distinguish the value of the variable upon loop exit. The loop exit η gating function used in the Program Dependence Web [BMO90] serves exactly this purpose. While we don't feel we need all the generality of the PDW, we are investigating adding some of its elements to the factored use-def chains used in our compiler internal representation.

In one other place the SSA representation is less precise than we would like. The SSA form of the monotonic variable in loop L15 (where we add a few more uses of k is shown in Figure 10. In this example, the compiler can easily find the SCR in the SSA graph, including the assignments to $\{k_2, k_3, k_4\}$. The loop entry value is k_2, and the ϕ-function for k_4 has two different offsets, k_2 and $k_2 + 1$; thus this is not a linear induction variable. However, all variables in the SCR are monotonically increasing. Even stronger, we can say that k_3 is monotonically *strictly* increasing, since if the k_3 assignment occurs more than once, it must assign a larger value each time. Thus, the dependence due to the assignment and reuse of array `B` will have dependence direction (=) (see discussion in the next section); on the other hand, since k_2 and k_4 are only monotonic, the flow dependence due to array `F` has dependence direction ($\leq$) (and there is an anti-dependence with direction (<)). However, we would also like to notice and take advantage of the fact that within the body of the conditional statement (*e.g.* at the assignment to array `C`), k_2 also must be strictly monotonic. One way to detect this would be to notice that any uses of k_2 in this region are *post-dominated* by the strictly monotonic assignment. Another way would be to again use elements of the Program Dependence Web, in this case to add a *switch* at the conditional; this would essentially give a unique name for each value entering a new control region.

6 Use in Dependence Testing

The driving force for classifying the variables in loops as shown in this paper is to improve the generality of dependence testing in loops, generating more precise dependence graphs and allowing more aggressive optimizations. Dependence testing for linear induction variables is generally well-covered in the literature [AK87, BCKT79, GKT91, MHL91]. Banerjee presents some algorithms for handling polynomial induction variables in his MS thesis [Ban76]. After a brief review, we focus on dependence with wrap-around variables, monotonic variables and periodic variables.

The algorithm used to classify variables will actually classify each subexpression as one of the generalized variable types. Thus, each subscript expression will be classified as an induction expression, monotonic expression, etc. Dependence testing in such a system involves constructing a dependence equation from the expressions. For instance, in the program:

```
       i = 0
       j = 3
L21: loop
         i = i + 1
         A(i) = A(j-1)
         j = j + 2
     endloop
```

the left hand side subscript will be classified as the linear induction expression $\langle L21, 1, 1 \rangle$, while the right hand subscript will be classified as $\langle L21, 2, 2 \rangle$. From this, the compiler can immediately read off the coefficients to get the dependence equation:

$$1i' + 1 = 2i'' + 2$$

The dependence decision algorithm will determine whether there are integer values of the free variables i', i'' that solve the dependence equation and lie within the loop limits. Often, dependence distance or direction information can be found, determining that the solution only occurs when (for instance) $i'' - i' = 1$ or $i' < i''$ [WB87]. This information is critical to many optimization algorithms.

In the case where one of the expressions has the wrap-around attribute, the same dependence equation can be constructed and solved, but the dependence relation should be flagged as holding only after k iterations, the order of the wrap-around variable. This allows the compiler to decide whether the loop can be optimized before going through the headache of peeling off the first k iterations of the loop.

If the subscript expressions are members of the same periodic variable family, such as:

```
     j = 1
     k = 2
     l = 3
L22: loop
        A(2*j) = A(2*k)
        temp = j
        j = k
        k = l
        l = temp
     endloop
```

the dependence equation should be constructed in terms of j and k:

$$2j = 2k$$

The dependence solvers determine whether there are integer values of j and k such that the dependence equation has a solution, and may determine distance or direction information in terms of j and k. What we need is to translate that distance or direction information into the appropriate information in terms of the loop iteration numbers. Suppose, as in this case, the decision algorithm determines that there is a solution when $j = k$. Let j_h refer to the value of j during iteration h. Because of the periodic nature of the variables, the compiler also knows that $j_{h'} = k_{h''}$ only when $h' \neq h''$. Thus, the $=$ direction for the dependence equation translates into a $\neq$ direction for the dependence relation; this is exactly the information needed to optimize the relaxation codes described earlier.

For monotonic variables, a similar situation occurs. The dependence equation is constructed in terms of the monotonic variables; if m is monotonic increasing, and the dependence equation is

$$2m' = 2m''$$

the dependence solver will find that there is dependence only when $m' = m''$. Now the compiler needs to translate this into direction information for the loop; since m is monotonic, $m_{h'} = m_{h''}$ can occur when $h' = h''$ or when $h' < h''$ (since m may not be incremented every iteration). Similar cases hold for strictly monotonic and monotonic decreasing variables.

6.1 Loop Normalization

Loop normalization is a linear transformation on the index set of a **for** loop to change the sequence of values of the loop variable to start at zero (or one) with a step of one; thus the loop:

```
for i = 2 to 11 by 3 loop
    ... A(i) ...
```

will be changed to:

```
for i = 0 to (11-2)/3 loop
    ... A(i*3+2) ...
```

This transformation was initially designed to simplify the formulation of data dependence testing algorithms [BCKT79]. Since normalization always puts the loop lower limits into subscript expressions, it can complicate life for simple dependence analyzers when the lower limit contains other variables, as shown by the work on Parafrase [SLY90]. For this reason, and because it can adversely affect the kinds of transformations allowed in programs (such as loop interchanging), this author has in the past argued against implementing loop normalization [Wol86]. It is interesting to note that this formulation of induction variables essentially normalizes all loops. One example used to argue against normalization is:

```
L23: for i = 1 to n loop
L24:     for j = i+1 to n loop
            A(i,j) = A(i-1,j)
```

Modern dependence analysis applied to this example will typically find a dependence *distance vector*, with one distance computed for each nested loop; see the tons of literature on this subject for further details [AK87, BCKT79, GKT91, MHL91]. In this case, the distance vector is $(1, 0)$, meaning distance one in the i loop and distance zero in the j loop. Normalizing the inner loop (to a lower limit of one) changes it to:

```
L23':for i = 1 to n loop
L24':    for j = 1 to n-i loop
            A(i,j+i) = A(i-1,j+i)
```

The computation in the loop hasn't changed, but the dependence distance vector has; now the distance vector is $(1, -1)$. While this may seem innocuous, some important transformations (such as loop interchanging) are prevented by this case.

In our framework, however, the shape of the loop iteration space is not part of the induction variable recognition strategy; in fact, *both* examples above will have the same results after induction variable recognition:

```
L23: for i = ··· loop
L24:     for j = ··· loop
             A(⟨L23,1,1⟩,⟨L24,⟨L23,2,1⟩,1⟩)
               = A(⟨L23,0,1,⟨L24,⟨L23,2,1⟩,1⟩)
```

Intuitively, this strategy implicitly normalizes all induction variables with respect to a simple loop counter with initial value zero and step one (recall $h = \langle L14, 0, 1\rangle$). One strategy would be to keep the induction expression corresponding to the lower loop limits and factor these into the dependence equations. More likely, use of this induction variable representation will force compilers to abandon the *direction vector* dependence representation, which has been criticized by many researchers as too coarse [IT88]. A direction vector encodes the *sign* of the elements of the distance vector; while less precise in general, it can be used effectively when the distance vector is not constant. It may also force compilers to implement *loop skewing* and *loop interchanging* as a single transformation [Wol86]; this has been formulated in the past as a linear transformation on the index set [KMW67], and is currently in vogue as "unimodular transformations" [WL91, Ban91].

7 Summary and Conclusions

We have shown a fast and simple algorithm for classifying all induction variables in a loop; this algorithm is linear in the size of the SSA graph, not iterative. The algorithm is a somewhat obvious application of Tarjan's SCR algorithm on the SSA graph. It has several advantages, such as finding basic and non-basic induction variables in one pass. While usually used for applying strength reduction, we focus here on induction variable detection for dependence testing.

More importantly, we use the same algorithm to classify many different types of integer variables in loops, including polynomial and geometric induction variables, as well as flip-flop, periodic, wrap-around and monotonic variables. While some of these cases have been classified before, they were done by special case analysis instead of in a unified framework.

We have shown that the classification scheme is efficient, and how to use this information in data dependence testing. We have implemented the part of this algorithm that detects linear induction variables in our research compiler, and are adding the full algorithm at this time.

References

[ACK81] F. E. Allen, John Cocke, and Ken Kennedy. Reduction of operator strength. In Steven S. Muchnick and Neil D. Jones, editors, *Program Flow Analysis: Theory and Applications*, pages 79–101. Prentice-Hall, 1981.

[AK87] John R. Allen and Ken Kennedy. Automatic translation of Fortran programs to vector form. *ACM Trans. on Programming Languages and Systems*, 9(4):491–542, October 1987.

[ASU86] A. V. Aho, R. Sethi, and J. D. Ullman. *Compilers: Principles, Techniques, and Tools*. Addison-Wesley, Reading, MA, 1986.

[AWZ88] B. Alpern, M.N. Wegman, and F.K. Zadeck. Detecting equality of variables in programs. In *Conf. Record 15th Annual ACM Symp. Principles of Programming Languages* [POP88], pages 1–11.

[Ban76] Utpal Banerjee. Data dependence in ordinary programs. M.S. thesis UIUCDCS-R-76-837, Univ. Illinois, Dept. Computer Science, November 1976.

[Ban91] Utpal Banerjee. Unimodular transformations of double loops. In Nicolau et al. [NGGP91], pages 192–219.

[BCKT79] Utpal Banerjee, Shyh-Ching Chen, David J. Kuck, and Ross A. Towle. Time and parallel processor bounds for Fortran-like loops. *IEEE Trans. on Computers*, C-28(9):660–670, September 1979.

[BMO90] Robert A. Ballance, Arthur B. Maccabe, and Karl J. Ottenstein. The program dependence web: A representation supporting control-, data-, and demand-driven interpretation of imperative languages. In *Proc. ACM SIGPLAN '90 Conf. on Programming Language Design and Implementation*, pages 257–271, White Plains, NY, June 1990.

[CFR+91] Ron Cytron, Jeanne Ferrante, Barry K. Rosen, Mark N. Wegman, and F. Kenneth

Zadeck. Efficiently computing static single assignment form and the control dependence graph. *ACM Trans. on Programming Languages and Systems*, 13(4):451–490, October 1991.

[CK77] John Cocke and Ken Kennedy. An algorithm for reduction of operator strength. *Communications ACM*, 20(11):850–856, November 1977.

[EHLP92] Rudolf Eigenmann, Jay Hoeflinger, Zhiyuan Li, and David Padua. Experience in the automatic parallelization of four Perfect benchmark programs. In Utpal Banerjee, David Gelernter, Alexandru Nicolau, and David A. Padua, editors, *Languages and Compilers for Parallel Computing*. Springer-Verlag, 1992. (to appear).

[FL88] Charles N. Fischer and Richard J. LeBlanc, Jr. *Crafting a Compiler*. Benjamin-Cummings, Menlo Park, CA, 1988.

[GKT91] Gina Goff, Ken Kennedy, and Chau-Wen Tseng. Practical dependence testing. In *Proc. ACM SIGPLAN '91 Conference on Programming Language Design and Implementation* [SIG91], pages 15–29.

[IT88] François Irigoin and Rémi Triolet. Supernode partitioning. In *Conf. Record 15th Annual ACM Symp. Principles of Programming Languages* [POP88], pages 319–329.

[KMW67] Richard M. Karp, Raymond E. Miller, and Shmuel Winograd. The organization of computations for uniform recurrence equations. *J. ACM*, 14(3):563–590, July 1967.

[MHL91] Dror E. Maydan, John L. Hennessy, and Monica S. Lam. Efficient and exact data dependence analysis. In *Proc. ACM SIGPLAN '91 Conference on Programming Language Design and Implementation* [SIG91], pages 1–14.

[NGGP91] Alexandru Nicolau, David Gelernter, Thomas Gross, and David Padua, editors. *Advances in Languages and Compilers for Parallel Computing*. Research Monographs in Parallel and Distributed Computing. MIT Press, Boston, 1991.

[POP88] *Conf. Record 15th Annual ACM Symp. Principles of Programming Languages*, San Diego, CA, January 1988.

[PW86] David A. Padua and Michael Wolfe. Advanced compiler optimizations for supercomputers. *Communications ACM*, 29(12):1184–1201, December 1986.

[RWZ88] B.K. Rosen, M.N. Wegman, and F.K. Zadeck. Global value numbers and redundant computations. In *Conf. Record 15th Annual ACM Symp. Principles of Programming Languages* [POP88], pages 12–27.

[SIG91] *Proc. ACM SIGPLAN '91 Conference on Programming Language Design and Implementation*, Toronto, June 1991.

[SLY90] Zhiyu Shen, Zhiyuan Li, and Pen-Chung Yew. An empirical study of Fortran programs for parallelizing compilers. *IEEE Trans. Parallel and Distributed Systems*, 1(3):356–364, July 1990.

[Tar72] R. Tarjan. Depth-first search and linear graph algorithms. *SIAM J. Comput.*, 1(2):146–160, June 1972.

[WB87] Michael Wolfe and Utpal Banerjee. Data dependence and its application to parallel processing. *International J. Parallel Programming*, 16(2):137–178, April 1987.

[WL91] Michael E. Wolf and Monica S. Lam. An algorithmic approach to compound loop transformations. In Nicolau et al. [NGGP91], pages 243–259.

[Wol86] Michael Wolfe. Loop skewing: The wavefront method revisited. *International J. Parallel Programming*, 15(4):279–294, August 1986.

[WZ91] Mark N. Wegman and F. Kenneth Zadeck. Constant propagation with conditional branches. *ACM Trans. on Programming Languages and Systems*, 13(2):181–210, April 1991.

A General Framework for Iteration-Reordering Loop Transformations (Technical Summary)

Vivek Sarkar
IBM Palo Alto Scientific Center
1530 Page Mill Road
Palo Alto, CA 94304
(vivek@paloalto.vnet.ibm.com)

Radhika Thekkath *
Dept. of Comp. Science and Eng. FR-35
University of Washington
Seattle, WA 98195
(radhika@cs.washington.edu)

Abstract

This paper describes a general framework for representing iteration-reordering transformations. These transformations can be both matrix-based and non-matrix-based. Transformations are defined by rules for mapping dependence vectors, rules for mapping loop bound expressions, and rules for creating new initialization statements. The framework is extensible, and can be used to represent any iteration-reordering transformation. Mapping rules for several common transformations are included in the paper.

1 Introduction

Iteration-reordering transformations are a special class of program transformations that only change the execution order of loop iterations in a perfect loop nest without changing the contents of the loop body. Iteration-reordering transformations are used extensively by restructuring compilers for optimizing vector execution, parallel execution, and data locality. Prior work on iteration-reordering loop transformations can mainly be classified as either a) proposing new iteration-reordering transformations, or b) developing a unified system for matrix-based iteration-reordering transformations (also known as unimodular transformations). Several iteration-reordering transformations have been proposed over the years (e.g. interchange, reversal, permutation, skewing, parallelization, strip-mining, blocking, coalescing, interleaving); however, these transformations were defined in isolation, without a framework to help combine them together. Likewise, a lot of work has been done on developing a unified framework for matrix-based iteration-reordering loop transformations. However, the set of matrix-based transformations is too restrictive to suffice for a practical compiler system e.g. none of parallelization, blocking, coalescing, interleaving can be represented by a transformation matrix.

The success of past work on unification of unimodular transformations arose from the special properties of unimodular matrices[1] that represent these transformations. From these properties it follows that multiplication of two unimodular matrices results in a unimodular matrix. This ability to compose unimodular transformations by multiplying the transformation matrices gives rise to a natural unifying framework. Thus, a sequence of unimodular transformations can be combined into a single transformation matrix, and then applied only once to the loop nest, instead of repeatedly applying each transformation in the sequence to the loop nest to obtain the final form. However, as mentioned earlier, the unimodular framework is restrictive because it cannot represent iteration-reordering transformations such as parallelization, blocking, coalescing, or interleaving.

In this paper, we present a general framework for iteration-reordering transformations. We define an iteration-reordering transformation to be a sequence of template instantiations from a small but extensible kernel set of transformation templates. A transformation template is defined by rules for mapping dependence vectors, rules for mapping loop bound expressions, and rules for creating new initialization statements. The mapping rules for an iteration-reordering transformation are derived automatically from the mapping rules for its constituent kernel transformations. It is easy to see that our transformation system is closed under composition, since the composition of two transformations can simply be represented by the concatenation of their sequences of template instantiations. The effect of a transformation is to map an input perfect loop nest into an output perfect loop nest (possibly with a different number of loops). Our framework provides a systematic way for testing legality and generating code for a given sequence of iteration-reordering loop transformations. It frees the

*R.Thekkath supported partly by NSF PYI Award #MIP-9058-439.

ACM SIGPLAN '92 PLDI-6/92/CA
© 1992 ACM 0-89791-476-7/92/0006/0175...$1.50

[1] A matrix is unimodular if it satisfies the following three properties, 1) It is a square matrix, 2) All its elements are integers, and 3) Its determinant is ± 1. The three most commonly used unimodular transformations are loop reversal, loop interchange and loop skewing.

compiler writer from the burden of dealing with various iteration-reordering transformations in isolation, and allows her/him to concentrate her/his efforts on the problem of selecting transformations to satisfy a given optimization goal.

The rest of the paper is organized as follows. Section 2 provides a description of our framework and describes the set of kernel transformation templates considered in this paper. Section 3 defines the mapping rules for sets of data dependence vectors, and shows how the rules are used to test if a given transformation is legal for a given loop nest. Section 4 defines the mapping rules for loop bounds expressions, and shows how the rules are used to test if a given transformation is legal for a given loop nest. Section 4 also provides code generation rules for the transformations; these rules can be composed together to generate code for any arbitrary sequence of transformations. Section 5 discusses related work, and briefly outlines some of the advantages of using this general framework. Section 6 contains our conclusions. Appendix A uses a matrix multiply loop nest as an example to show the application of a non-trivial iteration-reordering loop transformation.

2 The Sequence Representation in the Framework

We define an iteration-reordering transformation to be a sequence of template instantiations from a small but extensible kernel set of transformation templates. A *transformation template* has parameters and providing specific values for these parameters creates a particular instantiation of this transformation template. The set of transformation templates used in the framework is called the *kernel set of loop transformation templates.* The optimizer selects templates from this kernel set and instantiates them with specific values so as to build a desired iteration-reordering transformation as a sequence of template instantiations.

The transformation template specifies rules for mapping dependence vectors, mapping loop bound expressions, and creating initialization statements for a transformed loop nest. The dependence vectors of a loop nest are used to test the legality of applying a transformation, with respect to the data dependence constraints of the original loop nest. When the loop nest is transformed, its dependence vectors will also change, as specified by the dependence vector mapping rules. This avoids recomputing the dependence vectors for the transformed loop nest, which is in general an expensive operation. The mapping rules for dependence vectors are discussed in greater detail in Section 3. Transformation of loop bounds and creation of initialization statements are actions required to generate code for the transformed loop nest. The preconditions in the loop bounds mapping rules are used to test the legality of applying a transformation, with respect to the loop bounds constraints. The mapping rules for loop bounds are discussed in greater detail in Section 4.

The kernel set of transformation templates assumed in this paper is shown in Table 1 along with a description of their parameters. The power of our framework lies in the following unifying principles:

1. *Template instantiation*
   An *instantiation* of a loop transformation template is obtained by supplying values for the parameters required by the template. For example, the parameter required by the `Parallelize` transformation template are n = loop nest size, and *parflag* = set of loops to be parallelized.

2. *Sequence representation for loop transformations*
   An iteration-reordering loop transformation is defined to be a *sequence*, $T =< t_1, \ldots, t_k >$, where each t_i is an instantiation of a kernel loop transformation template. Informally, the effect of transformation T is the cumulative effect of first applying t_1, then applying t_2, and so on up to t_k. Therefore, a mapping rule for transformation T is derived by composing the corresponding mapping rules for kernel transformations, t_1, t_2, etc.

   Using the sequence representation, the composition of transformations $T =< t_1, \ldots, t_k >$ and $U =< u_1, \ldots, u_l >$ is defined by sequence concatenation to be $U \circ T =< t_1, \ldots, t_k, u_1, \ldots, u_l >$. For the sake of efficiency, the concatenated sequence can be reduced in length by composing t_k and u_1 into a single template instantiation, whenever it is possible to do so. For example, if t_k and u_1 are both instantiations of the `Unimodular` template, then their composition can be replaced by a single `Unimodular` template instantiation with a transformation matrix that equals the product of u_1 and t_k's transformation matrices.

3. *Legality test*
   There is a uniform method to test if a given loop transformation sequence, $T =< t_1, \ldots, t_k >$, is legal for a given loop nest N. This legality test consists of two parts:

   (a) *Dependence vector test*
   Using the dependence vector mappings for the template instantiations (t_i's) contained within transformation T, check if the transformed set of N's dependence vectors contains a lexicographically negative[2] tuple. If so, transformation T is illegal for loop nest N. This legality test does not require each individual template instantiation in T to be legal when applied, only that the entire sequence be legal (see Section 3 for more details).

   (b) *Loop bounds test*
   Using the loop bound expression mappings for the template instantiations (t_i's) contained within transformation T, check if any of t_i's loop bounds

[2] Lexicographically negative is defined in Section 3, with an example.

Kernel Set of Templates	*Description*
`Unimodular`(n, M)	n is the input loop nest size (in all templates). M is the $n \times n$ *unimodular transformation matrix* specifying the desired transformation [4].
`ReversePermute`$(n, rev, perm)$	rev is a *reverse mask* such that $rev[i]$ = `true` implies loop i should be reversed, and $perm$ is a *permutation map* indicating that loop i should be moved to position $perm[i]$ after all reversals have been done.
`Parallelize`$(n, parflag)$	$parflag[i]$ = `true` means that loop i is to be parallelized.
`Block`$(n, i, j, bsize)$	The range $i \ldots j$ specifies a set of contiguous loops to be blocked (tiled), and $bsize$ is a vector such that $bsize[k]$ contains an expression for the block size of loop k. Blocking can be viewed as a combination of strip mining and interchanging [15].
`Coalesce`(n, i, j)	The range $i \ldots j$ specifies a set of contiguous loops to be *coalesced* (or collapsed) into a single loop [11].
`Interleave`$(n, i, j, isize)$	The contiguous range $i \ldots j$ specifies all loops to be *interleaved*. The value $isize[k]$ defines the *interleave factor* for loop k. This is similar to `Block`. In both, the outer loop iterates between blocks and the inner loop iterates between the elements of this block. In the `Block` transformation, every block is a set of contiguous iterations in the original loop, while in the `Interleave` transformation, a block consists of non-contiguous iterations from the original loop, based on the interleave factor.

Table 1: Kernel Set of Transformation Templates

preconditions is violated. If so, transformation T is illegal for loop nest N. This legality test requires the loop bounds preconditions to be satisfied for each individual template instantiation in T (see Section 4 for more details).

The basic algorithm for the legality test remains the same, regardless of the kernel set of loop transformation templates, K, the loop transformation, T, or the loop nest, N.

4. *Code generation for the transformed loop nest*
There is a uniform method to generate code for the transformed loop nest, N', obtained by applying transformation $T = < t_1, \ldots, t_k >$ on loop nest N. This method consists of two parts:

   (a) *Generate new loop bound expressions*
   For each transformation template t_i in the sequence T, apply its rules for mapping loop bounds expressions starting with the loop nest N, to finally obtain the transformed loop nest N'. Note that N' need not have the same number of loops as N. In general, the index variables used for loop nest N' will be different from those used for loop nest N.

   (b) *Generate new initialization statements*
   Many transformations change the names of the index variables or create additional index variables. Thus, statements in the loop body that use these index variables as array subscripts or otherwise must be modified, or initialization statements must be inserted at the the top of the loop body to initialize the old index variables as functions of the new index variables. Our framework uses the latter approach. Figure 1(a) contains a simple loop nest that is transformed by skewing the j loop with respect to the i loop and then interchanging the two loops. Figure 1(b) shows the transformed loop, when it is generated using initialization statements (the approach used by our framework).

   The initialization statements are automatically generated for loop nest N by applying the rules for each template instantiation t_i. The set of initialization statements, $INIT_i$, for template instantiation t_i defines t_i's input index variables as functions of t_i's output index variables. Therefore, the sets of initializations statements for the sequence $t_1, \ldots, t_k$, should be emitted in the order $INIT_k, \ldots, INIT_1$.

3 Data Dependence Vectors

In section 3.1 we define the dependence vector representation assumed by our framework. In section 3.2, we discuss the legality tests and mapping rules for dependence vectors.

```
do i = 2, n-1
  do j = 2, n-1
     a(i,j) = (a(i,j)+a(i-1,j)+
     a(i,j-1)+a(i+1,j)+a(i,j+1))/5
  enddo
enddo
```

The transformation is to skew the j loop w.r.t the i loop and then interchange the two loops.

Figure 1(a): Loop nest and transformation

```
do jj = 4, n+n-2
  do ii = max(2,j-n+1), min(n-1,j-2)
     j = jj - ii
     i = ii
     a(i,j) = (a(i,j)+a(i-1,j)+
     a(i,j-1)+a(i+1,j)+a(i,j+1))/5
  enddo
enddo
```

Figure 1(b): Transformed loop with init statements

3.1 Understanding Dependence Vectors

Following prior work in the area of iteration-reordering loop transformations, we represent the data dependence constraints for a loop nest by a *set of dependence vectors* D:

Definition 3.1 A *dependence vector* for a loop nest of size n is an n-tuple, $\vec{d} = (d_1, \ldots, d_n)$, where entry d_k corresponds to the kth loop (counting from outermost to innermost). In practice, there are two kinds of values for d_k that are of interest [9]:

1. *Distance* — d_k is an integer value, $d_k = y \in \mathcal{Z}$.
2. *Direction* — d_k is one of the six values, '$+$' (positive), '$-$' (negative), '$\not-$' (non-negative), '$\not+$' (non-positive), '$\pm$' (non-zero), '$*$' (any) [3]. □

Let us use $S(d_k)$ to denote the set of integer values that is represented by d_k. In the case of a distance value, $S(d_k)$ is a singleton set, i.e. $S(d_k) = \{y\}$. When d_k is one of the six possible direction values, then $S(d_k) = \{x | x \in \mathcal{Z} \wedge$ x's sign is contained in $d_k\}$. A direction value is used when the exact dependence distance is unknown. Hence it is an imprecise notation that is used to denote the direction of the dependence flow and represents all possible integer values in that direction.

The *set of integer tuples* denoted by dependence vector $\vec{d} = \{d_1, \ldots, d_n\}$ is given by Tuples($\vec{d}$) $= S(d_1) \times \ldots \times S(d_k)$ i.e. the Cartesian product of the integer sets corresponding to $d_1, \ldots, d_k$. If D is the set of all the dependence vectors for a loop nest, then Tuples(D) is simply the union of the tuple sets for each dependence vector in D, that is, Tuples(D) $= \bigcup_{\vec{d} \in D}$ Tuples($\vec{d}$).

Definition 3.2 An integer tuple, $\vec{a} = (a_1, \ldots, a_n)$ is lexicographically negative (positive) if and only if its first non-zero element, a_i, is negative (positive) i.e. $a_j = 0,\ \forall 1 \leq j < i$ and $a_i < 0$ ($a_i > 0$). □

Definition 3.3 An *execution instance* of a loop nest of size n is defined as a n-tuple, $\vec{a} = (a_1, \ldots, a_n)$, where a_k specifies the iteration number of the kth loop. □

The set of dependence vectors for a loop nest, D, enforces a partial order on the execution instances of the loop nest; for any two distinct execution instances $\vec{a}$ and $\vec{b}$, if their difference $\vec{b} - \vec{a}$ belongs to Tuples(D), then instance $\vec{b}$ must be executed after instance $\vec{a}$. This partial order summarizes all the iteration-reordering constraints imposed by data dependences. We assume that the original execution order satisfies this partial order. This implies that Tuples(D) cannot contain a lexicographically negative integer tuple for the original loop nest (otherwise the original execution order can be shown to violate some data dependence constraint). Further, if D' is the set of dependence vectors that result after a loop transformation is applied, and Tuples(D') contains a lexicographically negative tuple, then the transformed loop nest can be shown to violate some data dependence constraint and so the transformation must be illegal. This fact forms the basis of the data dependence legality test discussed in subsection 3.2.

The original set of dependence vectors for a perfect loop nest is computed using standard data dependence analysis techniques [4, 15, 10, 6, 12]. To obtain the best precision possible, it is recommended that a dependence vector containing summary direction values (i.e. one of '$\not-$', '$\not+$', '$\pm$', '$*$') be expanded into an equivalent set of dependence vectors that contain no summary direction values.

3.2 Transformation of Dependence Vectors

In this subsection, we describe how a set of dependence vectors is transformed by a given iteration-reordering loop transformation. Consider a set of dependence vectors D, and an iteration-reordering loop transformation $T = < t_1, \ldots, t_k >$. Using the sequence structure defined in Section 2, we compute the transformed set of dependence vectors as $T(D) = D_k$, where each $D_i = t_i(D_{i-1})$ is computed by applying the dependence vector mapping rules for kernel transformation t_i on $D_{i-1}\ \forall 1 \leq i \leq k$, and $D_0 = D$ is the initial set of dependence vectors for a loop nest, N. If we determine that Tuples($T(D)$) contains a lexicographically negative tuple[4], then we return $IsLegal(T, N)$ = `false`. Note that each individual transformation stage need not be legal, only that the final result be legal. This is because the final set of tuples denotes the final

[3] An alternate notation for the six direction values is to use the relational operators, '<', '>', '≤', '≥', '≠', and '*' respectively [15]. We do not represent an '=' direction in our framework because it is equivalent to a zero distance.

[4] Given a transformed dependence vector $\vec{d'} \in D'$, it is easy to determine by examining $\vec{d'}$ whether or not Tuples($\vec{d'}$) contains a lexicographically negative tuple.

execution order of the loop nest iterations, and the execution order in an intermediate transformation step is immaterial.

Table 2 outlines the dependence vector mapping rules for all the transformation templates considered in this paper. In general, an instantiation of a transformation template maps an input dependence vector set, D, into an output dependence vector set, D'. In fact, all transformation templates in Table 2, except `Block` and `Interleave`, map a given dependence vector $\vec{d} \in D$ into a single dependence vector, $\vec{d'} \in D'$; the `Block` and `Interleave` transformations may map $\vec{d} \in D$ into as many as 2^{j-i+1} dependence vectors in D' (this is one reason why they cannot be represented by a matrix).

Figure 2(a) shows a sample loop nest and its dependence vectors. Figure 2(b) shows a simple `ReversePermute` transformation and the result of applying the corresponding rules to the original vectors. This interchange transformation is illegal because it creates a lexicographically negative dependence vector, $(-1, 1)$. However, note that first reversing loop j makes interchange legal; this new `ReversePermute` operation is shown along with the resulting dependence vectors in Figure 2(c).

We require all data dependence mapping rules to be *consistent*. A dependence vector mapping rule is said to be *consistent* if and only if it preserves data dependences among execution instances. This idea is formalized in the following definition:

Definition 3.4 A *dependence vector mapping rule*, $D \mapsto D'$, for transformation template t is *consistent* if and only if $\text{Tuples}(D') \supseteq \{t(\vec{b}) - t(\vec{a}) | \vec{b} - \vec{a} \in \text{Tuples}(D)\}$, where $t(\vec{a})$ and $t(\vec{b})$ are executions instances in the transformed loop nest corresponding to execution instances $\vec{a}$ and $\vec{b}$ in the original loop nest. □

Theorem 3.5 All the dependence vector mapping rules in Table 2 are consistent. □

The proof for Theorem 3.5 is omitted due to space limitations.

The consistency property for mapping rules ensures that a mapping rule does not remove any dependence constraints. Another important property for mapping rules is *precision*, i.e., does the mapping rule introduce any extra cross-iteration dependences? Informally, we can say that mapping rule $D \mapsto D'$ is "equivalent to or more precise than" mapping rule $D \mapsto D''$, if $\text{Tuples}(D') \subseteq \text{Tuples}(D'')$ is always true. If all dependence vectors in D only contain direction values, then we can prove that all mapping rules in Table 2 are "as precise as possible". If only distance values are present in D, then the result applies to the `ReversePermute` and `Parallel` mapping rules; in all other cases, there is a loss of precision when distance values are approximated by direction values. *Proofs omitted due to space limitations.*

4 Transformation of Loop Bounds Expressions

In section 4.1, we discuss the legality constraints imposed by loop bounds, as well as our classification of loop bounds that makes it convenient to test the legality constraints. In section 4.2, we define the preconditions and mapping rules for all the transformation templates considered in this paper. In subsection 4.3, we outline the matrix-based representation used to support efficient transformation of loop bounds expressions

Figure 3 shows the general structure of how a loop nest of size n is transformed into a loop nest of size n' by a kernel template instantiation. To obtained the combined effect of a sequence of template instantiations, this kind of transformation is repeated for each template instantiation in the sequence such that the output loop bounds and loop body from one template instantiation serve as the input for the next template instantiation. Expressions l_k, u_k, s_k in Figure 3 contain the lower, upper, and step bounds expressions for the original loop nest. A bounds expression for loop k may depend on index variables $x_1, \ldots, x_{k-1}$. We assume that no bounds expression for loop $k > 1$ has a side effect (if a bounds expression for loop $k > 1$ had a side effect, it would make loops $k-1$ and k imperfectly nested). $loop_k \in \{\texttt{do}, \texttt{pardo}\}$ indicates if input loop k is sequential or parallel. Expressions l'_k, u'_k, s'_k contain the lower, upper, and step bounds expressions for the transformed loop nest. $loop'_k \in \{\texttt{do}, \texttt{pardo}\}$ indicates if transformed loop k is sequential or parallel. In general, the transformed loop nest will have n initialization statements to initialize the original index variables, $x_1, \ldots, x_n$, as functions of the new index variables, $x'_1, \ldots, x'_{n'}$. We make a special effort to reuse original index variable names by avoiding initialization statements of the form $x_i = x'_j$.

4.1 Loop Bounds Legality Constraints

The lower bound, upper bound or step in a loop statement is generally an expression that involves constants, index variables of outer loop statements, and other terms that are invariant in the loop nest. A transformation may be applied to a given loop nest only if these expressions satisfy the *preconditions* for applying this transformation. For example, consider the doubly-nested triangular loop in Figure 4(a) and assume that there are no data dependence constraints. These loop bounds satisfy the preconditions for a `Unimodular` transformation, so it is legal to permute the loops (say), and the resulting loop nest is shown in Figure 4(b).

Figure 4(c) contains a triply-nested loop for computing the matrix product of a dense matrix (`b`) and a sparse matrix (`c`), with the result stored in a dense matrix (`a`). The lower and upper bounds of loop `k` are nonlinear functions of `j` thus making it illegal to interchange loops `j` and `k`. However, the preconditions for the `ReversePermute` transformation

Transformation template	Dependence vector mapping rule
`Unimodular`(n, M)	$D' = \left\{ \vec{d'} \mid \vec{d} \in D \wedge \vec{d'} = M \times \vec{d} \right\}$ where $M \times \vec{d}$ is a matrix-vector product, appropriately extended for direction values [9, 14].
`ReversePermute` $(n, perm, rev)$	$D' = \{ \ (d'_1, \ldots, d'_n) \mid (d_1, \ldots, d_n) \in D \wedge d'_{perm[k]} = (rev[k] \ ?\ reverse(d_k) : d_k) \ \}$ where $reverse(d_k)$ is computed as follows: $\begin{array}{c\|\|c\|c\|c\|c\|c\|c\|c} d_k & \text{'+'} & \text{'}-\text{'} & \text{'}\not+\text{'} & \text{'}\not-\text{'} & \text{'}\pm\text{'} & \text{'*'} & x \in \mathcal{Z} \\ \hline reverse(d_k) & \text{'}-\text{'} & \text{'+'} & \text{'}\not-\text{'} & \text{'}\not+\text{'} & \text{'}\pm\text{'} & \text{'*'} & -x \end{array}$
`Parallel`$(n, parflag)$	$D' = \{ \ (d'_1, \ldots, d'_n) \mid (d_1, \ldots, d_n) \in D \wedge d'_k = (parflag[k] \ ?\ parmap(d_k) : d_k) \ \}$ where $parmap(d_k) = \begin{cases} 0 & \text{if } d_k = 0 \\ \text{'*'} & \text{if } d_k \neq 0 \end{cases}$
`Block`$(n, i, j, bsize)$	$D' = \{ \ (d_1, \ldots, d_{i-1}, d'_i, \ldots, d'_j, d''_i, \ldots, d''_j, d_{j+1}, \ldots, d_n) \mid (d_1, \ldots, d_n) \in D \wedge (d'_k, d''_k) \in blockmap(d_k) \ \forall i \leq k \leq j \ \}$ where $blockmap(d_k) = \begin{cases} \{ (0,0) \} & \text{if } d_k = 0 \\ \{ (\text{'*'}, \text{'*'}) \} & \text{if } d_k = \text{'*'} \\ \{ (0, d_k), (d_k, \text{'*'}) \} & \text{if } d_k = 1 \text{ or } -1 \\ \{ (0, d_k), (dir(d_k), \text{'*'}) \} & \text{otherwise} \end{cases}$ and $dir(d_k) = \begin{cases} d_k & \text{if } d_k \text{ is a direction value or if } d_k = 0 \\ \text{'+'} & \text{if } d_k \text{ is a positive distance value} \\ \text{'}-\text{'} & \text{if } d_k \text{ is a negative distance value} \end{cases}$
`Coalesce`(n, i, j)	$D' = \{ \ (d_1, \ldots, d_{i-1}, d', d_{j+1}, \ldots, d_n) \mid (d_1, \ldots, d_n) \in D \wedge d' = mergedirs(dir(d_i), \ldots, dir(d_j)) \ \}$ where the function *mergedirs* is evaluated by a pairwise merging of its arguments, for example, $mergedirs(+, -) = \pm$, and so on.
`Interleave`$(n, i, j, isize)$	Similar to `Block`, but use *imap* instead of *blockmap* $\begin{array}{c\|\|c\|c\|c\|c} d_k & 0 & \text{'+'}, \text{'}\not+\text{'}, x \in \mathcal{Z}^+ & \text{'}-\text{'}, \text{'}\not-\text{'}, x \in \mathcal{Z}^- & \text{'}\pm\text{'}, \text{'*'} \\ \hline imap(d_k) & \{ (0,0) \} & \{ (\text{'}\not+\text{'}, \text{'}\not+\text{'}), (\text{'}-\text{'}, \text{'+'}) \} & \{ (\text{'}\not-\text{'}, \text{'}\not-\text{'}), (\text{'+'}, \text{'}-\text{'}) \} & \{ (\text{'*'}, \text{'*'}) \} \end{array}$

Table 2: Dependence vector mapping rules for kernel transformations in K

allow loop `i` to be moved to the innermost position since the bounds of loop `k` are invariant in `i`.

To maintain precise information about the nature of loop bounds expressions, we define a function $type(expr_j, x_i)$ that captures how index variable x_i is used in bounds expression $expr_j$ (i.e., one of l_j, u_j, or s_j), for $i < j$:

$$type(expr_j, x_i) = \begin{cases} \texttt{const}, & \text{if } expr_j \text{ is a compile-time constant} \\ \texttt{invar}, & \text{if } expr_j \text{ is invariant in } x_i \\ \texttt{linear}, & \text{if } expr_j \text{ is linear in } x_i \\ & \text{(and the coefficient of } x_i \text{ in } expr_j \\ & \text{is a compile-time constant)} \\ \texttt{nonlinear}, & \text{otherwise} \end{cases}$$

The *type* values form a totally ordered lattice in which `const` $\sqsubseteq$ `invar` $\sqsubseteq$ `linear` $\sqsubseteq$ `nonlinear`; a predicate expression of the form "$type(expr_j, x_i) \sqsubseteq V$" will therefore be satisfied by any *type* value that is equal to or below V in the lattice. The first column in Tables 3 and 4 shows the preconditions for applying a given template instantiation. As an example, looking at the `Unimodular` template, we see that one of the preconditions says that $type(l_j, x_i) \sqsubseteq$ **`linear`**. If we examine the type of the lower bound expression for loop `k` in example Figure 4(c) as a function of `j`, we see that it has $type =$ **`nonlinear`**; hence the precondition is violated and the `Unimodular` transformation cannot be applied to this example.

For a given loop nest N and transformation sequence T, if a precondition is violated for any kernel transformation contained within $T = \langle t_1, \ldots, t_k \rangle$, then we return $IsLegal(T, N) =$ `false`. When testing for legality, we do not actually generate the new loop bounds expressions and initialization statements for each t_k in the sequence T;

```
do i = 2, n-1
    do j = 2, n-1
        a(i,j) = b(j)
        if (...) b(j) = a(i-1,j+1)
    enddo
enddo
```

$D = \{(1,-1),(+,0)\}$

Figure 2(a): Loop nest and dependence vectors

$\texttt{ReversePermute}(n, perm, rev)$
$n = 2, rev = [0\ 0], perm = [1\ 0]$
$D' = \{(-1,1),(0,+)\}$

Figure 2(b): Illegal Transformation

$\texttt{ReversePermute}(n, perm, rev)$
$n = 2, rev = [0\ 1], perm = [1\ 0]$
$D' = \{(1,1),(0,+)\}$

Figure 2(c): Legal Transformation

$$
\begin{array}{l}
loop_1\ x_1 = l_1, u_1, s_1 \\
\quad \vdots \\
\quad loop_n\ x_n = l_n(x_1,\ldots,x_{n-1}), u_n(x_1,\ldots,x_{n-1}), s_n(x_1,\ldots,x_{n-1}) \\
\quad\quad \ldots \\
\Longrightarrow \\
loop'_1\ x'_1 = l'_1, u'_1, s'_1 \\
\quad \vdots \\
\quad loop'_{n'}\ x'_{n'} = l'_{n'}(x'_1,\ldots,x'_{n'-1}), u'_{n'}(x'_1,\ldots,x'_{n'-1}), s'_{n'}(x'_1,\ldots,x'_{n'-1}) \\
\quad\quad x_1 = f_1(x'_1,\ldots,x'_{n'}) \\
\quad\quad \vdots \\
\quad\quad x_n = f_n(x'_1,\ldots,x'_{n'}) \\
\quad\quad \ldots
\end{array}
$$

Figure 3: General structure of Transformed Loop Bounds Expressions and Initialization Statements

instead, we use a matrix-based representation (outlined in subsection 4.3) to carry sufficient information to evaluate the *type* predicates in the preconditions.

Though max and min are nonlinear functions, there are special cases in which loop bounds that are max or min functions of linear terms will themselves be classified as *type* = **linear**. Specifically, if the step is positive and the lower bound expression is a max function of linear terms and/or the upper bound expression is a min function of linear terms, then each term of the max or min function can be treated as a separate linear inequality [14] (if the step is negative, then the special case occurs when the lower bound is a min function and the upper bound is a max function). This classification is useful for transforming loop nests with this special form of max/min functions, a form that is frequently obtained as the output of the Unimodular and Blocking transformations. *Due to space limitations, the code generation details for transforming max/min loop bounds were omitted in Tables 3 and 4.*

4.2 Transformation Rules

The second column in Tables 3 and 4 depicts the output form of the input loop nest structure of Figure 3. This output form is obtained by applying the rules for mapping loop bounds expressions and creating initialization statements. To clarify some notation, when the output loop nest refers to "$loop_k$", this indicates the $loop_k$ value (do or pardo) from the input loop nest. A use of "$loop'_k$" indicates a loop in the output loop nest.

The rules for the Unimodular transformation have been studied in detail in the literature [7, 14] and are omitted here. The preconditions and mapping rules for the ReversePermute transformation template are shown in Table 3; this template partially overlaps with the Unimodular template. The preconditions for ReversePermute require the lower and upper bounds expressions to be invariant (rectangular), but do not require the step expressions to be compile-time constants. The preconditions for Unimodular allow the lower and upper bounds expressions to be linear, but require the step expressions to be compile-time constants. For cases in which ReversePermute and Unimodular can achieve the same result, it is preferable to use ReversePermute because a) step expressions are not normalized to +1, b) index variable names are reused without creating initialization statements, and c) matrix computations are avoided on dependence vectors.

The Coalesce transformation [11] includes normalization of the *lower bound* and the *step* expression as part of the transformation mapping. The Block transformation (Table 4) takes special care to bound the iteration space

Transformation template	Loop nest mapping
`Unimodular`(n, M) **Preconditions:** $\forall\, 1 \le i < j \le n$, 1. $type(l_j, x_i) \sqsubseteq$ `linear` 2. $type(u_j, x_i) \sqsubseteq$ `linear` 3. $type(s_j, x_i) \sqsubseteq$ `const` **Output loop nest size:** $n' = n$	The transformation of loop bounds expressions and the creation of initialization statements have been studied in detail for this case [7, 14]. If the (constant) step value is $\neq 1$, then the bounds are normalized to step $= 1$ before applying the unimodular transformation.
`ReversePermute`$(n, perm, rev)$ (Partial overlap with Unimodular) **Preconditions:** $type(expr_j, x_i) \sqsubseteq$ `invar`, where $expr_j$ is one of l_j, u_j or s_j, $\forall\, i < j$ s.t. $perm[i] > perm[j]$. **Output loop nest size:** $n' = n$	$loop_{perm[1]}\ x_{perm[1]} = l'_1, u'_1, s'_1$ $\vdots$ $loop_{perm[n]}\ x_{perm[n]} = l'_n, u'_n, s'_n$ where, for $1 \le k \le n$, $l'_k, u'_k, s'_k = \begin{cases} l_{perm[k]}, u_{perm[k]}, s_{perm[k]} & rev[k] = F \\ U_{perm[k]}, l_{perm[k]}, -s_{perm[k]} & rev[k] = T \end{cases}$ $U_{perm[k]} =$ $u_{perm[k]} - \mathrm{sgn}(s_{perm[k]}) * \mathrm{mod}(\mathrm{abs}(u_{perm[k]} - l_{perm[k]}), \mathrm{abs}(s_{perm[k]}))$
`Parallel`$(n, parflag)$ **Preconditions:** none **Output loop nest size:** $n' = n$	$loop'_1\ x_1 = l_1, u_1, s_1$ $\vdots$ $loop'_n\ x_n = l_n, u_n, s_n$ $loop'_k = \begin{cases} loop_k & parflag[k] = \texttt{false} \\ \texttt{pardo} & parflag[k] = \texttt{true} \end{cases}$ $\quad \forall\, 1 \le k \le n$,
`Coalesce`(n, i, j) **Preconditions:** $type(expr_m, x_k) \sqsubseteq$ `invar`, where $expr_m$ is one of l_m, u_m or s_m $\forall i \le k < m \le j$ **Output loop nest size:** $n' = n - (j - i)$	$loop_1\ x_1 = l_1, u_1, s_1$ $\vdots$ $loop^c\ x^c = 1, U, 1$ $\vdots$ $loop_n\ x_n = l_n(x_1, \ldots, f_i(x^c), \ldots, f_j(x^c), \ldots), \ldots$ $x_i = f_i(x^c)$ $\vdots$ $x_j = f_j(x^c)$ $\ldots$ $U = \prod_{k=i}^{j} U^k$, where $U^k = \max\left(1 + \left\lfloor \frac{(u_k - l_k)}{s_k} \right\rfloor, 0\right)$ $loop^c = \begin{cases} \texttt{do} & \text{if } \exists k, i \le k \le j, \text{ such that } loop_k \neq \texttt{pardo} \\ \texttt{pardo} & \text{otherwise} \end{cases}$ for $i \le k \le j$ $f_k(x^c) = l_k + \left(\left\lceil \frac{x^c}{\prod_{p=k+1}^{j} U^p} \right\rceil - U^k \left\lfloor \frac{x^c - 1}{\prod_{p=k}^{j} U^p} \right\rfloor - 1\right) s_k$
`Interleave`$(n, i, j, isize)$ **Preconditions:** $\forall i \le k < m \le j$, 1. $type(l_m, x_k) \sqsubseteq$ `linear` 2. $type(u_m, x_k) \sqsubseteq$ `linear` 3. $type(s_m, x_k) \sqsubseteq$ `const` **Output loop nest size:** $n' = n + (j - i + 1)$	$loop_1\ x_1 = l_1, u_1, s_1$ $\vdots$ $loop_i\ x'_i = 0, isize[i] - 1, 1$ $\vdots$ $loop_j\ x'_j = 0, isize[j] - 1, 1$ $loop_i\ x_i = l_i + x'_i * s_i, u_i, isize[i] * s_i$ $\vdots$ $loop_j\ x_j = l_j + x'_j * s_j, u_j, isize[j] * s_j$ $\vdots$ $loop_n\ x_n = l_n, u_n, s_n$

Table 3: Loop nest mapping for kernel transformations in K

```
do i = 1, n
  do j = i, n
    ...
```

Figure 4(a): Triangular

```
do j = 1, n
  do i = 1, j
    ...
```

Figure 4(b): Interchanged

```
do i = 1, n
  do j = 1, n
    do k = colstr(j), colstr(j+1)-1
      a(i,j) += b(i,rowidx(k))*c(k)
```

Figure 4(c): Nonlinear bounds

Transformation template	Loop nest mapping
`Block`$(n, i, j, bsize)$ **Preconditions:** $\forall\, i \le k < m \le j$, 1. $type(l_m, x_k) \sqsubseteq$ `linear` 2. $type(u_m, x_k) \sqsubseteq$ `linear` 3. $type(s_m, x_k) \sqsubseteq$ `const` **Output loop nest size:** $n' = n + (j - i + 1)$	$loop_1\ x_1 = l_1, u_1, s_1$ $\vdots$ $loop_i\ x'_i = l'_i, u'_i, s_i * bsize[i]$ $\vdots$ $loop_j\ x'_j = l'_j, u'_j, s_j * bsize[j]$ $loop_i\ x_i = L'_i, U'_i, s_i$ $\vdots$ $loop_j\ x_j = L'_j, U'_j, s_j$ $\vdots$ $loop_n\ x_n = l_n, u_n, s_n$ ... where $\forall\ i \le k \le j$ and $i \le h < k$ $l'_k = l_k(x_1 \ldots x_{i-1}, x'_{min}[k,i] \ldots x'_{min}[k, k-1])$ $u'_k = u_k(x_1 \ldots x_{i-1}, x'_{max}[k,i] \ldots x'_{max}[k, k-1])$ $x'_{min}[k,h] = \begin{cases} x'_h - bsize[h], & \text{if the coeff. of } x_h \text{ in any term of } l_k \text{ is} < 0 \\ x'_h, & \text{otherwise} \end{cases}$ $x'_{max}[k,h] = \begin{cases} x'_h + bsize[h], & \text{if the coeff. of } x_h \text{ in any term of } u_k \text{ is} > 0 \\ x'_h, & \text{otherwise} \end{cases}$ $L'_k = \begin{cases} \max(x'_k, l_k), & s_k > 0 \\ \min(x'_k, l_k), & s_k < 0 \end{cases}$ $U'_k = \begin{cases} \min(x'_k + s_k * (bsize[k] - 1), u_k), & s_k > 0 \\ \max(x'_k + s_k * (bsize[k] - 1), u_k), & s_k < 0 \end{cases}$

Table 4: Loop nest mapping for kernel transformations in K

so that only tiles with some work are created (the only exception occurs when there is a `max` or `min` function in the loop bounds and not all the function's terms are monotonic in the same direction). This is unlike the solution in [14] that creates a rectangular boundary around a trapezoidal iteration space, and hence may create many tiles with no work. The blocking scheme proposed in [15] requires that all block sizes be equal for the algorithm to only create tiles with some work. A more general code generation algorithm is given in [3], based on scanning polyhedra (e.g. it can be used to generate code for non-rectangular tiling); however, this algorithm can also create more tiles than necessary.

4.3 Representation of Loop Bound Expressions

To efficiently transform the loop bound expressions through each template instantiation in a transformation sequence, we use a matrix-based representation for loop bound expressions. Specifically, this representation consists of three matrices, `LB`, `UB`, `STEP`, for the *lower bound*, *upper bound*, and *step* expressions respectively. Let n be the number of loops in the loop nest for which the bounds are to be represented. These coefficient matrices have the shape $(1 \ldots n) \times (0 \ldots n)$. Matrix entry (i, j) is only defined when $i \ge j$. Figure 5 shows a sample loop nest and its `LB`, `UB` and `STEP` matrices. We represent multiple linear bounds constraints for `max` and `min` functions by allowing each matrix entry to contain a list of coefficient values, one per inequality. For example in the figure, the `LB` matrix has an

```
do i = max(n,3), 100, 2
   do j = 1, min(2, i+512), 1
      do k = sqrt(i)/2, 2*j, i
         . . .
      enddo
   enddo
enddo
```

$type(u_2, i) =$ `linear`
$type(l_3, i) =$ `nonlinear`
$type(u_3, j) =$ `linear`
$type(s_3, i) =$ `linear`
$type =$ `invar` or `const`, in all other cases.

$$\mathtt{LB} = \begin{bmatrix} \max < \mathtt{n,\ 3} > & \perp & \perp & \perp \\ 1 & 0 & \perp & \perp \\ \mathtt{sqrt(i)/2} & 0 & 0 & \perp \end{bmatrix}$$

$$\mathtt{UB} = \begin{bmatrix} \mathtt{100} & \perp & \perp & \perp \\ \min < \mathtt{2,\ 512} > & \min < \mathtt{0,\ 1} > & \perp & \perp \\ 0 & 0 & 2 & \perp \end{bmatrix}$$

$$\mathtt{STEP} = \begin{bmatrix} 2 & \perp & \perp & \perp \\ 1 & 0 & \perp & \perp \\ 0 & 1 & 0 & \perp \end{bmatrix}$$

Figure 5: A sample loop nest and its LB, UB and STEP matrices.

entry $\max < \mathtt{n,\ 3} >$.

Each matrix entry has a *type* tag. The $(i, 0)$ entry represents the loop-invariant part of the bounds expression for loop i; this entry may contain an arbitrary expression that is only evaluated at run-time. The (i, j) entry represents the constant (integer) coefficient of index variable j in the bounds expression for loop $i > j$, assuming that $type(i, j) \sqsubseteq$ `linear`. If $type(i, j) =$ `nonlinear`, then the (i, j) entry is set to zero, and the terms involving index variable j are combined into the $(i, 0)$ entry of the matrix. This is a convenient way to store both linear and nonlinear terms in the matrix representation. For an example of the `nonlinear` representation, look at the `LB` matrix entry for loop `k` as a function of `i`. *Further details on the loop bounds representation have been omitted due to space limitations.*

5 Related Work

There are several papers related to iteration-reordering transformations that have been published in the literature, often with a fair amount of overlap in the material presented. Space limitations prevent us from discussing all these references; instead, we outline a representative subset that, to the best of our knowledge, covers the prior work related to our paper. We focus on discussing prior work in the area of *frameworks* for iteration-reordering transformations, rather than other (orthogonal) topics like data dependence analysis techniques, or optimization algorithms that use iteration-reordering transformations, or loop transformations that reorder statements as well as iterations.

Lamport [9] introduced the *hyperplane method* and the *coordinate method* for parallel execution of iterations in a loop nest. Both methods are special forms of iteration-reordering transformations. The framework used in [9] included dependence vectors that contain distance or direction values, and iteration-reordering transformations that can be represented by $\mathcal{Z}^n \mapsto \mathcal{Z}^n$ linear mappings. Further, the legality test for a linear mapping was based on the existence of a lexicographically negative tuple in the set of transformed dependence vectors. However, the focus on the paper was on the two methods for rewriting a sequential loop nest into a form containing parallel loops, and the framework was only developed to the extent needed by these transformations. The framework in our paper is much more general—we support linear and non-linear transformations, allow input and output loop nest sizes to be different, and permit all iteration-reordering transformations to be composed together in a general way.

Wolfe [15] introduced a comprehensive *data dependence graph*, with edges labeled by *direction vectors*, as the basis for a loop transformation framework. Several iteration-reordering transformations were supported by this framework e.g. *loop interchanging*, *iteration space tiling* (blocking), *loop skewing*, *vectorization*, and *concurrentization*. However, each transformation had its own special legality test based on the direction vectors and on the nature of loop bounds expressions. Our framework is more general in several ways: we provide a single legality test for all iteration-reordering transformations, we support a larger class of iteration-reordering transformations (e.g. we allow transformations of parallel loops), we allow dependence vectors to contain both distance and direction values, and we treat transformations as independent entities, separate from the data dependence graph.

Allen and Kennedy [1, 2] introduced the notion of *loop-carried* and *loop-independent* dependences, and defined legality tests for parallelization and interchange based on the idea of the *level* of a loop-carried dependence. They also coined the term, "reordering transformation"; we instead use the term, "iteration-reordering transformation", so as to be more specific. Our work can be viewed as a generalization of the results in [1, 2] that relate to iteration-reordering (reordering) transformations, since our legality test accommodates many other transformations apart from parallelization and interchange, and since we also base our legality test on the nature of the loop bounds expressions.

Irigoin and Triolet [8] describe a framework for iteration-reordering transformations based on *supernode partitioning*, an aggregation technique achieved by hyperplane partitioning, followed by iteration space tiling across hyperplane boundaries. In this framework, data dependences are represented by *dependence cones* rather than dependence vectors. They also provide a general code generation algorithm for any linear transformation that corresponds to a unimodular change of basis [7]. Their framework incorporates loop interchange, hyperplane partitioning, and loop tiling (blocking) in a unified way, for loop nests with linear bounds expressions. Our framework takes its inspiration from this kind of unified approach to loop transformations, but is more general in that it incorporates other non-linear transformations like loop parallelization and loop coalescing, and it allows transformation of loop nests with non-linear loop bounds expressions by maintaining precise information on the loop bounds constraints. Our framework is also more practical, because it is based on dependence vectors rather than dependence cones, and because it incurs the overhead of general linear (unimodular) transformations only when strictly necessary.

Recently, *unimodular transformations* have begun gaining popularity as a practical framework for iteration-reordering transformations. Banerjee [5] shows how transformations like loop interchange, loop reversal, and loop skewing, can be represented by a unimodular transformation matrix; however, the results in the paper are proved only for loop nests of size = 2, and containing constant loop bounds. Wolf and Lam [14] also show how unimodular transformations can be used to unify loop interchange, loop reversal, and loop skewing; the results in their paper are applicable to loop nests of arbitrary size and with linear bounds constraints. They also incorporate the tiling (blocking) transformation into their framework by proposing a two-step approach, where a unimodular transformation is followed by a tiling transformation. The unifying aspect of the unimodular frameworks in [5, 14] is similar in scope to the unifying approach of Irigoin and Triolet. However, the unimodular frameworks are more practical since they are based on dependence vectors (as in [9]), rather than dependence cones. Our framework is superior to the unimodular frameworks in several ways: we support a larger class of iteration-reordering transformations (e.g. loop parallelization, loop coalescing, loop reversal/interchange with unknown strides) while still maintaining a uniform legality test and code generation scheme, we allow transformation of loop nests with non-linear loop bounds expressions by storing precise information on the loop bounds constraints, and we incur the overhead of unimodular transformations only when strictly necessary.

Whitfield and Soffa [13] define a specification language (called GOSpeL) for global optimizations, in which an optimization is specified by *preconditions* and *actions*. An optimization can only be enabled when all its preconditions are satisfied; if enabled, the actions specify how the program representation should be updated to materialize the optimization. They also describe an optimizer generator tool (called GENesis) that can be used to automatically generate an optimizer from a GOSpeL specification. The precondition and action rules in GOSpeL are not powerful enough to specify general iteration-reordering loop transformations, as described in this paper. However, our framework for iteration-reordering loop transformations would be a natural extension to a GENesis-like system since the legality tests for a loop transformation sequence define the preconditions for its applicability, and the code generation rules for a loop transformation sequence define the actions to be performed.

Perhaps the biggest advantage of our framework is that it treats a transformation as an independent entity, distinct from the loop nests on which it may be applied. Thus, transformations may be created, instantiated, composed, and destroyed, without being tied to a particular loop nest. The advantage of this approach is that it makes it easy to consider several alternative transformations for a loop nest, where each transformation could be an arbitrarily complex sequence of template instantiations from the kernel set. Note that a loop nest remains unchanged while the transformation system considers the legality and effectiveness of applying various alternative transformations; the loop nest only needs to be updated when code generation is finally requested for a particular transformation. This flexibility is useful for supporting arbitrary levels of search and "undo" in an automatic transformation system, and can also be used to exploit parallel processing in the compiler by concurrently evaluating the effectiveness of alternative transformations for a loop nest.

6 Conclusions and Future Work

We have described a novel unified framework for *all* iteration-reordering transformations. The key strengths of this framework are:

- Single legality test for all iteration-reordering loop transformations.
- Ease of addition of new transformations by specifying new rules.
- Separation of transformations from loop nests.
- Treatment of `Parallel` as just another iteration-reordering transformation in the framework.
- Special attention to the constraints imposed by loop bounds expressions.
- An efficient and general implementation of the `ReversePermute` transformation, a case that occurs frequently in practice.
- Generation of efficient code when blocking trapezoidal loops.

We believe that our framework supports iteration-reordering transformations in their full generality. The main direction for future work would be in using this framework in an automatic transformation system, so as to optimize loop nests for data locality, parallel execution, and vector execution. Another avenue for future work lies in extending this framework to include other transformations like loop distribution or loop unrolling that reorder both iterations and statements.

Finally, we observe that the kernel transformation mapping rules for dependence vectors and loop bounds expressions were derived "by hand" from the iteration mapping defined by the transformation. An interesting area of future theoretical work would be to explore the possibility of deriving the dependence vector and loop bounds mapping rules automatically from a given iteration mapping function. This may be feasible today for the `Unimodular` transformation, but to do so for something like the `Block` transformation (where iteration mapping is defined using the `mod` and `div` operators) would indeed be a great challenge.

Acknowledgements

The authors would like to thank Ann Campbell, Ray Ellersick, Ping Liao, John Ng, Khoa Nguyen, Edith Schonberg, Jin-Fan Shaw, and Morgan Young for their support and technical assistance at IBM. We also thank Fran Allen, David Callahan, Michael Wolf, and people from the compiler seminar class at the University of Washington for their many comments and suggestions on improving the paper.

References

[1] John R. Allen. *Dependence Analysis for Subscripted Variables and its Application to Program Transformation.* PhD thesis, Rice University, 1983.

[2] Randy Allen and Ken Kennedy. Automatic translation of fortran programs to vector form. *ACM Transactions on Programming Languages and Systems*, 9(4):491–592, October 1987.

[3] Corinne Ancourt and François Irigoin. Scanning polyhedra with DO loops. *Third ACM Symposium on Principles and Practice of Parallel Programming*, pages 39–50, April 1991.

[4] Utpal Banerjee. *Dependence Analysis for Supercomputing.* Kluwer Academic Publishers, Norwell, Massachusetts, 1988.

[5] Utpal Banerjee. Unimodular transformations of double loops. *Proceedings of the Third Workshop on Languages and Compilers for Parallel Computing*, August 1990.

[6] Gina Goff, Ken Kennedy, and Chau-Wen Tseng. Practical dependence testing. *Proceedings of the ACM SIGPLAN '91 Conference on Programming Language Design and Implementation*, 26(6):15–29, June 1991.

[7] François Irgoin. Code generation for the hyperplane method and for loop interchange. Technical report, Ecole Nationale Superieure des Mines de Paris, October 1988. Report ENSMP-CAI-88-E102/CAI/I.

[8] François Irigoin and Remi Triolet. Supernode partitioning. *Conference Record of Fifteenth ACM Symposium on Principles of Programming Languages*, pages 319–329, 1988.

[9] L. Lamport. The parallel execution of do loops. *Communications of the ACM*, pages 83–93, February 1974.

[10] Dror E. Maydan, John L. Hennessy, and Monica S. Lam. Efficient and exact data dependence analysis. *Proceedings of the ACM SIGPLAN '91 Conference on Programming Language Design and Implementation*, 26(6):1–14, June 1991.

[11] Constantine D. Polychronopoulos and David J. Kuck. Guided self-scheduling: A practical scheduling scheme for parallel supercomputers. *IEEE Transactions on Computers*, C-36(12):1425–1439, December 1987.

[12] William Pugh. The omega test: a fast and practical integer programming algorithm for dependence analysis. *Proceedings of Supercomputing '91*, pages 4–13, November 1991.

[13] Deborah Whitfield and Mary Lou Soffa. Automatic generation of global optimizers. *ACM SIGPLAN '91 Conference on Programming Language Design and Implementation*, pages 120–129, June 1991.

[14] Michael E. Wolf and Monica S. Lam. A loop transformation theory and an algorithm to maximize parallelism. *IEEE Transactions on Parallel and Distributed Systems*, 2(4):452–471, October 1991.

[15] Michael J. Wolfe. *Optimizing Supercompilers for Supercomputers.* Pitman, London and The MIT Press, Cambridge, Massachusetts, 1989. In the series, Research Monographs in Parallel and Distributed Computing This monograph is a revised version of the author's Ph.D. dissertation published as Technical Report UIUCDCS-R-82-1105, U. Illinois at Urbana-Champaign, 1982.

A Matrix multiply example

In this section, we use a matrix multiply loop nest as an example to illustrate the effect of a non-trivial iteration-reordering transformation defined as a sequence of five kernel transformations. Figure 6 shows the input loop nest. Figure 7 shows how the dependence vectors and loop bounds expressions are updated by the sequence of template instantiations.

```
do i = 1, n
      do j = 1, n
            do k = 1, n
                  A(i, j) = A(i, j) + B(i, k) * C(k, j)
            enddo
      enddo
enddo
```

Figure 6: Matrix Multiply example–input loop nest.

Transform	Dep.Vectors	Index	LB	UB	STEP	loop
START	$(=,=,+)$	i	1	n	1	do
		j	1	n	1	do
		k	1	n	1	do
ReversePermute	$(=,+,=)$	j	1	n	1	do
n = 3		k	1	n	1	do
rev=[F F F]		i	1	n	1	do
perm=[3 1 2]						
Block	$(=,=,=,=,+,=)$	jj	1	n	bj	do
n = 3	$(=,+,=,=,*,=)$	kk	1	n	bk	do
i = 1		ii	1	n	bi	do
j = 3		j	jj	$\min(n, jj + bj - 1)$	1	do
bsize=[bj bk bi]		k	kk	$\min(n, kk + bk - 1)$	1	do
		i	ii	$\min(n, ii + bi - 1)$	1	do
Parallelize	$(=,=,=,=,+,=)$	jj	1	n	bj	pardo
n = 6	$(=,+,=,=,*,=)$	kk	1	n	bk	do
parflag=[1 0 1 0 0 0]		ii	1	n	bi	pardo
		j	jj	$\min(n, jj + bj - 1)$	1	do
		k	kk	$\min(n, kk + bk - 1)$	1	do
		i	ii	$\min(n, ii + bi - 1)$	1	do
ReversePermute	$(=,=,=,=,+,=)$	jj	1	n	bj	pardo
n = 6	$(=,=,+,=,*,=)$	ii	1	n	bi	pardo
rev=[F F F F F F]		kk	1	n	bk	do
perm=[1 3 2 4 5 6]		j	jj	$\min(n, jj + bj - 1)$	1	do
		k	kk	$\min(n, kk + bk - 1)$	1	do
		i	ii	$\min(n, ii + bi - 1)$	1	do
Coalesce	$(=,=,=,+,=)$	jic	1	$\lfloor \frac{n-1+bi}{bi} \rfloor * \lfloor \frac{n-1+bj}{bj} \rfloor$	1	pardo
n = 6	$(=,+,=,*,=)$	kk	1	n	bk	do
i = 1		j	tmp_j	$\min(n, \mathrm{tmp}_j + bj - 1)$	1	do
j = 2		k	kk	$\min(n, kk + bk - 1)$	1	do
		i	tmp_i	$\min(n, \mathrm{tmp}_i + bi - 1)$	1	do

$$\mathrm{tmp}_j = 1 + \left(\lceil \mathrm{jic} / \lfloor (n-1+bi)/bi \rfloor \rceil - \lfloor (n-1+bj)/bj \rfloor * \left(\frac{\mathrm{jic} - 1}{\lfloor (n-1+bj)/bj \rfloor * \lfloor (n-1+bi)/bi \rfloor} \right) - 1 \right) * bj$$

$$\mathrm{tmp}_i = 1 + \left(\mathrm{jic} - \lfloor (n-1+bi)/bi \rfloor * \left(\frac{\mathrm{jic} - 1}{\lfloor (n-1+bi)/bi \rfloor} \right) - 1 \right) * bi$$

Figure 7: Matrix Multiply example–shows the change in the loop nest for each transformation in the sequence.

Relaxing SIMD Control Flow Constraints using Loop Transformations*

Reinhard v. Hanxleden Ken Kennedy

Department of Computer Science
Rice University
Houston, TX 77251-1892

Abstract

Many loop nests in scientific codes contain a parallelizable outer loop but have an inner loop for which the number of iterations varies between different iterations of the outer loop. When running this kind of loop nest on a SIMD machine, the SIMD-inherent restriction to single program counter common to all processors will cause a performance degradation relative to comparable MIMD implementations. This problem is not due to limited parallelism or bad load balance, it is merely a problem of control flow.

This paper presents a loop transformation, which we call *loop flattening*, that overcomes this limitation by letting each processor advance to the next loop iteration containing useful computation, if there is such an iteration for the given processor. We study a concrete example derived from a molecular dynamics code and compare performance results for flattened and unflattened versions of this kernel on two SIMD machines, the CM-2 and the DECmpp 12000. We then evaluate loop flattening from the compiler's perspective in terms of applicability, cost, profitability, and safety. We conclude with arguing that loop flattening, whether performed by the programmer or by the compiler, introduces negligible overhead and can significantly improve the performance of scientific codes for solving irregular problems.

*This research was supported by the Center for Research on Parallel Computation, a National Science Foundation Science and Technology Center. Use of the DECmpp 12000 was provided by the Center for Research on Parallel Computation under NSF Cooperative Agreement No. CCR-8809615 with support from Digital Equipment Corporation.

ACM SIGPLAN '92 PLDI-6/92/CA
© 1992 ACM 0-89791-476-7/92/0006/0188...$1.50

1 Introduction

In the process of parallelizing scientific programs, it is common to find loop nests in which the outer loop can run in parallel but the amount of computation in the inner loop varies for different iterations of the outer loop. This causes a load balancing problem because the outer loop iterations have to be partitioned among the processors in such a manner that each processor has a roughly equal amount of work to do. Load balancing is a difficult problem in itself which has been frequently addressed in the literature [1, 9, 11]. Once this problem is solved, we can usually expect good performance when running such a loop nest on a shared-memory or distributed-memory MIMD (Multiple Instruction, Multiple Data) machine.

However, this kind of loop nest causes special problems for SIMD (Single Instruction, Multiple Data) architectures because of the restricted control flow on these machines [4]. If the number of iterations of the inner loops varies from one outer loop iteration to the next, then the restriction to a common program counter makes a naïve SIMD implementation inefficient. As observed in a case study implementing an image processing algorithm on the Massively Parallel Processor [23, page 143]: "... the complexity of each iteration in the SIMD environment is dominated by the largest region in the image. This is due to the fact that the synchronous execution of instructions forces each processor to either perform the operation or wait in an idle state until all processors have completed the operation." To overcome this limitation, we propose a new technique, which we call *loop flattening*, that, roughly speaking, amounts to lifting the innermost loop body up into the outer, parallel loop by merging the control of the inner loops with the control of the outer loop.

This paper is organized as follows. Section 2 describes the different variants of pseudo Fortran which we will use throughout this document. Section 3 presents a small example to illustrate the kind of problem we are interested in and gives a first glance at loop flattening, which Section 4 elaborates at at a more general level. Section 5 examines the applicability of loop flattening for a nonbonded force kernel, taken from a typical molecular dynamics program, which we implemented on both the CM2 and the DECmpp. Section 6 evaluates loop flattening from the compiler perspective. We conclude with a discussion of related work in Section 7.

2 Languages

The concepts introduced here apply to a broad range of languages. We will give program examples in different variants of pseudo Fortran:

F77 - Strictly sequential Fortran 77 (possibly a "dusty deck" program).

F77D - F77 enhanced with distribution statements as proposed in Fortran D [8] and High Performance Fortran [12]. An important goal of F77D is to provide a basis for efficient compilation towards both MIMD and SIMD distributed memory machines, so it should not contain any constructs which are specific to either architecture.

$F77_{MIMD}$ - A Fortran 77 version to run on a MIMD machine, which assumes a separate name space for each processor.

$F90_{SIMD}$ - A Fortran 90 version to run on a SIMD machine, similar to Connection Machine Fortran [21] or MasPar Fortran [16]. There are two important differences to the F77 variants:

- By default, scalars of the F77 version will be *replicated* in the $F90_{SIMD}$ version; *i.e.*, they will be declared as vectors of size P, where processor p owns the p-th element.
- In keeping with Fortran 90 convention, omitted array indices refer to all elements of an array dimension, and an unsubscripted array reference refers to all array elements.

For enhancing readability of the $F90_{SIMD}$ examples, we extend the language constructs which are typically implemented by vendors in several ways:

- The FORALL construct cannot only be applied to single statements, but also to blocks. The general form of this extension can be interpreted differently depending on the semantics chosen for the case where different iterations modify the same set of data; our examples, however, will avoid these access interferences.
- DO-ENDDO's, DO-WHILE's, IF's, WHERE's, and FORALL's can be nested freely within each other.

```
C    P1 – sequential version
     DO i = 1, K
       DO j = 1, L(i)
         X(i,j) = i * j
       ENDDO
     ENDDO
```

Figure 1: Original loop nest `EXAMPLE`.

```
C    P2 – Fortran D version
     DECOMPOSITION XD(K,Lmax), LD(K)
     ALIGN X with XD, L with LD
     DISTRIBUTE XD(BLOCK,*), LD(BLOCK)

     DO i = 1, K
       DO j = 1, L(i)
         X(i,j) = i * j
       ENDDO
     ENDDO
```

Figure 2: `EXAMPLE` in F77D.

- WHILE loops can be controlled by an array of booleans (instead of just a scalar boolean), if the different array elements are guaranteed to have identical values.

3 Example of Loop Flattening

Consider the contrived F77 loop nest in Figure 1, henceforth called `EXAMPLE`. This clearly is a dependence free, parallelizable loop, where the number of inner loop iterations depends on the current iteration of the outer loop. Let K be 8 and let $L(1{:}8)$[1] have the values 4,1,2,1,1,3,1,3, respectively. Assuming $P = 2$ processors and the *owner computes rule*, where in all assignment statements the right hand side expression is computed by the processor which "owns" the left hand side variable, we can in this case just distribute L and the rows of X blockwise to achieve perfect load balance. This is illustrated in the F77D program in Figure 2, which assigns $L(1{:}4)$, $X(1{:}4,1{:}4)$ to the first processor and $L(5{:}8)$, $X(5{:}8,1{:}4)$ to the second processor. The owner computes rule results in partitioning the iteration space among the two processors, so each processor executes only some iterations of the outer loop.

For a MIMD machine, the Fortran D compiler would derive the $F77_{MIMD}$ program shown in Figure 3. Each processor executes the loop nest independently, needing a total of

$$TIME_{MIMD} = \max_{p=1,2} \sum_{i=1}^{4} L(i + 2(p-1)) = 8 \qquad (1)$$

[1] Fortran 90 notation for the array elements $L(1) \ldots L(8)$.

```
C   P3 - MIMD version
  DO i = 1, 4
    DO j = 1, L'(i)
      X'(i,j) = i * j
    ENDDO
  ENDDO
```

Figure 3: `EXAMPLE` in $F77_{MIMD}$. X and L are renamed to X' and L' to reflect that there is no common name space any more. On processor p, $p = 1, 2$, $L'(i)$ corresponds to $L(i + 4(p-1))$, and $X'(i,j)$ corresponds to $X(i + 4(p-1), j)$.

Time	1	2	3	4	5	6	7	8
i_1	1	1	1	1	2	3	3	4
j_1	1	2	3	4	1	1	2	1
i_2	1	2	2	2	3	4	4	4
j_2	1	1	2	3	1	1	2	3

Figure 4: MIMD execution trace for `EXAMPLE` loop' i_p and j_p denote i and j on processor p.

inner loop iterations. This is illustrated in the trace in Figure 4.

A $F90_{SIMD}$ version could be derived from the F77D program by just changing the outer DO loop to a FORALL loop. This would result in a partitioning of the iteration space, similar to the F77D version. For expository reasons, we will give a slightly different but equivalent $F90_{SIMD}$ version which takes the data decomposition and the number of processors already into account and thus directly reflects the control flow for $K = 8$ and $P = 2$. As in the $F77_{MIMD}$ version, we change the upper bound of the outer loop from $K = 8$ to $K/P = 4$ and let each processor execute all iterations of the loop. We continue to use the loop index i in control flow related statements; to allow the different processors to operate on different data, we introduce an auxiliary induction variable, i', which replaces i in non-control flow statements. The result is shown in Figure 5.

Note how we had to transform the inner DO loop

```
C   P4 - naive SIMD version
  DO i = 1, 4
    i' = i + [0,4]
    DO j = 1, max(L(i'))
      WHERE (j ≤ L(i')) X(i',j) = i' * j
    ENDDO
  ENDDO
```

Figure 5: `EXAMPLE` in $F90_{SIMD}$. [0,4] denotes the two-element vector containing 0 and 4.

```
C   P5 - flattened SIMD version
  i = [1,5]
  K = [4,8]
  j = 1
  WHILE ANY(i ≤ K)
    WHERE (i ≤ K)
      X(i,j) = i * j
      WHERE (j = L(i))
        i = i + 1
        j = 1
      ELSEWHERE
        j = j + 1
      ENDWHERE
    ENDWHERE
  ENDWHILE
```

Figure 7: `EXAMPLE` in flattened $F90_{SIMD}$.

due to the single SIMD control flow. To make sure that each processor can perform all of its iterations, the upper bound $L(i')$ had to be changed into the maximum of $L(i')$ over all processors. This in turn necessitated a guard for the loop body which tests whether this processor is still involved in the current inner loop iteration or whether it is masked out and sits idle, possibly to participate again in later iterations.

We will refer to this transformation, which can be applied to other loop types as well, as *SIMDizing* a loop. It is a straightforward consequence of the SIMD restricted control flow, yet it is the crucial motivation for the concepts introduced in this paper. The outer loop does not have to be SIMDized in this particular case because we know that each processor works on exactly four rows of X and therefore has to execute the outer loop the same number of times. Loop SIMDizing has the effect that our $F90_{SIMD}$ program has to execute

$$TIME_{SIMD} = \sum_{i=1}^{4} \max_{p=1,2} L(i + 4(p-1)) = 12 \qquad (2)$$

iterations. Roughly speaking, our time bound has increased from a maximum over sums to a sum over maxima. This becomes apparent when considering the execution trace shown in Figure 6.

Since the equivalent MIMD implementation performs significantly better, this bad running time can not be explained with lack of parallelism or bad load balance. To overcome this purely control flow related problem, we apply *loop flattening*, which will be introduced at a more general level in the next section. The result is shown in Figure 7. Now we can achieve the same time bound as in the MIMD implementation, needing only eight steps as shown in the trace in Figure 4.

The reader might have noticed that the loop body shown in Figure 7 is now always executed at least once for each outer loop iteration, which is equivalent to

Time	1	2	3	4	5	6	7	8	9	10	11	12
i_1	1	1	1	1	2			3	3	4		
j_1	1	2	3	4	1			1	2	1		
i_2	1				2	2	2	3		4	4	4
j_2	1				1	2	3	1		1	2	3

Figure 6: Execution trace for unflattened example loop; i_p, j_p denote the actual iteration counts of processor p, no entry means "idle."

```
init1                    i = 1
WHILE test1              WHILE (i ≤ K)
  init2                    j = 1
  WHILE test2              WHILE (j ≤ L(i))
    BODY                     X(i,j) = i * j
    increment2               j = j + 1
  ENDWHILE                 ENDWHILE
  increment1               i = i + 1
ENDWHILE                 ENDWHILE
```

Figure 8: Generic loop nest **GENNEST** (left) and corresponding **EXAMPLE** (right); original version after normalization.

assuming $L(i) \geq 1$ for all i. Even though this is correct in our example, a more general loop flattening does not rely on this assumption, as we will see in the next section.

4 General Loop Flattening

Assume that we are given two fully parallelizable nested loops like in the previous section; an extension of the following to deeper loop nests is straightforward. Each of the loops might be structured as a WHILE loop, a DO-WHILE loop, a simple DO or FORALL loop, or it might use conditional GOTO's. The transformation described here can be done either at the F77/ F77D level or at the $F90_{SIMD}$ level. For simplicity and generality, we will present it here on the F77 level. A corresponding $F90_{SIMD}$ version can always be directly derived by SIMDizing loops and replacing IF's with WHERE's.

As a first step, we *normalize* both loops by breaking their control pattern into three *phases* for each nesting level l; an initialization phase $init_l$, a guard $test_l$, and an incrementing step $increment_l$. For example, a control pattern like `DO var = lo, hi, stride` would be broken into $init_l \equiv$ `var = lo`, $test_l \equiv$ `(var ≤ hi)`, and $increment_l \equiv$ `var = var + stride`. The resulting loop nest **GENNEST** is shown in Figure 8, along with the corresponding version of the **EXAMPLE** from the previous section (of course, we usually expect $\mathcal{BODY}$ to contain more computational work than in **EXAMPLE**).

Since **GENNEST** conservatively tests for loop completion before entering the loop body, all loops can be brought into this normal form. To estimate the running time of the above code on P processors, for processor p let K_p be the number of outer loop iterations and L_p^i be the number of inner loop iterations for the i-th outer loop iteration. A straightforward MIMD version would then finish after

$$TIME_{MIMD} = \max_{p=1 \ldots P} \sum_{i=1}^{K_p} L_p^i \qquad (1')$$

iterations.

A $F90_{SIMD}$ version could be derived by SIMDizing both WHILE loops and would execute

$$TIME_{SIMD} = \sum_{i=1}^{\max_{p=1}^{P} K_p} \max_{p=1 \ldots P} L_p^i \qquad (2')$$

iterations. Again, if the number of iterations of the inner loop varies from one outer loop iteration to the next, then the restriction to a common program counter makes this SIMD implementation inefficient.

Since we do not know whether the evaluation of $test_l$ has any side effects, we introduce flags t_l to store the results of evaluating the conditions $test_l$ before we make any other transformations, see Figure 9. So far, control flow is still unchanged.

The key idea of loop flattening is to make sure that each processor has a chance to advance to the next loop iteration where it participates in the execution of $\mathcal{BODY}$ before the control flow actually reaches $\mathcal{BODY}$. One requirement which follows immediately is that control variables (iteration counts etc.) are replicated to allow individual processors to advance independently to the next outer loop iteration whenever they are done with the current inner loop. Furthermore, we have to take $\mathcal{BODY}$ out of the part of the loop nest which handles the transition between different iterations of the inner and outer loop. Each processor should be able to execute $\mathcal{BODY}$ whenever it has still work left to do in this loop nest and the control flow reaches $\mathcal{BODY}$. In other words, $\mathcal{BODY}$ should be executed whenever t_1 is true, independent of t_2. The

```
init1                         i = 1
t1 = test1                    t1 = (i ≤ K)
WHILE t1                      WHILE t1
  init2                         j = 1
  t2 = test2                    t2 = (j ≤ L(i))
  WHILE t2                      WHILE t2
    BODY                          X(i,j) = i * j
    increment2                    j = j + 1
    t2 = test2                    t2 = (j ≤ L(i))
  ENDWHILE                      ENDWHILE
  increment1                    i = i + 1
  t1 = test1                    t1 = (i ≤ K)
ENDWHILE                      ENDWHILE
```

Figure 9: `GENNEST/EXAMPLE`, with guard variables.

```
init1                         i = 1
t1 = test1                    t1 = (i ≤ K)
IF t1 THEN init2              IF t1 then j = 1
WHILE t1                      WHILE t1
  t2 = test2                    t2 = (j ≤ L(i))
  WHILE (t1 ∧¬ t2)              WHILE (t1 ∧¬ t2)
    increment1                    i = i + 1
    t1 = test1                    t1 = (i ≤ K)
    IF t1 THEN                    IF t1 THEN
      init2                         j = 1
      t2 = test2                    t2 = (j ≤ L(i))
    ENDIF                         ENDIF
  ENDWHILE                      ENDWHILE
  IF t1 THEN                    IF t1 THEN
    BODY                          X(i,j) = i * j
    increment2                    j = j + 1
  ENDIF                         ENDIF
ENDWHILE                      ENDWHILE
```

Figure 10: `GENNEST/EXAMPLE`, after flattening.

flattened loop version meeting these goals is shown in Figure 10.

As the reader might verify, we still execute exactly the same instructions in the same order and the same number of times as we did in the original loop nest. We also still have two nested loops. However, $\mathcal{BODY}$ is lifted out of the inner loop. The inner loop now contains just the control structure to let each processor advance to the next iteration in which it actually executes $\mathcal{BODY}$. In other words, *the processors still have to run through $\mathcal{BODY}$ and the rest of the loop nest in lockstep, but now they may be executing effectively different loop iterations.*

The above transformation is the most general, conservative one. It can be optimized for several special cases; one common case is that

```
init1                         i = 1
init2                         j = 1
WHILE test1                   WHILE (i ≤ K)
  BODY                          X(i,j) = i * j
  increment2                    j = j + 1
  IF NOT test2 THEN             IF NOT(j ≤ L(i))
    increment1                    i = i + 1
    init2                         j = 1
  ENDIF                         ENDIF
ENDWHILE                      ENDWHILE
```

Figure 11: `GENNEST/EXAMPLE`, flattened and optimized.

```
init1                         i = 1
init2                         j = 1
WHILE test1                   WHILE (i ≤ K)
  BODY                          X(i,j) = i * j
  IF done2 THEN                 IF (j = L(i))
    increment1                    i = i + 1
    init2                         j = 1
  ELSE                          ELSE
    increment2                    j = j + 1
  ENDIF                         ENDIF
ENDWHILE                      ENDWHILE
```

Figure 12: `GENNEST/EXAMPLE` after further optimization.

1. $test_1$, $test_2$ and $init_2$ have no side effects, and that
2. for each outer loop iteration, the inner loop is executed at least once.

Then we can safely transform the code into the simpler version shown in Figure 11.

If it further is the case that

3. we can replace the guard $test_2$ with a test whether we are in the last inner iteration, $done_2$ (for example, in `DO var = lo, hi, stride`, we can replace $test \equiv$ `(var` $\leq$ `hi)` with $done \equiv$ `(var = hi)`),

then we can save the last execution of $increment_2$, as shown in Figure 12. The SIMDized equivalent `EXAMPLE` of this version was shown in Figure 7.

5 Case Study with Molecular Dynamics

The transformation described in the previous section should be profitable whenever some processors sit idle in an inner loop and still have work to do in later iterations of the outer loop. This seems to be a situation potentially occurring in many scientific programs solving

```
DO At1 = 1, N
  F(At1) = 0
  DO pr = 1, pCnt(At1)
    At2 = partners (At1, pr)
    F(At1) = F(At1) + Force (At1, At2)
  ENDDO
ENDDO
```

Figure 13: F90$_{SIMD}$ version of the nonbonded force calculation NBFORCE.

irregular problems [2, 19, 22, 23]. One example is the GROMOS molecular dynamics program, which contains several interesting kernels of this kind [6, 7, 10]. Here we want to focus on the calculation of the nonbonded forces between individual pairs of atoms.

5.1 The application

Since the nonbonded forces between pairs of atoms quickly decrease as the distances between them increase, they are usually approximated by considering only pairs of atoms which are closer together than a predefined *cutoff* radius; typical values are in the order of 10 Å. Still, in the GROMOS code this kernel typically accounts for about 90% of the overall simulation cost. For atom i, the atoms close enough to i are precomputed into an array $partners(i, 1{:}pCnt(i))$. This precomputation can be quite expensive in itself and is usually done only every k simulation steps, where $k = 10$ is one common value [20].

Figure 13 shows a F77 version NBFORCE for calculating the nonbonded forces between N atoms. This code can be parallelized by partitioning the set of all atoms into P disjoint subsets and assigning one subset to each processor p. To achieve load balancing, the sum over the number of the partners of the atoms in a processor's subset should be roughly equal across the processors. Furthermore, to achieve locality and scalability, the atoms within each subset should be closely together in space.

Figure 14 shows a F90$_{SIMD}$ program which lays out the data in a cyclic fashion. If we assume for simplicity that P divides N, then each processor computes the nonbonded forces for N/P atoms. The uneven atom density results in varying values of $pCnt$; therefore, the inner loop with the (relatively expensive) force calculation often has to be executed with processors masked out even though they still have work to do in later iterations, just as it was the case in the EXAMPLE in Section 3. All processors have to go through

$$TIME_{SIMD} = \sum_{i=1}^{N/P} \max_{p=1 \ldots P} pCnt(Atom_p^i) \qquad (2'')$$

iterations, where $Atom_p^i$ is the i-th Atom of processor p.

```
F = 0
At1 = [1 : P]
lastAt = [N-P+1 : N]
WHILE ANY (At1 ≤ lastAt)
  WHERE (At1 ≤ lastAt)
    DO pr = 1, max(pCnt(At1))
      WHERE (pr ≤ pCnt(At1))
        At2 = partners (At1, pr)
        F(At1) = F(At1) + Force (At1, At2)
      ENDWHERE
    ENDDO
    At1 = At1 + P
  ENDWHERE
ENDWHILE
```

Figure 14: F90$_{SIMD}$ version of NBFORCE.

```
F = 0
At1 = [1 : P]
lastAt = [N-P+1 : N]
pr = 1
WHILE ANY (At1 ≤ lastAt)
  WHERE (At1 ≤ lastAt)
    At2 = partners (At1, pr)
    F(At1) = F(At1) + Force (At1, At2)
    WHERE (pr = pCnt(At1))
      At1 = At1 + P
      pr = 1
    ELSEWHERE
      pr = pr + 1
    ENDWHERE
  ENDWHERE
ENDWHILE
```

Figure 15: Flattened F90$_{SIMD}$ version of NBFORCE. We take into account that $pCnt(i) \geq 1$ for all i.

This can be improved on by applying loop flattening, where we take into account that each atom has at least one interaction partner. The result is shown in Figure 15. Now each processor can loop through its atoms individually, so this code achieves the same time bound as a MIMD implementation:

$$TIME_{SIMD}^{flat} = \max_{p=1 \ldots P} \sum_{i=1}^{N/P} pCnt(Atom_p^i), \qquad (1'')$$

which is only limited by the quality of our workload distribution.

5.2 The hardware used

We implemented the nonbonded force kernel taken from the GROMOS program suite on two SIMD machines and one workstation. Our implementation models the behavior of the actual GROMOS routine by reading in the arrays $pCnt$ and $partners$ as produced by GROMOS and then generating the calls to a force routine for each interaction pair. To exclude communication time from our measurements, we assume that the *pCnt* and *partners* arrays and the molecular configuration data (including the coordinates of atoms we are interacting with) are already locally available when calling the force routines.

The **DECmpp 12000 model 8B** (Digital Equipment Corporation), which is identical to the MasPar MP-1200 series model, consists of 8192 processors (up to 16384 available), which are arranged in a mesh topology. It has 64 Kbytes main memory per processor, which gives 512 Mbytes total. Based on clock cycle counts, the individual processors are rated at 1.8 Mips. They are joined by an array control unit rated at 14 Mips. The MPFortran version we had on site (1.0) did not allow the use of indirect array addressing in FORALL statements, so the timing results we present here are achieved using an α-version of the 2.0 compiler at MasPar which does not have this restriction.

The **CM-2** (Thinking Machines Corporation) consists of 8192 one-bit processors (up to 65536 available), arranged in a hypercube topology. These are enhanced with 128 64-bit vector Floating Point Accelerators (FPA's) which use vector registers of length four. Each FPA is shared by two processor nodes of 32 processors each. The processors have 256 Kbits memory per processor, yielding a total of 268 Mbytes. The performance measured for a BYTE ADD is 500 Mips. We compiled our codes using the Slicewise 1.1 CMFortran compiler which lays out the data "slicewise" across the one-bit processors and uses the FPA's directly.

We also implemented the kernel on the **Sparc 2** (Sun Microsystems, Inc.), which is rated at 28 Mips and whose 16 Mbytes memory allowed us to run the smaller test cases. We compiled our program with the Sun f77 compiler.

One additional interesting machine parameter is the *data granularity* which measures how small an array can be if we want to distribute it across *all* processors. This granularity, *Gran*, is particularly important on SIMD machines since whenever a certain array has to be manipulated by some processors, all processors have to step through the operation and they will be merely masked out if they do not actually own part of the array. Furthermore, this potential waste of processing time can not only occur for small arrays, but it is encountered whenever array sizes are not exact multiples of *Gran* [15]. On the CM-2, using the slicewise compiler results in $Gran = P * 4/32 = P/8$ (32 processors per FPA, vector length 4); *i.e.*, we can economically use arrays whose total sizes are arbitrary multiples of $P/8$. This is a major advantage of the Slicewise model over the Paris model, which allocates data per one-bit processor. The corresponding data granularity on the DECmpp is simply $Gran = P$, and on the Sparc it is obviously $Gran = 1$.

Furthermore, the SIMD machines differ in the way they distribute data across the processors, which is significant if a dimension larger than *Gran* is distributed. The difference can be summarized as a cyclic ("cut-and-stack") data layout on the DECmpp and a block-wise layout on the CM-2.

5.3 Implementation experience

The DECmpp program and the CM-2 program used a single source, annotated with two sets of compiler directives, one for each machine. This worked relatively well; the only exception in our code was the `reshape` intrinsic. (The CMFortran convention for the argument order of this function is `mold` argument first, `source` argument second; MPFortran calls the `mold` argument `shape`, and has the order reversed. This combination of incompatibilities necessitated separate include files when using `reshape`; another option we tried was to replace the `reshape`'s with explicit `forall` statements, which caused a slight performance degradation on both machines.) The Sparc implementation shared the code for performing I/O and gathering timing statistics.

On the DECmpp, a compiler switch is used to recompile for different machine sizes. No compiler switch is needed for CM-2 since it uses a *virtual processor* model which adjusts automatically to the actual machine size. However, we can still obtain significant performance improvements if compile time constants are used to adjust array dimensions to actual machine configurations.

The indirect addressing used in the flattened loop version frequently required resorting to FORALL's in the source code. For example, the statement

```
forall(i=1:P) at2(i) = partners(i,l(i),pr(i))
```

cannot be expressed with indirection vectors as

```
at2 = partner(:,l,pr)
```

since this expression would yield a three-dimensional array with `at2(i,j,k) = partners(i,l(j),pr(k))` instead of the desired one-dimensional array computed in the `forall` statement. However, implementing the $F90_{SIMD}$ code from Figure 15 was still relatively straightforward. The initial flattened loop version, L_f, ran well on both machines without further tuning; it is shown in Figure 16. `Lrs` is the number of *memory layers* (or *virtual processor slices*) which are in actual use; it is `Lrs` $= \lfloor 1+(N-1)/Gran \rfloor$. The dimensions indexed with `1:Lrs` are of size `maxLrs` $= \lfloor 1 + (N_{max} - 1)/P \rfloor$; for our implementation, the maximal number of atoms simulated is $N_{max} = 8192$. For example, for $Gran = 128$ and the $N = 6968$ atom test case described in Subsection 5.4, it is `Lrs` $= 55$ and `maxLrs` $= 64$; for $Gran = 8192$, we have `Lrs` $=$ `maxLrs` $= 1$.

Our experience with the implementation of the unflattened loop version was very different. The initial

```
      subroutine AllFFlat()
C     Formal parameters omitted here;
C     F, pCnt, partners are distributed
C     in first dimension

      integer at1(P),at2(P),l(P),pr(P),m(P)
      real Force(P)
cmf$  layout Force,at1,at2,l,pr,m
cmpf  ondpu Force,at1,at2,l,pr,m

      F = 0
      l = 1
      pr = 1
      at1 = [1:P]
      do while(any(l.le.Lrs))
        forall(i=1:P) at2(i) =
     .        partners(i,l(i),pr(i))
        call OneFFlat(Force, at1, at2)
        forall(i=1:P, l(i).le.Lrs)
     .        F(i,l(i)) = F(i,l(i)) + Force(i)
        forall(i=1:P) m(i) =
     .       (pCnt(i,l(i)).ge.pr(i))
        where (m)
          pr = pr + 1
        elsewhere
          pr = 1
          l = l + 1
          at1 = at1 + P
        endwhere
      enddo
```

Figure 16: Actual implementation of the flattened $F90_{SIMD}$ version of NBFORCE.

```
      subroutine AllF()
C     Formal parameters omitted here;
C     F, pCnt, partners are distributed
C     in first dimension

      integer at1(P,maxLrs),at2(P,maxLrs)
      real Force(P,maxLrs)
cmf$  layout Force(:news,:serial)
cmf$  layout at1(:news,:serial)
cmf$  layout at2(:news,:serial)
cmpf  ondpu Force,at1,at2
cmpf  map Force(allbits,memory)
cmpf  map at1(allbits,memory)
cmpf  map at2(allbits,memory)
      integer pr

      F = 0
      at1 = reshape(shape = [P,maxLrs],
     .      source = [1:Nmax])
      maxPCnt = maxval(pCnt)
      do pr = 1, maxPCnt
        at2(:,1:Lrs) = partners(:,1:Lrs,pr)
        call OneF(Force,at1,at2)
        where (pCnt.ge.pr)
          F(:,1:Lrs) = F(:,1:Lrs) +
     .        Force(:,1:Lrs)
        endwhere
      enddo
```

Figure 17: Actual implementation of the unflattened CMFortran/MPFortran version of NBFORCE.

implementation of the pseudocode in Figure 14 was trivial to write, but its performance was roughly an order of magnitude worse than the flattened version on both machines and required significant performance debugging. We tried several different implementations using interface blocks, layout directives, inlining, different compiler switches, etc.; parameter arrays were automatic, fixed size, or passed in COMMON blocks; the dimension corresponding to different atom numbers was either left as a single dimension (as in Force(1:Nmax)), or split up into physical processor number and memory layer (as in Force(1:P,1:maxLayers)); we tried DO-WHILE loops (as in do while(any(pr.le.pCnt))) and DO-ENDDO loops with precomputed loop bounds (do pr = 1, maxPCnt); we also tried vectorizing the code in the dimension indexed by pr, but this was unfeasible due to the size of partners.

We here present timing results for two different unflattened versions; the first version, L_u^1, is shown in Figure 17. The other version, L_u^2, differs from L_u^1 in that all explicit "1:Lrs" indices are replaced with just a ":" referring to the whole dimension. Note that the dimension indexed with 1:Lrs is actually laid out serially into local memory. Theoretically the machine front end could take advantage of the explicit subscripts of the L_u^1 version by pruning the number of processed memory layers. However, in practice it turns out that, at least on the CM-2, the processors will always cycle through *all* layers of memory. Doubling N_{max} (and therefore doubling maxLrs) and leaving all other parameters fixed results therefore not only in doubling execution time of the L_u^2 version on both machines, but on the CM-2, it also doubles running time of the L_u^1 version. On the DECmpp, the L_u^1 time increases by about 5%, while the running time of L_f stays unaffected on both machines, which is a nice side effect of loop flattening. Therefore, using the L_u^1 loops does not automatically result in any savings by reducing the number of processed layers; however, we have to pay the additional overhead of checking on each layer whether it is active [5]. This overhead is saved in the L_u^2 version.

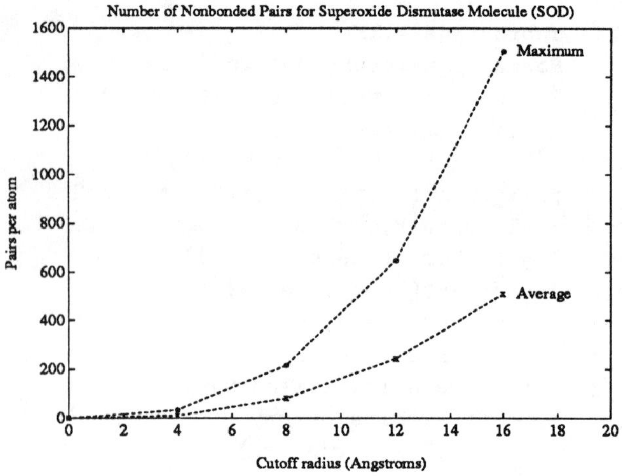

Figure 18: Maximum and average number of non-bonded force interaction partners per atom for the superoxide dismutase molecule, using different cutoff radii.

5.4 The input data

We ran our test case for the bovine superoxide dismutase molecule (*SOD*), which has $N = 6968$ atoms. SOD is a catalytic enzyme composed of two identical subunits, each with 151 amino-acid residues and two metal atoms [20].

Figure 18 shows maximal and average numbers of interaction partners, $pCnt_{max}$ and $pCnt_{ave}$, which indicate the computational workloads for different cutoff radii. As expected, both values increase cubicly with the cutoff radius. As indicated in Equations 1″ and 2″, the difference between maximum and average number of partners gives us an upper bound on how much improvements we can expect from loop flattening.

5.5 The results

Table 1 gives performance results for the CM-2 and the DECmpp 12000, which are also displayed in Figure 19. For comparison, the running times on the Sparc were 3.86 seconds for 4 Å case and 31.43 seconds for 8 Å case. All runs were done several times, the differences in running times were usually less than 0.01%.

All loop versions were also timed with inlined calls to the force routine. On the CM-2, the effect was marginal; on the DECmpp, fluctuations were within 5%, roughly evenly distributed in both directions.

Table 2 gives the number of calls to Force routine for the flattened and the unflattened loop versions (the latter number scaled up by `Lrs` to account for the different argument sizes of `OneF()` and `OneFFlat()`) for different data granularities, along with their ratios. Note that the counts given in the last row are actually the maxima of $pCnt$ for the corresponding cutoff radii, as given in Figure 18. The given L_u/L_f ratios are bounded by the $pCnt_{max}/pCnt_{ave}$ ratios, which are 3.347, 2.689, 2.665, and 2.949 for cutoffs 4 Å, 8 Å, 12 Å, and 16 Å, respectively.

5.6 Interpretation

Considering the different computing powers per individual processor, the overall speedups of the parallel codes over the Sparc code version were satisfactory. However, we have to take into account that we excluded communication costs from our study. Due to the irregular nature of the problem, these communication costs might be relatively high; but as indicated earlier, the communication requirements are not changed by our transformation.

When comparing Tables 1 and 2, loop flattening fulfills the expectations given by Equations 1″ and 2″. Despite the significant effort on speeding up the unflattened loop versions (as described in Subsection 5.3), the improvements of the flattened version often went beyond what we predicted from the $pCnt_{max}/pCnt_{ave}$ ratios, in particular on the DECmpp. We assume that this is largely due to the side effect mentioned in Subsection 5.3, namely that loop flattening makes actual running times less dependent on array sizes if we do not access all parts of the array; *i.e.*, we can increase N_{max} without automatically making L_f slower (unlike for L_u^2 and even L_u^1). This we consider a significant advantage in practice, since this allows to compile programs with provision for maximal problem sizes without paying a penalty on smaller sizes.

Moreover, it turned out that the effort of expressing array bounds in terms of actual machine sizes improved the unflattened loop versions as well. This was particularly beneficial for the virtual processor model of the CM-2.

It is important to keep in mind that the slicewise compiler for the CM-2 actually generates code with a data granularity of $Gran = P/8$, as discussed in Subsection 5.2. This coarser granularity results in more atoms per processor and therefore better applicability of loop flattening. As the table and the graph indicate for the CM-2, several cases could be run with the L_f version with reasonable performance while they could not be run at all in L_u^1 or L_u^2 because of stack overflows; large temporary arrays were needed in L_u^1 and L_u^2 even in loop versions which forward substituted intermediate results.

The differences between the two unflattened loop versions L_u^1 and L_u^2 were larger on the CM-2 than on the DECmpp, as mentioned in Subsection 5.3. However, even on the DECmpp L_u^2 performed better than L_u^1 when `Lrs` approached `maxLrs`.

P/Gran	4Å L_u^1	4Å L_u^2	4Å L_f	8Å L_u^1	8Å L_u^2	8Å L_f	12Å L_u^1	12Å L_u^2	12Å L_f	16Å L_u^1	16Å L_u^2	16Å L_f
1024/128			3.89			27.03						
2048/256	6.57	3.86	2.13	42.91	25.13	14.72						
4096/512	3.22	1.83	1.11	21.02	11.95	7.65			24.78			
8192/1024	1.72	0.99	0.64	11.19	6.46	4.57			13.31			27.17
1024/1024	0.910	0.934	0.390	5.36	5.85	2.81	15.91	17.45	8.19	36.86	40.45	16.84
2048/2048	0.638	0.481	0.266	3.35	3.00	1.69	9.96	8.95	4.98	23.07	20.71	10.68
4096/4096	0.352	0.269	0.157	1.86	1.55	1.05	5.18	4.59	3.14	11.96	10.58	6.51
8192/8192	0.145	0.129	0.104	0.683	0.715	0.671	1.92	2.09	2.00	4.42	4.82	4.66

Table 1: Performance results for the CM-2 (upper half) and the DECmpp (lower half). Running times (in seconds) are listed for different cutoff radii and different loop versions. L_u^1: unflattened loop selecting memory layers, L_u^2: unflattened loop using all memory layers, L_f: flattened loop.

Gran	4Å L_u	4Å L_f	4Å L_u/L_f	8Å L_u	8Å L_f	8Å L_u/L_f	12Å L_u	12Å L_f	12Å L_u/L_f	16Å L_u	16Å L_f	16Å L_u/L_f
128		722			5076							
256	924	397	2.327	6048	2754	2.196						
512	462	224	2.063	3024	1559	1.940		4649				
1024	231	125	1.848	1512	906	1.669	4536	2642	1.717	10528	5436	1.937
2048	132	86	1.535	864	545	1.585	2592	1606	1.614	6016	3434	1.752
4096	66	51	1.210	432	357	1.210	1296	1069	1.212	3008	2222	1.354
8192	33	33	1	216	216	1	648	648	1	1504	1504	1

Table 2: Number of calls to Force routine, flattened/unflattened version. The data granularity, *Gran*, is equal to P for the DECmpp and $P/8$ for the CM-2. L_u counts are multiplied with `Lrs`.

6 Loop Flattening from the Compiler's Perspective

The discussion so far seems to advocate a certain style of SIMD programming for applications which can benefit from loop flattening, just as a certain style of programming emerged when vector machines became popular. However, this would be contrary to existing efforts to make programming independent from machine idiosyncrasies, as for example the development of the Fortran D language. For non-SIMD machines, it still seems natural and efficient to have the inner loop bodies contained in the inner loops, even though flattened loops should run well on these machines also. Therefore, we suggest to make loop flattening part of the optimizing repertoire of SIMD compilers.

Applicability is ensured whenever there are multiple loops fully contained in each other, *i.e.*, there are not several loops on the same nesting level. This can be easily derived from the abstract syntax tree. Furthermore, the normalized version always tests the loop guard $test_l$ before executing $\mathcal{BODY}$, so we cover all loop constructs. The transformation itself is relatively straightforward; for example, there are no parameters to adjust, unlike in loop skewing. The first step of the transformation is to identify the three phases *init*, *test*, and *increment*.

WHILE/DO-WHILE loops: The relevant phases can be identified from their position between the WHILE/ENDWHILE keywords. Since $increment_2$ and $\mathcal{BODY}$ stay together throughout the transformation, we actually do not need to separate these two phases.

DO/FORALL loops: The phases can be derived directly from the loop header, as exemplified earlier.

GOTO loops: Similarly to WHILE loops, we can identify the phases by their position between labels and jumps.

After normalization, the introduction of flags t_l and the actual code rearrangement follow straightforwardly. As described in Section 4, we also can often detect opportunities for further optimizations, for example when we are transforming simple DO/FORALL loops.

In evaluating *profitability*, we note that the additional overhead caused by loop flattening is, in the worst case, to manipulate two flags and to perform two

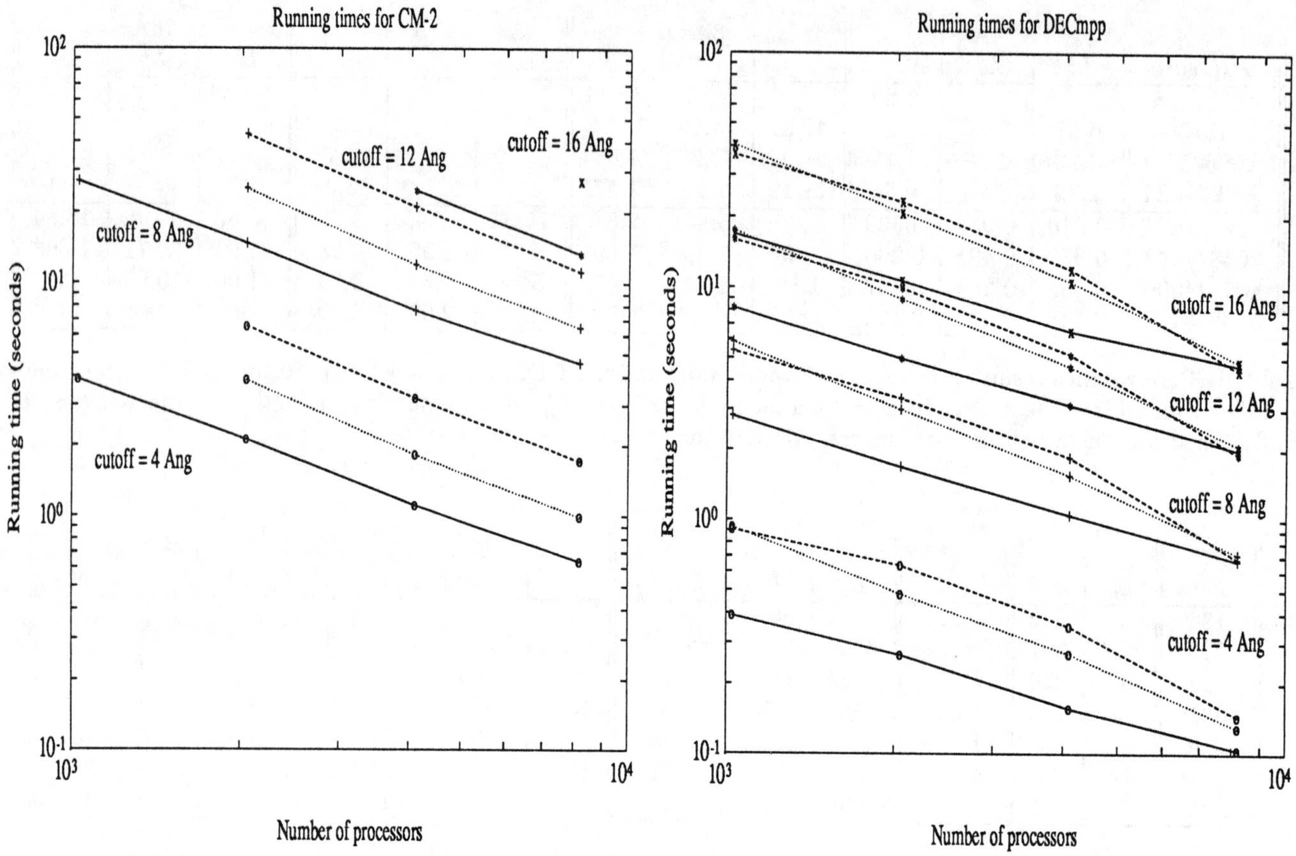

Figure 19: Performance results for the CM-2 and the DECmpp 12000. Different loop versions vary in line style; dashes: unflattened loop selecting memory layers; dots: unflattened loop using all memory layers; solid lines: flattened loop. Different cutoff radii are indicated by point styles; circles: 4 Å, plusses: 8 Å; stars: 12 Å; crosses: 16 Å. For judging speedups, note the log-log scale and the aspect ratio.

conditional jumps. So we can relatively safely assume profitability whenever the inner loop bounds may vary across the processors.

As with many code transformations, the hardest problem in automating loop flattening is to determine its *safety*. A sufficient condition is that the loop into which we lift an inner loop body can be parallelized, which might be hard to detect, especially if indirect addressing occurs. However, this is already a necessary condition for parallelizing loops in general, and therewith a standard problem for parallelizing compilers [13]. The same technology developed there can be applied here.

When safety is ensured, either by user information (like a FORALL loop header) or by "heroic dependence analysis," we expect that the systematic loop flattening transformation, as described in Section 4, can be implemented efficiently into compilers like the Fortran D compiler in the ParaScope programming environment [14].

7 Related Work

The restricted control flow of pure SIMD programming has been addressed by several researchers. Phillipsen et al. introduce two variants of a FORALL statement, a synchronous version and an asynchronous one [17]. The *asynchronous FORALL* allows multiple threads of control to coexist. This can either be emulated using stacks of MASK bits, or it can be implemented directly in an MSIMD machine which contains multiple program counters. In either case, their proposal is mainly concerned with allowing the concurrent execution of both branches in IF-THEN-ELSE constructs; it does not directly apply to inner loops with varying bounds.

Loop flattening can also be used to process multiple array *segments* of different lengths per processor, as introduced in Blelloch's *V-RAM model* [3]. Thus it can be viewed as a generalization of substituting direct addressing with *indirect addressing* as Tomboulian and Pappas did for computing the Mandelbrot set [22].

Loop flattening bears similarities to *loop coalescing*

in that it also manipulates loop control flow, but it is very different in its motivation and final outcome [18]. Loop coalescing merges iteration variables to achieve a higher degree of parallelism and to allow a more flexible distribution of inner loop iterations among the processors. Although loop flattening can also simplify load balancing, the transformation per se does not change *which* loop iterations a processor executes. Instead, it gives it more freedom as to *when* it executes them.

To conclude, the relative performance difference between conventional and flattened $F90_{SIMD}$ programs will depend on the variance of the cost of the inner loops for different outer loop iterations. We expect the difference to be significant in many cases, as it was for the application described in this paper. Furthermore, we believe that current compiler technology can automate this transformation effectively. If this were done, it would represent another significant step toward compiler support of architecture independent parallel programming for a large class of irregular scientific problems.

Acknowledgements

We are very grateful to Terry Clark and Ridgway Scott for providing detailed knowledge and experience about parallelizing molecular dynamics codes. Terry also supplied us with the pairlist data for the SOD molecule simulated in our experiments. Special thanks to Jim Armstrong from MasPar, who was an invaluable source of information and very helpful with the DECmpp implementation. Mark Mazina assisted with both the DECmpp and the CM-2 programming. We also wish to thank Chuck Koelbel and Jerry Roth for many profitable discussions about solving irregular problems on parallel computers and about SIMD related problems. Matthias Felleisen gave helpful comments on the submitted abstract.

References

[1] T. Bemmerl, A. Bode, O. Hansen, and T. Ludwig. A testbed for dynamic loadbalancing on distributed memory multiprocessors. PUMA Working Paper 14, Technical University Munich, München, Germany, August 1990.

[2] H. Berryman, J. Saltz, W. Gropp, and R. Mirchandaney. Krylov methods preconditioned with incompletely factored matrices on the CM-2. *Journal of Parallel and Distributed Computing*, 8:186–190, 1990.

[3] G. E. Blelloch. *Vector Models for Data-Parallel Computing.* The MIT Press, 1990.

[4] T. Bräunl. Structured SIMD programing in Parallaxis. *Structured Programming*, 10(3):121–132, 1989.

[5] P. Christy. Virtual processors considered harmful. In *Proceedings of the 6th Distributed Memory Computing Conference*, Portland, OR, April 1991.

[6] T. W. Clark, R. v. Hanxleden, K. Kennedy, C. Koelbel, and L. R. Scott. Evaluating parallel languages for molecular dynamics computations. In *Scalable High Performance Computing Conference*, Williamsburg, VA, April 1992.

[7] T. W. Clark, R. v. Hanxleden, J. A. McCammon, and L. Ridgway Scott. From sequential to parallel molecular dynamics. In *Intel Supercomputer University Partners Conference*, Timberline Lodge, Mt. Hood, OR, April 1992.

[8] G. C. Fox, S. Hiranandani, K. Kennedy, C. Koelbel, U. Kremer, C. Tseng, and M. Wu. Fortran D language specification. Technical Report TR90-141, Dept. of Computer Science, Rice University, December 1990. Revised April, 1991.

[9] G. C. Fox, M. Johnson, G. Lyzenga, S. Otto, J. Salmon, and D. Walker. *Solving Problems on Concurrent Multiprocessors.* Prentice-Hall, 1988.

[10] W. F. van Gunsteren and H. J. C. Berendsen. GROMOS: GROningen MOlecular Simulation software. Technical report, Laboratory of Physical Chemistry, University of Groningen, Nijenborgh, The Netherlands, 1988.

[11] R. v. Hanxleden and L. R. Scott. Load balancing on message passing architectures. *Journal of Parallel and Distributed Computing*, 13:312–324, 1991.

[12] *Proceedings of the High Performance Fortran Forum*, Houston, TX, January 1992.

[13] S. Hiranandani, K. Kennedy, and C. Tseng. Compiler support for machine-independent parallel programming in Fortran D. In J. Saltz and P. Mehrotra, editors, *Compilers and Runtime Software for Scalable Multiprocessors.* Elsevier, Amsterdam, The Netherlands, to appear 1992.

[14] K. Kennedy, K. S. McKinley, and C. Tseng. Analysis and transformation in the ParaScope Editor. In *Proceedings of the 1991 ACM International Conference on Supercomputing*, Cologne, Germany, June 1991.

[15] K. Knobe, J. Lukas, and G. Steele, Jr. Data optimization: Allocation of arrays to reduce communication on SIMD machines. *Journal of Parallel and Distributed Computing*, 8(2):102–118, February 1990.

[16] MasPar Computer Corporation, Sunnyvale, CA. *MasPar Fortran Reference Manual.*

[17] M. Phillipsen and W. F. Tichy. Modula-2* and its compilation. In *First International Conference of the Austrian Center for Parallel Computation*, Salzburg, Austria, September 1991.

[18] C. D. Polychronopoulos. Loop coalescing: A compiler transformation for parallel machines. In S. Sahni, editor, *Proceedings of the 1987 International Conference on Parallel Processing*, St. Charles, IL, August 1987. Pennsylvania State University Press.

[19] J. Saltz, S. Petiton, H. Berryman, and A. Rifkin. Performance effects of irregular communication patterns on massively parallel multicomputers. ICASE Report 91-12, Institute for Computer Application in Science and Engineering, Hampton, VA, January 1991.

[20] J. Shen and J. A. McCammon. Molecular dynamics simulation of Superoxide interacting with Superoxide Dismutase. *Chemical Physics*, 158:191–198, 1991.

[21] Thinking Machines Corporation, Cambridge, MA. *CM Fortran Reference Manual.*

[22] S. Tomboulian and M. Pappas. Indirect addressing and load balancing for faster solutions to the Mandelbrot set on SIMD architectures. In *Frontiers90: The 3rd Symposium on the Frontiers of Massively Parallel Computation*, pages 443–450, College Park, MD, October 1990.

[23] M. Willebeek-LeMair and A. P. Reeves. Solving nonuniform problems on SIMD computers: Case study on region growing. *Journal of Parallel and Distributed Computing*, 8:135–149, 1990.

A Dynamic Scheduling Method for Irregular Parallel Programs

Steven Lucco*

Computer Science Division, 571 Evans Hall
UC Berkeley, Berkeley CA, 94720

Abstract

This paper develops a methodology for compiling and executing *irregular* parallel programs. Such programs implement parallel operations whose size and work distribution depend on input data. We show a fundamental relationship between three quantities that characterize an irregular parallel computation: the total available parallelism, the optimal grain size, and the statistical variance of execution times for individual tasks. This relationship yields a dynamic scheduling algorithm that substantially reduces the overhead of executing irregular parallel operations.

We incorporated this algorithm into an extended Fortran compiler. The compiler accepts as input a subset of Fortran D which includes blocked and cyclic decompositions and perfect alignment; it outputs Fortran 77 augmented with calls to library routines written in C. For irregular parallel operations, the compiled code gathers information about available parallelism and task execution time variance and uses this information to schedule the operation. On distributed memory architectures, the compiler encodes information about data access patterns for the runtime scheduling system so that it can preserve communication locality.

We evaluated these compilation techniques using a set of application programs including climate modeling, circuit simulation, and x-ray tomography, that contain irregular parallel operations. The results demonstrate that, for these applications, the dynamic techniques described here achieve near-optimal efficiency on large numbers of processors. In addition, they perform significantly better, on these problems, than any previously proposed static or dynamic scheduling algorithm.

1 Introduction

The aim of our research is to achieve efficient execution of parallel programs. Compiler research toward this goal has focused on four main areas: discovery of parallelism [2, 3, 25], static scheduling [8, 10, 24], linear transformation of iteration spaces to improve data locality or expose parallelism [31, 33, 34], and improved compiler technology to support the first three activities [7, 9]. In this paper we focus on a particularly intractable class of parallel programs for which static techniques such as these are not sufficient to generate highly efficient code. This is not a deficiency of the static techniques, which are often a prerequisite for efficient execution, but a property of the programs themselves. Such programs, which we call *irregular*, contain parallel operations whose size and work distribution depend on input data. Because of this property, a static schedule that performs well on one set of input data may perform poorly on others. Further, even static schedules that use random task assignments to avoid bias will have only moderate efficiency if the individual tasks have significant execution time variance.

Many basic computational techniques, such as adaptive mesh refinement [5], time-step subdivision [1, 20], tree traversal [12], and monte-carlo methods[30], yield irregular parallel programs. To execute such pro-

*Supported in part by an IBM Fellowship. Email address: lucco@cs.Berkeley.EDU. Research sponsored in part by the Defense Advanced Research Projects Agency (DoD), monitored by Space and Naval Warfare Systems Command under Contract N00039-88-C-0292

ACM SIGPLAN '92 PLDI-6/92/CA
© 1992 ACM 0-89791-476-7/92/0006/0200...$1.50

grams efficiently, we generate code that assigns tasks to processors dynamically. We require that a dynamic scheduling policy have two properties: adaptivity and statelessness. The latter property means that current scheduling decisions do not use information about past decisions; this implies that the scheduling policy will function correctly under the addition and subtraction of processors, and the addition of new tasks to the set of tasks being scheduled. An adaptive scheduling policy gathers runtime information about the distribution of task execution times, and uses this information to improve the efficiency of the schedule. No previously proposed dynamic scheduling policies have both these properties; however, we believe both are necessary for efficient execution of irregular problems. In this paper, we develop an adaptive, stateless dynamic scheduling algorithm and describe how we incorporated the algorithm into a compiler for shared and distributed memory architectures.

The remainder of the paper is organized as follows. Section 2 gives some examples of irregular programs and illustrates how different types of execution time distributions can arise. Section 3 presents our basic compilation framework and describes how we modified it to incorporate dynamic scheduling. Section 4 illustrates some important properties of previously proposed scheduling algorithms. In section 5.1, we prove a new property of multiprocessor scheduling and use this property to derive a relationship between optimal grain size, available parallelism and task execution time variance. In section 5.2, we develop our probabilistic dynamic scheduling algorithm and extend it for execution on distributed memory machines. Finally, section 6 presents efficiency results for a set of application programs.

2 Irregular Programs

First we give some examples which illustrate how irregular work distributions can arise in programs. We define a parallel operation as a set of N independent tasks, such as the iterates of a DOALL loop. In an *irregular* parallel operation, task execution times vary significantly and unpredictably. Consider the irregular Fortran loop shown in figure 1.

```
      DOALL 10 I=1,N
        IF (C{0.9,0.1}) THEN
          {200}
        ELSE
          {60000}
        ENDIF
10      CONTINUE
```

Figure 1: A Sample Irregular Loop

The numbers in brackets indicate execution costs for sequential sections of the loop. The conditional statement is labeled with the probabilities of the true and false branches respectively. Even given this information it is impossible (except for very large N) to compute a schedule for this loop statically that is efficient in the average case.

Suppose that we randomly assign tasks to processors. Since the execution costs of the tasks are themselves random, we can just assign successive contiguous blocks of N/p tasks to each processor (this is equivalent to using the owner computes rule [14] for a blocked decomposition). Figure 2 shows the efficiency of this method for executing our loop example, given different values of N/p. No static method can beat the average case behavior of random assignment.

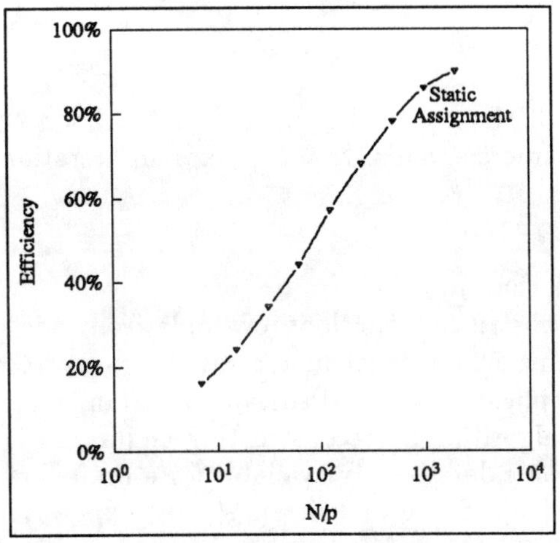

Figure 2: Efficiency of Static Assignment

This result is not limited to this example, but applies to any parallel operation with significant variance in task execution times. The expected finishing time of a chunk of N/p tasks is $N\mu/p$, where μ is the mean task cost. However, given no restriction on task cost distribution, the best bound on the finishing time of p such chunks is $N\mu/p+\sigma\sqrt{N/2}$ where σ is the standard deviation of task costs [11]. For an important class of distributions (including normal, uniform, and exponential), Kruskal [16] demonstrates the tighter bound $N\mu/p + \sigma\sqrt{2N \ln p/p}$. However, either bound leaves room for substantial inefficiency.

Since the expected inefficiency (the second term in these expressions) grows as the square root, while the expected completion time grows linearly, random assignment will be efficient for large N/p; however, we will demonstrate that it is only more efficient than dynamic methods when $\sigma \ll \mu$ (*i.e.* the tasks do not differ much in cost) or the scheduling overhead is much

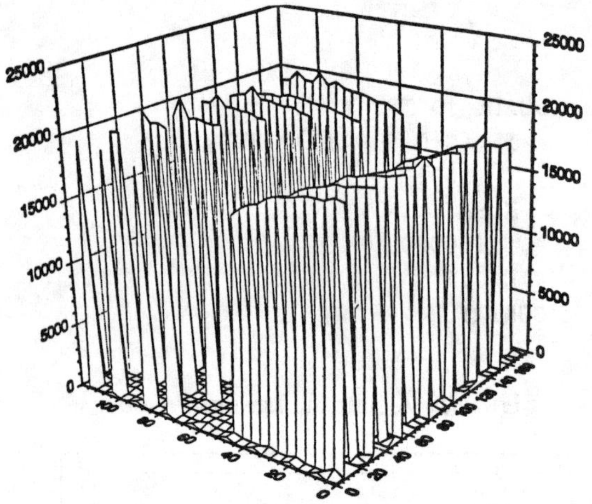

Figure 3: Execution Profile of Psirrfan Loop Nest. Z axis is microseconds; X and Y axes are iteration numbers.

greater than μ.

We abstracted our loop example from one of the programs in our benchmark set, an x-ray tomography application called Psirrfan. Psirrfan implements a new algorithm for reconstructing an image where tomographic data is only available for a limited range of angles [13]. Some of Psirrfan's most expensive operations are executed only when input data is missing. Figure 3 shows an execution profile for an important loop nest involved in implementing the image reconstruction.

In addition, Psirrfan contains another type of irregular operation. In this type of operation, the body of one loop computes the bounds for another. In Psirrfan, this gives rise to a normal work distribution; we have also seen instances where computed bounds give rise to uniform distributions.

Another application program whose measurements are reported in section 6 is the UCLA General Circulation Model [6]. Variants of this program are used widely to model trends in climate. We studied a section of this program, COMP3, that represents about 60% of the total execution time and is highly irregular. In this case, the irregularity arises during the simulation, rather than directly from the original input data. COMP3 contains several physics modules which are only invoked when certain atmospheric conditions exist. For example, in the cumulus clouds over Kenya, COMP3 models the thermal properties of water vapor; in the clear skies over the Sahara, it does not. To make matters worse, weather systems travel large distances across the Earth's surface, dragging along their special atmospheric conditions. As with Psirrfan, these computational irregularities are expressed as function calls and inner loops protected by conditionals.

The climate model has an additional important property. It updates its simulation state using a two dimensional 5x5 stencil (over latitude and longitude). This means that any scheduling algorithm must preserve the program's communication locality by mapping most adjacent grid elements to the same processor.

3 Context

This section gives a brief overview of our extended Fortran 77 compiler, and describes how we modified it to generate efficient code for irregular parallel programs, using the scheduling methods described in section 5.

The compiler recognizes the following two extensions for explicitly specifying parallelism: DOALL and PARALLEL SECTION. DOALL denotes that all iterates of a loop can execute simultaneously. PARALLEL SECTION identifies sequences of program statements that can execute independently. In addition, the compiler recognizes a subset of the Fortran D extensions for specifying data decomposition [14]. It handles BLOCKED and CYCLIC decompositions in one or two dimensions, and perfect alignment. The target architectures discussed in this paper are the Ncube-2 distributed memory multiprocessor (512 processors) and the Cray Y/MP shared memory vector multiprocessor (8 processors).

Compilation proceeds in four pipelined phases. In phase one, parallel operations are transformed to improve data locality and to reduce synchronization overhead. The compiler uses transformations including loop interchange [4] and loop skewing [34] to expose coarse grained parallelism [32]. In addition, phase one performs tiling transformations to improve the data locality of loop nests [31].

When compiling for distributed memory machines, phase one also generates code to partition arrays among processors according to programmer-specified decompositions. Following the convention of the Rice Fortran D compiler [14], our compiler uses the *owner computes* rule to make an initial assignment of loop iterations to processors. Under this rule, if an array element is the left hand side of an assignment statement, the processor holding that array element computes the right hand side of the statement.

Our runtime scheduling system uses the distributed algorithm described in section 5.2 to transfer ownership of array segments and their associated computations. This algorithm operates under the assumption that data has been laid out to maximize communication locality. When re-assigning computations, the algorithm avoids excessive data scattering by maintaining a minimum grain size, K_{min}. K_{min} determines the minimum number of iterations that can be transferred as a block from one processor to another. This minimum grain size constrains the scheduler not to exceed the bandwidth requirements of the machine. On machines like the Ncube, which have a large message startup cost, the minimum grain size must also be large enough to keep the average number of messages per processor reasonably low.

Phase two of the compiler generates calls to the runtime communication library. It uses the dataflow algorithms described in [14] to compute *send* and *receive* sets for each parallel operation, and then uses this information to generate communication code. To support transfer of ownership, all messages follow a forwarding protocol [19] to find their actual destinations.

In phase three, the compiler generates *code blocks* for each parallel operation. The code blocks are parameterized by grain size. Phase four generates *scheduling templates* for each parallel operation. There are four types of scheduling templates: *sequential, static, profile,* and *sample.* The first of these executes the operation sequentially. The second uses the owner computes rule on distributed memory machines, and allocates tasks to processors evenly on shared memory machines.

The latter two use the dynamic scheduling algorithms described below. They differ in how they gather information about the distribution of task execution times. Profile templates use information gathered from previous runs of the program to estimate execution time mean and variance [27]. Sample templates begin with a rough estimate of these two quantities and refine the estimates through runtime sampling of task execution times. On the Ncube and Cray Y/MP, the code performs sampling by reading a memory-mapped microsecond clock. The scheduling algorithm preserves the output of sampled tasks, so that no repeated task execution is necessary.

4 Properties of Previous Approaches

Researchers have proposed many different approaches to scheduling parallel operations. Regular loops in scientific programs have been scheduled using delay insertion [8] or combinatorial exploration of possible processor assignments [24]. These approaches are not applicable to irregular parallel operations because they require loop bounds and loop body execution times to be known at compile time.

Sarkar and Hennessy have used execution time estimates and a critical path algorithm to partition parallel programs statically [28]. Our algorithm for determining a minimum grain size is similar to Sarkar's partitioning algorithm in that it balances communication costs against execution time estimates. Also, we use the algorithm reported in [27] to estimate execution time variance. Our scheduling algorithm is different in that it uses runtime information about execution time variance to determine the grain size at which a parallel operation is scheduled.

A somewhat different approach to scheduling is *load balancing*[26]. Load balancing algorithms run in parallel with a computation; their goal is to re-assign tasks such that each processor ends up with the same number of pending tasks. There are two main types of load balancing algorithms: *local* and *global.* Local algorithms attempt to achieve overall balance through communication among neighboring processors. In global algorithms, a central manager gathers *load indices* from each processor and directs the transfer of tasks.

These algorithms have two features which make them more applicable to distributed operating systems than to the scheduling of a single parallel program. First, they disregard communication relationships between tasks. Second, the goal of these load balancing algorithms is to maintain even numbers of pending tasks on each processor. In contrast, the goal of the algorithms presented here is to have all processors finish a parallel operation at the same time. Load balancing algorithms keep throughput high when parallelism is abundant, but lack the precision necessary to make a single parallel operation efficient.

Yew and Tang have proposed a dynamic scheduling method called self-scheduling [29]. Self-scheduling follows the *first available* rule in assigning tasks to processors. Whenever a processor finishes executing a task, it becomes available and requests a new task. Self-scheduling produces even processor finishing times, even with uneven processor starting times. However, if the cost of scheduling a task is h then the expected finishing time for N tasks is $N(\mu + h)/p$. For $\mu = h$, the contribution of scheduling overhead doubles the expected finishing time.

Self-scheduling can be generalized so that processors are given a *chunk* of K tasks whenever they become available. Kruskal and Weiss suggest a technique [16] for determining the optimal value of K, given N, p, σ, and μ. However, any method that uses a single chunk size K has expected unevenness of $K\mu/2$ in its processor finishing times. If we choose a large value of K, this unevenness will be significant. If we choose a small value, we incur a large total scheduling overhead.

We would like to find a strategy that combines the low runtime overhead of large chunk sizes with the even finishing times of self-scheduling. In the next section, we investigate the finishing times of *tapering* methods, which use the first available rule but reduce runtime overhead by scheduling large chunks at the beginning of a parallel operation and successively smaller chunks as the computation proceeds. In theory, the smaller chunks should smooth out uneven finishing times left by the larger chunks.

Polychronopoulis and Kuck suggest a tapering method, guided-self-scheduling (GSS) [23], that chooses chunk size $K_i = \lceil R_i/p \rceil$ where R_i is the number of tasks remaining after the $i-1^{st}$ chunk has been scheduled ($R_1 = N$). The goal of this tapering rule is to smooth out uneven processor start times. It is optimal when $\sigma = 0$, but does not address the problem of variable task execution times.

5 Tapering Methods

In this section, we present our method for selecting a chunk size K_i, given the number of remaining tasks R_i, number of processors p, and distribution(μ,σ). The method selects K_i using an expression of the form $K_i = \max\left(K_{min}, f(\frac{\sigma}{\mu}, K_{min}, \frac{R_i}{p}, h)\right)$, where K_{min} is the minimum chunk size and f is a function we will derive below. This expression yields GSS as a special case when $\sigma = 0$.

The goal of any tapering method is to achieve optimally even finishing times while scheduling the smallest possible number of chunks. When scheduling the ith chunk, we would like to pick the largest possible number of tasks K_i such that our expected maximum finishing time does not increase. Define $finish_{i,j}$ to be the time at which processor j has finished with any chunks numbered less than or equal to i. Let $fmax_i = \max_j(finish_{i,j})$, and $lag_i = \sum_j(fmax_i - finish_{i,j})$ (lag_0 is the initial unevenness in processor start times). If we schedule n chunks then $fmax_n$ is the finishing time of the computation, and lag_n measures the total amount of processor idle time (the inefficiency) during the computation (see figure 4 for an example).

5.1 The Fill Lemma

First, we introduce a lemma that illustrates a key property of the first available rule. The goal of this lemma is to show how lag_{i+1} depends on lag_i. That is, given a particular unevenness in finishing times after scheduling chunk i, the lemma tells whether the scheduling of chunk $i+1$ will cause smoothing or increase unevenness, and by how much. In the following, $cost_i$ denotes the execution time of chunk i (note that the size of all chunks could be 1, so this lemma applies to the scheduling of individual tasks).

Lemma 1 If $fmax_{i+1} = fmax_i$ then $lag_{i+1} = lag_i - cost_{i+1}$. Otherwise, $lag_{i+1} \leq (p-1)cost_{i+1}$.

Proof. **Case I:** $fmax_{i+1} = fmax_i$:
The condition for this case states that the maximum

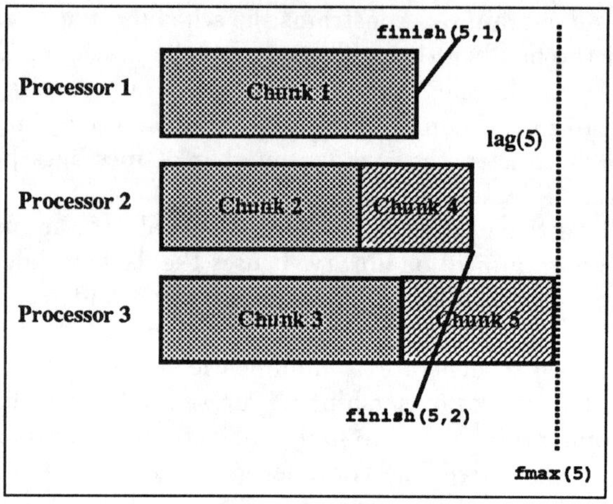

Figure 4: A Scheduling Scenario

finishing time does not increase as a result of the scheduling of chunk $i+1$. But, if this is true, there is some processor j such that $finish_{i+1,j} = finish_{i,j} + cost_{i+1}$ and $finish_{i+1,j} \leq fmax_i$. If chunk $i+1$ is assigned to processor j then for $k \neq j, finish_{i+1,k} = finish_{i,k}$. Thus,

$$\begin{aligned} lag_{i+1} &= \textstyle\sum_{k\neq j}(fmax_i - finish_{i,k}) + \\ & \quad fmax_i - (finish_{i,j} + cost_{i+1}) \\ &= lag_i - cost_{i+1} \qquad \square \end{aligned}$$

Case II: $fmax_{i+1} > fmax_i$:
When the maximum finishing time, $fmax_{i+1}$ *does* increase, then there is some processor q such that $finished_{i,q} = \min_j(finished_{i,j})$ and $finished_{i+1,q} = finished_{i,q} + cost_{i+1} = fmax_{i+1}$. Since $finished_{i,q}$ is the minimum finishing time after chunk i and only processor q's finish time changes as a result of the scheduling of chunk $i+1$, $\sum_j(fmax_{i+1} - finish_{i,j}) \leq (p-1)cost_{i+1}\square$.

We call Case I the *fill-in* rule, and Case II the *excess* rule. The point of this lemma is that, whenever the excess rule applies (*i.e.* $fmax_{i+1} > fmax_i$), we can bound lag_{i+1} independent of lag_i.

Corollary 1 *Let l be the index of the last chunk for which $fmax_l > fmax_{l-1}$. Then we can bound lag_n independent of $lag_{i|i<l}$. Further,*

$$lag_n = lag_l - \sum_{j=l+1}^{n} cost_j$$

Corollary 1 suggests that our analysis need only consider the state of the computation from the last time the excess rule applies. Corollary 2 gives us a procedure for deciding when a chunk can be the last chunk for which the excess rule applies.

Corollary 2 *If* $(lag_i - \sum_{j=i+1}^{n} cost_j) < 0$ *then chunk* i *can not be the last chunk for which the excess rule applies.*

5.2 Probabilistic Tapering

We can use the fill lemma as the basis for a probabilistic tapering method. Given execution time variance, we cannot know the exact time necessary to execute any task or group of tasks. Therefore, given a bound b that expresses the maximum allowable inefficiency, we seek a scheduling method that makes $lag_n < b$ with high probability. We will express the new scheduling method as a rule for computing a set of chunk sizes $K_1, \ldots, K_n$ such that, if tasks are handed out with these chunk sizes, $lag_n < b$ with high probability.

We denote as $fill_i$ the term $\sum_{j=i+1}^{n} cost_j$ in Corollary 2 and assert a final corollary to Lemma 1. This corollary is what makes a probabilistic analysis of tapering methods tractable.

Corollary 3 $lag_n \leq \max_i((p-1)cost_i - fill_i)$

We can use this expression to limit the effect of each chunk K_i on lag_n such that lag_n is less than the given bound b with high probability. Suppose that at time i, there are R_i tasks remaining and that our tapering method chooses to schedule a chunk containing K_i tasks. Then we can rewrite corollary 3 as $lag_n \leq \max_i((p-1)t(K_i) - t(R_{i+1}))$, where $t(K_i)$ and $t(R_{i+1})$ are random variables representing the actual time taken to execute K_i and R_{i+1} tasks, respectively.

Let $Z_i = (p-1)t(K_i) - t(R_{i+1})$. We would like to find the largest value of K_i such that $\Pr[Z_i > b] < \epsilon$ for a given bound b and probability ϵ. Using Chebychev's inequality we find $\Pr[Z_i - \mathcal{E}(Z_i) > a] < \sigma^2_{Z_i}/a^2$, where $\sigma^2_{Z_i}$ is the variance of Z_i and $\mathcal{E}(Z_i)$ is the expected value of Z_i. If we let $a = b - \mathcal{E}(Z_i)$, then we have $\Pr[Z_i > b] < \sigma^2_{Z_i}/(b - \mathcal{E}(Z_i))^2$. Let $\Pr[Z_i > b] = \epsilon$. Substituting $\mathcal{E}(Z_i) = (pK_i - R_i)\mu$ (using $R_{i+1} = R_i - K_i$) and $\sigma^2_{Z_i} = \sigma^2(((p-1)^2 - 1)K_i + R_i)$ (where σ^2 and μ are the variance and mean of the original task cost distribution), we have

$$\epsilon < \sigma^2(((p-1)^2 - 1)K_i + R_i)/(b - (pK_i - R_i)\mu)^2 \quad (1)$$

The partial derivative of (1)'s right hand side with respect to K_i is always positive. Thus, if we set the right hand side of (1) equal to ϵ and solve for K_i, we will find the largest K_i such that $((p-1)cost_i - fill_i) < b$ with probability at least $1 - \epsilon$.

A Practical Algorithm Chebychev's inequality is valid for all distributions. In practice, this means that it yields a needlessly conservative value for K_i. Note that both $t(K_i)$ and $t(R_{i+1})$ are sums of individual task costs. By the Central Limit Theorem, the sum of K independent variates approaches a normal distribution as K increases. For the distributions found in irregular programs (normal, multinomial, uniform, exponential) this approach is rapid.

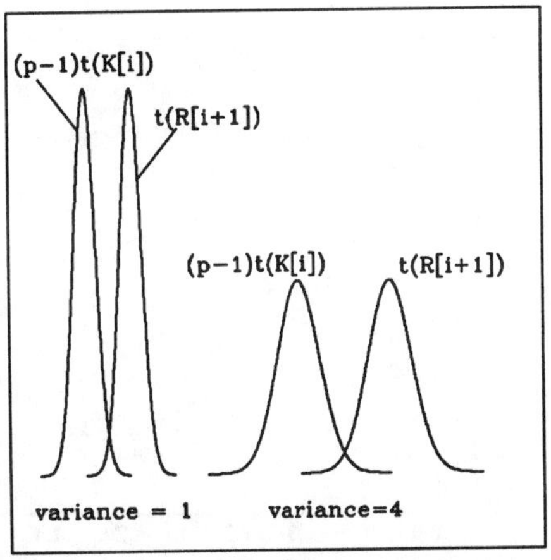

Figure 5: Illustration of K_i selection.

Our current runtime system uses the following method for choosing K_i, based on the assumption that the distribution of Z_i is normal. Using a table we can find a value α such that $\Pr[Z_i - \mathcal{E}(Z_i) > \alpha\sigma_{Z_i}] < \epsilon$ for a given value of ϵ. Put simply, we are guessing that Z_i will not exceed its expected value by more that α standard deviations. Since we want $\Pr[Z_i > b] < \epsilon$ for some bound b, we have $\mathcal{E}(Z_i) + \alpha\sigma_{Z_i} = b$. Substituting for $\mathcal{E}(Z_i)$ and σ_{Z_i} as before and letting $b = 0$ we have

$$(R_i - pK_i)\mu = \alpha\sigma\sqrt{((p-1)^2 - 1)K_i + R_i} \quad (2)$$

Let $T_i = R_i/p$, and $v_\alpha = \alpha\sigma/\mu$. Then (2) becomes $T_i - K_i = v_\alpha\sqrt{\frac{((p-1)^2-1)}{p^2}K_i + \frac{R_i}{p^2}}$. Intuitively, K_i is less than $T_i = R_i/p$ by an amount related to the variance of the work distribution. If we approximate $((p-1)^2 - 1)/p^2$ as 1 and R_i/p^2 as 0, then solving for K_i yields

$$K_i = \left\lceil T_i + \frac{v_\alpha^2}{2} - v_\alpha\sqrt{2T_i + v_\alpha^2/4} \right\rceil \quad (3)$$

Figure 5 shows how equation (3) maintains the invariant $\Pr[Z_i > 0] < \epsilon$. Z_i is the difference between two random variables $(p-1)t(K_i)$ and $t(R_{i+1})$. Expression (3) sets the distance between the means of these two variables to be some number of standard deviations, specifically α. When $\sigma = 0$ then the expression sets the means to be the same value: $(p-1)R_i/p$ (like GSS). As the variance increases (3) increases the distance between the means to maintain the invariant.

Thus, for a given scheduling event i, we can ensure that $\Pr[Z_i > 0] < \epsilon$ for any ϵ by selecting the corresponding number of standard deviations, α, from a table. However, we would like to derive a single value of α

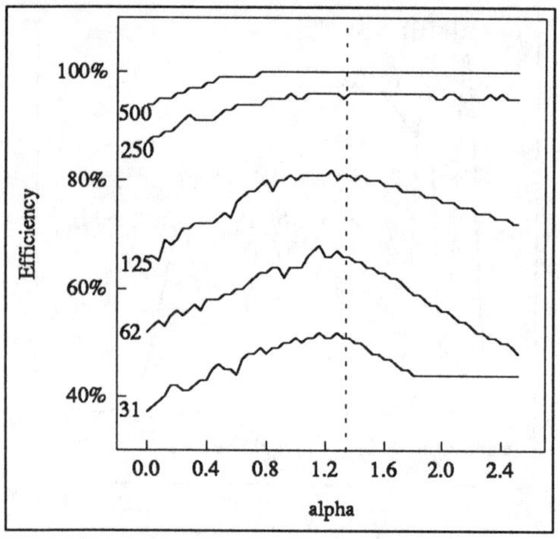

Figure 6: Effect of α. Lines labeled with N/p.

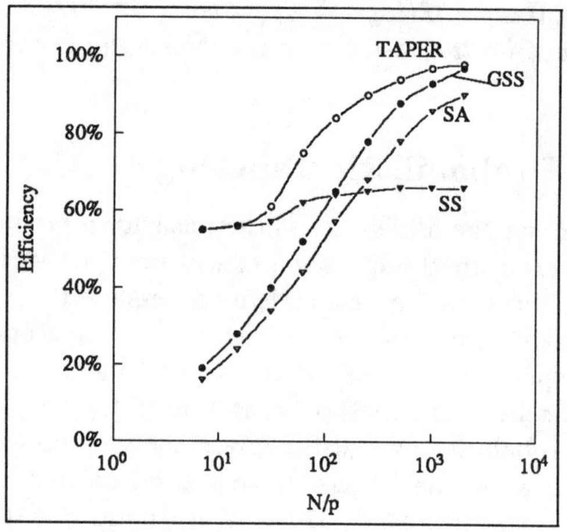

Figure 7: Binomial Distribution Pr[60000]=0.1, Pr[200]=0.9

for the entire parallel operation. To do this we require an expression that, given ϵ, yields $\Pr[\max_i(Z_i) > b]$. It is an open question whether such an expression can be found; without it, determining the best value for α is analytically intractable.

In practice, it is possible to discover a sufficiently accurate value for α empirically. Two parameters, the scheduling overhead (h) and the ratio of tasks to processors (N/p) can affect the optimum value of α. Using a normal distribution, we measured the optimum value of α over the entire possible range of both parameters, varying h from 0 to ∞ and N/p from 1 to ∞. Figure 6 summarizes the results for some typical values of N/p and with $h = 1$. Over all combinations of h and N/p, we found that the value $\alpha = 1.3$ was within 3% of optimum. All of the performance results reported in this paper were obtained using this single value for α.

Figure 6 also indicates that a scheduling method using (3) can withstand considerable inaccuracy in the value of $\frac{\sigma}{\mu}$, since v_α in (3) is just the scaled coefficient of variation $\alpha\frac{\sigma}{\mu}$. For example, we found that for all of the benchmark applications discussed in section 6, simply using (3) and setting $v_\alpha = 3$ yielded better performance than the other scheduling methods tested. In all cases, runtime measurement of $\frac{\sigma}{\mu}$ further improved performance.

Incorporating Overhead Equation (3) implicitly addresses overhead by selecting the largest number of tasks K_i that meets the constraint $\Pr[Z_i > 0] < \epsilon$. If we explicitly account for overhead, we can improve our value for K_i. We represent overhead through the parameter K_{min}, the minimum chunk size. To determine K_{min}, we use two additional parameters: K_{band} and K_{sched}.

We noted in section 3 that the compiler computes the minimum chunk size, K_{band}, necessary to ensure that communication between processors containing logically adjacent chunks does not exceed the bandwidth requirements of the machine (K_{band} is zero on shared memory multiprocessors). The other parameter, K_{sched}, is smallest chunk size such that the mean time to execute K_{sched} tasks exceeds h, the overhead of scheduling a chunk. We set $K_{min} = \min(K_{band}, K_{sched}, N/p)$.

When $K_{min} = N/p$, we can't improve on a static schedule for the parallel operation. However, we can modify equation (3) such that it yields a dynamic scheduling method that outperforms static scheduling whenever $K_{min} < N/p$. We know that if all chunks contain K_{min} or more tasks, the average value for lag_n will be will be at least $K_{min}p\mu/2$. Hence, there is no reason to require $Z_i \leq 0$ and therefore b (the bound on acceptable lag_n) $= 0$ in the derivation above. If we set $b = K_{min}p\mu/2$, then equation (3) still holds, provided we set $T_i = \frac{R_i}{p} + K_{min}/2$. Our final expression for computing K_i becomes

$$K_i = \max\left(K_{min}, \left\lceil T_i + \frac{v_\alpha^2}{2} - v_\alpha\sqrt{2T_i + v_\alpha^2/4}\right\rceil\right) \tag{4}$$

Combining our techniques for selecting α and K_{min} with equation (4) we have an algorithm for dynamic scheduling. We call the algorithm TAPER. Figures 7 through 9 compare the performance of TAPER with guided self-scheduling (GSS), self-scheduling (SS), and static assignment (SA) for some synthetic work distributions.

Even Starting Times The derivation and simulation results given above demonstrate that TAPER yields a near-optimal schedule assuming only $lag_0 < N$ (*i.e.* processors can start at different times) and that task costs are independent random variables. Further,

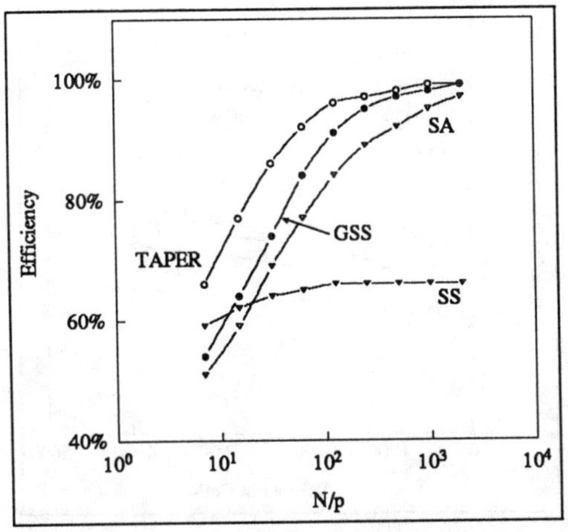

Figure 8: Uniform Distribution on [0,10]. Overhead = 0.5μ.

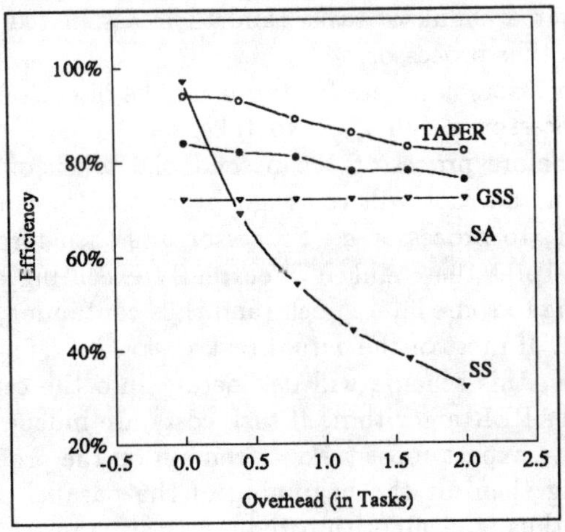

Figure 9: Performance on Pr[10] = 0.9, Pr[1] = 0.1 for different overheads.

TAPER is stateless. Adding tasks only increases $fill_i$; removing processors only decreases $(p-1)t(K_i)$.

If the scheduling algorithm is given additional information about processor starting times, it can do better. For example, suppose we know that p processors will execute the entire parallel operation and that all processors start at the same time. We can use this information to choose larger chunk sizes than TAPER. Let s_i be the time at which the ith chunk is assigned. Let $D_i = \frac{N}{p} - \frac{s_i}{\mu}$. This is the distance in tasks between s_i and the expected finishing time of the computation. Taking into account the variance in possible finishing times yields $K_i = \max(K_{min}, \lceil D_i - v_\alpha\sqrt{D_i}\rceil)$.

We call this method for selecting K_i the DISTANCE method. The difference between DISTANCE and TAPER is greatest for the first p chunks scheduled. Further, it is expensive to maintain globally meaningful values for s_i. For these reasons, we use a hybrid method (called EVENSTART) in situations where all processors begin simultaneously. This method uses DISTANCE for the first p chunks and TAPER thereafter. Figure 10 illustrates how EVENSTART maintains a small unevenness in chunk finish times throughout a parallel operation.

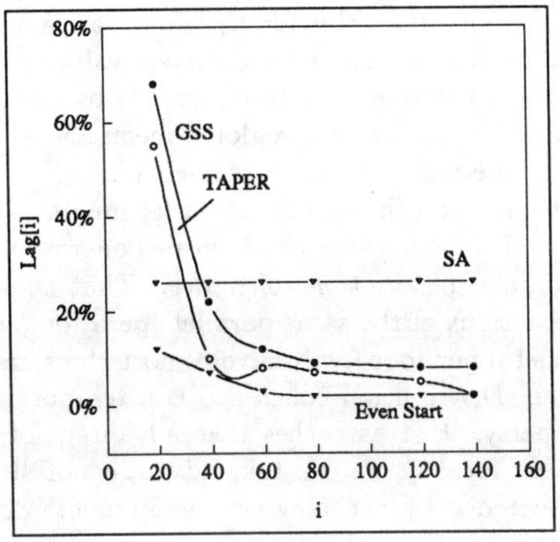

Figure 10: As chunks are scheduled, lag_i decreases.

Determining the Distribution When profiling information is not sufficient to provide values for μ and σ, we need to discover these values at runtime. This is done by having each processor randomly select a few tasks from its large initial chunk and measure the execution times for these tasks. This information is accumulated as processors request later chunks. We therefore need a method to pick the first p chunk sizes. One technique is to use $K_i = N/2p$ for the first p chunks, since TAPER will always allocate more than half the work in the first p chunks. Hummel and Shoenberg have proposed a similar scheduling rule based on a different analysis [15]. This method is excessively conservative for large N/p. We chose instead to estimate that $\frac{\sigma}{\mu} = 3$. This *ad hoc* technique works well in practice because the estimate is quickly updated on each processor as sampling information accumulates.

Nonindependent Task Costs The above discussion assumes that task execution times are independent random variables. If execution times are correlated, then we have two choices. First, we can randomize the iteration space. That is we can randomly permute the tasks of a parallel operation so that we can use the independence assumption. This is possible for some programs like Psirrfan, where there is little communication locality. For the COMP3 benchmark, communication requirements make this transformation counterproductive.

Second, we can do additional sampling of the task costs to build a *cost function*. A cost function estimates task execution times as a function of iteration number. When determining K_i we begin with the estimate $K_i = \lceil R_i/p \rceil$. We then use the cost function to determine the distribution over the particular set of K_i tasks selected. Given the distribution estimate (μ,σ), we refine the value for K_i and obtain a new distribution estimate. To find the correct value for K_i we must scale the value we obtain from (4) by $s = \mu_g/\mu_c$. In this expression, μ_g is the global mean and μ_c is the mean for the tasks in the current chunk.

We have found the cost function technique to be extremely effective because most parallel operations have considerable *distribution coherence*. That is, successive executions of the same parallel operation (such as a parallel inner loop) will have almost the same cost function. Distribution coherence is a temporal locality property. Just as caches take advantage of memory access locality, we can take advantage of distribution coherence by cacheing our assignments of tasks to processors. On distributed memory machines, this cacheing takes the form of transferring blocks of array elements between processors. On shared memory machines, each processor stores its own task assignments.

Distributed Memory On distributed memory machines, we can no longer model the effect of scheduling a chunk of tasks with a fixed overhead h. Each task may require a certain amount of data for its computation, so there will be a per-task as well as a per-chunk transfer cost. Further, we need to preserve communication locality by maintaining a minimum chunk size, K_{min}. We solve this problem by beginning with some original data decomposition and assigning tasks to processors according to the owner computes rule. As we gain information about the work distribution, we refine the data decomposition.

In the distributed algorithm the p processors are logically connected as a binary tree with p leaves. Some of the processors act as both leaves and internal nodes of the tree. We modify TAPER so that it chooses chunk sizes in *epochs* of p chunks. Adding this constraint to the derivation above yields the scheduling rule $K_j = \max(K_{min}, \lceil \frac{2}{3}T_j - v_\alpha\sqrt{3T_j + v_\alpha^2/4} \rceil)$ (where K_j is the number of tasks in the p chunks of the jth epoch).

All processors start in epoch 0. When a processor begins executing a chunk it sends its current epoch value (called a *token*) to its parent, which passes the token to its parent (possibly combining messages from both children). When the root receives p tokens from the same epoch, it increments the global epoch value and broadcasts (through the tree) a message to all processors. The message tells the processors to increment

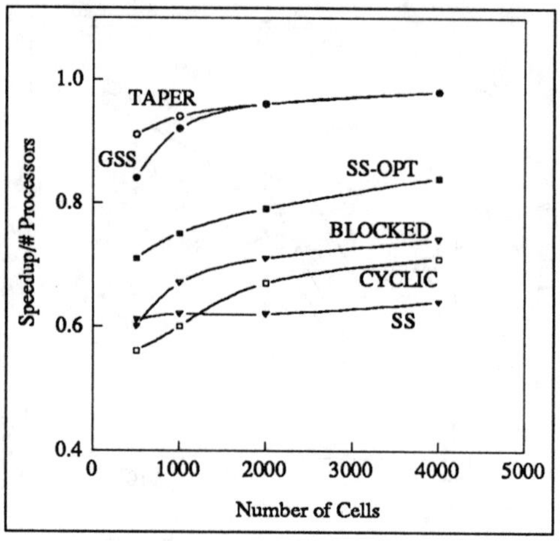

Figure 11: AMR on Ncube

their epoch value and may also tell some processors to transfer a chunk of tasks (and their associated data) to another processor.

Processors compete for the p chunks of each epoch. If processor a can get two tokens of value i to the root before processor b can send one token of value i, then the root will re-assign processor b's chunk of size K_i to processor a. Processor b is then forced to re-interpret the chunk it is currently executing as belonging to some later epoch (and thus containing fewer tasks). If most of the actual task cost is on a few processors, this scheme will degenerate into the centralized TAPER algorithm. If task costs are independent then we expect most tasks to remain on the processor owning them at the beginning of the parallel operation; thus, the algorithm reduces task transfer costs and maintains communication locality.

6 Benchmarks

This section gives performance results for several real applications that contain irregular parallel operations. For each application we give a brief description of its computational characteristics. The appendix gives graphs comparing the performance of GSS, SS, SS with optimal single chunk size (SS-OPT), static assignment (SA or BLOCKED and CYCLIC decompositions), and TAPER on each application. Efficiencies are reported against optimized sequential code. Cray results are for 8 processors, Ncube results are for 512 processors. To be fair to SS and GSS, we modified these methods to use the distributed algorithm given in section 5.2.

Our first application, AMR, is an adaptive vortex method for computing fluid flow [5]. The method uses a finer grid size wherever vortices are present. Its computational structure is similar to our climate example, but it has more floating point operations per memory

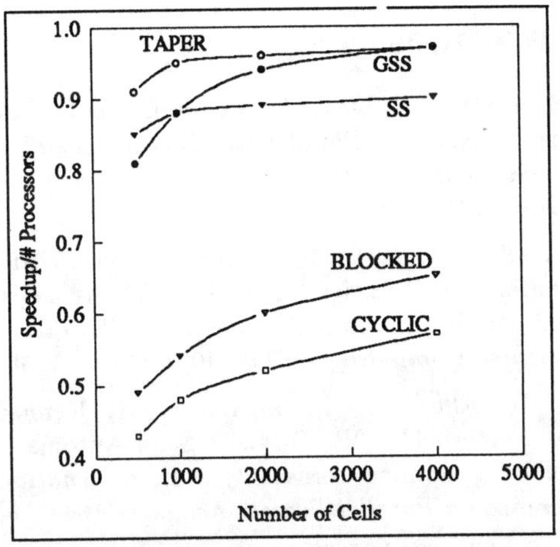

Figure 12: AMR on Cray Y/MP

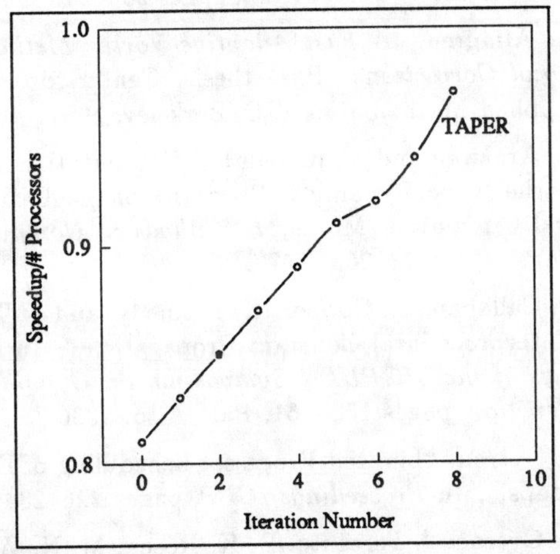

Figure 13: First few iterations of AMR inner loop on Ncube.

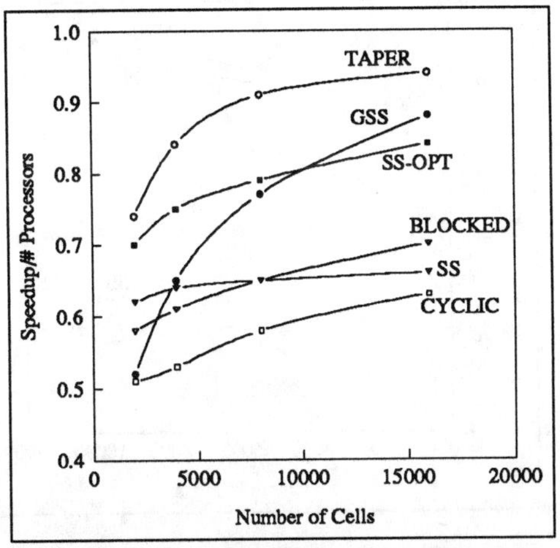

Figure 14: COMP3 on Ncube

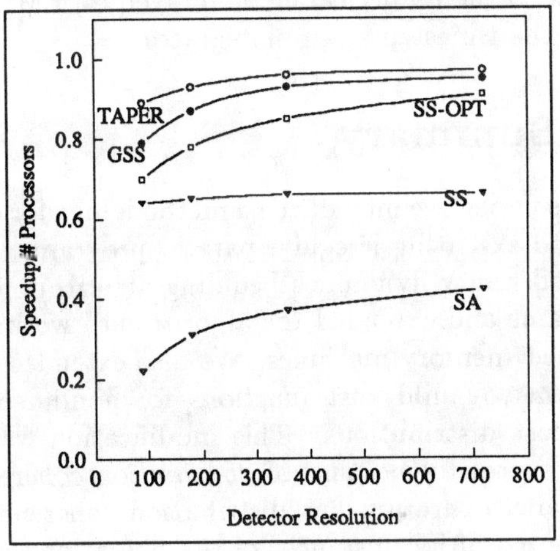

Figure 15: Psirrfan on Ncube

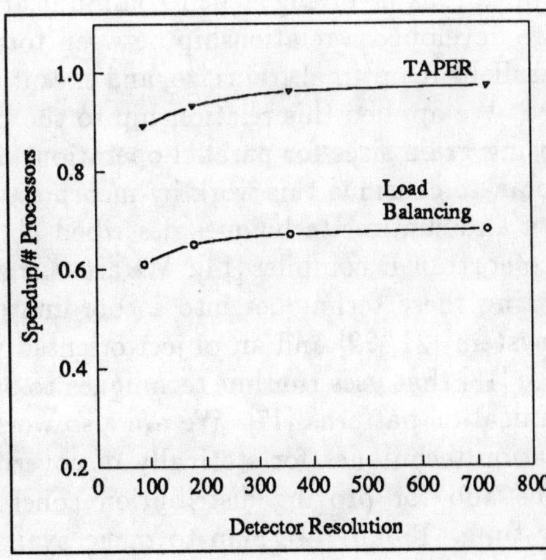

Figure 16: Psirrfan Load Balancing Comparison

access. This example illustrates the power of distribution coherence. For the first few seconds of the short computation, TAPER builds the cost function. Then it reaches a point of maximum efficiency where the cost function needs only incremental improvement (see figure 13).

We have already introduced the features of COMP3, a section of the UCLA General Circulation Model [6]. Note that, for small data sizes, no method can execute COMP3 efficiently because of the climate model's communication requirements. We have also introduced Psirrfan, an x-ray tomography application. For Psirrfan, we include a comparison with a representative local load balancing algorithm [26].

Our final application, EMU, is a timing simulator that is part of the MULGA circuit design system [1, 20]. Unlike the applications seen thus far, EMU has an exponential work distribution. EMU divides a circuit into regions; elements of a particular region are connected by pass transistors. For each region, EMU

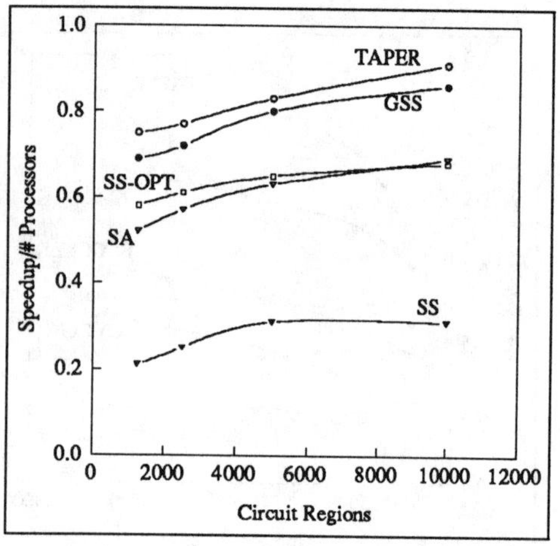

Figure 17: EMU on Ncube

uses a backward Euler integration to update voltage values. If the numerical method diverges, EMU subdivides the timestep and re-integrates.

7 Summary

In this paper, we introduced a methodology for compiling and executing irregular parallel programs. We developed a new dynamic scheduling algorithm for such programs and extended the algorithm to work on distributed memory machines. We also extended the algorithm to build *cost functions* for nonindependent task cost distributions. This modification was especially successful because of *distribution coherence*. If a parallel operation has distribution coherence, successive execution instances of the operation will have nearly identical work distributions. We modeled the effect of communication locality through a minimum grain size K_{min}; this method was sufficient for three real applications involving stencil communication. Finally, we developed a relationship between total available parallelism, optimal grain size, and execution time variance. We applied this relationship to the problem of choosing grain sizes for parallel operations.

We plan to continue this work by incorporating the compiler and runtime techniques described above into the Rice Fortran D compiler [14]. We are currently incorporating these techniques into a coordination language system [21, 22] and an object-oriented parallel language [18] that uses runtime techniques to optimize communication patterns [17]. We are also working on compilation techniques for statically discovering cost functions and for proving distribution coherence at compile-time. Finally, we plan to make available, in conjunction with the Advanced Computing Research Facility at Argonne National Labs, a benchmark suite of irregular programs.

References

[1] B. Ackland, S. Lucco, T. London, and E. DeBenedictis. "CEMU: A Parallel Circuit Simulator,". In *Proceedings of the International Conference on Computer Design*, October 1986.

[2] F. Allen, M. Burke, P. Charles, R. Cytron, and J. Ferrante. "An Overview of the PTRAN Analysis System for Multiprocessing,". *Journal of Parallel and Distributed Computing*, 5:617–640, October 1988.

[3] J. R. Allen, D. Baumgartner, K. Kennedy, and A. Porterfield. "PTOOL: A Semi-Automatic Parallel Programming Assistant,". In *International Conference on Parallel Processing*, pages 164–170, 1986.

[4] J. R. Allen and K. Kennedy. "Automatic Loop Interchange,". In *Proceedings of the SIGPLAN Symposium on Compiler Construction*, pages 233–246, June 1984.

[5] A. Almgren. *A Fast Adaptive Vortex Method Using Local Corrections.* PhD thesis, Center for Pure and Applied Mathematics, UC/Berkeley, 1991.

[6] A. Arakawa and V. R. Lamb. "Computational Design of the Basic Dynamical Processes of the UCLA General Circulation Model,". *Methods in Computational Physics*, 17:173–265, 1977.

[7] D. Callahan, K. Cooper, K. Kennedy, and L. Torczon. "Interprocedural Constant Propagation,". In *Proceedings of the SIGPLAN Symposium on Compiler Construction*, pages 152–161, Palo Alto, 1986.

[8] R. Cytron. "Limited Processor Scheduling of Doacross Loops,". In *Proceedings ICPP*, pages 226–234, 1987.

[9] R. Cytron, J. Ferrante, B. K. Rosen, M. N. Wegman, and K. Zadeck. "An Efficient Method of Computing Static Single Assignment Form,". In *ACM Conference on Principles of Programming Languages*, pages 25–35, 1989.

[10] M. Girkar and C. Polychronopoulos. "Partitioning Programs for Parallel Execution,". *1988 International Conference on Supercomputing (ICS)*, pages 217–229, July 1988.

[11] E. Gumbel. "The Maxima of the Mean of the Largest Value of the Range,". *Annals of Mathematics and Statistics*, 25, 1954.

[12] O. Hansson and A. Mayer. "Heuristic Search as Evidential Reasoning,". In *Proceedings of the Fifth Workshop on Uncertainty in AI*, August 1989.

[13] K. A. Heiskanen. *Tomography with Limited Data in Fan Beam Geometry.* PhD thesis, UC/Berkeley, 1990.

[14] S. Hiranandani, K. Kennedy, and C.-W. Tseng. "Compiler Support for Machine-Independent Parallel Programming in Fortran D,". Technical Report TR91-149, Rice University, March 1991.

[15] S. F. Hummel, E. Schonberg, and L. E. Flynn. "Factoring: A Practical and Robust Method for Scheduling Parallel Loops,". Technical Report 74172, IBM Research Division, 1991.

[16] C. Kruskal and A. Weiss. "Allocating Independent Subtasks on Parallel Processors,". *IEEE Transactions on Software Engineering*, SE-11, October 1985.

[17] S. Lucco. "A Heuristic Linda Kernel for Hypercube Multiprocessors,". In *Proceedings of the Second Conference on Hypercube Multiprocessors*, September 1987.

[18] S. Lucco. "Parallel Programming in a Virtual Object Space,". In *Conference on Object-Oriented Programming Systems, Languages, and Applications*, October 1987.

[19] S. Lucco and D. Anderson. "Tarmac: A Language System Substrate Based on Mobile Memory,". In *International Conference on Distributed Computing Systems*, 1990.

[20] S. Lucco and K. Nichols. "A Performance Analysis of Three Parallel Programming Methodologies in the Context of MOS Timing Simulation,". In *Digest of Papers: IEEE Compcon*, pages 205–210, 1987.

[21] S. Lucco and O. Sharp. "Delirium: An Embedding Coordination Language,". In *Proceedings of Supercomputing '90*, pages 515–524, November 1990.

[22] S. Lucco and O. Sharp. "Parallel Programming With Coordination Structures,". In *ACM Conference on the Principles of Programming Languages*, January 1991.

[23] C. Polychronopoulis and D. Kuck. "Guided Self-Scheduling: A Practical Scheduling Scheme for Parallel Supercomputers,". *IEEE Transactions on Computers*, C-36(12), December 1987.

[24] C. Polychronopoulos and U. Banerjee. "Speedup Bounds and Processor Allocation for Parallel Programs on a Multiprocessor,". *Proceedings of the 1986 International Conference on Parallel Processing*, pages 961–968, August 1986.

[25] C. Polychronopoulos, M. Girkar, M. R. Haghighat, C. L. Lee, B. Leung, and D. Schouten. "Parafrase-2: An Environment for Parallelizing, Partitioning, Synchronizing, and Scheduling Programs on Multiprocessors,". In *Proceedings of the International Conference on Parallel Processing*, volume II, pages 39–48, 1989.

[26] L. Rudolph, M. Slivkin-Allalouf, and E. Upfal. "A Simple Load Balancing Scheme for Task Allocation in Parallel Machines,". In *ACM Symposium on Parallel Algorithms and Architectures*, 1991.

[27] V. Sarkar. "Determining Average Program Execution Times and their Variance,". In *SIGPLAN Conference on Programming Language Design and Implementation*, June 1989.

[28] V. Sarkar and J. Hennessey. "Partitioning Parallel Programs for Macro Dataflow,". In *ACM Conference on Lisp and Functional Programming*, pages 202–211, Cambridge, Mass., 1986.

[29] P. Tang and P.-C. Yew. "Processor Self-Scheduling for Multiple Nested Parallel Loops,". *Proceedings of the 1986 International Conference on Parallel Processing*, pages 528–535, August 1986.

[30] S. Ulam and N. Metropolis. "The Monte Carlo Method,". *Journal of the American Statistics Association*, 44:335ff, 1949.

[31] M. E. Wolf and M. S. Lam. "A Data Locality Optimizing Algorithm,". In *SIGPLAN Conference on Programming Language Design and Implementation*, pages 30–44, June 1991.

[32] M. E. Wolf and M. S. Lam. "A Loop Transformation Theory and an Algorithm to Maximize Parallelism,". *IEEE Transactions on Parallel and Distributed Systems*, 2(4):452–471, October 1991.

[33] M. Wolfe. *Optimizing Supercompilers for Supercomputers*. PhD thesis, University of Illinois at Urbana-Champaign, October 1982.

[34] M. Wolfe. "More Iteration Space Tiling,". In *Proceedings of Supercomputing*, pages 655–664, 1989.

How to Analyze Large Programs Efficiently and Informatively

Dhananjay M. Dhamdhere*
dmd @ kailash.ernet.in

Barry K. Rosen†
bkr @ watson.ibm.com

F. Kenneth Zadeck‡
fkz @ cs.brown.edu

Elimination of partial redundancies is a powerful optimization that has been implemented in at least three important production compilers and has inspired several similar optimizations. The global data flow analysis that supports this family of optimizations includes some bidirectional problems. (A bidirectional problem is one in which the global information at each basic block depends on both control flow predecessors and control flow successors.) This paper contributes two ways to simplify and expedite the analysis, especially for large programs.

- *For each global data flow question, we examine only the places in the program where the question might have an answer different from a trivial default answer. In a large program, we may examine only a small fraction of the places conventional algorithms would examine.*
- *We reduce the relevant bidirectional problems to simpler unidirectional problems. These bidirectional problems can be solved by applying a quick correction to a unidirectional approximation.*

1 Introduction

Elimination of partial redundancies (*EPR*) [MR79] is a powerful optimization that has been implemented in at least three important production compilers (COMPASS Compiler Engine, MIPS, and IBM PL.8) and has inspired several similar optimizations [Cho88, JD82a, JD82b]. While these optimizations have been useful in practice, they account for a significant portion of the time and space devoted to optimization. This paper contributes two ways to simplify and expedite the data flow analysis that supports this family of optimizations, which we call *EPR-like*.

- For each global data flow question, we examine only the places in the program where the question *might* have an answer different from a trivial default answer. For reasons explained later in this section, the technique is called *slotwise analysis* and is also useful for some less powerful but more common optimizations. For EPR-like optimizations, where most expressions are not redundant and move only a short distance, the potential savings from using a sparse method such as slotwise analysis can be substantial.
- We show how to reduce the bidirectional problems posed by the various EPR-like optimizations to simpler unidirectional problems. (A bidirectional problem is one in which the global information at each basic block depends on both control flow predecessors and control flow successors.) These bidirectional problems can be solved by first solving a unidirectional approximation and then applying a quick correction.

These contributions are described below and more fully explained in the following sections, which also discuss relevant previous work in detail.

Standard algorithms for data flow analysis [ASU86] process a program of size n in $O(n^2)$ bit-vector steps (worst case) or $O(n)$ bit-vector steps (typical cases). In the most natural formulations of many problems, the lengths of the bit vectors are proportional to the size of the program and each bit-vector step takes $O(n)$ time. For example, a program of size n has about n candidates for redundancy elimination. Each candidate deserves its own *slot* in a bit vector. (Slots are also known as "components" or "elements" or "positions".) With long bit vectors, standard algorithms are $O(n^3)$ at worst and $O(n^2)$ at best. The algorithm presented here is $O(n^2)$ at worst. For some problems, our algorithm is effectively $O(n)$ despite the fact that n vectors of length n would have a total of n^2 slots.

More precisely, the time devoted to the i-th slot is $O(p_i)$, where $p_i \leq n$ is the size of the part of the program visited while computing the i-th slot of each of the bit vectors at *some* of the basic blocks in the program. Each slot is computed only in its own relevant part of the program. Elsewhere, it is known to take on a given default value. Our method is thus a member of the broad family of *sparse* algorithms. Let p be the average of p_i as i varies over n slots. Then the total time is $O(pn)$, with $p = n$ at worst. For some problems, p is typically a small fraction of n. In particular, for EPR-like problems, experience with the COMPASS Compiler Engine suggests that bit vectors typically have the default value for about 99% of the bits.[1]

On a machine with 32-bit words, treating each slot separately will be faster than standard bit-vector methods

---

*Dept. of Computer Science and Engineering, Indian Institute of Technology, Powai, Bombay 400 076 INDIA

†Mathematical Sciences Dept., IBM Research Division, P.O. Box 218, Yorktown Heights, NY 10598 USA

‡Computer Science Dept., P.O. Box 1910, Brown University, Providence, RI 02912 USA This author was supported in part by the Office of Naval Research and the Defense Advanced Research Projects Agency (under Contracts N00014-83-K-0146 and ARPA order 6320, and N00014-91-J-4052 and ARPA Order 8225) and in part by the National Science Foundation under grant CCR-9015988.

ACM SIGPLAN '92 PLDI-6/92/CA
© 1992 ACM 0-89791-476-7/92/0006/0212...$1.50

[1] We thank Bob Morgan (personal communication, November 7, 1990) for this information.

whenever $32p < n$, and in some other cases as well. Details are given in §2, which also discusses the few other sparse algorithms in data flow analysis.

One important application is treated in detail here: placement analysis to support elimination of partial redundancies. (Moving invariant code out of loops is an important special case of this optimization.) The standard equations for this problem are *bidirectional*: along a control flow edge (x, y), some of the information flows *forward* (from x to y) while some of it flows *backward* (from y to x). Most efficient analysis algorithms deal only with unidirectional flow, as in the forward-only flow of ordinary redundancy elimination. We show how to perform placement analysis by a unidirectional approximation followed by a quick correction. This unidirectional approximation uses our slotwise analysis.

Solving an arbitrary bidirectional problem would require multiple corrections, but placement analysis and the other EPR-like problems are not arbitrary. The complicated equations have some simple properties that imply quick convergence, if one is careful about where to start. Details are in §3, which is formulated to be read *either* from a bit-vector viewpoint *or* from a general lattice-theoretic viewpoint. An example is worked in §4. The techniques applied in §4 to one particular formulation of placement analysis are equally applicable to other formulations and to the other EPR-like optimizations [Cho88, JD82a, JD82b]. Finally, §5 explains how our method of placement analysis can be exploited by a compiler that detects *second-order* effects: elimination of partial redundancies involving one expression can create new opportunities involving other expressions.

2 Classical Bit-Vector Problems

Being a sparse algorithm, slotwise analysis for each bit-vector slot visits only the nodes where the bit in that one slot might be different from a trivial default value. Depending on the problem in question, the default is either 0 or 1. To handle both cases simultaneously, we review three ways to classify problems.

1. Information may flow either forward or backward along edges. In each classical problem, the flow is in only one of these possible directions. Section 2.1 treats forward flow in detail. The backward case is an easy transformation of the forward case, as §2.2 explains.

2. At a join node (in a forward problem) or at a branch node (in a backward problem), previous algorithms need to *merge* together information propagated to the node along several edges. The merge operation (denoted $\sqcap$) is either bitwise AND (denoted $\wedge$) or bitwise OR (denoted $\vee$). Let $\bot$ be the bit value that *controls* the merge: for any x, $x \sqcap \bot = \bot$. Thus, $\bot = 0$ if $\sqcap$ is $\wedge$ but $\bot = 1$ if $\sqcap$ is $\vee$. In both cases, let $\top$ be the other bit value. The merge rule defines a partial ordering of the bit vectors, with $x \sqsubseteq y$ whenever each slot with $\top$ in x has $\top$ in y.

3. At the **Entry** node (in a forward problem) or at the **Exit** node (in a backward problem), each slot has a given *default value*. For example, the problem of available expressions has the default $EntryInfo = 0 = \bot$ because nothing is available at **Entry**.[2] On the other hand, the problem of reaching definitions has the default $EntryInfo = 0 = \top$ because nothing reaches **Entry**. The same bit 0 has different significance in these two problems because the merge operators are different.

2.1 Forward Problems

Associated with each edge (x, y) is a *flow function* $f = Flow(x, y)$ that tells how to transform a bit vector ξ at x to a bit vector η at y when control flows from x to y. The equations to be solved are

$$Info(\texttt{Entry}) = EntryInfo$$

and, for each node $y \neq$ **Entry**,

$$Info(y) = \bigsqcap_{x \in Pred(y)} [Flow(x, y)](Info(x)).$$

The desired solution to these equations is the one that could be obtained by iterating from an initial guess of all $\top$ bits.

By solving for each slot in *Info* separately, we simplify the flow functions. There are only four ways to map from {0,1} to {0,1}, and only three of them make sense in data flow analysis. Along any edge (x, y), the flow function is one of those displayed in Figure 1. For example, consider

function	behavior	comment
START	$0 \mapsto 1$ $1 \mapsto 1$	constant at 1
STOP	$0 \mapsto 0$ $1 \mapsto 0$	constant at 0
PROPAGATE	$0 \mapsto 0$ $1 \mapsto 1$	passes arg. along

Figure 1. Possible flow functions on a single bit.

whether an expression E is available on entry to a basic block. The code within the block x may START availability of E by computing E and not assigning to any operand of E thereafter. Otherwise, x may STOP availability of E by assigning to an operand of E or may just PROPAGATE to y whatever was true on entry to x. With only three possibilities to consider, we can examine the flow functions to help decide the order in which to visit nodes. Standard algorithms, on the other hand, consider n slots at once and cannot enumerate 3^n possibilities.

In order to treat problems with $\bot = 0$ and problems with $\bot = 1$ simultaneously, it is convenient to stipulate that LOWER is whichever of START, STOP has value $\bot$ and RAISE is whichever of START, STOP has value $\top$. Edges are considered to be PROPAGATE edges by default. Local analysis for the slot of current interest flags the exceptional (RAISE and LOWER) edges and puts them in two lists. At the end of global analysis for the current slot, these lists are traversed and the flags are reset, so as to be ready for local analysis of the next slot. Similar resetting is done for other information. In particular, the global bit of information for each basic

[2] This standard assumption is adopted here for ease of presentation but is not important to our method. More extensive optimization is sometimes possible with other assumptions. For example, an expression whose only variables are local temporaries may be considered available at Entry. Without interprocedural information, on the other hand, the standard assumption is definitely needed for any expression whose only variables are globals or parameters.

block defaults to the given value $EntryInfo$ associated with the Entry node. This value may be either $\top$ or $\bot$, but we assume it is the same for each slot. The general case is easily handled by applying our method twice, once for slots with $EntryInfo = \top$ (*high* information) and once for slots with $EntryInfo = \bot$ (*low* information).

2.1.1 High Information at Entry

Initialize the set N_1 of visited nodes to hold all targets of LOWER edges. Initialize a worklist to hold these same nodes. Whenever a node is taken off the worklist, every successor z reached by a PROPAGATE edge is examined. If z is not already in N_1, then z is put in N_1 and put on the worklist.

Let N_0 be the full set of nodes. Then $Info(x) = \top$ for $x \in N_0 - N_1$ and $Info(x) = \bot$ for $x \in N_1$. Thus all the $Info$ bits have been determined at cost $O(\|N_1\|)$, where the *extended size* $\|...\|$ of a set of nodes counts edges that touch the nodes as well as the nodes themselves.

2.1.2 Low Information at Entry

Initialize the first set N_1 of visited nodes to hold all targets of RAISE edges. Initialize a worklist to hold these same nodes. Whenever a node is taken off the worklist, every successor z reached by a PROPAGATE edge is examined. If z is not already in N_1, then z is put in N_1 and put on the worklist.

Let N_0 be the full set of nodes. We already know that $Info(x) = \bot$ for $x \in N_0 - N_1$, so there is no need to examine these nodes. Nodes in N_1 might have either $\bot$ or $\top$. These nodes are classified by a second worklist search. Initialize the second set N_2 of visited nodes to hold every node $y \in N_1$ such that, for some inedge $e = (x, y)$, either e LOWERS information or $x \notin N_1$ and e does not RAISE information. Initialize a worklist to hold these same nodes y. Whenever a node is taken off the worklist, every successor z reached by a PROPAGATE edge is examined. If z is in N_1 but is not already in N_2, then z is put in N_2 and put on the worklist. Once the second search is complete, we know that $Info(x) = \top$ for $x \in N_1 - N_2$ and $Info(x) = \bot$ for $x \in N_2$. Thus all the $Info$ bits have been determined at cost $O(\|N_1\|)$, with about twice as much work as in the easier case of high information at entry.

2.2 Backward Problems

With both forward and backward problems, it is customary to say that the global information "at" a basic block is what is known on *entry* to the block, so the flow function associated with an edge from x to y is determined by the code inside x and has nothing to do with the code inside y. After the flow functions have been found, backward problems are solved by the mirror image of the method for forward problems. Whenever a node is taken off the worklist, its predecessors (rather than successors) are examined. The Exit node plays the role of Entry. The given value $ExitInfo$ may be either $\top$ or $\bot$. Just as with forward problems, $\top$ needs one search while $\bot$ needs two.

2.3 Discussion

After discussing proper accounting for lengths of bit vectors when analyzing various algorithms for live (also known as "upwards-exposed") variables, Kou [Kou77] proposed that live variables be found by the backwards version of the simple worklist algorithm in §2.1.1. Apart from more elaborate (but still quadratic) algorithms oriented toward incremental analysis [MR90, Zad84], Kou's algorithm has had little influence. Standard algorithms are effectively quadratic in practice, and the 32-way parallelism of standard bit vector operations is still attractive, even when the vectors are long.

The way compilers use information about available expressions differs in three ways from the way they use information about live variables for tasks like register allocation:

1. *The information in any one slot can be computed, used, and discarded before computing the information in any other slot.* To eliminate redundant computations of an expression E, we only need availability information for E. To build an interference graph for register allocation, on the other hand, we need liveness information for all variables.

2. *The information in many of the slots is the default bit value at many of the basic blocks in a large program.* Many expressions E are unavailable throughout much of the program.

3. *The default value is* $\bot$. The information at Entry (since this is a forward problem) is 0 in every slot, and 0 is the controlling value for the merge operation.

Differences 1 and 2 make a slotwise approach much more attractive, while difference 3 makes the previous slotwise approach [Kou77] inapplicable. Our new algorithm in §2.1.2 handles difference 3. Difference 1 has the interesting consequence that using the information for one expression may improve the information for another expression. Details are in §5.

The following subsections compare slotwise analysis with two other nontraditional approaches.

2.3.1 Incremental Analysis

Incremental analysis has a focus quite unlike that of slotwise (or any other sparse) analysis. An incremental algorithm assumes that the data flow information (and perhaps some auxiliary information) has already been computed everywhere. It tries to respond to a change in the input with work related more to the corresponding change in the output than to the size of the whole problem. A sparse algorithm, on the other hand, has no previous solution of the problem to update: it starts from scratch.

2.3.2 Building Sparse Graphs

Choi, Cytron, and Ferrante [CCF91] generalized static single assignment form [CFR+91] to derive a sparse representation of any given problem. The original graph is replaced by a collection of smaller graphs such that many of the flow functions in each graph are either constants or the identity function. The combined cost of constructing all of the sparse graphs and solving the problem separately on each of them may be less than the cost of solving the problem directly.

Building sparse graphs is much more complicated than slotwise analysis and is asymptotically slower. When an analytic mistake inherited from [CFR+89] is corrected [CFR+91], the worst-case complexity for constructing each sparse graph is $O(n^3)$. Slotwise analysis is $O(n^2)$ for solving the entire problem.[3] Most bit-vector problems are more amenable to either slotwise or traditional analysis than to building sparse graphs.

One important potential advantage of sparse analysis, however, is its algebraic generality. The information at each

[3]The pessimism in worst-case bounds is more severe for building sparse graphs than for slotwise analysis, so the real difference may be less than the worst-case bounds suggest.

$$Info(y) \quad = \quad \mathcal{F}(y) \sqcap \mathcal{B}(y) \tag{1}$$

$$\mathcal{F}(y) \stackrel{\text{def}}{=} \begin{cases} EntryInfo & \text{if } y = \mathbf{Entry} \\ \displaystyle\bigsqcap_{x \in Pred(y)} [ForwFlow(x,y)](Info(x)) & \text{if } y \neq \mathbf{Entry} \end{cases} \tag{2}$$

$$\mathcal{B}(y) \stackrel{\text{def}}{=} \begin{cases} ExitInfo & \text{if } y = \mathbf{Exit} \\ \displaystyle\bigsqcap_{z \in Succ(y)} [BackFlow(y,z)](Info(z)) & \text{if } y \neq \mathbf{Exit} \end{cases} \tag{3}$$

Figure 2. The information at y is the merge of auxiliary information propagated forward and backward to y.

slot in a vector is not required to be a bit. For data flow analysis problems like degrees of availability [Ros81], where *bit* vectors are inappropriate but slots can be partitioned to yield many identity or constant flow functions, it is likely that building sparse graphs would be useful.

3 Bidirectional Problems

As defined here, bidirectional problems are a natural generalization of the classical unidirectional problems. Section 4 shows that this generalization covers some important practical problems. As with any formal definition, however, the possibility remains that an intuitively "bidirectional" problem may not fit the definition. Indeed, one such problem is considered briefly at the end of this section. Our formal definition is *an* appropriate one, and it would be futile to agonize over *the* appropriate one.

Notations like $\sqcap$ or $\sqsubseteq$ in this section may be read in two ways:

1. The information assigned to each node is a pair of bits, and notations from §2 are overloaded in the natural way. The Boolean operations applied by a flow function may $\wedge$ or $\vee$ the argument with local information, but may not negate the argument. This reading covers placement analysis (§4.1) and the other analyses that support other EPR-like optimizations [Cho88, JD82a, JD82b].

2. The information assigned to each node is an element of a lattice[4] where every descending chain is of finite length and there are designated top ($\top$) and bottom ($\bot$) elements. The flow functions are *monotonic*: if $\xi \sqsubseteq \eta$ then $f(\xi) \sqsubseteq f(\eta)$.

Informally, the word "bidirectional" is appropriate for any problem where the information at a node depends on both predecessors and successors. Just as classical unidirectional analysis restricts attention to the simple way that $Info(y)$ depends on $Info(x)$ for $x \in Pred(y)$ in §2.1, our bidirectional analysis restricts attention to the simple way that $Info(y)$ depends on $Info(x)$ for $x \in Pred(y)$ and on $Info(z)$ for $z \in Succ(y)$ in Figure 2. Formally, a *bidirectional problem* associates *two* flow functions $ForwFlow(x,y)$ and $BackFlow(x,y)$ with each edge (x,y). The equations to be solved are as shown in Figure 2, and the desired solution to these equations is the one that could be obtained by iterating from an initial guess of $Info(y) = \top$ for all y.

For arbitrary bidirectional problems, iteration is much less attractive than for unidirectional problems. When the nodes are visited in a well-chosen order [HU75], unidirectional bit-vector problems can be solved in just three or four passes on the graphs that occur in practice. The corresponding strategy for bidirectional problems would be to visit nodes alternately in postorder and in reverse postorder. Even an *acyclic* graph with n nodes needs $\Omega(n)$ passes in the worst case because a change from $\top$ to $\bot$ can propagate alternately forward and backward along edges. The known bidirectional problems of practical importance, however, are all easily shown to satisfy the simple algebraic conditions explained in §3.1, despite the superficial complexity of the specific equations for each problem. Moreover, the problems need only be solved for control flow graphs where certain edges have been split, as explained in §3.2. Edge splitting and algebra combine to make the important bidirectional problems easy to solve, as explained in §3.3. An intermediate step approximates the actual problems as unidirectional bit-vector problems. These problems (and some auxiliary unidirectional problems that are solved to determine their flow functions) have the properties (discussed in §2.3) that make the slotwise method preferable over standard methods.

3.1 Algebraic Assumptions

We list three possible assumptions about the flow functions in Figure 2. Consider any two outedges (x,y) and (x,z) from a node x. Then

$$BackFlow(x,y) = BackFlow(x,z). \tag{4}$$

Consider any backward function b. Then all ξ, η satisfy

$$b(\xi \sqcap \eta) = b(\xi) \sqcap b(\eta). \tag{5}$$

Consider any backward function b, any forward function f, and any result ξ of $\sqcap$-ing together some values of forward functions. Then all η satisfy

$$\begin{aligned} \eta \;\sqsubseteq\; f(b(\eta)) &= f(b(\eta) \sqcap \xi) \\ &= f(b(\eta) \sqcap EntryInfo). \end{aligned} \tag{6}$$

The *clustering*(4) and *distributivity*(5) assumptions are familiar from unidirectional data flow analysis, where they are often made, seldom really used, and sometimes false. In this paper, they are both used and true. The assumption

[4] If the word "lattice" is unfamiliar, then reading the notations in terms of pairs of bits is recommended. Though lattices have been put to good use in data-flow analysis, it is difficult to write an introduction to lattice theory for these purposes [Ros81].

that forward functions are *largish* (6) has no obvious intuitive significance. It just happens to be true for the important bidirectional problems.

3.2 Edge Splitting

We consider a simple transformation of the control flow graph underlying the bidirectional problem in Figure 2. To *split* a control flow edge (x, y) is to replace (x, y) by two new edges (x, u) and (u, y), where u is a new node representing an empty basic block. (In the course of optimization, some code may be moved into u.) Without any splitting, placement analysis would yield weaker information that misses chances to improve the compiled code [MR79, Fig. 6] [RWZ88, p. 18]. Once the principle of splitting has been accepted, there are still the questions of which edges to split and when to split them. Our splitting criteria are simple and independent of the optimizations to be performed:

- Any edge that runs directly from a branch node to a join node is to be split.
- Splitting is to be done *before* analysis begins.

Many papers have considered some form of edge splitting, usually with other splitting criteria. Dhamdhere and Isaac [DI80], for instance, considered edge splitting when placing code in light of execution-frequency information. For elimination of partial redundancies, the splitting criteria given above were used by Rosen, Wegman, and Zadeck [RWZ88, p. 17] and may have been used earlier. Sorkin [Sor89] proposed (incorrectly) that splitting to create loop preheaders would suffice. The fact that splitting is more widely needed was implicitly recognized by Morel and Renvoise [MR79, Fig. 6].

Alternatively, one can decide in the course of analysis which edges to split. This strategy was proposed independently, for different variations on the original placement analysis [MR79], by Dhamdhere [Dha88] and by Drechsler and Stadel [DS88]. Analysis predicts what *will* hold at each old node, then determines which edges need to be split in order to validate the predictions. For an ambitious compiler that tries to seize many of the opportunities that one optimization creates for another, splitting as needed complicates the compiler, especially if the compiler writer is unwilling to bear the expense of a separate call on the memory allocator for each split edge. Once code has been moved into a new block created by splitting for the sake of one optimization, the new block effectively becomes an old block for later optimizations, and a new edge to (from) the new block may need to be split later.

Because old basic blocks may become empty in the course of optimization, a late optimization that removes empty blocks is needed anyway. Our splitting criteria make the graph somewhat larger,[5] but much of the splitting we do will be done eventually, if not by one optimization then by another. Occasionally, we split an edge but never put anything into the new basic block. In this case, the edge will be restored as a byproduct of removing empty basic blocks.

[5] For example, we effectively add a dummy `else` to each `if-then` without one.

3.3 Some Problems Are Easy

The bidirectional problem in Figure 2 is *mostly backward* if the information at each node y satisfies

$$Info(y) \;=\; \mathcal{F}_C(y) \sqcap \mathcal{B}_A(y), \tag{7}$$

where $\mathcal{B}_A$ and $\mathcal{F}_C$ are defined as follows. Replacing $Info(z)$ with $\mathcal{B}(z)$ in (3), we get an ordinary backward problem that can be solved to yield the *backward approximation* $\mathcal{B}_A$ to $Info$. Then we visit each node y in any convenient order and use $\mathcal{B}_A(x)$ in place of $Info(x)$ in (2) to compute the *forward correction* $\mathcal{F}_C(y)$.

Solving a mostly backward problem is only slightly more work than solving the backward approximation, which can share storage with the final answer. The following result shows that placement analysis and other important bidirectional problems are indeed mostly backward.

Theorem 1 *Consider any bidirectional problem (Figure 2) such that (thanks to edge splitting) no edge runs from a branch node to a join node. Suppose the forward functions are largish and the backward functions are clustered and distributive. Then the problem is mostly backward.*

Proof. For each node z, let

$$\mathcal{M}(z) \stackrel{\text{def}}{=} \mathcal{F}_C(z) \sqcap \mathcal{B}_A(z).$$

Because $Info(z) \sqsubseteq \mathcal{B}_A(z)$ (and thus $Info(z) \sqsubseteq \mathcal{F}_C(z)$), we already have $Info(z) \sqsubseteq \mathcal{M}(z)$. To show that $\mathcal{M}(z) \sqsubseteq Info(z)$, we show that every edge (x, y) has

$$\mathcal{M}(y) \sqsubseteq f(\mathcal{M}(x)) \quad \text{where} \quad f = ForwFlow(x, y); \tag{8}$$

$$\mathcal{M}(x) \sqsubseteq b(\mathcal{M}(y)) \quad \text{where} \quad b = BackFlow(x, y). \tag{9}$$

Because $Info$ is the largest way to assign information to nodes such that similar $\sqsubseteq$ relations hold, these imply $\mathcal{M}(z) \sqsubseteq Info(z)$. Proving (8) and (9) thus implies that the problem is mostly backward.

Consider any edge (x, y). Let f and b be as in (8) and (9). Thanks to clustering and distributivity, the definition of $\mathcal{B}_A$ implies

$$\mathcal{B}_A(x) \;=\; b\left(\bigsqcap_{z \in Succ(x)} \mathcal{B}_A(z)\right) \tag{10}$$

In particular, $\mathcal{B}_A(x)$ has the form $b(\eta)$. Moreover, $\mathcal{F}_C(x)$ is either $EntryInfo$ or the result of $\sqcap$-ing together some values of forward functions. Thus

$$\begin{array}{rcll} \mathcal{F}_C(y) & \sqsubseteq & f(\mathcal{B}_A(x)) & \text{by definition of } \mathcal{F}_C \\ & = & f(\mathcal{B}_A(x) \sqcap \mathcal{F}_C(x)) & \text{because } f \text{ is largish} \\ & = & f(\mathcal{M}(x)) & \text{by commutativity} \end{array}$$

But $\mathcal{M}(y) = (\mathcal{F}_C(y) \sqcap \ldots) \sqsubseteq \mathcal{F}_C(y)$, so $\mathcal{M}(y) \sqsubseteq f(\mathcal{M}(x))$ and (8) holds.

For (9), the argument depends on whether or not y is a join node. Suppose first that y is a join node. Thanks to edge splitting, $Succ(x) = \{y\}$. Thus (10) implies $\mathcal{B}_A(x) = b(\mathcal{B}_A(y))$. Similarly, any other predecessor z of y

has $\mathcal{B}_A(z) = b(\mathcal{B}_A(y))$. Therefore

$$\begin{aligned}
\mathcal{B}_A(y) &= \bigsqcap_{z \in Pred(y)} \mathcal{B}_A(y) && \text{because } \sqcap \text{ is idempotent}^6 \\
&\sqsubseteq \bigsqcap_{z \in Pred(y)} ForwFlow(z,y)[b(\mathcal{B}_A(y))] && \text{because } ForwFlow(z,y) \text{ is largish} \\
&= \bigsqcap_{z \in Pred(y)} ForwFlow(z,y)(\mathcal{B}_A(z)) && \text{because } \mathcal{B}_A(z) = b(\mathcal{B}_A(y)) \\
&= \mathcal{F}_C(y) && \text{by definition of } \mathcal{F}_C
\end{aligned}$$

Therefore

$$\begin{aligned}
\mathcal{M}(x) &\sqsubseteq \mathcal{B}_A(x) && \text{by definition of } \mathcal{M} \\
&= b(\mathcal{B}_A(y)) && \text{because } Succ(x) = \{y\} \\
&= b(\mathcal{F}_C(y) \sqcap \mathcal{B}_A(y)) && \text{by } \mathcal{B}_A(y) \sqsubseteq \mathcal{F}_C(y) \\
&= b(\mathcal{M}(y)) && \text{by definition of } \mathcal{M}
\end{aligned}$$

and (9) holds if y is a join node.

Now suppose that y is not a join node. Then

$$\begin{aligned}
\bigsqcap_{z \in Succ(x)} \mathcal{B}_A(z) &\sqsubset fb\left(\bigsqcap_{z \in Succ(x)} \mathcal{B}_A(z)\right) && \text{because } f \text{ is largish} \\
&= f(\mathcal{B}_A(x)) && \text{by (10)} \\
&= \mathcal{F}_C(y) && \text{by } Pred(y) = \{x\}
\end{aligned}$$

Therefore (10) implies $\mathcal{B}_A(x) \sqsubseteq b(\mathcal{F}_C(y))$. But $\mathcal{B}_A(x) \sqsubseteq b(\mathcal{B}_A(y)$ also, yielding

$$\begin{aligned}
\mathcal{B}_A(x) &\sqsubseteq b(\mathcal{F}_C(y)) \sqcap b(\mathcal{B}_A(y)) \\
&= b(\mathcal{F}_C(y) \sqcap \mathcal{B}_A(y)) = b(\mathcal{M}(y)).
\end{aligned}$$

Therefore $\mathcal{M}(x) \sqsubseteq \mathcal{B}_A(x) \sqsubseteq b(\mathcal{M}(y))$ and (9) also holds if y is not a join node. □

Corollary 1 *Under the hypothesis of Theorem 1, suppose also that y is either a join node or a node with $\mathcal{B}_A(y) = \bot$. Then $Info(y) = \mathcal{B}_A(y)$ and the forward functions along inedges of y have no effect on the solution.*

Proof. By the theorem, $Info(y) = \mathcal{F}_C(y) \sqcap \mathcal{B}_A(y)$. Suppose first that y is a join node. The argument for (9) in the proof of the theorem shows that $\mathcal{B}_A(y) \sqsubseteq \mathcal{F}_C(y)$ and hence that $Info(y) = \mathcal{B}_A(y)$. Now suppose instead that $\mathcal{B}_A(y) = \bot$. Then $Info(y) = \ldots \sqcap \bot = \bot = \mathcal{B}_A(y)$. In both cases, $Info(y)$ is found without applying any forward functions along inedges of y. These functions were already known to have no effect on $Info(z)$ for any $z \neq y$, so they have no effect at all on the solution. □

Drechsler and Stadel [DS88, p. 638] implicitly derived another corollary of Theorem 1 for one particular version of placement analysis. If enough of the basic blocks are empty, then the forward correction can be shown to be unnecessary at the nonempty blocks. A compiler using this corollary needs a separate round of edge splitting for each EPR-like optimization, to replenish the supply of empty blocks. With Theorem 1, on the other hand, we sometimes need the forward correction but never need to split an edge created by earlier splitting.

Dhamdhere and Patil [DP90, Dha91] considered a variant of placement analysis where forward-flowing information is merged with $\vee$ while backward-flowing information is merged with $\wedge$. They showed that this variant could be solved by a backward approximation followed by a variant of interval-based forward data flow analysis. In our result, on the other hand, the merge is the same in both directions, as is more common. The forward correction is a simple traversal in any convenient order. Our result also applies to irreducible control flow and to *any* bidirectional problem (as defined here) that satisfies the conditions explained in §3.1. Similar conditions, with the roles of forward and backward functions reversed, suffice to make a problem be mostly forward.

[6] For all ξ, $\xi \sqcap \xi = \xi$.

4 Worked Example

In this section we first present the details of placement analysis [MR79] as later refined by [Cho83, JD82a] and then work through a small example in detail.

4.1 Placement Analysis

We begin by reviewing of some auxiliary unidirectional problems whose solutions are treated like local information by the actual placement analysis. For most of this section, we consider a single expression E and the problem of where best to place the computations of E in the given program.

4.1.1 Availability

For each basic block x, let AVGEN(x) be 1 if the code in x generates the availability of E by computing E and not assigning to any operand of E thereafter. Let NONE(x) be 1 if x assigns to none of the operands of E. It is customary in [MR79]-inspired analysis to associate two global availability bits with each node y:

$$\text{AVIN}(y) = \begin{cases} 0 & \text{if } y = \text{Entry}; \\ \bigwedge_{x \in Pred(y)} \text{AVOUT}(x) & \text{if } y \neq \text{Entry}; \end{cases}$$

$$\text{AVOUT}(y) = \text{AVGEN}(y) \vee [\text{AVIN}(y) \wedge \text{NONE}(y)].$$

Substituting for AVOUT(x) in the equation for AVIN(y) yields equation (11) in Figure 3. This equation involves only the AVIN bits and exemplifies §2.1 with $\bot = 0$ and low information at Entry.

4.1.2 Partial Availability

The same local information used in §4.1.1 can also be used to determine *partial* availability, which says that E is available along some (perhaps not all) paths to a node y:

$$\text{PAVIN}(y) = \begin{cases} 0 & \text{if } y = \text{Entry}; \\ \bigvee_{x \in Pred(y)} \text{PAVOUT}(x) & \text{if } y \neq \text{Entry}; \end{cases}$$

$$\text{PAVOUT}(y) = \text{AVGEN}(y) \vee [\text{PAVIN}(y) \wedge \text{NONE}(y)].$$

Substituting for PAVOUT(x) in the equation for PAVIN(y) yields equation (12) in Figure 3. This equation involves only

$$\text{AVIN}(y) = \begin{cases} 0 & \text{if } y = \textbf{Entry} \\ \bigwedge_{x \in Pred(y)} \text{AVGEN}(x) \vee [\text{AVIN}(x) \wedge \text{NONE}(x)] & \text{if } y \neq \textbf{Entry} \end{cases} \tag{11}$$

$$\text{PAVIN}(y) = \begin{cases} 0 & \text{if } y = \textbf{Entry} \\ \bigvee_{x \in Pred(y)} \text{AVGEN}(x) \vee [\text{PAVIN}(x) \wedge \text{NONE}(x)] & \text{if } y \neq \textbf{Entry} \end{cases} \tag{12}$$

$$\text{PPIN}(y) = \begin{cases} 0 & \text{if } y = \textbf{Entry} \\ \left(\begin{array}{l} \text{PAVIN}(y) \ \wedge \ (\text{CB4}(y) \vee [\text{PPOUT}(y) \wedge \text{NONE}(y)]) \ \wedge \\ \quad \bigwedge_{x \in Pred(y)} [\text{PPOUT}(x) \vee \text{AVOUT}(x)] \end{array} \right) & \text{if } y \neq \textbf{Entry} \end{cases} \tag{13}$$

$$\text{PPOUT}(y) = \begin{cases} 0 & \text{if } y = \textbf{Exit} \\ \bigwedge_{z \in Succ(y)} \text{PPIN}(z) & \text{if } y \neq \textbf{Exit} \end{cases} \tag{14}$$

$$\text{INSERT}(y) \stackrel{\text{def}}{=} \text{PPOUT}(y) \wedge \sim \text{AVOUT}(y) \wedge \sim (\text{PPIN}(y) \wedge \text{NONE}(y)) \tag{15}$$

$$\text{DELETE}(y) \stackrel{\text{def}}{=} \text{PPIN}(y) \wedge \text{CB4}(y) \tag{16}$$

Figure 3. Placement analysis in a fairly conventional formulation.

$$Info(y) = \mathcal{F}(y) \ \wedge \ \mathcal{B}(y) \tag{17}$$

$$\mathcal{F}(y) \stackrel{\text{def}}{=} \begin{cases} \langle 0, 1 \rangle & \text{if } y = \textbf{Entry} \\ \bigwedge_{x \in Pred(y)} [ForwFlow(x,y)](Info(x)) & \text{if } y \neq \textbf{Entry} \end{cases} \tag{18}$$

$$\mathcal{B}(y) \stackrel{\text{def}}{=} \begin{cases} \langle [NodeBack(y)](0), 0 \rangle & \text{if } y = \textbf{Exit} \\ \bigwedge_{z \in Succ(y)} [BackFlow(y,z)](Info(z)) & \text{if } y \neq \textbf{Exit} \end{cases} \tag{19}$$

$$[ForwFlow(x,y)](\xi) \stackrel{\text{def}}{=} \eta \quad \text{where} \quad \left\langle \begin{array}{c} \eta_{in} \\ \eta_{out} \end{array} \right\rangle = \left\langle \begin{array}{c} \xi_{out} \vee \text{AVOUT}(x) \\ 1 \end{array} \right\rangle \tag{20}$$

$$[BackFlow(y,z)](\zeta) \stackrel{\text{def}}{=} \eta \quad \text{where} \quad \left\langle \begin{array}{c} \eta_{in} \\ \eta_{out} \end{array} \right\rangle = \left\langle \begin{array}{c} [NodeBack(y)](\zeta_{in}) \\ \zeta_{in} \end{array} \right\rangle \tag{21}$$

Figure 4. Equations (13) and (14) from placement analysis reformulated in terms of pairs of bits, using the functions $NodeBack(y)$ from bits to bits defined by $[NodeBack(y)](\beta) \stackrel{\text{def}}{=} \text{PAVIN}(y) \wedge (\text{CB4}(y) \vee [\beta \wedge \text{NONE}(y)])$.

the PAVIN bits and exemplifies §2.1 with $\bot = 1$ and low information at Entry. Indeed, finding the PAVIN bits by the method of §2.1.1 is precisely the first step in finding the AVIN bits by the method of §2.1.2. Traditional algorithms, on the other hand, would not exploit the similarity between partial availability and availability.

4.1.3 Placement Possible Bits

One more bit of local information is used here. Let CB4(x) be 1 if E is computed in x before any assignments to operands of E. The global *placement possible* bits have the more complicated equations (13) and (14) in Figure 3.[7] Substituting for PPOUT(...) in the equation for PPIN(y) would not be helpful, but the somewhat more elaborate formal manipulations in §4.1.5 help reveal the direct applicability of §3 and the indirect applicability of §2.

4.1.4 Insertion and Deletion Points

Once the PPIN(...) and PPOUT(...) bits have been computed, it is easy to determine where to insert new computations of the expression and where to delete old ones that become fully redundant after the insertions. The last two equations in Figure 3 do this.

4.1.5 Pairs of Bits

When several expressions are considered, PPIN(y) and PPOUT(y) become two bit vectors, each of which has a slot for each expression. This representation is convenient for performing many operations, but not for reasoning about the results. Mathematically, it is more convenient to consider a single vector whose slots hold pairs of bits $\langle \mathrm{PPIN}(y), \mathrm{PPOUT}(y)\rangle$. The bitwise notations $(\wedge, \vee, \sqcap, \bot, \top, \sqsubseteq)$ from §2 are overloaded in the natural way, so as to apply to pairs of bits as well as to single bits. Unlike a flow function on a bit vector of length 2, however, a flow function applied to a pair of bits $\xi = \langle \xi_{in}, \xi_{out}\rangle$ may use both argument bits for each result bit:

$$f(\xi) = \eta \quad \text{where} \quad \left\langle \begin{array}{c} \eta_{in} \\ \eta_{out} \end{array} \right\rangle = \left\langle \begin{array}{c} f_{in}(\xi_{in}, \xi_{out}) \\ f_{out}(\xi_{in}, \xi_{out}) \end{array} \right\rangle .$$

Equations (13) and (14) in Figure 3 can now be written in terms of pairs of bits, where $\sqcap$ is $\wedge$ and $\bot$ is $\langle 0, 0\rangle$. A pair $Info(y)$ is associated with each node y. This information depends on a pair $\mathcal{F}(y)$ flowing forward from predecessors of y and a pair $\mathcal{B}(y)$ flowing backward from successors of y, as shown in Figure 4 and discussed below.

The derivation of Figure 4 from Figure 3 is typical of what is needed for the analyses that support EPR-like optimizations. The equations in Figure 4 are of interest only because they have been chosen to be equivalent to equations (13) and (14) in Figure 3:

$$Info(y) = \langle \mathrm{PPIN}(y), \mathrm{PPOUT}(y)\rangle .$$

Consider any node $y \neq$ Entry. The local information associated with y determines the function $NodeBack(y)$ defined in the figure caption, and this function tells how to use PPOUT(y) in computing PPIN(y). Thus, (13) for $y \neq$ Entry can be rewritten as

$$\mathrm{PPIN}(y) = [NodeBack(y)](\mathrm{PPOUT}(y)) \wedge \bigwedge_{x \in Pred(y)} [\bullet\bullet\bullet].$$

[7] The original equations [MR79] are even more complicated; we have incorporated later refinements [Cho83, JD82a].

To model this with (17), we want

$$\begin{aligned} \mathcal{F}(y)_{in} &= \bigwedge_{x \in Pred(y)} [\mathrm{PPOUT}(x) \vee \mathrm{AVOUT}(x)]; \\ \mathcal{B}(y)_{in} &= [NodeBack(y)](\mathrm{PPOUT}(y)). \end{aligned}$$

To get the $\mathcal{F}(y)_{in}$ desired, we choose each $[ForwFlow(x, y)_{in}]$ as displayed in (20). To get the $\mathcal{B}(y)_{in}$ desired if $y \neq$ Exit, we observe that $NodeBack(y)$ distributes over the $\wedge$ in (14). Then we choose each $[BackFlow(y, z)_{in}]$ as displayed in (21). To get the $\mathcal{B}(y)_{in}$ desired if $y =$ Exit, we apply $NodeBack(y)$ to the value PPOUT(y) = 0 and obtain PAVIN(y) $\wedge$ CB4(y) as the appropriate $ExitInfo_{in}$ in (19).

Consider any node $y \neq$ Exit. We proceed as above, but now the formulas happen to be simpler. In particular, (14) for $y \neq$ Exit can be rewritten as

$$\mathrm{PPOUT}(y) = 1 \wedge \bigwedge_{z \in Succ(y)} \mathrm{PPIN}(z).$$

To model this with (17), we want

$$\begin{aligned} \mathcal{F}(y)_{out} &= 1; \\ \mathcal{B}(y)_{out} &= \bigwedge_{z \in Succ(y)} \mathrm{PPIN}(z). \end{aligned}$$

To get the $\mathcal{F}(y)_{out}$ desired if $y \neq$ Entry, we choose each $[ForwFlow(x, y)_{out}]$ as displayed in (20). To get the $\mathcal{F}(y)_{out}$ desired if $y =$ Entry, we choose $EntryInfo_{out} = 1$ in (18). To get the wanted $\mathcal{B}(y)_{out}$, we choose each $[BackFlow(y, z)_{out}]$ as displayed in (21).

Two choices remain in Figure 4. To model (13) for $y =$ Entry, we choose $EntryInfo_{in} = 0$ in (18). To model (14) for $y =$ Exit, we choose $ExitInfo_{out} = 0$ in (19).

4.1.6 Algebraic Properties

Now that the PP equations have been cast into the general form of Figure 2, we can verify the algebraic assumptions in §3.1. In the definition (21) of the backward flow functions, the Boolean operations applied to ζ_{in} are independent of the outedge chosen. These operations also distribute over $\wedge$, so (4) and (5) hold. For (6), consider also the definition (20) of the forward flow functions. When a forward function is applied after a backward function, the result $\omega = f(b(\eta))$ has

$$\left\langle \begin{array}{c} \omega_{in} \\ \omega_{out} \end{array} \right\rangle = f\left(\left\langle \begin{array}{c} \bullet\bullet\bullet \\ \eta_{in} \end{array} \right\rangle\right) = \left\langle \begin{array}{c} \eta_{in} \vee \bullet\bullet\bullet \\ 1 \end{array} \right\rangle .$$

Thus $\eta \sqsubseteq f(b(\eta))$. Moreover, because f ignores the *in*-component of its argument, any ξ with $\xi_{out} = 1$ has $f(b(\eta)) = f(b(\eta) \wedge \xi)$. In particular, $EntryInfo$ and all values of forward functions have $\xi_{out} = 1$, so (6) follows.

4.2 The Worked Example

Figure 5 contains a small program fragment and its control flow graph. Code motion guided by placement analysis eliminates partial redundancies, as shown in Figure 6. Local data flow information for this analysis is in Figure 7. Figure 8 shows the placement information found by the steps detailed in the rest of this section. In each column in Figure 8, the "–" entries represent nodes where bits are known to have the default value *because* the nodes were never visited in computing that column. While the number of such nodes is small here, it should be quite large in practice. Had there been more of the program between Entry and node 1 or between 6 and Exit in the example, our algorithm would not have visited any of those nodes.

We compute PAVIN by the algorithm in §2.1.1, using the substituted form in (12). For the computation of PAVIN, the controlling bit value is $\perp = 1$ and we have high information ($\top = 0$) at Entry. Thus, LOWER = START and any edge with AVGEN = 1 at its source node is a LOWER edge. Similarly, RAISE = STOP and any edge with AVGEN = 0 and NONE = 0 at its source node is a RAISE edge. The remaining edges are PROPAGATE edges.

The set of LOWER edges is {(4,5), (4,6)}; the set of RAISE edges is {(2,4)}. The set N_1 is initialized to {5, 6}. After propagation, 1, 2, 3, 4, 7, and Exit are also in N_1. Thus, PAVIN is 1 at nodes 1, 2, 3, 4, 5, 6, 7, Exit and 0 elsewhere.

We compute AVIN by the algorithm in §2.1.2, using the substituted form in (11). For the computation of AVIN, the controlling bit value is $\perp = 0$ and we have low information at Entry. Thus, RAISE = START and any edge with AVGEN = 1 at its source node is a RAISE edge. Similarly, LOWER = STOP and any edge with AVGEN = 0 and NONE = 0 at its source node is a LOWER edge. The remaining edges are PROPAGATE edges.

The set of RAISE edges is {(4,5), (4,6)}; the set of LOWER edges is {(2,4)}. From the calculation of PAVIN, we already know that N_1 is {1, 2, 3, 4, 5, 6, 7, Exit}. The set N_2 is initialized to {1, 4}. After propagation, 2 and 3 are also in N_2. Thus, AVIN is 1 at nodes {5, 6, 7, Exit} and 0 elsewhere.

The next step is to attack the PPIN, PPOUT system. By applying the transformations in §3.3 to equations (18) and (19) in Figure 4, we obtain the forward correction (22) to the backwards approximation (23) in Figure 9.

Substitution for *BackFlow* in (23) yields a system where all of the bits $\mathcal{B}_A()_{in}$ can be computed before computing any of the bits $\mathcal{B}_A()_{out}$ (see (24) and (25) in Figure 9). Problem (24) can be solved by the backwards version of the algorithm in §2.1.2. Since $\perp = 0$, RAISE = START and LOWER = STOP. The RAISE edges are { (4,5), (4,6) }; the LOWER edges are {(Entry,1), (2,4)}. The remaining edges are PROPAGATE edges.

We have low information at Exit because CB4(Exit) = 0. We initialize N_1 as {4}, then add 1, 3, 5, 6, and 7 to it. We initialize N_2 as {1}, then add 6 and 7 to it. Thus, the set of nodes y with $\mathcal{B}_A(y)_{in} = 1$ is { 3, 4, 5 }. The set of nodes z with $\mathcal{B}_A(z)_{out} = 1$ is { 2, 3, 5 }.

Substitution for *ForwFlow* in (22) yields a system where the bits $\mathcal{F}_C()_{out}$ are already known (see (26) and (27) in Figure 9). Thus, the set of nodes y with $\mathcal{F}_C(y)_{in} = 1$ is { 4, 5, 6, 7, Exit}. The equations for INSERT and DELETE in Figure 3 tell us to insert new computations in nodes 2 and 3 while deleting the old computation in node 4. The resulting program is indeed as shown in Figure 6.

5 Second Order Effects

Traditional EPR [MR79] performs placement analysis for all expressions "simultaneously" with a bit-vector algorithm but then rearranges the computations for each separate expression E. Several implementors have noticed that moving one expression may provide an opportunity to move other expressions. Slotwise analysis is well suited to detecting and exploiting such *second-order effects* without excessive work.

```
1   repeat
1     if P
2       then A ← 0
4     repeat
4       ... ← A + B
4     until Q
6   until R
```

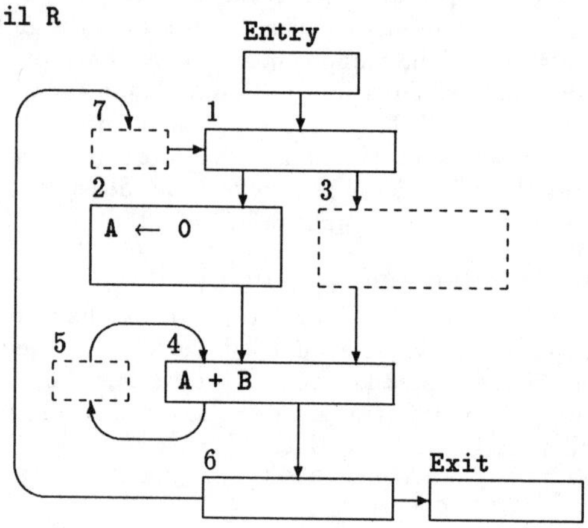

Figure 5. A sample program and its control flow graph. Edge splitting inserted the dashed line nodes.

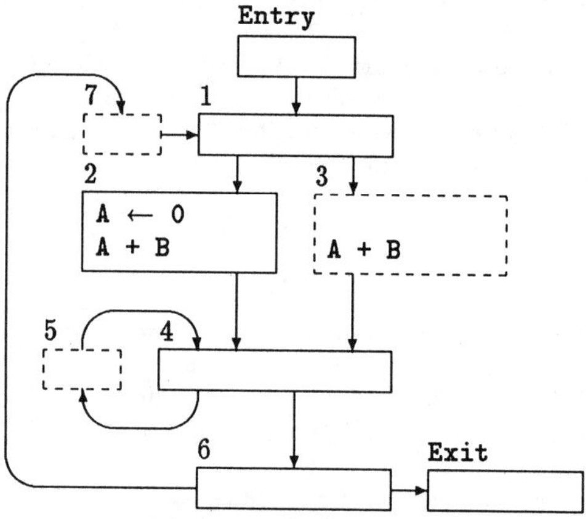

Figure 6. Effect of code motion on Figure 5.

Node	NONE	AVGEN	CB4
Entry	1	0	0
1	1	0	0
2	0	0	0
3	1	0	0
4	1	1	1
5	1	0	0
6	1	0	0
7	1	0	0
Exit	1	0	0

Figure 7. Local information for Figure 5.

Node	PAVIN	PAVOUT	AVIN	AVOUT	$\mathcal{B}_A()_{in}$	$\mathcal{B}_A()_{out}$	$\mathcal{F}_C()_{in}$	INSERT	DELETE
Entry	-	0	-	0	-	0	0	0	0
1	1	1	0	0	0	0	0	0	0
2	1	0	0	0	-	1	0	1	0
3	1	1	0	0	1	1	0	1	0
4	1	1	0	1	1	0	1	0	1
5	1	1	1	1	1	1	1	0	0
6	1	1	1	1	0	0	1	0	0
7	1	1	1	1	0	0	1	0	0
Exit	1	1	1	1	-	0	1	0	0

Figure 8. Global information for Figure 5. Default values (shown as "-") are 0 for PAVIN, AVIN, $\mathcal{B}_A()_{in}$.

$$\mathcal{F}_C(y) = \begin{cases} \langle 0,1\rangle & \text{if } y = \texttt{Entry} \\ \bigwedge_{x \in Pred(y)} [ForwFlow(x,y)](\mathcal{B}_A(x)) & \text{if } y \neq \texttt{Entry} \end{cases} \tag{22}$$

$$\mathcal{B}_A(y) = \begin{cases} \langle \mathrm{PAVIN}(y) \wedge \mathrm{CB4}(y), 0 \rangle & \text{if } y = \texttt{Exit} \\ \bigwedge_{z \in Succ(y)} [BackFlow(y,z)](\mathcal{B}_A(z)) & \text{if } y \neq \texttt{Exit} \end{cases} \tag{23}$$

$$\mathcal{B}_A(y)_{in} = \begin{cases} \mathrm{PAVIN}(y) \wedge \mathrm{CB4}(y) & \text{if } y = \texttt{Exit} \\ \bigwedge_{z \in Succ(y)} \mathrm{PAVIN}(y) \wedge (\mathrm{CB4}(y) \vee \lfloor \mathcal{B}_A(z)_{in} \wedge \mathrm{NONE}(y) \rfloor) & \text{if } y \neq \texttt{Exit} \end{cases} \tag{24}$$

$$\mathcal{B}_A(y)_{out} = \begin{cases} 0 & \text{if } y = \texttt{Exit} \\ \bigwedge_{z \in Succ(y)} \mathcal{B}_A(z)_{in} & \text{if } y \neq \texttt{Exit} \end{cases} \tag{25}$$

$$\mathcal{F}_C(y)_{in} = \begin{cases} 0 & \text{if } y = \texttt{Entry} \\ \bigwedge_{x \in Pred(y)} [\mathcal{B}_A(x)_{out} \vee \mathrm{AVOUT}(x)] & \text{if } y \neq \texttt{Entry} \end{cases} \tag{26}$$

$$\mathcal{F}_C(y)_{out} = 1 \tag{27}$$

Figure 9. Application of Theorem 1 to the equations in Figure 4.

We deal with the expressions separately *throughout* EPR, using a worklist. Before explaining the details, we review the (sometimes tacit) assumptions about intermediate code that underlie data flow analysis in general and placement analysis in particular.

To a first approximation, the intermediate code consists of assignments of one of two kinds. The simpler kind is just a *copy*:

$$\langle variable_{\mathrm{dest}} \rangle \leftarrow \langle variable_{\mathrm{source}} \rangle.$$

The more complex kind is a *computation*:

$$\langle variable \rangle \leftarrow \langle expression \rangle,$$

where $\langle expression \rangle$ is often, but not always, the application of a binary operator to a pair of variable or constant operands. The actual syntax of expressions is irrelevant here, so long as the operands are visible and so long as any possible changes to variables of interest are displayed as assignments to those variables.

Various practical complications can be handled by allowing the left-hand side of a computation to be a tuple of variables, each of which is assigned from an expression in a tuple on the right-hand side. For example, the target machine might not separate computing `X + Y` from computing a condition code to support branching on the sign of `X + Y`. Doing one entails doing the other, and both are moved or inserted or deleted at once. For a target machine

T1 ← A + B	T_{A+B} ← A + B T1 ← T_{A+B}	T_{A+B} ← A + B
T2 ← T1 * C	T2 ← T1 * C	T2 ← T_{A+B} * C
...	...	
T3 ← A + B	T_{A+B} ← A + B T3 ← T_{A+B}	T_{A+B} ← A + B
T4 ← T3 * C	T4 ← T3 * C	T4 ← T_{A+B} * C

Figure 10. Code that exploits the modifications to take advantage of second-order effects.

that does addition this way, the intermediate code actually manipulated by EPR might include assignments like

$$\langle \texttt{A}, \texttt{CC} \rangle \leftarrow \langle \texttt{X} + \texttt{Y}, \texttt{Condition(``+'', X, Y)} \rangle,$$

where A, X, Y are numerical variables and CC is a condition code variable. Many more examples are in [CFR+91, §3.1]. Each "expression" considered by placement analysis is actually a tuple of expressions that appears on the right-hand side of a computation.

Once one sees that the major oversimplification in the first approximation *is* the presumption that all tuples are of length 1, it becomes fairly safe (as well as quite convenient) to use the approximation. Optimizations that seem to be restricted to simple computations like A ← X+Y are usually more general, but involve some small loops over the components of tuples when written out in general form. Omitting these loops simplifies the presentation in the following subsections. We also assume that local (within one basic block) redundancies have already been removed in the obvious way. Thus, a block may compute an expression E at most once before all assignments to operands of E and at most once after all assignments to operands of E. (There may also be computations of E interspersed with assignments to operands of E.) Section 5.1 deals with ordinary intermediate code. Section 5.2 deals with intermediate code in SSA form [CFR+91], which permits more extensive optimization in exchange for introducing another kind of copy operation and many more variables.

5.1 Ordinary Intermediate Code

Consider any expression E computed in the intermediate code, perhaps in several different basic blocks. This expression forms one slot for placement analysis. Initially, the worklist contains all of the slots. On each iteration of the algorithm, a slot is taken from the worklist and the equations in Figure 3 are solved for that one slot. If some INSERT or DELETE bits are nonzero, then the intermediate code is changed, as described below (this may entail adding another slot to the worklist). The algorithm terminates when the worklist empties.

If some of the INSERT or DELETE bits for the current slot E are nonzero, then the intermediate code is changed as follows:

1. A new unique temporary name T_E is created.

2. Consider any basic block where AVGEN = 1 and DELETE = 0. The last old computation $V \leftarrow E$ in the block is replaced by a new computation $T_E \leftarrow E$ followed by a copy $V \leftarrow T_E$.

3. Consider any basic block where DELETE = 1. The first old computation $V \leftarrow E$ in the block is replaced by a copy $V \leftarrow T_E$.

4. Consider any basic block where INSERT = 1. A new computation $T_E \leftarrow E$ is inserted into the block, after any assignments to operands of E that may occur in the block.

The example in Figure 10 illustrates several points. On the left of this figure is an intermediate code fragment. Initially there are three slots, one for each of the expressions A + B, T1 * C, and T3 * C. If the slots for the last two expressions happen to be taken off the worklist first, then no changes are made to the intermediate code until the slot for A + B is considered. The middle part of the figure shows the results of processing the A + B slot. Two copy statements are added. The code on the right shows the results of copy propagation [ASU86]. Now the expression T_{A+B} forms a new slot that is put on the worklist and leads to further optimization when its turn comes.

In this example, the copy propagation changes the expressions T1 * C and T3 * C to T_{A+B}*C. Not only must a new slot be created for the new expression, but also the slots for T1 * C and T3 * C must be added to the worklist, since the deletion (caused by copy propagation) of one instance of the expression may change the placement of the other instances of the expression.

5.2 SSA Form Intermediate Code

If the intermediate code is in static single assignment (SSA) form [CFR+91], then EPR can be more extensive though more complex. We plan to submit a longer version of this paper, with details for SSA-form intermediate code, to a journal. The rest of this section outlines some of the issues.

When a program is in SSA form, each variable is assigned a value at exactly one point in the program text. If the original intermediate code has several assignments to the same variable V, then each of them becomes an assignment to a new unique variable V_i. To preserve the original flow of values, SSA form introduces a new kind of copy operation at some of the join nodes.

A *ϕ-function* at a join node y has the form

$$var_{dest} \leftarrow \phi(var_{source1}, var_{source2}, \ldots),$$

where there is one operand for each control flow inedge of y. The operands are listed in the same (arbitrary) order used to list the inedges. If control passes to y along the K-th inedge (x, y), then the value of the corresponding operand $var_{sourceK}$ is copied to var_{dest} and the other operands are ignored.

With SSA form, copy propagation can always eliminate every ordinary copy $var_{dest} \leftarrow var_{source}$ from one variable to another. All uses of var_{dest}, including uses as operands of ϕ-functions, can safely be replaced by uses of var_{source}. Details are in [RWZ88], where it is shown that the resulting expressions act like "global value numbers" - if two occurrences of expressions E_1 and E_2 in the original program become occurrences of the very same expression $E_1' \equiv E_2'$ with SSA variables, then redundancy elimination can put those two occurrences in the same slot, even though the original E_1 and E_2 may look different.

Eliminating redundancies between two expressions that look different but compute the same value is useful. Unfortunately, translation to SSA form sometimes hides other opportunities for EPR when it replaces one expression E, computed in many different places with operands that have many different values, by many different computations of expressions $E', E'', \ldots$ with different SSA variables as the operands. Rosen, Wegman, and Zadeck [RWZ88] try to seize the new opportunities without losing the old ones, but their algorithm is complicated and restricted to reducible control flow. Moreover, there are some cases where the original EPR [MR79] moves an invariant out of a loop with multiple exits but [RWZ88] does not.[8] These cases suggest that SSA-based EPR should be done more along the lines of §5.1, but with some provision for putting several different expressions $E', E'', \ldots$ in the same slot whenever SSA form would hide old opportunities.

[8] An invariant expression E may be computed along some, but not all, paths through the loop body. It may also be computed along all paths starting from some, but not all, of the loop exits. If the end result is that E is computed along all paths after entering the loop, then [MR79] replaces all these computations of E by a new computation in the loop preheader.

References

[ASU86] A. V. Aho, R. Sethi, and J. D. Ullman. *Compilers: Principles, Techniques, and Tools.* Addison-Wesley, 1986.

[CCF91] J. Choi, R. Cytron, and J. Ferrante. Automatic construction of sparse data flow evaluation graphs. *Conf. Rec. Eighteenth ACM Symp. on Principles of Programming Langs.*, pages 55–66, January 1991.

[CFR+89] R. Cytron, J. Ferrante, B.K. Rosen, M.N. Wegman, and F. K. Zadeck. An efficient method of computing static single assignment form. *Conf. Rec. Sixteenth ACM Symp. on Principles of Programming Langs.*, pages 25–35, January 1989.

[CFR+91] R. Cytron, J. Ferrante, B.K. Rosen, M.N. Wegman, and F. K. Zadeck. Efficiently computing static single assignment form and the control dependence graph. *ACM Trans. on Programming Langs. and Systems*, 13(4):451–490, October 1991.

[Cho83] F. C. Chow. A portable machine-independent global optimizer - design and measurements. Technical Report 83-254 (PhD Thesis), Computer Systems Laboratory, Stanford U. Stanford, CA, December 1983.

[Cho88] F. C. Chow. Minimizing register usage penalty at procedure calls. *Proc. SIGPLAN'88 Symp. on Compiler Construction*, pages 85–94, June 1988. Published as *SIGPLAN Notices* Vol. 23, No. 7.

[Dha88] D. M. Dhamdhere. A fast algorithm for code movement optimization. *SIGPLAN Notices*, 9(3):243–273, August 1988.

[Dha91] D. M. Dhamdhere. Practical adaptation of the global optimization algorithm of morel and renvoise. *ACM Trans. on Programming Langs. and Systems*, 13(2):291–294, April 1991.

[DI80] D. M. Dhamdhere and J. R. Isaac. A composite algorithm for strength reduction and code movement optimization. *Int. J. of Computer and Information Sci.*, 23(10):172–180, 1980.

[DP90] D. M. Dhamdhere and H. Patil. An efficient algorithm for bidirectional data flow analysis. Technical Report TR-016-90, Dept. of Computer Sci. and Eng., Indian Inst. of Technology, 1990. Revision to appear in *ACM Trans. on Programming Langs. and Systems.*

[DS88] K.-H. Drechsler and M. P. Stadel. A solution to a problem with Morel and Renvoise's "Global Optimization by Suppression of Partial Redundancies". *ACM Trans. on Programming Langs. and Systems*, 10(4):635–640, October 1988.

[HU75] M. S. Hecht and J. D. Ullman. A simple algorithm for global data flow analysis problems. *SIAM J. Computing*, 4(4):519–532, Dec. 1975.

[JD82a] S. M. Joshi and D. M. Dhamdhere. A composite hoisting-strength reduction transformation for global program optimization (part I). *Int. J. of Computer Math.*, pages 22–41, 1982.

[JD82b] S. M. Joshi and D. M. Dhamdhere. A composite hoisting-strength reduction transformation for global program optimization (part II). *Int. J. of Computer Math.*, pages 111–126, 1982.

[Kou77] L. T. Kou. On live-dead analysis for global data flow problems. *J. ACM*, 24(3):473–483, July 1977.

[MR79] E. Morel and C. Renvoise. Global optimization by suppression of partial redundancies. *Comm. ACM*, 22(2):96–103, February 1979.

[MR90] T. J. Marlowe and B. G. Ryder. An efficient hybrid algorithm for incremental data flow analysis. *Conf. Rec. Seventeenth ACM Symp. on Principles of Programming Langs.*, pages 184–196, January 1990.

[Ros81] B. K. Rosen. Degrees of availability as an introduction to the general theory of data flow analysis. In S. S. Muchnick and N. D. Jones, editors, *Program Flow Analysis*, chapter 2, pages 55–76. Prentice Hall, 1981.

[RWZ88] B. K. Rosen, M. N. Wegman, and F. K. Zadeck. Global value numbers and redundant computations. *Conf. Rec. Fifteenth ACM Symp. on Principles of Programming Langs.*, pages 12–27, January 1988.

[Sor89] A. Sorkin. Some comments on "A Solution to a Problem with Morel and Renvoise's 'Global Optimization by Suppression of Partial Redundancies' ". *ACM Trans. on Programming Langs. and Systems*, 11(4):666–668, October 1989.

[Zad84] F. K. Zadeck. Incremental data flow analysis in a structure program editor. *Proc. SIGPLAN'84 Symp. on Compiler Construction*, pages 132–143, June 1984. Published as *SIGPLAN Notices* Vol. 19, No. 6.

Lazy Code Motion

Jens Knoop*
CAU Kiel†
jk@informatik.uni-kiel.dbp.de

Oliver Rüthing‡
CAU Kiel†
or@informatik.uni-kiel.dbp.de

Bernhard Steffen
RWTH Aachen§
bus@zeus.informatik.rwth-aachen.de

Abstract

We present a bit-vector algorithm for the *optimal* and *economical* placement of computations within flow graphs, which is as *efficient* as standard uni-directional analyses. The point of our algorithm is the *decomposition* of the bi-directional structure of the known placement algorithms into a sequence of a backward and a forward analysis, which directly implies the efficiency result. Moreover, the new compositional structure opens the algorithm for modification: two further uni-directional analysis components exclude any unnecessary code motion. This *laziness* of our algorithm minimizes the register pressure, which has drastic effects on the run-time behaviour of the optimized programs in practice, where an economical use of registers is essential.

Topics: data flow analysis, program optimization, partial redundancy elimination, code motion, bit-vector data flow analyses.

1 Motivation

Code motion is a technique to improve the efficiency of a program by avoiding unnecessary recomputations of a value at run-time. This is achieved by replacing the original computations of a program by auxiliary variables (registers) that are initialized with the correct value at suitable program points. In order to preserve the semantics of the original program, code motion must additionally be *safe*, i.e. it must not introduce computations of new values on paths. In fact, under this requirement it is possible to obtain *computationally optimal* results, i.e. results where the number of computations on each program path cannot be reduced anymore by means of safe code motion (cf. Theorem 3.9). Central idea to obtain this optimality result is to place computations *as early as possible* in a program, while maintaining safety (cf. [Dh2, Dh3, KS2, MR1, St]). However, this strategy moves computations even if it is *unnecessary*, i.e. there is no run-time gain[1]. This causes superfluous *register pressure*, which is in fact a major problem in practice.

In this paper we present a *lazy* computationally optimal code motion algorithm, which is unique in that it

- is as *efficient* as standard uni-directional analyses and
- avoids any unnecessary register pressure.

The point of this algorithm is the *decomposition* of the bi-directional structure of the known placement algorithms (cf. "Related Work" below) into a sequence of a backward analysis and a forward analysis, which directly implies the efficiency result. Moreover, the new compositional structure allows to avoid any unnecessary code motion by modifying the standard computationally optimal computation points according to the following idea:

- Initialize "as late as possible" while maintaining computational optimality.

Together with the suppression of initializations, which are only going to be used at the insertion point it-

*Part of the work was done, while the author was supported by the Deutsche Forschungsgemeinschaft grant La 426/9-2.

†Institut für Informatik und Praktische Mathematik, Christian-Albrechts-Universität, Preußerstraße 1-9, D-2300 Kiel 1.

‡The author is supported by the Deutsche Forschungsgemeinschaft grant La 426/11-1.

§Lehrstuhl für Informatik II, Rheinisch-Westfälische Technische Hochschule Aachen, Ahornstraße 55, D-5100 Aachen.

ACM SIGPLAN '92 PLDI-6/92/CA
© 1992 ACM 0-89791-476-7/92/0006/0224...$1.50

[1] In [Dh3] unnecessary code motions are called *redundant*.

self, this characterizes our approach of *lazy code motion*. Figure 1 displays an example, which is complex enough to illustrate the various features of the new approach. It will be discussed in more details during the development in this paper. For now just note that our algorithm is unique in performing the optimization displayed in Figure 2, which is exceptional for the following reasons: it eliminates the partially redundant computations of "a+b" in node **10** and **16** by moving them to node **8** and **15**, but it does not touch the computations of $a+b$ in node **3** and **17** that cannot be moved with run-time gain. This confirms that computations are only moved when it is profitable.

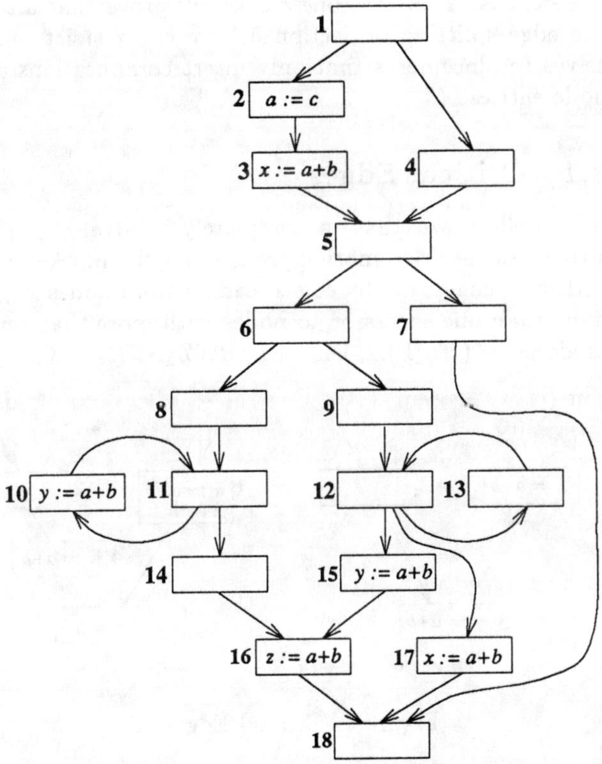

Figure 1: The Motivating Example

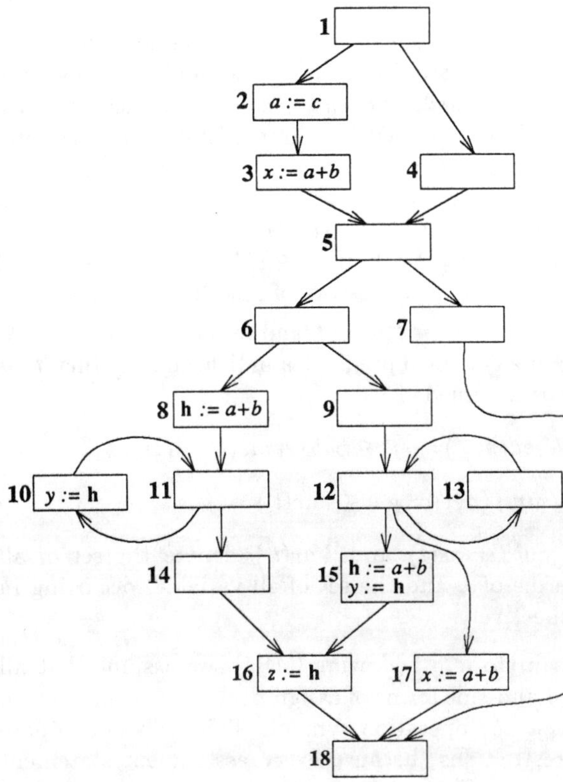

Figure 2: The Lazy Code Motion Transformation

Related Work

In 1979 Morel and Renvoise proposed a bit-vector algorithm for the suppression of partial redundancies [MR1]. The bi-directionality of their algorithm became model in the field of bit-vector based code motion (cf. [Ch, Dh1, Dh2, Dh3, DS, JD1, JD2, Mo, MR2, So]). Bi-directional algorithms, however, are in general conceptually and computationally more complex than uni-directional ones: e.g. in contrast to the uni-directional case, where reducible programs can be dealt with in $O(n\,log(n))$ time, where n characterizes the size of the argument program (e.g. number of statements), the best known estimation for bi-directional analyses is $O(n^2)$ (cf. [Dh3]). The problem of unnecessary code motion is only addressed in [Ch, Dh2, Dh3], and these proposals are of heuristic nature: code is unnecessarily moved or redundancies remain in the program.

In contrast, our algorithm is composed of *uni-directional* analyses[2]. Thus the same estimations for the worst case time complexity apply as for uni-directional analyses (cf.[AU, GW, HU1, HU2, Ke, KU1, Ta1, Ta2, Ta3, Ull]). Moreover, our algorithm is *conceptually simple*. It only requires the sequential computation of the four predicates `D-Safe`, `Earliest`, `Latest`, and `Isolated`. Thus our algorithm is an extension of the algorithm of [St], which simply computes the predicates `D-Safe` and `Earliest`. The two new predicates `Latest` and `Isolated` prevent any unnecessary code motion.

2 Preliminaries

We consider *variables* $v \in \mathbf{V}$, *terms* $t \in \mathbf{T}$, and *directed flow graphs* $G=(N,E,\mathrm{s},\mathrm{e})$ with node set N and edge set E. Nodes $n \in N$ represent *assignments* of the

[2] Such an algorithm was first proposed in [St], which later on was interprocedurally generalized to programs with procedures, local variables and formal parameters in [KS2]. Both algorithms realize an "as early as possible" placement.

form $v := t$ and edges $(m, n) \in E$ the nondeterministic branching structure of G[3]. $\mathbf{s}$ and $\mathbf{e}$ denote the unique *start node* and *end node* of G, which are both assumed to represent the empty statement *skip* and not to possess any predecessors and successors, respectively. Every node $n \in N$ is assumed to lie on a path from $\mathbf{s}$ to $\mathbf{e}$. Finally, $succ(n) =_{df} \{ m \mid (n, m) \in E \}$ and $pred(n) =_{df} \{ m \mid (m, n) \in E \}$ denote the set of all successors and predecessors of a node n, respectively.

For every node $n \equiv v := t$ and every term $t' \in \mathbf{T} \setminus \mathbf{V}$ we define two local predicates indicating, whether t' is used or modified[4]:

- $Used(n, t') =_{df} t' \in SubTerms(t)$ and
- $Transp(n, t') =_{df} v \notin Var(t')$

Here $SubTerms(t)$ and $Var(t')$ denote the set of all subterms of t and the set of all variables occurring in t, respectively.

Conventions: Following [MR1], we assume that all right-hand-side terms of assignment statements contain at most one operation symbol. This does not impose any restrictions, because every assignment statement can be decomposed into sequences of assignments of this form. As a consequence of this assumption it is enough to develop our algorithm for an arbitrary but fixed term here, because a global algorithm dealing with all program terms simultaneously is just the independent combination of all the "term algorithms". This leads to the usual bit-vector algorithms that realize such a combination efficiently (cf. [He]).

In the following, we fix the flow graph G and the term $t \in \mathbf{T} \setminus \mathbf{V}$, in order to allow a simple, unparameterized notation, and we denote the computations of t occurring in G as *original computations*.

3 Computationally Optimal Computation Points

In this section we develop an algorithm for the "as early as possible" placement, which in contrast to previous approaches is composed of *uni-directional* analyses. Here, *placement* stands for any program transformation that introduces a new auxiliary variable $\mathbf{h}$ for t, inserts at some program points assignments of the form $\mathbf{h} := t$, and replaces some of the original computations of t by $\mathbf{h}$ provided that this is *correct*, i.e. that $\mathbf{h}$ represents the same value. Formally, two computations of t represent the *same value* on a path if and only if no operand of t is modified between them. With this formal notion of value equality, the correctness condition above is satisfied for a node n if and only if on every path leading from $\mathbf{s}$ to n there is a last initialization of $\mathbf{h}$ at a node where t represents the same *value* as in n.

This definition of placement obviously leaves the freedom of inserting computations at node entries and node exists. However, one can easily prove that after the edge splitting of Section 3.1 we can restrict ourselves to placements that only insert computations at node entries.

3.1 Critical Edges

It is well-known that in completely arbitrary graph structures the code motion process may be blocked by "critical" edges, i.e. by edges leading from nodes with more than one successor to nodes with more than one predecessor (cf. [Dh2, Dh3, DS, RWZ, SKR1, SKR2]).

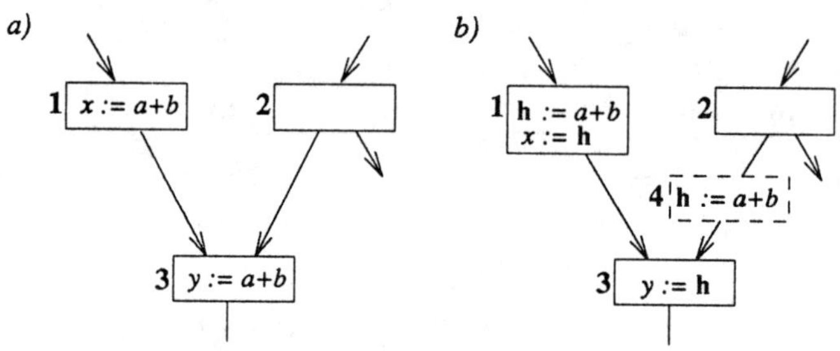

Figure 3: Critical Edges

In Figure 3(a) the computation of "$a+b$" at node **3** is partially redundant with respect to the computation of "$a+b$" at node **1**. However, this partial redundancy cannot safely be eliminated by moving the computation of "$a+b$" to its preceding nodes, because this may introduce a new computation on a path leaving node **2** on the right branch. On the other hand, it can safely be eliminated after inserting a synthetic node **4** in the critical edge $(\mathbf{2}, \mathbf{3})$, as illustrated in Figure 3(b).

We will therefore restrict our attention to programs having passed the following edge splitting transformation: every edge leading to a node with more than one predecessor has been split by inserting a synthetic node[5]. This simple transformation certainly implies that all critical edges are eliminated. Moreover, it sim-

[3] We do not assume any structural restrictions on G. In fact, every algorithm computing the fixed point solution of a uni-directional bit-vector data flow analysis problem may be used to compute the predicates `D-Safe`, `Earliest`, `Latest`, and `Isolated` (cf. [He]). However, application of the efficient techniques of [AU, GW, HU1, HU2, Ke, KU1, Ta1, Ta2, Ta3, Ull] requires that G satisfies the structural restrictions imposed by these algorithms.

[4] Flow graphs composed of *basic blocks* can be treated entirely in the same fashion replacing the predicate *Used* by the predicate *Antloc* (cf. [MR1]), indicating whether the computation of t is locally anticipatable at node n.

[5] In order to keep the presentation of the motivating example simple, we omit synthetic nodes that are not relevant for the Lazy Code Motion Transformation.

plifies the subsequent analysis, since it allows to obtain programs that are computationally and lifetime optimal (Optimality Theorem 4.9) by inserting all computations uniformly at node entries (cf. [SKR1, SKR2])[6].

3.2 Guaranteeing Computational Optimality

A placement is

- *safe*, iff every computation point n is an n-*safe* node, i.e.: a computation of t at n does not introduce a new value on a path through n.

  This property is necessary in order to guarantee that the program semantics is preserved by the placement process[7].

- *earliest*, iff every computation point n is an n-*earliest* node, i.e. there is a path leading from $\mathbf{s}$ to n where no node m prior to n is n-safe and delivers the same value as n when computing t.

A safe placement is

- *computationally optimal*, iff the results of any other safe placement always require at least as many computations at run-time.

In fact, safety and earliestness are already sufficient to characterize a computationally optimal placement:

⋆ A placement is computationally optimal if it is safe and earliest.

However, we consider the following stronger requirement of safety which leads to an equivalent characterization and allows simpler proofs:

A placement is

- *down-safe*, iff every computation point n is an n-*down-safe* node, i.e. a computation of t at n does not introduce a new value on a terminating path starting in n.

  Intuitively, this means that an initialization $\mathbf{h} := t$ placed at the entry of node n is justified on every terminating path by an original computation occurring before any operand of t is modified[8].

As safety induces earliestness, down-safety induces the notion of *ds-earliestness.* The following lemma states that it is unnecessary to distinguish between safety and down-safety in our application, and that the notions of earliestness and ds-earliestness coincide.

[6] Splitting critical edges only, would require a placement procedure which is capable of placing computations both at node entries and node exits.

[7] In particular, a safe placement does not change the potential for run-time errors, e.g. "division by 0" or "overflow".

[8] In [MR1] down-safety is called *anticipability*, and the dual notion to down-safety, *up-safety*, is called *availability*.

Lemma 3.1 *A placement is*

1. *earliest if and only if it is ds-earliest*
2. *safe and earliest if and only if it is down-safe and ds-earliest*

Proof: ad 1): Earliestness implies ds-earliestness. Thus let us assume an n-ds-earliest computation point $n \neq \mathbf{s}$. This requires a path from $\mathbf{s}$ to n where no node m prior to n is n-down-safe and delivers the same value as in n when computing t. In particular, there is no original computation on this path before n that represents the same value. Thus a node m prior to n on this path where a computation of t has the same value as in n cannot be n-up-safe[9] and consequently not n-safe either[10]. Hence node n is n-earliest.

ad 2): Due to 1) it remains to show that a safe and earliest placement is also down-safe. This follows directly from the fact that an n-earliest computation point n is not n-up-safe, which has been proved in 1). □

Let n be a computation point of a down-safe and earliest placement. Then the n-down-safety of n yields that every terminating path $p = (n_1, .., n_k)$ starting in n has a prefix $q = (n_1, \ldots, n_j)$ which satisfies:

a) $Used(n_j)$

b) $\neg Used(n_i)$ for all $i \in \{1, \ldots, j-1\}$

c) $Transp(n_i)$ for all $i \in \{1, \ldots, j-1\}$

In the remainder of the paper the prefixes q are called *safe-earliest first-use paths* (SEFU-paths). They characterize the computation points of safe placements in the following way:

Lemma 3.2 *Let pl_{se} be a safe and earliest placement, pl_s a safe placement and $q = (n_1, \ldots, n_j)$ a SEFU-path. Then we have:*

1. *pl_{se} has no computation of t on $(n_2, \ldots, n_j)$.*
2. *pl_s has a computation of t on q.*

Proof: In order to prove 1) let n_i be a computation point of pl_{se} with $i \in \{2, \ldots, j\}$. Then we are going to derive a contradiction to the earliestness of pl_{se}. According to Lemma 3.1 we conclude that pl_{se} is down-safe and, in particular, that n_i is n-down-safe. Moreover, every predecessor m of n_i is n-down-safe too: this is trivial in the case where n_i has more than one predecessor, because then they must all be synthetic nodes. Otherwise, n_{i-1} is the only predecessor of n_i. In this case its n-down-safety follows from the

[9] n-*up-safety* of a node is defined in analogy to n-down-safety.

[10] Note that a node is n-safe if and only if it is n-down-safe or n-up-safe.

properties a) – c) of q and the n-down-safety of n_1. Consequently, n_i is not n-ds-earliest and therefore due to Lemma 3.1 not n-earliest either.

2) follows immediately from the n-earliestness of n_1, and the safety of pl_s. □

As an easy consequence of Lemma 3.2 we obtain:

Corollary 3.3 *No computation point of a computationally optimal placement occurs outside of a SEFU-path.*

The central result of this section, however, is:

Theorem 3.4 *A placement is computationally optimal if it is down-safe and earliest.*

Proof: Applying Lemma 3.2, which is possible because of Lemma 3.1, we obtain that any safe placement has at least as many computations of t on every path p from s to e as the down-safe and earliest placement. □

In the following we will compute all program points that are n-down-safe and n-earliest.

3.2.1 Down-Safety

The set of n-down-safe computation points for t is characterized by the greatest solution of Equation System 3.5, which specifies a backward analysis of G.

Equation System 3.5 (Down-Safety)

$$\textbf{D-SAFE}(n) = \begin{cases} \textit{false} & \textit{if } n = \mathrm{e} \\ \textit{Used}(n) \lor \\ \textit{Transp}(n) \land \prod_{m \in succ(n)} \textbf{D-SAFE}(m) & \textit{otherwise} \end{cases}$$

Let `D-Safe` be the greatest solution of Equation System 3.5. Then we have (see Figure 4 for illustration):

Lemma 3.6 (Down-Safe Computation Points) *A node n is* n-*down-safe if and only if* `D-Safe`(n) *holds.*

Proof: "only if": Let **D** denote the set of nodes that are n-down-safe and **U** the set of nodes satisfying *Used*. Then all successors of a node in **D****U** are again in **D**. Thus a simple inductive argument shows that for all nodes $n \in$ **D** the predicate **D-SAFE**(n) remains constantly true during the maximal fixed point iteration.

"if": This can be proved by a straightforward induction on the length of a terminating path starting in n. □

3.2.2 Earliestness

Earliestness, which according to Lemma 3.1 is equivalent to ds-earliestness, is characterized by the least solution of Equation System 3.7, whose solution requires a forward analysis of G.

Equation System 3.7 (Earliestness)

$$\textbf{EARLIEST}(n) = \begin{cases} \textit{true} & \textit{if } n = \mathrm{s} \\ \sum_{m \in pred(n)} (\neg \textit{Transp}(m) \lor \\ \quad \neg\texttt{D-Safe}(m) \land \textbf{EARLIEST}(m)) & \textit{otherwise} \end{cases}$$

Let `Earliest` denote the least solution of Equation System 3.7. Along the lines of Lemma 3.6 we can prove:

Lemma 3.8 (Earliest Computation Points) *A node n is* n-*earliest if and only if* `Earliest`(n) *holds.*

Figure 4 shows the predicate values of `Earliest` for our motivating example. It illustrates that `Earliest` is valid at the start node and additionally at those nodes that are reachable by a path where no node prior to n is n-down-safe and delivers the same value as n when computing t. Of course, computations cannot be placed earlier than in the start node, which justifies `Earliest`(**1**) in Figure 4. Moreover, no node on the path (**1**, **4**, **5**, **7**, **18**) is n-down-safe. Thus `Earliest`({**2**, **4**, **5**, **6**, **7**, **18**}) holds. Finally, evaluating t at node **1** and **2** delivers a different value as in node **3**, which yields `Earliest`(**3**).

`D-Safe` and `Earliest` induce the Safe-Earliest Transformation:

The Safe-Earliest Transformation

- Introduce a new auxiliary variable **h** for t.
- Insert at the entry of every node n satisfying `D-Safe` and `Earliest` the assignment **h** := t.
- Replace every original computation of t in G by **h**.

Whenever `D-Safe`(n) holds there is a node m on every path p from s to n satisfying `D-Safe`(m) and `Earliest`(m) such that no operand of t is modified between m and n. Thus all replacements of the Safe-Earliest Transformation are correct, which guarantees that the Safe-Earliest Transformation is a placement. Moreover, according to Lemma 3.1, Lemma 3.6 and Lemma 3.8 the Safe-Earliest Transformation is down-safe and earliest. Together with Theorem 3.4 this yields:

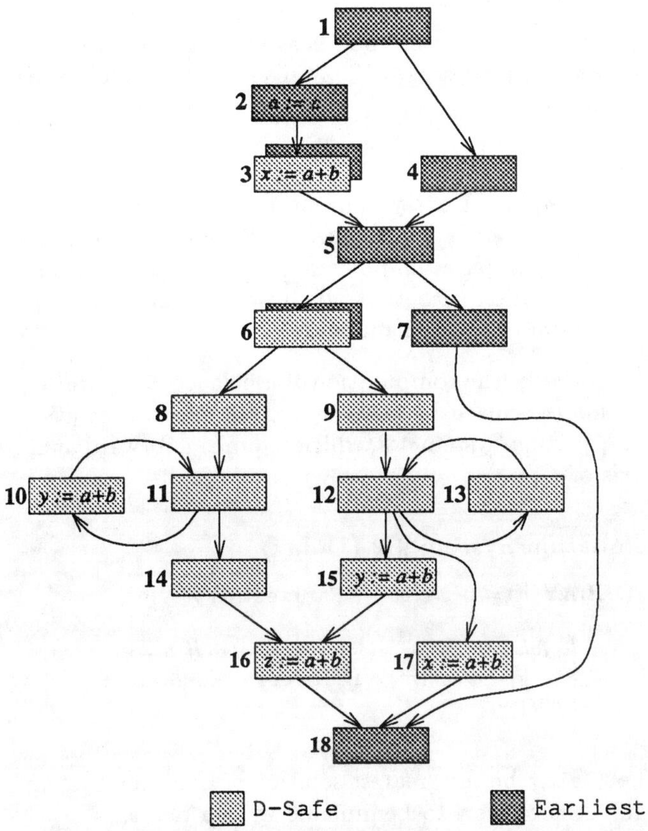

Figure 4: The D-Safe and Earliest predicate values

Theorem 3.9 (Computational Optimality)
The Safe-Earliest Transformation is computationally optimal.

Figure 5 shows the result of the Safe-Earliest Transformation for the motivating example of Figure 1, which is essentially the same as the one delivered by the algorithm of Morel and Renvoise [MR1][11]. In general, however, there may be more deviations, since their algorithm inserts computations at the end of nodes, and it moves computations only, if they are partially available. Introducing this condition can be considered as a first step in order to avoid unnecessary code motion. However, it limits the effect of unnecessary code motion only heuristically. For instance, in the example of Figure 5 the computations of node 10, 15, 16 and 17 would be moved to node 6, and therefore more than necessary. In particular, the computation of node 17 cannot be moved with run-time gain at all.

In the next section we are going to develop a procedure that completely avoids any unnecessary code motion.

[11] In the example of Figure 1 the algorithm of [MR1] would not insert a computation at node 3.

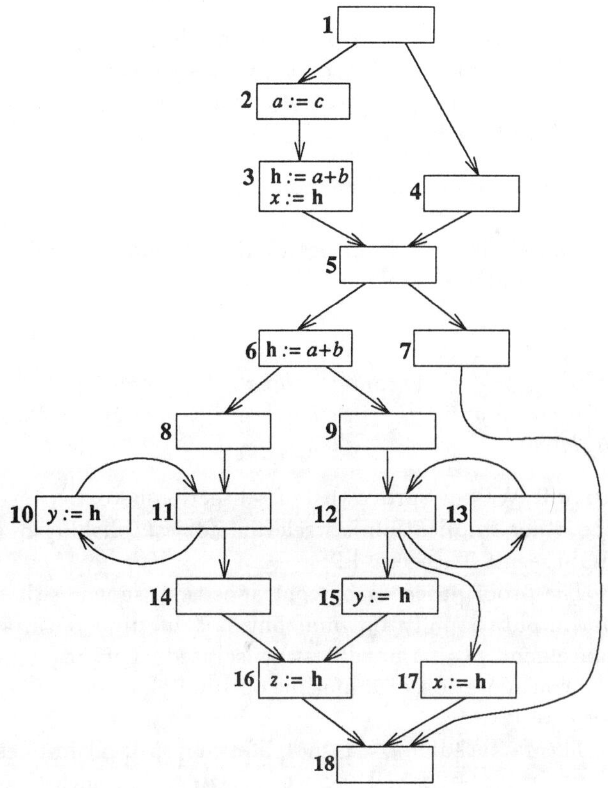

Figure 5: The Safe-Earliest Transformation

4 Suppressing Unnecessary Code Motion

In order to avoid unnecessary code motion, computations must be placed as *late* as possible while maintaining computational optimality. We therefore define:

A computationally optimal placement *pl* is

- *latest*, iff every computation point *n* is an n-*latest* node, i.e.:
  - *n* is a computation point of some computationally optimal placement and
  - on every terminating path *p* starting in *n* any following computation point of a computationally optimal placement occurs after an original computation on *p*.

  Intuitively, this means no other computationally optimal placement can have "later" computation points on any path.

- *isolated*, iff there is a computation point *n* that is an n-*isolated* node with respect to *pl*, i.e. on every terminating path starting in a successor of *n* every original computation is preceded by a computation of *pl*.

Essentially, this means that an initialization $\mathbf{h} := t$ placed at the entry of n reaches a second original computation at most after passing a new initialization of $\mathbf{h}$.

- *lifetime optimal* (or economic), iff any other computationally optimal placement always requires at least as long lifetimes of the auxiliary variables (registers).

We have:

Theorem 4.1 *A computationally optimal placement is lifetime optimal if and only if it is latest and not isolated.*

Proof: We only prove the "if"-direction here, because the other implication is irrelevant for establishing our main result Theorem 4.9.

The proof proceeds by contraposition, showing that a computationally optimal but not lifetime optimal placement pl_{co} is not latest or isolated. This requires the consideration of a lifetime optimal placement pl_{lto} for comparison.

The fact that pl_{co} is not lifetime optimal implies the existence of a SEFU-path $q = (n_1, .., n_j)$ such that pl_{co} has an initialization in a node n_c which precedes a computation of pl_{lto} in a node n_l with $c \leq l$. Now we have to distinguish two cases:

Case 1: $c < l$. Applying property b) of q, we obtain that the path $(n_c, .., n_{l-1})$ is free of original computations. Thus n_c is not n-latest and consequently pl_{co} not latest.

Case 2: $c = l$. Obviously, this implies $c = l = j$, and that the computation of pl_{lto} in n_l is an original one.

Thus it remains to show that n_l is n-isolated with respect to pl_{co}, i.e. that on every terminating path starting in a successor n of n_j the first original computation is preceded by a computation of pl_{co}.

We lead the assumption that n_j is not n-isolated, i.e. that there exists a path $p = (n, \ldots, m)$ without computations of pl_{co} but with an original computation at m, to a contradiction. Under this assumption Lemma 3.2(2) delivers that p is also free of computations of the Safe-Earliest Transformation, which yields that every node of p appears outside a SEFU-path. Thus, according to Corollary 3.3, p is also free of computations of pl_{lto}, which implies that pl_{lto} does not initialize $\mathbf{h}$ on either q or p. Moreover, because of the n-earliestness of n_1, it is also impossible that $\mathbf{h}$ is initialized on every path from $\mathtt{s}$ to n_1 after the last modification of an operand of t. This contradicts the placement property of pl_{lto}, and therefore implies that n_j is n-isolated with respect to pl_{co} as desired. □

Intuitively, lifetime optimal placements can be obtained by successively moving the computations from their earliest safe computation points in direction of the control flow to "later" points as long as computational optimality is preserved. This gives rise to the following definition:

A placement is

- *delayed*, iff every computation point n is an n-*delayed* node, i.e. on every path from $\mathtt{s}$ to n there is a computation point of the Safe-Earliest Transformation such that all subsequent original computations of p lie in n.

Technically, the computation of n-delayed computation points is realized by determining the greatest solution of Equation System 4.2, which requires a forward analysis of G.

Equation System 4.2 (Delay)

$$\mathbf{DELAY}(n) = \texttt{D-Safe}(n) \wedge \texttt{Earliest}(n) \vee$$

$$\begin{cases} \mathit{false} & \mathit{if}\ n = \mathtt{s} \\ \prod_{m \in pred(n)} \neg \mathit{Used}(m) \wedge \mathbf{DELAY}(m) & \mathit{otherwise} \end{cases}$$

Let $\texttt{Delay}$ be the greatest solution of Equation System 4.2. Analogously to Lemma 3.6 we can prove:

Lemma 4.3 *A node n is n-delayed if and only if $\texttt{Delay}(n)$ holds.*

Furthermore we have:

Lemma 4.4

1. *A computationally optimal placement is delayed.*
2. *A delayed placement is down-safe.*

Proof: ad 1): We have to show that every computation point n of a computationally optimal placement is n-delayed. This can be deduced from Corollary 3.3 and property b) of SEFU-paths, which deliver that every path from $\mathtt{s}$ to n goes through a computation point of the Safe-Earliest Transformation such that all subsequent original computations of p lie in n.

ad 2): According to Lemma 3.6 and Lemma 4.3 it is enough to show that $\texttt{Delay}(n)$ implies $\texttt{D-Safe}(n)$ for every node n. This can be done by a straightforward induction on the length of a shortest path from $\mathtt{s}$ to n. □

Based on the predicate $\texttt{Delay}$ we define $\texttt{Latest}$ by:

$$\texttt{Latest}(n) =_{df} \texttt{Delay}(n) \wedge (\mathit{Used}(n) \vee \neg \prod_{m \in succ(n)} \texttt{Delay}(m))$$

The predicate values of $\texttt{Delay}$ and $\texttt{Latest}$ are illustrated for our motivating example in Figure 6.

We have:

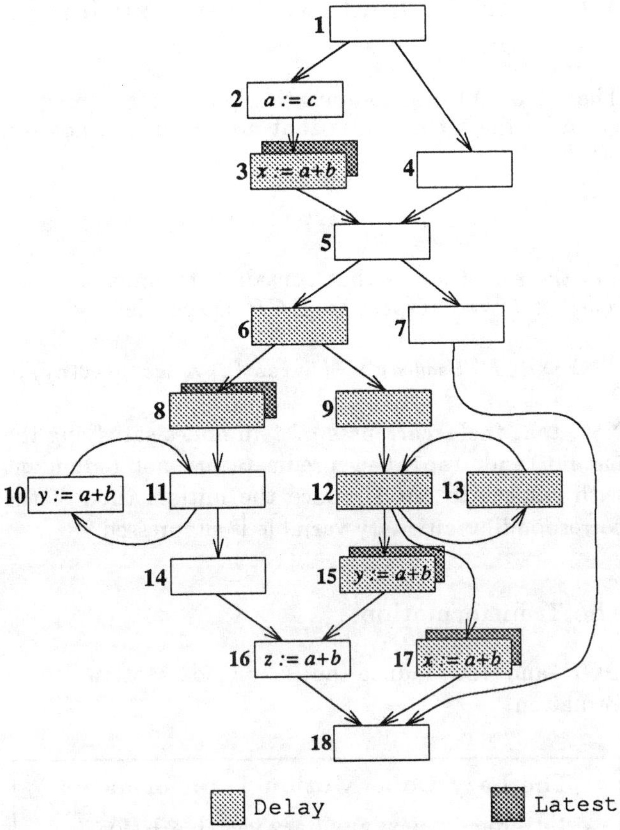

Figure 6: The `Delay` and `Latest` predicate values

Lemma 4.5 *A node n is* n-*latest if and only if* `Latest`(n) *holds.*

Proof: We will concentrate here on the part of the proof being relevant for the proof of Theorem 4.9, which is the "if"-direction for nodes that occur as computation points of some computationally optimal placement. This is much simpler than the proof for the general case.

Thus let us assume a computation point n of a computationally optimal placement satisfying `Latest`. Then it is sufficient to show that on every terminating path p starting in n any following computation point of a computationally optimal placement occurs after an original computation on p.

Obviously, this is the case if n itself contains an original computation. Thus we can reduce our attention to the other case, in which ¬`Delay`(m) must hold for some successor m of n. This directly yields that n is a synthetic node with m being its only successor, because m must have several predecessors.

Now assume a terminating path p starting in m, and a node l that occurs not later than the first node with an original computation. Then it remains to show that l is not a computation point of a computationally optimal placement.

Lemma 3.2(1) implies that there does not exist any computation point of the Safe-Earliest Transformation prior to l on p, because n is n-delayed due to Lemma 4.3. Moreover Lemma 4.3 yields that m is not n-delayed. Thus l cannot be n-delayed either. According to Lemma 4.4(1) this directly implies that l is not a computation point of any computationally optimal placement. □

As `D-Safe` and `Earliest` also `Latest` specifies a program transformation. We have:

Lemma 4.6 *The* Latest Transformation *is a computationally optimal placement.*

Proof: Whereas the safety property holds due to Lemma 4.3 and Lemma 4.4, the proof that the Latest Transformation is a placement and that it is computationally optimal can be done simultaneously by showing that (1) every SEFU-path contains a node satisfying `Latest` and that (2) nodes satisfying `Latest` do not occur outside SEFU-paths. This is straightforward from the definition of `Delay`. □

Figure 7 shows the result of the Latest Transformation for the motivating example.

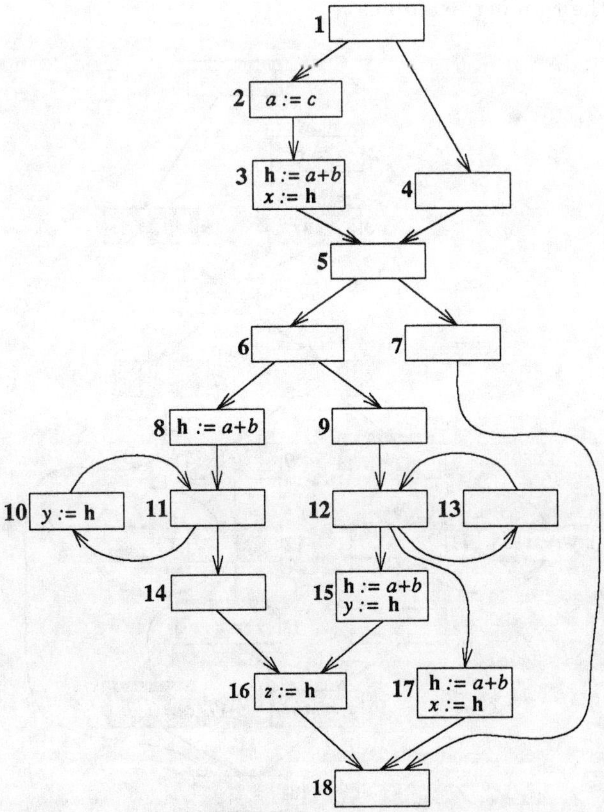

Figure 7: The Latest Transformation

The Latest Transformation is already more economic than any other algorithm proposed in the literature.

However, it still contains unnecessary initializations of **h** in node **3** and **17**. In order to avoid such unnecessary initializations, we must identify all program points where an inserted computation would only be used in the insertion node itself. This is achieved by determining the greatest solution of Equation System 4.7, which specifies a backward analysis of G.

Equation System 4.7 (Isolation)

$$\mathbf{ISOLATED}(n) = \prod_{m \in succ(n)} (\texttt{Latest}(m) \vee \neg Used(m) \wedge \mathbf{ISOLATED}(m))$$

Let $\texttt{Isolated}(n)$ be the greatest solution of Equation System 4.7. Then we can prove in analogy to Lemma 3.6:

Lemma 4.8 *A node n is* n-*isolated with respect to the Latest Transformation if and only if* $\texttt{Isolated}(n)$ *holds.*

Figure 8 shows the predicate values of `Isolated` for the running example.

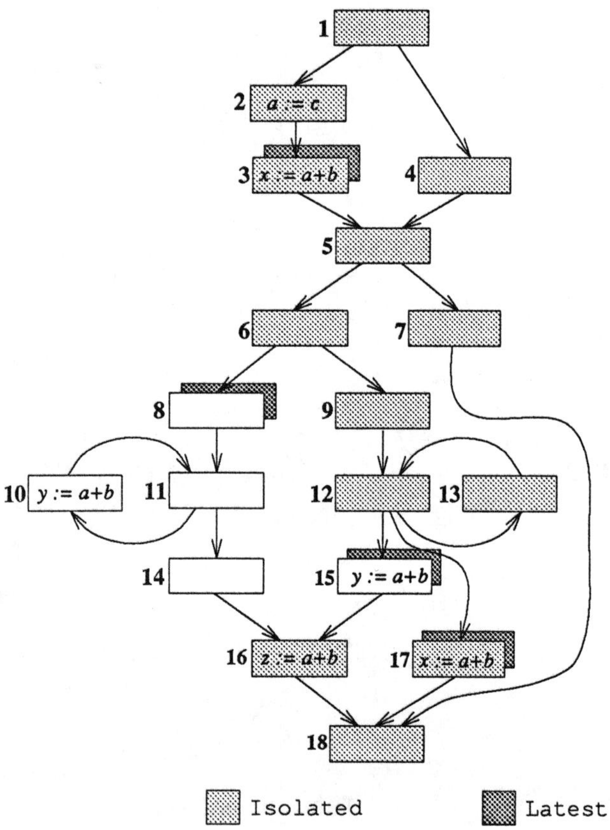

Figure 8: The `Isolated` and `Latest` predicate values

4.1 The Optimal Program Transformation

The set of optimal computation points for t in G is given by the set of nodes that are *latest*, but not *isolated*

$$\mathbf{OCP} =_{df} \{ n \mid \texttt{Latest}(n) \wedge \neg \texttt{Isolated}(n) \}$$

and the set of nodes that contain a redundant occurrence of t with respect to **OCP** is specified by

$$\mathbf{RO} =_{df} \{ n \mid Used(n) \wedge \neg(\texttt{Latest}(n) \wedge \texttt{Isolated}(n)) \}$$

Note that the occurrences of t in nodes satisfying the `Latest` and `Isolated` predicate are not redundant with respect to **OCP**, since the initialization of the corresponding auxiliary variable is suppressed.

The Transformation

OCP and **RO** induce the Lazy Code Motion Transformation.

The Lazy Code Motion Transformation

- Introduce a new auxiliary variable **h** for t.
- Insert at the entry of every node in **OCP** the assignment **h** $:= t$.
- Replace every original computation of t in nodes of **RO** by **h**.

Our main result states that this transformation is optimal:

Theorem 4.9 (Optimality Theorem)

The Lazy Code Motion Transformation is computationally and lifetime optimal.

Proof: Following the lines of Lemma 4.6 we can prove that the Lazy Code Motion Transformation is a computationally optimal placement. According to Lemma 4.5 and Lemma 4.8 it is also latest and not isolated (Lemma 4.8 can be applied since the Lazy Code Motion Transformation has the same computation points as the Latest Transformation.). Thus Theorem 4.1 completes the proof. □

The application of the Lazy Code Motion Transformation to the flow graph of Figure 1 results in the promised flow graph of Figure 2.

5 Conclusions

We have presented a bit-vector algorithm for the *computationally* and *lifetime optimal* placement of computations within flow graphs, which is as *efficient* as standard uni-directional analyses. Important feature of this algorithm is its *laziness*: computations are placed as *early as necessary* but as *late as possible*. This guarantees the lifetime optimality while preserving computational optimality.

Fundamental was the decomposition of the typically bi-directionally specified code motion procedures into uni-directional components. Besides yielding clarity and reducing the number of predicates drastically, this allows us to utilize the efficient algorithms for uni-directional bit-vector analyses. Moreover, it makes the algorithm modular, which supports future extensions: in [KRS] we present an extension of our lazy code motion algorithm which, in a similar fashion as in [JD1, JD2], uniformly combines code motion and strength reduction, and following the lines of [KS1, KS2] a generalization to programs with procedures, local variables and formal parameters is straightforward. We are also investigating an adaption of the *as early as necessary* but *as late as possible* placing strategy to the semantically based code motion algorithms of [SKR1, SKR2].

References

[AU] Aho, A. V., and Ullman, J. D. Node listings for reducible flow graphs. In *Proceedings 7th STOC*, 1975, 177 - 185.

[Ch] Chow, F. A portable machine independent optimizer – Design and measurements. Ph.D. dissertation, Dept. of Electrical Engineering, Stanford University, Stanford, Calif., and Tech. Rep. 83-254, Computer Systems Lab., Stanford University, 1983.

[Dh1] Dhamdhere, D. M. Characterization of program loops in code optimization. *Comp. Lang. 8*, 2 (1983), 69 - 76.

[Dh2] Dhamdhere, D. M. A fast algorithm for code movement optimization. *SIGPLAN Not. 23*, 10 (1988), 172 - 180.

[Dh3] Dhamdhere, D. M. Practical adaptation of the global optimization algorithm of Morel and Renvoise. *ACM Trans. Program. Lang. Syst. 13*, 2 (1991), 291 - 294.

[DS] Drechsler, K. H., and Stadel, M. P. A solution to a problem with Morel and Renvoise's "Global optimization by suppression of partial redundancies". *ACM Trans. Program. Lang. Syst. 10*, 4 (1988), 635 - 640.

[GW] Graham, S. L., and Wegman, M. A fast and usually linear algorithm for global flow analysis. *Journal of the ACM 23*, 1 (1976), 172 - 202.

[He] Hecht, M. S. Flow analysis of computer programs. Elsevier, North-Holland, 1977.

[HU1] Hecht, M. S., and Ullman, J. D. Analysis of a simple algorithm for global flow problems. In *Proceedings 1st POPL*, Boston, Massachusetts, 1973, 207 - 217.

[HU2] Hecht, M. S., and Ullman, J. D. A simple algorithm for global data flow analysis problems. In *SIAM J. Comput. 4*, 4 (1977), 519 - 532.

[JD1] Joshi, S. M., and Dhamdhere, D. M. A composite hoisting-strength reduction transformation for global program optimization – part I. *Internat. J. Computer Math. 11*, (1982), 21 - 41.

[JD2] Joshi, S. M., and Dhamdhere, D. M. A composite hoisting-strength reduction transformation for global program optimization – part II. *Internat. J. Computer Math. 11*, (1982), 111 - 126.

[Ke] Kennedy, K. Node listings applied to data flow analysis. In *Proceedings 2nd POPL*, Palo Alto, California, 1975, 10 - 21.

[KRS] Knoop, J., Rüthing, O., and Steffen, B. Lazy strength reduction. To appear.

[KS1] Knoop, J., and Steffen, B. The interprocedural coincidence theorem. Aachener Informatik-Berichte Nr. 9127, Rheinisch-Westfälische Technische Hochschule Aachen, Aachen, 1991.

[KS2] Knoop, J., and Steffen, B. Efficient and optimal interprocedural bit-vector data flow analyses: A uniform interprocedural framework. To appear.

[KU1] Kam, J. B., and Ullman, J. D. Global data flow analysis and iterative algorithms. *Journal of the ACM 23*, 1 (1976), 158 - 171.

[KU2] Kam, J. B., and Ullman, J. D. Monotone data flow analysis frameworks. *Acta Informatica 7*, (1977), 309 - 317.

[Mo] Morel, E. Data flow analysis and global optimization. In: Lorho, B. (Ed.). Methods and tools for compiler construction, Cambridge University Press, 1984.

[MR1] Morel, E., and Renvoise, C. Global optimization by suppression of partial redundancies. *Commun. of the ACM 22*, 2 (1979), 96 - 103.

[MR2] Morel, E., and Renvoise, C. Interprocedural elimination of partial redundancies. In: Muchnick, St. S., and Jones, N. D. (Eds.). Program flow analysis: Theory and applications. Prentice Hall, Englewood Cliffs, NJ, 1981.

[RWZ] Rosen, B. K., Wegman, M. N., and Zadeck,F. K. Global value numbers and redundant computations. In *Proceedings 15th POPL*, San Diego, California, 1988, 12 - 27.

[So] Sorkin, A. Some comments on A solution to a problem with Morel and Renvoise's "Global optimization by suppression of partial redundancies". *ACM Trans. Program. Lang. Syst. 11*, 4 (1989), 666 - 668.

[St] Steffen, B. Data flow analysis as model checking. In *Proceedings TACS'91*, Sendai, Japan, Springer-Verlag, LNCS 526 (1991), 346 - 364.

[SKR1] Steffen, B., Knoop, J., and Rüthing, O. The value flow graph: A program representation for optimal program transformations. In *Proceedings 3rd ESOP*, Copenhagen, Denmark, Springer-Verlag, LNCS 432 (1990), 389 - 405.

[SKR2] Steffen, B., Knoop, J., and Rüthing, O. Efficient code motion and an adaption to strength reduction. In *Proceedings 4th TAPSOFT*, Brighton, United Kingdom, Springer-Verlag, LNCS 494 (1991), 394 - 415.

[Ta1] Tarjan, R. E. Applications of path compression on balanced trees. *Journal of the ACM 26*, 4 (1979), 690 - 715.

[Ta2] Tarjan, R. E. A unified approach to path problems. *Journal of the ACM 28*, 3 (1981), 577 - 593.

[Ta3] Tarjan, R. E. Fast algorithms for solving path problems. *Journal of the ACM 28*, 3 (1981), 594 - 614.

[Ull] Ullman, J. D. Fast algorithms for the elimination of common subexpressions. *Acta Informatica 2*, 3 (1973), 191 - 213.

A Safe Approximate Algorithm for Interprocedural Pointer Aliasing*

William Landi (landi@cs.rutgers.edu)
Barbara G. Ryder (ryder@cs.rutgers.edu)

Department of Computer Science
Rutgers University, New Brunswick, NJ 08903

Abstract

During execution, when two or more names exist for the same location at some program point, we call them *aliases*. In a language which allows arbitrary pointers, the problem of determining aliases at a program point is $\mathcal{P}$-space-hard [Lan92]. We present an algorithm for the Conditional May Alias problem, which can be used to safely approximate Interprocedural May Alias in the presence of pointers. This algorithm is as precise as possible in the worst case and has been implemented in a prototype analysis tool for C programs. Preliminary speed and precision results are presented.

1 Introduction

Programming language environments feature software tools that improve the quality, efficiency, understandability, and reusability of code. Optimizers, debuggers, testers and parallelizers use *data flow analysis* to statically extract semantic information from programs to increase their efficacy. Aliases represent important semantic information whose precision can greatly affect the quality of optimized code and the precision of various compile-time interprocedural analyses [Cal88, CK89, PRL91].

An *alias* occurs at some program point during program execution when two or more names exist for the same location. The aliases of a particular name at a program point t are all other names that refer to the same memory location on some path to t. When this execution path traverses more than one procedure, we are solving the Interprocedural May Alias Problem.

While the calculation of aliases for FORTRAN is well understood [Ban79, Coo85, CK89, Mye81], aliasing in C is different than aliasing in Fortran in two respects. First, aliases can change due to side effects of intraprocedural execution flow. Second, aliases created during execution of a called procedure can affect aliases which hold on return to the calling procedure. Arbitrary pointers cause the problem of computing aliases to become $\mathcal{P}$-space-hard; currently, there are no good approximation algorithms.

In this paper, we present an approximation algorithm for interprocedural pointer-induced aliasing based upon Conditional May Alias information that describes aliasing within a procedure assuming certain conditions hold at its entry. We report data on algorithm performance and accuracy on real C programs. We define a appropriate precision measure and show that our algorithm is as precise as possible in the worst case.

2 Related Work

Weihl devised an approximation algorithm for finding aliases in the presence of pointers [Wei80], which unfortunately was very imprecise. Our attempts to use his

*The research reported here was supported, in part, by Siemens Research Corporation and NSF grant CCR-8920078.

ACM SIGPLAN '92 PLDI-6/92/CA
© 1992 ACM 0-89791-476-7/92/0006/0235...$1.50

algorithm for interprocedural analysis of C programs in ISMM [Ryd89] were unsuccessful because of the degree of imprecision in the reported aliases. Chow and Rudmik [CR82] also presented an algorithm for finding aliases in the presence of pointers; however, their algorithm traced non-executable interprocedural execution paths and handled local variables incorrectly. Coutant [Cou86] extended Weihl's work by keeping his restriction of finding program aliases, but allowing the tracing of aliases through more than one level of dereference and adding additional language constructs (e.g., structures and arrays). Benjamin Cooper [Coo89] developed an algorithm which used *alias histories* to insure that a procedure returns to the call site that invoked it.

There also has been some work [Deu90, Deu92, NPD87] in detecting aliases in higher order programming languages. [NPD87] only considers programs with single level dereferences and has the added difficulty of tracking the binding of functions to names. The problem addressed by [Deu90] is an order of magnitude complication over general aliasing; he allows closures (partially evaluated functions) and continuations (storing of runtime environment for later reuse). In [Deu92], an algorithm for finding aliases in polymorphically typed programs is presented.

The work done on dependence analysis and conflict detection in programs with recursive structures [CWZ90, Gua88, HA90, HN89, HPR89, JM82, LH88] is also related, although it is directed at finding access patterns into structures rather than explicitly finding aliases. A *conflict* [LH88] occurs between two statements when one statement writes a location and the other accesses (reads or writes) the same location (*loc*), thus preventing the possibility of those statements being executed in arbitrary order. A data dependence exists between two statements iff they conflict and there is an execution path from one program point to the other on which *loc* is not written.

```
int *g1, g2;
P()
{
  g1 = &g2;
}
main ()
{
  int **l1, *l2;
  l1 = &g1;
  P();
  l2 = &g2;
  P();
}
```

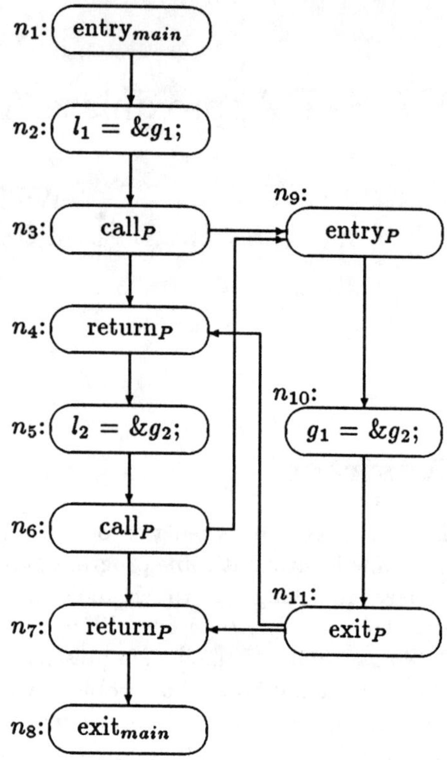

Figure 1: A program and its ICFG

3 Problem Representation

We analyze C-like imperative programming languages with sophisticated pointer usage and data structures, no type casting, explicit function calls (without function variables), and arrays which we treat as aggregates. We represent a program by an *Interprocedural Control Flow Graph* or *ICFG*[LR91] which intuitively is the union of statement-level control flow graphs for each procedure augmented by call, return, entry and exit nodes. Call nodes are connected to the entry nodes of procedures they invoke; exit nodes are connected to return nodes corresponding to these calls. A sample ICFG can be found in Figure 1.

Objects are locations that can store information, and *object names* provide ways to refer to objects. An object name is a variable and a (possibly empty) sequence of dereferences and field accesses. Object names can be defined by three simple BNF rules:

- *object_name* → **object_name*
- *object_name* → *object_name.field_of_structure*
- *object_name* → *variable*

If there are any recursively defined data structures (e.g., linked lists) then the number of object names is potentially infinite. We will limit to some constant, k, the number of dereferences allowable in any object name and obtain a finite number of potential object names. We consider any object name with $l > k$ dereferences to be represented by the object name obtained by ignoring the last $l-k$ dereferences yielding a unique k-limited name. Thus, for $k = 1$, $p\text{->}f_1\text{->}f_2$ would be represented by $p\text{->}f_1$ (and not by $*p$). We borrow terminology from [JM79] and call this *k-limiting*, because their process is analogous even though they *k-limit* dynamic structures while we *k-limit object names.* We need the following functions for object names:

is_prefix(on_1, on_2) returns *true* iff on_1 can be transformed into on_2 by a (possibly empty) sequence of dereferences and field accesses.

apply_trans(on_1, on_2, on_3): *is_prefix*(on_1, on_2) must be *true*. The function applies to on_3 the sequence of dereferences and field accesses necessary to transform on_1 into on_2 and returns the result. For example, *apply_trans*($p\text{->}n$, $p\text{->}n\text{->}d$, r) returns $r\text{->}d$.

As in [LR91] we will represent *aliases* by unordered pairs of object names (e.g., $\langle v, *p\rangle$). The order is unimportant because the alias relation is symmetric. Since we have k-limited object_names, to safely represent aliases we must assume that $\langle a, b_k\rangle$ with k-limited component b_k, represents not only $\langle a, b_k\rangle$ but also any alias $\langle a, b'_k\rangle$ such that b_k can be transformed into b'_k by a sequence of dereferences and field accesses. Also $\langle a_k, b_k\rangle$ with two k-limited components represents itself and all aliases $\langle a'_k, b'_k\rangle$ such that a_k is a prefix of a'_k and b_k is a prefix of b'_k.

The following definitions will be used throughout the paper:

realizable: A path is **realizable** iff it is a path in the ICFG and whenever a procedure on this path returns, it returns to the call site which invoked it.

holds: Alias $\langle a, b\rangle$ **holds** on the realizable path $\rho n_1 n_2 ... n_i$ iff a and b refer to the same location after execution of program point n_i whenever the execution defined by the path occurs.

Interprocedural May Alias: The precise[1] solution for **Interprocedural May Alias** is $\{[n, \langle a, b\rangle] \mid \exists$ a realizable path, $\rho n_1 n_2 ... n_{i-1} n$, in the ICFG on which $\langle a, b\rangle$ holds$\}$.

visible: At a call site, an object name (e.g., $*x$) of the calling procedure is **visible** in the called procedure iff the called procedure is in the scope of the object name *and* at run time the object name refers to the same object in both the calling and called procedure. (e.g., If x is a local variable of procedure P, then the x in P before a recursive call is not visible after the call, since at execution time it is a different instantiation.)

4 Approximating May Alias

The may-hold Relation We have used our precise algorithm for computing aliases in the presence of single level pointers [LR91] as a basis for a safe interprocedural aliasing algorithm for arbitrary pointers. The key idea in both algorithms is to use **Conditional May Alias** information that answers the question: *If there is a path from program entry to the entry node of the procedure containing n_i on which every alias in the set $\mathcal{AA}$ holds, then may object name a be aliased to object name b on some path to n_i?* Fortunately, it is safe to consider only $\mathcal{AA}$ (sets of aliases) with cardinality less than or equal to one [Lan92]. To insure efficiency, we only concern ourselves with $\mathcal{AA}$ sets that actually occur. We use *may-hold*$([(n_i, \mathcal{AA}), \langle a, b\rangle])$ to encode the answer to the Conditional May Alias question:

may-hold$([(n_i, \mathcal{AA}), \langle a, b\rangle])$ is *true* iff $\langle a, b\rangle$ holds on some path from *entry*(n_i), the entry of the procedure containing n_i, to n_i assuming there is a path from entry of main to *entry*(n_i) on which the assumed alias $\mathcal{AA}$ holds **and there is a path from entry of main to the *entry*(n_i) on which $\mathcal{AA}$ holds.**

[1] We are using the standard data flow definition of precise which means "precise up to symbolic execution", assuming all paths through the program are executable [Bar78].

For even further efficiency gains we have designed our algorithm so that work is performed only when *may-hold*($[(n_i, \mathcal{AA}), \langle a, b\rangle]$) is *true*. Since most of the *may-holds* will be *false*, this improves the average time complexity of our algorithm considerably.

Finally, given Conditional May Alias, May Alias is easily computable;

may-alias(*node*) =

$$\{\mathcal{PA} \mid (\exists \mathcal{AA})\textit{may-hold}(node, AA, PA) = true\}.$$

This can be computed in time linear in the size of the *may-hold* solution; thus, we will only concern ourselves with the computation of *may-hold*.

Computing may-hold The algorithm for computing *may-hold* is simple at a high level. First, we find all the *may-hold* relations which are trivially true, (e.g., *may-hold*($[(\text{“}p = \&v\text{”}, \emptyset), \langle *p, v\rangle]$) is true). Once we have this initial set of *true may-holds*, we compute the set of all *true may-holds* using a worklist algorithm (Figure 2) which propagates alias information from exits of nodes to their immediate successors in the ICFG.

The remainder of this section gives details of this algorithm. We discuss our implementation of *may-hold*, parameter binding, and the functions used in Figure 2. We will use the following macro throughout:

```
make_true(node,AA,PA)
{  if may-hold([(node,AA),PA]) is false
   {  set may-hold([(node,AA),PA]) to true
      add (node,AA,PA) to the worklist
   }
}
```

Representation In order to have an efficient implementation for our alias algorithm, we must be able to do the following operations in constant time:

- Set *may-hold*($[(node, \mathcal{AA}), \mathcal{PA}]$) to *false* for all possible *node*, $\mathcal{AA}$, and $\mathcal{PA}$.
- Find the value of *may-hold*($[(node, \mathcal{AA}), \mathcal{PA}]$) for a given *node*, $\mathcal{AA}$, and $\mathcal{PA}$.
- Set the value of *may-hold*($[(node, \mathcal{AA}), \mathcal{PA}]$) for a given *node*, $\mathcal{AA}$, and $\mathcal{PA}$.

We use dynamic hashing [KS86] to do this, giving us constant time operations in the average case. We

```
find_aliases()
{ worklist = ∅
  /* Alias Introduction */
  for each node (N) in the ICFG
  { if N is an assignment to a pointer
      aliases_intro_by_assignment(N)
    if N is a call node
      aliases_intro_by_call(N)
  }
  /* Implied Aliases */
  while worklist is not empty
  { remove (N,AA,PA) from worklist
    if N is a call node
      aliases_at_call_implies(N,AA,PA)
    else if N is an exit node
      alias_at_exit_implies(N,AA,PA)
    else any_other_alias_implies(N,AA,PA)
  }
}
```

Figure 2: Computing may-hold

assume *may-hold* for any $[(node, \mathcal{AA}), \mathcal{PA}]$ triple is *false* if it is not in the hash table; otherwise it is *true* [Lan92].

Implicit Assumptions Consider the assignment “$p = q$” where p and q are pointers to linked lists. This assignment results in the following:

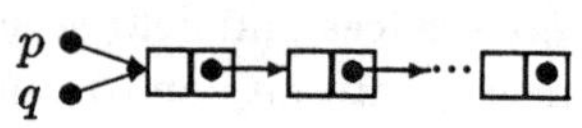

Thus yielding the aliases $\langle *p, *q\rangle$, $\langle$*p->next*, *q->next*$\rangle$, $\langle$*p->next->next*, *q->next->next*$\rangle$, and so on. However, these aliases depend on $*q$, *q->next*, and *q->next->next* being non-*NULL* before the assignment. Our algorithm implicitly assumes that this is the case, and we would create all of the above aliases that k-limiting allows. This assumption is not an inherent part of our algorithm and can be removed, but we use it here because it is generally reasonable and increases efficiency of the algorithm. For conciseness, throughout this paper, whenever we create an alias $\langle *p, *q\rangle$ we assume that the aliases $\langle$*p->next*, *q->next*$\rangle$, $\langle$*p->next->next*, *q->next->next*$\rangle$, ... are also created although we do not explicitly state this everywhere.

Modeling Parameter Bindings For interprocedural analysis, we need to model the affects of parameter bindings on aliases. We do this with a function $bind_{call}(\mathcal{PA})$. Intuitively, $bind_{call}(\emptyset)$ will be all the aliases on entry of a called procedure that must exist because of parameter bindings, while $bind_{call}(\langle a, b\rangle)$ will be the set of aliases at entry of a called procedure whose existence is implied by a being aliased to b at *call*.

Unfortunately, this definition is not sufficient because a procedure call can both create and destroy an alias in the *calling* procedure, involving an object name not visible in the called procedure. For example, the first call of P in Figure 1 creates the alias $\langle **l_1, g_2\rangle$ in main even though l_1 is not in the scope of P. However, only references to the visible object name in an alias pair can affect whether the alias holds on a path. A procedure has the same effect on all alias pairs which contain visible object name *w* and any non-visible object name. Therefore, we use the object name *non_visible* to represent all non-visible object names[2].

In the *bind* function, if any of the aliases in the bind set involve *non_visible*, we need to know the corresponding object name in the calling procedure. For example, assume q is global to *P*, r is not visible to *P*, and q,r, and f are all type "int *":

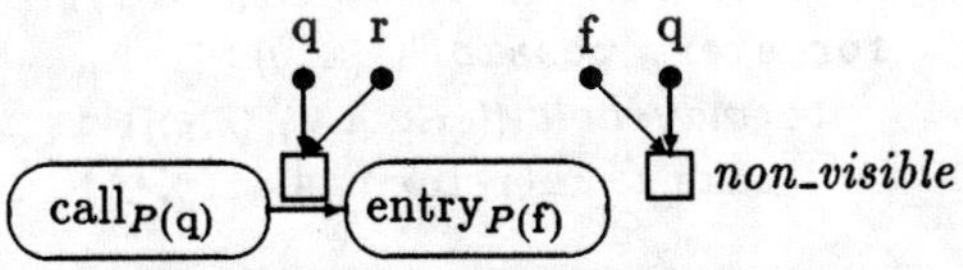

$$bind_{call_{P(q)}}(\emptyset) = \{\langle *q, *f\rangle\}$$

$$bind_{call_{P(q)}}(\langle *q, *r\rangle) = \left\{ \begin{array}{l} (\langle *f, *q\rangle, \text{-}), \\ (\langle *q, non\_visible\rangle, *r), \\ (\langle *f, non\_visible\rangle, *r) \end{array} \right\}$$

The occurrence of $(\langle *q, non\_visible\rangle, *r)$ in $bind_{call_{P(q)}}(\langle *q, *r\rangle)$ represents the fact that *q is aliased to non-visible object name $*r$ at the entry of the called procedure P.

Computing $bind_{call}(\emptyset)$*:* There are two ways aliases can be implied by parameter bindings. The first alias corresponds to a simple formal to actual pairing. For example, if P is a function with formal f of type "int *" and *call* is an invocation of P with actual a then $\langle *f, *a\rangle$[3] is in $bind_{call}(\emptyset)$. The second occurs if two distinct formals are passed two actuals where one actual is a prefix of the other. For example, if P is a function with two formals f_1 (type "int **") and f_2 (type "int *") and *call* is P(a,$*a$) then $\langle **f_1, *f_2\rangle$ is in $bind_{call}(\emptyset)$.

Computing $bind_{call}(\langle x, y\rangle)$*:* There are three ways that an alias at a call site may imply an alias on entry to a procedure. The first is trivial: if the two object names are global to the called procedure then they are also aliased on entry to the called procedure. The other two can be illustrated by the following example (both a_1 and a_2 are global to P):

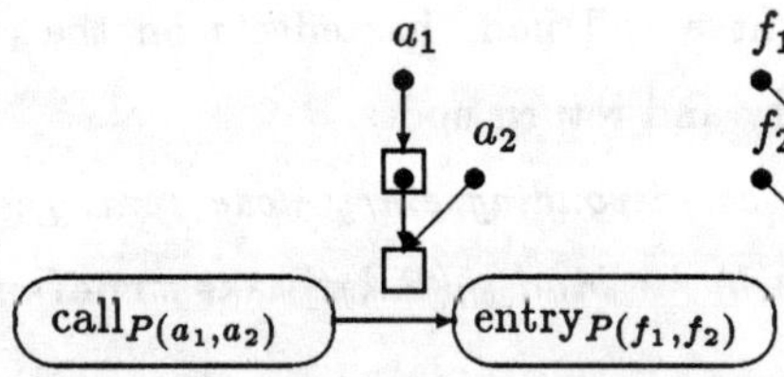

In this example, since $*a_2$ is aliased to $**a_1$ at $call_{P(a_1,a_2)}$, $*f_2$ is aliased to $**a_1$. This example can be generalized to the second way an alias at a call site can imply an alias at the entry of a procedure. Whenever an actual has an alias to an object name, its corresponding formal picks up an alias to that object name or *non_visible*, if the object name is not visible in the called procedure. Also in the example, since $*a_2$ is aliased to $**a_1$ at $call_{P(a_1,a_2)}$, $*f_2$ is aliased to $**f_1$ at $entry_{P(f_1,f_2)}$. This is typical of the third case; when two actuals are aliased at a call site, the corresponding formals are aliased on entry to the called procedure. The algorithm for computing $bind_{call}(\langle x, y\rangle)$ is a straightforward encoding of these three cases.

The remainder of this section gives a more detailed description of the algorithm in Figure 2 by discussing which *may-holds* are set to *true* by each its functions.

---

[2] In [LR91] we referred to *non_visible* as "·".

[3] $(\langle *f, non\_visible\rangle, *a)$ if a is not visible in P.

4.1 Aliases_intro_by_assignment(*node*)

Let *node* be the pointer assignment "$p = q$".[4] Clearly, *may-hold*($[(node, \emptyset), \langle *p, *q\rangle]$) is *true* unless p is a prefix of q. To understand this exception, consider the assignment "$p = p\text{->}next$". It does not create an alias $\langle *p, *(p\text{->}next)\rangle$ because p and $p\text{->}next$ both refer to different objects after this assignment but their alias relationship does not change.

4.2 Aliases_intro_by_call(*node*)

For each alias $\langle a, b\rangle$ in $bind_{call}(\emptyset)$, `make_true(`*entry*`,` $\langle a, b\rangle$`,`$\langle a, b\rangle$`)` where *entry* is the entry node corresponding to *call*.

4.3 Alias_at_call_implies(*call*,$\mathcal{AA}$,$\mathcal{PA}$)

A *may-hold* at a call node has effects on the corresponding entry and return nodes.

Effects on corresponding entry node (entry): For each alias $\langle a, b\rangle$ in $bind_{call}(\mathcal{PA})$, `make_true(`*entry*`,` $\langle a, b\rangle$`,`$\langle a, b\rangle$`)`.

Effects on corresponding return node (return): For simplicity assume that we are dealing with a programming language that has no local variables, and thus no formal parameters. We are interested in the relationship between *may-hold* at a return node and *may-hold* at its predecessors. Clearly, *may-hold* ($[(return, \mathcal{AA}), \langle a,b\rangle]$) is *true* if $\langle a, b\rangle$ holds at the corresponding *exit* node, conditional on $\mathcal{AA}'$ holding at its *entry* **and** $\mathcal{AA}'$, conditional on $\mathcal{AA}$, holds at the corresponding *call* node.

This situation can be generalized resulting in the equation in Figure 3. We have to introduce the functions *back-bind* and *back-bind'* which have the following definitions:[5]

back-bind$_{call}(\langle a, b\rangle)$ specifies the alias on any path to *call* that guarantees a is aliased to b after control flows to corresponding entry node.

back-bind$'_{call}(\langle a, non\_visible\rangle, o)$ specifies the alias on any path to *call* that guarantees a is aliased to the non-visible object name o after control flows to corresponding entry node.

These definitions imply:

back-bind$_{call}(\langle a, b\rangle) = \langle c, d\rangle$ iff $\langle a, b\rangle \in bind_{call}(\langle c, d\rangle)$

back-bind$'_{call}(\langle a, non\_visible\rangle, o) = \langle c, d\rangle$ iff $\langle a, non\_visible\rangle \in bind_{call}(\langle c, d\rangle)$ and *non_visible* represents o.

We can now proceed to describe the effects of *may-hold* ($[(call, \mathcal{AA}), \mathcal{PA}]$) at the corresponding return. To do a case analysis, let $\mathcal{PA} = \langle a, b\rangle$:

1. If a and b are both not visible in the called procedure then the procedure invocation does not affect this alias. The desired action is obviously `make_true(`*return*`,`$\mathcal{AA}$`,`$\langle a, b\rangle$`)`.

2. a and b are both visible in the called procedure. We know *may-hold*($[(call, \mathcal{AA}), \mathcal{PA}]$) ($\mathcal{PA} \equiv$ *back-bind*$_{call}(\mathcal{AA}')$) and we consider its relationship to *Rule 2*. From *call* we can get *exit* and *return* of *Rule 2*. From $\mathcal{PA}$ we can get $\mathcal{AA}'$.[6] This leaves *Rule 2* with one free variable $\langle x, y\rangle$, so the obvious action for *may-hold*($[(call, \mathcal{AA}), \langle a,b\rangle]$) would be[7]:

```
For each (AA',_) in bind_call(<a,b>)
  for every possible <x,y>:
    if may-hold([(exit,AA'),<x,y>]) is true
      make_true(return,AA,<x,y>)
```

However, this is not acceptable because it requires work to be done for every possible $\langle x, y\rangle$ even though most $\langle x, y\rangle$ are not necessary. Since in *Rule 2* we are performing a conjunction in which we know one half is true, instead of doing work for all $\langle x, y\rangle$, we would prefer to only do work for $\langle x, y\rangle$ such that *may-hold*($[(exit, \mathcal{AA}'), \langle x,y\rangle]$) is *true*. This can be done at the cost of maintaining an additional data structure[Lan92].

[4] "$p = \&x$" is handled similarly. Simply consider $q \equiv \&x$ and treat $*\&x \equiv x$.

[5] These functions recover the $\mathcal{PA}$ aliases from call-sites.

[6] $bind_{call}(back\text{-}bind_{call}(\mathcal{AA}')) = \mathcal{AA}'$.

[7] Strictly speaking this means if *may-hold*($[(exit, \emptyset), \langle x,y\rangle]$) was *true*, we make *may-hold*($[(return, \mathcal{AA}), \langle x,y\rangle]$) *true* for all possible $\mathcal{AA}$. However, in practice it is sufficient to only make *may-hold*($[(return, \emptyset), \langle x,y\rangle]$) *true*.

Rule 1 If x and y are both not visible in the called procedure:

$$may\text{-}hold([(return, \mathcal{AA}), \langle x,y\rangle]) = may\text{-}hold([(call, \mathcal{AA}), \langle x,y\rangle])$$

Rule 2 If x and y are both visible in the called procedure:

$$may\text{-}hold([(return, \mathcal{AA}), \langle x,y\rangle]) = may\text{-}hold([(exit, \emptyset), \langle x,y\rangle]) \vee \bigvee_{\mathcal{AA}' \in \mathcal{ASSUMED}^\dagger} \begin{pmatrix} may\text{-}hold([(exit, \mathcal{AA}'), \langle x,y\rangle]) \wedge \\ may\text{-}hold([(call, \mathcal{AA}), back\text{-}bind_{call}(\mathcal{AA}')]) \end{pmatrix}$$

Rule 3 If x is visible but y is not (the symmetric case is similar):

$$may\text{-}hold([(return, \mathcal{AA}), \langle x,y\rangle]) = \bigvee_{\langle o, non\_visible\rangle \in \mathcal{ASSUMED}^\dagger} \begin{pmatrix} may\text{-}hold([(exit, \langle o, non\_visible\rangle), \langle x, non\_visible\rangle]) \wedge \\ may\text{-}hold([(call, \mathcal{AA}), back\text{-}bind'_{call}(\langle o, non\_visible\rangle, y)]) \end{pmatrix}$$

† $\mathcal{ASSUMED}$ is the set of all possible assumed aliases.

Figure 3: *may-hold* relation at return nodes

3. Assume a is not visible in the called procedure but b is.

   This corresponds to *Rule 3* in Figure 3 and is analogous to the case where a and b are both visible in the called procedure, except now we need to fill in the *non_visible* at *exit* with a. Thus we would get the following action for $may\text{-}hold([(call, \mathcal{AA}), \langle a,b\rangle])$:

```
For each (AA', nv) in bind_call(<a, b>),
for every possible <x, y>:
(assume x contains non_visible^8):
    if may-hold([(exit, AA'), <x, y>]) is true
    { let x' = nv
      apply_trans(non_visible, x, x')
      make_true(return, AA, <x', y>) }
```

More Complex Effects on Return Nodes in Case 3: While the action described above is sufficient if only single level pointers are allowed, it is not sufficient in the general case. In general, it is possible to have an alias between two non_visible's. For example, the second call of P in Figure 1 creates the alias $\langle **l_1, *l_2\rangle$ at n_{10} even though neither l_1 nor l_2 are visible in P. Thus we must handle the case of creation in the called procedure of an alias between two non-visible object names. We will do this with a special case of *may-hold* with two assumed aliases:

$$may\text{-}hold([(exit, \begin{matrix}\langle o_1, non\_visible\rangle \\ \langle o_2, non\_visible\rangle\end{matrix}), \langle nv_1, nv_2\rangle])$$

[8] For example, $x = *non\_visible$.

This represents the fact that if o_1 is aliased to non-visible object name l_1 and o_2 is aliased to non-visible object name l_2 on a path to the entry of the procedure then, on some path to *exit*, nv_1 (where the non_visible portion represents l_1) is aliased to nv_2 (where the non_visible portion represents l_2). Thus,

$$may\text{-}hold([(n_{11}, \begin{matrix}\langle g_1, *non\_visible\rangle \\ \langle g_2, *non\_visible\rangle\end{matrix}), \langle *non\_visible, non\_visible\rangle])$$

represents the alias $\langle **l_1, *l_2\rangle$ at n_{11} because

- g_1 is aliased to $*non\_visible$ ($non\_visible \equiv l_1$) at n_9 when called from n_6 and
- g_2 is also aliased to $*non\_visible$ ($non\_visible \equiv l_2$) at n_9 when called from n_6.

The action for Case 3 given above must be modified to handle the special case where *may-holds* $([(call, \mathcal{AA}), \mathcal{PA}])$ implies one of the two assumed aliases needed for an alias with two non_visibles. Details can be found in [Lan92].

4.4 Alias_at_exit_implies($exit$,$\mathcal{AA}$,$\mathcal{PA}$)

An exit node can have any number of successors, however they are all return nodes. This function encodes the rules for return nodes in Figure 3 with the additional case of aliases between two non-visible object names. The encoding is analogous to that for `Alias_at_call_implies` and we omit a formal description of this routine.

4.5 Any_other_alias_implies(*node*,$\mathcal{AA}$,$\mathcal{PA}$)

The implications of *may-hold*([(*node*, $\mathcal{AA}$), $\mathcal{PA}$]) depend on its successors and must be considered separately for each successor. Since we have examined the cases where *node* is a call or exit node, the successors must be either a call, an exit, or a statement in the program.

Successor (succ) is a call node, exit node, or a program statement which is not an assignment to a pointer: These nodes simply collect *may-hold* information from their parents. When *succ* is of one of these types, the action for *may-hold*([(*node*, $\mathcal{AA}$), $\mathcal{PA}$]) is simply `make_true(`*succ*,$\mathcal{AA}$,$\mathcal{PA}$`)`.

Successor (succ) is an assignment to a pointer: This case encompasses the major intraprocedural affects of pointers on aliasing. The effects of *may-hold* ([(*node*, $\mathcal{AA}$), $\mathcal{PA}$]) depend on the relationship of the object names in $\mathcal{PA}$ and the object names involved in the pointer assignment. In the following discussion we will consider *succ* to the be statement "$p = q$", where p and q are arbitrary object names of pointer type. What follows is a case analysis; the algorithm applies all suitable cases. The cases are: 1. Does the assignment preserve the alias? 2. What are the effects of an alias of $*q$? 3. What are the effects of an alias of p?

1. $\mathcal{PA} = \langle y, z\rangle$ where p is a prefix of neither y nor z. (preserves the alias)
   In all cases, y and z point to the same object after the assignment as before since only p changes its value and the assignment has no effects on $\langle y, z\rangle$. The action in this case is simply `make_true(`*succ*`,` $\mathcal{AA}$`,`$\mathcal{PA}$`)`. This is clearly safe, but it can also be approximate.

2. $\mathcal{PA} = \langle y, z\rangle$ where **is_prefix_with_deref(**q,y**)**[9] (effects of an alias of $*q$).
   There are 3 different cases that need to be handled (the first two are mutually exclusive, but either can occur in conjunction with the third). They are: (i) *not* **is_prefix(**p,z**)**, (ii) **is_prefix(**p,z**)**, and (iii) the interaction of $\langle *q, z\rangle$ with other known aliases.

In general, the effects of the assignment on this alias depend on whether or not **is_prefix(**p,z**)** is true. The two types of effects are characterized by the following examples:

Case 2.i: $y \equiv *q$

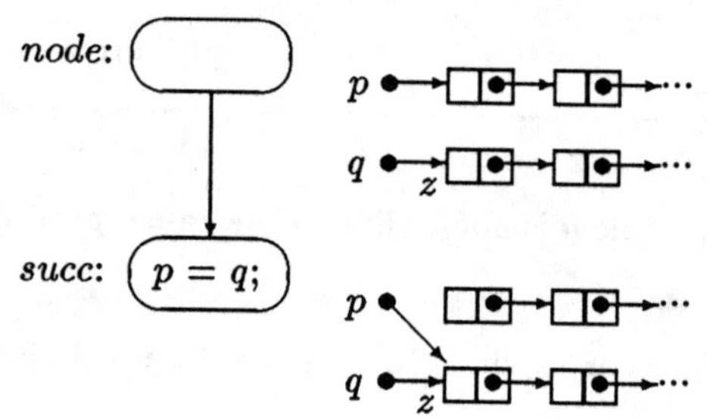

In case 2.i, *may-hold*([(*node*, $\mathcal{AA}$), $\langle *q, z\rangle$]) implies *may-hold*([(*succ*, $\mathcal{AA}$), $\langle *q, z\rangle$]) and *may-hold*([(*succ*, $\mathcal{AA}$), $\langle *p, z\rangle$]).

Case 2.ii: $y \equiv *q$, $z \equiv *(p\text{->}next)$

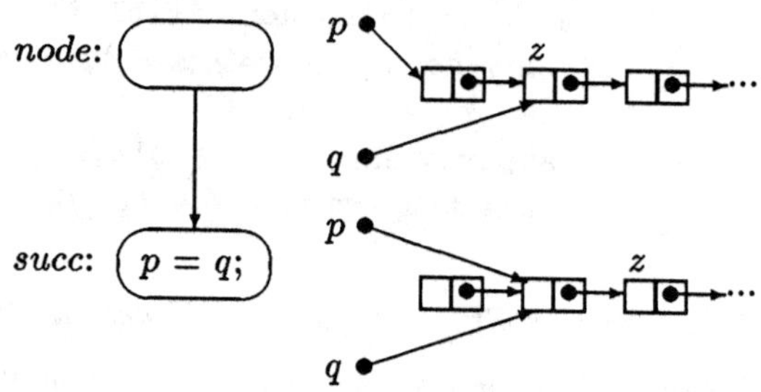

In case 2.ii, *may-hold*([(*node*, $\mathcal{AA}$), $\langle *q, *(p\text{->}next)\rangle$]) gives no information about the aliasing that occurs at *succ*[10]. Thus the action when *may-hold*([(*node*, $\mathcal{AA}$), $\langle y, z\rangle$]) is *true* for *succ* = "$p = q$" where is_prefix_with_deref(q,y) would appear to be:

```
if !is_prefix(p,z)
{ apply_trans(q,y,p')
  make_true(succ,AA,⟨p',z⟩) }
```

[9] **is_prefix_with_deref(**q,y**)** is the same as **is_prefix(**q,y**)** except that y must have at least one more deference than q.

[10] The only alias that holds at *succ* in case 2.ii, is $\langle *p, *q\rangle$ which holds regardless of the alias situation at *node*.

This can miss some aliases when p is not a prefix of z. Consider the following case 2.iii:

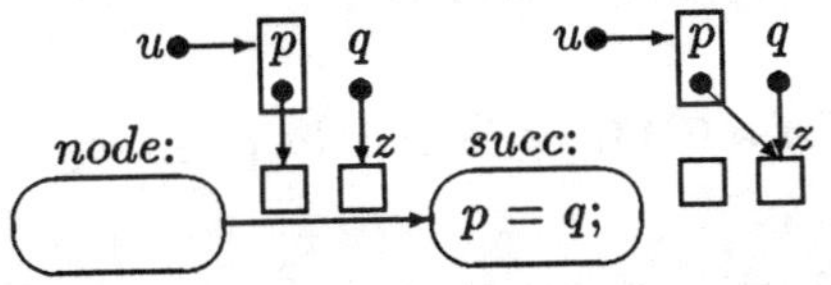

The problem is that the existence of the alias $\langle **u, z\rangle$ at *succ* does not necessarily follow from a single alias at *node*. Instead, $\langle **u, z\rangle$ can hold on $[entry_{main}]...[node]$ $[succ]$ if both $\langle *u, p\rangle$ and $\langle z, *q\rangle$ hold on the path $[entry_{main}]...[node]$. Unfortunately, we do not keep any information about pairs of aliases holding on the same path. Whenever we have $may\text{-}hold([(node, \mathcal{AA}), \langle *u, p\rangle])$ and $may\text{-}hold([(node, \mathcal{AA}'), \langle z, *q\rangle])$ we have to assume $may\text{-}hold([(\text{"}p = q\text{"}, \mathcal{AA}), \langle **u, z\rangle])$ in order for our solution to be safe. We must extend the above action to account for this situation. One notable feature of this extension which deserves mention is how to handle the case when $\mathcal{AA} \neq \mathcal{AA}'$ when both occur on the same path. We do not allow multiple assumptions, so we must safely approximate this situation. Clearly both assumptions are individually necessary and either can be safely chosen. In general, if one assumption contains *non_visible*, then use that one (so that we remember how to instantiate *non_visible*); otherwise use either.

3. $\mathcal{PA} = \langle p, v\rangle$ (effects of an alias of p)

   Again there are three cases to consider; (i) simple effects of $\langle p, v\rangle$, (ii) secondary effects of $\langle p, v\rangle$, and (iii) interaction of $\langle p, v\rangle$ with other known aliases.

   The effects of "$p = q$" on $\langle p, *u\rangle$ (i.e., $v \equiv *u$) are characterized by:

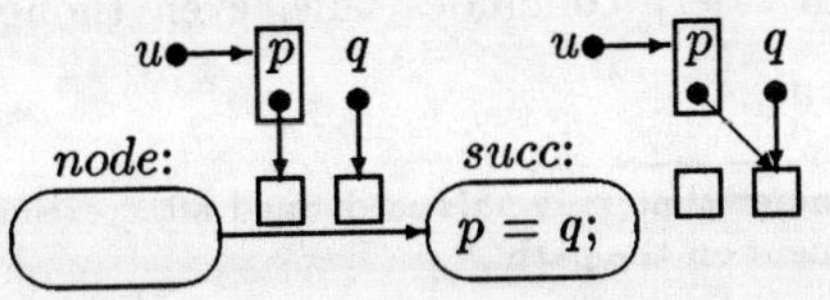

Case 3.i: $may\text{-}hold([(node, \mathcal{AA}), \langle p, *u\rangle])$ implies $may\text{-}hold([(succ, \mathcal{AA}), \langle p, *u\rangle])$ and, unless u or p is a prefix of q[11], $may\text{-}hold([(succ, \mathcal{AA}), \langle *q, **u\rangle])$.

Case 3.ii: An alias $\langle *p, o\rangle$ at *node* is, in general, implicitly killed. However, in the case where $\langle p, *u\rangle$ holds on some path to *node*, $\langle *p, **u\rangle$ will not be killed by the assignment "$p = q$" and we have to account for this.

Case 3.iii: The only other effect of $may\text{-}hold([(node, \mathcal{AA}), \langle p, *u\rangle])$ comes from handling the other half of case 2.iii and is handled in the same way.

5 Empirical Results

This section starts with a theoretical examination of the worst case precision of our algorithm. We next discuss our implementation of the algorithm and empirically compare our solution to Weihl's solution. We then report empirical data on algorithm precision.

Precision Throughout this paper we have used k-limiting to deal with infinite sets of object names, and we now apply that notion to precision.

$$limit_k(solution) = \left\{ (node, \langle a', b'\rangle) \;\middle|\; \begin{array}{l} (node, \langle a, b\rangle) \in solution, a' \text{ is} \\ \text{the k-limited representation} \\ \text{for } a, \text{ and } b' \text{ is the k-limited} \\ \text{representation for } b \end{array} \right\}$$

We use the following definition for the precision of a safe algorithm A when analyzing program P:

$$precision_k(A, P) = \frac{|limit_k(\{A\text{'s solution for } P\})|}{|limit_k(\{\text{precise solution for } P\})|}$$

Consider the program *all-or-none* in Figure 4 for any given n. This program has the unfortunate property that if no aliases hold before it is executed then the precise solution under the common assumptions of static

[11] when u or p is a prefix of q, we do not want to create $\langle *u, *q\rangle$ for the same reason we do not want to create $\langle *p, *(p\text{->}next)\rangle$ for "$p = p\text{->}next$".

```
while (-)
{ #for all k, 1 ≤ k ≤ n:
    if (-)
    {  vk = b;
       b = NULL;
    }
  #end for all
  if (-)
  { b = d;
    d = NULL;
  }
}
```

Figure 4: Program *all-or-none(n)*; n is a parameter determining the size of the program

analysis has $n+1$ program point aliases. However, if *just* the alias $\langle *\mathtt{b}, *\mathtt{d}\rangle$ holds before program *all-or-none* then, for all i and j $(1 \leq i, j \leq n)$, $*\mathtt{v}_i$ is aliased to $*\mathtt{v}_j$ on some path to all program points ($\mathcal{O}(n^3)$ of them). Any approximate algorithm can erroneously produce the alias $\langle *\mathtt{b}, *\mathtt{d}\rangle$. Thus when *all-or-none(n)* follows the creation of the erroneous $\langle *\mathtt{b}, *\mathtt{d}\rangle$ alias, the algorithm will report $\mathcal{O}(n^3)$ aliases[12] even though there are only $\Omega(n)$ aliases. For our algorithm, using the the precision measurement $precision_k$ this is the worst case.

Prototype Our prototype implementation, written in C, finds aliases for a reduced version of C that excludes: union types, nested structures, casting, pointers to functions, and exception handling. The first three of these omissions are not theoretically difficult to handle, but complicate the implementation. The other two require more theoretical examination. We do allow arrays and pointer arithmetic; however, we deal with these on a very simple and naive level and treat them as aggregates. For building ICFGs, we were fortunate to have access to *ptt*, a program developed by Siemens Research Corporation.

Empirical Comparison to Weihl's Algorithm Unfortunately, we can not directly compare our alias solution to Weihl's solution because we find program-point specific aliases and Weihl does not. Therefore let us define *program-aliases* as:

$$\{\langle a, b\rangle \mid (\exists n)\text{a ICFG node and } \langle a, b\rangle \in \mathit{may\text{-}alias}(n)\}$$

In Table 1 we compare our solution versus Weihl's solution. As expected Weihl's algorithm reports more program aliases than our algorithm. The timing for Weihl's algorithm is approximate because in our implementation of his algorithm, we were only able to time the second stage of his calculation (the transitive closure part) and not the total time taken. On average Weihl reported 30.7 times as many aliases and the timings are more or less comparable. The numbers reported here are based on an improved implementation of our algorithm. *make* was included in the original data set, but the new implementation does not yet handle it.

Measurement of Empirical Precision There are four distinct approximations in our alias algorithm (this is proved in [Lan92]). Our first source of approximation, k-limiting, is discussed in Section 2. A second source of approximation is illustrated by the following scenario. Suppose there is an assignment $p = x$ at program point t, alias pair $\langle p, *q\rangle$ holds on some path[13] to an immediate predecessor of t and $\langle *x, *y\rangle$ also holds on some path to an immediate predecessor of t. Does $\langle **q, *y\rangle$ hold on some path to t?

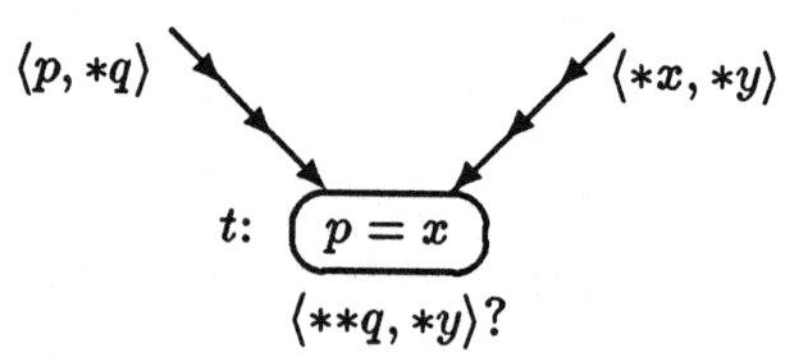

If both $\langle p, *q\rangle$ and $\langle *x, *y\rangle$ occur on the **same** path, then $\langle **q, *y\rangle$ holds on that path extended by t; our algorithm safely concludes this, even though it may not be true.

[12] the $\mathcal{O}(n^3)$ from *all-or-none(n)* plus some constant number form the program that erroneously generates $\langle *\mathtt{b}, *\mathtt{d}\rangle$

[13] Remember that *may-hold* is defined after execution of the last statement on the path.

Program	Lines	Weihl		*program-aliases*		Weihl / *program-aliases*	*program-aliases* / Weihl
		Number	Time	Number	Time	Number	Time
ul	523	4,851	3s	349	26s	13.8	8.7
pokerd	1,354	62,225	84s	352	4s	176.7	0.1
compress	1,488	6,316	4s	341	2s	18.5	0.5
loader	1,522	39,059	36s	496	7s	78.7	0.2
learn	1,642	61,845	46s	883	27s	70.0	0.6
ed	1,772	1,796	6s	1,455	42s	1.2	1.4
diff	1,793	44,366	58s	1,444	43s	30.4	0.7
tbl	2,545	4,401	10s	1,065	85s	4.1	8.5
lex	3,315	9,490	18s	1,240	50s	7.6	2.7

$program\text{-}aliases = \{\langle a, b\rangle \mid (\exists n) n \text{ is a node of the ICFG and } \langle a, b\rangle \in may\text{-}alias(n)\}$

Table 1: Comparison to Weihl

The third source of approximation is similar to the second. Consider the assignment $p = x$ at program point t. Suppose $\langle p, *q\rangle$ holds on some path to an immediate predecessor of t and $\langle **q, *z\rangle$ holds on some path to an immediate predecessor of t. Does $\langle **q, *z\rangle$ hold on some path to t?

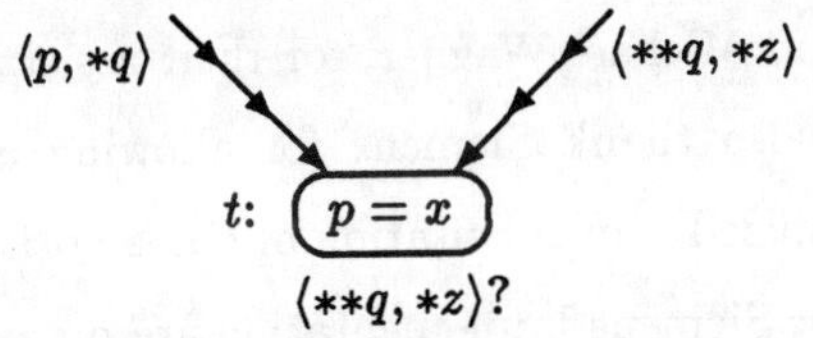

If on at least one path to an immediate predecessor of t $\langle **q, *z\rangle$ holds, and neither $\langle p, *q\rangle$ nor $\langle p, z\rangle$ does, then $\langle **q, *z\rangle$ holds on that path extended by t. However, if on all those paths $\langle **q, *z\rangle$ and $\langle p, *q\rangle$ both hold, then $\langle **q, *z\rangle$ does not necessarily hold on any path to t. Here, our algorithm safely assumes that $\langle **q, *z\rangle$ holds on some path to t.

The fourth approximation results from two distinct aliases of the LHS of an assignment.

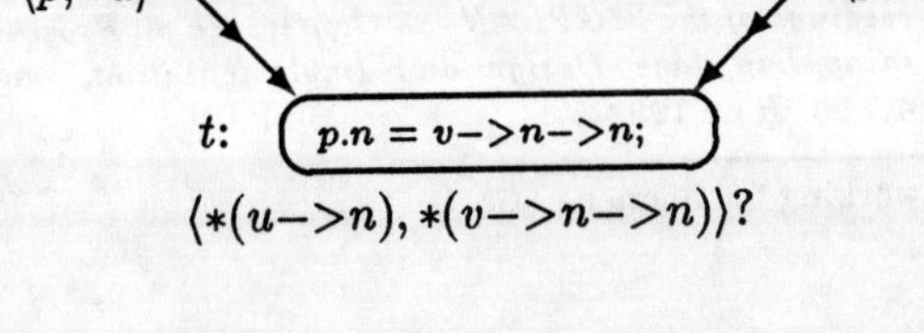

Normally, $\langle *(u{-}{>}n), *(v{-}{>}n{-}{>}n)\rangle$ should hold on a path to t because assigning $v{-}{>}n{-}{>}n$ to $p.n$ is also an assignment to $u{-}{>}n$ on paths on which $\langle p, *u\rangle$ holds. This, however, is not necessarily the case. If, for example, on the same path $\langle p, *v\rangle$ holds then $\langle *(u{-}{>}n), *(v{-}{>}n{-}{>}n)\rangle$ does not necessarily hold:

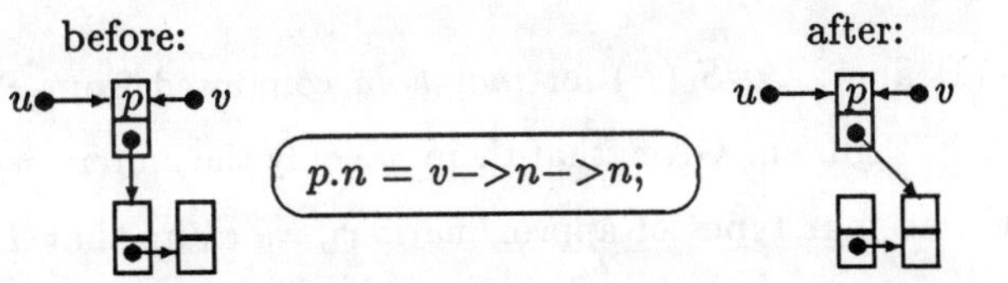

We've modified our algorithm to count the last three approximations. An alias is counted as possibly imprecise if it is the result of any of the last three types of the approximations or depends on the existence of another alias that is counted as possibly imprecise. In [Lan92], we prove that the four cases given above are the only ***base*** sources of imprecision in a variant our algorithm.[14]

There is one other source of approximation that is not a base source of approximation. Consider the fol-

[14] The algorithm presented here has the implicit assumption that the RHS of an assignment is not NULL on some path to the assignment, which can lead to imprecision. We consider this assumption reasonable, and have not counted this imprecision.

lowing (where s is some immediate predecessor of t):

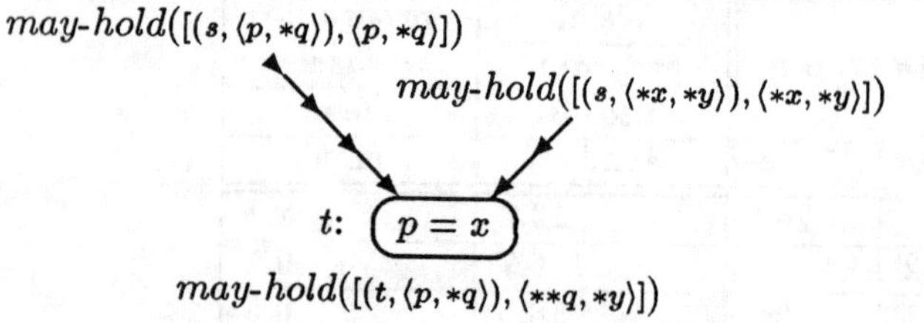

This is the second source of approximation mentioned above. Note that since *may-hold* at t depends on two assumptions we arbitrary chose one. Assume that the *may-hold* at t reaches the exit of the procedure so that we get *may-hold*$([(exit, \langle p, *q\rangle), \langle **q, *y\rangle])$. It is possible possible that the alias $\langle **q, *y\rangle$ does indeed hold on some path to t (and some path to *exit*) and hence is not imprecise. However, we will propagate $\langle **q, *y\rangle$ to a *return* if only the alias $\langle p, *q\rangle$ holds at the corresponding *call*. This can be inaccurate even though the original *may-hold* at t is accurate. Notice, however, that any such inaccuracies will be counted, because the *may-hold* at t will be counted as possibly inaccurate and since the *may-hold* at exit depends (indirectly) on *may-hold* at t, it too will be counted as possibly inaccurate.

Define $\%YES_k(P)$ for *may-hold* computed from P as in Figure 5. Given that there are only the aforementioned four types of approximations, we claim that $L \subseteq limit_k$(precise solution). Thus $\%YES_k(P) \leq 100 * (1/precision_k(landi, P))$ and can be used to bound precision.[15]

Table 2 presents empirical precision results for 18 C programs with the k-limit constant equal to three[16]. This suite contains all the programs that we compared to Weihl's algorithm in Section 5. These programs came from a pool of available C programs that was collected for an ongoing empirical study of the structure of C programs [RP88]. The sample is by no means large enough to draw general conclusions about algorithm behavior, but it is large enough to indicate that our algorithm performs well over a limited domain of C programs.

[15] *landi* refers to our approximate algorithm.

[16] In [Lan92] we've also examined these programs for k= 1 to 4.

6 Conclusions

Our development of an approximate algorithm for solving for Interprocedural May Alias has been promising. It justified the use of Conditional May Alias as a method for the interprocedural aspects of the alias problem. While it is not precise in the presence of arbitrary pointers, it is safe, erring conservatively. We showed that for at least one definition of precision, in the worst case no algorithm can be more precise than our algorithm. Our empirical investigations yielded encouraging precision results and showed great improvement over the extant technique [Wei80]. Our idea of using a conditional version of aliasing to solve for aliases has been extended to the Interprocedural Reaching Definitions Problem in C [PRL91].

Acknowledgments We thank our colleagues at Siemens Corporate Research, Hemant Pande, Michael Platoff, and Michael Wagner, for their assistance with *ptt*. We also thank Siemens for allowing us to use their optimized implementation of our algorithm. The timings for Siemens implementation are on average 13 times faster than our initial ones. Rita Altucher, Bruce Ladendrof, and William Landi[17] are primarily responsible for the improvements.

References

[Ban79] J. Banning. An efficient way to find the side effects of procedure calls and the aliases of variables. In *Conference Record of the Sixth Annual ACM Symposium on Principles of Programming Languages*, pages 29–41, January 1979.

[Bar78] J. M. Barth. A practical interprocedural data flow analysis algorithm. *Communications of the ACM*, 21(9):724–736, 1978.

[Cal88] D. Callahan. The program summary graph and flow-sensitive interprocedural data flow analysis. In *Proceedings of the SIGPLAN '88 Conference on Programming Language Design and Implementation*, pages 47–56, June 1988.

[17] while working for Siemens

$$\%YES_k(P) = 100 * \left(\frac{\left| L = \left\{ (node, \mathcal{PA}) \;\middle|\; \begin{array}{l} (\exists \mathcal{AA})\textit{may-hold}([(node, \mathcal{AA}), \mathcal{PA}]) = \text{YES} \\ \text{and not directly or indirectly the result} \\ \text{of a type 2, 3 or 4 approximation} \end{array} \right\} \right|}{|\{ (node, \mathcal{PA}) \mid (\exists \mathcal{AA})\textit{may-hold}([(node, \mathcal{AA}), \mathcal{PA}]) = \text{YES} \}|} \right)$$

Figure 5: Definition of $\%YES_k(P)$

Program	ICFG Nodes	May Aliases	$\%YES_k$ (*Program*)	Time
allroots	407	257	100†	1s
fixoutput	615	1,937	100†	1s
diffh	647	8,046	100†	1s
poker	896	3330	100†	2s
ul	1,625	101,273	100†	26s
lex315	1,204	5,163	100†	2s
loader	1,596	119,259	78†	24s
compress	1,914	8,656	67†	2s
tp	1,710	96,098	100†	9s

Program	ICFG Nodes	May Aliases	$\%YES_k$ (*Program*)	Time
pokerd	1,936	54,819	45	7s
learn	2,781	179,844	98†	27s
ed	3,299	127,502	100†	41s
assembler	3,631	1,260,582	10†	396s
diff	3,926	89,056	88†	40s
simulator	5,305	241,621	98†	31s
football	5,910	232,913	100†	23s
tbl	5,960	400,464	100†	80s
lex	6,792	420,268	96†	44s

† $\%YES_k(Program) \leq 100 * (1/precision_k(landi, Program))$

Table 2: Precision of our May Alias Solution ($k = 3$)

[CK89] K. Cooper and K. Kennedy. Fast interprocedural alias analysis. In *Conference Record of the Sixteenth Annual ACM Symposium on Principles of Programming Languages*, pages 49–59, January 1989.

[Coo85] K. Cooper. Analyzing aliases of reference formal parameters. In *Conference Record of the Twelfth Annual ACM Symposium on Principles of Programming Languages*, pages 281–290, January 1985.

[Coo89] B. G. Cooper. Ambitious data flow analysis of procedural programs. Master's thesis, University of Minnesota, May 1989.

[Cou86] D. S. Coutant. Retargetable high-level alias analysis. In *Conference Record of the Thirteenth Annual ACM Symposium on Principles of Programming Languages*, pages 110–118, January 1986.

[CR82] A. Chow and A. Rudmik. The design of a data flow analyzer. In *Proceedings of the ACM SIGPLAN Symposium on Compiler Construction*, pages 106–113, June 1982.

[CWZ90] D. R. Chase, M. Wegman, and F. K. Zadeck. Analysis of pointers and structures. In *Proceedings of the SIGPLAN '90 Conference on Programming Language Design and Implementation*, pages 296–310, June 1990. SIGPLAN Notices, Vol 25, No 6.

[Deu90] A. Deutsch. On determining lifetime and aliasing of dynamically allocated data in higher-order functional specifications. In *Conference Record of the Seventeenth Annual ACM Symposium on Principles of Programming Languages*, pages 157–168, January 1990.

[Deu92] Alain Deutsch. A storeless mode of aliasing and its abstractions using finite representation of right-regular equivalence relations. In *Proceedings of the IEEE 1992 Conference on Computer Languages*, April 1992.

[Gua88] C. A. Guarna. A technique for analyzing pointer and structure references in parallel restructuring compilers. In *Proceedings of the International Conference on Parallel Processing*, pages 212–220, 1988.

[HA90] W.L. Harrison III and Z. Ammarguellat. Parcel and miprac: Parallelizers for symbolic and numeric programs. In *International Workshop on Compilers for Parallel Computers*, December 1990.

[HN89] L. J. Hendren and A. Nicolau. Parallelizing programs with recursive data structures. In *Proceedings of the 1989 International Conference on Parallel Processing*, pages 49–56, August 1989.

[HPR89] S. Horwitz, P. Pfeiffer, and T. Reps. Dependence analysis for pointer variables. In *Proceedings of the ACM SIGPLAN Symposium on Compiler Construction*, pages 28–40, June 1989.

[JM79] N. Jones and S. Muchnick. Flow analysis and optimization of lisp-like structures. In S. Muchnick and N. Jones, editors, *Program Flow Analysis: Theory and Applications*, pages 102–131. Prentice Hall, 1979.

[JM82] N. D. Jones and S. S. Muchnick. A flexible approach to interprocedural data flow analysis and programs with recursive data structures. In *Conference Record of the Ninth Annual ACM Symposium on Principles of Programming Languages*, pages 66–74, January 1982.

[KS86] H. Korth and A. Silberschatz. *Database System Concepts*. McGraw-Hill, New York, NY, 1986.

[Lan92] W. Landi. *Interprocedural Aliasing in the Presence of Pointers*. PhD thesis, Rutgers University, January 1992. LCSR-TR-174.

[LH88] J. R. Larus and P. N. Hilfinger. Detecting conflicts between structure accesses. In *Proceedings of the*

SIGPLAN '88 Conference on Programming Language Design and Implementation, pages 21–34, July 1988. SIGPLAN NOTICES, Vol. 23, No. 7.

[LR91] W. Landi and B. G. Ryder. Pointer-induced aliasing: A problem classification. In *Conference Record of the Eighteenth Annual ACM Symposium on Principles of Programming Languages*, pages 93–103, January 1991.

[Mye81] E. M. Myers. A precise interprocedural data flow algorithm. In *Conference Record of the Eighth Annual ACM Symposium on Principles of Programming Languages*, pages 219–230, January 1981.

[NPD87] A. Neirynck, P. Panangaden, and A. Demers. Computation of aliases and support sets. In *Conference Record of the Fourteenth Annual ACM Symposium on Principles of Programming Languages*, pages 274–283, January 1987.

[PRL91] H.D. Pande, B. G. Ryder, and W. Landi. Interprocedural def-use associations in c programs. In *Proceedings of the Fifth Testing, Analysis, and Verification Symposium*, October 1991.

[RP88] B. G. Ryder and H. Pande. The interprocedural structure of c programs: An empirical study. Laboratory for Computer Science Research Technical Report LCSR-TR-99, Department of Computer Science, Rutgers University, February 1988.

[Ryd89] B. G. Ryder. Ismm: Incremental software maintenance manager. In *Proceedings of the IEEE Computer Society Conference on Software Maintenance*, pages 142–164, October 1989.

[Wei80] W. E. Weihl. Interprocedural data flow analysis in the presence of pointers, procedure variables and label variables. In *Conference Record of the Seventh Annual ACM Symposium on Principles of Programming Languages*, pages 83–94, January 1980.

Abstractions for Recursive Pointer Data Structures: Improving the Analysis and Transformation of Imperative Programs

Laurie J. Hendren*
School of Computer Science
McGill University

Joseph Hummel†
Alexandru Nicolau‡
Dept. of Information and Computer Science
UC-Irvine

Abstract

Even though impressive progress has been made in the area of optimizing and parallelizing programs with arrays, the application of similar techniques to programs with pointer data structures has remained difficult. In this paper we introduce a new approach that leads to improved analysis and transformation of programs with recursively-defined pointer data structures.

Our approach is based on a mechanism for the Abstract Description of Data Structures (ADDS), which makes explicit the important properties, such as dimensionality, of pointer data structures. Numerous examples demonstrate that ADDS definitions are both natural to specify and flexible enough to describe complex, cyclic pointer data structures.

We discuss how an abstract data structure description can improve program analysis by presenting an analysis approach that combines an alias analysis technique, *path matrix* analysis, with information available from an ADDS declaration. Given this improved alias analysis technique, we provide a concrete example of applying a software pipelining transformation to loops involving pointer data structures.

1 Introduction and Motivation

One of the key problems facing both optimizing and parallelizing compilers for imperative programming languages is *alias analysis*, that is, detecting when two distinct memory accesses may refer to the same physical memory location. Alias analysis is a critical component of such compilers, and the effectiveness of many compiler analysis techniques and code-improving transformations rely upon accurate alias analysis. Given the current trend towards vector, RISC, and superscalar architectures, where optimizing compilers are even more important for efficient execution, the need for more accurate analysis will grow.

Scientific codes have often been the target of optimizing and parallelizing compilers. Such codes typically use arrays for storing data, and loops with regular indexing properties to manipulate these arrays. A good deal of work has been done in the area of analysis and transformation in the presence of arrays and loops, and as a result numerous techniques have been developed; for example, invariant code motion, induction variable elimination, loop unrolling, and vectorization [Lov77, Kuc78, DH79, PW86, AK87, ASU87, ZC90], along with various instruction scheduling strategies such as software pipelining [RG82, AN88a, AN88b, Lam88, EN89]. Unfortunately, codes that utilize dynamically-allocated pointer data structures are much more difficult to analyze, and therefore there has not been as much progress in this area. This is problematic, since numerous data structures in imperative programs—linked-lists and trees for example—are typically built using recursively-defined pointer data structures. Furthermore, such data structures are used not only in symbolic processing, but also in some classes of scientific codes (e.g. computational geometry [Sam90] and the so-called *tree-codes* [App85, BH86]).

The goal of this paper is to: (1) investigate why the analysis of pointer data structures is more difficult than the analysis of array references, (2) suggest a new mechanism for describing pointer data structures, and (3) show how better descriptions of such data structures lead to improved analysis and transformation of imperative programs.

*This work supported in part by FCAR, NSERC, and the McGill Faculty of Graduate Studies and Research.

†Direct correspondence to this author, jhummel@ics.uci.edu.

‡This work supported in part by NSF grant CCR8704367 and ONR grant N0001486K0215.

ACM SIGPLAN '92 PLDI-6/92/CA
© 1992 ACM 0-89791-476-7/92/0006/0249...$1.50

1.1 The Problem

To motivate the problem, consider the two code fragments shown in Figure 1[1]. The upper code fragment adds the element `b[j]` to each element of array `a`. Since arrays have the property that `a[i]` and `a[j]` refer to different locations if $i \neq j$, the compiler can immediately determine from this code fragment that each iteration references a different location of `a`. Further, arrays are usually statically allocated, and it is straightforward to determine that the arrays `a` and `b` are different objects. Thus any reference to `a` will never refer to the same location as `b[j]`, implying that `b[j]` is loop invariant. These observations allow the compiler to perform a number of transformations, including (1) loading `b[j]` into a register before the loop begins, and (2) transforming the loop by perhaps unrolling or applying software pipelining.

```
for i = 1 to N
  a[i] = a[i] + b[j];


while p <> NULL
 { p->data = p->data + q->data;
   p = p->next;
 }
```

Figure 1: Arrays versus linked-lists.

Now consider the lower code fragment in Figure 1, which operates on a linked-list. This code traverses a list `p`, and at each step adds the value `q->data` to the node currently being visited. In this case, the properties of the structure are not obvious from the code fragment. For example, unless we can guarantee that the list is acyclic, we cannot safely determine that each iteration of the loop refers to a different node `p`. This makes the application of loop transformations difficult. Secondly, since the nodes are dynamically allocated, it is much more difficult to determine if `p` and `q` ever refer to the same node. Hence the compiler will be unable to detect if `q->data` is loop invariant. As a result, even though the code fragment performs a similar function to the array-based version, traditional optimizing and parallelizing compilers will be unable to apply similar transformations.

1.2 Previous Work

There are currently three approaches for dealing with the problem of alias analysis in the presence of pointer data structures: (1) assume the most conservative case, that all pointers and nodes are potential aliases, (2) analyze other parts of the program in an attempt to automatically discover the underlying properties of the data structures (and hence the relationship between all pointers and nodes), or (3) require code annotations.

Although approach (1) is far more common (perhaps with (3) as a backup), there has been significant work on approach (2). One class of solutions has been the development of advanced alias analysis techniques (also called structure estimation techniques) that attempt to statically approximate dynamically-allocated data structures with some abstraction. The most commonly used abstraction has been *k-limited* graphs [JM81], and variations on *k-limited graphs* [LH88a, LH88b, HPR89, CWZ90]. The major disadvantage of these techniques is that the approximation introduces cycles in the abstraction, and thus list-like or tree-like data structures cannot be distinguished from data structures that truly contain cycles. The work by Chase et al. [CWZ90] has addressed this problem to some degree; however, their method fails to find accurate structure estimates in the presence of general recursion. This is a serious drawback since programs with recursively-defined data structures often use recursion as well. Another method, *path matrix* analysis, was designed to specifically deal with distinguishing tree-like data structures from DAG-like (shared) and graph-like (cyclic) structures [HN90, Hen90]. This analysis uses the special properties exhibited by tree-like structures to provide a more accurate analysis of list-like and tree-like structures even in the presence of recursion. However, it has the disadvantage that it cannot handle cyclic structures (even if the cyclic nature would not hamper optimizing or parallelizing transformations). Related approaches include those based on more traditional dependence analysis (e.g. [Gua88], which assumes that structures do not have cycles) and abstract interpretation techniques (e.g. Harrison in [Har89] presents a technique designed for list-like structures commonly used in Scheme programs, while more recently he has been developing a uniform mechanism for handling both symbolic data and arrays using the notion of generalized iteration space [Har91]). In general, even though each of these methods work for certain classes of pointer data structures, they undoubtably fail in the presence of general, possibly cyclic structures and recursion.

Code annotations represent a compromise, since the programmer can specify what the compiler cannot determine. However, code annotations are often difficult to use, due to the varied kinds of information that must be conveyed to the compiler. For example, the programmer may need to specify the data dependencies [Lar89], the transformation to apply [CON], or the "distinctness" of data [KKK90]. Also, the compiler typically takes these annotations on blind faith, and so is unable to warn the programmer if a coding change invalidates an annotation; this is true for [Lar89, CON],

[1] Treat a, b, p, and q as local variables, where a and b are arrays of size N and p and q are pointers.

while in [KKK90] it was suggested that the system could perform dynamic checks provided that the *programmer* uniquely "tags" each node. Finally, such annotations must be repeated throughout the program to maximize performance.

2 Our Approach

Based on our past experience of developing alias analysis techniques for tree-like structures, and the failure of other techniques to find accurate information for more general structures, we believe that a lack of appropriate data structure descriptions is the most serious impediment to the further improvement of analysis techniques. After studying a wide range of imperative pointer data structures, we have developed an approach for describing what we feel are the important properties of such structures, important in the sense of enabling numerous optimizing and parallelizing transformations. Current imperative programming languages provide no mechanisms for expressing this kind of information[2].

Our approach, called **ADDS**, provides the programmer with a mechanism for the **A**bstract **D**escription of **D**ata **S**tructures. ADDS is a minor addition to most imperative programming languages, and was designed to:

- be simple for the programmer to use,
- minimize and localize program annotation,
- describe complex pointer data structures, and
- enable powerful transformations.

The properties expressed through such data structure descriptions are used to increase the accuracy and hence effectiveness of existing analysis techniques. This allows the application of powerful optimizing and parallelizing transformations, and may also lead to the development of new pointer-specific transformations.

Asking the programmer to specify some properties of his or her data structures should not be considered a radical change in our way of thinking about programming in imperative programming languages. In the pointer data structures domain, programmers already convey quite a bit of implicit information about their data structures. For example, consider the following two recursive type declarations:

```
type BinTree              type TwoWayLL
{ int       data;         { int        data;
  BinTree *left;            TwoWayLL *next;
  BinTree *right;           TwoWayLL *prev;
};                        };
```

[2] It should be noted that Larus in [Lar89] discussed a similar approach for Lisp; however, his approach required code (not type) annotations, described only acyclic structures, and could not be used in code fragments which might modify the structure.

Even though these type declarations appear identical to the compiler (each declares a record with three fields, one integer and two recursive pointers), the naming conventions imply very different structures to readers of the program. In addition, each structure has some very nice properties which the compiler could exploit. A binary tree naturally subdivides into two disjoint subtrees that can be operated on in parallel. A two-way linked-list has the property that a traversal in the forward direction using only the `next` field never visits the same node twice (likewise for traversals using only the `prev` field); this property of never visiting the same node twice enables the parallelization of node processing along the list. The idea of ADDS is simply to make this implicit information explicit to the compiler. Positive side-effects may be increased human understanding of programs, and the compiler's ability to generate run-time checks to ensure proper use of dynamic data structures.

Note that Fortran 90 has taken a similar stance in its treatment of pointers to variables. Variables accessible through pointers must be explicitly declared as either pointers or targets [MR90]. This simple declaration greatly improves the accuracy of alias analysis in the presence of pointers.

However, also note that the presence of a description mechanism such as ADDS is not enough by itself. Side-effects in imperative programs often rearrange the components of a data structure, causing a temporary but intentional invalidation of the properties we wish to exploit. Application of optimizing or parallelizing transformations (that rely on these properties) during such a time would be incorrect, and intolerable. Hence some form of data structure validation analysis, beyond alias analysis, is necessary not only to ensure correctness, but to enhance debugging as well.

In the remainder of this paper we present our viewpoint that:

1. recursive pointer data structures, regardless of their overall complexity, typically contain substructures that exhibit regular properties that can be exploited for the purpose of program analysis and transformation, and
2. the ability to express these properties explicitly is an important first step towards the long-term goal of accurate and efficient program analysis in the presence of cyclic pointer data structures.

The organization of the paper is as follows. In sections 3 and 4 we address the problem of expressing the regular properties of recursive pointer data structures. In section 3 we present ADDS through a series of intuitive, increasingly complex examples, and in section 4 we define the properties of ADDS data structures more formally. In section 5 we discuss how the information provided by ADDS can be used to improve the analysis and transformation of programs; in particular, we demonstrate how ADDS enables the application of software pipelining to a list-traversal loop. Finally, in section 6 we present our conclusions.

3 ADDS - Abstract Description of Data Structures

The transformation of codes involving data structures requires knowledge about the properties exhibited by that structure, e.g. shape, size, and method of element access. With arrays, these properties are readily identifiable. The shape of an array is fixed and declared at compile-time, its size is known at the time of creation (and often at compile-time), and locations are referenced using integer indices. For example, given a statement S of the form `i = i + c` ($c \neq 0$), the compiler is guaranteed that `a[i]` refers to different elements of `a` before and after the execution of S. Contrast this with user-defined pointer data structures, in which none of these properties are made explicit. Unlike the array example, even a simple traversal statement T such as `p = p->next` will prevent the compiler from determining whether `p` denotes a different "element" after the execution of T, or the same element.

In this section we shall present our mechanism—ADDS—for describing what we feel are the important properties of recursive pointer data structures: shape, and a sense of direction. We begin with an intuitive summary of these properties, and then demonstrate through a series of increasingly complex examples how such properties are captured using ADDS. We postpone a more formal definition of ADDS to section 4.

3.1 Dimensions, Directions in Pointer Data Structures

Suppose you have a recursive pointer data structure and you wish to describe its shape. Consider the structure in its general form, and select a node as the "origin"—it doesn't matter which node you choose, though some choices make more sense than others (e.g. the root of a tree versus a leaf). Next, think of your structure as having "dimensions," different paths emanating from the origin, with typically one dimension per path. Finally, select a node n other than the origin, and for each recursive pointer field f in n, decide which dimension f traverses and in which "direction." The "forward" direction implies traversing f moves one unit away from the origin, and "backward" implies traversing f moves one unit back towards the origin. A field is limited to traversing one dimension in only one direction[3].

[3] This restriction can be overcome by the programmer without too much difficulty.

By default, a structure has one dimension D, where it is assumed that all recursive pointer fields traverse D in an "unknown" direction. The idea is to override this default and provide more specific information. For example, we can specify that a singly linked-list has one dimension `X`, and one recursive pointer field `next` that traverses `X` in the forward direction. As illustrated below, a two-way linked-list is best described as having a single dimension `X`, with `next` traversing forward along `X` and `prev` traversing backward along `X`:

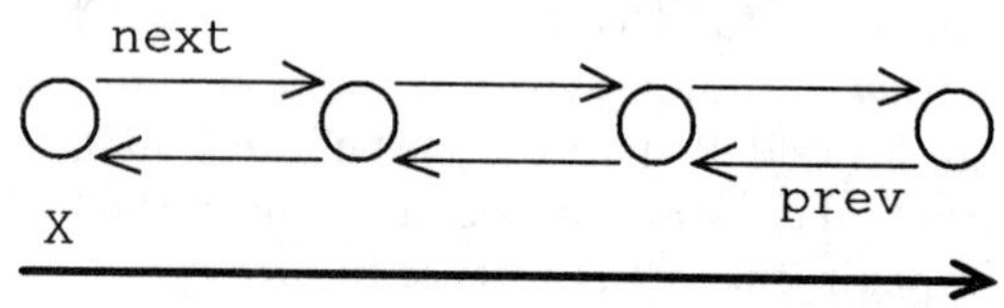

To differentiate such a list from a more general DAG-like list, e.g.

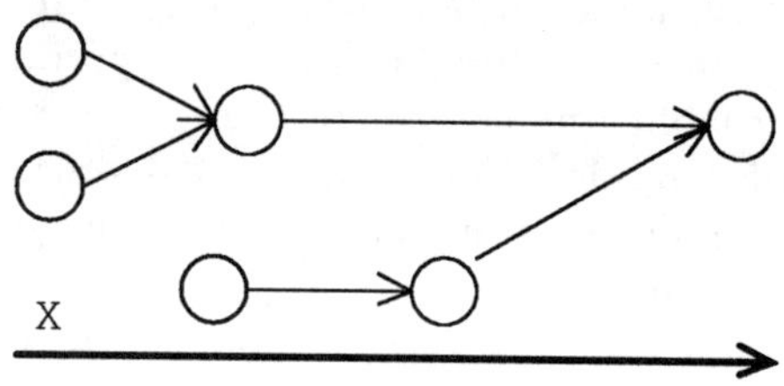

we introduce the notion of a field f traversing "uniquely forward," which implies that for any node n, at most one node n' ($n' \neq n$) points to n using f. Syntactically, the ADDS declaration of a two-way linked-list would then look like:

```
type TwoWayLL [X]
  { int        data;
    TwoWayLL *next is uniquely forward along X;
    TwoWayLL *prev is backward along X;
  };
```

A binary tree can be thought of as having two dimensions `left` and `right`, but for reasons soon to be apparent, we shall consider a binary tree as having only one dimension, `down`. The important property of a binary tree (and of trees in general) is that for any node n, all subtrees of n are disjoint. This information can be expressed by saying that the `left` and `right` fields "combined" traverse `down` in a uniquely forward manner. More formally, `left` and `right` exhibit the property that at most one `left` *or* one `right` points to any node n, but not both. The motivation for choosing one dimension to describe a binary tree is to support the notion of parent pointers, a field that refers from either a left or right child back to its parent. Pictorially, we view a binary tree with parent pointers as:

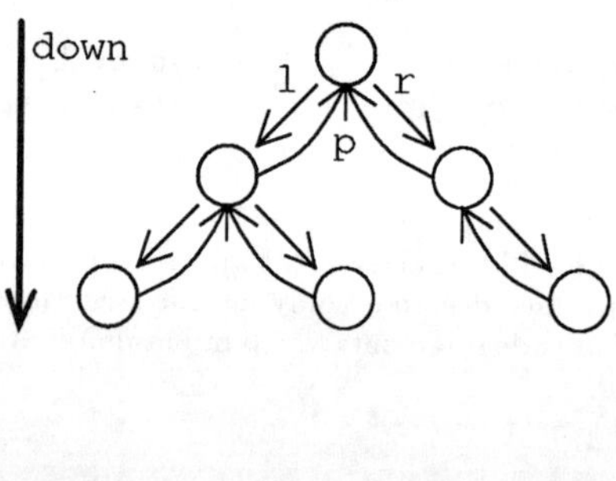

Its ADDS declaration would thus be:

```
type PBinTree [down]
 { int       data;
   PBinTree *left, *right
              is uniquely forward along down;
   PBinTree *parent
              is backward along down;
 };
```

Note that by declaring `left` and `right` together, we are expressing this notion of a combined traversal.

The flexibility of ADDS is illustrated by more exotic recursive pointer data structures. Typically such structures exhibit multiple dimensions, where dimensions are either "independent" (disjoint) or "dependent." For example, an *orthogonal list* [Sta80], used to implement sparse matrices, has two dependent dimensions `X` and `Y` (much like the two-dimensional array it represents):

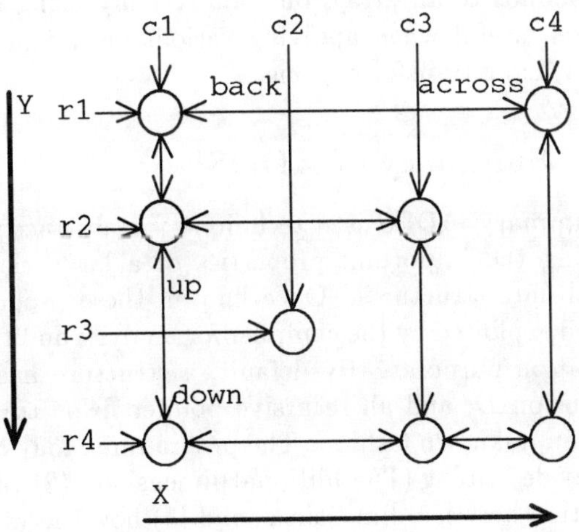

We say `X` and `Y` are dependent since one traversal along `X` and another traversal along `Y` may lead to a common node or substructure. For example, traversing along `X` from `r4` and along `Y` from `c3` may lead to the same node. However, even though the dimensions are dependent, notice that *orthogonal lists* still possess regular properties. For example, traversing forward along `X`, or forward along `Y`, is guaranteed never to visit the same node twice. Further, each row is disjoint, so that parallel traversals of different rows along `X` will never visit the same node (likewise for columns and the Y dimension). These properties are captured in the following ADDS declaration by declaring that the fields `across` and `down` are uniquely forward:

```
type OrthL [X][Y]
 { int     data;
   OrthL *across is uniquely forward along X;
   OrthL *back   is backward along X;
   OrthL *down   is uniquely forward along Y;
   OrthL *up     is backward along Y;
 };
```

Note that unless stated otherwise, dimensions (in this case `X` and `Y`) are considered dependent. Such conservative nature is intentional.

A similar data structure that has two independent dimensions is a list of lists. Consider the following which illustrates a list of lists, including back pointers along each dimension:

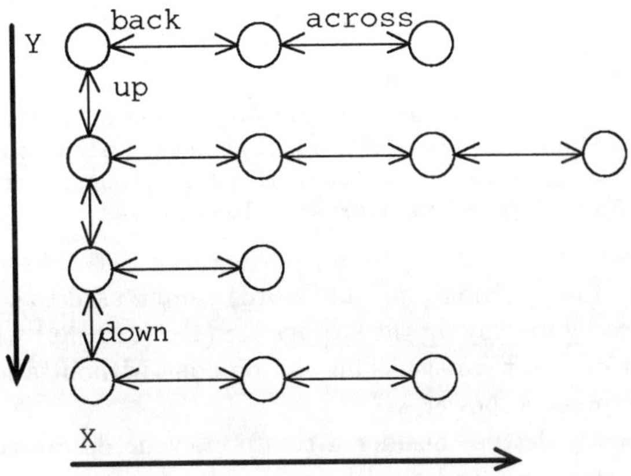

Note that each node may be accessed by a forward traversal along **either** the `X` dimension **or** the `Y` dimension, but not both; this is identical to the situation for binary trees. Hence `X` and `Y` are considered independent, which is conveyed using `||` in the following ADDS declaration:

```
type LoLs [X][Y] where X || Y
 { int    data;
   LoLs *across is uniquely forward along X;
   LoLs *back   is backward along X;
   LoLs *down   is uniquely forward along Y;
   LoLs *up     is backward along Y;
 };
```

An interesting three-dimensional structure that has both dependent and independent dimensions is the *two-dimensional range tree* [Sam90], used to answer queries such as "find all points within the interval x1...x2" or "find all points within the bounding rectangle (x1,y1) and (x2,y2)." As illustrated below, it is a binary tree of binary trees, where the leaves of each tree are linked together to form a two-way linked list:

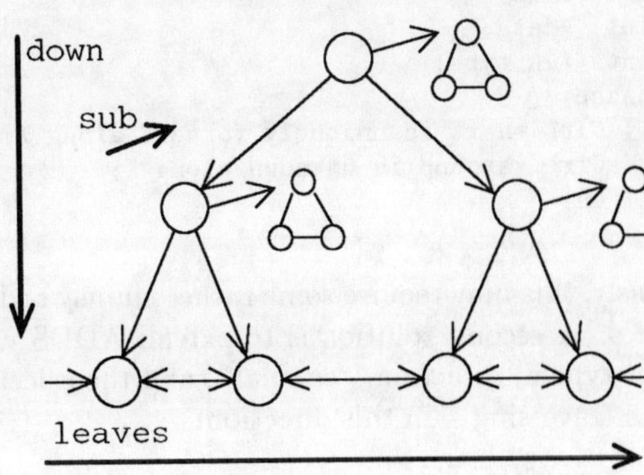

The dimensions `down` and `leaves` are dependent; each leaf node can be reached by a forward traversal along both the **down** dimension and the **leaves** dimension. However, observe that **sub** is independent of both **down** and **leaves**. That is, any node that can be accessed by a forward traversal along **sub**, cannot be accessed by a forward traversal along **down** nor along **leaves**. This leads to the following declaration:

```
type TwoDRT [down][sub][leaves]
                         where sub||down, sub||leaves
 { int     data;
   TwoDRT *left, *right
              is uniquely forward along down;
   TwoDRT *subtree is uniquely forward along sub;
   TwoDRT *next is uniquely forward along leaves;
   TwoDRT *prev is backward along leaves;
 };
```

Note that a union (variant record) can be used to save space by overlaying the storage for (**left**, **right**) with that of (**next**, **prev**). This can be done without a loss of expressive power.

Lastly, let us consider a common cyclic data structure, the circular linked-list:

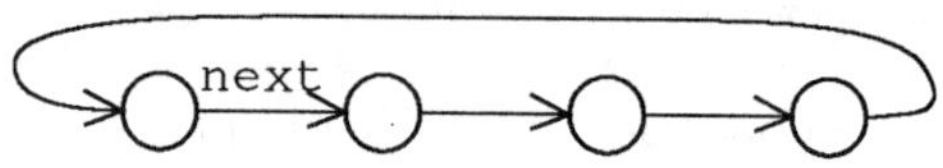

This type of structure can be problematic, since a single field **next** is used for what are essentially two purposes, (1) traversing uniquely forward and (2) circling around. One declaration is thus:

```
type CirL [X]
 { int   data;
   CirL *next is unknown along X;
 };
```

This is equivalent to saying nothing at all (the default), and the unknown nature of **next** prevents the compiler from performing possible optimizing or parallelizing transformations (e.g. given the statement `p = q->next` the compiler must conservatively assume that `p` and `q` are aliases). One solution is to provide a more explicit declaration that more accurately reflects the properties of a circular list:

```
type CirL [X]
 { int   data;
   int   un_type;
   union
    { CirL *next is uniquely forward along X;
      CirL *around is unknown along X;
    } un;
 };
```

Obviously, this may require some rather clumsy coding practices. A second solution is to extend ADDS with another type of direction, "circular", and then declare **next** as traversing **X** in this direction:

```
type CirL [X]
 { int   data;
   CirL *next is circular along X;
 };
```

This solution is more desirable, since the declaration does not require a change in the coding of the program. However, one needs to know the length of the list in order to perform accurate alias analysis, which is generally unavailable at compile-time. This implies information must be collected and maintained at run-time, which is not considered in this paper.

3.2 Speculative Traversability

In all cases, a data structure declared using ADDS is required to be *speculatively traversable* [HG92]. This property allows one to traverse past the "end" of a data structure without causing a run-time error. It can be automatically supported by the compiler, and places no additional burden on the programmer (except good programming practices—e.g. in C, they must use the name **NULL** and not an arbitrary integer). This property is analogous to *computing* an array index outside the bounds of an array, but not actually using it. It is often useful when applying various optimizing and parallelizing transformations.

3.3 Summary of ADDS

In summary, ADDS is a technique for abstractly describing the important properties of a large class of useful data structures. Once known, these properties can be exploited by the compiler for analysis and transformation purposes. By default, a structure has one dimension D, and all recursive pointer fields traverse D in an unknown fashion. The programmer may refine this by describing (1) additional dimensions, (2) the interaction between dimensions, and (3) how the various fields traverse the dimensions. As illustrated with our examples, the choice of dimensions and directions is quite intuitive, and the use of ADDS does not place a heavy burden upon the programmer.

It should be noted that a programming language and its compilers could directly support data structures such as **TwoWayLL** and **PBinTree** via predefined, abstract data types (e.g. see [Gro91] for a tool that generates, from a context-free grammar description, ADTs for graph-like structures, and [Sol90] for an implementation of parallelizable lists). However, a quick survey of the literature (or a data structures text [Sta80]) would reveal a wide variety of important pointer data structures. Implementations for these structures can differ widely as well. Thus, instead of trying to predefine the most common types of pointer data structures (and constrain the implementation), we chose the opposite approach, namely to develop a technique which allows the programmer to define and implement *their own* data structures. We believe ADDS is flexible enough to describe the important properties of nearly all pointer data structures, while providing the compiler with the information necessary to enable powerful optimizing and parallelizing transformations.

4 Formal Properties of ADDS

In this section we present an overview of the formal properties of ADDS data structures. These definitions are not crucial to the understanding of the ideas, but they do show that our ADDS approach has some well-specified properties. For each definition we summarize the importance of the property being defined. If the reader is comfortable with the intuitive definitions presented in section 3, this section can be safely skipped.

Let N be a data structure declaration with n recursive pointer fields, $n \geq 1$. Let k be the number of programmer-specified dimensions over N, $1 \leq k \leq n$. The dimensions of N are denoted by $d_1, \ldots, d_k$, and the recursive pointer fields of N are denoted by $f_1, \ldots, f_n$. A recursive pointer field f may traverse along only one dimension d, and in only one of three directions: forward, backward, or unknown. pN denotes a dynamically-allocated node of type N, and $pN.f$ is either NULL[4] or denotes the dynamically-allocated node of type N reached by traversing the pointer stored in field f of pN. Traversing a series of non-NULL fields is denoted using a regular expression notation, e.g.

- $pN(.f)^2$ denotes the node $pN.f.f$,
- $pN(.f)^+$ denotes any one of the nodes $pN.f$, $pN.f.f$, $\ldots$,
- $pN((.f)+(.g))^*$ denotes any one of the nodes pN, $pN.f$, $pN.g$, $pN.f.f$, $pN.f.g$, $pN.g.f$, $pN.g.g$, $\ldots$.

For any such regular expression R, R denotes a list of nodes which may or may not contain duplicates. If this list is **run-time finite** (i.e. for all fields f in R, there exists a node pN' denoted by R such that $pN'.f$ is NULL), then there are no duplicates. Otherwise R denotes a **run-time infinite** list of nodes, in which case there must be duplicates.

All nodes pN can be thought of as forming a single data structure pDS of type N. pDS is considered **well-behaved** if the abstraction defined for N is valid. In cases where pDS is not well-behaved (e.g. pDS is under modification) the abstraction must be ignored at these points in the program[5]. The definitions presented here assume a well-behaved data structure.

Def 4.1: if N is **speculatively traversable**, then for all fields f and for all nodes pN, if $pN.f =$ NULL then $pN.f.f$ is a valid traversal and also yields NULL.

[Implication: legal to traverse past what would normally be thought of as the "end" of a structure.]

Def 4.2: if f traverses d in the **forward** direction, then for all nodes pN, the list of nodes denoted by $pN(.f)^*$ is run-time finite.
[Implication: f is acyclic, traversing f never visits a node twice.]

Def 4.3: if f traverses d in a **uniquely forward** direction, then Def 4.2 holds for f, and for all distinct nodes pN and pN', either

1. $pN.f = pN'.f =$ NULL, or
2. $pN.f \neq pN'.f$.

[Implication: f is acyclic and list-like, traversing f from different nodes never visits the same node.]

Def 4.4: if f traverses d in an **unknown** direction, then there may exist a node pN such that the list of nodes denoted by $pN(.f)^*$ is run-time infinite.
[Implication: f is potentially cyclic, traversing f is unpredictable and could visit a node twice.]

Def 4.5: if a field b traverses d in the **backward** direction, then there exists a field f that traverses d in the forward direction.

Def 4.6: if f traverses d in a uniquely forward direction and b traverses d in the backward direction, then for all nodes pN, either:

1. $pN.f =$ NULL,
2. $pN.f.b =$ NULL, or
3. $pN.f.b = pN$.

[Implication: traversing f then b forms a cycle, otherwise f or b is NULL.]

Def 4.7: if f and g ($f \neq g$) traverse d in a **combined uniquely forward** direction, then Def 4.3 holds for f, Def 4.3 holds for g, and for all distinct nodes pN and pN',

1. $pN.f \neq pN'.g$ or $pN.f = pN'.g =$ NULL, and
2. $pN.g \neq pN'.f$ or $pN.g = pN'.f =$ NULL.

[Implication: f and g are tree-like, they separate a structure into disjoint substructures.]

Def 4.8: if fields $f_1, f_2, \ldots, f_m$ $(2 < m \leq n)$ traverse d in a combined uniquely forward direction, then for all f_i and f_j, $1 \leq i, j \leq m$ and $i \neq j$, Def 4.7 holds for f_i and f_j.
[Implication: generalization of Def 4.7—the m fields separate a structure into m disjoint substructures.]

Def 4.9: (a) let d_i and d_j be dimensions of N $(i \neq j)$. If d_i and d_j are **independent**, then for any field f traversing d_i in the forward direction, for any field g traversing d_j in the forward direction, and for all distinct nodes pN and pN',

[4] Treat NULL as denoting a typeless node that is dynamically-allocated by the system at startup.

[5] The problem of validation is discussed in section 5.

1. $pN.f \neq pN'.g$ or $pN.f = pN'.g =$ NULL, and
2. $pN.g \neq pN'.f$ or $pN.g = pN'.f =$ NULL.

(b) Further, for any field uf traversing d_i in a uniquely forward direction and for any field b traversing d_i in the backward direction, either

3. $pN.uf =$ NULL, or
4. for all pN'' in the list denoted by $pN.uf(.g)^*$, $pN''.b = pN$ or $pN''.b =$ NULL.

[Implication: (a) d_i and d_j separate a structure into disjoint substructures, (b) uniquely forward/backward cycles hold across an independent dimension.]

Def 4.10: let d_i and d_j be dimensions of N $(i \neq j)$. If d_i and d_j are not independent, then they are **dependent** and Def 4.9 does not hold for d_i and d_j.
[Implication: traversal along d_i and d_j could lead to the same node/substructure.]

5 Analysis and Transformation using ADDS

The principal goal of ADDS is to improve the analysis of codes utilizing pointer data structures. As discussed in section 1.2, existing analysis-only approaches exhibit various limitations when faced with such structures. Our approach is to use the information available in the ADDS declarations to guide the analysis. This synergy between the abstract data structure descriptions and the analysis technique provides a more general and more accurate approach. For example, by using information about the dimensionality and direction of field traversals, the abstraction approximations are freed from estimating needless cycles (such as those formed by the forward and backward directions along the same dimension), and can therefore avoid making needless conservative approximations.

Let us make this idea more concrete. Analysis-only approaches begin with initial assumptions about what properties are important to estimate, and then tailor the approximation domain and analysis rules appropriately. For example, by choosing k-limited graphs as the approximation domain, one is forced to conservatively approximate non-cyclic structures with cycles, which implies the approximation cannot distinguish tree-like structures from cyclic ones. To further illustrate how the choice of analysis depends on the type of data structure under consideration, consider once again the following two data types, `BinTree` and `TwoWayLL`:

```
type BinTree                type TwoWayLL
{ int       data;           { int         data;
  BinTree *left;              TwoWayLL *next;
  BinTree *right;             TwoWayLL *prev;
};                          };
```

Without additional information, these types will appear identical to the compiler, and thus the same sort of analysis must be applied. Clearly however, there are some analyses that will be more appropriate for one structure than the other; after all, binary trees exhibit much different properties than two-way linked-lists.

In the case of two-way linked-lists, the appropriate approximation for the paths between two nodes p and q is the number of `next` links from p to q. In addition, the analysis rules for traversing `next` links from q (`q = q->next`) should lengthen paths between p and q, while analysis rules for traversing `prev` links from q (`q = q->prev`) should shorten paths. Both the approximation domain and the appropriate rules for traversals can be easily inferred from an ADDS declaration that says (1) there is one dimension, (2) the field `next` traverses `uniquely forward`, and (3) the field `prev` traverses `backward`.

Now consider binary trees. In this case, the appropriate approximation of paths is that of going `left`, `right` or `down` (where `down` is a conservative approximation for going either `left` or `right`). Traversing along either the `left` or `right` fields lengthens paths; there is no field for which a traversal shortens a path. This information can be expressed by an ADDS declaration that which states that `left` and `right` traverse `uniquely forward` along the same dimension. This in turn can be used to build an appropriate approximation domain, and set of analysis rules, for binary trees.

Thus, the problem is that initial assumptions bias program analysis. If the analysis starts with very weak assumptions, then the resulting analysis will be overly conservative; this is the current situation with structure estimation techniques. If the initial assumptions are valid for only one class of data structures, then applying the analysis to other classes will lead to inaccurate and conservative analysis; this is the case of applying ordinary path matrix analysis to cyclic structures. Hence it appears crucial that in order to perform accurate analysis in the presence of a wide variety of data structures, we must begin with accurate information about the structure. This is the essence behind ADDS, and our approach.

In this section we show how the properties of ADDS data structures can be used to improve the accuracy of program analysis, and thus enable the application of powerful optimizing and parallelizing transformations. In particular, we present in section 5.1 a new approach combining ADDS with an existing analysis technique. Then in section 5.2 we demonstrate a new application of software pipelining made possible by our approach.

5.1 Program Analysis

As discussed earlier, the presence of a description mechanism such as ADDS is not enough in itself to enable optimizing and parallelizing transformations in the presence of pointer data structures. Imperative programs routinely rearrange components of such a structure, and it is during these points in a program that the abstraction (or parts thereof) must be ignored by the compiler. Otherwise transformations may be applied that are based on invalid assumptions, causing incorrect code generation. Hence some form of abstraction validation analysis is required to enable a given transformation; this is in addition to more traditional alias analysis which is needed to ensure that the transformation is safely applied.

Our approach to the analysis problem is a combined one, in which safe analysis techniques are used in conjunction with ADDS declarations. In particular, we are developing an approach to the static analysis of ADDS data structures that is an extension of *path matrix* analysis [HN90, Hen90], called *general path matrix* analysis. Path matrix analysis was originally designed to automatically discover and exploit the properties of acyclic data structures. With the help of ADDS, general path matrix analysis is capable of handling cyclic data structures as well.

General path matrix analysis computes, at each program point, a path matrix PM which estimates the relationship between every pair of live pointer variables; PM is thus a function of the current path matrix and the program statement under analysis. The entry $PM(p,q)$ denotes an explicit path or alias, if any, from the node pointed to by p to the node pointed to by q. The analysis does not attempt to express all possible paths between two nodes, since cyclic data structures would soon overwhelm the matrix. Instead, the paths explicitly traversed by the program are captured in the PM, while the remaining paths and aliases are deduced from the current state of the path matrix and the ADDS declarations.

5.1.1 Abstraction Validation Analysis

In order to validate an ADDS declaration, the effect of certain pointer statements on the path matrix must be compared with the original ADDS declaration. In particular, statements of the form `p->f = q` may change the shape of the data structure. This in turn may result in a violation of the declared abstraction. However, this is generally not an error in an imperative program, and so is not treated as one. Instead, we note that the abstraction is invalid at this point in the program, and we do not perform any transformations that rely on the validity of the necessary ADDS properties[6].

Though the actual process of validation is beyond the scope of this paper, the idea is as follows. The ADDS declaration is encoded as a series of relationships between the various pointer fields of the node. During analysis, if the path matrix ever denotes a relationship between two fields that is illegal, this part of the abstraction is deemed invalid and an entry is added to the path matrix encoding the violation. Later, if another program statement fixes the relationship between these two fields, the entry is removed and the abstraction is once again considered valid.

A common example of a temporary break in an abstraction is the moving of a subtree from one node to another within a binary tree. Here is a possible code fragment:

```
dest->left = src->left;
src->left  = NULL;
```

After analysis of the first statement, it is obvious that `src` and `dest` share a common subtree, even though this violates the disjointness property of a binary tree. However, the violation is immediately corrected, as is usually the case.

5.1.2 Alias Analysis

Alias analysis is best explained via example. Consider the following code fragment, in which the pointer variable `hd` denotes the head of a two-way linked-list of nodes. Each node represents a point in 2D space, and contains its x and y coordinates. The code shifts the origin from (0, 0) to (`hd->x`, 0) by subtracting the x-coordinate of this first point from all remaining points:

```
p = hd->next;
while p <> NULL
  { p->x = p->x - hd->x;
    p = p->next;
  }
```

	hd	p	p'
hd	$=$	$=?$	$=?$
p	$=?$	$=$	$=?$
p'	$=?$	$=?$	$=$

Alias Matrix AM

If the compiler fails to discover that `next` traverses a list in the forward direction (i.e. that Def 4.2 holds for `next`), then its analysis of the above code will be overly conservative—the compiler must assume that `next` is cyclic, and hence that `hd` and all values of `p` are potential aliases for the same node. The effect of this conservative alias analysis is summarized above in "alias matrix" form[7]. The p' entries are used to denote aliasing during the loop, where definite aliases are indicated by $=$ and possible aliases are indicated by $=?$. Observe that all the entries denote some form of aliasing. In particular, the entry $AM[hd,p']$ indicates that `hd` is a possible alias for the iterative values of `p`. As discussed in section 1.1, this prevents a number of useful loop transformations.

Now suppose the programmer declared his or her linked-list using the ADDS declaration `TwoWayLL`, as

[6] Of course, such a violation could in fact be an error. Warning the programmer, or providing a compiler switch to enable these warnings, would be a useful debugging tool.

[7] Please note that this is just a convenient way of expressing aliases, and is not the result of path matrix analysis.

given in section 3.1. Assuming general path matrix analysis determines that the structure abstraction is well-behaved (valid) at the start of this code fragment, the compiler can use the acyclic nature of the **next** field (from Def 4.2) to infer that the statement `p = p->next` never visits the same node twice. As a result, general path matrix analysis would produce the following path matrices, which denote (from top to bottom): just before the loop, after one iteration, and after the loop analysis has reached a fixed point. The important difference between these path matrices and the previous alias matrix AM is the replacement of the =? entires with more accurate information about paths.

	hd	p
hd	$=$	$next$
p		$=$

	hd	p	p'
hd	$=$	$next^2$	$next$
p		$=$	
p'		$next$	$=$

	hd	p	p'
hd	$=$	$next^+$	$next^+$
p		$=$	
p'		$next$	$=$

An entry in the path matrix like $next^+$ indicates a path of one or more **next** links; all paths are either explicitly encoded within an entry, implicitly encoded within other entries and the ADDS declarations, or both. All aliases are explicitly encoded, so an empty entry guarantees that the two pointers are not aliases. Thus, we see that the ADDS declaration and general path matrix analysis have captured the desired property in the PM necessary for performing numerous optimizing and parallelizing transformations, namely that **hd**, **p** and p' are never aliases.

5.2 Transformations

Optimizing and parallelizing transformations come in many forms, including:

- fine-grain transformations (e.g. improved instruction scheduling),
- loop transformations (e.g loop unrolling or software pipelining), and
- coarse-grain transformations (e.g. parallel execution of code blocks).

The application of such transformations typically requires accurate alias analysis. As shown in the previous subsection, ADDS and general path matrix analysis provide such accuracy. This will clearly aid in fine-grain transformations where dependency analysis is crucial. When transforming code that operates on a data structure, loop transformations typically require the structure to exhibit list-like properties, while coarse-grain transformations typically require tree-like properties. Such properties are all expressible using ADDS.

Earlier work [HG92] has shown the applicability of loop unrolling [DH79] on scalar architectures. For example, a simple loop to initialize every node of a linked-list showed 47% speedup on the MIPS architecture for a list of size 100 with 3-unrolling (see [HG92] for more details and timings). In this section we present an example of a more powerful loop transformation, software pipelining [RG82, AN88a, AN88b, Lam88, EN89]. Given the current trend towards machines supporting higher degrees of parallelism, e.g. VLIW and superscalar, this type of optimization offers larger speedups.

Once again, consider the code fragment discussed in the previous subsection 5.1.2, which manipulates a two-way linked-list of points. The following is an equivalent loop body written in pseudo-assembly code:

```
S1   if p==NULL goto done
S2   load   p->x,R1
S3   load   hd->x,R2
S4   sub    R1,R2,R3
S5   store  R3,p->x
S6   load   p->next,p
S7   goto   S1
```

As we saw earlier, if the compiler's analysis is overly conservative, then the compiler will incorrectly assume that **hd** and all values of **p** are potential aliases for the same node. In this case the data dependency graph shown in Figure 2 is constructed, with false loop-carried dependencies from S5 to S2 and S3. The result is that the loop appears to exhibit very little parallelism between iterations. However, as we also discussed, if the data structure is declared as a **TwoWayLL**, general path matrix analysis will be able to determine that in fact **hd** and all the iterative values of **p** are never aliases. This will eliminate these false dependencies, and the loop now appears as a sequence of nearly independent, parallelizable iterations.

To exploit this parallelism, we can apply software pipelining. First we need to minimize the effect of the loop-carried dependence from S6 to S1. By renaming, we can move S6 above S2, calling it S1.6, and then replace S6 with a copy statement. The result is the following semantically equivalent loop:

```
S1   if p==NULL goto done
S1.6 load   p->next,p'
S2   load   p->x,R1
S3   load   hd->x,R2
S4   sub    R1,R2,R3
S5   store  R3,p->x
S6   move   p',p
S7   goto   S1
```

The next iteration of the loop can now begin as soon as S1.6 of the current iteration completes, allowing the

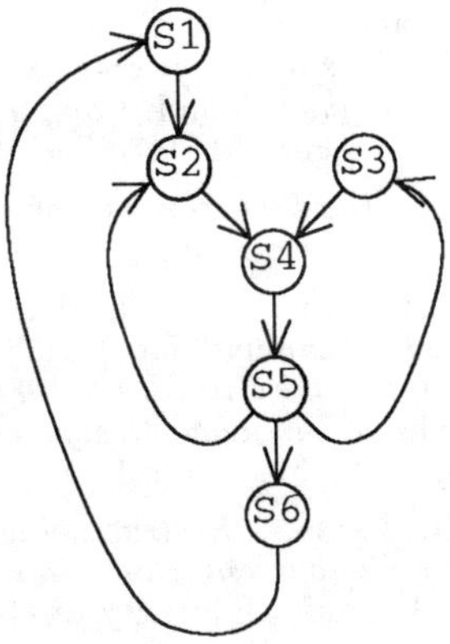

Figure 2: Dependency graph for pseudo-code.

loop bodies to nearly overlap in execution. But in addition, since the list must be speculatively traversable (by Def 4.1), it is safe to swap S1 and S1.6, further increasing the amount of available parallelism. Finally, since `hd` and `p` are never aliases, we can deduce that `hd->x` is loop invariant. Hence S3 can be moved outside and above the loop.

The code below incorporates the above-mentioned transformations, producing a semantically equivalent loop:

```
S0   load    hd->x,R2
S1   load    p->next,p'
S2   if p==NULL goto done
S3   load    p->x,R1
S4   sub     R1,R2,R3
S5   store   R3,p->x
S6   move    p',p
S7   goto    S1
```

This loop can be pipelined as follows (the columns denote different iterations, rows denote statements executing in parallel):

```
S1
S2  S1
S3  S2  S1
S4  S3  S2  S1
S5  S4  S3  S2  S1
    S5  S4  S3  S2
        S5  S4  S3
            S5  S4
                S5
```

The boxed "statement" represents the new parallel pipelined body of the loop. As a result, the code exhibits a theoretical speedup of 5. Note that the copy statement S6 is removed as part of the pipelining process, via (enhanced) copy propagation [NPW91].

In general, software pipelining can lead to even larger speedups, depending on the characteristics of the loop body. Obviously, the actual speedup also depends heavily on the target machine's architecture.

6 Conclusions

As we have shown with numerous examples, many recursively-defined pointer data structures exhibit important properties which compilers can exploit for optimization and parallelization purposes. These properties are often known to the programmer—conveyed implicitly e.g. through the use of appropriate identifiers—and yet unavailable to the compiler. This lack of information hinders the accuracy of alias analysis and thus restricts the transformations that can be applied to codes using pointer data structures.

In this paper we have proposed an abstract description technique, ADDS, which allows the programmer to state such properties explicitly. The description of a recursive pointer data structure using ADDS is quite intuitive, and does not place an excessive burden on the programmer. By combining ADDS and general path matrix analysis, we demonstrated that the resulting approach enables more accurate and more general alias analysis, and hence the application of powerful optimizing and parallelizing transformations. As we have seen, software pipelining is one such transformation.

ADDS represents an important first step in our long-term goal of efficient compiler analysis of codes involving cyclic pointer data structures. ADDS is a simple extension to most any imperative programming language, and yet can lead to analysis and transformations that are otherwise not possible using traditional methods. With the increasing use of languages that support pointers and recursively-defined pointer data structures, the importance of such an approach will no doubt increase.

References

[AK87] Randy Allen and Ken Kennedy. Automatic translation of FORTRAN programs to vector form. *ACM Transactions on Programming Languages and Systems*, 9(4), October 1987.

[AN88a] A. Aiken and A. Nicolau. Optimal Loop Parallelization. In *Proceedings of the SIGPLAN 1988 Conference on Programming Language Design and Implementation*, pages 308–317, June 1988.

[AN88b] A. Aiken and A. Nicolau. Perfect Pipelining: A new loop parallelization technique. In *Proceedings of the 1988 European Symposium on Programming.* Springer Verlag Lecture Notes in Computer Science No.300, March 1988.

[App85] Andrew W. Appel. An Efficient Program for Many-Body Simulation. *SIAM J. Sci. Stat. Comput.*, 6(1):85–103, 1985.

[ASU87] Alfred V. Aho, Ravi Sethi, and Jeffrey D. Ullman. *Compilers: Principles, Techniques, and Tools*. Addison-Wesley, 1987.

[BH86] Josh Barnes and Piet Hut. A Hierarchical O(NlogN) Force-Calculation Algorithm. *Nature*, 324:446–449, 4 December 1986. The code can be obtained from Prof. Barnes at the University of Hawaii.

[CON] CONVEX Computer Corporation. CONVEX C and FORTRAN Language Reference Manuals. 1990.

[CWZ90] D.R. Chase, M. Wegman, and F.K. Zadek. Analysis of pointers and structures. In *Proceedings of the SIGPLAN '90 Conference on Programming Language Design and Implementation*, pages 296–310, 1990.

[DH79] J.J. Dongarra and A.R. Hinds. Unrolling loops in FORTRAN. *Software-Practice and Experience*, 9:219–226, 1979.

[EN89] Kemal Ebcioglu and Toshio Nakatani. A New Compilation Technique for Parallelizing Loops Loops with Unpredictable Branches on a VLIW Architecture. In *Proceedings of the Second Workshop on Programming Languages and Compilers for Parallel Computing*, Research Monographs in Parallel and Distributed Computing. MIT-Press, 1989.

[Gro91] Josef Grosch. Tool support for data structures. *Structured Programming*, 12(1):31–38, January 1991.

[Gua88] Vincent A. Guarna Jr. A technique for analyzing pointer and structure references in parallel restructuring compilers. In *Proceedings of the International Conference on Parallel Processing*, volume 2, pages 212–220, 1988.

[Har89] W. Ludwell Harrison III. The interprocedural analysis and automatic parallelization of scheme programs. *Lisp and Symbolic Computation*, 2(3/4):179–396, 1989.

[Har91] W. Ludwell Harrison III. Generalized iteration space and the parallelization of symbolic programs. In Ian Foster and Evan Tick, editors, *Proceedings of the Workshop on Computation of Symbolic Languages for Parallel Computers*. Argonne National Laboratory, October 1991. ANL-91/34.

[Hen90] Laurie J. Hendren. *Parallelizing Programs with Recursive Data Structures*. PhD thesis, Cornell University, April 1990. TR 90-1114.

[HG92] Laurie J. Hendren and Guang R. Gao. Designing Programming Languages for Analyzability: A Fresh Look at Pointer Data Structures. In *Proceedings of the 4th IEEE International Conference on Computer Languages (to appear, also available as ACAPS Technical Memo 28, McGill University)*, April 1992.

[HN90] Laurie J. Hendren and Alexandru Nicolau. Parallelizing Programs with Recursive Data Structures. *IEEE Trans. on Parallel and Distributed Computing*, 1(1):35–47, January 1990.

[HPR89] Susan Horwitz, Phil Pfeiffer, and Thomas Reps. Dependence analysis for pointer variables. In *Proceedings of the SIGPLAN '89 Conference on Programming Language Design and Implementation*, pages 28–40, June 1989.

[JM81] N. D. Jones and S. S. Muchnick. *Program Flow Analysis, Theory and Applications*, chapter 4, Flow Analysis and Optimization of LISP-like Structures, pages 102–131. Prentice-Hall, 1981.

[KKK90] David Klappholz, Apostolos D. Kallis, and Xiangyun Kang. Refined C: An Update. In David Gelernter, Alexandru Nicolau, and David Padua, editors, *Languages and Compilers for Parallel Computing*, pages 331–357. The MIT Press, 1990.

[Kuc78] D.J. Kuck. *The Structure of Computers and Computations: Volume I*. Wiley, 1978.

[Lam88] Monica Lam. Software Pipelining: An Effective Scheduling Technique for VLIW Machines. In *Proceedings of the SIGPLAN 1988 Conference on Programming Language Design and Implementation*, pages 318–328, June 1988.

[Lar89] James R. Larus. *Restructuring Symbolic Programs for Concurrent Execution on Multiprocessors*. PhD thesis, University of California, Berkeley, 1989.

[LH88a] James R. Larus and Paul N. Hilfinger. Detecting conflicts between structure accesses. In *Proceedings of the SIGPLAN '88 Conference on Programming Language Design and Implementation*, pages 21–34, June 1988.

[LH88b] James R. Larus and Paul N. Hilfinger. Restructuring Lisp programs for concurrent execution. In *Proceedings of the ACM/SIGPLAN PPEALS 1988 - Parallel Programming: Experience with Applications, Languages and Systems*, pages 100–110, July 1988.

[Lov77] D.B. Loveman. Program Improvement by Source-to-Source Transformation. *Journal of the ACM*, 24(1):121–145, January 1977.

[MR90] Michael Metcalf and John Reid. *Fortran 90 Explained*. Oxford University Press, 1990.

[NPW91] A. Nicolau, R. Potasman, and H. Wang. Register Allocation, Renaming and their impact on Fine-grain Parallelism. In *Proceedings of the Fourth Workshop on Languages and Compilers for Parallel Computing*, August 1991.

[PW86] David A. Padua and Michael J. Wolfe. Advanced compiler optimization for supercomputers. *Communications of the ACM*, 29(12), December 1986.

[RG82] B. R. Rau and C. D. Glaeser. Efficient Code Generation for Horizontal Architectures: Compiler Techniques and Architectural Support. In *Proceedings of the 9th Symposium on Computer Architecture*, April 1982.

[Sam90] Hanan Samet. *The Design and Analysis of Spatial Data Structures*. Addison-Wesley, 1990.

[Sol90] Jon A. Solworth. The PARSEQ Project: An Interim Report. In David Gelernter, Alexandru Nicolau, and David Padua, editors, *Languages and Compilers for Parallel Computing*, pages 490–510. The MIT Press, 1990.

[Sta80] Thomas A. Standish. *Data Structure Techniques*. Addison-Wesley, 1980.

[ZC90] Hans Zima and Barbara Chapman. *Supercompilers for Parallel and Vector Computers*. ACM Press, 1990.

Alphonse: Incremental Computation as a Programming Abstraction

Roger Hoover*

The more things change, the more they remain the same. *Alphonse Karr* [Kar49]

Abstract

Alphonse is a program transformation system that uses dynamic dependency analysis and incremental computation techniques to automatically generate efficient dynamic implementations from simple exhaustive imperative program specifications.

1 Overview

In most computer applications there are numerous properties that the underlying algorithms maintain as the program data changes. Consider, for example, an application that utilizes a search tree. After additions or deletions to this tree's data, an efficient search algorithm may require the property that the tree be balanced. The Alphonse system described in this paper automates the maintenance of such properties using procedurally coded specifications.

These computational properties typically can be established by a straightforward *exhaustive* algorithm that examines and adjusts all of the relevant data. For example, a binary tree can be balanced with a simple recursive pass over the tree. We could execute the exhaustive algorithm after each change to the data, but this would be unnecessarily inefficient. In a dynamic or interactive setting where the property must be maintained after each of many small data modifications, a complex algorithm is typically used to avoid the redundant computation inherent to many repeated invocations of this exhaustive algorithm. The Alphonse program transformation system generates efficient dynamic implementations from simple exhaustive program specifications. It transforms these programs to use dynamic dependency analysis and incremental evaluation techniques in order to automatically maintain the Alphonse properties.

Alphonse can be used with programs written in a conventional imperative language. The Alphonse properties are also written in this language, with procedures and data associated in an object oriented style. Pragmas are used to indicate the procedures that comprise the Alphonse properties. While these program specifications would produce the correct result if compiled by a traditional compiler, they would be inefficient due to the repeated evaluations induced by running the exhaustive algorithm at every step. The Alphonse system translates these inefficient programs into efficient ones that *dynamically* analyze the dependencies between the operations of the exhaustive algorithm and *incrementally* execute the portions of the computation that are different from those executed before recent data modifications.

The advantage of this approach is that program specifications are substantially simpler, making them easier to program, debug, prove correct, understand, maintain, and modify. In large interactive applications, where programmers have difficulty reasoning about the complex dependencies that arise from the interaction of several algorithms over a set of changing data, Alphonse takes on this responsibility, allowing the construction of more sophisticated software systems. In addition, the dependency information maintained by Alphonse programs enables a host of other benefits including eager evaluation, sophisticated debugging, and parallel execution.

This paper is organized as follows: Section 2 describes how incremental computation techniques are used in Alphonse. Section 3 discusses the language used for Alphonse and gives an example. Our dynamic analysis technique is covered in Section 4 and Section 5 gives the program transformations that adapt Alphonse programs to perform this dynamic analysis. A number of optimizations are given in Section 6. Section 7 gives three examples. Our implementation effort is described in Section 8, Section 9 analyzes time and space requirements. Finally, Section 10 compares Alphonse with similar systems.

2 Incremental Computation

The model of incremental computation is as follows: First, a computation is performed to establish some property. Then, a small change is introduced to the program or data, requiring a slightly different computation. The previous computation needs subsequent alterations in order to reflect the result dictated by this change.

Incremental computation is used in Alphonse between two parts of the program: The *mutator* is a normal imperative program that performs arbitrary imperative operations. The *Maintained portion* is an imperative exhaustive program that establishes a property P on the program data.

*IBM T.J. Watson, P.O. Box 704, Yorktown Heights, NY 10598, rhoover@watson.ibm.com

ACM SIGPLAN '92 PLDI-6/92/CA

The interface between these two parts consists of a set of *Alphonse procedures* called by the mutator, along with a collection of storage locations that are referenced by both portions. The mutator performs modifications to the state of these storage locations, and the Maintained portion reacts to these changes to re-establish property P. The mutator accesses the results of the Alphonse computation by performing calls to the Alphonse procedures.

While the Maintained portion specifies a property that must hold when a given Alphonse procedure returns, this property is not necessarily established upon the call to the Alphonse procedure. If the state change introduced by the mutator does not affect the property specified by the given Alphonse procedure, no computation is required. Otherwise, the programmer specified *evaluation method* is used. With *eager evaluation*, the computation may be performed at any time after the state change. Even when using *demand evaluation*, which lazily updates the procedures, some or even all of the computation may have been performed earlier in time in order to maintain some other Alphonse property.

Well established incremental computation techniques are used to maintain Alphonse properties. We use a combination of two such techniques, quiescence propagation[1] and function caching[2] [Pug88, PT89].

Quiescence propagation is an incremental update technique that allows the reuse of large networks of interrelated computations that are expressed as directed graphs. Each node of the graph represents an intermediate step of the entire computation and directed edges connect two intermediate computation nodes u and v if v uses data computed by u. After a change to the computation graph, intermediate computation steps are performed beginning at the change points and continuing toward dependent computations. Propagation becomes *quiescent* when the new result of intermediate computations matches the old value cached from before the computation graph change. The amount of computation is minimized when done in a topological order with respect to the graph, and much research has been directed at algorithms to compute this order in the presence of graph changes.

Function caching is a technique that captures the computation of individual function calls for later reuse. A table is kept for each function with an entry for each different function call, indexed by the argument values. Subsequent calls with identical arguments are not re-computed—a cached return value is used instead. The technique requires that the functions be deterministic as well as be combinators (that is, depend only upon their arguments).

In Alphonse, we make two contributions to incremental computation research: First, we give program transformations that adapt an imperative program to automatically maintain the graph structure necessary for quiescence propagation. Second, we combine function caching with quiescence propagation to allow functions that are not combinators (i.e., functions that examine global state). We compare Alphonse with other incremental systems in Section 10.

3 Specification Language

Alphonse programs are written in an imperative language L that has been extended with pragmas to form *Alphonse-L*. While we make a few reasonable assumptions about this *base language* L in Section 3.1, all L programs are valid *Alphonse–L* programs. Alphonse properties are also written in L, but are denoted by pragmas.

[1] Referred to as *change propagation* in [Rep84].

[2] Also known as memoizing.

3.1 Base Language

Alphonse can be used in conjunction with any imperative programming language with the following properties:

- Record types (we will refer to instances of record types as *objects*[3]), with:
  - Data fields,
  - Pointer fields (we assume that pointers are well behaved), and
  - Procedure valued fields (which we apply to the containing objects and refer to as *methods*);
- Dynamic Allocation (for object creation); and
- Pragmas (which are used to indicate which procedures and methods comprise Alphonse properties).

By well behaved, we mean that we can create, dereference, and assign pointers. We do not allow pointer constants and pointer arithmetic such as in C as they significantly complicate the automatic detection of change required to maintain Alphonse properties. (It is possible that static analysis techniques for pointers, or a safe subset of C, could reduce the need to track changes at potentially every memory location and allow its use with Alphonse.)

We refer to functions and variables accessible to the outer language scope as *top-level*. While we assume dynamic allocation, one can perform maintained property computations in this system without the ability to dynamically create objects. This limitation, however, severely reduces expressibility. One would want to provide a standard facility to dynamically allocate objects out of a fixed array or heap.

3.2 Language Notation

We will use the following notation in our examples.[4]

- Object types are declared as follows.

```
TYPE SubType = SuperType OBJECT
  Field1 : FType1;
  ...
METHODS
  Method1 (arg, ...) : MType1 := MProc1;
  ...
OVERRIDES
  Override1 := OProc1;
  ...
END
```

  This notation declares an object type (called *SubType* here), that inherits both fields and methods from *SuperType* and contains *Field*$_1$,... as new fields. In addition, methods *Method*$_1$,... are added to the type with implementations provided by procedures *MProc*$_1$,.... Overrides replace the implementations of inherited methods.

[3] Although we use the terminology of object oriented programming, we are assuming nothing more than what is explicitly stated here.

[4] This is Modula-3 [Nel91].

- Objects of type T are dynamically allocated through the use of the NEW statement:

  NEW(T)

- Pragmas are denoted:

  ⟨*PRAGMA NAME AND ARGUMENTS*⟩

3.3 Alphonse Notation

Alphonse properties are specified as procedures (including functions) in the base imperative language L. There are two pragmas that are used to distinguish Alphonse procedures from the remainder of the program.

1. Inserting the ⟨*MAINTAINED*⟩ pragma before method or override declarations indicates that these procedures are not to be executed if they produce results identical to their previous executions.
2. The ⟨*CACHED*⟩ pragma is placed before a procedure declaration to denote a procedure whose return value is to be remembered and returned for future calls to the procedure with identical arguments. Note that if the procedure has accessed nonlocal storage, mutations of this storage may require updating the cache (see Section 4.2). Additional pragma arguments allow the specification of the caching technique, cache size, and the replacement algorithm.

An optional argument to the maintained and cached pragmas allows the programmer to specify the evaluation strategy. With DEMAND evaluation, the value of a procedure is updated lazily upon calls to that procedure. EAGER evaluation updates values *before* subsequent procedure call requests, and is useful in applications with computation cycles available due to input/output, etc.

Let p be a procedure call $proc(a_0, \ldots, a_k)$, where *proc* is a cached procedure, or *proc* implements a maintained method call $a_0.m(a_1, \ldots, a_k)$. We call p an *incremental procedure instance* and define $R(p)$, the set of *referenced arguments* of p, to be the set of all values external to *proc* that are accessed (both read *and* write) by the call. This set includes any incremental procedure instances or top-level variables that are transitively referenced through *non*incremental procedure calls. Procedure parameters a_i are not included in $R(p)$ if passed by value, but storage pointed to by VAR and pointer parameters must be included in $R(p)$ if it is dereferenced.[5]

3.4 Example

As an example of how Alphonse is used, consider Algorithm 1. We use the object type *Tree* and the maintained method *height* to maintain the property that the height in the tree is computed for each node of a binary tree. A single object of type TreeNil is pointed to by tree nodes with less than two children.

Implemented by the procedure *Height*, the *height* method computes the height in the tree from the bottom up. Beginning with a height of 0 for the TreeNil object at the leaves, the height at each node is computed as the maximum child height plus one.

[5] We discuss methods for limiting the set of referenced arguments in Section 6.4.

```
TYPE Tree = OBJECT left, right: Tree;
  METHODS (*MAINTAINED*) height := Height;
END;

TYPE TreeNil = Tree OBJECT
  OVERRIDES (*MAINTAINED*) height := HeightNil;
END;

PROCEDURE Height(t : Tree) : INTEGER=
  BEGIN
    RETURN MAX(t.left.height(), t.right.height())+1
  END Height;

PROCEDURE HeightNil(t : Tree) : INTEGER=
  BEGIN RETURN 0 END HeightNil;
```

Algorithm 1: Maintained Height Tree

Let $subtree(t)$ be the subtree rooted at vertex t. As the procedure that implements the *height* method calls itself recursively to perform its computation, non-incremental execution of $t.height$ requires $O(|subtree(t)|)$ time. When the method is maintained, $O(|subtree(t)|)$ time is used for the first call. Subsequent *height* calls on t or any of its descendents, however, will require $O(1)$ time, since the result values are cached. Changes to a child field pointing to node x in the tree will require $O(\text{height})$ time (plus the bookkeeping cost of the quiescence propagation algorithm) to update all of the cached values on the new and former paths from x to the tree root. Changes to many pointers in the tree, however, are batched by the evaluation algorithm and result in $O(|AFFECTED|)$ (plus quiescence propagation bookkeeping) computations, where $AFFECTED$ is the set of height values that are different.

Examples of the notation in the previous subsection: The dynamic allocation of an object t of type *Tree* will result in the creation of an incremental procedure instance, $t.height()$. The referenced argument set $R(t.height())$ includes $t.left$, $t.left.height()$, $t.right$, and $t.right.height()$. $R(n.height()) = \emptyset$ where n is the *TreeNil* object.

3.5 Restrictions

We place the following restrictions on each Alphonse procedure p.

DET p must implement a deterministic function. That is, when called with the same formal and referenced arguments, it must have the same behavior and return the same value. This restriction is necessary to insure that p's result will be identical if executed under identical conditions, the essential property that allows us to avoid subsequent executions of p until predicated by change. DET precludes Alphonse procedures from true non-deterministic behavior or the use of internal static state to simulate it (as in pseudorandom number generators).

TOP p must be a top-level procedure and may access only top-level or local data. TOP insures that p is always available for execution by the evaluator and that the data accessed by p changes only by assignment and not through the pushing and popping of automatic stack variables. We can relax this restriction if the compiler generates the code necessary to perform cache invalidation at the end of a variable's lifetime.

OBS If p has an eager evaluation strategy in program P, p may not produce side effects such that spurious executions of p (at procedure call boundaries) can affect the result of P's computation. OBS limits the side effects produced by an eager procedure p so that the eager evaluation of p is not observed in the program output, or through program anomalies that would abort or infinitely delay the execution of P.

The above restrictions are not automatically enforced by the Alphonse compiler. Instead, we require the programmer to prove that the Alphonse procedures are compliant (A proof example is given in Section 7.3). While it is possible to insure that these restrictions are not violated by imposing simple conservative assumptions (e.g. (no eager side affects)⇒OBS), it is not decidable in general whether or not a given program P obeys these restrictions.

Traditional input (output) is modeled as the removal from (concatenation to) a top-level stream variable containing the input (output) string, and obviously violates the OBS restriction if included in eager procedures. We model other I/O, such as pointer device input and bit mapped display, as reads from (or writes to) special top-level variables and these actions can often be incorporated in eagerly evaluated procedures.

3.6 Expressibility

While the Alphonse–L language retains the exact semantics of the imperative language L, the efficiency provided by incremental evaluation gives rise to *enhanced expressibility* despite the restrictions of the previous section. Because the programmer is free from reasoning about the explicit ordering of computation steps, he or she can specify the computation more clearly and succinctly. While these programs can be executed by L without Alphonse, the difference in execution speed can be large enough that these algorithms are not practical without incremental evaluation. Thus, incremental computation has effectively *extended* the language to allow a declarative style of programming that specifies *what* to compute without giving the precise execution order.

4 Dynamic Analysis

In order to maintain Alphonse properties with quiescence propagation, it is important that we know about *change* and *dependence* as it relates to the Maintained portion. Change becomes relevant when modifications are made to variables examined by all Alphonse procedures. These changes must be made known to the computation in order to update Alphonse procedures (transitively) dependent upon the change. Dependence between Alphonse procedures and the program state must therefore also be known. In this Section, we give our dynamic dependence analysis technique. Section 5 details the program transformations that are used insert this algorithm into the Alphonse program.

It is important to note why dynamic analysis is necessary in Alphonse, given that other incremental systems [Yeh83, RT88, Hud86, HK89] utilize static dependency analysis. These systems are based on grammars and have the property that for any given intermediate computation, only a small fixed set of the program state can be examined. Alphonse procedures, on the other hand, are not limited to a local set of references. Instead, these procedures may traverse data structures, examine global data, and call other functions. A static determination of the exact set of referenced arguments is, in general, undecidable. Thus, we are limited to two choices: a *conservative* approximation to this set, or an exact, *dynamically* maintained, set. With the inclusion of pointer types in the imperative language, conservative approximations become unacceptly imprecise using existing static analysis techniques [CWZ90, Hen90]. We use dynamic analysis with static optimizations when appropriate (see Section 6).

4.1 Dependence

Dependence information in Alphonse is stored in a *dependency graph*. Nodes of this graph are created to represent each incremental procedure instance, as well as each global variable location accessed by these procedure instances. Edges of this graph connect nodes u to v if the procedure instance represented by v depends on the procedure instance or variable represented by u. Thus, $succ(u)$, the successor set of u, would contain v. We also maintain the reverse edges, with $u \in pred(v)$. The cached variable or procedure return value is stored in $value(u)$. The boolean field $consistent(u)$ stores the cache status.

4.2 Caching with Propagation

We integrate quiescence propagation and function caching through the use of dependency graph nodes to represent both maintained methods and cached procedures. In the following, let p be an incremental procedure instance (that is, a maintained method call $o.m(a_1, \ldots, a_k)$ or a cached procedure call $f(a_1, \ldots, a_k)$), represented by dependency graph node u.

Edges to u in the dependency graph come from the nodes representing elements of $R(p)$. Since $R(p)$ does not contain $a_1, \ldots, a_k$, the dependence of p upon any given a_i is not represented by dependency graph edges. Instead, calls to the given method or procedure ($o.m$ or f) are stored in a table known as the *argument table*. This table contains all nodes that represent calls to p, one for each distinct argument vector $\langle a_1, \ldots, a_k \rangle$, and is indexed by this vector. (For efficiency, the argument table can be eliminated if $k = 0$. While cached procedures of zero arguments are rare, methods with zero arguments are quite common).

Changes in an element of $R(p)$ result in the propagation of change to p for both cached procedures as well as maintained methods. Changes of argument value (say a'_i instead of a_i) between successive executions of a given call, on the other hand, result in the remapping of edges from $(u \rightarrow n)$ to $(u' \rightarrow n)$, where u' represents the incremental procedure instance with arguments $\langle a_1, \ldots a_{i-1}, a'_i, a_{i+1}, a_k \rangle$.

The advantage of this organization is that it eliminates the combinator restriction of traditional function caching (Section 2). As all of the state accessed by a cached procedure is encoded in $R(p)$ and $\langle a_1, \ldots, a_k \rangle$, a change to $r, r \in R(p)$, can be effectively translated into an update of the cached return value.

4.3 Recording Dependence

In order to record the dependence between Alphonse procedures and the storage that they access, we need to be able to represent the correspondence between these runtime objects and their dependency graph nodes. We do this by allocating pointer fields that relate storage and procedures with their dependency graph nodes (and vice versa) as follows: We refer to each typed storage location allocated for the executing program as an *abstract location*. We provide a dependency graph pointer field for each top-level abstract location l, the address of which is obtained by *nodeptr*(l). This address is *nil* if l does not represent top-level storage. Procedures are mapped into dependency graph nodes with pointer field, the address of which is returned by *tableptr*(p), where p is an Alphonse procedure. *tableptr*(p) evaluates to *nil* if the procedure is not cached or maintained. The expression *ref*(n) gives a pointer back to the corresponding abstract location or procedure represented by dependency graph node n.

Dependencies are dynamically recorded as follows. A stack, *CallStack*, stores the graph nodes of currently executing Alphonse procedures. *top*(*CallStack*) is the graph node representing the most recently called incremental procedure instance, and is *nil* at other times when no such procedures are executing. Upon a call to an incremental procedure instance p, p's dependency graph node is pushed on *CallStack*, and is removed upon the completion of p.

At the point of call to an Alphonse procedure p' or a reference to nonlocal storage s, a check is made to *top*(*CallStack*) to see if an Alphonse procedure is currently executing. If the stack is not *nil* it will contain a graph node v representing this procedure. Let u be the graph node that represents the accessed storage s or called procedure p' (we create u if it does not exist). An edge is then added from u to v. Note that p is dependent upon storage s that is *written* as well as read—should s be rewritten in the future, a subsequent execution of p must have the effect of setting it back.

If p has been executed previously, it has a set of dependent edges from Alphonse procedures and storage locations that were accessed during the previous execution. These edges (contained in the *pred*(v) set) are removed before subsequent executions. Thus, the dependency graph contains a snapshot of all dependencies that influenced the result of the most recent computation of the Maintained portion of the program.

4.4 Change

Change in the Alphonse computation must be accurately tracked, since quiescence propagation assumes that previous results of procedures are still valid if their input did not change. The set of storage changes that could potentially affect the computation are those that have been accessed (directly or transitively) by Alphonse procedures. By the dependency graph construction above, each of these variables will have an associated dependency graph node. We therefore check *nodeptr*(v) $\uparrow$ upon every operation that writes a variable v that is potentially accessible to Alphonse procedures. If *nodeptr*(v) $\uparrow=$ *nil* (or *node*(v) $=$ *nil* if v happens not to be top-level), program execution proceeds in the conventional manner. Otherwise, if *node*(v) $\uparrow= u$, the procedures represented by *succ*(u) could perform operations that are different from their previous executions. If the new value of v is different from the previously cached value in *value*(u), u is placed into a global *inconsistent set*.

4.5 Evaluation

Upon subsequent calls to Alphonse procedures, a check is made for dependency graph nodes in the inconsistent set. If this set is not empty, program execution is preempted by the evaluation routine. Inconsistent nodes are removed and processed until the inconsistent set is empty. An element u is processed as follows:

- If u represents a storage location, all elements of *succ*(u) are added to the inconsistent set.
- If u represents a demand incremental procedure instance, if *consistent*(u) is true, then we set it to false and add all elements of *succ*(u) to the inconsistent set.
- If u represents an eager incremental procedure instance p, p is re-executed. If the result value is different from *value*(u), all elements of *succ*(u) are added to the inconsistent set.

The selection of u from the set is done using an algorithm such as [Hud86, Hoo86, Hoo87, AHR$^+$90]. Note that the evaluation routine should be called whenever cycles are available (input/output, etc) and can be preempted when necessary.

5 Transformations

We capture the relevant activities of imperative languages with the following operations:

access(v), where v is an expression that can be resolved to a variable location, returns the value of that variable.

modify(l, v), where l is an expression that can be resolved to a variable location and v is some value, updates l to contain value v.

call($p, a_1, \ldots, a_k$), where p is a procedure or method valued expression with k arguments, returns the result of the procedure.

Program transformations are used to insert these operations into the base language program as follows:

- Each read access to storage l is replaced by *access*(v), if l is top-level (or cannot be statically determined to not be top-level). Pointer dereferencing (including the dereferencing of VAR parameters) counts as a read access to the pointer storage.
- Each assignment to storage l of value v is replaced by *modify*(l, v), if l is top-level (or cannot be statically determined not to be top-level).
- Each non-method procedure call $p(a_1, \ldots, a_k)$ is replaced with *call*($p, a_1, \ldots, a_k$), if p is top-level (or cannot be statically determined not to be top-level).
- Each method call $o.m(a_1, \ldots, a_k)$ is replaced with *call*($o.m, a_1, \ldots, a_k$).

We illustrate this translation here with an example (Algorithm 2). Note that pointers must be accessed twice, once for the pointer once for the location it points to. In addition, observe the difference in treatment in the call to *p2* for a (local), b (top-level), and c (formal parameter).

We transform the program further by replacing each *access*, *modify*, and *call* operation by the code template shown in Algorithms 3, 4, and 5 respectively. The transformation can be done either at the compiler level, or by using a source to source translation. The *nodeptr* and *tableptr* fields can either be generated by a modified compiler, or alternatively at the expense of a level of indirection, additional transformations can be used to change each variable type into a record structure with two fields, one for the real storage location, the other for the dependency graph node

```
PROCEDURE p1(c: INTEGER): INTEGER=
    BEGIN
      FOR a:=1 TO 10 DO
        p↑ := p2(a+b+c, y↑)
      END;
      RETURN p↑
    END
becomes:
  PROCEDURE p1(c: INTEGER): INTEGER=
    BEGIN
      FOR a:=1 TO 10 DO
        modify(access(p), call(p2,
          a+access(b)+c, access(access(y))))
      END;
      RETURN access(access(p))
    END
```

Algorithm 2: Transformed Program

```
access(v) →
  IF nodeptr(v) ≠ NIL THEN
    IF top(CallStack) ≠ NIL THEN
      IF nodeptr(v)↑ = NIL THEN
        nodeptr(v)↑ := NEW(DepGraph);
        ref(nodeptr(v)↑) := v
      END;
      CreateEdge(top(CallStack), nodeptr(v)↑)
    END
  END;
  RETURN v
```

Algorithm 3: Access Transformation

access pointer. Likewise, the code for *access*, *modify*, and *call* can be emitted directly by the code generator, or they can encoded as procedures, customized for each variable type and procedure signature.

The result of this algorithm is the dynamic construction and maintenance of a dependency graph for program P.

Theorem 5.1 *Given an Alphonse program P, Alphonse execution of P will produce the same output as a conventional execution of P.*

Proof: If the Alphonse execution of P produces different output from a conventional execution of P, then either:

1. At some point in the Alphonse execution there exists a *first* expression $e = x$ whose value is different than the expression $x', x \neq x'$ computed in the conventional execution, or

```
modify(l, v) →
  access(l); l := v;
  IF nodeptr(l) ≠ NIL THEN
    IF nodeptr(l)↑ ≠ NIL THEN
      IF value(nodeptr(l)↑) ≠ v THEN
        SetAdd(Inconsistent, nodeptr(l)↑)
      END
    END
  END;
```

Algorithm 4: Modify Transformation

```
call(p, a_1, ..., a_k) →
  IF tableptr(p) = NIL THEN RETURN p(a_1, ... a_k) END;
  IF tableptr(p)↑ = NIL THEN
    tableptr(p)↑ := NEW(ArgTable)
  END;
  n := TableFind(tableptr(p)↑, ⟨a_1, ..., a_k⟩);
  IF n = NIL THEN
    n := TableAdd(tableptr(p)↑, ⟨a_1, ..., a_k⟩);
    ref(n) := p; consistent(n) := FALSE
  ELSE
    IF SetSize(Inconsistent) > 0 THEN
      Evaluate(Inconsistent)
    END
  END;
  IF top(CallStack) ≠ NIL THEN
    CreateEdge(top(CallStack), n)
  END;
  IF consistent(n) THEN RETURN value(n)
  ELSE
    RemovePredEdges(n); StackPush(CallStack, n);
    consistent(n) := TRUE ; retval := p(a_1, ... a_k);
    value(n) := retval; StackPop(CallStack);
    RETURN retval
  END;
```

Algorithm 5: Call Transformation

2. The Alphonse execution produced a program anomaly (e.g. infinite loop, run time exception, etc.) that the conventional execution did not (or vice versa).

Case 1: Expression e must be the result of a procedure call or a memory read, since Alphonse affects only procedure calls, memory reads, and memory writes. Say e is a procedure call p. If p was executed upon the evaluation of e and returned a value x, than either restriction DET has been violated, or there was a prior expression that evaluated differently prior to e. If, instead, x was the cached value for p, restriction TOP and the inconsistent marking of the Alphonse algorithm insure that all subexpressions computed by p were consistent and the above holds as well.

Assume e is a read of abstract memory location l containing the value x. The Alphonse execution must have either (a) failed to write x' to l, or (b) caused some spurious write to set l to be x.

Case 1a: Since the only statements that Alphonse avoids are incremental procedure executions whose referenced arguments are consistent, the write to l must be in an Alphonse procedure call p that had been executed previously. DET requires p to have written l in the prior execution if a second execution of p would write l. Thus, l must have been overwritten by some other assignment. However, l is in $R(p)$, l would be marked inconsistent, and p would have been re-executed.

Case 1b: The write to l must have been caused by the execution of an incremental procedure p. Demand procedures are only executed when called (thus the conventional execution would also write l), and the writing of l by an eager procedure violates OBS.

Case 2: Either the (missing) program anomaly must be in an avoided Alphonse procedure (like case 1a), or the (extra) program anomaly was introduced by an Alphonse procedure (like case 1b). ∎

6 Optimizations

There are a number of optimizations that are necessary to facilitate the efficient application of dynamic dependence analysis in conjunction with imperative programs. We discuss these techniques in this section.

6.1 Limiting Runtime Checks

Each access, modify, and call operation, as expanded in Section 5, performs several checks to determine whether or not a variable or procedure is involved in an Alphonse computation. The uniform application of these tests would result in a substantial performance decrease. We use dataflow analysis to identify the many variables and procedures where the results of these tests are statically known. These optimizations are of vital importance for embedded applications, as much of the computation will be independent of the Maintained portion and should not be penalized by the Alphonse overhead.

6.2 Static Graph Construction

Production based incremental systems, such as attribute grammar systems, have low dependency graph manipulation overhead due to statically computed dependency subgraphs for each production. The dependency graph is inferred from the composition of these subgraphs dictated by the production interconnectivity.

As the referenced argument set for many Alphonse procedures is static, the compiler could generate a similar subgraph. Our dependency graph structure can be extended to allow this representation.

6.3 Graph Partitioning

With eager quiescence propagation, one does not blindly keep the dependency graph consistent after every change. Unless extra CPU cycles are available, the set of inconsistent nodes accumulates. This delay allows multiple changes to be batched and re-evaluated together. If, upon the call to an Alphonse procedure, this set is not empty, we must suspend the caller and force propagation.

However, the inconsistencies represented in the inconsistent set do not necessarily affect the requested value. In some cases, if the dependency graph is not fully connected, this value may not even be dependent upon the changes. To avoid waiting in this case, we maintain the dependency graph as a set of unconnected components, each representing a separate instance of quiescence propagation.

The first division is achieved using static analysis. First, we construct a *connectivity graph* of types declared by the program. Each type t is represented by a node $C(t)$, and directed edges are added from nodes $C(t_1)$ to $C(t_2)$ if t_1 has a pointer field that can point to an object of type t_2. Second, we augment this graph nodes $C(p)$ for each procedure call site p that could be an incremental procedure instance. Edges are then added from $C(p)$ to $C(t)$ for each type t that could be potentially accessed by p.

The resulting connectivity graph is separated into disconnected components. Upon the creation of a new dependency graph node for a top-level variable or incremental procedure, it is statically placed in a dependency graph partition based upon the location of the representative node in this division.[6]

A further refinement is possible using a dynamic analysis. For each of the above dependency graph partitions, we keep disjoint sets of unconnected nodes using the union/find algorithm [AHU74]. New dependency graph nodes are placed in their own unique set. Upon adding an edge from x to y, we perform a union between the sets that contain x and y.

The result of this analysis is many small dependency graphs, each with their own inconsistent set. This will decrease the likelyhood that eager evaluation will be forced due to irrelevant changes and thus will allow more inconsistencies to be batched.

6.4 Reducing the Argument Set

The programmer sometimes has semantic knowledge that is not derivable by the system, but can be utilized to improve the efficiency of the computation. This is manifested in Alphonse by referenced arguments of a procedure that the programmer knows cannot affect the value of the computation.

For example, consider a lookup procedure in a balanced search tree, where the programmer can often show that the lookup is dependent upon the found item, but not dependent upon the log(n) *access* operations needed to locate it. We provide an additional pragma, ⟨*UNCHECKED*⟩, to allow this knowledge to be specified on an expression basis, eliminating these dependencies from the Alphonse computation.

7 Examples

We illustrate the power of Alphonse programming with three examples.

7.1 Attribute Grammars

In this section, we show how all attribute grammars can be represented as Alphonse data types. We also give an example of this translation.

Attribute grammars [Knu68] are defined in terms of a context free grammar. For each nonterminal in a given production, equations are used to define attributes as a function of other attributes of other nonterminals of the production.

$$\mathrm{N}_0 ::= \mathrm{N}_1 \ldots \mathrm{N}_n$$
$$\mathrm{N}_{n_0}.a_0 = f(\mathrm{N}_{n_1}.a_1, \ldots, \mathrm{N}_{n_k}.a_k)$$

There are two types of attributes. Attributes defined for left hand side nonterminals (N_0) are *synthesized*. Attributes defined for right hand side nonterminals ($\mathrm{N}_1 \ldots \mathrm{N}_n$) are *inherited*.

We represent each production P in the grammar with an object type T, which we name after the left hand side nonterminal. This type contains:

- A pointer to the parent production,
- Pointers to objects of the types representing each right hand side nonterminal $p(\mathrm{N}_i)$,
- Fields representing the values of right hand side terminal symbols, and

[6] It is possible that static pointer analysis techniques [LH88, Hen90, CWZ90] might make this analysis less conservative.

```
ROOT ::= EXP
  ROOT.value = EXP.value
  EXP.env = EmptyEnv()

EXP0 ::= EXP1 '+' EXP2
  EXP0.value = EXP1.value+EXP2.value
  EXP1.env = EXP0.env
  EXP2.env = EXP0.env

EXP0 ::= 'let' ID '=' EXP1 'in' EXP2 'ni'
  EXP0.value = EXP2.value
  EXP1.env = EXP0.env
  EXP2.env = UpdateEnv(EXP0.env,ID,EXP1.value)

EXP ::= ID
  EXP.value = LookupEnv(EXP.env,ID)

EXP ::= INT
  EXP.value = INT
```

Algorithm 6: AG Expression Trees

- Methods implementing all attribute equations in production P.

A dynamically allocated instance O of type T represents a production instance generated by the grammar.

To complete the construction, we must show how to construct the attribute equations. We directly translate each equation into an imperative procedure, replacing each attribute reference $(\mathrm{N}_{n_i}.a_i)$ by a method call to the method $O.p(\mathrm{N}_i).a_i()$. Synthesized attribute equations are represented by methods with no arguments,[7] implemented by this procedure.

Inherited attributes, however, require us to determine the context of the right hand nonterminal inheriting the value. Say N is a nonterminal appearing one or more times on the right hand side of production P. We represent all attribute equations for $\mathrm{N}.a$ in a single method with one argument. The object representing the right hand side production is passed as the argument and a case analysis is done to determine the appropriate context of N. Each arm of this case analysis contains the code for the given nonterminal context.

The above translation is illustrated by the attribute grammar example shown in Algorithm 6. We assume a representation of environments[8] with *EmptyEnv*, *UpdateEnv*, and *LookupEnv* operations.

The result of the translation is as follows. First, we assume integers for our value type *Val*, and assume *Env*, a translation of the environment type and related operations that were unspecified in the attribute grammar. Productions *Prod* are objects with a production parent. An expression production *Exp* is a production with maintained methods for value *value*() and environment *env*(). As described above, the inherited attribute *env* is translated into a method with a single argument to distinguish the nonterminal context. These basic types are illustrated in Algorithm 7.

Each production is then written as a subtype of *Exp*, adding right hand side nonterminals and terminals as well as overriding the *value*() and *env*() methods. These types are shown in Algorithm 8 and the method implementations

[7] Other than the object O.

[8] That is, a keyed set of ⟨identifier,value⟩ pairs.

```
TYPE Val = INTEGER;
TYPE Env = ...;

TYPE Prod = OBJECT parent : Prod; END;

TYPE Exp = Prod OBJECT
  METHODS
    <*MAINTAINED*> value() : Val;
    <*MAINTAINED*> env(c : Exp) : Env;
END;
```

Algorithm 7: Basic Types

```
TYPE RootExp = Exp OBJECT exp : Exp;
  OVERRIDES
    <*MAINTAINED*> value := ExpVal;
    <*MAINTAINED*> env := NullEnv;
END;

TYPE PlusExp = Exp OBJECT exp1, exp2 : Exp;
  OVERRIDES
    <*MAINTAINED*> value := SumVal;
    <*MAINTAINED*> env := PassEnv;
END;

TYPE LetExp = Exp OBJECT
    exp1, exp2 : Exp;
    id : TEXT;
  OVERRIDES
    <*MAINTAINED*> value := Exp2Val;
    <*MAINTAINED*> env := LetEnv;
END;

TYPE IdExp = Exp OBJECT id : TEXT;
  OVERRIDES <*MAINTAINED*> value := IdVal;
END;

TYPE IntExp = Exp OBJECT int : INTEGER;
  OVERRIDES <*MAINTAINED*> value := IntVal;
END;
```

Algorithm 8: Types for Productions

are given in Algorithm 9. Note that the procedure *LetEnv* illustrates the technique for encoding inherited attributes for a given nonterminal context.

7.2 Spreadsheet

We can extend the previous attribute grammar into a spreadsheet as follows. First, we define a Cell object consisting of an expression tree of type Exp (from Section 7.1), and a maintained method value that simply returns the value of the expression tree. An array of Cell objects represents the spreadsheet.

In order to allow the cell functions to reference the values of other cells, we add a CellExp production to our expression trees. This production uses two integer valued terminal fields to select another cell in the array and return the result of its value method. The program for this is shown in Algorithm 10. Note that this example shows the use of top-level data references and illustrates how one Alphonse program can be used to construct another.

```
PROCEDURE ExpVal(o : Exp) : Val =
  BEGIN RETURN o.exp.value() END ExpVal;

PROCEDURE NullEnv(o,c : Exp) : Env =
  BEGIN RETURN EmptyEnv() END NullEnv;

PROCEDURE SumVal(o : PlusExp) : Val =
  BEGIN
    RETURN o.exp1.value()+o.exp2.value()
  END SumVal;

PROCEDURE PassEnv(o,c : Exp) : Env =
  BEGIN RETURN o.parent.env(o) END PassEnv;

PROCEDURE Exp2Val(o : PlusExp) : Val =
  BEGIN RETURN o.exp2.value() END Exp2Val;

PROCEDURE LetEnv(o,c : Exp) : Env =
  BEGIN
    IF c=o.expl THEN RETURN o.parent.env(o)
    ELSE RETURN UpdateEnv(o.parent.env(o),
                 id,o.expl.value())
    END
  END LetEnv;

PROCEDURE IdVal(o : IdExp) : Val =
  BEGIN
    RETURN LookupEnv(o.parent.env(o),id)
  END IdVal;

PROCEDURE IntVal(o : IntExp) : Val =
  BEGIN RETURN o.int END IntVal;
```

Algorithm 9: Method Implementations

```
TYPE Cell = OBJECT func : Exp;
  METHODS (*MAINTAINED*) value() := ExpVal;
END;

PROCEDURE ExpVal(o : Cell) : Val =
  BEGIN RETURN o.exp.value() END ExpVal;

cells : ARRAY [1..100], [1..100] of Cell;

TYPE CellExp = Exp OBJECT x,y : INTEGER;
  OVERRIDES (*MAINTAINED*) value := CellVal;
END;

PROCEDURE CellVal(o : CellExp) : Val =
  BEGIN RETURN cells[o.x,o.y].value() END CellVal;
```

Algorithm 10: Spreadsheet

7.3 Dynamic Data Structures

Another powerful use of Alphonse is the construction of *dynamic data structures*. For example, a balanced search tree insertion routine can be thought of as an algorithm that takes a balanced tree and produces a new balanced tree containing the added element. Of course, an efficient insertion algorithm will produce *incrementally* only the changes necessary to derive the output from the input. These changes are then applied to the input structure. In this section, we illustrate how Alphonse can be used to implement dynamic data structures by showing a simple implementation of AVL binary search trees [AVL62, HS82]. (AVL trees are balanced binary trees where, for every node x, the height of the children of x differs by at most one.)

We begin by extending the *Tree* data type of Algorithm 1 with an additional maintained method, *balance*, resulting in the *Avl* data type shown in Algorithm 11. As in the *Tree* data type, a special subtype is used to represent missing leaf pointers—*balance* here simply returns the object. For interior nodes, however, the *balance* method performs the tree rotations necessary to balance the subtree (according to the AVL definition). Thus, balance on the tree root will result in a balanced tree.

Not shown, are procedures for lookup, insert, and delete. However, since the data structure is self balancing, these operations are exactly the same as for an *unbalanced* binary tree. The programmer is simply required to call the *balance* method prior to performing a search operation, in order to insure that the tree is balanced and guarantee $O(\log n)$ behavior.

Note that the recursion in *Balance* admits to the possibility of multiple changes. Thus, the algorithm allows arbitrary operations (e.g. splitting, joining, subtree insertion) as well as multiple change operations between each tree balancing. The programmer simply must ensure that the structure is in fact a tree and the nodes are ordered as required. Thus, the algorithm is both an *off-line* as well as *on-line* algorithm.

Theorem 7.1 *Algorithm 11 is an Alphonse program.*

Proof: We need to show that Algorithm 11 obeys the restrictions of Section 3.5.

DET There is no static local storage nor any nondeterministic language constructs used in the program.

TOP All procedures are top-level and no local storage is passed via pointer or VAR parameters.

OBS *Balance* is the only Alphonse procedure that causes side effects, namely the tree rotations. Since these rotations preserve the tree order, tree searches will return the same result regardless of when *Balance* is executed. We must also show that the enclosing program uses AVL trees only for searching and does not have behavior that depends upon the structure of the tree (height, relative node positions, etc.).

∎

8 Implementation

We are currently building an implementation of Alphonse–Modula-3, using source to source translation: The program

```
TYPE Avl = Tree OBJECT
  METHODS (*MAINTAINED*) balance := Balance;
END;

TYPE AvlNil = Avl OBJECT
  OVERRIDES
    (*MAINTAINED*) height := HeightNil;
    (*MAINTAINED*) balance := BalanceNil;
END;

PROCEDURE Balance(t : Avl) : Avl =
  BEGIN
    t.left := t.left.balance();
    t.right := t.right.balance();
    IF Diff(t) > 1 THEN
      IF Diff(t) = 2 AND Diff(t.left) = -1 THEN
        t.left := RotateLeft(t.left)
      END;
      t := RotateRight(t).balance()
    ELSIF Diff(t) < -1 THEN
      IF Diff(t) = -2 AND Diff(t.right) = 1 THEN
        t.right := RotateRight(t.right)
      END;
      t := RotateLeft(t).balance()
    END;
    RETURN t
  END Balance;

PROCEDURE BalanceNil(t : Avl) : Avl =
  BEGIN RETURN t END BalanceNil;

PROCEDURE Diff(t : Avl) : INTEGER=
  BEGIN
    RETURN t.left.height()-t.right.height()
  END Diff;

PROCEDURE RotateRight(t : Avl) : Avl =
  VAR s,b : Avl;
  BEGIN
    s := t.left; b := s.right; s.right := t; t.left := b;
    RETURN s
  END RotateRight;

PROCEDURE RotateLeft(t : Avl) : Avl =
  VAR s,b : Avl;
  BEGIN
    s := t.right; b := s.left; s.left := t; t.right := b;
    RETURN s
  END RotateLeft;
```

Algorithm 11: AVL Trees

is parsed and an abstract syntax tree is generated containing nodes for the Alphonse pragmas. Program transformations are then applied to the tree to insert the *call*, *access*, and *modify* operations as described in Section 5, while removing the Alphonse pragmas. Unparsing the syntax tree will then yield a pure Modula-3 program containing the code fragments of Section 5 and references to evaluation routines contained in an auxiliary module. We are also considering a second implementation in an object oriented database system.

9 Analysis

There are two ways to compare the resources required by an Alphonse program A to those required by conventional programs. We can either compare the space and time required by A to the time and space required by an equivalent program to A designed to run efficiently in the conventional model, or we could compare A to the time and space required by a conventional execution of A.

Making concrete statements about a comparison of A to an equivalent efficient conventional program is difficult, as there is nothing to limit the programmer from constructing a program that uses all of the applicable Alphonse techniques as well as other techniques that apply only to the problem at hand. Alphonse is not designed to compete with programmers willing to embed detailed caching strategies in their code. Alphonse is for programmers who seek the efficiency of incremental computation, but are unwilling to embrace the high cost of incremental programming. Instead, we must examine each application and ask how A relates to the program that the programmer would be likely to write.

Consider the example from Algorithm 1. When faced with the problem of maintaining the height at each node, an ambitious programmer might create a height field in each node, and upon each pointer change in the tree, travel to the root of the tree updating all pointers on the path. While this is roughly what the Alphonse program A would do (and is what the dependencies dictate), A would have the advantage of:

- Batching the computations spurred by each change,
- Performing the batched operations together to avoid duplicate updates at nodes that are ancestors of multiple changes, and
- Computing the updates with different threads of control to utilize computing cycles available before the next request for the height of a node.

While the programmer could choose to add any of these items to the competing code, the result would be substantial complication and the increased opportunity for errors. The Alphonse program A yields these benefits safely.

The cost of executing A is made up of the cost of the dynamic translation plus the cost of performing the incremental evaluation. We will refer the reader to the appropriate literature for the cost of applying the underlying incremental techniques [Rep84, Hud86, Hoo86, Hoo87, AHR+90], and focus on the costs of translating the algorithm into the incremental intermediate form. Thus, we consider the time and space required by the dynamic dependence analysis (Section 4) as compared to the time and space required to run the program under the conventional execution model.

9.1 Space

Let M be the maximum amount space required by an Alphonse program when executing under the conventional (that is, non-incremental) execution model. We analyze the space needed in terms of M.

We require space for the call stack of incremental procedure instances, as well as space for the dependency graph, both nodes and edges. The procedures on the call stack are a subset of the conventional procedure call stack, and therefore require $O(M)$ space. Dependency graph nodes (and *node* pointers) are required for top-level variables and incremental procedure instances. If we assume a constant sized cache for each cached procedure, this too can be stored in $O(M)$ space.

The edges of the dependency graph, however, could require $O(M^2)$ space if dependencies between top-level variables and incremental procedure instances grows dense. While it is easy to exhibit this behavior (each Alphonse procedure scans $O(M)$ data, it is our experience that such dense dependence is not encountered in applications that can benefit from incremental computation. In the $O(M^2)$ case, essentially every part of the computation is dependent upon the entire computation. Thus, every change will trigger the re-execution of $O(M)$ incrementally maintained procedures resulting in zero speedup with incremental evaluation.

In many Alphonse applications, the Alphonse procedures have constant sized referenced argument sets, and thus an $O(M)$ space requirement. Maintaining properties that perform search operations in balanced trees would require $O(M \log M)$ space, but this could be reduced to $O(M)$ space usage through the use of the techniques of Section 6.4.

9.2 Time

Let T be the time required to execute an Alphonse algorithm under the conventional, non-incremental execution model. We argue that dynamic dependence analysis can be performed in $O(T)$.

If we assume that object creation is a constant time operation, then clearly, creation of dependency graph nodes upon the first access to a top-level variable or incrementally maintained procedure does not add to asymptotic running time of the program. Likewise, since individual edges are added upon the access of data, the creation of edges falls within this bound.

We must show, however, that the edge removal at procedure calls in Algorithm 5 is constant time per edge. This is the case if we use a doubly linked list of bidirectional edges to represent successors and predecessors in the dependency graph. Thus, the $O(1)$ cost of removing each edge can be charged to the edge creation.

If the dynamic dependency graph partitioning algorithm of Section 6.3 is used, the time bound is slightly increased to $O(T \times G(M))$, where $G()$ is the inverse Ackermann's function. We expect the actual performance of the algorithm to be substantially faster than $O(T)$, due to the performance gains of incremental computation. The exact performance, of course, will depend upon the amount of computation reuse with the programmers partitioning of the problem into incrementally maintained procedures.

10 Related Research

The major goal of Alphonse is to improve the construction, understanding, and correctness of incremental algorithms by automatically generating much of the intricate algorithm detail. RAPTS [Pai86] is another program transformation system with a similar goal. However, our approaches are quite different. RAPTS uses a specification terms of high level abstract operations such as set manipulation. This program is transformed into an efficient implementation through the automatic substitution of efficient precanned low level algorithms for these abstract operations. In contrast, the focus of Alphonse is on the construction of such low level algorithms, which are impossible to efficiently write in RAPTS.

Alphonse is much closer in spirit with other *automatic incremental systems*, which generate incremental implementations that automatically perform the bookkeeping necessary to track change and dependence. Such systems include attribute grammar systems such as the Synthesizer Generator [RT88], the graph grammar system of [Kap86], the message passing framework of [DRZ85], as well as the boxes and cables method of [ACR+88] and its implementation in the Cactis object oriented database system [HK89]. We briefly describe Alphonse's advantages and contributions over these systems.

Most of these systems are based upon grammars, which place practical limitations upon their applicability in many applications. In addition, grammar based systems suffer from the local communication and aggregation problems [RMT86, Hoo86, Hoo87]. The specification languages used by the above systems tend to be somewhat unusual, and the runtime environment imposes additional limitations (i.e. the Synthesizer Generator uses an editing paradigm, Cactis, a database paradigm). As a result, it is difficult to embed their programs inside conventional ones.

When compared to other incremental systems, Alphonse has the following advantages:

- Alphonse subsumes grammar based languages (see Section 7.1).
- The language is a familiar one, especially for object-oriented programmers.
- It is not limited to local communication. Incrementally maintained procedures are allowed to look at global information and navigate arbitrary data structures. This ability also side steps the aggregation problem.
- It uses the conventional compile/execute runtime environment.
- Incremental subproblems can be embedded inside arbitrary programs with a consistent, procedure call and data structure interface.

While it is beyond the scope of this paper, the dynamic dependence information gathered by Alphonse can also be used for additional advantage, such as in debugging and scheduling parallel execution.

11 Conclusions

The Alphonse system presents a powerful new programming technique. Through the use of *dynamic analysis* and the integration of quiescence propagation and *function caching*, it advances the automatic specification of incremental algorithms. It is systems of this type that will deliver the benefits of incremental computation to the general purpose programming community.

I would like to thank John Field, Martin Odersky, Tom Marlowe, and Dan Yellin for invaluable conversations that helped to shape Alphonse.

References

[ACR+88] B. Alpern, A. Carle, B. Rosen, P. Sweeney, and K. Zadeck. Graph attribution as a specification paradigm. In *Proceedings of the ACM SIGSOFT/SIGPLAN Software Engineering Symposium on Practical Software Development Environments*, pages 121–129, Boston, Massachusetts, November 1988.

[AHR+90] B. Alpern, R. Hoover, B. Rosen, P. Sweeney, and K. Zadeck. Incremental evaluation of computational circuits. In *Proceedings of the First Annual ACM-SIAM Symposium on Discrete Algorithms*, pages 32–42, San Francisco, California, January 1990.

[AHU74] A. Aho, J. Hopcroft, and J. Ullman. *The Design and Analysis of Computer Algorithms.* Addison-Wesley, Reading, Massachusetts, 1974.

[AVL62] G. Adel'son-Velskii and Y. Landis. An algorithm for the organization of information. *Dokl. Akad. Nauk SSSR*, 146:263–266, 1962. English translation in *Soviet Math. Dokl.* 3, pp. 1259–1262.

[CWZ90] D. Chase, M. Wegman, and F.K. Zadeck. Analysis of pointers and structures. In *Proceedings of the SIGPLAN '88 Conference on Programming Language Design and Implementation*, pages 296–310, White Plains, New York, June 1990.

[DRZ85] A. Demers, A. Rogers, and F. Zadeck. Attribute propagation by message passing. In *Proceedings of the ACM SIGPLAN '85 Symposium on Language Issues in Programming Environments*, pages 43–59, Seattle, Washington, June 1985.

[Hen90] L. Hendren. *Parallelizing Programs with Recursive Data Structures.* PhD thesis, Cornell University, Ithaca, New York, April 1990.

[HK89] S. Hudson and R. King. Cactis: A self-adaptive, concurrent implementation of an object-oriented database management system. *ACM Transactions on Database Systems*, 14(3):291–321, September 1989.

[Hoo86] R. Hoover. Dynamically bypassing copy rule chains in attribute grammars. In *Proceedings of the Thirteenth Annual ACM Symposium on Principles of Programming Languages*, pages 14–25, St. Petersburg, Florida, January 1986.

[Hoo87] R. Hoover. *Incremental Graph Evaluation.* PhD thesis, Cornell University, Ithaca, New York, May 1987.

[HS82] E. Horowitz and S. Sahni. *Fundamentals of Data Structures.* Computer Science Press, Rockville, Maryland, 1982.

[Hud86] S. Hudson. *A User Interface Management System Which Supports Direct Manipulation.* PhD thesis, University of Colorado, August 1986.

[Kap86] S. Kaplan. Incremental attribute evaluation on graphs. Technical Report UIUC-DCS-86-1309, University of Illinois, Urbana-Champaign, Illinois, December 1986.

[Kar49] A. Karr. Les Guêpes, Janvier 1849. Plus ça change, plus c'est la même chose.

[Knu68] D. Knuth. Semantics of context-free languages. *Mathematical Systems Theory*, 2(2):127–145, June 1968.

[LH88] J. Larus and P. Hilfinger. Restructuring lisp programs for concurrent execution. In *Proceedings of the ACM/SIGPLAN Parallel Programming: Experience with Applications, Languages and Systems*, pages 100–110, New Haven, Connecticut, July 1988.

[Nel91] G. Nelson, editor. *Systems Programming with Modula-3.* Prentice-Hall, Englewood Cliffs, New Jersey, 1991.

[Pai86] R. Paige. Programming with invariants. *IEEE Software*, 3(1):56–69, January 1986.

[PT89] W. Pugh and T. Teitelbaum. Incremental computation via function caching. In *Proceedings of the Sixteenth Annual ACM Symposium on Principles of Programming Languages*, pages 315–328, Austin, Texas, January 1989.

[Pug88] W. Pugh. *Incremental Computation and the Incremental Evaluation of Function Programs.* PhD thesis, Cornell University, Ithaca, New York, August 1988.

[Rep84] T. Reps. *Generating Language-based Environment.* MIT Press, Cambridge, Massachusetts, 1984.

[RMT86] T. Reps, C. Marceau, and T. Teitelbaum. Remote attribute updating for language-based editors. In *Proceedings of the Thirteenth Annual ACM Symposium on Principles of Programming Languages*, pages 1–13, St. Petersburg, Florida, January 1986.

[RT88] T. Reps and T. Teitelbaum. *The Synthesizer Generator.* Springer-Verlag, Berlin, Heidelberg, New York, 1988.

[Yeh83] D. Yeh. On incremental evaluation of ordered attributed grammars. *BIT*, 23:308–320, 1983.

Compiler Support for Garbage Collection in a Statically Typed Language*

Amer Diwan *Eliot Moss* *Richard Hudson* †

Object Systems Laboratory
Department of Computer Science
University of Massachusetts
Amherst, MA 01003

Abstract

We consider the problem of supporting compacting garbage collection in the presence of modern compiler optimizations. Since our collector may move any heap object, it must accurately locate, follow, and update all pointers and values derived from pointers. To assist the collector, we extend the compiler to emit tables describing live pointers, and values derived from pointers, at each program location where collection may occur. Significant results include identification of a number of problems posed by optimizations, solutions to those problems, a working compiler, and experimental data concerning table sizes, table compression, and time overhead of decoding tables during collection. While gc support can affect the code produced, our sample programs show no significant changes, the table sizes are a modest fraction of the size of the optimized code, and stack tracing is a small fraction of total gc time. Since the compiler enhancements are also modest, we conclude that the approach is practical.

1 Introduction

As part of ongoing efforts to implement orthogonal persistence [1] and garbage collection for Modula-3 [2], we have designed and implemented compiler techniques to assist the garbage collector and the persistent memory manager. Our work has been done in the context of Modula-3, but is applicable to other statically typed languages.[1] In the remainder of this section we describe the requirements we had to meet to support garbage collection in our context.

*This project is supported by National Science Foundation Grant CCR-8658074, Digital Equipment Corporation, Apple Computer, and GTE Laboratories.

†The authors can be reached electronically via Internet addresses {diwan,moss,hudson}@cs.umass.edu.

[1] The Modula-3 type system allows some dynamism, but type safety of all constructs (except those permitted only in UNSAFE modules) can be checked at compile time.

ACM SIGPLAN '92 PLDI-6/92/CA
© 1992 ACM 0-89791-476-7/92/0006/0273...$1.50

With regards to persistence, our scheme must allow objects to be moved, and possibly removed from main memory altogether, for buffer management [3, 4] purposes. Moreover, since orthogonality allows *any* object to become persistent, *all* objects need to be movable. This requirement is also essential for fully compacting garbage collection (cf. [5, 6]), which yields good locality and fast object allocation time.

Portability to a wide variety of hardware and software platforms is one of the key goals for Persistent Modula-3. Therefore our scheme must not rely on any special hardware support (such as hardware pointer tags).

Our scheme must have minimal impact on run-time performance. Our work is being done in the context of a highly-optimizing compiler.[2] Thus we must not defeat or disallow any compiler optimizations. This is a challenge since the compiler and optimizer are not bound by the rules of the source language and may introduce complex pointer manipulations. We also want to avoid tagging objects except when explicitly required by the language.

In a statically typed language, the compiler knows which global variables contain pointers. It also knows which stack locations and registers contain pointers at any point in a program. In the following sections we describe a technique that exploits this compile-time knowledge to assist the garbage collector in locating and updating pointers in the stack and in the registers, and at the same time meets our requirements: the ability to move objects, portability, and minimal impact on performance. After describing the scheme, we present some experimental results.

2 Basic Problems

Unambiguous full copying collection (cf. [8, 5, 6]) must be able to determine if an object is reachable from other live objects or from the roots. Moreover, the garbage collector must be able to find all pointers to a given object so that they may be updated when the object is moved. These requirements translate to a number of low level requirements on the collector: (i) it must be able to determine the size of heap allocated objects, so that they can be copied; (ii) it must be

[2] Our compiler is based on gcc 2.0 and uses its optimizer [7].

able to locate pointers contained in heap objects, so they they can be both traced and updated; (iii) it must be able to locate pointers in global variables; (iv) it must be able to find all references in the stack and in the registers at any point in the program at which collection may occur; (v) it must be able to find objects that are referred to by values created as a result of pointer arithmetic; (vi) and it must be able to update these values when the objects involved are moved.

Modula-3 requires type descriptors in heap objects which makes it straightforward to determine the size of heap allocated objects and to find pointers within them. Thus it is easy to trace the heap. Since Modula-3 is a statically typed language, compile-time location of pointers in global variables is also simple. Locating pointers in the stack and in registers is more difficult, because the stack layout and register assignments may vary even within a procedure. We must also be able to handle compiler temporaries containing pointers, in the stack and in registers.

Updating and following pointers is complicated if pointers do not always point directly to objects. We say a pointer is *tidy* if it points at the object header (or some standard fixed offset from the header). Untidy pointers may be introduced by language features or by compiler optimizations. In Modula-3, pointers to the interior of objects are created by the `VAR` parameter passing mechanism, by the `WITH` statement, and by `SUBARRAY` expressions. Here are examples of optimizations that create untidy pointers:[3]

Strength Reduction: The body

```
A[i] := 13;
INC (i);
```

of an array initialization loop can be turned into `*p++ = 13`, with `p` appropriately initialized.

Virtual Array Origin: If `A` is an array of type `ARRAY [7..13] OF INTEGER`, the obvious method of accessing `A[i]` is:
`*(&A[7] + (i - 7) * sizeof (int))`
The subtraction can be avoided by creating an (untidy) pointer to `A[0]` and using it to index into the array.

Common Subexpression Elimination: The code

```
A[i,j] := 10;
A[i,k] := 20;
```

may be compiled into

```
t = &A[i];
*(t + j * sizeof (int)) = 10;
*(t + k * sizeof (int)) = 20;
```

if the optimizer can determine that `t` is being computed twice and that `i` is not updated.

[3]In our examples we present source code in Modula-3 and compiler/optimizer output in C. Note, though, that our Modula-3 compiler generates assembly code.

Double Indexing: The code

```
A[i] := 1;
B[i] := 2;
```

may be optimized to

```
t1 = &A[0] + (i * sizeof(int));
t2 = &B[0] - &A[0];
*t1 = 1;
*(t1 + t2) = 2;
```

which is useful on machines that have addressing modes with two or more index registers, such as the SPARC.

We use the term *derived value* for any value created by pointer arithmetic, and the term *base value* for any value participating in the derivation. Note that a derived value may be an untidy pointer to the interior of an object (strength reduction example), an untidy pointer that points outside the object to which it refers (virtual array origin example), or even a non-pointer value (double indexing example), and the examples given above may not exhaust the possibilities. In Section 3, we describe a scheme that handles a broad class of pointer arithmetic, which includes all optimizations performed by `gcc`.

3 Solutions

We construct tables at compile time to assist the collector in locating and updating all pointers in the stack and in the registers. We construct one set of tables per *gc-point*. A gc-point is a program point where a collection might occur.[4] An alternative is to use tags or type descriptors in the stack. We decided against tagging stack allocated objects because the stack layout is relatively static, and thus amenable to tabular description, and stack frames are created and destroyed at a high rate, so the overhead of maintaining any kind of descriptors in the stack is likely to be unacceptable.

We construct three kinds of tables for each gc-point in a procedure: *stack pointers*, *register pointers*, and *derivations*. The stack pointers table encodes the locations in the procedure's stack frame that contain live tidy pointers at the gc-point. Likewise, the register pointers table encodes the registers that contain live tidy pointers at that gc-point. The derivations table describes the derivation of all derived values live at the gc-point. In this section we concentrate on the conceptual contents and usage of the tables, and defer consideration of implementation issues to Section 5.

At garbage collection time, the first task is to locate the tables for each frame on the stack. This is done by extracting return addresses from frames and using them to search a table that maps gc-points to gc tables. We can use the stack pointers table directly. Using the register pointers table requires additional information about which registers were

[4]We give details on choosing these points in Section 5.

a →

Base Location	Relation
b1	+
b2	−
b3	+

Figure 1: Derivations table for a at program point p

saved at each call point, so that the register contents can be reconstructed as of the time of the call.

The derivations tables are needed for updating derived values when their base values change. At each gc-point, each live derived location is associated with a table that describes its derivation at that point. For example, Figure 1 shows the derivation table for a variable whose value is derived as:

```
a := b1 + b3 - b2 + E
```

where E is some integer expression that does not use pointers or derived values.

There are two steps to updating the derived values. The first step occurs immediately after all the tables have been located. In this step, the value of E is calculated and stored in a. To calculate E we adjust a by applying the inverse operation for each base value of a:

```
a := a - b1 - b3 + b2
```

Note that the order in which derived values are updated is crucial: a derived value must be updated *before* any of its base values. Thus, if a base value is a derived value itself, then its value must be adjusted *after* that of any values derived from it and *before* any values from which it is derived. We take two measures to ensure this ordering. First, we visit the derivations table of a callee before that of its caller. Second, the derivations tables for a given gc-point are ordered such that the derivations table of a derived value comes before the derivations tables of its base values. Note that circular dependencies cannot occur because derivations are always made from previously calculated base values.

The second step of the update occurs after garbage collection has completed. Its purpose is to reconstruct the derived values from the updated bases. This step uses the new base values to re-derive a. In the above example the new values of b1 and b3 are added to a while that of b2 is subtracted. Once again the order in which updates occur is important; a value needs to be updated before any values derived from it. This order is exactly the reverse of that required in the previous step.

We have made two assumptions in the design of the derivations table. First, we assume that the base values are live whenever values derived from them are live. This is necessary for us to be able to update the derived values. In Section 4 we show how we ensure this property. As a side effect of this requirement, we never need to follow derived values to find reachable objects. This is because we require the lifetime of a base value to include that of its derived values. Hence, any object reachable via a derived value is also reachable via a non-derived value. Second, we assume that the operations used in the derivation (+ and − in this example) have inverses. Invertibility allows us to use the technique outlined above to adjust a derived value if one (or more) of its base values change as a result of collection. In the above example, invertibility allowed us to update a given only the base values; no information about E was needed. Our current implementation handles two kinds of operations in a derivation (+ and −),[5] but it can easily be extended to handle other invertible operations as well. Thus, we currently handle all deriving expressions of the form:

$$\sum_i p_i - \sum_j q_j + E$$

where p_i and q_i are pointers or derived values, and E does not involve either pointers or derived values. To handle non-commutative operations, we would need to be careful about the order of the base values in the table for each derivation. To handle non-invertible operations the tables would have to be redesigned to allow the entire deriving expression to be recomputed at run time.

4 Some Complications

The job of the compiler would be simple if it could correctly, statically, and unambiguously identify the base values for each derived value at any given point in the program. Unfortunately, this is not the case for at least three scenarios: (i) when a base value dies before a value derived from it, (ii) when multiple derivations of a value reach a gc-point, and (iii) when indirect references are used as base values in a derivation. In this section we describe each of these problems and present our solutions to them.

The following example illustrates the *Dead Base* problem:

SOURCE

```
A: REF ARRAY [1..10] OF INTEGER;
FOR i := 1 TO LAST (A^) DO
  s := s + A^[i];
END;
```

OPTIMIZED

```
for (i = 1; i <= 10; i++) {
  s = s + *A++;
    <gc-point>
}
```

[5] These are the only operations exploited by the gcc optimizer.

If data flow analysis can determine that `A` is dead after the loop, then the compiler may use `A` to efficiently step through the array. In this code, `A`'s base value (the original value of `A`) is not available to the collector inside the loop. Hence, if collection is triggered at `gc-point` then the collector will be unable to update `A`.

We solve this problem by making our compiler consider a use of a derived value as a use of each of its base values.[6] This forces the compiler to retain the base values for the lifetime of the values derived from them. While this can affect performance by increasing the lifetime of variables, which in turn can increases register pressure, we try to minimize its impact by careful selection of base values. When multiple copies of a base value are available, we give preference to stack allocated base values over register allocated ones (to reduce register pressure), and to values in user declared variables over values in compiler temporaries (to shorten temporary lifetimes).

The problem of *Ambiguous Derivations* occurs when multiple derivations of a derived value reach a program point. This is illustrated in the following example:

SOURCE

```
i := 1;
WHILE (cond)
  IF (inv) THEN
    PRINT (P[i]);
  ELSE
    PRINT (Q[i]);
  END;
  INC (i);
END;
```

OPTIMIZED

```
i = 1;
if (inv)
  t = &P[0] + 1;
else
  t = &Q[0] + 1;
while (cond)
  PRINT (*(t + i++));
```

If `inv` is invariant in the loop, the optimizer may hoist the conditional out of the loop causing `t`'s derivation to be ambiguous inside the loop; `t` is derived from either `&P[0]` or `&Q[0]`.

We solve this problem by introducing *path variables* for each ambiguously derived value. The path variable encodes which one of the possible derivations actually happened. The following code segment illustrates it for the example above:

[6] We need to do this only if the derived value is live at some later gc-point.

```
i = 1;
if (inv) {
    t' = <path 1 taken>
    t = &P[0] + 1;
}
else {
    t' = <path 2 taken>
    t = &Q[0] + 1;
}
while (cond)
  PRINT (*(t + i++));
```

When our compiler detects an ambiguous derivation, it emits tables for each possible derivation; the appropriate derivations table is chosen at run time based on the value of the path variable.

An alternative solution to the ambiguous derivations problem is to use *Path Splitting* similar to Chambers and Ungar [9]. Figure 2 demonstrates this technique. In Figure 2, the body of the loop is duplicated such that the derivation of `t` in each copy of the loop body is unambiguous.

Currently we use the path variable scheme to disambiguate derivations. Both solutions have overheads. The path variable technique adds assignments to the program; the path splitting technique increases the code size and is also more complicated than the path variable scheme. We selected the path variable scheme because it is simpler and we believe ambiguous derivations are rare, and thus the run-time overhead is not significant.

The problem of *Indirect References* occurs when the location of a base value is not known at compile time. This can happen if the base value is obtained by an indirect reference.

SOURCE

```
a:  REF ARRAY [1..5] OF
      REF ARRAY [5..9] OF INTEGER;
foo (a^[2]^[6]);
```

COMPILED

```
foo ( *(a + sizeof (int))
       + sizeof (int))
```

In the example, if the parameter to `foo` is passed by reference, then the expression pushed on the stack is derived from the value in memory location `a + sizeof (int)`. Hence, we cannot determine the location of the base value at compile time. We solve this problem by preserving the intermediate reference in a stack slot or register, thus causing the derivation to refer to a value in a compile-time known location. Indirect references pose a problem only for machines with complicated addressing modes. We expect that this problem will not arise for load/store architectures.

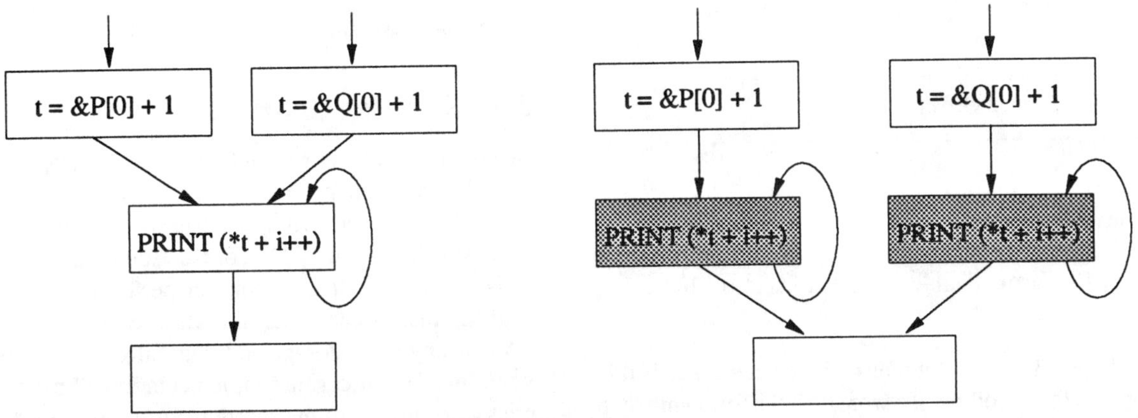

Figure 2: Disambiguating derivations by path splitting

5 Implementation Issues

The organization of the tables and the selection of gc-points might have a significant impact on the performance of our scheme. The tables should be as small as possible but at the same time the collector must be able to extract the information it needs efficiently; compactly encoded tables are likely to have higher decoding overhead. Since tables are emitted at each gc-point, the number of gc-points affects the space overhead of our scheme. Selection of gc-points is especially relevant in a pre-emptive multi-threaded environment. Since a thread switch can occur at any time, we must be prepared to handle a collection when a thread is not at a gc-point. In Sections 5.1, 5.2, and 5.3, we survey some possible solutions to these concerns and justify the choices we have made.

5.1 Table Organization

Storing a list of all live tidy pointers in the stack at each gc-point in a procedure is likely to be expensive. We expect that the variation in stack layout at different gc-points is usually small and thus we consider using *delta* tables at gc-points. A delta table encodes how the information at a given gc-point differs from the information in some other table (called its *ground* table). Our implementation uses a scheme called *δ-main*.

In the *δ-main* scheme, each procedure has a *main* table which describes all slots in the frame of that procedure that contain pointers at some gc-point. Given this, a delta table merely describes which entries of the main table are valid at the gc-point. Since the delta table needs to contain only liveness information, only one bit per entry in the main table is needed per gc-point.

Our current implementation uses the *δ-main* main scheme for stack allocated non-derived pointers only. The registers table has 1 bit per hard register; any attempt to compact this information further is likely to yield little or no improvement. We do not use a delta scheme for the derivations table because in our experience derived values are rare; moreover, they tend to have short lifetimes and thus the information varies

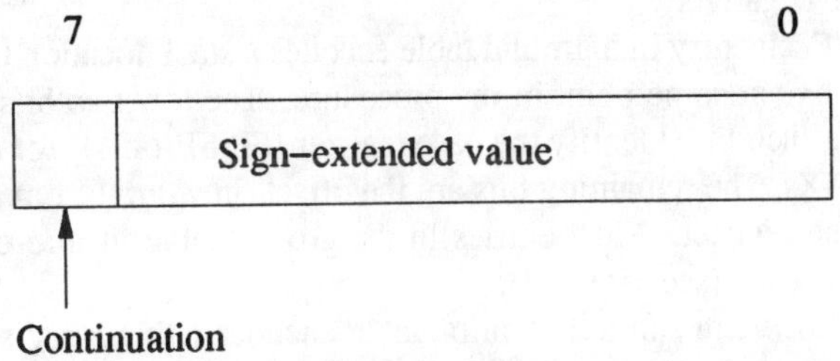

Figure 3: Packing words into bytes.

widely between gc-points. For instance, an important source of derived values in Modula-3 is call-by-reference, which creates derived values that are live at only one gc-point (the call). We therefore store full information for derived values at each gc-point.

In our measurements we observed that delta and registers tables for adjacent gc-points are often identical. Also, many registers tables, many delta tables, and most derivations tables are empty. We keep a descriptor at each gc-point which indicates if any of the tables at that gc-point are empty, or if they are identical to the table at the preceding gc-point.

5.2 Compressing the tables

Despite the compact representation provided by the *δ-main* scheme, we found that the tables were unacceptably large: about 45% of the size of optimized code (see Section 6.1). In this section, we describe the packing techniques that we use to reduce the table sizes to about 16% of the optimized code size.

The stack tracing tables are generated in two phases. The first phase produces tables of 32 bit words. Each memory location is encoded into a word, and the delta tables and register pointers tables occupy an integral number of words.[7] The second phase goes through the table of words and packs

[7] The number of words used for a delta or a register pointers table depends on either the number of entries in the ground table or the number of hard registers.

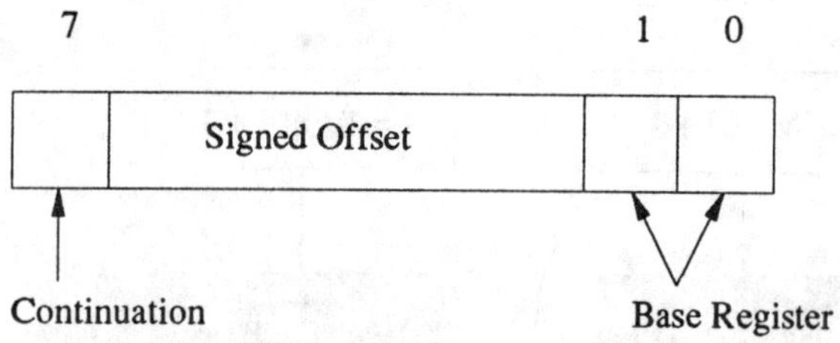

Figure 4: A ground table entry that fits into 1 byte.

them into bytes. The high bit of each byte determines if it is the last byte in the encoding of a word or if the following byte is also part of the word (see Figure 3). The bytes are stored from most- to least-significant, and the first byte is sign-extended, since many offset (and hence many word values) are negative.

Each entry in a ground table encodes a stack location that is live at some point in the procedure. The low two bits of the encoding identify the base register (FP, SP, or AP, for the VAX). The remaining bits are the offset (in words) from the base register. Most entries in the ground table fit into one byte each (see Figure 4).

Each entry in a derivation table encodes either a register or a memory location. This encoding is more involved than that of the ground table because entries in this table are not restricted to {FP, SP, AP} $\pm$ offset. Thus, most entries in the derivations table require 2 bytes.

The register pointers table contains 1 bit per hard register; most of these tables compact to 1 or 2 bytes each. The delta table contains 1 bit per entry in the ground table. Most of our procedures had fewer than 8 stack allocated pointers, allowing most delta tables to be compressed to 1 byte. Besides the above mentioned tables, we have a descriptor at each gc-point that encodes whether any of the tables at the current gc-point are empty or are identical to those at the previous gc-point. This information packs into 1 byte per gc-point.

At each gc-point we find the appropriate tables by using a mapping from program counter values to gc tables. We compress this by using distances between gc-points in conjunction with the start address of the enclosing module, instead of using 32 bits for the program counter value at each gc-point. The distances are not available until link time; our compiler assumes that distances between adjacent gc points can fit in two bytes. If the distances had been available to our compiler, we would have been able to compress most distances to 1 byte, yielding an additional savings of 1 byte per gc-point.

There is one important consideration that our current implementation does not handle: each pointer contained in an array is treated as a separate variable. We have no way of indicating patterns (e.g., starting from address a, the next 200 stack location are pointers). We have a design for compact descriptions of arrays, and it will be simple to add it to the implementation. Our benchmarks did not use any such arrays, so adding this space optimization would not affect the result we report here.

5.3 Selecting GC-Points

Selecting gc-points in a single threaded environment is easy: all calls can be considered gc-points since all allocation is done via a call and hence collection will never be triggered at a non-call point.[8] Of course, some calls do not need to be gc-points. If the compiler performs inter-procedural analysis then it can determine that some procedures never allocate any heap storage and thus calls to them need not be gc-points. In our current implementation all calls except for ones to *non-allocating* procedures are considered gc-points. The non-allocating procedures are statically determined (for instance run-time error reporting routines) rather than via inter-procedural analysis. We may explore refinements in future work.

Selecting gc-points in a multi-threaded environment with pre-emptive scheduling is more challenging since collection may be triggered while threads are suspended at non-gc-points. In our approach, if a thread triggers collection then the suspended threads that are not at gc-points are resumed and allowed to run until they all reach gc-points. We accomplish this by ensuring that resumed threads reach (and block on) a gc-point in a bounded amount of time, and that they do not do any allocations. Ensuring that a resumed thread does not allocate any memory before it reaches a gc-point requires that most calls be gc-points. To avoid an unbounded wait for threads to become ready for collection, we insert a gc-point in all loops that do not have a *guaranteed gc-point* in them. A loop has a guaranteed gc-point if an allocating-procedure or a nested loop is executed at each iteration of the loop, regardless of the path taken through loop. In addition to gc-points at calls and in loops, we need gc-points at places where a thread can block.[9]

6 Results

This paper is not about a fast garbage collection technique. It is about how garbage collection can be assisted by compile-time acquisition of information, and have minimum impact on compiler optimizations. As such, our results are not timings for the garbage collector; they are measurements of the sizes of the compile-time tables generated, the effect our schemes have on compiler optimizations, and the time required to decode the generated tables. In Section 6.1 we give the table sizes for each of our benchmarks, in Section 6.2 we describe the effects of our scheme on the quality of generated code , and in Section 6.3 we report the time required to decode the tables at garbage collection time.

[8] This will not work if allocation is done inline, in which case we must include inline allocations as gc-points.

[9] In most systems these points are call points so they do not need special treatment.

6.1 Table Sizes

We measured table sizes for 4 Modula-3 programs: `typereg`, `FieldList` [10], `takl` [11] and `destroy` [12]. `typereg` implements type registration and type comparisons using structural equivalence for our Modula-3 run-time system. `FieldList` implements command parsing for a UNIX shell. We considered `typereg` and `FieldList` to be good programs to use for our measurements for two reasons. First, they are "real" programs rather than synthetic benchmarks. Second, they consist of a number of short routines with frequent calls. Since we consider most calls as gc-points, we felt that this would represent a worst case scenario. We chose `takl` because it is a well known benchmark. We chose `destroy` because it is heavily recursive and triggers garbage collection frequently, and thus stresses the code that decodes the tables at garbage collection time.

In Table 6.1 we list relevant data about each of the benchmark programs. (The `-opt` suffix indicates that compiler optimizations were turned on.) In Table 6.1 we give the corresponding table sizes, under both the full information and the *δ-main* schemes, with and without each of byte and identical-to-previous compression. Here is the key for interpreting the columns of these tables:

Size Program size in bytes.

NGC Number of gc-points that had non-empty tables.

NPTRS Total number of pointers.

NDEL Number of delta tables emitted.

NREG Number of register pointers tables emitted.

NDER Number of derivations tables emitted.

Plain Table sizes as a percentage of *code size* with no compression.

Previous Table sizes as a percentage of *code size* when a descriptor is used to indicate that a table is identical to that at the previous gc-point.

Packing Table sizes as a percentage of *code size* when byte level packing is used.

PP Table sizes as a percentage of *code size* when both *Previous* and *Packing* are used.

None of our benchmarks had any ambiguous derivations and therefore the compiler introduced no path variables.

From Table 6.1 it can be seen that storing full information at each gc-point (with packing) generally produces larger tables than those produced by *δ-main* (with packing). However the difference is not great. *δ-main* is based on the assumption that procedures have many non-empty gc-points and many live stack allocated pointers at each gc-point. If this is not the case, then storing full information at each gc-point can yield table sizes comparable to *δ-main* without the extra run-time decoding overhead of *δ-main*. However, our measurements indicate that the run-time overhead of decoding these tables is small, so there is little practical benefit to storing full information at each gc-point (see Section 6.3).

For the *δ-main* scheme, both *Packing* and *Previous* tend to reduce table sizes. Applying both *Packing* and *Previous* reduces the table size from about 45% of the size of the optimized code to about 16%.

6.2 Effects on the optimized code

Our schemes have no effect on the *optimized code* produced for any of our benchmarks. There are, however, some instructions introduced in the *unoptimized code.* Most of the differences result from needing to preserve indirect references at gc-points. There are 12 cases where this occurs in `typereg` for the VAX and 32 cases in `FieldList` for the VAX; here is a typical case:

Without gc restrictions

```
addl2 (r7),r0
```

With gc restrictions

```
movl (r7),r1
addl2 r1,r0
```

Our solution to the dead base pointer problem adds two moves to the unoptimized `FieldList`; both are inserted to preserve a clobbered base value.

Note that gc-safety, as proposed by Boehm[10] [13], encounters the same requirement, so this is a basic safety concern rather than a result of our approach. Also, this particular code effect is not likely to occur on load/store architectures.

Compiler support for garbage collection may have other effects on the generated code besides the ones described above. In particular, most generational schemes perform *store checks* [14] when pointers might be written into heap locations. This is a property of the garbage collection scheme[11] and therefore we do not "charge" this overhead to our scheme.

6.3 Timings

While good compression of the gc tables is important for our scheme to be practical, the time to decode those tables must also be reasonable. We do not yet have a complete implementation of the garbage collection run-time, but we have an initial version of stack tracing which we timed on the `destroy` benchmark. `destroy` builds a complete tree of specified branching factor and depth. It then repeatedly builds a new subtree at some fixed intermediate depth, and

[10] Actually, Boehm does not appear to have recognized the indirect reference problem in the work we cite above. He focused on situations that extend the lifetime of a derived pointer but did not address cases where the lifetime of a base pointer might be shortened, e.g., by its being overwritten in the heap.

[11] For instance, page traps could be used instead of store checks to implement generational schemes.

Program	Size	NGC	NPTRS	NDEL	NREG	NDER
typereg	3154	59	87	58	26	3
typereg-opt	2289	52	122	39	41	0
FieldList	4594	51	103	45	18	11
FieldList-opt	3330	82	319	61	70	11
takl	457	8	11	8	6	0
takl-opt	437	9	18	6	9	0
destroy	1240	12	14	11	2	0
destroy-opt	552	14	18	4	13	0

Table 1: Statistics of each of the benchmark programs

	Full Info		δ-*main*			
Program	Plain	Packing	Plain	Previous	Packing	PP
typereg	45.5	14.3	35.0	28.2	12.3	10.6
typereg-opt	51.4	17.2	41.6	35.5	16.0	14.0
FieldList	30.3	11.1	16.4	14.8	6.1	5.6
FieldList-opt	64.7	22.9	53.0	47.6	20.8	18.7
takl	51.6	17.9	41.1	34.1	16.0	14.2
takl-opt	55.8	19.7	43.9	37.5	17.6	15.6
destroy	17.1	5.9	17.1	15.2	6.6	6.1
destroy-opt	46.4	17.4	42.8	38.4	18.1	16.5

Table 2: Table sizes as a percentage of code size

replaces a randomly chosen subtree of the same height with the new subtree. We ran `destroy` in our Smalltalk system, which uses the accurate scavenging scheme [15] we plan to install in the Modula-3 run-time. We found that collections averaged 280 ms of elapsed time. We coded the benchmark in Modula-3 as similarly as possible, and caused "collections" at approximately the same points. To determine stack tracing costs, we ran two versions of the Modula-3 program, one with "collection" being a stack trace, the other with "collection" being a null call, and calculated stack tracing to take 470 μs per collection. However, the difference between the runs was small, and the variance significant even with many repetitions in a system running in single-user mode, so the 90% confidence limit is that stack tracing takes less than 1710 μs per collection for this program. The corresponding numbers per stack frame traced are 27 μs and 98 μs, respectively. We ran these tests on a VAXStation 3500, which is generally rated at 3 to 5 VAX MIPS, suggesting that our current code executes on the order of 100 to 400 VAX instructions per frame traced. We believe we can tighten this up measurably.

Whether one uses the 470 μs per collection figure or the 1710 μs one, there are two additional factors to take into account in comparing stack tracing overhead with overall gc time. First, the `destroy` benchmark is unusually gc intensive. Programs that create a lot of objects, but where most do not survive to the next collection, exhibit something like five times lower gc cost. Also, a Modula-3 collector may be faster than a Smalltalk collector since for Modula-3 we can generate type-specific routines for tracing heap objects, and avoid Smalltalk's object and pointer decoding overhead. We will be generous and allow a factor of two speed up for Modula-3, though we doubt the advantage is really that great. Thus, in less gc-intensive Modula-3 programs, we estimate the ratio of stack tracing time to total gc time to be less than 1710/28000 = 6% (470/28000 = 1.7%). We conclude that stack tracing overhead is only a small part of gc time, even in a high performance scavenging collector.

7 Related Work

Algol-68 implementations were the first to produce compiler generated routines to assist in garbage collection. In the Branquart and Lewi scheme [16], tables are produced that map stack locations to the appropriate garbage collection routine. Unlike our scheme, these tables have to be updated every time a reference to the heap is created on the stack.

Goldberg's compiler [17] produces stack tracing routines. The return address in a call is used to locate a routine that knows how to trace the frame of the caller. His work is not done in the context of an optimizing compiler and thus he does not address many of the issues we handle.

Boehm [13, 18] is currently incorporating garbage collection support in a C compiler. He is using an ambiguous roots collector and his main concern is ensuring that all live objects have at least one pointer to their headers (i.e., there are no live objects that are reachable only from derived values). This problem is similar to our dead base pointer and indirect references scenarios described in Section 4. Since he never moves objects he does not need to deal with the issues in updating derived values.

Exception handling implementations in CLU, Trellis, and Modula-3 also use compiler generated tables. In our Modula-3 implementation [19] tables are generated for each point where an exception may be raised. The tables contain the addresses of handlers for the exceptions that can be raised at that point.

Zurawski and Johnson [20] emit compile-time tables to allow them to construct the unoptimized state of the program from the optimized state. Like us, they have to deal with the effects of pointer arithmetic introduced by the optimizer. Their focus, however, is on debugging; some optimizations are disallowed to make debugging possible. There is a general similarity between the simpler kinds of information we need for garbage collection and what is needed for symbolic debugging in the presence of optimization. Debuggers do not need to update values or handle the derived value cases that we do, however.

8 Conclusions

We have described and evaluated compiler techniques for supporting fully compacting garbage collection in a statically typed language. We started with the following requirements: the ability to move any object, portability, and low run-time overhead. We met these requirements by making extensive use of the information available to the compiler. While we are not the first to recognize the availability of the compile-time information, we believe that we are the first to exploit it so thoroughly in a *highly optimizing compiler*.

9 Acknowledgements

Tony Hosking provided us with garbage collection measurements from the UMass Smalltalk system. We would also like to thank Chuck Lins for his extensive comments on a draft of the paper.

References

[1] M. Atkinson, K. Chisolm, and P. Cockshott, "PS-Algol: an Algol with a persistent heap," *ACM SIGPLAN Not.*, vol. 17, pp. 24–31, July 1982.

[2] G. Nelson, ed., *Systems Programming in Modula-3*. New Jersey: Prentice Hall, 1991.

[3] J. E. B. Moss, "Implementing persistence for an object oriented language," COINS Technical Report 87-69, University of Massachusetts, Amherst, MA 01003, Sept. 1987.

[4] A. L. Hosking, "Main memory management for persistence," Oct. 1991. Position paper for OOPSLA '91 Workshop on Garbage Collection.

[5] J. F. Bartlett, "Compacting garbage collection with ambiguous roots," Research Report 88/2, Western Research Laboratory, Digital Equipment Corporation, Feb. 1988.

[6] J. F. Bartlett, "Mostly-copying garbage collection picks up generations and C++," Technical Note TN-12, Western Research Laboratory, Digital Equipment Corporation, Palo Alto, CA 94301, Oct. 1989.

[7] R. M. Stallman, *GCC*. Free Software Foundation, Cambridge, MA.

[8] H.-J. Boehm and M. Weiser, "Garbage collection in an uncooperative environment," *Software: Practice and Experience*, vol. 18, pp. 807–820, Sept. 1988.

[9] C. Chambers and D. Ungar, "Making pure object oriented languages practical," in *Proceedings of the Conference on Object-Oriented Programming Systems, Languages, and Applications*, (Phoenix, Arizona, Oct. 1991), pp. 1–15, *ACM SIGPLAN Not. 26*, 11 (Nov. 1991).

[10] S. Harbison. Personal Communication, 1992.

[11] R. P. Gabriel, *Performance and Evaluation of Lisp Systems*. Cambridge, MA: MIT Press, 1985.

[12] A. L. Hosking, J. E. B. Moss, and D. Stefanović, "A comparative performance evaluation of write barrier implementations." Submitted for publication, Feb. 1992.

[13] H.-J. Boehm, "A proposal for GC-safe C compilation," Oct. 1991. Position paper for OOPSLA '91 Workshop on Garbage Collection.

[14] D. Ungar, "Generation scavenging: A non-disruptive high performance storage reclamation algorithm," in *Proceedings of the ACM SIGSOFT/SIGPLAN Software Engineering Symposium on Practical Software Development Environments*, (Pittsburgh, Pennsylvania, Apr. 1984), pp. 157–167, *ACM SIGPLAN Not. 19*, 5 (May 1984).

[15] R. L. Hudson, J. E. B. Moss, A. Diwan, and C. F. Weight, "A language-independent garbage collector toolkit," COINS Technical Report 91-47, University of Massachusetts, Amherst, MA 01003, Sept. 1991. Submitted for publication.

[16] P. Branquart and J. Lewi, "A scheme for storage allocation and garbage collection in Algol-68," in *Algol 68 Implementation* (J. E. L. Peck, ed.), North-Holland Publishing Company, 1971.

[17] B. Goldberg, "Tag-free garbage collection in strongly typed programming languages," in *Proceedings of the ACM SIGPLAN '91 Conference on Programming Language Design and Implementation*, (Toronto, Ontario, Canada, June 1991), pp. 165–176, *ACM SIGPLAN Not. 26*, 6 (June 1991).

[18] H.-J. Boehm, "Personal communication," July 1991.

[19] A. Diwan, "Exception handling in Modula-3." Internal OOS Document, 1990.

[20] L. W. Zurawski and R. E. Johnson, "Debugging optimized code with expected behavior," *ACM Trans. Programming Languages and Systems*, To appear.

Register Allocation for Software Pipelined Loops

B. R. Rau, M. Lee, P. P. Tirumalai, M. S. Schlansker
Hewlett Packard Laboratories
1501 Page Mill Road
Palo Alto, CA 94303

Abstract

Software pipelining is an important instruction scheduling technique for efficiently overlapping successive iterations of loops and executing them in parallel. This paper studies the task of register allocation for software pipelined loops, both with and without hardware features that are specifically aimed at supporting software pipelines. Register allocation for software pipelines presents certain novel problems leading to unconventional solutions, especially in the presence of hardware support. This paper formulates these novel problems and presents a number of alternative solution strategies. These alternatives are comprehensively tested against over one thousand loops to determine the best register allocation strategy, both with and without the hardware support for software pipelining.

Keywords: register allocation, modulo scheduling, software pipelining, instruction scheduling, code generation, instruction-level parallelism, multiple operation issue, VLIW processors, Very Long Instruction Word processors, superscalar processors, pipelining

1 Introduction

1.1 Software pipelining

Software pipelining [5] is a loop scheduling technique which yields highly optimized loop schedules. Algorithms for achieving software pipelining fall into two broad classes:

- modulo scheduling as formulated by Rau and Glaeser [15] and,
- algorithms in which the loop is continuously unrolled and scheduled until a situation is reached which allows the schedule to wrap back on itself without draining the pipelines [13].

Although, to the best of our knowledge, there are no published measurements on this issue, it is our belief that the second class of software pipelining algorithms can cause unacceptably large code size. Consequently, our interest is in modulo scheduling. In general, this is an NP-complete problem and subsequent work has focused on various heuristic strategies for performing modulo scheduling ([9, 11, 12, 10] and the as yet unpublished heuristics in the Cydra 5 compiler [6]). Modulo scheduling of loops with early exits is described by Tirumalai, et al. [19]. Modulo scheduling is applicable to RISC, CISC, superscalar, superpipelined, and VLIW processors, and is useful whenever a processor implementation has parallelism either by having pipelined operations or by allowing multiple operations to be issued per cycle.

ACM SIGPLAN '92 PLDI-6/92/CA
© 1992 ACM 0-89791-476-7/92/0006/0283...$1.50

This paper describes methods for register allocation of modulo scheduled loops that were developed at Cydrome over the period 1984-1988, but which have not as yet been published. These techniques are applicable to VLIW processors such as the Cydra 5 [18]. The processor model supports the initiation of multiple operations in a single cycle where each operation may have latency greater than one cycle. The use of hardware features, that specifically support the efficient execution of modulo scheduled loops, is assumed. These features include rotating register files (register files supporting compiler-managed hardware renaming, which were termed the MultiConnect in the Cydra 5), predicated execution, and the Iteration Control Register (ICR - a boolean register file that holds predicates) [6, 18]. This paper also considers register allocation of modulo scheduled loops on processors having no special support for modulo scheduling.

Our discussion is limited to register allocation following modulo scheduling. Register allocation prior to modulo scheduling places unacceptable constraints on the schedule and, therefore, results in poor performance. Concurrent scheduling and register allocation is preferable, but achieving this, in the context of modulo scheduling, is not understood. This paper does not attempt to describe a complete scheduling-allocation strategy. For instance, little will be said on the important issue of what to do if the number of registers required by the register allocation exceeds the number available. Instead, the focus is on studying the relative performance of various allocation algorithms with respect to the number of registers that they end up using and their computational complexity.

In the rest of this section, we provide a brief overview of certain terms associated with modulo scheduling, descriptions of predicated execution and rotating register files, and of modulo scheduled code structure in the presence of this hardware support. We also examine the nature of the lifetimes that the register allocator must deal with for modulo scheduled loops. Section 2 discusses the various register allocation strategies and code schemas that can be employed, and the interdependencies between them. In the context of these alternatives, the register allocation problem is formulated in Section 3 and the candidate register allocation algorithms are laid out in Section 4. Section 5 describes the experiments performed and examines the data gathered from those experiments, finally, Section 6 states our conclusions.

1.2 A quick overview of modulo scheduling

A **rotating register file** is addressed by adding the register specifier in the instruction to the contents of the Iteration Control Pointer (ICP) modulo the number of registers in the rotating register file. A special loop control operation, brtop, decrements the ICP amongst other actions. As a result of the brtop operation, a register that was previously specified as r_i is specified as r_{i+1}, and a different register now corresponds to the specifier r_i. Lifetimes of a value generated by an operation in one iteration co-exist with the corresponding values generated in previous and subsequent iterations. Newly generated values are written to successive locations in the rotating register file and do not overwrite previously generated values even though exactly the same code is being executed repeatedly. This also introduces the need for the compiler to perform value tracking; the same value, each time it is used, may have to be referred to by a different register specifier depending on the number of brtop operations that lie between that use and the definition [6].

The **Iteration Control Register** file, ICR, is a rotating register file that stores boolean values called predicates. **Predicated execution** allows an operation to be conditionally executed based on the value of the predicate associated with it. For example, the operation

$$a = op(b,c) \text{ if } p_i$$

executes if the predicate p_i is one, and is nullified if p_i is zero. The primary motivation for predicated execution is to achieve effective modulo scheduling of loops containing conditional branches [6, 18]. If-conversion [1] may use predicates to eliminate all branches from the loop body. The resulting branch-free loop body can now be modulo scheduled. In the absence of predicated execution, other techniques must be used which require either multiple versions of code corresponding to the various combinations of branch conditions [7, 13] or restrictions on the extent of overlap between successive iterations [11]. A secondary benefit of predicated execution, the one relevant to this study, is in controlling the filling and draining of the software pipeline in a highly compact form of modulo scheduled code known as kernel-only code.

The number of cycles between the initiation of successive iterations in a modulo schedule is termed the **initiation interval** (II). The schedule for an iteration can be divided into **stages** consisting of II cycles each. The number of stages in one iteration is termed the **stage count** (SC). If the schedule length is SL cycles, the number of stages is given by

$$SC = \left\lceil \frac{SL}{II} \right\rceil .$$

Figure 1 shows the record of execution of five iterations of the modulo scheduled loop with a stage count of 4. The execution of the loop can be divided into three phases: ramp up, steady state, and ramp down. In Figure 1, the first 3*II cycles, when not all stages of the software pipeline execute, constitute the ramp up phase. The steady state portion begins when the fourth and last stage of the first iteration coincides with the first stage of the fourth iteration. During the steady state phase, one iteration completes for every one that starts. The steady state phase ends when the first stage of the last iteration has completed at time 5*II. Thereafter, in the ramp down phase, one iteration completes every II cycles until the execution of the loop completes at time 8*II.

In generating code for a modulo schedule, one can take advantage of the fact that exactly the same pattern of operations is executed in each stage of the steady state portion of the modulo schedule's execution. This behavior is achieved by looping on a piece of code corresponding to one stage of the steady state portion of the record of execution. This code is termed the **kernel**. The record of execution leading up to the steady state is implemented with a piece of code called the **prologue**. The **epilogue**, implements the record of execution following the steady state.

In Figure 1, the number of stages in the prologue and the epilogue are each equal to SC-1. In general, depending on whether or not hardware support is provided, the register allocation strategy employed and the nature of the loop, the number of stages in the prologue and epilogue can be more or less than SC-1. For DO-loops, with hardware support in the form of the rotating register file and predicated execution, it is not necessary to have explicit code for the prologue and the epilogue. Instead a single copy of the kernel is sufficient to execute the entire modulo scheduled loop. This is called **kernel-only** (KO) code. Consider the KO code depicted in Figure 2a. All the operations from the same stage of the same iteration are logically grouped by attaching them to the same predicate. The KO code is repeatedly executed every II cycles. The predicates take on values as shown in Figure 2b. Operations in a stage S_i are executed when the corresponding predicate P_i is one. Five iterations each consisting of four stages are swept out diagonally in Figure 2b. P_0 is the predicate pointed to by the ICP. This predicate is set to 1 by the brtop operation during the ramp up and steady state phases, and is set to 0 during the ramp down phase. Because brtop decrements the ICP, a different physical register P_0 is written into every II cycles. A detailed description of the operation of kernel-only code is provided in [6, 17].

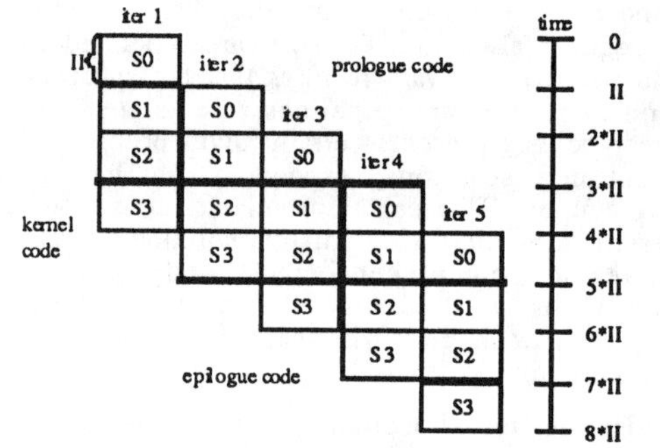

Figure 1. Software pipelined loop execution

1.3 Lifetimes of values within loops

Each value produced in the loop has one producer and one or more consumers. The lifetime of a value starts when the producer is issued and ends when all of the consumers have finished. This definition of lifetime is required if the VLIW code is to be interruptible and re-startable with a hardware model in which operations, that have been issued, always go to completion before the interrupt is handled. Otherwise, the lifetime could start when the producer finishes and end when the last consumer begins.

Lifetimes correspond either to loop-invariant variables or to loop-variant variables. Loop-invariants are repeatedly used but never modified during loop execution. Loop-invariants, which are referenced in the loop, are assumed to have already been allocated in the (non-rotating) GPR file using conventional register allocation techniques. This is not the topic of this paper.

A new value is generated in each iteration for a loop-variant and, consequently, there is a different lifetime corresponding to each iteration. Loop-variants can be further categorized based on whether or not the value defined in one iteration is used in a subsequent one, and on whether or not a value defined in one of the last few iterations is used after the loop. That a loop-variant is used by a subsequent iteration is equivalent to saying that each iteration uses a value defined by a previous iteration. In the case of the first few iterations, these previous iterations do not exist, and the expected values must be generated before the loop is entered and, therefore, are live-in to the loop. Likewise, if a value that is defined in one of the last few iterations is used after the loop, it will be live-out from the loop.

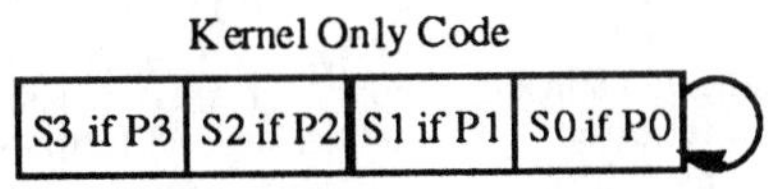

(a)

P3	P2	P1	P0
0	0	0	1
0	0	1	1
0	1	1	1
1	1	1	1
1	1	1	1
1	1	1	0
1	1	0	0
1	0	0	0

Predicate values as controlled by brtop

			S0
		S1	S0
	S2	S1	S0
S3	S2	S1	S0
S3	S2	S1	S0
S3	S2	S1	
S3	S2		
S3			

Stages as enabled by predicates

(b)

Figure 2. Kernel-only code

FORTRAN example

```
subroutine foo(a,s)
real a(10), s
do i = 1,35
   s = s + a(i)
   a(i) = s * s * a(i)
enddo
stop
end
```

Modulo scheduled code

```
time  index  operation
 0    OP0    vr34:-m2read(vr33[1] lit: 0)
13    OP1    vr35:-fadd(vr34 vr35 [1])
15    OP2    vr36:-fmpy(vr35 vr35)
18    OP3    vr37:-fmpy(vr36 vr34)
20    OP4   $vr38:-m1write(vr37 vr33[1] lit: 0)
 0    OP5    vr33:-aladd(vr33[1] vr32)
 0    OP6   $vr39:-brtop(slit: 'L.4-foo')
21    ---    ** schedule for iteration completes **
```

Figure 3. Modulo scheduled loop example

Figure 3 shows a FORTRAN DO-loop example, and the corresponding pseudo-code after scheduling. The latencies of the operations are given in Table 3. The schedule has an initiation interval, II, of 2 cycles. The issue time for each operation is indicated in the left hand column. A single iteration completes in 21 cycles. In the loop shown in Figure 3, virtual register vr32, which is used in the address add (operation OP5), is a loop-invariant. It is allocated to the GPR file and has the value 4 written into it prior to entering the loop. The lifetime corresponding to a loop-invariant such as vr32 extends through all iterations of the loop. Virtual register vr37 is a loop-variant. It represents a new value of a(i) computed in each iteration of the loop. This value is produced by operation OP3 and has only one consumer, operation OP4, which belongs to the same iteration. Virtual register vr35 is also a loop-variant. It is produced by operation OP1 and represents a new value of s computed in each iteration. This value has two consumers, operations OP2 and OP1. Operation OP2 uses the value produced in the same iteration whereas operation OP1 uses the value produced one iteration earlier, indicated by the "[1]" after the vr35 operand. For loop variants like vr35 and vr37, there is a different lifetime corresponding to each iteration.

Recurrences always result in live-in loop-variants, and it is common for the last definition of a loop-variant to be live-out. Furthermore, compiler optimizations that eliminate loads and/or stores can also result in live-in and live-out values. When a load from (store to) a particular memory location in one iteration is followed by a load from that same memory location in a subsequent iteration, the latter load is redundant; the value may be used directly from the register to (from) which it was loaded (stored). The first few iterations require that the appropriate registers be pre-loaded with the proper live-in values prior to loop entry. Likewise, when multiple stores from separate iterations can be proven to access the same memory location, all the stores, except for the last one, are redundant and can be eliminated. This assumes that that last store actually occurs. In the case of the last few iterations, the supposedly redundant store, that was supposed to be covered by a store in a subsequent iteration, is, in fact, not redundant since the iteration containing the covering store is not executed. The last value that should have been stored must be stored after exiting the loop and, so, must be live-out. Such load-store optimizations, of scalar as well as subscripted references, were performed by the Cydra 5 compiler [6, 14] and have also been studied by Callahan, et al. [3].

In the loop example in Figure 3, load/store optimization has been done with respect to s (vr35). In the absence of this optimization, each loop iteration would have contained a load and a store of s. The optimizer recognizes that only the load in the first iteration and the store in the last iteration are required, and that intermediate values can be held in registers. The initial load is moved out of the loop and is executed prior to loop entry establishing the value of s (vr35) for the first iteration. The initial value is, therefore, live-in to the loop. Subsequent iterations use the values generated one iteration earlier (vr35[1]). Correspondingly, the store in the last iteration is moved out of the loop and is executed after loop exit. The value of s calculated in the last iteration is required by this store and, therefore, must be live-out.

After optimization and scheduling, the set of lifetimes corresponding to a single loop-variant is presented to the register allocator as a 4-tuple. Each 4-tuple is of the form (start, end, omega, alpha). The parameters start and end specify, respectively, the issue time of the producer of a value and the latest completion time amongst all the operations that consume that value. Both start and end are expressed relative to the initiation time of the iteration containing the producer. Omega is one less than the highest numbered iteration that uses the value defined by the first iteration, i.e., it is the number of iterations spanned by that value. It is also the number of live-in values for the loop-variant. Alpha specifies the number (counting back) of iterations from the end of the loop in which the earliest live-out value was defined. It is also the number of live-out values for the loop variant. For instance, if alpha = 1, the only live-out value was defined in the last iteration; if alpha = 2, the values of the loop variant defined in the last two iterations are both live-out. Even if we want *only* the value from the second last iteration (and not that from the last iteration), we define alpha to be 2.

The example in Figure 3 has five loop-variants which are shown in Figure 4. The first and the fifth have an omega = 1 indicating that there is one live-in value for each. The live-in value for loop-variant 1 is the initial value of s, and that for loop-variant 5 is the initial address of a(i), i.e., the address of a(1). These two values must be pre-loaded into the appropriate registers prior to loop entry. Loop-variant 1 also has an alpha = 1 indicating that the value computed in the last iteration is live-out . This is the final value of s which must be stored after loop exit.

```
Number of loop invariants = 1
II = 2
five loop variants:

#  Start  End   Omega  Alpha
1  13     16    1      1  <--- vr35 (s)
2  18     20    0      0  <--- vr37
3  15     19    0      0  <--- vr36
4   0     19    0      0  <--- vr34 (a(i))
5   0     22    1      0  <--- vr33 (addr of a(i))
```

Figure 4. Loop-variant lifetimes for the program in Figure 3.

Figure 5 shows a space-time diagram generated by the register allocator for the 35 iterations of the example in Figure 3. The horizontal axis represents time in clock cycles advancing from the far left (cycle 0) to the far right (cycle 89). The vertical axis denotes physical register space. The number of rows in the chart indicates the number of registers used in the achieved allocation. Once a value is generated into a physical register r_i, it occupies that register until the lifetime ends. The same loop-variant produced in the next iteration is generated into physical register r_{i-1} due to the decrementing of the ICP (even though the register specifier used is the same). If r_i is 0, r_{i-1} will be the highest numbered register. As iterations are initiated every II cycles, the start times of these two lifetimes are II cycles apart. This gives rise to the **wand** portion (the diagonal band) of the set of lifetimes for a loop-variant as each iteration yields a lifetime which is lower by one register and to the right by II cycles from the lifetime in the previous iteration. The lifetime generated by the first iteration is shown in boldface. Live-in values, which are pre-loaded prior to loop entry, must remain in the registers until their lifetimes end. This adds a **leading blade** to the wand of recurring values which extends, on the left, all the way through cycle 0. For example, the leading blade for loop-variant 1 occupies register 18 from cycle 0 to cycle 14. Note that the blade lifetime need not always be longer than the wand lifetime. For instance, the leading blade for loop-variant 5, which occupies register 13, is shorter than the lifetime for the first iteration, which is in register 12. This is because for this loop-variant start is less than II. As discussed, the lifetimes of live-out values, which are used after loop exit, must be extended until the loop completes. This adds a **trailing blade** to the wand of recurring values. For example, the trailing blade for loop-variant 1 occupies register 11 from cycles 85 through 89. The thicknesses of the leading and trailing blades depend on the values of omega and alpha, respectively. For example, if loop-variant 1 had omega = 2, the leading blade would include register 19 from cycles 0 through 12 as indicated by the asterisks in Figure 5.

When the possibility for confusion is present, we shall refer to a single lifetime (single live range) as a **scalar lifetime** and to the set of lifetimes corresponding to a loop-variant, across the entire execution of the loop, as a **vector lifetime**. The register allocation problem involves packing these vector lifetimes (wands with or without leading or trailing blades) as tightly as possible in the space-time plane.

2 Code Generation Strategies

For our purposes here, three activities are involved in generating code for modulo scheduled loops: modulo scheduling, register allocation and determining the correct code schema to use. Register allocation is the topic of this paper. However, the manner in which this is done depends both on the presence or absence of rotating register files as well as the code schema used. Any code schema can be assembled from the following components [17], for each of which the corresponding notation is also listed:

- prologue code (P),
- kernel code (K),
- unrolled kernel code (K^n),
- epilogue code (E),
- multiple-epilogue code (E^n),
- a sequential, preconditioning loop (S).

For instance, a specific code schema consisting of a prologue, an unrolled kernel, and multiple epilogues would be denoted by (PK^nE^n) whereas one with a preconditioning loop, a prologue, unrolled kernel, and epilogue would be denoted by (SPK^nE). In the special case when the code schema consists of only the kernel or unrolled kernel code, we add the suffix O (KO, K^nO). We have two schemes for handling the overlapping lifetimes for a loop-variant that are encountered in modulo scheduled code:

- static renaming via modulo variable expansion, (MVE), and
- dynamic remapping via the use of rotating register files (DR).

Lastly, we shall consider two styles of register allocation:

- blades allocation, (BA), and
- wands-only allocation (WO).

```
   000000000011111111112222222222333333333344444444445555555555666666666677777777778888888888
   012345678901234567890123456789012345678901234567890123456789012345678901234567890123456789
  |------------------------------------------------------------------------------------------
 1|                  222 5555555555555555555555511113333344444444444444444444222
 0|44444444444444444444222 5555555555555555555555511113333344444444444444444444222
27|  44444444444444444444222 5555555555555555555555511113333344444444444444444444222
26|    44444444444444444444222 5555555555555555555555511113333344444444444444444444222
25|      44444444444444444444222 5555555555555555555555511113333344444444444444444444222
24|        44444444444444444444222 5555555555555555555555511113333344444444444444444444222
23|          44444444444444444444222 5555555555555555555555511113333344444444444444444444222
22|            44444444444444444444222 5555555555555555555555511113333344444444444444444444
21|              44444444444444444444222 55555555555555555555555111133333
20|                44444444444444444444222 55555555555555555555555111133333
19|*************     44444444444444444444222 55555555555555555555555111133333
18|1111111111111113333344444444444444444444222 55555555555555555555555111133333
17|             11113333344444444444444444444222 55555555555555555555555111133333
16|               11113333344444444444444444444222 55555555555555555555555111133333
15|                 11113333344444444444444444444222 55555555555555555555555111133333
14|                   11113333344444444444444444444222 55555555555555555555555111133333
13|5555555555555555555551111333334444444444444444444422 55555555555555555555555111133333
12|5555555555555555555555511113333344444444444444444444222 55555555555555555555555111133333
11|  5555555555555555555555511113333344444444444444444444222 55555555555555555555555111111111
10|    5555555555555555555555511113333344444444444444444444222 55555555555555555555555
 9|      5555555555555555555555511113333344444444444444444444222 55555555555555555555555
 8|        5555555555555555555555511113333344444444444444444444222 55555555555555555555555
 7|          5555555555555555555555511113333344444444444444444444222 55555555555555555555555
 6|            5555555555555555555555511113333344444444444444444444222 5555555555555555555555
 5|              5555555555555555555555511113333344444444444444444444222
 4|                5555555555555555555555511113333344444444444444444444222
 3|                  5555555555555555555555511113333344444444444444444444222
 2|                    5555555555555555555555511113333344444444444444444444222
  |------------------------------------------------------------------------------------------
   000000000011111111112222222222333333333344444444445555555555666666666677777777778888888888
   012345678901234567890123456789012345678901234567890123456789012345678901234567890123456789

                                          time --->
```

Figure 5. Space-time register allocation chart

All of these are elaborated upon below. The code schema, the renaming scheme and the style of register allocation cannot be selected independently. For instance, wands-only allocation precludes kernel-only code and vice versa, whereas blades allocation is compatible with both the kernel-only schema as well as the PKE schema. Modulo variable expansion always requires kernel unrolling. Furthermore, the choice of code schema is influenced and limited by the nature of the loop (DO-loop or WHILE-loop) and whether predicated execution or rotating register files or both are present [17].

Table 1. Selected combinations of code schema / renaming scheme / register allocation style.

Hardware Features	Register allocation strategy for DO-loops
None	PK^nE^n / MVE / WO
	SPK^nE / MVE + WO
Predicated execution and rotating register files	PKE^n / DR / WO
	PKE / DR / BA
	KO / DR / BA

A **register allocation strategy** is a specific combination of the register allocation style, renaming scheme and code schema. In this paper, we shall only discuss in detail DO-loops with either no hardware support or with both predicated execution and rotating register files. Table 1 lists the legal register allocation strategies under these circumstances. We shall examine three of these in detail:

- KO/DR/BA,
- PKE^n/DR/WO, and
- PK^nE^n/MVE/WO or SPK^nE/MVE/WO.

When there is no risk of confusion, we shall abbreviate and refer to the first two strategies as the BA and WO strategies, respectively, and to both variations of the third one, collectively, as the MVE strategy.

2.1 Code generation with hardware support

With hardware support in the form of rotating register files and predicated execution, it is not necessary to have explicit code for the prologue and the epilogue. Instead a single copy of the kernel is sufficient to execute the entire modulo scheduled loop. This is called **kernel-only** (KO) code (Figure 2). Since the ramp up, steady state and ramp down phases of the loop execution are all effected with the same code, the kernel code, the register allocator for the kernel must take into account all the scalar lifetimes corresponding to a loop-variant, over the complete execution of the loop, i.e., the vector lifetimes, including the blades. It does so by spacing the vector lifetimes adequately far apart in the register file to ensure that no part of one vector lifetime overlaps any part of another (Figure 5). We shall refer to this style of register allocation as **blades allocation** (BA). KO code is attractive in that it is very compact, but there is the possibility that the requisite BA style of allocation requires more registers due to the constraints imposed by the leading and trailing blades. Since, in general, each vector lifetime has a different shape to its blade, it might be expected that the quality of the packing of the vector lifetimes in the space-time plane will be relatively poor.

A second code generation strategy avoids this problem by peeling off an appropriate number of iterations of the kernel at the beginning and end of the loop to form a prologue and epilogue, respectively. The prologue is designed to be long enough that all the non-wand portions of the leading blades are in the prologue, and the epilogue is made long enough that all the non-wand portions of trailing blades are in the epilogue. The amount of prologue peeling to ensure this is

$$LPS = \max\left\{0, \left\lceil \frac{start}{II} \right\rceil - 1\right\}$$

over all loop-variants with omega > 0. Similarly, the amount of epilogue peeling needed to ensure that trailing blades need not be considered during register allocation is

$$LES = \max\left\{0, SC - \left\lfloor \frac{end}{II} \right\rfloor + alpha - 1\right\}$$

over all loop-variants with alpha > 0. (Since the length of the prologues and epilogues are determined solely by the live-in and live-out values, and not by the requirement of achieving a steady-state schedule, this may not correspond to the SC-1 stages shown in Figure 1). The corresponding style of register allocation is termed the **wands-only** (WO) style since blades can be ignored during register allocation for the kernel. The register allocator need only ensure that the wands do not overlap. Register allocation for the prologue and epilogue is done separately, honoring the constraints imposed by the allocation for the kernel. By construction, the prologue and epilogue are long enough to ensure that any conflict with a blade can only occur in the prologue or epilogue where the lifetimes can be re-allocated independently of the way in which the lifetimes for the same loop-variant were allocated in the kernel. However, now that the register assignments in the prologue and epilogue are different, multiple epilogues are needed to handle loop exits from the prologue. One epilogue can no longer serve in all cases since the register assignments are different. Note, also, that the amount of prologue and epilogue peeling given above is sufficient but not necessary to ensure that a register allocator which disregards leading and trailing blades will produce a correct allocation; an inspection of the register assignments *after* register allocation may reveal that less unpeeling is adequate based on the specific way in which the vector lifetimes have been packed. In this study, however, we treat the above formulae as if they are both necessary and sufficient.

2.2 Code generation without hardware support

When no hardware support is available, modulo scheduling can be accomplished by **modulo variable expansion** (MVE), i.e., unrolling the kernel and renaming the multiple copies that now exist of each virtual register definition [11]. The unrolling and renaming is required to prevent successive lifetimes, corresponding to the same loop-variant, from overwriting one another in the same register. Register allocation consists of packing the scalar lifetimes together compactly--a more traditional register allocation task, except that we would expect to see a much larger fraction of lifetimes live across the back-edge than we would with a sequential loop. The minimum degree of unroll, K_{min}, is determined by the longest lifetime among the loop-variants. Because iterations are initiated every II cycles, K_{min} can be calculated as:

$$K_{min} = \underset{i}{MAX}\left(\left\lceil \frac{(end_i - start_i)}{II} \right\rceil\right).$$

By unrolling the kernel more than K_{min} times, there is the possibility that fewer registers might be required in the modulo scheduled code, but at the cost of increasing the generated code size and the compile time of the allocation process. With MVE code, prologue and epilogue peeling of SC-1 stages are required to ramp up and ramp down the software pipeline. In addition to this requirement, live-in and live-out values also impose prologue and epilogue peeling constraints as explained for the WO strategy above. For the MVE renaming scheme, the number of stages of prologue and epilogue are given by

$$PS = \max\{SC\text{-}1, LPS\}, \text{ and}$$
$$ES = \max\{SC\text{-}1, LES\}, \text{ respectively.}$$

As a result the blades may be ignored while performing register allocation for the kernel. We shall refer to this register allocation strategy as the MVE strategy.

```
/*loop precondition code*/
while ((N<(PS+K+ES-SC+1)) or ((N-PS-ES+SC-1) mod K ≠ 0))
   N = N-1
   sequential loop body (stages A,B,C,D)
end while
/*MVE software pipeline code*/
lc = N-1
if lc ≥ 0 then do
   MVE modulo scheduled code
end do
```

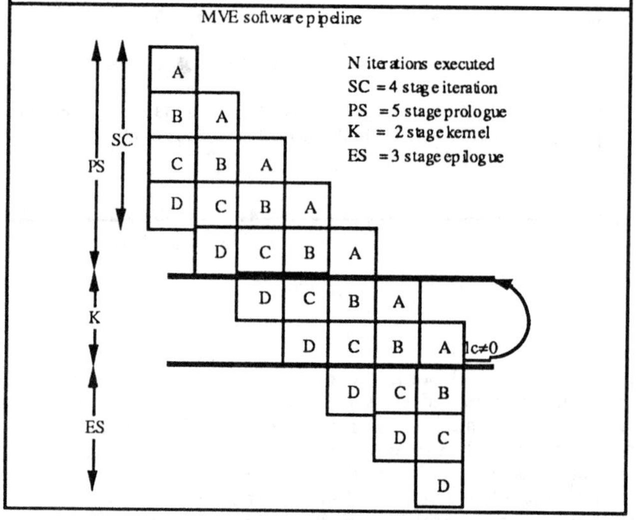

Figure 6. Preconditioned MVE code

With MVE, either additional epilogues or loop preconditioning are required in addition to the prologue, epilogue and unrolled kernel. The software pipelined code can execute only certain integer numbers of iterations. Assume that PS stages are peeled away from the beginning of the loop, ES stages are peeled away from the end of the loop, the kernel is unrolled K times, and the schedule for an iteration has SC stages (Figure 6). The code, as described above, can only execute PS+ES-SC+1+i*K iterations for i ≥ 1 if the only way of exiting the loop is at the end of the last stage of the unrolled kernel.

One code generation schema adds a sequential, non-modulo scheduled version of the loop known as the preconditioning code. The preconditioning code ensures that the pipelined part is entered with an appropriate trip count so that the loop will need to exit only after the last stage of the unrolled kernel. The loop counter, LC, is initialized with this trip count prior to entering the modulo scheduled loop and must be decremented by K each time through the unrolled kernel (every K*II cycles). The iteration of the kernel terminates when LC is 0.

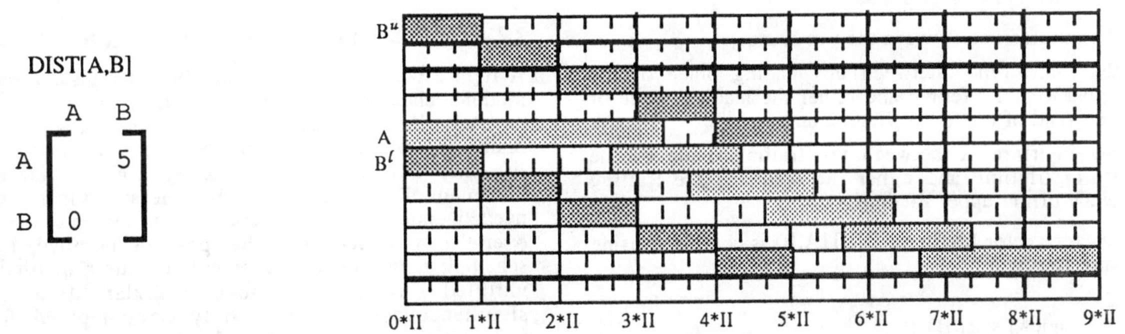

Figure 7. Distance matrix calculation

Preconditioning does not work for WHILE-loops and loops with early exits where the trip count is not known prior to beginning the execution of the loop. Also, it decreases the performance of DO-loops because of the need to process residual iterations serially. This effect is particularly noticeable with short trip counts. Preconditioning can be avoided by placing a branch, which decrements and tests LC, in each stage of the prologue and kernel. The loop is, therefore, exited after the correct number of iterations. However, each of these exit points now requires distinct epilogue code to complete the iterations in progress at the time of exiting the software pipeline. This will result in some amount of increase in code size and code generation complexity. At the same time, it yields the highest performance code with the MVE strategy. In this paper, we shall study the code size of both code schemas for the MVE strategy.

A more detailed discussion of code schema for modulo scheduled loops is provided in [17]. For the sake of brevity, we have limited our discussion to only a quarter of all the possibilities. It should be noted that WHILE-loops can be handled in a very similar manner as long as certain additional details are addressed.

3 Formulation of the register allocation problem

Informally, the register allocation task for modulo scheduled loops with hardware support consists of packing together the space-time shapes, that correspond to the vector lifetimes, so as to take up a minimum number of registers. An allocation is legal if, out of all the scalar lifetimes that make up all of the vector lifetimes, no two scalar lifetimes that overlap in time are allocated to the same register. This bin packing takes place on the surface of a cylinder with time corresponding to the axis and the registers corresponding to the circumference. So, the task is to pack the vector lifetimes together so that they fit on the surface of a cylinder having the smallest possible circumference. In describing the allocation algorithms, we shall need to refer to the linear ordering of registers, and it is important to bear in mind that if, for instance, we have 64 registers, it is equally correct to refer to the register below 0 as either -1 or as 63.

When discussing a vector lifetime, we shall use the lifetime produced by the first iteration of the loop as the point of reference. Thus, a vector lifetime has been allocated to physical register 7 if the defining operation in the first iteration writes its result to physical register 7. Iterations 2, 3, etc., would write their results to physical registers 6, 5, and so on. Note that, in this discussion, when we refer to registers, we refer to the the absolute addresses of registers which are different for each iteration. However, assuming the presence of the kind of register renaming that is provided by the rotating register file, the register specifier in the instruction would be invariant. Also, the start and finish times of a vector lifetime refer to those of the scalar lifetime corresponding to the first iteration.

As another point of terminology, when we say that one vector lifetime is allocated "above" another one, we mean that the wand of the first lifetime lies above (and to the right) of the wand for the second lifetime in the space-time diagram (see Figure 5). Note that this does *not* mean that the first lifetime is allocated to a higher location than is the second. If the start time for the first lifetime is sufficiently later than the start time for the second, then it can be allocated to a lower location even though it is "above" the second lifetime in the space-time diagram. For scalar lifetimes, "above" and "higher location" are synonymous.

3.1 The register allocation constraint

Allocation constraints for modulo scheduled loops can be abstracted in order to simplify the formulation of the problem and the implementation of the allocation algorithms. Given four parameters for each vector lifetime (start, end, omega, alpha), we construct the matrix, DIST, which has one row and one column for each vector lifetime. Each off-diagonal element specifies the minimum distance (in registers) allowable between a pair of lifetimes when they are allocated in the rotating register file. In Figure 7, vector lifetimes A and B for a schedule with II = 3 are shown in a space-time diagram. (Two possible allocations for B are shown in Figure 7, labelled B^{ℓ} and B^{u}.) A loop with five iterations is shown. Lifetime A has: (start = 8, end = 13, omega = 1, alpha = 1). Lifetime B has: (start = 0, end = 3, omega = 0, alpha = 0). The shapes of the lifetimes A and B are completely specified by these four parameters. Whereas lifetime B is a wand, i.e., a simple diagonal shape, lifetime A is not, and must carry a value live-in and live-out due to the value of the parameters: omega = 1 and alpha = 1.

Assume that lifetime A has been allocated to some register in the rotating register file. Lifetime B can be allocated adjacent to A either "below" A (B^{ℓ}) or "above" A (B^{u}) in Figure 7. When lifetime B^{ℓ} is moved as high as is possible without interfering with the scalar lifetime that constitutes the leading blade of A, it ends up being allocated to the same register as A. (Recall that a vector lifetime is said to be allocated to the register to which the scalar lifetime corresponding to the first iteration is allocated). Therefore, DIST[B,A] has the value 0. Similarly, when lifetime B^{u} is moved to the lowest position possible, it ends up being allocated 5 registers higher than A. Therefore, DIST[A,B] has the value 5. All off-diagonal elements of the DIST matrix are defined likewise. In this example, the distance between A and B^{ℓ} was limited by the interference between the leading blade of A and the wand of B^{ℓ}, and the distance between A and B^{u} was limited by the interference between the wand of A and the wand of B". In general, there are three different possible interferences, any one of which can limit the minimum distance between two blades:

1. the interference between the two wands,
2. the interference between the leading blade of the upper vector lifetime and either the leading blade or the wand of the lower lifetime and,
3. the interference between the trailing blade of the lower lifetime and either the wand or the trailing blade of the upper lifetime.

Accordingly, for vector lifetimes, DIST[A,B] is computed using the following formulae:

$$d_1 = \left\lceil \frac{\text{end(A)-start(B)}}{\text{II}} \right\rceil$$

$$d_2 = \begin{cases} d_1, & \text{if omega(B)} = 0 \\ \max(d_1, \text{omega(A)}), & \text{otherwise} \end{cases}$$

$$d_3 = \begin{cases} d_2, & \text{if alpha(A)} = 0 \\ \max(d_2, \text{alpha(A)}), & \text{otherwise} \end{cases}$$

For WO, DIST[A,B] = d_1. For BA, DIST[A,B] = d_3.

The DIST matrix for scalar lifetimes, with the MVE strategy, is much simpler. If two scalar lifetimes X and Y are live simultaneously, then DIST[X,Y] = DIST[Y,X] = 1. Otherwise, DIST[X,Y] = DIST[Y,X] = 0.

The register allocation problem is to pack the lifetimes, whether vector or scalar, on the surface of a cylinder with the minimum circumference while honoring the minimum distance requirements, as specified by the DIST matrix, between every pair of lifetimes. The appropriate definition of the DIST matrix is used depending on whether the register allocator is working with vector or scalar lifetimes and depending on the register allocation algorithm being used.

3.2 A lower bound on the number of registers

A tight lower bound on the number of registers needed for a modulo scheduled loop is useful in assessing the success of the register allocation. A simple, yet surprisingly tight, lower bound is obtained by calculating the total number of scalar lifetimes that are live during each cycle and taking the maximum of these totals. Clearly, at least this many registers are needed under all circumstances. This maximum is computed over the entire length of the (possibly unrolled) kernel after scheduling. In view of the repetitive pattern of lifetimes in an unrolled kernel, the number of scalar lifetimes that are simultaneously live need only be computed for any II consecutive cycles of the kernel.

4 Register Allocation Algorithms

The nature of the overall register allocation process is described in Figure 8. The set of lifetimes to be allocated are presented to the register allocator in some arbitrary order by the compiler. One can choose either to retain that order or to put it into a better order which improves the quality of the allocation achieved by a one-pass allocation algorithm. The choice of ordering heuristic is controlled by the variable OrderingAlgorithm. Zero, one or multiple heuristics may be selected simultaneously. The allocation process consists of repeatedly selecting an as yet unallocated lifetime, in the order imposed by the ordering heuristics, and allocating it. The choice of register location into which this lifetime is allocated is determined by the allocation algorithm. The variable that controls this is AllocationAlgorithm. In this study, we only consider one-pass register allocation algorithms, i.e., algorithms in which each lifetime is allocated exactly once with no back-tracking or iteration.

```
procedure Allocate;

begin
  case OrderingAlgorithm of
    0: {do nothing};
    1: order by start time;
    2: order by conflict;
    3: order by conflict and start time with appropriate priorities;
    4: order by adjacency;
    5: order by adjacency and start time with appropriate priorities;
    6: order by adjacency and conflict with appropriate priorities;
    7: order by adjacency, conflict and start time with appropriate priorities;
    end { case };
  Lifetimes[1].location := 0;
  LastLT := 1;
  update the set of disallowed allocations for every unallocated lifetime;
  for SelectedLT := 2 to NumberOfLifetimes do
    begin
      case AllocationAlgorithm of
        1: BestFit(SelectedLT, SelectedLocation);
        2: FirstFit(SelectedLT, SelectedLocation);
        3: EndFit(SelectedLT, LastLT, SelectedLocation);
        end { case };
      Lifetimes[SelectedLT].location := SelectedLocation;
      LastLT := SelectedLT;
      update the set of disallowed allocations for every unallocated lifetime;
    end { for SelectedLT := 2 to NumberOfLifetimes do };
end;
```

Figure 8. Overview of the register allocation algorithm

```
procedure BestFit (SelectedLT, BestLocation);
{ Find the "best" location, BestLocation, in which to allocate }
{ the selected lifetime, SelectedLT. }

begin
  FirstLocation := minimum over all allocated lifetimes, i, of
                   Lifetime[i].location - Dist[SelectedLT,i];
  LastLocation := maximum over all allocated lifetimes, i, of
                  Lifetimes[i].location + Dist[i,SelectedLT];
  BestFitSoFar := infinity;
  for TrialLocation := FirstLocation to LastLocation do
    begin
      if SelectedLT can be allocated to TrialLocation then
        begin
          ThisFit := number of registers needed if SelectedLT is
                     allocated to TrialLocation;
          ThisFOM := FOM(SelectedLT, TrialLocation); { figure-of-merit for    }
                                                     { allocating SelectedLT }
                                                     { to TrialLocation      }

          if (ThisFit < BestFitSoFar) or
            ((ThisFit = BestFitSoFar) and (ThisFOM > BestFOM)) then
            begin
              BestFitSoFar := ThisFit;
              BestFOM := ThisFOM;
              BestLocation := TrialLocation;
            end; { if }
        end; { if }
    end; { for }
end;
```

Figure 9. The best fit algorithm

```
procedure FirstFit (SelectedLT, FirstLocation);
{ Find the first (lowest) location, FirstLocation, in which }
{ the selected lifetime, SelectedLT, can be allocated. }

begin
  FirstLocation := 0;
  while SelectedLT cannot be allocated at FirstLocation do
    FirstLocation := FirstLocation + 1;
end;
```

Figure 10. The first fit algorithm

```
procedure EndFit (SelectedLT, LastLT, SelectedLocation);
{ Find the location, SelectedLocation, in which to allocate }
{ the selected lifetime, SelectedLT. }

begin
  SelectedLocation := Lifetime[LastLT].location + Dist[LastLT,SelectedLT];
  while SelectedLT cannot be allocated at SelectedLocation do
    SelectedLocation := SelectedLocation + 1;
end;
```

Figure 11. The end fit algorithm

4.1 Register allocation algorithms

The **best fit** algorithm (Figure 9) is an attempt to come up with the best allocation possible without an exhaustive search, backtracking or iteration, i.e., once a lifetime is allocated to a particular register, it stays allocated to that same register. As with all the allocation algorithms considered here, the lifetimes are allocated one by one in the order prescribed by the conjunction of the selected sorting heuristics (see below). Initially, allocation is performed on an infinite plane (unbounded registers). With best fit, every location is examined starting with the highest, permissible location that is "below" all the previously allocated lifetimes up through the lowest, permissible location that is "above" all of the previously allocated lifetimes. It is possible to allocate the current lifetime in between a pair of previously allocated lifetimes. For each candidate location to which it is possible to allocate the lifetime, the minimum number of registers needed to permit this allocation is computed. This is done by wrapping the infinite plane into a cylinder of minimum circumference, i.e., minimum number of registers, while respecting the minimum distance requirements between every pair of lifetimes. The location that is finally selected is the one that minimizes the number of registers needed. Ties are broken using an additional heuristic, FOM. Each time a lifetime is allocated, some number of locations are made unavailable to the as yet unallocated lifetimes because of conflicts with the lifetime just allocated.

```
procedure AdjacencyOrder;

begin
  put all lifetimes in the set NotSetAside;
  initialize OutputList to empty;
  remove lifetime 1 from NotSetAside and append it to OutputList;
  LastLT := 1;
  for i := 2 to NumberOfLifetimes do
    begin
      MinDistance := infinity;
      SelectedLT := null;
      CurrentSet := empty;
      for j := 1 to NumberOfLifetimes do
        if j in NotSetAside then
          begin
            if WO or BA strategies then
              begin
                ThisDistance := (start[j] - end[LastLT]) + DIST[LastLT,j] * II;
                if ThisDistance < MinDistance then
                  begin
                    SelectedLT := j;
                    MinDistance := ThisDistance;
                  end;
              end
            else { if MVE strategy then }
              begin
                conflict[j] := false;
                ThisDistance := start[j] - end[LastLT];
                if lifetime[j] conflicts with any lifetime in CurrentSet then
                  begin
                    conflict[j] := true;
                    ThisDistance := ThisDistance + penalty;
                  end;
                if ThisDistance < MinDistance then
                  begin
                    SelectedLT := j;
                    MinDistance := ThisDistance;
                  end;
              end;
          end; { if j in NotSetAside then }
      remove SelectedLT from NotSetAside and append it to OutputList;
      LastLT := SelectedLT;
      if MVE strategy then
        if conflict[SelectedLT] then
          CurrentSet := {SelectedLT}
        else
          CurrentSet := CurrentSet ∪ {SelectedLT};
    end; { for i := 2 to NumberOfLifetimes do }
end;
```

Figure 12. The adjacency ordering algorithm

However, in general, some subset of these were already unavailable due to the previously allocated lifetimes. The figure-of-merit, FOM, is inversely proportional to the number of additional locations that are made unavailable if SelectedLT is allocated to TrialLocation.

The **first fit** algorithm (Figure 10) proceeds in a similar fashion except that it always begins its search at location 0 and terminates as soon as a location is found to which the lifetime can be allocated.

The **end fit** algorithm (Figure 11) is intended to be used primarily with the adjacency ordering heuristic (see below), with each lifetime being allocated, "above" the last lifetime allocated, to the lowest possible location. Consequently, the search for a location starts with the lowest location such that the current lifetime is both above the previously allocated lifetime and does not cause a conflict with it. This location is specified by the DIST matrix. The search ends at the first legal location that is encountered, i.e., one which has no conflict with *any* of the previously allocated lifetimes.

4.2 Lifetime ordering heuristics

Three ordering heuristics are considered here: start-time ordering, adjacency ordering and conflict ordering. **Start-time ordering** is motivated primarily by the scalar lifetime case. For a single, non-loop basic block, every lifetime consists of a single interval. In this case, it can be shown that allocating scalar lifetimes in increasing order of start time, to the lowest available register, yields an optimal allocation. (A sketch of the proof of this theorem is provided in [16].)

This procedure is not necessarily optimal for a loop, especially a modulo scheduled one, in which lifetimes extend across the back-edge of the loop yielding discontiguous lifetimes, i.e., live at the beginning and end of the loop body but not in between. It can, however, be shown that an upper bound on the number of registers needed is L+M, where L and M are the maximum and minimum number of lifetimes, respectively, that are live simultaneously [8]. In any event, ordering by start time was viewed as a potentially successful heuristic to use even in this situation and, in fact, was used as the secondary ordering heuristic for vector lifetime allocation in the Cydra 5 compiler.

The primary ordering heuristic in the Cydra 5 compiler was what we shall term **adjacency ordering**. This greedy heuristic was used in conjunction with the end fit allocation algorithm. At each step, that lifetime is selected which minimizes the horizontal distance, in the space-time diagram (Figure 5), between the lifetime that was allocated last and the one just selected. Bearing in mind that the horizontal dimension is time, we see that this heuristic attempts to minimize the amount of time that any given register is idle.The adjacency ordering algorithm (Figure 12) is quite straightforward for vector lifetimes. Lifetime 1 is selected first. Thereafter, the lifetime, B, that is selected at each step is the one for which

$$(start[B] - end[A]) + DIST[A,B]*II$$

is minimum, where A is the lifetime that was previously selected. Note that (start[B] - end[A]) is the horizontal distance in the space-time diagram if A and B were allocated to the same register. DIST[A,B]*II is the additional gap given that B must be allocated to a register that is at least DIST[A,B] higher than the one to which A has been allocated. This heuristic is quite similar to the one used with the Travelling Salesman Problem and, in fact, in the WO case, register allocation can be formulated as a Travelling Salesman Problem.

For scalar lifetimes, too, an attempt is made to minimize the time that a register is idle. In fact, the adjacency ordering algorithm essentially performs a quick-and-dirty allocation. At any point in time, CurrentSet is the set of lifetimes that are tentatively allocated to the same register--the same row in the space-time diagram. This heuristic keeps appending lifetimes to the right-hand side of the row, always selecting at each step the lifetime that minimizes the gap between the end of the previous lifetime and the selected lifetime. When it is impossible to add an additional lifetime without conflicting with one of the lifetimes in that row (taking into account the wrap-around of the lifetime at K*II), a new row is started.

Conflict ordering is motivated by a register allocation strategy which is to vector lifetimes what graph coloring [4] is to scalar lifetimes. This strategy reduces to the graph coloring approach in the case of scalar lifetimes. The basic idea is to establish, for each lifetime, a reasonably tight upper bound on the number of registers to which this lifetime cannot be allocated due to interference with the rest of the lifetimes, across all possible allocations for the rest of the lifetimes. This upper bound is referred to as the total conflict for that lifetime. The total conflict plus one is guaranteed to be an adequate number of registers to ensure the allocatability of that lifetime. The lifetime with the smallest total conflict is set aside and the total conflict is re-computed ignoring all lifetimes that have been set aside. This process is repeated until all lifetimes have been set aside. The lifetimes are ordered in the reverse order in which they were set aside. The conflict ordering algorithm is shown in Figure 13.

The total conflict is computed using the CONFLICT matrix. For vector lifetimes,

$$CONFLICT[i,j] = DIST[i,j] + DIST[j,i] - 1 \quad \text{for all } i \neq j.$$

For scalar lifetimes,

$$CONFLICT[i,j] = DIST[i,j] = DIST[j,i] \quad \text{for all } i \neq j.$$

The total remaining conflict for lifetime i at any point in time is the sum of all CONFLICT[i,j] such that i≠j and j has not yet been set aside.

Each ordering heuristic takes the incoming list of lifetimes and reorders them in accordance with the heuristic. Multiple heuristics may be employed in conjuction with one another. When this is done, it is necessary to decide which heuristic is the primary one, which one is secondary (i.e., is used to break ties when the primary one cannot discriminate between two lifetimes), and so on. When two heuristics are used together, there are two possible prioritizations and, when all three are used together, there are six possible prioritizations. The success of the register allocator is sensitive to the specific prioritization selected. For each combination of allocation strategy and allocation algorithm, all possible prioritizations were evaluated using the input data set described in Section 5. The best prioritization in each case is listed in Table 2.

```
procedure ConflictOrder;
{ Definition:  RemainingTotalConflict[i] is defined to be the sum of    }
{              Conflict[i,j] over all j, i<>j, which have not yet been }
{              set aside.                                               }

begin
  initialize RemainingTotalConflict for all lifetimes;
  put all lifetimes in the set NotSetAside;
  while NotSetAside ≠ empty do
    begin
      MinConflict := infinity;
      for i:= 1 to NumberOfLifetimes do
        if i in NotSetAside then
          if RemainingTotalConflict[i] ≤ MinConflict then
            begin
              MinConflict := RemainingTotalConflict[i];
              SelectedLT := i;
            end; { if }
      remove SelectedLT from NotSetAside;
      for all lifetimes j which are in NotSetAside do
        update RemainingTotalConflict[j];
    end; { while }
  order the lifetimes in the reverse order of removal from NotSetAside;
end;
```

Figure 13. The conflict ordering algorithm

Table 2. Prioritization of ordering heuristics when used in conjunction with one another. The order in which the heuristics are listed is primary heuristic first, then secondary heuristic etc.

Allocation Strategy	Allocation Algorithm	Priority of Ordering Heuristics
MVE	Best Fit First Fit	conflict, start start, adjacency conflict, adjacency conflict, start, adjacency
	End Fit	conflict, start adjacency, start adjacency, conflict adjacency, start, conflict
WO BA	Best Fit First Fit End Fit	start, conflict adjacency, start adjacency, conflict adjacency, start, conflict

In the context of the taxonomy that we have defined, the Cydra 5 compiler generates kernel-only code and performs blades allocation using the end fit allocation algorithm along with adjacency (primary) and start-time (secondary) ordering.

4.3 Computational Complexity

The worst-case computational complexity for register allocation depends upon the specific combination of ordering heuristics and allocation algorithm that is employed. From an inspection of the algorithms (Figures 8-13) one can see that the worst-case complexity of the three ordering heuristics and the three register allocation algorithms is:

start time	$O(n^2)$
conflict	$O(n^2)$
adjacency	$O(n^2)$
best fit	$\max(O(n^2), O(n^2r))$
first fit	$\max(O(n^2), O(n^r))$
end fit	$\max(O(n^2), O(n))$

where n is the number of lifetimes (either scalar or vector) to be allocated and r is the number of registers required to do so. (Note that for the MVE strategy, the number of lifetimes will be K_{min} times greater than for the other strategies.) Empirically, we found that r was a linear function of n (approximately 0.61*n+14.5) over the range of values of n for which there was statistical significance. So, effectively, best fit, first fit and end fit are $O(n^3)$, $O(n^2)$ and $O(n^2)$, respectively. Since the ordering heuristics are $O(n^2)$, it is the selected allocation algorithm that dominates the complexity of the register allocation phase. Note that in the conflict ordering algorithm, updating RemainingTotalConflict[j] for all j that are still in NotSetAside is an $O(n)$ operation.

When multiple ordering heuristics are used together, the lowest priority ordering is performed first, and the highest priority one last. It is necessary, therefore, that each sorting algorithm have the property that it maintains the relative ordering of all lifetimes that are equal under the sorting criterion that is currently being applied. Consequently, a simplistic sort of $O(n^2)$ complexity was used for start-time ordering instead of using heapsort which is $O(n \log n)$. The complexity expressions for the allocation algorithms contain two terms, the greater one of which determines the complexity. The $O(n^2)$ term is caused by having to update the disallowed locations for each as yet unallocated lifetime each time a lifetime is allocated (Figure 8). The updating process is $O(n)$ in complexity, and it is invoked n times. The other term is dependent on the allocation algorithm selected. In understanding these, one should note that each of the procedures in Figures 9-11 are invoked $O(n)$ times and that the loops in Figures 9 and 10 are executed $O(r)$ times on each invocation. Lastly, the function FOM that is called from within the loop in the best fit algorithm is itself $O(n)$ in complexity.

The worst-case complexity is generally quite pessimistic compared to what is actually experienced because in many cases, the iterations of the loops are guarded by IF-statements that are often not executed. So, we also have measured the empirical computational complexity for each combination. This is presented in Section 5. Counters were placed at the entry point as well as in every innermost loop of every relevant procedure. These counters count the total number of times that that point in the program is visited. In the spirit of worst-case complexity analysis, we used the largest of the counts as the indicator of empirical computational complexity.

5 Experimental Results

Measurements were taken to examine the effectiveness of the allocation algorithms described in the previous section. To this end, over one thousand FORTRAN DO-loops from the SPEC [20] and PERFECT Club [2] benchmark suites were modulo scheduled on a hypothetical machine similar to the Cydra 5 [18]. Only measurements on DO-loops were performed, even though all the register allocation algorithms discussed are fully applicable to WHILE-loops and loops with early exits. This is due to the limitation of the Cydra 5 compiler which was used to generate the input to the register allocator and which is unable to recognize loops which are not DO-loops. Also, only those DO-loops with no conditional branching were selected so as to permit a meaningful comparison between MVE (which assumes no predicated execution) and the other two allocation strategies. Apart from the relative code sizes for the three allocation strategies, we do not expect any of the conclusions regarding the relative merits of the various allocation algorithms and ordering heuristics to be different across the broader set of loops.

Table 3. Relevant details of the machine model used by the compiler for this study.

Pipeline	Number	Operations	Latency
Memory port	2	Load Store	13 1
Address ALU	2	Address add / subtract	1
Adder	1	Floating point add / subtract Integer add / subtract	1 1
Multiplier	1	Floating point multiply Integer multiply	2 2
Instruction pipeline	1	Branch	2

The relevant details of this hypothetical machine are shown in Table 3. The machine model permits the issue of up to seven operations per cycle. All the functional unit pipelines read their inputs and write their results to a common rotating register file. The 13 cycle load latency reflects an access that bypasses the first-level cache. (Our experience has been that locality of reference is often missing within innermost loops. Until compiler algorithms are devised which reliably ascertain whether or not a sequence of references in a loop has locality, it is preferably to have the deterministic albeit longer latency that comes from consistently bypassing the first-level cache.)

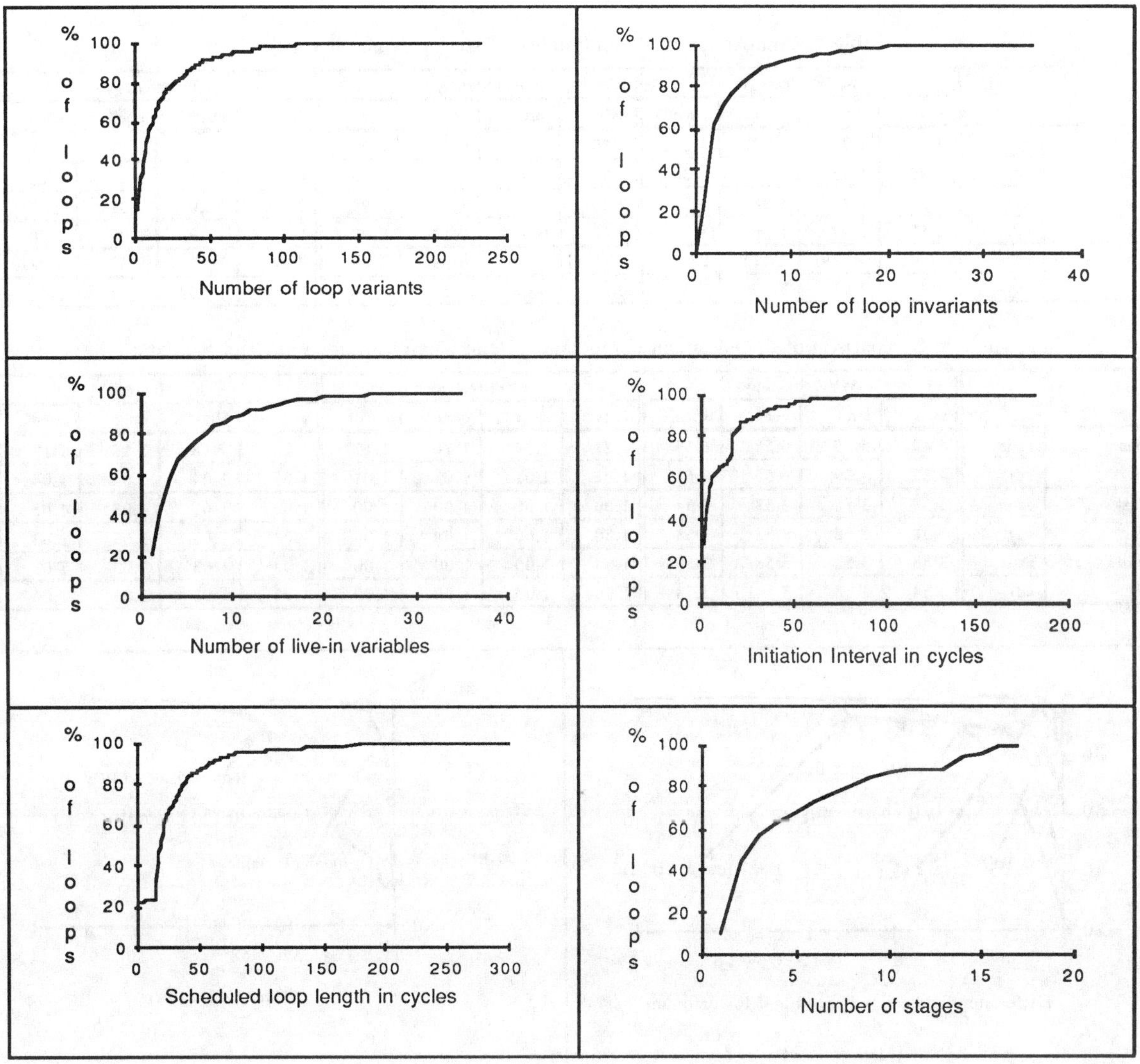

Figure 14. Cumulative distribution functions for key statistics of the input loops

The Cydra 5 compiler was used to generate a modulo schedule for each loop and then output a set of lifetime descriptions for all the loop-variants. The lifetime descriptions were used as input to a program that applied all combinations of ordering heuristics and allocation algorithms to each input set in turn. The register allocation program outputs various data for each input data set and for each combination of algorithms and heuristics. The data include the number of registers needed by the loop-variants, a lower bound on the number required, the code size, and the empirical computational complexity.

The characteristics of the loops that were analyzed in our experiment are shown in Figure 14. Each graph is a cumulative distribution. From Figure 14 it can be seen that most loops in our sample set had fewer than 80 loop-variants, although there were a few that had more than 200. In contrast, most loops had fewer than 10 loop-invariants with a few having more than 30. Every loop had at least one live-in variable, most having less than 15, and a few having over 30. Live-out variables were less frequent; not shown in Figure 14 is that 80% had no live-out variables and, of the remaining, about half had one live-out and the rest had two live-outs. The graph for the initiation interval indicates that most loops had an II less than 40 cycles. Nearly 60% of the loops had an II less than 8 cycles. Schedule lengths are generally less than 90 cycles, but a few loops had schedules several hundred cycles long. The number of stages in the software pipeline was 10 or less 90% of the time.

Tables 4-6 contains data on the various heuristics and strategies. All combinations were studied. For each combination

- Table 4 shows the optimality, i.e., the average of the difference between the achieved number of registers and the lower bound,
- Table 5 shows the average measured empirical computational complexity relative to the lowest average empirical computational complexity across all combinations (that for WO with end fit), and
- Table 6 shows the average code size in operations. For MVE, two code sizes are shown: with multiple epilogues and with preconditioning. (In the context of VLIW machines, a distinction needs to be made between an operation and an instruction. An instruction consists of multiple operations, whereas an operation is a unit of computation equivalent to a RISC instruction. The code size is proportional to the number of operations for both VLIW and RISC processors.)

Table 4. Comparison of the optimality of strategies and heuristics

		MVE Strategy				WO Strategy				BA Strategy			
		as is	strt t	conf	st/cnf	as is	strt t	conf	st/cnf	as is	strt t	conf	st/cnf
best	as is	3.21	1.71	1.32	1.30	0.89	0.52	0.52	0.51	1.23	0.58	0.62	0.59
fit	adj	2.40	1.75	1.30	1.30	0.27	0.08	0.14	0.08	0.49	0.24	0.27	0.23
first	as is	3.36	1.77	1.36	1.36	2.46	0.99	1.16	0.99	3.86	2.20	2.31	2.17
fit	adj	2.55	1.82	1.36	1.36	0.18	0.08	0.14	0.08	1.38	1.49	1.27	1.40
end	as is	16.42	35.79	27.75	28.80	5.65	6.52	6.59	6.79	7.08	7.72	8.34	7.98
fit	adj	3.30	2.51	3.00	2.37	0.18	0.08	0.14	0.08	1.40	1.56	1.37	1.48

Table 5. Comparison of the empirical computational complexity of strategies and heuristics

		MVE Strategy				WO Strategy				BA Strategy			
		as is	strt t	conf	st/cnf	as is	strt t	conf	st/cnf	as is	strt t	conf	st/cnf
best	as is	4.44	5.39	6.58	6.69	1.21	1.14	1.10	1.12	1.24	1.18	1.13	1.17
fit	adj	4.35	5.39	6.65	6.68	1.01	1.01	1.01	1.01	1.05	1.04	1.04	1.04
first	as is	3.58	3.58	3.58	3.58	1.00	1.00	1.00	1.00	1.03	1.03	1.03	1.03
fit	adj	3.58	3.58	3.58	3.58	1.00	1.00	1.00	1.00	1.03	1.03	1.03	1.03
end	as is	3.58	3.58	3.58	3.58	1.00	1.00	1.00	1.00	1.03	1.03	1.03	1.03
fit	adj	3.58	3.58	3.58	3.58	1.00	1.00	1.00	1.00	1.03	1.03	1.03	1.03

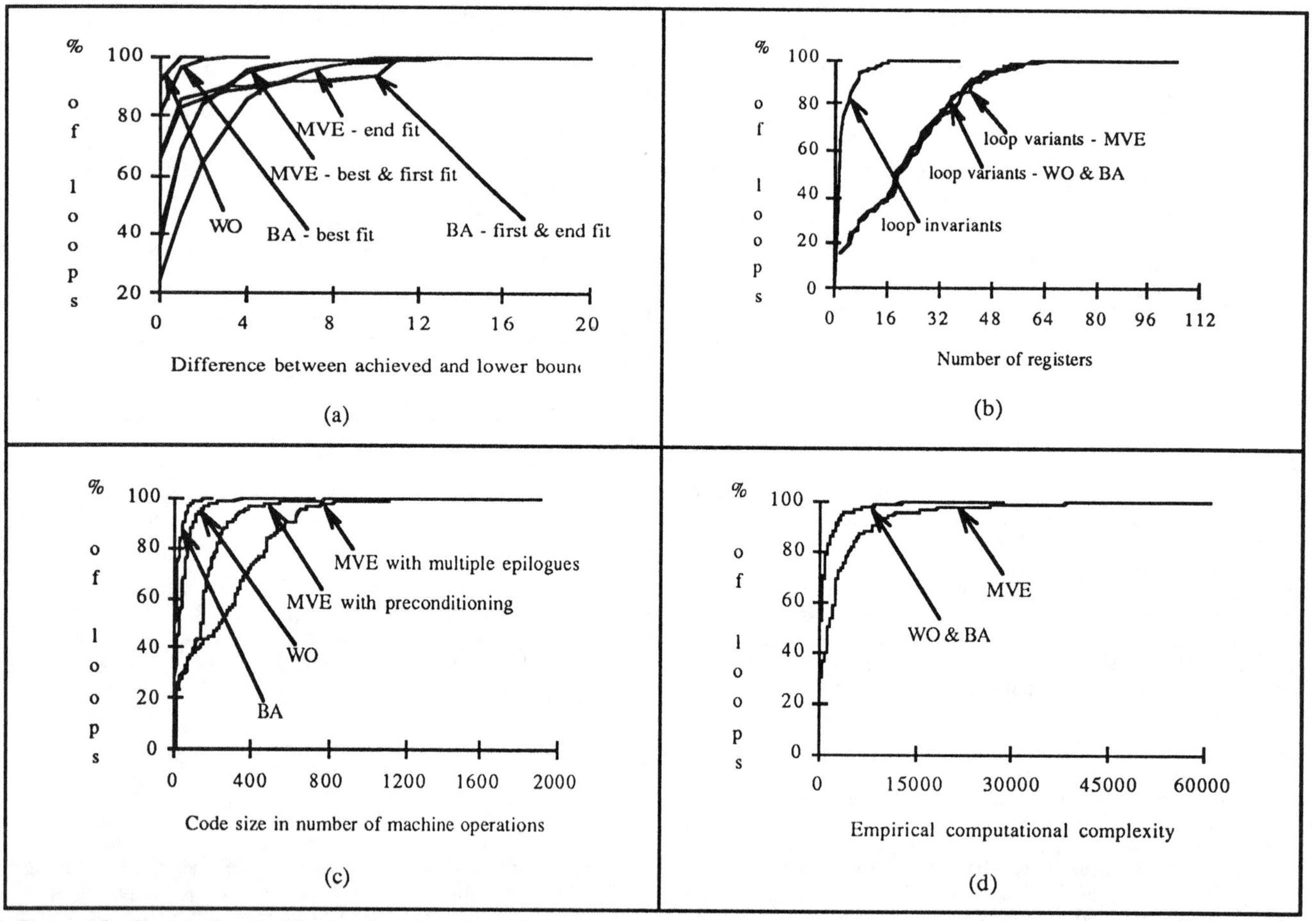

Figure 15. Cumulative distribution functions for (a) the degree of optimality (b) the number of registers used (c) the code size for the loop (d) the empirical computational complexity.

For the MVE strategy, fewest excess registers were used on the average by best fit allocation, using conflict ordering in conjunction with one or both of start-time and adjacency ordering. If first fit allocation were to be employed instead of best fit, but using the same ordering heuristics, marginally poorer allocation is obtained (< 5% worse) but with almost a halving of the empirical computational complexity. The WO strategy achieves near-optimal results when it uses adjacency and start-time heuristics (with or without the use of the conflict heuristic) and regardless of which allocation algorithm is used. For the BA strategy, best results were obtained with best fit allocation using adjacency, start-time and conflict ordering. This only had slightly higher empirical computational complexity (by 1%) than first fit or end fit.

Figure 15a shows the cumulative distribution of the difference between the actual number of registers used and the lower bound, i.e., the extent of the deviation from the lower bound. It should be noted that the deviation from optimality may be less since even the optimal allocation may require more registers than the lower bound. A separate plot is shown for each of the nine combinations of allocation strategy and allocation algorithm. In each case, the results corresponding to the best combination of ordering heuristics were selected. The three plots for WO are indistinguishable. Over 90% of the loops yield optimal allocation, and almost all of the rest require only one register over the lower bound. BA with best fit is almost as good. 80% of the loops are optimal, another 15% require an additional register, and very few need more than two registers over the lower bound. First fit and end fit for BA are very similar to each other, and significantly different from best fit. Especially interesting is the "plateau" between 1 and 10 registers; over 80% of the loops need at most one additional register, and almost 10% require 11 additional registers, with the rest of the loops requiring some intermediate number of registers. This suggests an interesting, hybrid allocation algorithm in which one first attempts first fit allocation and then, if too many additional registers end up being required, performs best fit allocation. For MVE, best fit and first fit are almost indistinguishable. 40% of the loops are optimal, and rarely are more than 6 additional registers required. End fit for MVE is significantly worse.

On the average, all three strategies, when they employ the best combination of allocation algorithm and ordering heuristics, are able to achieve extremely good register allocation; On the average, WO is near-optimal, BA requires 0.24 registers more than the lower bound, and MVE requires 1.3 registers over the lower bound. The differences lie in their empirical complexity and the resulting code size.

Table 6. Comparison of the code size of strategies

	Code size
MVE - multiple epilogues	258.51
MVE - preconditioning	142.43
WO	42.30
BA	18.21

If we limit our discussion to only the best combinations for each strategy, WO has the lowest empirical complexity, BA is about 4% worse, and MVE is worse by a factor of 6.6. This factor drops to 3.6 if first fit, instead of best fit, is used for MVE. With respect to code size, BA is clearly the best. WO and MVE require code that is 2.3 and 14.2 times larger, respectively. If preconditioned code is used with MVE, the factor drops to 7.8 (but at the cost of reduced performance, especially for small trip counts). It must be noted, however, that these results correspond only to the modulo scheduled innermost loops. The relative code size and compilation time increases for the complete program would be less depending on what fraction of the code consists of innermost loops. Furthermore, the increase in the static code size is relatively unimportant; what matters is the effect of code size on instruction cache performance. The extent to which this is a problem requires further study.

For each combination of allocation strategy and allocation algorithm, Table 7 lists the set of preferred ordering heuristics. The combination of ordering heuristics selected is the one that yields the best register allocation, on the average. When different combinations of heuristics yield results that are very close in terms of optimality, the least expensive combination, computationally, is selected as the preferred one. In comparing the best fit and first fit algorithms for MVE, one sees that the two are very close in terms of optimality (a difference of 0.06 registers on the average) but that first fit has about half the empirical complexity of best fit. Consequently, in Table 7, first fit is underlined to indicate that it is preferred over best fit. With WO, all three allocation algorithms are equally optimal. So, we prefer end fit since it is the least expensive. With BA, best fit is significantly better than the other two for very little added complexity. Accordingly, best fit is the preferred allocation algorithm for BA.

Table 7. The preferred allocation algorithm for each allocation strategy and the preferred ordering heuristics for each allocation algorithm.

Allocation Strategy	Allocation Algorithm (Preferred)	Preferred Ordering Heuristics
MVE	Best Fit	conflict
	First Fit	conflict
	End Fit	adjacency, start, conflict
WO	Best Fit	adjacency, start
	First Fit	adjacency, start
	End Fit	adjacency, start
BA	Best Fit	adjacency, start
	First Fit	adjacency, conflict
	End Fit	adjacency, conflict

Comparing the WO and BA strategies (Tables 4-6), it can be seen that the number of registers used and the measured computational complexity are not very different, but the average code size for strategy WO is 2.3 times larger. If one is concerned about instruction cache performance, it may be preferable to use BA register allocation, and generate KO code. This also allows one to avoid the complexities involved with WO in generating the correct code schema for PKE^n code [17]. The performance degradation of BA relative to WO is limited to the lost opportunity in percolating outer loop computation into the prologue and epilogue. (In both cases, it is assumed that hardware support is available in the form of the rotating register file and predicated execution.)

With the MVE strategy, degrees of unroll greater than K_{min} were attempted. Larger degrees of unroll resulted in higher empirical computational complexity and code size, and provided little to no reduction in the number of registers used. For over 80% of the loops, unrolling by more than K_{min} saved at most one register. Very few cases were found where the savings were more than three registers. Furthermore, the number of registers needed does not decrease monotonically as the degree of unroll is increased. Additional unrolling beyond K_{min} is not worthwhile.

Figure 15b-d show the cumulative distributions for the number of registers used, the code size and the empirical computational complexity for the preferred allocation algorithm and ordering heuristics for each strategy. For the machine model used, 98% of the loops required less than 64 registers for loop-variants, and less than 12 registers for loop-invariants. The difference between the strategies is hardly noticeable in Figure 15b, but the MVE strategy performs slightly worse than the other two. Figure 15c and Figure 15d show the cumulative distributions of the code size and empirical computational complexity, respectively. The relative ordering of MVE, WO and BA is the same for the variance and maximum of the code size distribution as it is for the mean: MVE is larger than WO which is larger than BA. The same is true for the empirical computational complexity; the mean, variance and maximum for MVE are all greater than the corresponding values for BA which, in turn, are marginally greater than those for WO.

6 Conclusion

When hardware support is present, in the form of predicated execution and the rotating register file, the kernel-only, blades allocation strategy is to be preferred over the wands-only strategy requiring prologue-kernel-epilogue code. It results in about 55% less code size, and with insignificant increases in the average number of registers used or in the empirical computational complexity. The best combination of heuristics to use with best fit allocation is adjacency and start-time ordering heuristics.

The absence of hardware support for modulo scheduling necessitates prologue and epilogue code, kernel unrolling, modulo variable expansion, and either a sequential preconditioning loop or multiple epilogues. Our experimental data indicate that first fit allocation with conflict ordering is the best choice. Unrolling the kernel more than the minimum number of times necessary does not significantly reduce the number of registers required; instead it increases both the empirical computational complexity and the average code size. Our recommendation would be to employ the minimum degree of unroll.

The measurements of computational complexity and average code size lend some weight to arguments in favor of hardware support for modulo scheduling, in the form of the rotating register file and predicated execution. Without it, the increased empirical computational complexity (by a factor of 3 to 6) results in longer compile times. The increased average code size (by a factor of 7 to 14) can have a negative effect on the instruction hit rate in cache and, hence, on performance. The sequential execution of the residual iterations in preconditioned code can further degrade performance for realistic trip counts.

In this paper, we have studied the optimality of various allocation algorithms and heuristics. This serves as a useful guide in selecting the best algorithm for each situation with an objective to minimizing the number of registers needed. A different objective, and one that is equally important, is the issue of how one performs register allocation so as to make do with the number of registers that are available. The best algorithm from the first viewpoint is best from the second viewpoint, too. However, once modulo scheduling has been performed, if the register allocator fails to find a solution requiring no more registers than are available, some additional action must be taken. The options include one of the following actions:

- increasing the II,
- introducing spill code, or
- splitting the loop into smaller loops

followed by another modulo scheduling and register allocation pass. The issues and the difficulties in so doing are elaborated upon in [16].

Acknowledgements

The end fit allocation algorithm and the adjacency ordering heuristic, described in this paper, were conceived of by Ross Towle who, along with Warren Ristow and Jim Dehnert, implemented register allocation for vector lifetimes in the Cydra 5 compiler.

References

1. Allen, J.R., et al. Conversion of control dependence to data dependence. In *Proceedings of the Tenth Annual ACM Symposium on Principles of Programming Languages*, (January, 1983).

2. Berry, M., et al. The Perfect Club Benchmarks: Effective Performance Evaluation of Supercomputers. *The International Journal of Supercomputer Applications*, 3 (1989), 5-40.

3. Callahan, D., Carr, S., and Kennedy, K. Improving Register Allocation for Subscripted Variables. In *Proceedings of the ACM SIGPLAN '90 Conference on Programming Language Design and Implementation*, (June, 1990), 53-65.

4. Chaitin, G.J. Register allocation and spilling via graph coloring. In *Proceedings of the SIGPLAN82 Symposium on Compiler Construction*, (June, 1982), 201-207.

5. Charlesworth, A.E. An Approach to Scientific Array Processing: The Architectural Design of the AP-120B/FPS-164 Family. *IEEE Computer 14*, 9 (September, 1981), 18-27.

6. Dehnert, J.C., Hsu, P.Y.-T., and Bratt, J.P. Overlapped loop support in the Cydra 5. In *Proceedings of the Third International Conference on Architectural Support for Programming Languages and Operating Systems*, (Boston, Mass., April, 1989), 26-38.

7. Ebcioglu, K., and Nakatani, T. A new compilation technique for parallelizing loops with unpredictable branches on a VLIW architecture. In *Proceedings of the Second Workshop on Programming Languages and Compilers for Parallel Computing*, (Urbana-Champaign, 1989), 213-229.

8. Hendren, L.J., et al. Register Allocation using Cyclic Interval Graphs: A New Approach to an Old Problem. ACAPS Technical Memo 33. Advanced Computer Architecture and Program Structures Group, McGill University, Montreal, Canada, 1992.

9. Hsu, P.Y.T. Highly Concurrent Scalar Processing. CSG-49. Coordinated Science Lab., University of Illinois, Urbana, Illinois, 1986.

10. Jain, S. Circular scheduling: A new technique to perform software pipelining. In *Proceedings of the ACM SIGPLAN '91 Conference on Programming Language Design and Implementation*, (June, 1991), 219-228.

11. Lam, M. Software pipelining: an effective scheduling technique for VLIW machines. In *Proceedings of the ACM SIGPLAN '88 Conference on Programming Language Design and Implementation*, (June, 1988), 318-327.

12. Lee, R.L., Kwok, A.Y., and Briggs, F.A. The floating point performance of a superscalar SPARC processor. In *Proceedings of the Fourth International Conference on Architectural Support for Programming Languages and Operating Systems*, (Santa Clara, California, April, 1991), 28-37.

13. Nicolau, A., and Potasman, R. Realistic scheduling: compaction for pipelined architectures. In *Proceedings of the 23th Annual Workshop on Microprogramming and Microarchitecture*, (Orlando, Florida, November, 1990), 69-79.

14. Rau, B.R. Data flow and dependence analysis for instruction level parallelism. In *Proceedings of the Fourth Workshop on Languages and Compilers for Parallel Computing*, (Santa Clara, August, 1991).

15. Rau, B.R., and Glaeser, C.D. Some scheduling techniques and an easily schedulable horizontal architecture for high performance scientific computing. In *Proceedings of the Fourteenth Annual Workshop on Microprogramming*, (October, 1981), 183-198.

16. Rau, B.R., et al. Register Allocation for Modulo Scheduled Loops: Strategies, Algorithms and Heuristics. HP Labs Technical Report HPL-92-48. Hewlett-Packard Laboratories, Palo Alto, California, 1992.

17. Rau, B.R., et al. Code Generation Schema for Modulo Scheduled DO-Loops and WHILE-Loops. HP Labs Technical Report HPL-92-47. Hewlett-Packard Laboratories, Palo Alto, California, 1992.

18. Rau, B.R., et al. The Cydra 5 departmental supercomputer: design philosophies, decisions and trade-offs. *IEEE Computer 22*, 1 (January, 1989).

19. Tirumalai, P., Lee, M., and Schlansker, M.S. Parallelization of loops with exits on pipelined architectures. In *Proceedings of the Supercomputing '90*, (November, 1990), 200-212.

20. Uniejewski, J. SPEC Benchmark Suite: Designed for Today's Advanced Systems. *SPEC Newsletter 1*, 1 (Fall, 1989).

Probabilistic Register Allocation

Todd A. Proebsting and Charles N. Fischer*
University of Wisconsin-Madison†

Abstract

A new global register allocation technique, *probabilistic register allocation*, is described. Probabilistic register allocation quantifies the costs and benefits of allocating variables to registers over live ranges so that excellent allocation choices can be made. Local allocation is done first, and then global allocation is done iteratively beginning in the the most deeply nested loops. Because local allocation precedes global allocation, probabilistic allocation does not interfere with the use of well-known, high-quality local register allocation and instruction scheduling techniques.

1 Introduction

The dominant paradigm in modern register allocation is graph coloring ([CAC+81], [CH90], [BCKT89], [LH86]). Unfortunately, graph coloring does not really address the issue of register allocation, but rather a related issue—register assignment. That is, graph coloring tells us how to assign registers so that simultaneously live values aren't assigned the same register. The harder problem—which values to put in *some* register—is not directly addressed. Hence there is always a spilling heuristic that reduces register demand until coloring (register assignment) can succeed.

A famous political maxim states that "All politics is local," and we believe that much the same is true for register allocation. Ultimately, when an operand is actually used it must be in a register, and once a value is in a register, it is easy to reuse within a basic block. Simple, fast and nearly optimal local register allocators are known [HFG89]. Once local register needs are met, the effects of global allocation can be estimated ([Bea74], [Mor91]). In particular, a good global allocation improves upon good local allocation by eliminating unnecessary loads at the entrance to a basic block and by eliminating unnecessary stores at the exit from a basic block. An initial load of `v` is unnecessary if all predecessors exit with `v` in a register, and a terminal store of `w` is unnecessary if `w` is dead or all succeeding loads of `w` can be replaced with a reference to `w`'s register.

Of course we do not initially know which values will ultimately be allocated to registers, so we take a probabilistic approach. At the basic block level, we know values loaded locally into a register and not overwritten have a 100% probability of exiting in a register. The probability of other values residing in a register on exit depends on their probability of residing in a register upon entrance and the number of unused registers in a block. The probability that a value will be in a register upon entrance to a block depends on the probabilities it will exit in a register from all predecessor blocks.

Once initial estimates of the probability of register allocation are made, these estimates are weighted by the net benefit gained by allocating a given value to a register and the most promising candidate is allocated to a register. Probabilities are recomputed and again the most promising candidate is allocated to a register. This continues until all registers are allocated. The resulting technique is simple and fast (no backtracking ever occurs) and yet identifies those values that can readily and profitably reside in a register.

2 Graph Coloring Allocators

For most of the last decade, global register allocation research has concentrated on graph color-

*This work was supported by NSF grant CCR-8908355.

†Author's address: Dept. of Computer Sciences, 1210 W. Dayton St., Madison, WI 53706. Email: {todd,fischer}@cs.wisc.edu

ACM SIGPLAN '92 PLDI-6/92/CA

ing techniques ([CAC+81], [Cha82], [CH90], [LH86], [BCKT89], [CK91]). These techniques allocate registers by attempting to solve the related problem of assigning registers. The basic graph coloring technique involves creating a register interference graph and then pruning nodes from that graph that can be trivially colored (assigned a physical register). Given enough registers to "color" all register candidate values, this technique works well. However, once the interference graph is reduced to a graph for which the node pruning heuristic blocks, each technique must act so that register assignment may continue. Various graph coloring techniques differ precisely in what they do when pruning blocks.

Chaitin's techniques ([CAC+81], [Cha82]) take the simplest approach to handling such pruning blocks. A node (register candidate) is picked based on a cost measure, removed from the graph, and assigned permanently to a memory location. All subsequent references to that value must be from memory.

Priority based coloring ([CH90], [LH86]) also builds an interference graph and attempts to color it by pruning nodes. If this pruning blocks, a heuristic is employed to split large, costly live ranges into smaller ranges in an attempt to produce a graph that can be further pruned. Complex heuristics are used to split live ranges to minimize the costs of spilling and reloading the values across the boundaries to the new, smaller live-ranges. This mechanism is repeated until the all register candidates are assigned registers.

Callahan and Koblenz allocate registers globally by doing graph coloring "hierarchically" [CK91]. They treat the program as a hierarchy of nested "tiles." Tiles may be basic blocks, conditionals, or loops. They assign registers using graph pruning techniques, but start by assigning registers in innermost tiles and progressively assigning registers in enclosing tiles. This technique succeeds in isolating some local register needs from global register usage so that variables referenced within deeply nested loops will be assigned a register before a variable that is not referenced within the loop. If, however, within a tile, the graph pruning algorithm fails to find a coloring, their technique resorts to the graph-coloring spill techniques outlined in [BCKT89]. Therefore, while succeeding in biasing register allocation within a loop to variables used within that loop, spill decisions must still be made via *ad hoc* heuristic methods.

None of these graph coloring techniques do local (basic block level) register allocation as well as established algorithms ([HFG89], [Fre74], [FL88]) because local register allocation techniques are able to use information about the simple sequential nature of register usage in the block to minimize local spill code. This information is lost when register allocation is cast as a graph coloring problem.

3 Probabilistic Register Allocation

Our technique, Probabilistic Register Allocation, utilizes graph coloring techniques to assign registers, not to allocate them. Allocation is done prior to assignment based on quantified measures of the costs and benefits of having particular values in registers. Separating allocation from assignment allows our algorithm to concentrate on the important problem of determining which values will profitably be held in registers at different points in the program.

Probabilistic global allocation follows local allocation. Global allocation proceeds from inner loops to outer loops so that values used within a loop are routinely allocated a register for that loop.

3.1 Local Register Allocation & Probabilities

Most local register allocators share the basic principle of deciding what should stay in a register (or when a spill is necessary) by checking the closeness of the next use of the values already in registers ([HFG89], [Fre74], [FL88]). If a value in a register has only distant next uses then it will be spilled before a value to be used sooner. The intuitive explanation for such a heuristic is simple: the farther a potential use of a value is from a program point, the *less likely* the value is to remain in a register all the way to that use, thereby decreasing the expected value of retaining register residence. The likelihood of a value being able to stay register-resident can be viewed as roughly *inversely proportional* to the distance that value would have to stay register-resident. Therefore, heuristics choose to spill the value that seems likely to lose its register anyway. Conversely, one can view retaining a register allocation over a long distance as *more likely* to result in spills of other register values—another motivation for spilling those values with only distant uses.

The terms "less likely" and "inversely proportional" come from probability. To avoid the NP-Complete problems of optimal local register allocation, such heuristics use a simpler, *probabilistic* summary of the local circumstances to drive register allocation and spill decisions. We believe that a formal characterization of these algorithms as probabilistic has been ignored because in straight-line code, distance is always directly related to the probability of either being spilled or causing other values to be spilled.

Block X

Instr #	Instruction	Local Needs	Δ-Probabilities A	B	C	D	E	Comments
1	load A, v1	1	1*	2/3	2/3	2/3	2/3	
2	load B, v2	2	$\underline{1}$	1*	1/2	1/2	1/2	
3	add v1, v2, v3	1	0	$\underline{1}$	1	1	1	`A` is dead
4	load C, v4	2	-	0	1*	1	1	`B` is dead
5	load D, v5	3	-	-	$\underline{1}$	1*	0	All registers in use
6	add v4, v5, v6	2	-	-	1/2	1/2	-	Reuse either v4 or v5
7	add v3, v6, v7	1	1*	-	1	1	-	Reuse v3's register
8	store v7, A	1	$\underline{1}$	-	1	1	-	
9	load E, v8	2	$\underline{1}$	-	1	1	1*	Reuse v6's register
10	add v7, v8, v9	1	2/3	1*	2/3	2/3	2/3	
11	store v9, B	0	1	$\underline{1}$	1	1	1	
Probability Value in Register			2/3	$\underline{1}$	1/3	1/3	2/3	

Figure 1: Δ-Probabilities (3 Registers available for locals and globals)

3.2 Global Register Allocation & Probabilities

The use of probabilistic summary information to drive global register allocation has not been previously studied. Probabilities present the foundation for a global register allocator that combines the advantages of excellent local allocation with fast and effective global allocation. Probabilistic register allocation avoids the problems of live-range splitting that plague graph-coloring techniques [Cha82], [BCKT89], [CH90] by implicitly (and automatically) splitting ranges where the probability and benefit of residing in a register are low.

3.2.1 Calculating Global Register Probabilities

The probability that a register value will continue to exist in that register at a more distant point in straight-line code can be seen as inversely proportional to the distance to that point. This is not exact, but is intuitively plausible.

Approximating global probabilities requires the ability to handle control flow. Loops and conditionals complicate matters because a (variable's) value in a register may originate in many different locations and reach many different uses—there is not necessarily a unique next use or a single defining point. Simple data-flow analysis can determine all of the definitions that reach a particular use. The question to answer is "What is the probability that the value will remain in a register over all paths reaching a particular use from all the reaching definitions?"

A simple estimate of the probability can be derived by extending our local, basic block heuristic—count the total number of intervening instructions on all of the paths from definitions to the use in question. (No instruction should be counted twice, even if it appears on paths from two different definitions.)

Unfortunately, in practice this yields a relatively poor measure of probability because not all intervening instructions equally affect the probability that a register will need to be spilled. In addition, global register values need only be spilled when there are too few registers for both local needs and live global values. If along some path from a definition to a use the local allocator requires *all* of the registers, it would be impossible for the global value to be in a register along that path and hence the probability of the value being in a register at the use would be 0.

The *global* probability that a value will reside in a register at a given use (load) is computed from the local "Δ-probabilities" for that variable in the blocks that reach the load. Δ-probabilities are computed locally (for each live variable) based on local allocations and live variable analysis. Δ-probabilities are computed on a per instruction basis, and indicate the probability that a variable's value will continue to reside in a register after that instruction's register needs are resolved *if* the value had been in a register upto that instruction.

The example in Figure 1 illustrates how local allocation, liveness analysis and probabilities interact for potential register variables. (It is based on the program whose flow graph is shown in Figure 3.) The example assumes that there are 3 registers available to be allocated among the 5 variables and the intra-block temporary values. After the first instruction, local allocation requires 1 register, so 1 of the 3 registers must be allocated to `A` at this point, and only 2 of the remaining 3 registers will keep their values on entry. Therefore, the others (`B`–`E`) have a 2/3 chance of retaining a register. (We assume that if a value is live on entry, then it *may* be in a register, and we must ran-

Block Y

Instr #	Instruction	Local Needs	Δ-Probabilities A	B	C	D	E	Comments
12	load B, v10	1	2/3	1^*	2/3	2/3	2/3	
13	load E, v11	2	1/2	**1**	1/2	1/2	1^*	
14	add v10, v11, v12	1	1^*	**1**	1	1	0	E is dead (global info)
15	store v12, A	0	**1**	**1**	1	1	-	
Probability Value in Register			**1**	**1**	1/3	1/3	0	

Block Z

Instr #	Instruction	Local Needs	Δ-Probabilities A	B	C	D	E	Comments
16	load A, v13	1	1^*	2/3	2/3	2/3	2/3	
17	load C, v14	2	**1**	1/2	1^*	1/2	1/2	
18	add v13, v14, v15	1	2/3	2/3	2/3	2/3	1^*	
19	store v15, E	0	1	1	1	1	**1**	
Probability Value in Register			2/3	2/9	2/3	2/9	**1**	

Figure 2: Δ-Probabilities (3 Registers available for locals and globals)

domly choose one to give up its register when the local allocator needs an extra register. For simplicity, in the algorithm as implemented, we do not take "*distance to next use*" into account when calculating spill probabilities.) A "1^*" indicates that the variable was either loaded or calculated into a register at this instruction and therefore must exist in a register. A bold-face "**1**" indicates that the value has been allocated a register through that instruction.

The next instruction (#2) requires another register, so one of the remaining variables must be spilled—but not `A` because the local allocator keeps it in a register for a local use (#3). Because #2 requires 1 of the 2 remaining registers to be spilled, each candidate has a 1/2 chance of retaining a register. Instruction #3 does not lower the probability of any live variable because the local allocator recognizes that `A`'s value is dead and therefore reuses the register allocated to `A` for the result of the addition. Of course, `A`'s probability is 0 at this point because the local allocator has reallocated its register. It is impossible (probability = 0) for `E` to be register-resident at #5 because the instruction sequence #1–5 requires all 3 registers.

The bottom row of the table in Figure 1 indicates the probability that a variable will be in a register on exit. These values were calculated by multiplying together all the Δ-probabilities of the variable from the last point it was certain to be in a register to the end of the block.

It is also possible to calculate the conditional probabilities for variables that are not referenced within a basic block. If such a variable is in a register on entry to a block, the product of the Δ-probabilities for the entire block is the probability that it will be in a register on exit.

Figure 2 gives two example basic blocks with such "pass-through" values. In the top example (**Block Y**), the exit probabilities for `A`, `B`, and `E` are absolute probabilities (because the variables are referenced within the block). The probabilities for `C` and `D` are conditional—they are the probability that the value will still be in a register on exit if it was in a register on entry.

The computation of the Δ-probabilities at #14 (Figures 2 and 3) demonstrates the powerful interaction of local allocation and global data flow analysis. Global data-flow analysis indicates that the value of `E` is dead after #14, and, therefore, the local allocator may reallocate its register to hold the value of the computation (`A`). Because no additional registers were needed by the local allocator, the Δ-probabilities of `B`, `C`, and `D` are 1, reflecting no competition for registers (at that instruction).

Given the Δ-probabilities for each variable at each instruction, it is a simple matter to determine the probability that a variable will be available in a register at a particular use. That probability is the product of all the Δ-probabilities for that variable along all the paths from the points of definition that reach the use. Although the same instruction may appear along more than one path, its Δ-probability should only be factored in once.

The inner loop in Figure 3 has been annotated with global probabilities of register residence at each load assuming there are 3 registers available. (Blocks **X**, **Y**, and **Z** are given in Figures 1 and 2.) For instance, the probability of `C` being in a register at #4 is equal to

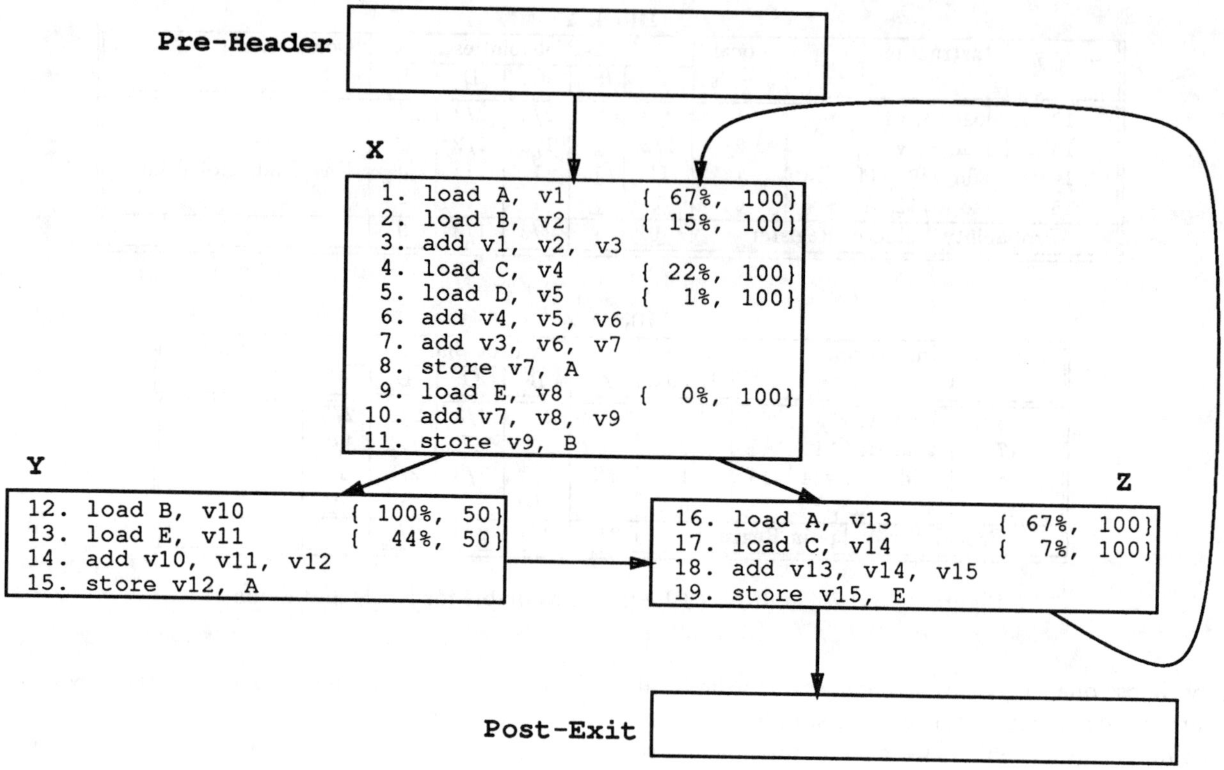

Figure 3: Sample Inner Loop with Global Probabilities (Assuming 3 Registers). The loads are annotated with {*probability, benefit*} pairs.

the product of the Δ-probabilities for #18, #19, #1, #2, and #3 (the path from the last register use of `C` is at #17, and we assume the variable can be placed in a register from the **Pre-Header** if necessary). The probability is, therefore,

$$2/3 * 1 * 2/3 * 1/2 * 1 = 2/9 \approx 22\%$$

The load of `C` at #4 has a greater global probability than the load of `B` at #2 even though it follows #2 in the basic block. This can be explained intuitively by observing that `B` must be register-resident through more of the loop (#13–19, #1) than `C` (#18–19, #1–3).

The extremely low probability (1%) for the "`load D, v5`" at #5 is a consequence the fact that for `D` to be available in a register at that location, it must be in a register for the entire loop.

4 Using Probabilities to Guide Global Register Allocation

Our global register allocation algorithm uses local probabilities combined with a measure of benefit to determine which variable uses should be globally allocated registers. Uses with large benefit and high probability are given the greatest register allocation priority.

The benefit of allocating a register to a use (and hence to all the paths reaching that use) is determined by estimating how often the use will be executed, and hence how many cycles may be saved if the value is accessed from a register rather than from memory. This can be determined heuristically from loop and conditional nesting levels, or empirically through profiling information from previous executions of the program [BL92].

Once a particular use has been allocated a register, there is no need to do a load of the variable at that use, thus saving time and space. Allocating a register causes the probabilities for many of the other inter-block variables to change. This follows from the observation that if a register becomes allocated at some point in the program, it must have a probability of 1 at that point. To make room for this fixed probability (1), the probabilities of any competing candidates must change.

If, for example, `B` and `E` in block **Z** become allocated, then after the load of `A` at #16 all three of the registers will be in use. Therefore the probability that `C` could be in a register at #17 must drop to 0. Because `E` is dead at #17, its register will be allocated to C when C is loaded.

Because the probabilities and allocations interact, global allocation is done iteratively. A greedy algorithm finds the best candidate for register allocation based on both its probability and benefit, and allocates a register to that use. We combine probability and benefit by multiplying them together to get a figure of merit for removing a particular load. Then the probabilities are recalculated, and another register is allocated. This process is repeated until there are no remaining uses with probability greater than 0.

4.1 Improving Probabilistic Register Allocation

Probabilistic register allocation carefully determines which candidates for registers show the greatest promise to benefit the program. Additional techniques complete the register allocation process. Our algorithm allocates registers *inside-out*, from the most deeply nested regions to the outermost, thereby emphasizing allocation in the code most likely to be executed often. The algorithm assumes that all variables initially reside in memory until they are allocated a register. After local allocation, the algorithm locates loads that can be removed by allocating a register along all paths from reaching definitions to the chosen load. After loads are removed, it is possible that some stores may be removed—those whose values are no longer referenced from memory. In addition, some loads and stores may be removed from a loop by placing them outside the loop in a pre-header or post-exit to increase loop speed. Local allocation, followed by load and store removal, provides a mechanism for global allocation that avoids the difficulties of splitting live-ranges or isolating spill candidates.

4.2 Example

The example in Figure 3 illustrates a simplified version of our algorithm (again, assuming 3 registers). Loads will be examined for removal in order of benefit and probability. The second number of each tuple is the *benefit* of removing the load—a value of 100 indicates the load will be executed on all of the 100 iterations of the loop whereas a value of 50 represents an estimate that that branch of the conditional will only execute half as often. (We assume that the probability that a value resides in a register from the **Pre-Header** is 100% because that can be made so by adding a load of the value there.)

Because #12 has a 100% probability of finding B in a register, its consideration could be deferred indefinitely—it is certain to be in a register! This 100% chance is easily deduced by recognizing that block **Y** has only **X** as a predecessor, and #10 (in **X**) left B in a register. (This is information that a graph coloring algorithm could not readily provide.) Delaying allocation (and the subsequent removal of the load) would, however, contribute spurious Δ-probabilities to the calculation of global probabilities for other uses; we therefore remove it immediately.[1]

The loads of A at #1 and #16 will be removed next because they have the highest probabilities (67%) of those loads with a benefit of 100 (and hence the highest "merit" value of 67). In order to remove the load at #1, it is necessary to insure that A's value will be in a register on the incoming control-flow arc from the **Pre-Header** by putting a load of A there.

After registers have been allocated in order to remove these three loads (#1, #12, #16), the probabilities for the remaining loads are recalculated. The new Δ-probabilities are given in Figure 4, and the new global probabilities (calculated using these Δ's) are given in Figure 5.

The Δ-probabilities for block **Y** of Figure 4 have undergone a dramatic change after the allocation of a registers for A and B. Because A is allocated a register upon entry, and because A is dead at #13, the register allocator can reuse that register for the load of E. Therefore, the Δ-probabilities for C and D are 1 throughout the block. The summary "*Probability Value in Register*" seems to indicate that 4(!) values have a 100% probability of being in a register at the end of the block. This result can be explained by recognizing that the probabilities for C and D are conditional—the value of C (or D) is in a register on exit *only if* it is in a register on entry. Since at most one of the two could have been in a register upon entry, we have not erroneously calculated that 4 values could fit in 3 registers.

Now, four remaining loads have the highest "figure of merit" (25) for removal: three loads with benefit of 100 and a probability of 25% (#2(B), #4(C), and #17(C)), and one load with benefit of 50 and a probability of 50% (#13(E)). For simplicity, we will arbitrarily choose to allocate a register to C at #4—this too requires an initial load of C in the **Pre-Header**. After this allocation, the remaining probabilities change again—only two of the remaining load instructions have probability greater than 0: #13 and #17. Fortunately, both of these loads can be removed.

It is useful to recognize how probabilities could determine that D could not be in a register at #5 after removing the load of C at #4. It might appear that

[1] All loads with 100% probability of register allocation are removed immediately, regardless of their benefit. Only this situation of 100% probability (*certainty*) is special-cased and it is done to insure accurate Δ-probability computations.

Block X

Instr #	Instruction	Local Needs	Δ-Probabilities A	B	C	D	E	Comments
1	-	0	1	-	-	-	-	*Removed*
2	load B, v2	1	1	1*	1/2	1/2	1/2	
3	add v100, v2, v3	1	0	1	1	1	1	A is dead
4	load C, v4	2	-	0	1*	1	1	B is dead
5	load D, v5	3	-	-	1	1*	0	
6	add v4, v5, v6	2	-	-	1/2	1/2	-	
7	add v3, v6, v100	1	1*	-	1	1	-	
8	store v100, A	1	1	-	1	1	-	
9	load E, v8	2	1	-	1	1	1*	
10	add v100, v8, v200	1	1	1*	1/2	1/2	1/2	
11	store v200, B	0	1	1	1	1	1	
Probability Value in Register			1	1	1/4	1/4	1/2	

Block Y

Instr #	Instruction	Local Needs	Δ-Probabilities A	B	C	D	E	Comments
12	-	0	1	1	-	-	-	*Removed*
13	load E, v11	1	0	1	1	1	1*	A is dead
14	add v200, v11, v100	0	1*	1	1	1	0	E is dead
15	store v100, A	0	1	1	1	1	-	
Probability Value in Register			1	1	1	1	0	

Block Z

Instr #	Instruction	Local Needs	Δ-Probabilities A	B	C	D	E	Comments
16	-	0	1	-	-	-	-	*Removed*
17	load C, v14	1	1	1/2	1*	1/2	1/2	
18	add v100, v14, v15	1	1	1/2	1/2	1/2	1*	
19	store v15, E	0	1	1	1	1	1	
Probability Value in Register			1	1/4	1/2	1/4	1	

Figure 4: Δ-Probabilities after 2 Allocations for `A` (`v100`), and 1 allocation for `B` (`v200`).

only 2 of the 3 registers are allocated at the entrance to block **X** (for registers `A` and `C`), but prior to loading `D` it is necessary to load `B` without destroying `A` or `C` and this uses all three registers. Similarly, `B` cannot be in a register at #2 because all three registers must be in use at the end of block **Z** holding the values of `A`, `C`, and `E` thus preventing the value of `B` from being held in a register over that control flow path.

After the loads are removed, simple data flow analysis indicates that further improvements can be made by removing the stores of `A` (at #8 and #15). If `A` is live on exit to the loop, a store of `A` must be added to the **Post-Exit**.

Note that removal of the "`load B, v10`" at #12 was possible *without* allocating a register to `B` for its entire live-range. `B` must be stored at #11 so that it may be loaded at #2 in a subsequent iteration, but probability analysis indicated that the value stored at #11 would be available at #12 in a register, so the load could be removed. (Graph coloring algorithms do not indicate this level of register availability information.)

After register allocation, `A` and `C` were effectively allocated registers for the inner region, and a load of `B` was removed. In total, 5 of 8 loads and 2 of 4 stores were removed from the loop. Figure 6 gives the code as it would appear after allocation and assignment with the register contents after each instruction given in parenthesis.

Our implementation actually gives a better allocation than the one described above by removing instructions #1, 2, 8, 11, 12, 13, 15, and 16 for an estimated cost of 50 fewer instruction. The better allocation was found because the implementation chose to remove instruction #2 whereas the previous (hand-calculated)

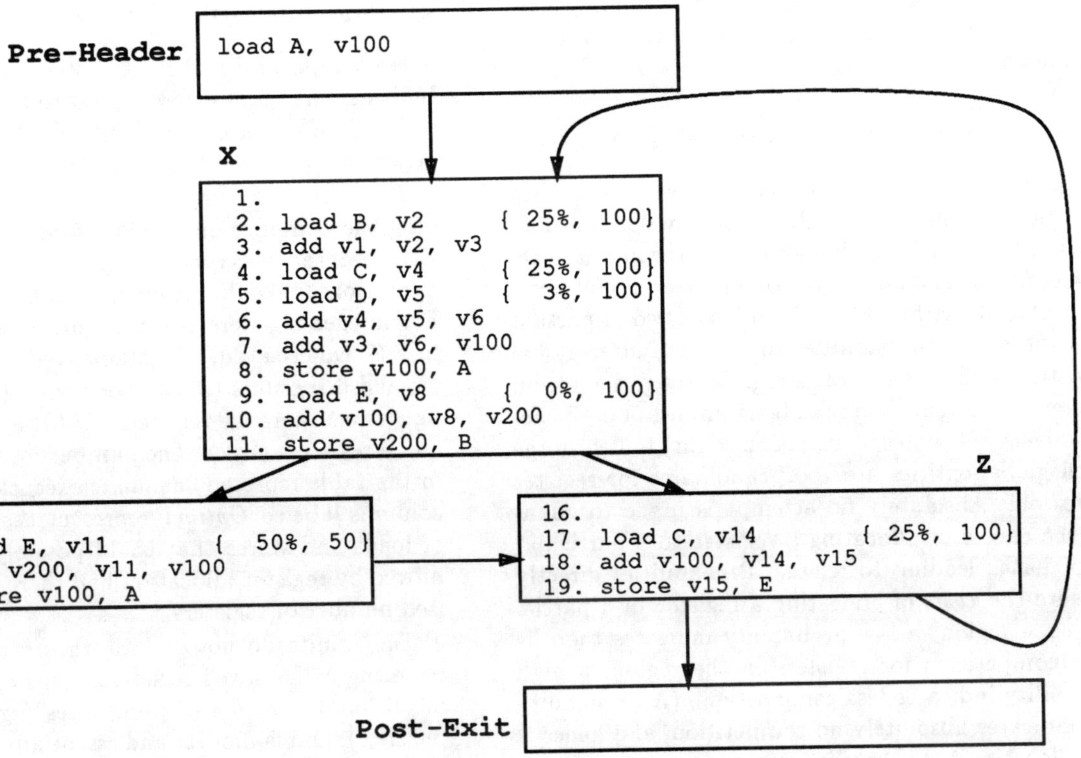

Figure 5: Global Probabilities after 3 Allocations

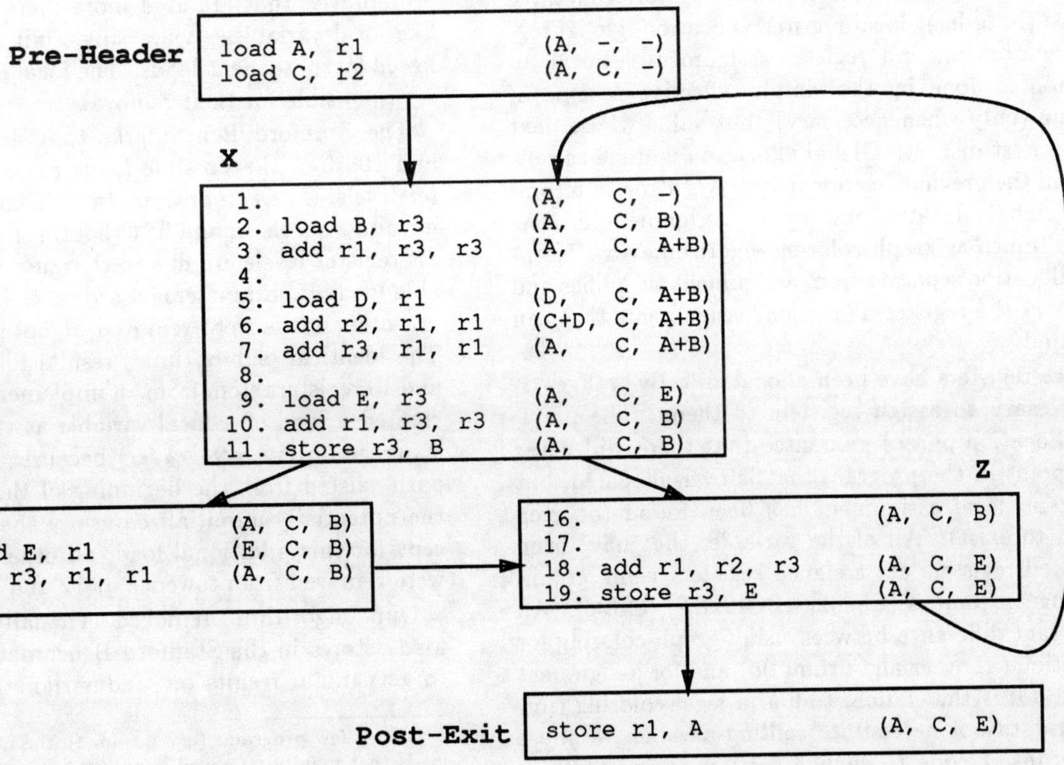

Figure 6: Code After Register Allocation and Assignment (Register Assignments in Parenthesis)

example chose #4. The implementation simply happened to break the tie among the candidates of merit 25 differently.

4.3 Probabilities Improve Beatty's Algorithm

Our algorithm is an improvement to Beatty's register allocation scheme [Bea74]. His algorithm does local allocation followed by global allocation through the removal of loads and stores to loop pre-header and post-exits. Our algorithm differs from his in two important ways: ours uses probabilities to provide better global allocation, and ours separates register assignment from register allocation. Beatty's algorithm uses only benefit analysis (estimates of execution count) to determine which global entities are good candidates for register allocation. Absolutely no attempt is made to quantify the effects of allocating a register to a particular set of paths leading to a use. Probabilities directly measure the *costs* of allocating a register in a particular code region; a low probability indicates there is great competition for registers in the region, a high probability indicates less competition. (A probability of 1 indicates absolutely no competition, and hence a *free* allocation.) Probabilistic cost measures improve Beatty's algorithm by guiding it to make good allocation decisions by balancing benefit **and** cost estimates.

Our probabilistic register allocator works in three phases (in order): local register allocation, global register allocation, and register assignment. Local allocation is done by the simple, effective scheme of spilling (only when necessary) that value whose next use is most distant. Global allocation is done as outlined in the previous sections. Beatty's algorithm combines global allocation and register assignment into one phase (much as graph coloring algorithms do). Keeping allocation separate from assignment simplifies and improves the register allocation/assignments that can be found.

Once registers have been allocated to live-ranges, it is necessary to assign registers to them. The previous allocation phases guarantee that there will never be a point in the program that is over-allocated, but so far no legal assignment has been found (or even shown to exist). All of the variables that have been allocated registers are assigned registers using graph-coloring techniques [Cha82], [BCKT89], [CH90]. An important difference between using graph-coloring for allocation (as other algorithms do) and for assignment (as we do) is that failure to find a legal coloring (unlikely) does not necessitate spilling a value; we must simply insert code to change register assignments or duplicate a code fragment with a new set of register assignments.

5 Implementation Results

A prototype probabilistic register allocator has been built as part of an experimental code generator for an ANSI C compiler ("`lcc`" [FH91b] [FH91a]). The code generator produces MIPS R2000 assembler.

The table in Figure 7 summarizes the results of running the compiler on the Stanford benchmarks suite. Each program was run with three different register configurations for both integer and floating point registers. For integer registers the configurations were 19 registers (9 caller-saved, 10 callee-saved), 12 registers (6, 6), and 6 registers (3, 3). For floating point, the configurations were 11 registers (5, 6), 8 registers (4, 4), and 4 registers (2, 2). The numbers of loads and stores in the table represent *dynamic* execution counts. The columns labeled *Optimal* represent the actual number of loads and stores that could possibly have been removed by register allocation had there been an unlimited number of registers.[2]

The results do not include the cost of saving and restoring callee-saved registers. This cost is negligible in all but the recursive procedures (eg. towers.c and puzzle.c), and is modest and essentially unavoidable in those.

The great number of locally removed loads and stores is the result of the fact that all basic block level temporaries that are used more than once are treated like local variables—via a single initializing store followed by subsequent loads. The local register allocator is responsible for their removal.

The Stanford Benchmarks that are not listed all had 100% of the possible loads removed at *all* register levels. The sub-optimal (and identical) results for intmm.c, queens.c, and fft.c (floating) at the two greatest register levels are due to charging for the unavoidable loads of parameters passed on the stack—100% of the other loads were removed at both register levels. The identical (sub-optimal) results for towers.c at 12 and 19 registers stem from an implementation bug that created a load of a local variable at the beginning of a procedure (its *pre-header*) because a definition-free path existed from the beginning of that procedure to the potentially uninitialized use of that variable. Except for this additional load, all other possible loads were removed from towers.c at 12 and 19 registers.

Our algorithm removed virtually all of the loads/stores in the Stanford Benchmarks. We expect to get similar results on "industrial strength" bench-

[2]For a few programs (eg. intmm.c), the number of possible loads that may be removed is *overstated* because the statistics do not reflect the fact that an initial load of a parameter passed on the stack is unavoidable. This, of course, results in an *understatement* of our algorithm's effectiveness.

		Load Removal (Execution Counts)				Store Removal (Execution Counts)			
Program	Registers (integer)	Optimal	Locally Removed	Globally Removed	Percent	Optimal	Locally Removed	Globally Removed	Percent
intmm.c	19	977854	521726	454528	99.8	272247	192002	80245	100.0
	12	977854	521726	454528	99.8	272247	192002	80245	100.0
	6	977854	457726	200128	67.3	272247	128002	75445	74.7
queens.c	19	696950	220450	465200	98.4	183401	5650	177751	100.0
	12	696950	220450	465200	98.4	183401	5650	177751	100.0
	6	696950	220450	288100	73.0	183401	5650	155151	87.7
quick.c	19	734725	273098	461627	100.0	213785	101453	112332	100.0
	12	734725	273098	461627	100.0	213785	101453	112332	100.0
	6	734725	257468	414742	91.5	213785	101453	58032	74.6
towers.c	19	614192	458887	138908	97.3	311413	180258	131155	100.0
	12	614192	458887	138908	97.3	311413	180258	131155	100.0
	6	614192	450696	138908	96.0	311413	180258	114772	94.7
fft.c	19	2036794	1598413	438221	99.9	479938	401267	78491	99.9
	12	2036794	1598413	392001	97.7	479938	401267	73191	98.9
	6	2036794	1352023	303859	81.3	479938	360181	67849	89.2
	(floating)								
fft.c	11	11090	5170	5895	99.8	1496	1024	446	98.3
	8	11090	5170	5895	99.8	1496	1024	446	98.3
	4	11090	5170	5850	99.6	1496	1024	425	96.7

Figure 7: Results on Selected Stanford Benchmarks.

marks such as the SPEC Benchmarks when we do more exhaustive tests of the code generator. Unfortunately, `lcc` does not do any global optimizations such as alias analysis or global common subexpression elimination that would create many additional candidates for global register allocation and, therefore, test our techniques more strenuously. (`Lcc` only considers temporaries, and scalar local variables and parameters as candidates for register allocation.) We have, therefore, chosen to create a similar register scarcity artificially by lowering the number of available registers. While not a perfect measure of how the algorithm would do in an optimizing compiler, the numbers are impressive nonetheless.

5.1 Compiler Performance

The current register allocator is a prototype implementation that slows `lcc`'s compilation rate from over 1000 lines/sec. to about 10 lines/sec. Modestly tuning this prototype implementation would certainly increase compilation speed by 20 to 50 times.

The naive implementation recomputes dataflow and Δ-probability information for the current loop after each load is removed. Doing this recomputation incrementally would likely increase the allocation speed dramatically.

Alternatively, a quicker, but less accurate, allocation heuristic could be built that would not recompute these values, but would instead use a static "snapshot" of the probabilities. This would avoid recomputing the Δ-probabilities after each load is removed. The static initial probabilities would still serve as an accurate metric of the relative scarcity of registers faced by each register candidate.

6 Other Uses for Probabilities

Register probabilities are general enough to help graph-coloring algorithms site spills and split live-range. For instance, presently graph coloring heuristics prune the interference graph by making the trivial observation that any live range with fewer conflicts than available registers can be removed from the graph and subsequently assigned a register. Probability analysis can additionally indicate, for those live ranges with too many conflicts, which will *probably* be allocated a register—thus intelligently directing further pruning of the interference graph.

Similarly, probabilistic register allocation could be used *after* graph-coloring techniques have exploited all the trivial pruning opportunities available. If the pruning stage fails to allocate registers to every node in the graph, our probabilistic algorithm could be used to allocate registers among the (presumably) many fewer remaining register candidates.

7 Conclusion

Using probabilities to guide global register allocation after a local allocation phase provides a simple and effective algorithm that avoids complex graph-coloring spill heuristics. It focuses attention on the problem of *allocating* registers over *assigning* registers—a weakness inherent to previous graph coloring schemes. Graph coloring algorithms awkwardly handle splitting live-ranges when registers are exhausted, but probabilistic global allocation completely subsumes this concern. Finally, because of the clean separation between local allocation and global allocation, our probabilistic algorithm allows existing excellent local register allocation and instruction scheduling algorithms to run unconstrained by global allocation policies.

8 Acknowledgements

David Callahan, Chris Fraser, Robert Henry, and Brian Koblenz provided comments that improved the content and accuracy of this paper.

References

[BCKT89] Preston Briggs, Keith D. Cooper, Ken Kennedy, and Linda Torczon. Coloring heuristics for register allocation. In *Proceedings of the SIGPLAN '89 Conference on Programming Language Design and Implementation*, pages 275–284, 1989.

[Bea74] J. C. Beatty. Register assignment algorithm for generation of highly optimized object code. *IBM Journal of Research and Development*, 18(1):20–39, January 1974.

[BL92] Thomas Ball and James R. Larus. Optimally profiling and tracing programs. In *Proceedings of the 19th Annual Symposium on Principles of Programming Languages*, pages 59–70, January 1992.

[CAC+81] G. J. Chaitin, M. A. Auslander, A. K. Chandra, J. Cooke, M. E. Hopkins, and P. W. Markstein. Register allocation via graph coloring. *Computer Languages*, 6:47–57, January 1981.

[CH90] Fred C. Chow and John L. Hennessy. The priority-based coloring approach to register allocation. *ACM Transactions on Programming Languages and Systems*, 12(4):501–536, January 1990.

[Cha82] G. J. Chaitin. Register allocation & spilling via graph coloring. In *Proceedings of the ACM SIGPLAN '82 Symposium on Compiler Construction*, pages 98–101, June 1982.

[CK91] David Callahan and Brian Koblenz. Register allocation via hierarchical graph coloring. In *Proceedings of the SIGPLAN '91 Conference on Programming Language Design and Implementation*, pages 192–203, 1991.

[FH91a] Christopher W. Fraser and David R. Hanson. A code generation interface for ANSI C. *Software—Practice and Experience*, 21(9):963–988, September 1991.

[FH91b] Christopher W. Fraser and David R. Hanson. A retargetable compiler for ANSI C. *SIGPLAN Notices*, 26(10), October 1991.

[FL88] Charles N. Fischer and Richard J. Leblanc, Jr. *Crafting a Compiler*. Benjamin/Cummings, Menlo Park, California, 1988.

[Fre74] R. A. Freiburghouse. Register allocation via usage counts. *Communications of the ACM*, 17(11), November 1974.

[HFG89] Wei-Chung Hsu, Charles N. Fischer, and James R. Goodman. On the minimization of loads/stores in local register allocation. *IEEE Transactions on Software Engineering*, 15(10):1252–1260, 1989.

[LH86] J. R. Larus and P. N. Hilfinger. Register allocation in the SPUR lisp compiler. In *Proceedings of the SIGPLAN '86 Symposium on Compiler Construction*, pages 255–263, 1986.

[Mor91] W. G. Morris. CCG: A prototype coagulating code generator. In *Proceedings of the SIGPLAN '91 Conference on Programming Language Design and Implementation*, pages 45–58, 1991.

Rematerialization

Preston Briggs
Keith D. Cooper
Linda Torczon

Department of Computer Science*
Rice University
Houston, TX 77251–1892

Abstract

This paper examines a problem that arises during global register allocation – *rematerialization*. If a value cannot be kept in a register, the allocator should recognize when it is cheaper to recompute the value (rematerialize it) than to store and reload it. Chaitin's original graph-coloring allocator handled simple instances of this problem correctly. This paper details a general solution to the problem and presents experimental evidence that shows its importance.

Our approach is to tag individual values in the procedure's SSA graph with information specifying how it should be spilled. We use a variant of Wegman and Zadeck's *sparse simple constant* algorithm to propagate tags throughout the graph. The allocator then splits live ranges into values with different tags. This isolates those values that can be easily rematerialized from values that require general spilling. We modify the base allocator to use this information when estimating spill costs and introducing spill code.

Our presentation focuses on rematerialization in the context of Chaitin's allocator; however, the problem arises in any global allocator. We believe that our approach will work in other allocators – while the details of implementation will vary, the key insights should carry over directly.

1 Introduction

In the past decade, the literature on register allocation has focused largely on *global* allocation – methods that factor information about the entire procedure into the decision process. Because the problem of optimal register allocation is NP-complete [19], compilers employ heuristic techniques to approximate its solution. In general, today's generation of global allocators produces "good" approximations; however, careful examination of the output of these allocators reveals that there is still room for improvement.

This paper examines a specific problem that arises in global register allocation – *rematerialization*. When a value must be spilled, the allocator should recognize those cases when it is cheaper to recompute the value than to store and retrieve it from memory. While our discussion is set in the context of a Chaitin-style graph-coloring allocator [6, 5, 3, 1], the same questions seem to arise in all global allocators.

Consider the code fragments shown in Figure 1 (the notation $[p]$ means "the contents of the memory location addressed by p"). Examining the *Source* column, we note that p is constant in the first loop, but varying in the second loop. The register allocator should take advantage of this situation.

Imagine that high demand for registers in the first loop forces p to be spilled; the *Ideal* column shows the desired result. In the upper loop, p is loaded just before it is needed (using some sort of "load-immediate" instruction). For the lower loop, p is loaded just before the loop, again using a load-immediate.

The *Chaitin* column illustrates the code that would be produced by a Chaitin-style allocator. The entire live range of p has been spilled to memory, with loads inserted before uses and stores inserted after definitions.

The final column shows code we would expect from a "splitting" allocator [8, 17, 16, 4]; the actual code might be worse. In fact, our work on rematerialization was motivated by problems observed during our own experiments with live range splitting. Unfortunately, examples of this sort are not discussed in the literature on splitting allocators and it is unclear how best to extend these techniques to achieve the *Ideal* solution.

We begin our discussion with a brief review of Chaitin-style allocators. Section 3 gives a high-level view of our approach to rematerialization. Section 4 describes the low-level modifications to the allocator required to support our approach. Experimental results are presented in Section 5. Subsequent sections suggest extensions and make comparisons with other work.

*This work has been supported by DARPA through ONR grant N00014-91-J-1989 and by the IBM Corporation.

ACM SIGPLAN '92 PLDI-6/92/CA
© 1992 ACM 0-89791-476-7/92/0006/0311...$1.50

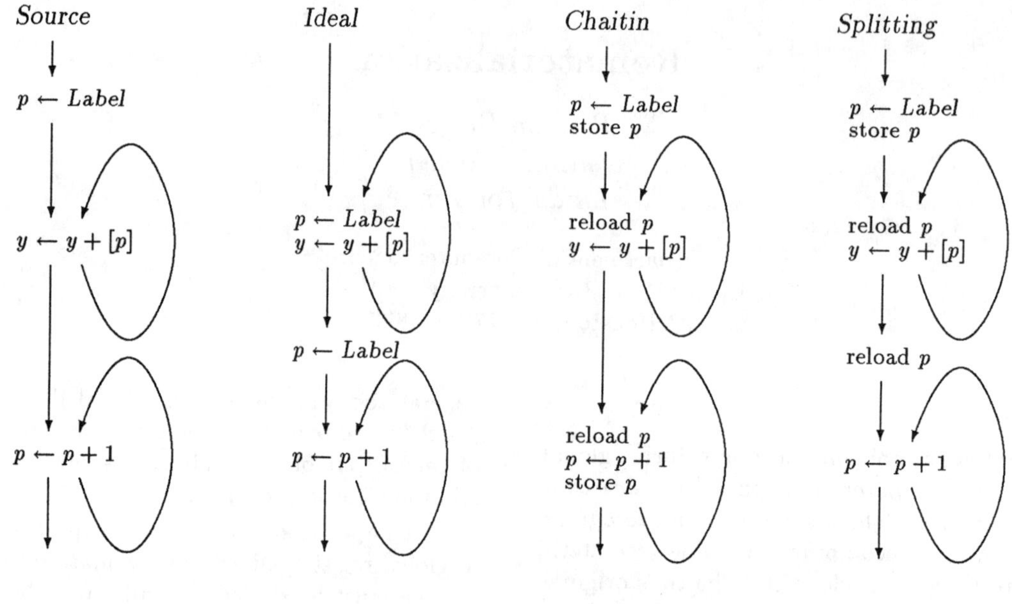

Figure 1: Rematerialization versus Spilling

2 Background

The notion of modeling register allocation as a graph coloring problem descends from very early work on storage allocation [18]. The first actual implementation was done by Chaitin *et al.* in the PL.8 compiler [6]. Chow and Hennessy described a priority-based scheme built on a coloring paradigm [8]. Our own work has built on Chaitin's approach [3]. To distinguish our allocator from Chaitin's, we call it the *optimistic* allocator.

Throughout this paper, we assume that the allocator works on either low-level intermediate code or assembly code. Before allocation, the code can reference an unlimited number of virtual registers. A single virtual register can have disconnected lifetimes in distinct parts of the procedure. Rather than map virtual registers directly onto physical registers, the allocator discovers the distinct *live ranges* in a procedure and allocates them to physical registers.

To model register allocation as a graph coloring problem, the compiler first constructs an interference graph G. Nodes in G represent live ranges; edges represent *interferences.* Thus, there is an edge from node i to node j if and only if live range l_i *interferes* with live range l_j; that is, they are simultaneously live at some point and cannot occupy the same register. Live ranges that interfere with l_i are its *neighbors* in the graph; the *degree* of l_i is the number of neighbors it has in the graph.

To find an allocation from G, the compiler looks for a k-coloring of G; that is, an assignment of k colors to the nodes of G such that neighboring nodes always have distinct colors. If we choose k to match the number of machine registers, then we can map a k-coloring for G into a feasible register assignment for the underlying code. Because finding a k-coloring of an arbitrary graph is NP-complete, the compiler uses a heuristic method to search for a coloring; it is not guaranteed to find a k-coloring for all k-colorable graphs. If a k-coloring is not discovered, some live ranges are *spilled*; *i.e.*, the values are kept in memory rather than registers.

Spilling one or more live ranges changes both the code and the interference graph. The compiler proceeds by iteratively spilling some live ranges and attempting to color the resulting new graph. This process is guaranteed to terminate. In practice, this process converges quickly [5, 3] (see also Table 2). Figure 2 illustrates the overall flow of the optimistic allocator.

Renumber finds the live ranges and gives them unique names. It creates a new live range for each definition point and unions together the live ranges that reach each use point.

Build constructs the interference graph using the dual representations, a triangular bit-matrix and a set of adjacency vectors, advocated by Chaitin [5].

Coalesce attempts to combine live ranges. Two live ranges l_i and l_j are combined, giving l_{ij}, if the initial definition of l_j is a copy from l_i and there is no interference between l_i and l_j. This has several beneficial effects; most importantly, it eliminates the copy and reduces the total degree of the graph. Since some coalesces can preclude others, the allocator should work "inside out," examining deeply-nested blocks first.

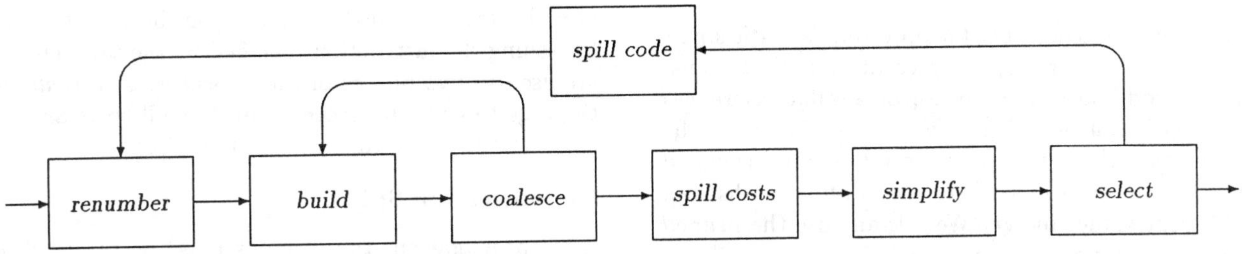

Figure 2: The Optimistic Allocator

Spill Costs estimates the cost associated with spilling each live range. Spill cost is computed as the cost of the memory accesses required to spill the live range, each weighted by 10^d where d is the instruction's loop nesting depth.

Simplify constructs an ordering of the nodes. It removes nodes with current degree less than k from G, pushes them on a stack, and decrements the degree of their neighbors. If all remaining nodes have k or more neighbors, it chooses a *spill candidate*, removes it from G, and pushes it on the stack.

The metric for picking spill candidates is critical. Chaitin suggested choosing the node that minimizes spill cost divided by degree [5].

Select assigns colors to the nodes of G in the order determined by *simplify*. *Select* repeatedly pops a node from the stack and attempts to give it a color distinct from its colored neighbors. If no color is available for a node, it is left uncolored. If all nodes receive colors, allocation is complete.

Spill Code is invoked if *select* left a node uncolored. It converts each such node into a collection of tiny live ranges by inserting a load or store at each use and definition.

Detailed descriptions of these processes can be found in Chaitin's work and our earlier paper [5, 6, 3].

3 Rematerialization

Chaitin *et al.* discuss several ideas for improving the quality of spill code [6]. They point out that certain values can be recomputed in a single instruction and that the required operands will always be available for the computation. They call these exceptional values *never-killed* and note that such values should be recalculated instead of being spilled and reloaded. They further note that an uncoalesced copy of a never-killed value can be eliminated by recomputing it directly into the desired register [6]. Together, these techniques are termed *rematerialization.* In practice, opportunities for rematerialization include:

- immediate loads of integer constants and, on some machines, floating-point constants,
- computing a constant offset from the frame pointer or the static data area pointer,
- loads from a known constant location in either the frame or the static data area, and
- loading non-local frame pointers from a *display*.

The values must be cheaply computable from operands that are available throughout the procedure.

It is important to understand the distinction between *live ranges* and *values.* A live range may comprise several values connected by common uses. In the *Source* column of Figure 1, p denotes a single live range composed from three values: the address *Label*, the result of the expression $p+1$, and (more subtly) the merge of those two values at the head of the second loop.

Chaitin's allocator correctly handles rematerialization when spilling live ranges with a single value, but cannot handle more complex cases; *e.g.*, the variable p in Figure 1. Our task is to extend Chaitin's work to take advantage of rematerialization opportunities for complex, multi-valued live ranges. Our approach is to tag each value with enough information to allow the allocator to handle it correctly. To achieve this, we

1. split each live range into its component values,
2. propagate rematerialization tags to each value, and
3. form new live ranges from connected values having identical tags.

This approach allows correct handling of rematerialization, but introduces the new problem of minimizing unnecessary splits. The following sections describe how to find values, how to propagate tags, how to split the live ranges, and how to remove unproductive splits.

3.1 Discovering Values

To find values, we construct the procedure's *static single assignment* (SSA) graph, a representation that transforms the code so that each use of a value references exactly one definition [11]. To achieve this goal, the construction technique inserts special definitions called ϕ-nodes at those points where control-flow paths join and different values merge. We actually use the *pruned* SSA, with dead ϕ-nodes eliminated [7].

A natural way to view the SSA graph for a procedure is as a collection of values, each composed of a single definition and one or more uses. Each value's definition is either a single instruction or a ϕ-node that merges two or more values. By examining the defining instruction for each value, we can recognize never-killed values and propagate this information throughout the SSA graph.

3.2 Propagating Rematerialization Tags

To propagate tags, we use an analog of Wegman and Zadeck's *sparse simple constant* algorithm [21]. We modify their lattice slightly to represent the necessary rematerialization information. The new lattice elements may have one of three types:

$\top$ *Top* means that no information is known. A value defined by a copy instruction or a ϕ-node has an initial tag of $\top$.

inst If a value is defined by an appropriate instruction (*never-killed*), it should be rematerialized. The value's tag is simply a pointer to the instruction.

$\bot$ *Bottom* means that the value must be spilled and restored. Any value defined by an "inappropriate" instruction is immediately tagged with $\bot$.

Additionally, their *meet* operation $\sqcap$ is modified correspondingly. The new definition is:

$$\begin{array}{lllll} \text{any} & \sqcap & \top & = & \text{any} \\ \text{any} & \sqcap & \bot & = & \bot \\ inst_i & \sqcap & inst_j & = & inst_i \quad \text{if } inst_i = inst_j \\ inst_i & \sqcap & inst_j & = & \bot \quad \text{if } inst_i \neq inst_j \end{array}$$

Note that $inst_i = inst_j$ compares the instructions on an operand-by-operand basis. Since our instructions have at most 2 operands, this modification does not affect the asymptotic complexity of propagation.

During propagation, each value will be tagged with a particular *inst* or $\bot$. Values defined by a copy instruction will have their tags *lowered* to *inst* or $\bot$, depending on the value that flows into the copy. Tags for values defined by ϕ-nodes will be lowered to *inst* if and only if all the values flowing into the node have equivalent *inst* tags; otherwise, they are lowered to $\bot$.

This process tags each value in the SSA graph with either an instruction or $\bot$. If a value's tag is $\bot$, spilling that value requires a normal, heavyweight spill. If, however, its tag is an instruction, it can be rematerialized by issuing the instruction specified by the tag. The tags are used in two phases of the allocator: *spill costs* uses the tags to compute more accurate spill costs and *spill code* uses the tags to emit the desired code.

3.3 Inserting Splits

After propagation, the ϕ-nodes must be removed and values renamed to recreate an executable program. Consider the example in Figure 3. The *Source* column simply repeats the example introduced in Figure 1. The *SSA* column shows the effect of inserting a ϕ-node for p and renaming the different values comprising p's live range. The *Splits* column illustrates the copies necessary to distinguish the different values without ϕ-nodes. The final column (*Minimal*) shows the single copy required to isolate the never-killed value p_0 from the other values comprising p. We avoid the extra copy by noting that p_1 and p_2 have identical tags after propagation (both are $\bot$) and may be treated together as a single live range p_{12}. Similarly, two connected values with the same *inst* tag would be combined into a single live range.

For the purposes of rematerialization, the copies are placed perfectly – the never-killed value has been isolated and no further copies have been introduced. The algorithm for removing ϕ-nodes and inserting copies is described in Section 4.1. In Section 6, we discuss the possibility of including *all* the copies suggested in the *Splits* column.

3.4 Removing Unproductive Splits

Our approach inserts the minimal number of copies required to isolate the never-killed values. Nevertheless, coloring can make some of these copies superfluous. Recall the *Minimal* column in Figure 3. If neither p_0 nor p_{12} are spilled and they both receive the same color, the copy connecting them is unnecessary. Because it has a real run-time cost, the copy should be eliminated whenever possible. Of course, *coalesce* would remove *all* of the copies, losing the desired separation between values with different tags. So, we use a pair of limited coalescing mechanisms to remove unproductive copies:

Conservative coalescing is a straightforward modification of Chaitin's *coalesce* phase. Conceptually, we add a single constraint to *coalesce* – only combine two live ranges if the resulting single live range will not be spilled.

Biased coloring increases the likelihood that live ranges connected by a copy get assigned to the same register. Conceptually, *select* tries to assign the same color to two live ranges connected by a copy.

Taken together, these two mechanisms remove most of the unproductive copies.

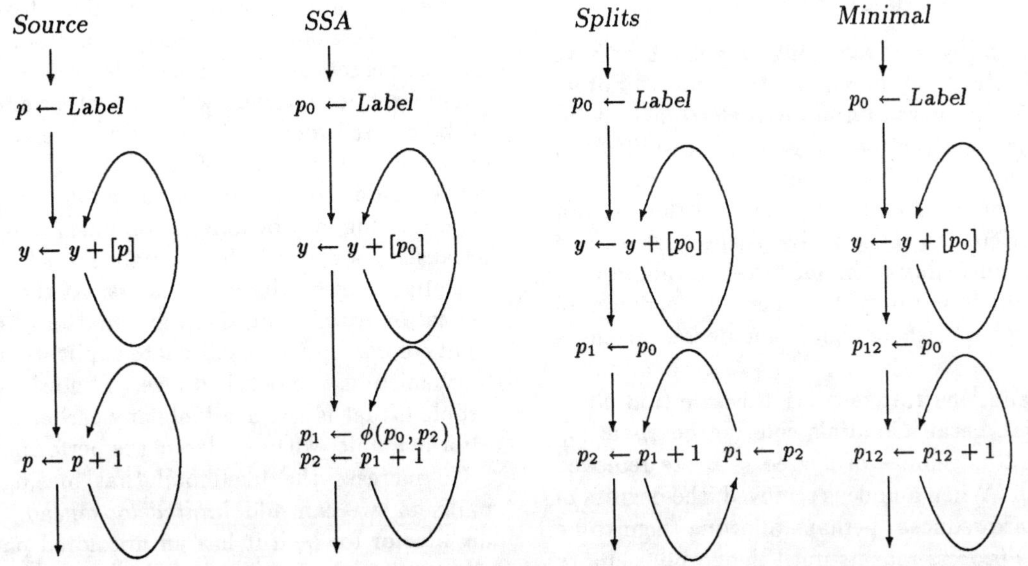

Figure 3: Introducing Splits

4 Implementation

Chaitin-style allocators can be extended naturally to accommodate our approach. The high-level structure depicted in Figure 2 is unchanged, but a number of low-level modifications are required. The next sections discuss the enhancements required in *renumber, coalesce,* and *select.*

4.1 Renumber

Chaitin's version of *renumber* (termed "getting the right number of names") was based on def-use chaining [6]. Long before our interest in rematerialization, we adopted an implementation strategy for *renumber* based on the pruned SSA graph. Conceptually, the old implementation has four steps:

1. Determine liveness at each basic block using a sparse data-flow evaluation graph [7].
2. Insert ϕ-nodes based on dominance frontiers [11]. Avoid inserting dead ϕ-nodes.
3. Renumber the operands in every instruction to refer to values instead of the original virtual registers. At the same time, accumulate availability information for each block. The intersection of *live* and *avail* is needed at each block to allow construction of a precise interference graph [6].
4. Form live ranges by unioning together all the values reaching each ϕ-node using a fast disjoint-set union. The disjoint-set structure is maintained while building the interference graph and coalescing (where coalesces are further union operations).

In our implementation, steps 3 and 4 are performed during a single walk over the dominator tree. Using these techniques, *renumber* completely avoids the use of *bit-vectored* flow analysis. Despite the apparent complexity of the algorithms involved, it is very fast in practice and requires only a modest amount of space.

Because *renumber* already uses the SSA graph, only modest changes are required to support rematerialization. The modified *renumber* has six steps:

1. Determine liveness at each basic block using a sparse data-flow evaluation graph.
2. Insert ϕ-nodes based on dominance frontiers, still avoiding insertion of dead ϕ-nodes.
3. Renumber the operands in each instruction to refer to values. At the same time, initialize the rematerialization tags for all values.
4. Propagate tags using the sparse simple constant algorithm as modified in Section 3.2.
5. Examine each copy instruction. If the source and destination values have identical *inst* tags, we can union them and remove the copy.
6. Examine the operands of each ϕ-node. If an operand value has the same tag as the result value, union the values; otherwise, insert a *split* (a distinguished copy instruction) connecting the values in the corresponding predecessor block.

Steps 5 and 6 are performed in a single walk over the dominator tree.

4.2 Conservative Coalescing

To prevent coalescing from removing the splits that have been carefully introduced in *renumber*, we must limit its power. Specifically, it should never coalesce a split instruction if the resulting live range may be spilled. In normal coalescing, two live ranges l_i and l_j are combined if l_j is defined by a copy from l_i and they do not otherwise interfere. In conservative coalescing, we add an additional constraint: combine two live ranges connected by a split if and only if l_{ij} has $< k$ neighbors of "significant degree," where significant degree means a degree $\geq k$.

To understand why this restriction is safe (indeed, it is conservative), recall Chaitin's coloring heuristic [5]. Before any spilling, nodes of degree $< k$ are removed from the graph. When a node is removed, the degrees of its neighbors are reduced, perhaps allowing them to be removed. This process repeats until the graph is empty or all remaining nodes have degree $\geq k$. Therefore, for a node to be spilled, it must have at least k neighbors with degree $\geq k$ in the initial graph.

In practice, we perform two rounds of coalescing. Initially, all possible copies are coalesced (but not split instructions). The graph is rebuilt and coalescing is repeated until no more copies can be removed. Then, we begin conservatively coalescing split instructions. Again, we repeatedly build the interference graph and attempt further conservative coalescing until no more splits can be removed.

In theory, we should not intermix conservative coalescing with unrestricted coalescing, since the result of an unrestricted coalesce may be spilled. For example, l_i and l_j might be conservatively coalesced, only to have a later coalesce of l_{ij} with l_k provoke the spilling of l_{ijk} (since the significant degree of l_{ijk} may be quite high). In practice, this may not prove to be a problem, permitting a simplification of the entire process.

Conservative coalescing directly improves the allocation. Each coalesce removes an instruction from the resulting code – a split instruction that was introduced by the allocator. In regions where there is little competition for registers (a region of low register pressure), conservative coalescing undoes all splitting. It cannot, however, undo all of the non-productive splits by itself.

4.3 Biased Coloring

The second mechanism for removing useless splits involves changing the order in which colors are considered for assignment. Before coloring, the allocator finds *partners* – values connected by splits. When *select* assigns a color to l_i, it first tries colors already assigned to one of l_i's partners. With a careful implementation, this is no more expensive than picking the first available color; it really amounts to biasing the spectrum of colors by previous assignments to l_i's partners.

The biasing mechanism can combine live ranges that conservative coalescing cannot. For example, l_i might have $2k$ neighbors of significant degree; but these neighbors might not interfere with each other and thus might all be colored identically. Conservative coalescing cannot combine l_i with any of its partners; the resulting live range would have too many neighbors of significant degree. Biasing may be able to combine l_i and its partners because it is applied after the allocator has shown that both live ranges will receive colors. At that late point in allocation, combining them is a matter of choosing the right colors. By virtue of its late application, the biasing mechanism uses a detailed level of knowledge about the problem that is not available any earlier in the process – for example, when coalescing is performed.

To increase the likelihood that biasing will match partners, we can add *limited lookahead.* When picking a color for l_i, if it has an uncolored partner l_j, the allocator can look for a color that is still available for l_j. On average, l_i has a small number of partners; thus, we can add *limited lookahead* to biased coloring without increasing the asymptotic complexity of *select*.

5 Experimental Results

To support our research, we have written an optimizing compiler for FORTRAN. The compiler is part of the ParaScope programming environment and includes support for interprocedural analysis and a variety of traditional optimizations [9]. We currently generate code for the IBM RT/PC and have experimental code generators for the Sparc, i860, and RS/6000. To experiment with register allocation, we have built a series of allocators that are independent of any particular architecture [2].

Our experimental allocators work with routines expressed in ILOC, a low-level intermediate language designed to allow extensive optimization. An ILOC routine that assumes an infinite register set is rewritten in terms of a particular target register set, with spill code added as necessary. The target register set is specified in a small table and may be varied to allow convenient experimentation with a wide variety of register sets.

After allocation, each ILOC routine is translated into a complete C routine. Each C routine is compiled and the resulting object files are linked into a complete program. There are several advantages to this approach:

- By inserting appropriate instrumentation during the translation to C, we are able to collect accurate, *dynamic* measurements.
- Compilation to C allows us to test a single routine in the context of a complete program running with real data.
- We are able to perform our tests in a machine-independent fashion, potentially using a variety of register sets.

```
LLE3:  nop                               LLE3:
LLA4:  ldi   r14   8                     LLA4:  r14 = (int) (8); i++;
       add   r9    r15   r11                    r9 = r15 + r11;
       mvf   f15   f0                           f15 = f0; c++;
       bc    L0023                              goto L0023;

L0023: lddrr f14   r14   r9              L0023: f14 = *((double *) (r14 + r9)); l++;
       dabs  f14   f14                          f14 = fabs(f14);
       dadd  f15   f15   f14                    f15 = f15 + f14;
       addi  r14   r14   8                      r14 = r14 + (8); a++;
       sub   r7    r10   r14                    r7 = r10 - r14;
       br    ge    r7    N6    N7               if (r7 >= 0) goto N6; else goto N7;
```

Figure 4: ILOC and C

Simply timing actual machine code is inherently machine-dependent and tends to obscure the effects of allocation. During the translation into C, we can add instrumentation to count the number of times any specific ILOC instruction is executed. For comparing register allocators, we are interested in the number of loads, stores, copies, load-immediates, and add-immediates.

Figure 4 shows a small sample of ILOC code and the corresponding C translation. Usually there is a one-to-one mapping between the ILOC statements and the C translations, though some additional C is required for the function header and declarations of the "register" variables; *e.g.*, `r14` and `f15`. Also note the very simple instrumentation appearing immediately after several of the statements. Of course, this code is very simple, but the majority of ILOC is no more complex.

5.1 The Target Machine

For the tests reported here, our target machine is defined to have sixteen integer registers and sixteen floating-point registers. Each floating-point register can hold a double-precision value, so no distinction is made between single-precision and double-precision values once they are held in registers. Up to four integer registers may be used to pass arguments (recall that arguments are passed by reference in FORTRAN; therefore, the argument registers hold pointers to the actual values); any remaining arguments are passed in the stack frame. Function results are returned in an integer or floating-point register, as appropriate. Ten of each register class are designated as callee-saves; the remaining six (including the argument registers) are not preserved by the callee.

When reporting costs, we assume that each load and store requires two cycles; all other instructions are assumed to require one cycle. Of course, these are only simple approximations of the costs on any real machine.

5.2 Spill Costs

Since our instrumentation reports dynamic counts of *all* loads, stores, *etc.*, we need a mechanism for isolating the instructions due to allocation. A difficulty is that some spills are profitable. In other cases, the allocator removes instructions; *e.g.*, copy instructions. Therefore, we tested each routine on a hypothetical "huge" machine with 128 registers, assuming this would give a nearly perfect allocation. The difference between the "huge" results and the results for one of the allocators targeted to our "standard" machine should equal the number of cycles added by the allocator to cope with insufficient registers.

5.3 The Test Suite

Our test suite is a collection of seventy routines contained in eleven programs. Eleven routines are from Forsythe, Malcolm, and Moler's book on numerical methods [13]. They are grouped into seven programs with simple drivers. The remaining fifty-nine routines are from the SPEC benchmark suite [20]. Four of the SPEC programs were used: `doduc` (41 routines), `fpppp` (12 routines), `matrix300` (5 routines), and `tomcatv` (1 routine). The two other FORTRAN programs in the suite (`spice` and `nasa7`) require language extensions not yet supplied by our front-end.

Table 1 summarizes the effect of our new approach to rematerialization. It compares two versions of the optimistic allocator that differ only in their handling of never-killed values. The column labeled *Optimistic* gives data for a version that uses Chaitin's limited approach to rematerialization. The column labeled *Rematerialization* gives data for a version incorporating our new method. The table shows only routines where a difference was observed.

The first two columns give the program and subroutine name. The third and fourth column give the observed spill costs for the two allocators being compared.

		Cycles of Spill Code		Percentage Contribution					
program	*routine*	*Optimistic*	*Rematerialization*	*load*	*store*	*copy*	*ldi*	*addi*	*total*
rkf45	fehl	68	50	26		7	−7		27
seval	spline	117	102	10	2	2	−1		13
solve	decomp	305	286	4	3		−1		6
svd	svd	1,977	1,966	1		0	−0		1
zeroin	zeroin	236	234	2		−1			1
doduc	bilan	1,046	966	5	3				8
	bilsla	16	15				6		6
	colbur	19	24	−11	−11	−5			−26
	ddeflu	335	375	−5	−7	1	1		−12
	debico	459	418	6	0	1	2		9
	deseco	4,957	4,636	7	2		−2	0	7
	drepvi	218	175	4	14	0	2		20
	drigl	32	31				3		3
	heat	34	31	6		1			9
	ihbtr	400	395	1	0		−0		1
	inideb	50	48				4		4
	inisla	31	28		6		3		10
	inithx	579	437	17	10		−2		25
	integr	502	372	18	12		−3		26
	lectur	221	166			2	23		25
	orgpar	39	35		5	−3	8		10
	paroi	1,433	1,383	8	0	−1	−4		4
	pastem	289	220	20	10	13	−19		24
	prophy	1,531	1,525		0		0		0
	repvid	599	404	9	13	11			33
fpppp	d2esp	35	34	6			−3		3
	main	210	199			0	5		5
	twldrv	11,311,624	11,198,058	2	0		−1		1
matrix300	sgemm	9,905	8,398	12	6		−3		15
tomcatv	tomcatv	367,995,733	355,039,258	4	0	−0			4

Table 1: Effects of Rematerialization

These costs are calculated from dynamic counts of instructions as described earlier. The last column (*total*) gives the percentage improvement in spill costs due to improved rematerialization – large positive numbers indicate significant improvements. The middle columns show the contribution of each instruction type to the total.

All percentages have been rounded to the nearest integer. Insignificant improvements are reported as 0 and insignificant losses are reported as −0. In cases where the result *is* zero, we simply show a blank. Since results are rounded, a *total* entry may not equal the sum of the contributing entries.

Consider the first row in Table 1. This row presents results for the routine `fehl` from the program `rkf45`. The optimistic allocator generated an allocation requiring 68 cycles of spill code; the enhanced allocator required only 50 cycles. 26% of the savings came from having to execute fewer loads and 7% arose from fewer copies. There was a 7% degradation due to more load-immediates. The total improvement was 27%.

From the entire suite of 70 routines, we observed improvements in 28 cases and degradations in only 2 cases. One loss was very small (2 loads, 2 stores, and an extra copy); the other was somewhat larger. Improvements ranged from tiny to reasonably large, with many greater than 20%. Of course, adjusting the relative costs of each instruction, especially loads and stores, will change the amount of improvement.

As expected, we see a pattern of fewer load instructions and more load-immediates. Typically, the number of stores and the number of copies are also reduced. The reduced number of copy instructions suggests that our heuristics for removing unhelpful splits are adequate in practice. Note that this reduction is obtained in spite of the extra copies introduced by *renumber*.

5.4 Allocation Costs

The improved support for rematerialization comes at a cost in allocation time. An extra pass over the code is required to initialize rematerialization tags before prop-

	repvid		tomcatv		twldrv	
Phase	*Old*	*New*	*Old*	*New*	*Old*	*New*
cfa	.00	.00	.00	.00	.01	.01
renum	.03	.05	.06	.10	.57	.91
build	.17	.17	.39	.43	10.27	8.81
costs	.01	.01	.02	.02	.16	.14
color	.02	.02	.04	.04	1.16	1.21
spill	.01	.01	.02	.02	.17	.16
renum	.02	.03	.02	.04	.10	.17
build	.06	.05	.09	.12	.63	.83
costs	.01	.01	.01	.01	.07	.06
color	.01	.02	.02	.03	.14	.21
spill	.01	.00	.01	.01	.03	.04
renum	.01	.03	.02	.04	.10	.17
build	.03	.06	.05	.09	.60	.82
costs	.01	.01	.01	.01	.07	.06
color	.01	.01	.02	.02	.13	.21
spill			.01	.01		
renum			.02	.03		
build			.05	.09		
costs			.01	.01		
color			.01	.02		
total	.40	.49	.89	1.13	14.19	13.80

Table 2: Allocation Times in Seconds

agation and further time is required to propagate the tags throughout the routine. Finally, at least one extra pass is required to accomplish *conservative coalescing.* On the other hand, the *build–coalesce* process may be slightly faster since we are able to eliminate some copies during *renumber* (recall step 5 in Section 4.1).

Table 2 shows comparative timings for the two allocators on three routines from the SPEC suite. Times are given in seconds and were measured with a 100 hertz clock on an unloaded IBM RS/6000 Model 540. Each run was repeated 10 times and the results averaged. The first column shows the phase of allocation, where *cfa* stands for control-flow analysis and includes the time required to compute forward and reverse dominators and dominance frontiers, *build* includes the entire *build–coalesce* loop, and *color* includes both *simplify* and *select.* Note that `tomcatv` required an additional round of spilling. For each routine, the *Old* column gives times required by the optimistic allocator with Chaitin's scheme and the *New* column gives times required by the same allocator with improved rematerialization.

We selected three routines to illustrate performance over a range of sizes. The first routine is `repvid`, from the program `doduc`, with 144 non-comment lines of FORTRAN. It compiles to a `.text` size of 1284 bytes using IBM's `xlf` compiler with full optimization. The second routine is `tomcatv`, with 133 lines and a `.text` size of 3064 bytes. The largest routine is `twldrv` from the program `fpppp`, with 881 lines and a `.text` size of 15,616 bytes. All three routines appear in Table 1.

An obvious conclusion to draw from the data in Table 2 is that support for rematerialization can require a small amount of additional compile-time. Occasionally, the new allocator may even be faster, though our experience suggests that `twldrv` is an exceptional case.

The results in Table 2 also illuminate a number of interesting details about the behavior of both allocators.

- The inital pass of the *build–coalesce* loop dominates the overall cost of allocation (as noted by Chaitin). In comparison, additional iterations of the *color–spill* process are quite inexpensive.
- In each case, the cost of *renumber* is higher for the *New* allocator, reflecting the cost of propagating rematerialization tags.
- In all but one case, the cost of the *build–coalesce* loop is higher for the *New* allocator, due to the additional passes of *conservative coalescing.*
- The very low costs of control-flow analysis illustrates the speed and practicality of the algorithm for calculating dominance frontiers [11].
- The higher cost of coloring in the first pass arises from the cost of choosing nodes to spill. While the cost of coloring is linear in the size of the graph, spill selection is $O(s \cdot n)$, where s is the number of spill choices and n is the number of nodes. With a large number of spills, this term dominates the cost of coloring.

We are pleased with the overall speed of both allocators. Our results appear to be slightly faster than the times reported by IBM's `xlf` compiler for register allocation and comparable to the times reported for optimization. In an extensive comparison with priority-based coloring, our allocators appeared much slower on very small routines, but much faster on very large routines [2]. Of course, these speeds are not competitive with the fast, local techniques used in non-optimizing compilers [14, 15]; however, we believe that global optimizations require global register allocation.

6 Extensions

Of course, rematerialization is not the only reason for splitting live ranges; others have observed that splitting a live range can improve the allocation [12, 8]. A natural extension to the scheme described in Section 3 is to split at *all* ϕ-nodes. This lets the allocator pick and choose among all the values in the SSA graph. The machinery used to support rematerialization can easily handle additional splitting.

While inserting copies at all ϕ-nodes introduces additional splitting, it misses a particularly important case. Consider the value p_0 in Figure 3. Because it is unmodified in the first loop, no ϕ-node is created at the loop header. Assume that additional code exists between the definition of p_0 and the first loop. If this causes p_0 to be spilled, we would like the allocator to consider the loop body separately from the code that precedes it, even though they are part of the same value in the SSA graph. If possible, the allocator should rematerialize p_0 in the loop header, where it will be defined exactly once. This suggests adding extra splits at the top of the loop.

We have experimented with a number of alternative splitting schemes. These include:

1. splitting all live ranges around all loops,
2. splitting all live ranges around outer loops,
3. splitting live ranges around the outermost loop where they are neither used nor defined,
4. splitting along the forward dominance frontiers (at all ϕ-nodes), and
5. splitting based on both forward and reverse dominance frontiers.

Conceptually, it seems easy to incorporate these ideas into our allocator; however, experience has shown that significant engineering is required.

The complete results of our experiments with loop-based splitting are presented in Briggs' thesis [2]. Each scheme had several major successes; each had several equally dramatic failures. While the improvements are large enough to warrant further study, the failures are significant enough to discourage adoption in a production compiler. Of course, we are holding the allocator to a high standard – the results of splitting are compared to the results presented in Section 5. Thus, we immediately notice both improvements and degradations. We intend to continue our search for a consistently profitable approach.

7 Related Work

Our work extends the work described by Chaitin *et al.* and recalls an approach suggested by Cytron and Ferrante. Chaitin et al. introduce the term *rematerialization* and discuss the problem briefly [6]. Because their allocator cannot split live ranges, they handle only the simple case where all definitions contributing to a live range are identical. Our work is a direct extension and is able to handle each component of a complete live range separately and correctly. Cytron and Ferrante suggest splitting based on (the equivalent of) the SSA [10]. Their goal is minimal coloring in polynomial-time – achieved at the cost introducing extra copies. There is no direct discussion of rematerialization; indeed, the discussion of spilling is very sketchy. In contrast, we are concerned primarily with quality of spill code.

It is also interesting to compare our approach to other published alternatives, particularly the splitting allocator of Chow and Hennessy and the hierarchical coloring allocator of Callahan and Koblenz [8, 4]. The published work does not indicate how they handle rematerialization. It is possible that they make no special provisions, trusting their splitting algorithm to do an adequate job. While we can imagine constructing implementations of their techniques to allow more direct comparisons, it is unlikely that the results would accurately reflect the potential of their schemes. In any case, it may be possible to modify their allocators to take advantage of our approach.

8 Summary

The primary contribution of this paper is a natural extension of Chaitin's ideas on rematerialization. In particular, we show how to handle complex live ranges that may be completely or partially rematerialized. We describe a technique for tagging the component values of a live range with correct rematerialization information. We introduce heuristics, especially conservative coalescing and biased coloring, that are required for good results. Finally, we present experimental results that show the effectiveness and practicality of our extensions.

9 Acknowledgements

Greg Chaitin, Ben Chase, John Cocke, Marty Hopkins, Bob Hood, Ken Kennedy, Chuck Lins, Peter Markstein, Tom Murtagh, Randy Scarborough, Rick Simpson, Tom Spillman, and Matthew Zaleski have all contributed to this work through encouragement and enlightened discussion. Our colleagues on the ParaScope project at Rice have provided us with an excellent testbed for our ideas. To all these people go our heartfelt thanks.

References

[1] David Bernstein, Dina Q. Goldin, Martin C. Golumbic, Hugo Krawczyk, Yishay Mansour, Itai Nahshon, and Ron Y. Pinter. Spill code minimization techniques for optimizing compilers. *SIGPLAN Notices*, 24(7):258–263, July 1989. *Proceedings of the ACM SIGPLAN '89 Conference on Programming Language Design and Implementation.*

[2] Preston Briggs. *Register Allocation via Graph Coloring.* PhD thesis, Rice University, April 1992.

[3] Preston Briggs, Keith D. Cooper, Ken Kennedy, and Linda Torczon. Coloring heuristics for register allocation. *SIGPLAN Notices*, 24(7):275–284, July 1989. *Proceedings of the ACM SIGPLAN '89 Conference on Programming Language Design and Implementation.*

[4] David Callahan and Brian Koblenz. Register allocation via hierarchical graph coloring. *SIGPLAN Notices*, 26(6):192–203, June 1991. *Proceedings of the ACM SIGPLAN '91 Conference on Programming Language Design and Implementation.*

[5] Gregory J. Chaitin. Register allocation and spilling via graph coloring. *SIGPLAN Notices*, 17(6):98–105, June 1982. *Proceedings of the ACM SIGPLAN '82 Symposium on Compiler Construction.*

[6] Gregory J. Chaitin, Marc A. Auslander, Ashok K. Chandra, John Cocke, Martin E. Hopkins, and Peter W. Markstein. Register allocation via coloring. *Computer Languages*, 6:47–57, January 1981.

[7] Jong-Deok Choi, Ron Cytron, and Jeanne Ferrante. Automatic construction of sparse data flow evaluation graphs. In *Conference Record of the Eighteenth Annual ACM Symposium on Principles of Programming Languages*, pages 55–66, January 1991.

[8] Fred C. Chow and John L. Hennessy. The priority-based coloring approach to register allocation. *ACM Transactions on Programming Languages and Systems*, 12(4):501–536, October 1990.

[9] Keith D. Cooper, Ken Kennedy, and Linda Torczon. The impact of interprocedural analysis and optimization on the $\mathbb{R}^n$ programming environment. *ACM Transactions on Programming Languages and Systems*, 8(4):491–523, October 1986.

[10] Ron Cytron and Jeanne Ferrante. What's in a name? The value of renaming for parallelism detection and storage allocation. In *Proceedings of the 1987 International Conference on Parallel Processing*, pages 19–27, August 1987.

[11] Ron Cytron, Jeanne Ferrante, Barry K. Rosen, Mark N. Wegman, and F. Kenneth Zadeck. Efficiently computing static single assignment form and the control dependence graph. *ACM Transactions on Programming Languages and Systems*, 13(4):451–490, October 1991.

[12] Janet Fabri. Automatic storage optimization. *SIGPLAN Notices*, 14(8):83–91, August 1979. *Proceedings of the ACM SIGPLAN '79 Symposium on Compiler Construction.*

[13] George E. Forsythe, Michael A. Malcolm, and Cleve B. Moler. *Computer Methods for Mathematical Computations.* Prentice-Hall, Englewood Cliffs, New Jersey, 1977.

[14] Christopher W. Fraser and David R. Hanson. A retargetable compiler for ANSI C. *SIGPLAN Notices*, 26(10):29–43, October 1991.

[15] Christopher W. Fraser and David R. Hanson. Simple register spilling in a retargetable compiler. *Software – Practice and Experience*, 22(1):85–99, January 1992.

[16] Rajiv Gupta, Mary Lou Soffa, and Tim Steele. Register allocation via clique separators. *SIGPLAN Notices*, 24(7):264–274, July 1989. *Proceedings of the ACM SIGPLAN '89 Conference on Programming Language Design and Implementation.*

[17] James R. Larus and Paul N. Hilfinger. Register allocation in the SPUR Lisp compiler. *SIGPLAN Notices*, 21(7):255–263, July 1986. *Proceedings of the ACM SIGPLAN '86 Symposium on Compiler Construction.*

[18] S. S. Lavrov. Store economy in closed operator schemes. *Zhurnal Vychislitel'noi Matematiki i Matematicheskoi Fiziki*, 1(4):687–701, 1961. English translation in *U.S.S.R. Computational Mathematics and Mathematical Physics* 3, 1962.

[19] Ravi Sethi. Complete register allocation problems. *SIAM Journal on Computing*, 4(3):226–248, 1975.

[20] SPEC release 1.2, September 1990. Standards Performance Evaluation Corporation.

[21] Mark N. Wegman and F. Kenneth Zadeck. Constant propagation with conditional branches. *ACM Transactions on Programming Languages and Systems*, 13(2):181–210, April 1991.

Avoiding Unconditional Jumps by Code Replication

Frank Mueller and David B. Whalley

Department of Computer Science, B-173
Florida State University
Tallahassee, Florida 32306-4019
e-mail: whalley@cs.fsu.edu

Abstract

This study evaluates a global optimization technique that avoids unconditional jumps by replicating code. When implemented in the back-end of an optimizing compiler, this technique can be generalized to work on almost all instances of unconditional jumps, including those generated from conditional statements and unstructured loops. The replication method is based on the idea of finding a replacement for each unconditional jump which minimizes the growth in code size. This is achieved by choosing the shortest sequence of instructions as a replacement. Measurements taken from a variety of programs showed that not only the number of executed instructions decreased, but also that the total cache work was reduced (except for small caches) despite increases in code size. Pipelined and superscalar machines may also benefit from an increase in the average basic block size.

1 Introduction

Unconditional jumps occur often in programs. Depending on the environment, execution frequencies between 4% and 10% have been reported [Pe77,Cl82]. Common programming constructs such as loops and conditional statements are translated to machine code using unconditional jumps, thus resulting in relatively compact code. Code size, however, has become less important since the introduction of caches. For instance, inlining [Da88] and loop unrolling [He90] can obtain improvements while increasing the code size.

This study describes a method of replacing unconditional jumps uniformly by replicating a sequence of instructions from the jump destination. To perform this task, an algorithm is proposed which is based on the idea of following the shortest path within the control flow when searching for a replication sequence. The effect of code replication is shown by capturing measurements from the execution of a number of programs.

The document is structured as follows. Section 2 gives an overview of research on related topics. Section 3 illustrates the advantages of using code replication for optimizing various programming constructs. Section 4 provides an informal description of the algorithms used to implement code replication. Section 5 discusses the results of the implementation by comparing the measurements of numerous programs with and without code replication. Section 6 gives an overview of future work and Section 7 summarizes the results.

2 Related Work

Several optimizations that attempt to improve code by replicating instructions have been implemented. Loop unrolling [He90] replicates the body within a loop. This reduces the number of compare and branch instructions that are executed. Also, more effective scheduling may be achieved for pipelined and multiple issue machines since some of the basic blocks comprising the loop contain more instructions after unrolling.

Inlining, an optimization method studied by Davidson and Holler [Da88], results in replicated code when a routine is inlined from more than one call site. Hwu and Chang [Hw89] used inlining techniques based on profiling data to limit the number of call site expansions and thereby avoid excessive growth. In general, a call to a non-recursive routine can be replaced by the actual code of the routine body. The procedure call can be viewed as an unconditional jump to the beginning of the body, and any return from the procedure can be viewed as an unconditional jump back to the instruction following the call.

Golumbic and Rainish [Go90] used the method of

ACM SIGPLAN '92 PLDI-6/92/CA

`i = 1; while (i++<n) x[i-1] = x[i];`				
		without replication		**with replication**
move 1 into data reg. 1 (variable i*)*		`d[1]=1;`		`d[0]=1;`
move addr. of x[] *into addr. reg. 0*		`a[0]=a[6]+x.;`		`d[1]=2;`
	L15			`NZ=d[0]?L[_n];`
copy data reg. 1 into data reg. 0		`d[0]=d[1];`		`PC=NZ>=0,L16;`
incr. index into x[]		`a[0]=a[0]+1;`		`a[0]=a[6]+x.+1;`
incr. data reg. 1 (variable i*)*		`d[1]=d[1]+1;`	L000	
compare data reg. 0 with variable n		`NZ=d[0]?L[_n];`		`B[a[0]]=B[a[0]+1];`
exit loop if greater/equal		`PC=NZ>=0,L16;`		`a[0]=a[0]+1;`
move x[i] *into* x[i-1]		`B[a[0]]=B[a[0]+1];`		`d[0]=d[1];`
jump unconditionally to L15		`PC=L15;`		`d[1]=d[1]+1;`
	L16	...		`NZ=d[0]?L[_n];`
				`PC=NZ<0,L000;`
			L16	...

Table 1: Exit Condition in the Middle of a Loop (RTLs for 68020)

replicating parts of basic blocks for instruction scheduling to exploit potential parallelism for a super-scalar processor. In their approach, it suffices to copy the number of instructions needed to avoid a pipeline stall from the block following a conditional statement. They expand natural loops similarly by replicating instructions from the top of the loop, negating the branch condition, and inserting another unconditional jump. Their goal was to increase the number of instructions that can be issued simultaneously.

3 Motivation

All replication techniques employed in the front-end of a compiler lack generality in reducing the number of unconditional jumps. Instances of unconditional jumps cannot always be detected due to interaction with other optimizations and a lack of information about the target architecture. Consequently, front-end methods for code replication cannot eliminate occurrences of unconditional jumps which are introduced by the optimization phase of a compiler.

The optimization evaluated in this study, code replication, was accomplished by modifying the back-end of the optimizing compiler VPO (Very Portable Optimizer) [Be88]. The algorithms to perform the optimization, except for a few small functions, are machine-independent. In general, RTLs[1] are searched for unconditional jumps. By determining the jump destination and using control flow information, a subset of the basic blocks in the function can be replicated, replacing the unconditional jump. Such an optimization can be applied to almost all occurrences of unconditional jumps. The following sections give examples of instances where code replication can be applied to applications written in C.

3.1 Loops

For while-loops, the front-end VPCC (Very Portable C Compiler) [Da89] generates intermediate code with an unconditional jump at the end of the loop. This unconditional transfer can be replaced by the instructions testing the termination condition of the loop with the termination condition reversed.

The intermediate code produced by the front-end for for-loops with an unknown number of iterations includes an unconditional transfer of control preceding the loop to the instructions comprising the termination condition, a portion of code placed at the end of the loop. This unconditional jump can also be replaced by the code which tests for the inverse termination condition. Thus, the code checking the termination condition would appear before the loop and at the end of the loop.

Often, the replication of the termination condition of while and for loops is performed by optimizing compilers. But when the exit condition is placed in the middle of a loop, most compilers do not attempt a replacement for the unconditional jump. An example for such a situation is given in Table 1. Code replication is used to replace the unconditional jump by the RTLs between label L15 and the conditional branch. The conditional branch is reversed and a new loop header is introduced at label L000. Afterwards, other optimizations such as common subexpression elimination are applied. In this example, one unconditional jump per loop iteration is saved. The method proposed in this study handles these cases as well as unstructured loops, which are typically not recognized as loops by an optimizer.

[1] Register Transfer Lists (RTLs) represent the effects of instructions of a target machine.

```
if (i>5)
   i = i / n;
else
   i = i * n;
return(i);
```

	without replication	with replication
compare i *and 5*	NZ=L[a[6]+i.]?5;	NZ=L[a[6]+i.]?5;
branch if less/equal	PC=NZ<=0,L22;	PC=NZ<=0,L22;
load i *into data reg. 0*	d[0]=L[a[6]+i.];	d[0]=L[a[6]+i.];
divide data reg. 0 by n	d[0]=d[0]/L[a[6]+n.];	d[0]=d[0]/L[a[6]+n.];
store data reg. 0 into i	L[a[6]+i.]=d[0];	L[a[6]+i.]=d[0];
jump unconditionally to L23	PC=L23;	a[6]=UK;
	L22	PC=RT;
load i *into data reg. 0*	d[0]=L[a[6]+i.];	L22
multiply data reg. 0 by n	d[0]=d[0]*L[a[6]+n.];	d[0]=L[a[6]+i.];
store data reg. 0 into i	L[a[6]+i.]=d[0];	d[0]=d[0]*L[a[6]+n.];
	L23	L[a[6]+i.]=d[0];
restore old frame pointer	a[6]=UK;	a[6]=UK;
return from subroutine	PC=RT;	PC=RT;

Table 2: If–Then–Else Statement (RTLs for 68020)

3.2 Conditional Statements

For the if-then-else construct an unconditional jump is generated at the end of the then-part to jump over the else-part. This unconditional jump can also be eliminated by code replication. There are two execution paths possible which are joined at the end of the if-then-else construct. The two execution paths can be separated completely or their joining can be at least deferred by replicating the code after the if-then-else construct, so that the unconditional jump is replaced by the copied instructions. Table 2 shows an example of replicating code where the two execution paths return from the function separately.[2] The method of code replication used for conditional statements can also be applied to *break* and *goto* statements, and conditional expressions in the C language (`expr?expr:expr`).

3.3 Sources for other Optimizations

Code replication also creates new opportunities for global optimizations by modifying the control flow of a function. The following paragraphs describe new opportunities for constant folding, instruction selection, common subexpression elimination, and code motion.

3.3.1 Constant Folding of Comparisons and Conditional Branches

After applying code replication, sources for constant folding may be introduced which did not exist before. For example, conditional branches, dependent on the comparison of two constants, may be introduced by changing the control flow during code replication. Depending on the result of the constant comparison, such a conditional branch can either be eliminated or replaced by an unconditional jump. In the later case, dead code elimination may remove instructions following the unconditional jump which can no longer be reached.

[2]Notice that nested if-then-else statements can cause code to be replicated very often, thus resulting in an disproportional growth in code size relative to the original code size.

3.3.2 Elimination of Instructions

In conjunction with code replication, common subexpression elimination can often combine instructions when an initial value is assigned to a register, followed by an unconditional jump. If the replication sequence uses the register, the use is replaced by the initial value so that the assignment to the register becomes redundant if there are no further uses or sets of the register. Similarly, instruction selection may combine instructions when the head of a loop is moved. For example, the second RTL in the replicated code of Table 1 is a simplification of the first and fifth RTLs in the code before replication.

3.3.3 Relocating the Preheader of Loops

After code replication the execution of some instructions may be avoided for an execution path. For instance, code motion is performed after an initial pass of code replication. This may result in a new location of the preheaders of loops. Thus, if a loop is not executed because the conditional branch preceding the loop is taken, the instructions in the preheader (following that branch) would not be executed. This may result in considerable savings when loops are nested. An example is the RTL preceding label L000 in the replicated code of Table 1 which is the loop preheader.

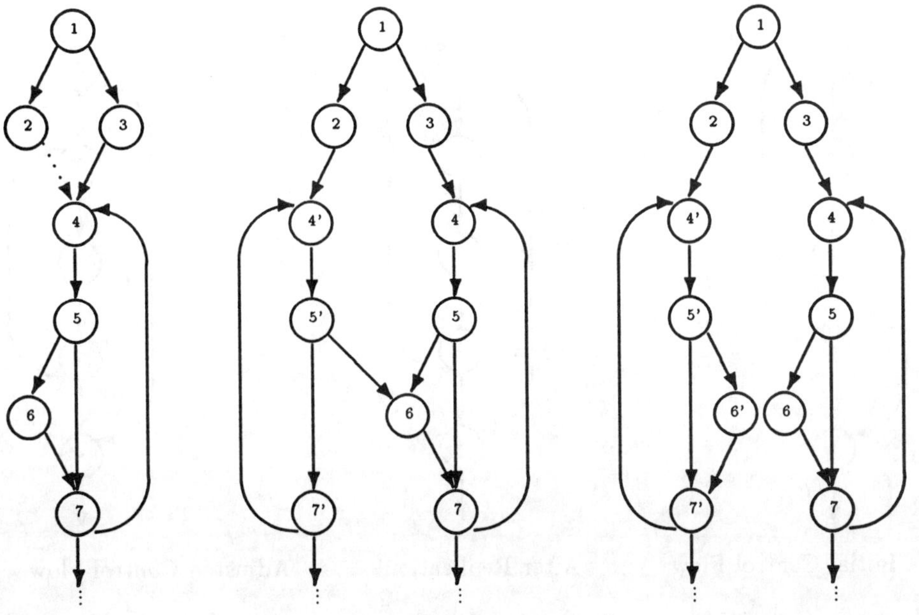

Figure 1: Interference with Natural Loops

4 JUMPS: An Algorithm for Code Replication

The task of code replication is to find a sequence of basic blocks to replace an unconditional jump. In order to avoid algorithms with a high degree of complexity, it was decided to make the initial assumption that only the shortest path between two basic blocks is examined. This constraint is motivated by the goal of limiting the size of code introduced by the replication process. The shortest path is determined with respect to the number of RTLs. Finding the shortest path in the control-flow graph with n blocks is accomplished by using Warshall's algorithm for calculating the transitive closure of a graph [Wa62] which has a complexity of $O(n^3)$. First, all legal transitions between any two distinct basic blocks are collected in a matrix. This initial pass creates a copy of the control flow graph but it excludes self-reflexive transitions and, optionally, other edges whose control flow is excluded explicitly. For example, the replication of indirect jumps has not yet been implemented at this point. Then, the non-reflexive transitive closure is calculated for all nodes with respect to the shortest path. The transitivity relation between two nodes is only recorded if it is the shortest connection found so far in terms of the number of RTLs in the traversed blocks [Fl62]. In the end, the matrix can be used to look up the shortest path between two arbitrary basic blocks in the table without having to recalculate it after each replication. The algorithm JUMPS is divided into the following steps:

1. Initially, the matrix used to find the shortest sequence of basic blocks to replace an unconditional jump is set up.
2. In the second step, the basic blocks within a function are traversed sequentially and unconditional jumps are replaced as follows. Either a sequence of blocks that ends with a return from the routine is replicated (*favoring returns*), or a sequence of blocks is chosen linking the current block containing the unconditional jump with the block positionally following the unconditional jump (*favoring loops*). In the latter case, the last block to be replicated will fall through to the next block. At this point, heuristics can be used to make the choice between these two options.
3. If a collected block (i.e. a block chosen for replication in the previous step) was detected to be the header of a natural loop and the block collected previously was not inside the same loop, then all blocks inside this loop are included in the replication sequence in their positional order. The example in Figure 1 has an unconditional jump from block 2 to block 4 before replication. Without replicating block 6, the original loop would have two entry points and would be unstructured.
4. Once a sequence of basic blocks is replicated, the control flow is adjusted accordingly. A conditional branch is reversed in the replicated path if the path does not follow the fall-through transition. New labels are introduced, and the destinations of conditional branches are modified. In addition, all

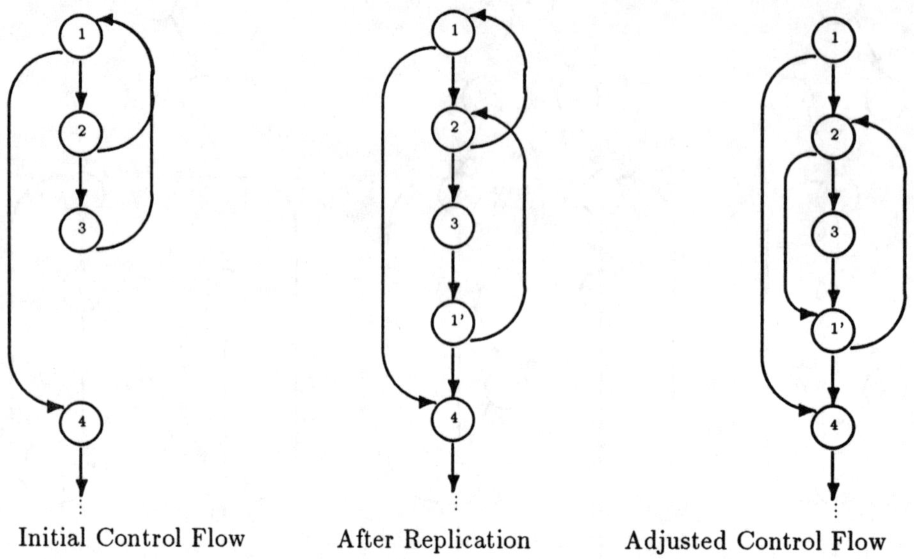

Figure 2: Partial Overlapping of Natural Loops

unconditional jumps that are found in the replicated code can be eliminated since the sequence of replicated blocks had to follow the control flow with fall-through transitions.

5. The adjustment of the control flow is extended, once again to preserve the structure of loops. When a replication is initiated from a block inside a loop, a portion of the loop can be copied without introducing unnatural loops. In addition, the control flow of all blocks in the loop which were not copied but branch conditionally to a block which was copied, is changed to the copied block. If a block occurs twice in the replication sequence, forward branches (positionally down) are favored over branches back to a previous block. These modifications are needed to avoid the introduction of natural loops which partially overlap and would complicate standard loop optimizations. An example is given in Figure 2. There is an unconditional transfer from block 3 to block 1 in the initial control flow. By changing the target of the conditional branch in block 2 after replication, the introduction of partially overlapping loops is avoided in the adjusted control flow.

6. Even with replication of entire natural loops, it is still possible for this algorithm to introduce new loops which are unstructured. Therefore, the control flow graph is checked to determine if it is still reducible. The replicated code is removed if it introduced a non-reducible flow graph. In this case, replication may be attempted using the longer block sequence (see step 2). Reducibility has to be preserved to ensure that the same optimizations can be applied to loops as without replication.

The algorithm JUMPS is applied to a function for each unconditional jump until no more unconditional jumps can be replaced. As a result of the replication process, blocks which cannot be reached by the control flow anymore can sometimes occur. Therefore, dead code elimination is invoked to delete these blocks.

5 Measurements

Static and dynamic frequency measurements and instruction cache performance measurements were taken from a number of well-known benchmarks, UNIX utilities, and one application (see Table 3). The code was generated for the Motorola 68020/68881 processor and

Class	Name	Description
Utilities	banner	banner generator
	cal	calendar generator
	compact	file compression
	deroff	remove nroff constructs
	grep	pattern search
	od	octal dump
	sort	sort or merge files
	wc	word count
Benchmarks	bubblesort	sort numbers
	matmult	matrix multiplication
	sieve	iteration
	queens	8-queens problem
	quicksort	sort numbers (iterative)
User code	mincost	VLSI circuit partitioning

Table 3: Test Set of C Programs

		static			dynamic		
		SIMPLE	LOOPS	JUMPS	SIMPLE	LOOPS	JUMPS
Sun SPARC	average	3.74%	2.40%	0.03%	3.28%	1.89%	0.10%
	std. deviation	1.78%	1.99%	0.12%	2.71%	2.56%	0.30%
Motorola 68020	average	5.08%	3.42%	0.04%	4.14%	2.47%	0.13%
	std. deviation	2.49%	2.83%	0.15%	3.48%	3.36%	0.43%

Table 4: Percent of Instructions that are Unconditional Jumps

the Sun SPARC processor, a RISC architecture. For the SPARC processor, delay slots after transfers of control were filled. The standard code optimization techniques such as branch chaining, instruction selection, register coloring, common subexpression elimination, constant folding, code motion, strength reduction, and constant folding at conditional branches were applied on the measured code. Library routines could not be measured since the source code was not available to be compiled by VPO.

The measurements were collected by using EASE (Environment for Architectural Study and Experimentation) [Da90-2] which is designed to measure the code produced by the optimizer VPO. When generating code, additional instructions are inserted to capture measurements during the execution of a program.

Each program was tested with three different sets of optimizations:

- SIMPLE: Only the standard optimizations were performed.
- LOOPS: Unconditional jumps preceding a loop or at the end of the loop are replaced by the termination condition of the loop and the replicated condition is reversed. Depending on the original layout of the loop, either one unconditional jump is removed at the entry point, or one unconditional jump is saved per loop iteration. This optimization is often implemented in conventional optimizers.
- JUMPS: This is the algorithm discussed previously. It is a generalized approach which attempts to replace any occurrences of unconditional jumps by replicating code.

5.1 Integration into an Optimizing Compiler

The code replication algorithms (JUMPS and LOOPS) are integrated into the optimizing back-end of the VPO compiler in the following manner. After performing initial branch optimizations such as branch chaining, code replication is performed to reduce the remaining number of unconditional jumps. When JUMPS is used for code replication, the compile-time overhead for the replication process itself is minimal, but the following optimization stages process more RTLs. The impact of LOOPS on the compile time is minimal.

Figure 3 summarizes the order in which the different optimization phases are invoked. Code replication is performed at an early stage so that the later optimizations can take advantage of the simplified control flow. In order to replace all unconditional jumps generated by constant folding at conditional branches or introduced by remote preheaders, code replication is reinvoked repeatedly. The final invocation of code replication replaces those unconditional jumps which remained in the code because replication would have resulted in a non-reducible flow graph.

```
branch chaining;
dead code elimination;
reorder basic blocks to minimize jumps;
code replication (either JUMPS or LOOPS);
dead code elimination;
instruction selection;
register assignment;
if (change)
  instruction selection;
do {
  register allocation by register coloring;
  instruction selection;
  common subexpression elimination;
  dead variable elimination;
  code motion;
  strength reduction;
  recurrences;
  instruction selection;
  branch chaining;
  constant folding at conditional branches;
  code replication (either JUMPS or LOOPS);
  dead code elimination;
} while (change);
filling of delay slots for RISCs;
```

Figure 3: Order of Optimizations

5.2 Static and Dynamic Behavior

Table 4 shows the number of unconditional jumps relative to the total number of instructions for the static and dynamic measurements. The number of unconditional jumps is reduced by 40-42% dynamically when LOOPS was applied, and with code replication practically no unconditional jumps are left. Thus, code replication results in a reduction of instructions executed by at least the number of unconditional jumps which could be avoided dynamically.

The few unconditional jumps left after code replication are due to indirect jumps, infinite loops, and interactions with other optimization phases (such as code motion) that may introduce unconditional jumps. Paths containing indirect jumps are excluded from replication in the current implementation. Infinite loops do not provide any opportunity to replace the unconditional branch. And interactions with other optimization phases are treated conservatively to avoid the potential of replication *ad infinitum*.

Table 5 illustrates the static and dynamic behavior of the programs. The columns SIMPLE indicate the total number of instructions and the other columns represent the change in the number of instructions relative to the SIMPLE version of each program. The static change is proportional to the growth of the code size. When LOOPS is applied, the number of instructions increases by only 2.6-4.0%. With generalized code replication, on the other hand, an average of about 53% more instructions are generated. The decrease in the number of instructions executed for LOOPS is less than half the decrease for JUMPS.

For the SPARC about 1.5 more instructions are found between branches after code replication was applied and 50% of the executed no-op instructions were eliminated. Thus, the opportunities for instruction scheduling may improve if code replication is applied for a pipelined machine. Also, in a multiple-issue processor more potential parallelism may be found [Ri72].

5.3 Impact on Instruction Caching

The cache performance was tested for cache sizes of 1Kb, 2Kb, 4Kb, and 8Kb. For each different cache size a direct-mapped cache with 16 bytes per line was simulated. Both the miss ratio and the fetch cost were measured in the experiment. The estimation of the fetch cost is based on the assumption that misses are ten times as expensive as hits. Thus, fetch cost is calculated as follows:

$$\begin{aligned} \textit{fetch cost} &= \textit{cache hits} * \textit{cache access time} + \\ &\quad \textit{cache misses} * \textit{miss penalty} \end{aligned}$$

where the cache access time is 1 time unit and the miss penalty is 10 units of time. Context-switches were simulated by invalidating the entire cache every 10,000 units of time. The estimates for the cache access time, the miss penalty, and the context-switching interval were adopted from Smith's cache studies [Sm82]. Notice that the overall fetch cost can decrease while the miss ratio increases for the same program. This can be explained by the reduced number of instructions executed after replication and illustrates the short-comings of the miss ratio as a measurement when the code in a program changes.

Table 6 shows the change of the miss ratio and fetch cost for varying sizes of direct-mapped caches. Each set of measurements with the same configuration is related to the corresponding values of the SIMPLE version. For example, for a 1Kb cache with context switches on the SPARC, the difference between the miss ratio of LOOPS and the miss ratio of the SIMPLE version was -0.05%, a slight decrease of misses.

The impact of context switching was minimal, and the miss ratio only increased slightly with context switching on.

For small caches, code replication (JUMPS) may be outperformed by loop replication (LOOPS). A program may initially fit in the cache, but after code replication is applied, it might not fit anymore. Therefore, capacity misses can be introduced. For example, for a 1Kb cache about 1% additional misses were caused by instruction fetches. But for larger caches the miss ratio changes only slightly.

Code replication places instructions together which are likely to be executed in a sequence but increases the distance between conditional branch instructions and their branch destinations. Nevertheless, the program's spatial locality can be improved by replicating code. Overall, code replication reduces the total number of instructions executed such that the average fetch cost is actually reduced except for small caches.

6 Future Work

The algorithm for code replication could be extended to copy indirect jumps and, for some architectures, their jump tables. If the table has to be replicated, the target addresses within the jump table should be revised. In either case, the jump destinations do not need to be copied. Thus, an indirect jump could terminate a replication sequence and provide yet another alternative besides replication paths favoring returns and favoring loops (see step 2 of algorithm JUMPS).

Furthermore, the increase in code size could be reduced by limiting the maximum length of a replication sequence to a specified number of RTLs. The improvements in the dynamic behavior of programs may drop slightly for this case while the performance of small caches should benefit.

Sun SPARC						
program	static instructions			dynamic instructions executed		
	SIMPLE	LOOPS	JUMPS	SIMPLE	LOOPS	JUMPS
cal	338	+3.25%	+21.89%	37,237	−2.95%	−3.15%
quicksort	321	+5.61%	+50.16%	836,404	−2.86%	−14.21%
wc	209	+0.96%	+58.37%	540,158	−0.00%	−1.96%
grep	968	+4.24%	+79.34%	1,930,791	−0.04%	−3.57%
sort	1,966	+4.63%	+89.17%	1,181,960	−0.71%	−10.49%
od	1,352	+4.59%	+95.19%	2,336,014	−8.84%	−10.22%
mincost	1,068	+6.84%	+30.99%	335,750	−0.59%	−3.91%
bubblesort	175	+7.43%	+5.14%	29,071,668	−0.05%	−0.07%
matmult	218	+4.59%	+3.67%	14,403,714	−0.08%	−0.28%
banner	169	+7.69%	+66.27%	2,565	−1.68%	−10.25%
sieve	93	+3.23%	+3.23%	2,184,965	−13.73%	−13.73%
compact	1,491	+1.07%	+75.18%	13,409,945	−1.94%	−4.86%
queens	114	+0.00%	+7.89%	263,518	−0.00%	−0.03%
deroff	7,987	+1.50%	+204.98%	448,581	−0.01%	−3.13%
average	1,176	+3.97%	+56.53%	4,784,519	−2.39%	−5.71%
Motorola 68020						
program	static instructions			dynamic instructions executed		
	SIMPLE	LOOPS	JUMPS	SIMPLE	LOOPS	JUMPS
cal	323	+3.72%	+24.77%	36,290	−3.09%	−3.17%
quicksort	245	+3.67%	+37.96%	536,566	−0.39%	−3.96%
wc	173	+0.58%	+56.65%	421,038	−0.00%	−5.32%
grep	775	+3.35%	+80.90%	1,309,586	−0.03%	−3.44%
sort	1,558	+3.98%	+63.67%	902,075	−1.49%	−12.43%
od	1,198	+2.92%	+85.73%	1,980,808	−9.45%	−10.30%
mincost	906	+3.20%	+35.98%	302,062	−1.10%	−5.13%
bubblesort	137	+3.65%	+2.92%	20,340,231	−18.92%	−18.92%
matmult	146	+3.42%	+3.42%	4,891,507	−0.21%	−0.21%
banner	177	+3.95%	+55.93%	2,473	−1.42%	−13.34%
sieve	70	+1.43%	+1.43%	1,759,088	−8.53%	−8.53%
compact	1,143	+0.70%	+73.93%	10,602,159	−1.54%	−5.26%
queens	94	+0.00%	+12.77%	189,518	−0.00%	−0.05%
deroff	5,730	+1.06%	+155.17%	360,051	−0.03%	−7.05%
average	905	+2.55%	+49.37%	3,116,675	−3.30%	−6.94%

Table 5: Number of Static and Dynamic Instructions

	cache size	1Kb		2Kb		4KB		8Kb	
processor	context sw.	LOOPS	JUMPS	LOOPS	JUMPS	LOOPS	JUMPS	LOOPS	JUMPS
		Cache Miss Ratio							
Sun	on	−0.05%	+1.07%	−0.22%	−0.07%	+0.03%	+0.25%	+0.01%	+0.11%
SPARC	off	−0.03%	+1.07%	−0.22%	−0.08%	+0.03%	+0.21%	+0.01%	+0.07%
Motorola	on	+0.08%	+1.26%	+0.04%	+0.75%	+0.01%	+0.09%	+0.01%	+0.07%
68020	off	+0.08%	+1.25%	+0.03%	+0.70%	+0.01%	+0.05%	+0.01%	+0.03%
		Instruction Fetch Cost							
Sun	on	−2.73%	+3.44%	−3.80%	−5.24%	−2.26%	−2.94%	−2.40%	−3.98%
SPARC	off	−2.64%	+3.68%	−3.87%	−5.33%	−2.24%	−3.13%	−2.47%	−4.30%
Motorola	on	−3.07%	+1.69%	−3.26%	−0.63%	−3.58%	−5.13%	−3.57%	−5.30%
68020	off	−3.04%	+1.86%	−3.28%	−0.71%	−3.61%	−5.48%	−3.60%	−5.66%

Table 6: Percent Change in Miss Ratio and Instruction Fetch Cost for Direct-Mapped Caches

7 Conclusions

A new global optimization method called code replication was developed which can be applied to eliminate almost all unconditional jumps in a program. The resulting programs are executing 5.7-6.9% less instructions in average. The number of instructions between branches is increased by 1.5 instructions on the average on the SPARC, so that the opportunities for instruction scheduling for pipelined or multi-issue machines are improved. The cache work decreases by about 4% except for small caches. The static number of instructions increases by an average of 53%. The generalized technique of code replication should be applied in the back-end of highly optimizing compilers if the execution time but not the program size is the major concern. The results of the test set also show that the replication of only the branch condition at natural loops, commonly performed in optimizing compilers, results in about 45% of the dynamic instruction savings which can be achieved by generalized code replication.

References

[Be88] M. E. Benitez, J. W. Davidson *A Portable Global Optimizer and Linker*, Proceedings of the SIGPLAN '88 Symposium on Programming Language Design and Implementation, Atlanta, GA, June 1988, pp. 329-338

[Cl82] D. W. Clark, H. M. Levy, *Measurement and Analysis of Instruction Use in the VAX-11/780*, Proceedings of the 9th Annual Symposium on Computer Architecture, April 1982, pp. 9-17

[Da88] J. W. Davidson, A. M. Holler, *A Study of a C Function Inliner*, Software, Vol. 18, No. 8, August 1988, pp. 775-790

[Da89] J. W. Davidson, D. B. Whalley, *Quick Compilers Using Peephole Optimizations*, Software – Practice and Experience, Vol. 19, No. 1, January 1989, pp. 195-203

[Da90-2] J. W. Davidson, D. B. Whalley, *Ease: An Environment for Architecture Study and Experimentation*, Proceedings of the SIGMETRICS 1990 Conference on Measurement and Modeling of Computer Systems, May 1990, pp. 259-260

[Fl62] R. W. Floyd, *Algorithm 97: Shortest Path*, Communications of the ACM, Vol. 5, No. 6, June 1962, p. 345

[Go90] M. C. Golumbic, V. Rainish, *Instruction Scheduling beyond Basic Blocks*, IBM Journal of Research Development, Vol. 34, No. 1, January 1990, pp. 93-97

[He90] J. L. Hennessy, D. A. Patterson, *Computer Architecture: A Quantitative Approach*, Morgan Kaufmann, 1990

[Hw89] W. W. Hwu, P. P. Chang, *Inlining Function Expansion for Compiling C Programs*, Proceedings of the ACM SIGPLAN 1989 Conference on Programming Language Design and Implementation, Vol. 24, No. 5, June 1989, pp. 246-257

[Pe77] B. L. Peuto, L. J. Shustek, *An Instruction Timing Model of CPU Performance*, Proceedings of the 4th Annual Symposium on Computer Architecture, March 1977, pp. 165-178

[Ri72] E. M. Riseman, C. C. Foster, *The Inhibition of Potential Parallelism by Conditional Jumps*, IEEE Transactions on Computers, Vol. 21, No. 12, December 1972, pp. 1405-1411

[Sm82] A. J. Smith, *Cache Memories*, Computing Surveys, Vol. 14, No. 3, September 1982, pp. 473-530

[Wa62] S. Warshall, *A Theorem on Boolean Matrices*, Journal of the ACM, No. 9, 1962, pp. 11-12

Simple and Efficient BURS Table Generation

Todd A. Proebsting*
University of Wisconsin-Madison†

Abstract

A simple and efficient algorithm for generating bottom-up rewrite system (BURS) tables is described. A small prototype implementation produces tables 10 to 30 times more quickly than the best current techniques. The algorithm does not require novel data structures or complicated algorithmic techniques. Previously published methods for on-the-fly elimination of states are generalized and simplified to create a new method, *triangle trimming*, that is employed in the algorithm.

1 Introduction

Tree pattern matching combined with dynamic programming can be used in code generators to create locally optimal code for expression trees [AGT89]. Code generators based on bottom-up rewrite system (BURS) theory can be extremely fast because all dynamic programming is done when the BURS automaton is built. At compile-time, it is only necessary to make two traversals of the subject tree: one bottom-up traversal to label each node with a *state* that encodes all optimal matches, and a second top-down traversal that uses these states to select and emit code. Fraser and Henry [FH91b] report that careful encodings can produce an automaton that executes fewer than 50 VAX instructions per node to do both traversals.

Two difficulties arise in creating a BURS-style code generator: efficiently generating the states and state-transition tables, and creating an efficient encoding of the automata for use in a compiler. A solution to the encoding problem is described by Fraser and Henry in [FH91b]. Because *all* potential dynamic programming decisions are done at table-generation time, they must be done efficiently. This paper describes a simple and efficient table generation algorithm whose implementation is an order of magnitude faster than the best current systems.

Simplicity has increased, not decreased, efficiency. Efficiency has been enhanced, and tables sizes kept small, by the development of a new technique, *triangle trimming*, for eliminating most redundant states. Triangle trimming is an uncomplicated optimization that, for complex grammars, reduces *both* the table generation time and table sizes by over 50%. We also describe optimizations that take advantage of special properties of BURS states.

2 Related Work

Naively generating BURS states and state-transition tables fails because the tables become too large. A typical CISC machine description will generate over 1000 states.[1] Directly encoding the transition table for a *single* binary operator would, therefore, require over 1,000,000 entries.

Chase [Cha87] discovered that many of the rows (and columns) of bottom-up pattern-matching transition tables are identical and proposed the idea of *index maps* to encode much smaller tables. Index maps are vectors that map states of the automaton to *representer states* for indexing a transition table. States may share a given row or column of a transition table through a single indirection. These maps can be produced on-the-fly during table generation so that no superfluous work will be performed.

Pelegri-Llopart, the originator of BURS theory ([PLG88], [PL88]), encorporated Chase's ideas into

*This work was supported by NSF grant CCR-8908355.

†Author's address: Dept. of Computer Sciences, 1210 W. Dayton St., Madison, WI 53706. Email: todd@cs.wisc.edu

ACM SIGPLAN '92 PLDI-6/92/CA
© 1992 ACM 0-89791-476-7/92/0006/0331...$1.50

[1] The integer *subset* of a Motorola 68000 grammar has over 800 states (Figure 6).

a system that added cost information for dynamic programming at table generation time. Balachandran, Dhamdhere, and Biswas [BDB90] also generalized Chase's ideas to use cost information.

Henry [Hen89] developed optimization techniques to limit the number of BURS states produced during table generation. With fewer states, a smaller automaton is produced more quickly. His techniques are much more aggressive than the simple index map techniques, but at the cost of increased complexity. In [Hen89], Henry states, "The table builder uses space and time voraciously, even though it uses very complex algorithms designed to minimize these resources." Our algorithm generalizes and simplifies his work. Our system can be directly compared to his on a variety of machine specifications, and shows a factor of 10 to 30 improvement in generation speed.

Previous algorithms rely on bit-vectors that encode information about pattern matching, and rely on auxiliary data structures to maintain cost information. Ours has a simple and efficient unified structure that maintains both cost and pattern matching information.

3 BURS Model

The input to a BURS code generator generator is a set of rules. Each rule indicates a tree pattern, a cost, a replacement symbol, and an action. The set of all the rules is called the *grammar*. Figure 1 gives a small sample grammar (without actions). The replacement symbol is a *nonterminal* on the left of the rule—the linearized tree pattern it derives is on the right. In the sample, *goal*, *reg* and *addr* are nonterminals. In addition to nonterminals, the grammar has *operators* of varying arities. In the sample, *Reg*, *Int*, *Fetch*, and *Plus* are operators with respective arities of 0, 0, 1, and 2.

A BURS pattern matcher finds a least-cost parse of a subject tree for the grammar that reduces to the *goal* nonterminal. Each tree node will be labeled with a state that encodes which rule is to be used when that node is to be reduced to a given nonterminal.

3.1 Normal Form Patterns

To simplify the generation of BURS tables, all patterns are put into the *canonical form* introduced in [BDB90]. This form requires that all patterns be of the form "$n \rightarrow m$" where both n and m are nonterminals, or of the form "$n_0 \rightarrow op(n_1, \ldots, n_k)$" where n_i are all nonterminals, $k \geq 0$, and op is an operator. This canonical form does not reduce the expressiveness of the grammars—any set of rules not in canonical form can be put into canonical form by introducing new nonterminals. Putting the previous rules into canonical form gives the rules on the right of Figure 1.

4 Algorithm to Generate BURS Tables

Our method of computing the states and state transition tables is an uncomplicated ***work-list*** algorithm. This algorithm is outlined below in procedure *Main*(). Initially, the states corresponding to each leaf operator (arity = 0) are computed, and added to the set of known states, *States*, and to the list of states to be processed, *WorkList*. One by one, states are removed from *WorkList* and processed. For each operator with arity greater than 0, the state must be examined to determine what transitions are induced by that state when combined with each of the already processed states. These transitions may create new states to be added to the *WorkList*.

```
procedure Main()
    States = ∅
    WorkList = ∅
    ComputeLeafStates()
    while WorkList ≠ ∅ do
        state = Pop(WorkList)
        ∀ op ∈ Operators do
            ComputeTransitions(op, state)
        end ∀
    end while
end procedure
```

4.1 Data Structures Used to Generate BURS Tables

The set of known states, *States*, is a table that maintains a one-to-one mapping from individual states to non-negative integers. These integers are used as indices into state transition tables via index maps.

States in a BURS code generator encode three pieces of information at any node in a subject tree: the nonterminals derived from patterns that match a rule at that node, the relative costs of those nonterminals, and which rules generated each nonterminal (at a minimal cost). Such triples are called *items*, and a collection of items describing a particular state is called an *itemset*. Itemsets are implemented as arrays of $\{cost, rule\}$ pairs that are indexed by a nonterminal. Itemsets are, therefore, states. A cost of infinity (∞) indicates that, in this state, no rule derives the given nonterminal. The empty state ($\emptyset$) has all costs equal to infinity. The relative costs are called *delta costs* and are always normalized so that the nonterminal with the lowest cost derivation has a delta cost of 0. Costs within an itemset are normalized by the routine *NormalizeCosts*() below.

Rule#	Simple Grammar LHS		RHS	Cost	Canonical Form LHS		RHS	Cost
1.	goal	→	reg	(0)	goal	→	reg	(0)
2.	reg	→	Reg	(0)	reg	→	Reg	(0)
3.	reg	→	Int	(0)	reg	→	Int	(0)
4.	addr	→	Plus(reg, Int)	(0)	addr	→	Plus(reg, n.1)	(0)
4a.					n.1	→	Int	(0)
5.	reg	→	Fetch(addr)	(2)	reg	→	Fetch(addr)	(2)
6.	reg	→	Plus(reg, reg)	(2)	reg	→	Plus(reg, reg)	(2)
7.	reg	→	Plus(Plus(reg, reg), reg)	(3)	reg	→	Plus(n.2, reg)	(3)
7a.					n.2	→	Plus(reg, reg)	(0)

Figure 1: Simple Grammar and Its Canonical Form

```
procedure NormalizeCosts(state)
    delta = min∀i {state[i].cost}
    ∀ n ∈ Nonterminals do
        state[n].cost = state[n].cost − delta
    end ∀
end procedure
```

4.2 Chain Rules

Itemsets are computed in a two-step process. *ComputeTransitions*() applies rules of the form "$n \rightarrow op(\ldots)$" to generate nonterminals in the initial itemset. Next, the algorithm computes the closure of this set by applying *chain rules*. Chain rules are rules of the form "$n \rightarrow m$" where both n and m are nonterminals. These rules may introduce new nonterminals into an itemset, or they may introduce cheaper ways of deriving nonterminals already in the set. Finding the closure of the set is done by iteratively trying all the chain rules and repeatedly applying those that add new or cheaper nonterminals, until no changes are made. *Closure*() below implements this procedure. Because all costs are non-negative, and because a change is made only if a strictly less expensive derivation is found, this process must terminate.

One nonterminal may be derived from another by zero or more chain rule applications. The least cost derivation is denoted "$n \stackrel{*}{\Rightarrow} m$." The cost of such least cost derivations, "$Cost(n \stackrel{*}{\Rightarrow} m)$," can be computed efficiently using a shortest path algorithm.

```
procedure Closure(state)
    repeat
        ∀ r : n → m such that m ∈ Nonterminals do
            cost = r.cost + state[m].cost
            if cost < state[n].cost then
                state[n] = { cost, r }
            end if
        end ∀
    until no changes to state
end procedure
```

4.3 Computing States and Transitions

The computation of the states and the state transition tables begins by generating a state for each leaf operator (with arity of 0) in the routine *ComputeLeafStates*(). These leaf states must be combined as children of each non-leaf operator, and new states will be created. Each new state is added to the *WorkList* and will be subsequently processed to determine what transitions it induces.

Computing the state to label each leaf is straightforward. Rules with a right hand side of the given leaf operator generate nonterminals directly into the itemset. Normalizing the costs and finding the closure of the itemset completes the computation of the state corresponding to the leaf operator.

For each dimension of a non-leaf operator,[2] an index map of *representer states* is maintained. Representer states are constructed from an itemset by retaining only those nonterminals that may contribute to a match in the given dimension for the given operator ([Cha87], [BDB90]). Suppose that, for a given grammar, there is no rule with a tree pattern for the binary operator, θ, that has a left child of nonterminal n. In this case, we would project n out of any state when that state is to be examined as a possible left child (in the 1st dimension) of θ.

Project() will retain only those nonterminals in a given state that may be used in determining the transitions that may be induced by that state as a given child of a particular operator. A representer state also discards the *rule* field of each item because that information does not affect transitions (only reductions). For each dimension, d, a table of representer states, $op.reps[d]$, is maintained that encodes a one-to-one mapping between those states and non-negative integers. Each dimension's $op.map[d]$ table maintains a mapping from global states to representer states ($op.map[d][s]$ is the representer state to which s maps

[2] Each operator of arity n has a transition table of n dimensions.

```
procedure ComputeLeafStates()
    ∀ leaf ∈ Leaves do
        state = ∅
        ∀ r : n → leaf do
            if r.cost < state[n].cost then
                state[n] = { r.cost, r }
            end if
        end ∀
        NormalizeCosts(state)
        Closure(state)
        WorkList = Append(WorkList, state)
        States = States ∪ {state}
        leaf.state = state
    end ∀
end procedure
```

```
function Project(op, i, state)
    pState = ∅
    ∀ n ∈ Nonterminals do
        if ∃ r : m → op(n_1,...,n_{i-1}, n, n_{i+1},...,n_{op.arity}) then
            // Nonterminal n may be used in the i^th dimension of op.
            pState[n].cost = state[n].cost
        end if
    end ∀
    NormalizeCosts(pState)
    return pState
end procedure
```

```
procedure ComputeTransitions(op, state)
    ∀ i ∈ 1..op.arity do
        pState = Project(op, i, state)
        op.map[i][state] = pState
        if pState ∉ op.reps[i] then
            op.reps[i] = op.reps[i] ∪ {pState}
            ∀ (s_1, ..., s_{i-1}, pState, s_{i+1}, ..., s_{op.arity}) such that each s_j ∈ op.reps[j] do
                result = ∅
                ∀ r : n → op(m_1,...,m_{op.arity}) do
                    cost = r.cost + pState[m_i].cost + Σ_{j≠i} s_j[m_j].cost
                    if cost < result[n].cost then
                        result[n] = { cost, r }
                    end if
                end ∀
                Trim(result)
                NormalizeCosts(result)
                if result ∉ States then
                    Closure(result)
                    WorkList = Append(WorkList, result)
                    States = States ∪ {result}
                end if
                op.transition[s_1, ..., s_{i-1}, pState, s_{i+1}, ..., s_{op.arity}] = result
            end ∀
        end if
    end ∀
end procedure
```

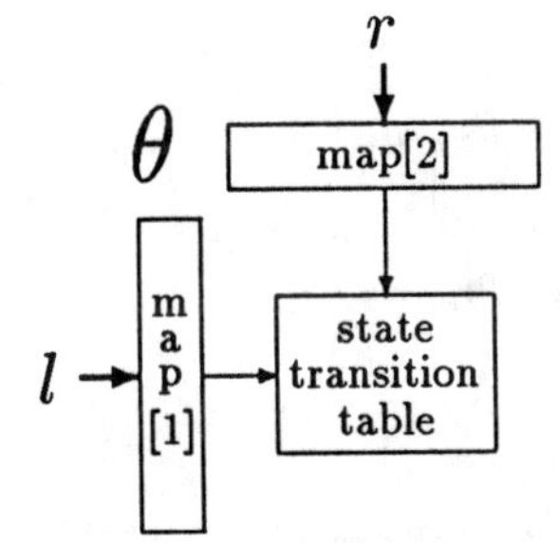

Figure 2: Computing Transitions for $\theta(l, r)$ Using Index Maps.

in the dth dimension of *op*).

Figure 2 illustrates the relationship between index maps and transition tables. Given the states l and r for the children of binary operator θ, an indirection is used to lookup the state transition for the θ node.

Transition tables are computed based on representer states, not on the original states. This reduces transition table size because many states may map to the same representer state. At tree-matching time the cost of using this technique is the extra level of indirection necessary to compute transitions. *ComputeTransitions*() (given below) finds all the transitions that each new state induces when used in combination with other known states for a given operator.

Each representer state is checked to see if it has already been processed. If the representer state has been previously processed, then no additional work must be done. If the representer state is new, the transition table must be extended along the given dimension for all possible combinations of the representer states of other dimensions (along with this representer state). This is done by generating all such combinations and then searching for all applicable rules. Once these rules have been applied, the delta costs are normalized, and the itemset is closed. If the generated state is new, then it is added to *States* and *WorkList*.

(The postponement of *Closure*() until after the check for the state's existence in *States* is an optimization justified in §5.4. *Trim*(), the routine responsible for reducing the number of states produced, is discussed in §4.4.)

4.4 State Trimming

Many of the states created by the *ComputeTransitions*() are nearly identical. The state-generation algorithm will run faster if it can increase the likelihood that two created states will be identical. Two states can often be made identical by trimming *unessential* nonterminals from the itemset. A nonterminal is unessential (in a particular state) if it can be proven that it will never be needed to produce a least-cost cover of any subject tree. Henry devised two *ad hoc* techniques, "sibling," and "demand" trimming [Hen89], to identify when one "{ *cost, rule* }" item (representing a nonterminal) can be safely removed from a state because another item subsumes it.

4.4.1 Triangle Trimming

By generalizing Henry's trimming techniques, we have developed *triangle trimming* for safely removing unessential nonterminals from an itemset. Triangle trimming considers all pairs of nonterminals in a particular itemset and determines if, given their respective costs, one of the nonterminals can be removed. A nonterminal can be removed if, in all dimensions of all rules where it is applicable, the other nonterminal can be used in a different rule to generate the same resulting nonterminal at no greater cost. Informally, a nonterminal, i, can be removed from an itemset if it can be shown that everywhere i can lead to a pattern match, another nonterminal, j, in the itemset can also lead to a comparable pattern match at no greater cost.

Determining if j subsumes i requires comparisons that have a *triangular* shape (see Figure 3). For a given operator, θ, and in a given dimension, d, two rules must be found such that both rules represent patterns for θ, and one rule, r, can employ i as its dth child, and the other rule, t, can employ j as its dth child. (It is not necessary that these rules use i and j directly—they may use nonterminals that are derived from i and j via chain rules.)

Since rule r reduces to nonterminal n_r, it must be shown that t can also produce n_r at no greater cost. We, therefore, start by assuming that rule r has matched. From this it can be determined if rule t can also match. Rule t can also match if its children in dimensions other than d can be derived via chain rules from the corresponding children of rule r. (All we are assuming is that r matches, therefore all we may assume in determining if $p_{t,k}$ exists for a match of rule t is whether $p_{t,k}$ may derived from $p_{r,k}$ via chain rules.)

Figure 3 shows how i and j, and the rules r and t must relate for j to subsume i. Once rule r is found to use i to derive n_r, a rule must be found that can employ j and can also derive n_r. Notice that for any rule r that employs i, it is only necessary to find one such rule t employing j for j to subsume i.

Subsumption is based not only on feasibility, but also on costs. A nonterminal cannot be removed if its removal would force more expensive reductions to be found than had it been retained. For the pair of rules, r and t, in Figure 3, it is possible to remove i from

$$
\begin{array}{lccccccccc}
 & & & & & i & & & & \\
 & & & & & \Downarrow * & & & & \\
\text{Rule } r\text{:} & n_r & \rightarrow & \theta(& p_{r,1}, & \ldots, & p_{r,d}, & \ldots, & p_{r,arity} &) \\
 & \Uparrow * & & & \Downarrow * & \Downarrow * & & \Downarrow * & \Downarrow * & \\
\text{Rule } t\text{:} & n_t & \rightarrow & \theta(& p_{t,1}, & \ldots, & p_{t,d}, & \ldots, & p_{t,arity} &) \\
 & & & & & & \Uparrow * & & & \\
 & & & & & & j & & &
\end{array}
$$

Figure 3: Triangle Trimming Relationship (for j to subsume i)

$$
\begin{array}{l}
state[i].cost + r.cost + Cost(p_{r,d} \overset{*}{\Rightarrow} i) \geq \\
state[j].cost + t.cost + Cost(p_{t,d} \overset{*}{\Rightarrow} j) + Cost(n_r \overset{*}{\Rightarrow} n_t) + \sum_{k \neq d} Cost(p_{t,k} \overset{*}{\Rightarrow} p_{r,k})
\end{array}
$$

Figure 4: Inequality that must hold for i to be removed if j is present.

the itemset containing j if the inequality in Figure 4 holds. The cost of using r is the sum of the cost of i, the cost of deriving $p_{r,d}$ from i, and the cost of r. Since our premise is only that rule r matches and that i and j are present in some itemset, the computation of the cost of using t with j to indirectly produce n_r will require not only the costs of t, j, and $p_{t,d} \overset{*}{\Rightarrow} j$, but will also require the costs of deriving the other $p_{t,k}$ from $p_{r,k}$ and the cost of deriving n_r from n_t.

The inequality in Figure 4 is the basis for finding the *minimal* cost difference between two nonterminals to allow one of them to be removed for a given rule. In general, to safely remove i, it is necessary to examine *all* contexts in which i can be used and find the cost difference that is sufficient to guarantee that i can be removed based on the relative costs of i and j. The routine, *Triangle*(), calculates this minimal difference for any pair of nonterminals. (When it is impossible for nonterminal j to be used in place of i, regardless of their respective costs, *Triangle*() returns ∞.)

4.4.2 Chain Rule Trimming

Two states are identical if they represent the same nonterminals at the same costs with each respective nonterminal generated by the same rule. Triangle trimming removes nonterminals from states whenever possible, thereby eliminating the possibility that two states differ on the particular costs or rules involving those nonterminals. To further minimize the number of states, it is necessary to bias the algorithm towards using the same rules whenever possible. Biasing the algorithm towards using chain rules whenever possible increases the likelihood that two states will have used the same rules to derive a given nonterminal. This bias can be forced by removing nonterminal entries from an itemset prior to closure when it can be determined that *Closure*() will restore those nonterminals at an equal or lesser cost using chain rules.

The routine, *Trim*(), uses both triangle and chain rule trimming to prune nonterminals from itemsets so that they will be more likely to be identical, thereby reducing the size of the generated tables and the table generation time.

5 Speed Optimizing Techniques

The previous routines provide many opportunities for speed optimization. Some of the improvements are general techniques not specific to BURS table generation; other improvements rely on subtle knowledge of BURS table generation.

5.1 Attempt Cheaper Alternatives First

It may appear that the two sets of nested loops in *Trim*() could be jammed into a single pair of nested loops for improved efficiency. Both loops have the intended side-effect of removing nonterminals from the states. Since the loops iterate over only the nonterminals that remain in the state, the second set of loops will normally iterate fewer times than the first set. Because triangle trimming is an expensive operation relative to chain rule trimming, it is more efficient to remove all possible nonterminals via chain rule trimming and then attempt triangle trimming only on the remaining nonterminals.

5.2 Precompute Values

In the previous routines, many situations exist where values can be computed once and used many times. For instance, *Project*() requires the knowledge of which nonterminals can appear in the ith dimension of oper-

```
// Compute C, such that if state[i].cost ≥ state[j].cost + C then i can safely be removed from state.
function Triangle(i, j)
    if i = Goal then
        return ∞        // Do not remove the goal nonterminal, tempting as it may be.
    end if
    Max = −∞
    ∀ n ∈ Nonterminals−{i} do
        if Max < Cost(n ⇒* j) − Cost(n ⇒* i) then
            Max = Cost(n ⇒* j) − Cost(n ⇒* i)
        end if
    end ∀
    ∀ op ∈ Operators do
        ∀ d ∈ 1..op.arity do
            ∀ r : n_r → op(p_{r,1}, ... ,p_{r,op.arity}) do
                C_i = Cost(p_{r,d} ⇒* i)
                if C_i < ∞ then
                    LocalMin = ∞
                    ∀ t : n_t → op(p_{t,1}, ... ,p_{t,op.arity}) do
                        C_{r,t} = Cost(n_r ⇒* n_t)
                        C_j = Cost(p_{t,d} ⇒* j)
                        C_k = Σ_{k≠d} Cost(p_{t,k} ⇒* p_{r,k})
                        C = C_{r,t} + C_j + C_k + t.cost − r.cost − C_i
                        if C < LocalMin then
                            LocalMin = C
                        end if
                    end ∀
                    if LocalMin > Max then
                        Max = LocalMin
                    end if
                end if
            end ∀
        end ∀
    end ∀
    return Max
end procedure
```

```
procedure Trim(state)
    ∀ n ∈ state do
        ∀ m ∈ state (m≠ n) do
            C = Cost(n ⇒* m)
            if state[n].cost ≥ state[m].cost + C then
                state[n] = { ∞, ⊥ } // Remove n from state.
            end if
        end ∀
    end ∀
    ∀ n ∈ state do
        ∀ m ∈ state (m≠ n) do
            C = Triangle(n, m)
            if state[n].cost ≥ state[m].cost + C then
                state[n] = { ∞, ⊥ } // Remove n from state.
            end if
        end ∀
    end ∀
end procedure
```

ator *op*. Because this list is invariant for a given rule set, it can be computed once and used repeatedly.

Efficiency is also enhanced if the list of rules is partitioned by the operator of the pattern, so that *ComputeTransitions*() will only iterate over the list of applicable rules.

The cost of transitive closure rules ($Cost(n \stackrel{*}{\Rightarrow} m)$) is precomputed advantageously since it is used often by *Trim*() and *Triangle*().

5.3 Lazy Computations

There are $O(N^2)$ possible pairs of nonterminals that may be used in a call to *Triangle*(), but in practice only very few pairs are ever used. Our original implementation precomputed the results of calling *Triangle*() with all possible combinations of nonterminals and then used table lookup for these values. Using this strategy, *Triangle*() consumed over 75% of the execution time generating tables for a VAX grammar. With 179 nonterminals in the (canonical form) grammar, *Triangle*() was called 32041 times, but fewer than 1000 of those values were ever referenced! Changing the program to compute those values by need increased the speed tremendously. Once computed, these values are cached for subsequent calls with the same arguments.

5.4 Defer Closure

If two itemsets are equal before closure, then they must be equal after closure. Because two itemsets are chain-rule trimmed before closure, it is also the case that if two itemsets are equal after closure, they must have been equal before closure. By maintaining both pre-closure and post-closure copies of an itemset in a table, we can check for the existence of an itemset in the table by comparing their pre-closure representations. This allows the closure computation to be deferred until it is known that the state is indeed new and must be added to the table.

5.5 Itemset Equivalence

Determining whether an itemset is already in a table of states is an expensive operation, and this test is done for every entry in every transition table. The integer subset 68000 grammar required over 425,000 calls to determine itemset equivalence. Making itemset equivalence testing efficient is extremely important. For two itemsets to be equal, they must be equal for all of their items. Fortunately, two observations make testing for equivalence much more efficient: two itemsets created as members of transition tables for different operators can never be equal, and for any given operator it is only necessary to compare the entries corresponding to the left-hand sides of the rules for that operator.

By keeping a reference to the generating operator as part of an itemset's representation, many itemsets can be determined to be unequal by recognizing that those entries differ. Should those entries be the same, it is only necessary to check that the nonterminal entries for the relevant nonterminals are equal for both itemsets. This check must be done after the states have been trimmed.

The same routines are used to implement the global *States* table, and each of the local *op.reps*[] tables. These tables are implemented as hash tables. Computing the hash function is also made more efficient by examining only the relevant nonterminals.

Calling *NormalizeCosts*() after *Trim*(), but before *Closure*(), allows it to limit the nonterminals it must inspect. Again, the same nonterminals that are relevant to determining itemset equivalence are those that must be normalized prior to a call to *Closure*().

5.6 Specialize Memory Allocation

Our program allocates and deallocates an enormous amount of memory during the computation of the itemsets and transition tables. The primary source of allocation and deallocation of memory in the algorithm is the tentative allocation of itemsets by *ComputeTransitions*() and *Project*(). Only after the itemset is allocated and computed can it be determined if an equivalent state has already been seen, thereby allowing the deallocation of the itemset. Redundant itemsets really *must* be deallocated—for a 68000 grammar the program computed over 100,000 redundant itemsets.

Fortunately, knowledge of the the allocation/deallocation pattern of particular data can lead to very efficient memory management [Han90]. This is the case with itemsets. Itemsets, after allocation, are computed and then either retained forever or immediately released. It can never be the case, therefore, that two itemset deallocations occur sequentially without an intervening allocation. This allows the creation of specialized deallocation and allocation routines for itemsets. The deallocation routine simply maintains a reference to the last discarded itemset, and does not return the space to the heap. Allocation checks this reference, and if the reference is not null, it returns the reference to the previously deallocated value (and clears the reference); only if the reference is null does the allocator request space from the heap.

5.7 Minimize space

On a machine without enormous amounts of RAM, it is important to avoid over-allocating memory and thrashing. The single biggest user of memory is the itemset representation for all of the computed states. Itemsets are kept as small as possible by minimizing the number of nonterminals in the canonical form grammar. A naive translation of a grammar into canonical form may produce too many nonterminals if it creates different nonterminals that represent identical patterns. It is important (and easy) to reuse previously created nonterminals.

6 Unprofitable Optimizations

Two additional techniques were not implemented because either the speed-up did not merit the additional complexity, or because the resulting code would only reduce the number of states, without also speeding up the code.

6.1 Closure Speedup

Because least-cost transitive chain rules are precomputed for use by *Trim*(), they are available for speeding up the *Closure*() routine. *Closure*(), however, represents less than 1% of the execution time of the program, and using these transitive rules only speeds that routine by 10-20%.

6.2 Post-pass State Minimization

It is possible to further eliminate states after they and the transition tables have been generated by isolating and removing states that differ only in the respective costs of each constituent nonterminal. State minimization for BURS is similar to DFA state minimization. Because state minimization is a post-pass, it cannot make the program faster—it must make it slower.[3] We decided the space savings was not worth the additional complexity or time and, therefore, did not attempt to add a state minimization pass.

7 Implementation Results

Our algorithm has been implemented in ANSI C [FHP91].[4] The input has two parts: a description of the operators (including the arity and identifying value of each), and a list of grammar rules. The operators are limited to being nullary (leaf), unary, or binary. (The arity was limited because the intended application required only nullary, unary, and binary operators.) Each rule includes an arbitrarily complex pattern, the nonterminal the pattern derives, its cost, and a unique external rule number (for identification). The front end of the table generator puts the rules into canonical form.

Function	Lines (C/Yacc)
Table Generation	1981
Front End	633
Table Output	1345
Total	3959

Figure 5: Code size for our BURS table generator

As output the program creates C routines and tables for labeling and reducing a subject tree. The program can output either a simple table-driven tree-labeler and reducer, or a hard-coded labeler and reducer. The hard-coded routines incorporate the time and space saving techniques in [FH91b].

The entire program is under 4000 lines of code that splits evenly between table generation routines and input/output routines. Figure 5 gives the number of lines of code used to implement the table generator.

Our program runs quickly on both simple and complex inputs. We compare our system to Henry's table generator that was derived from the CodeGen system [Hen89]. His system consists of over 20,000 lines of C code. It is not clear, however, how much of this code is a direct consequence of algorithm design, and how much is an indirect consequence of the fact that his BURS system was derived from the much bigger CodeGen distribution.

Figure 6 gives a description of 4 sample input grammars and the execution times for each system on each grammar. The first two grammars (used to generate code generators for `lcc` [FH91a]) are for the VAX and the MIPS R3000 RISC processor. Two others that were developed as part of the CodeGen project are integer (byte, word, and long) subsets of the VAX and Motorola 68000 processors. The timings were taken on a DECstation 5000 with 96Mb of RAM.[5]

The differences in the number of generated states between the two systems for the CodeGen grammars can be attributed to the presence of a state minimization post-pass in Henry's system that is not present in our system.

It should be noted that if triangle trimming is *disabled*, the number of states generated and the running times are about 100–200% higher than those reported here.

[3] Henry [Hen89] found that the additional time for the post-pass was negligible ($< 1\%$) in his system.

[4] The program, burg, is available via anonymous `ftp` from `kaese.cs.wisc.edu`. The compressed shar file `pub/burg.shar.Z` holds the complete distribution.

[5] The timings are *more* favorable towards our implementation on machines with limited amounts of RAM.

Grammar Description			Henry's System		Our System		Ratio
Machine	#Rules	#Nonterms	#States	Generation Time (seconds)	#States	Generation Time (seconds)	
vax	291	48	1017	467.7	1015	14.4	32
MIPS	136	9	125	21.4	125	0.6	36
vax.bwl	524	179	493	146.8	586	15.5	9
mot.bwl	462	80	499	251.5	838	14.4	14

Figure 6: Timings

8 Conclusion

The algorithm presented is a simple and efficient method of producing BURS tables. To the best of our knowledge our system is significantly faster than any other BURS system that does aggressive state trimming. The prototype implementation required fewer than 2000 lines of C code for producing the BURS automata. It was able produce these tables over 30 times more quickly than the previous "state of the art" optimizing system. Our system does not sacrifice table compaction optimizations to achieve this speed—to the contrary, the compaction techniques increase the overall speed of the implementation by reducing the number of states that must be examined.

The algorithm employs only simple data structures and routines to generate these tables quickly. We believe that, to a large degree, this design simplicity increases efficiency. To further increase speed, optimizations that exploit the specific nature of BURS table generation were isolated and are described here.

To reduce the number of states created a new technique of trimming states, triangle trimming, has been developed to isolate nonterminals that can be removed from a state. This trimming provides a many-fold reduction in the number of states and a commensurate speed-up in table generation.

9 Acknowledgements

We would like to thank Robert Henry for making his system available for comparison and explaining much of his early work in BURS table generation.

References

[AGT89] Alfred V. Aho, Mahedevan Ganapathi, and Steven W. K. Tjiang. Code generation using tree matching and dynamic programming. *ACM Transactions on Programming Languages and Systems*, 11(4):491–516, October 1989.

[BDB90] A. Balachandran, D. M. Dhamdhere, and S. Biswas. Efficient retargetable code generation using bottom-up tree pattern matching. *Computer Languages*, 15(3):127–140, 1990.

[Cha87] David R. Chase. An improvement to bottom-up tree pattern matching. In *Proceedings of the 14th Annual Symposium on Principles of Programming Languages*, pages 168–177, 1987.

[FH91a] Christopher W. Fraser and David R. Hanson. A code generation interface for ANSI C. *Software—Practice and Experience*, 21(9):963–988, September 1991.

[FH91b] Christopher W. Fraser and Robert R. Henry. Hard-coding bottom-up code generation tables to save time and space. *Software—Practice and Experience*, 21(1):1–12, January 1991.

[FHP91] Christopher W. Fraser, Robert R. Henry, and Todd A. Proebsting. BURG — fast optimal instruction selection and tree parsing. Technical Report 1066, University of Wisconsin, 1991.

[Han90] David R. Hanson. Fast allocation and deallocation of memory based on object lifetimes. *Software—Practice and Experience*, 20(1):5–12, January 1990.

[Hen89] Robert R. Henry. Encoding optimal pattern selection in a table-driven bottom-up tree-pattern matcher. Technical Report 89-02-04, University of Washington, 1989.

[PL88] Eduardo Pelegri-Llopart. *Rewrite Systems, Pattern Matching, and Code Generation.* Phd Thesis, Technical Report UCB/CSD 88/423, Computer Science Division, University of California, Berkeley, 1988.

[PLG88] Eduardo Pelegri-Llopart and Susan L. Graham. Optimal code generation for expression trees: An application of BURS theory. In *Proceedings of the 15th Annual Symposium on Principles of Programming Languages*, pages 294–308, 1988.

Eliminating Branches using a Superoptimizer and the GNU C Compiler

Torbjörn Granlund
Logic Programming and Parallel Systems Laboratory
Swedish Institute of Computer Science
Box 1263
S-164 28 Kista, Sweden
tege@sics.se

Richard Kenner
Ultracomputer Research Laboratory
New York University
715 Broadway, 10th Floor
New York, NY 10003
kenner@vlsi1.ultra.nyu.edu

1. Introduction

In 1987, Henry Massalin, of Columbia University, described a *superoptimizer* that generates optimal instruction sequences given a function to be performed [1]. The sequences are found by doing an exhaustive search over a subset of the instructions of the machine for which the optimization is made. Little or no mention of this important technique has occurred since. In the present work, we describe an alternative technique for constructing a superoptimizer, which will call the GNU Superoptimizer or GSO.

We believe this optimizer is faster and more versatile than Massalin's original work. We show how GSO was used to add patterns to GCC, the GNU C compiler, so it can eliminate many branch instructions when generating code for the IBM RS/6000. A number of surprising results were obtained, many of which were unknown to the architects of the RS/6000 processor.

In the first section we present some sample results of the superoptimizer. The next section discusses the basic design and structure of the GNU C compiler. Subsequently, we show how the results of the superoptimizer were used to enable the GNU C compiler to produce very compact code sequences on the RS/6000. After a brief discussion of the use of some specific RS/6000 instructions, the final two sections discuss how the GNU superoptimizer works and the limitations of superoptimization, and present a large number of instruction sequences generated by the superoptimizer for the RS/6000.

Although this paper uses the RS/6000 for all its examples, the techniques described here are applicable to most machines.

ACM SIGPLAN '92 PLDI-6/92/CA
© 1992 ACM 0-89791-476-7/92/0006/0341...$1.50

2. Sample Results of GSO

We first study the output produced by the superoptimizer when it searches for sequences that compute the value of the C expression `(signed int) a >= 0`. The input is assumed to be in register 3 and the output is placed in register 5.

The RS/6000 is a three-operand machine. Usually the presence of the letter "`i`" in an operation code signifies an immediate constant, "`il`", means that the operation is performed on the low-order 16 bits of a quantity, and "`iu`" means that the operation is performed on the high-order 16 bits.

Here is the superoptimizer output for the C expression `(signed int) a >= 0` on the RS/6000.

```
1:  sri     r4,r3,31
    xoril   r5,r4,1

2:  srai    r4,r3,31
    ai      r5,r4,1

3:  srai    r4,r3,31
    cal     r5,1(r4)

4:  xoriu   r4,r3,0x8000
    sri     r5,r4,31

5:  nand    r4,r3,r3
    sri     r5,r4,31

6:  sfi     r4,r3,-1
    sri     r5,r4,31
```

GSO found six ways to perform the operation, each of which takes two instructions. The first sequence computes `(a < 0)` by shifting the sign bit to the low-order bit, and then complements it by doing an `xor` with the constant one. The second and third sequences first duplicate the sign bit into the entire word (thus yielding –1 if `a` is negative, and 0 if `a` is greater than or equal to 0) and then add 1 to get the desired result. The difference between sequence two and three is in the instruction used to add 1. In the fourth sequence, the sign bit is first inverted and then shifted right into the low-order bit. The fifth and sixth sequences one's complement the entire value and then shift the sign bit into the low-order bit. They differ only in the manner in which the one's complement is computed. In the fifth sequence a logical operation is used, while an arithmetic operation is used in the sixth sequence.

These sequences do not use the **carry** bit. Therefore they are machine-independent and can be used on any machine that has logical negation and logical right shift instructions. Indeed, this particular method for computing `(signed int) a >= 0` has been known for quite some time. It is included here as an example of the superoptimizer output.

More interesting sequences involve use of the **carry** bit of a machine. On the RS/6000, the **carry** bit is simply the carry out of the high-order bit of the adder. A subtraction is defined as an addition of the minuend, the one's complement of the subtrahend, and either the **carry** bit or the constant one. The result of this *addition* determines the generated value of the **carry** bit.

When GSO is asked to compute the value of the expression `r3 == 0`, a single two-instruction sequence is found. It is

```
1:  sfi     r4,r3,0
    ae      r5,r4,r3
```

This sequence is quite typical of the type of **carry**-bit manipulations that occur in these types of conditional expressions. It works as follows: The first instruction computes the sum of the one's complement of `r3` and 1. It sets `r4` to the result of this addition, which is `-r3`, and sets the **carry** bit to the carry out of the high-order bit of the addition, which, in this case, has the effect of setting the **carry** bit to 1 if r3 equals zero, and to 0 otherwise. The second instruction sets `r5`, the final result, to `r4 + r3 +` **carry** `= -r3 + r3 +` **carry**, which is equal to the **carry** bit from the first instruction, or our desired final result.

More sequences will be presented throughout this paper and a large listing of sequences is presented in Section 8.

3. The GNU C Compiler

The GNU C compiler (GCC) is a highly portable, retargetable, optimizing C compiler. The recently released GCC version 2 supports virtually all general-purpose microprocessors currently in use and includes front ends for C, C++ and Objective-C, with front ends for FORTRAN and Ada under development. The code quality of GCC is quite competitive with commercial C compilers; in most cases the code produced for the Sparc and Motorola 88100 (and possibly others) runs faster than code produced by any other compiler. At least two vendors (NeXT and Data General) distribute GCC as the C compiler for their systems.

Rather than using a fixed intermediate language and compiling it for a variety of machines, GCC instead defines a representation called *RTL*, for *register transfer language*, in which the actual instructions of the target machine are represented. The source program is initially compiled directly into RTL representing the target machine instructions and using an unlimited number of registers. The remaining compilation phases perform optimizations and register allocation. The idea of using RTL and some of the optimizations came from the Portable Optimizer (PO), written at the University of Arizona by Jack Davidson and Christopher Fraser [3].

The implementation of GCC is much more fully described in [2]; here we summarize the points of interest to the remainder of the present paper.

Instructions in GCC, referred to as *insns*, are represented in RTL and are an expression tree consisting of the various RTL operators along with pointers to the next and previous insns and some dataflow information. RTL is usually written in a LISP-like notation; a typical add insn looks like:

```
(insn 11 10 12 (set (reg/i:SI 0)
                    (plus:SI (reg:SI 22)
                             (const_int 10)))
    152 {addsi3} (insn_list 9 (nil))
    (expr_list:REG_DEAD (reg:SI 22) (nil)))
```

This indicates that register 0 is set to the sum of register 22 and the constant integer 10. The unique number assigned to the insn is 11, the next insn is numbered 12, and the previous insn is 10. This insn matches pattern number 152 (named "addsi3") in the machine description file. The value used in this insn (register 22) was set in insn number 9 (and this is the first use) and register 22 dies in this insn.

Machine description files contain a list of *patterns*, which describe the instructions available on the machine and how to generate code for basic operations. A typical pattern, if named, says what RTL to generate for a particular operation (for example, **`addsi3`** means to do a three-operand addition of 4-byte integers). All patterns are used to specify what insns are valid and how to generate assembly code for the insn.

Each insn generated must match some pattern. The compiler ensures that all transformations applied to the insn chain as part of the optimization process continue to allow each insn to match some pattern. The `addsi3` pattern from the description file for the AMD 29000 (the pattern for the RS/6000 is slightly more complex) is as follows:

```
(define_insn "addsi3"
  [(set (match_operand:SI 0 "gen_reg_operand" "=r,r")
        (plus:SI (match_operand:SI 1 "gen_reg_operand" "%r,r")
                 (match_operand:SI 2 "add_operand" "rI,N")))]
  ""
  "@
   add %0,%1,%2
   sub %0,%1,%n2")
```

Since insns are represented as expression trees, the result of one insn can be substituted directly into its use in a second insn. If the insn that results from such a substitution matches a pattern in the machine description file, we are able to save an instruction in the compiled program. This transformation was originally done by the University of Arizona compiler and in GCC is done in a phase called the *combiner*. The combiner is also able to perform a wide variety of algebraic simplifications.

Typically, merging two or more insns together into one insn forms complex addressing modes on CISC machines. It is also used to form specialized instructions such as NOR or the various "multiply-accumulate" instructions that have become common.

Optimization phases of GCC which run before the combiner perform jump optimizations, common-subexpression elimination, and loop optimizations including strength reduction and loop unrolling. Following the combiner is instruction scheduling (to reduce data-dependent stalls on pipelined machines), register allocation, another jump optimization and instruction scheduling pass, and delay-slot filling.

4. Elimination of Conditional Jumps

In this section, we discuss the cost of conditional jumps, general methods used to eliminate them, and how we used the superoptimizer to produce efficient code on the RS/6000 that avoids jumps.

4.1. Costs of Jumps

Fundamentally, jumps interfere with the pipelined execution of instructions. Most modern processors have features that minimize this cost, for example by using delayed-branches, which require the compiler to find instructions to place in delay slots.

The RS/6000 uses a different, and quite novel, technique to streamline the execution of branch instructions. There are four execution units on the RS/6000: an integer unit, a floating-point unit, a condition-code unit, and a branch processor. Each cycle can fetch four instructions and dispatch them to the appropriate unit. Because of this structure, unconditional branches can be performed in parallel with other instruction execution at a net cost of zero cycles.

Conditional branches, however, often have a non-zero cost. The timing of conditional branches is quite complex and is described in more detail in [4]. Basically, the cost of a conditional branch depends on the number of cycles between the setting of the condition flag and the branch that tests it. If sufficient time has elapsed, the branch takes zero cycles. Otherwise, there is a delay of three cycles between the setting of the condition flag and the branch for taken branches and zero cycles for not taken branches (however, in the case of not taken branches, there must be a total of five cycles of instructions between the compare and the next branch after the not-taken branch to avoid additional delays).

On the RS/6000, instruction scheduling can sometimes be used to reduce the required delay, although this is usually not successful since most basic blocks are short and many scheduling algorithms only operate within one basic block. For machines with delay slots, delay slot scheduling can be used to reduce the cost of delay slots. GCC performs both optimizations.

Even when the cost of a branch can be reduced, it is nevertheless useful to eliminate as many jumps as possible. Not only has the branch cost not been reduced to zero by architectural features but it is desirable to increase the length of basic blocks. This is because optimizations are easier to perform within a single basic block; most of the optimizations in GCC, such as the combiner and instruction scheduling, only operate within a basic block.

The newly-announced DEC "Alpha" uses neither the technique used by the RS/6000 nor delay slots. Instead, it relies on branch-prediction techniques, and DEC warns that mis-predicted branches can cost ten cycles. Eliminating conditional jumps on the machine is therefore quite important.

4.2. Techniques for Elimination of Jumps

The techniques for eliminating jumps rely on the fact that jumps are often used to skip a relatively short section of code. These methods often involve what are sometimes called *set-condition code (scc)* instructions, which set a data register to one value if a comparison is true and to another value if the comparison is false. Machines that include instructions specifically for this purpose are the Motorola 68k and 88k families, the Intel i386 family, the AMD 29k family, the MIPS processors, and the newly-announced "Alpha" from DEC.

The "true" value is usually either plus or minus one but is sometimes a value consisting of just the sign bit. We sometimes want scc instructions that produce plus one for true and zero for false and sometimes want versions that yield minus one or zero. The following table shows how to obtain these values from all three versions of hardware instructions. Each entry shows the instruction required to convert the hardware "true" value into the desired representations.

Hardware Value	Desired Truth Value	
	+1	−1
+1	no-op	negate
−1	negate	no-op
sign bit	logical right shift	arithmetic right shift

In this section, we assume that all scc instructions return either plus one or zero, i.e., the value returned from a C relational expression.

The most straightforward application of scc instructions is to generate code for C relational operators assigned to a variable, for example, `a = (b >= c)`. To compile this statement, we simply apply the `ge` scc operation to `b` and `c` and place its output in `a`.

The compiler can also do this transformation if the statement is coded as `a = ((b >= c) ? 1 : 0)` or by a series of statements such as

```
if (b >= c)
  a = 1;
else
  a = 0;
```

This transformation is actually a special case of a more general principle. If an expression is to have the value zero if some condition is true and some other, possibly its previous, value if the condition is false, an scc instruction can also be used.

For example, consider the expression `a >= b ? c : 0`. We can evaluate this expression by taking a value consisting of all one bits when the condition is true and zero when it is false and performing a logical `and` of this value with `c`. That is, the given expression is equivalent to `c & -(a >= b)`. The transformation can also be done if the equivalent `if` statement is used. Even more generally, code such as

```
if (cond)
  foo = 0;
```

is equivalent to `foo &= -(! cond)`.

The next section will show how this general principle along with the use of GSO-generated sequences can result in quite compact code for some conditional expressions. However, this principle can be used even in the absence of scc operations, because of the algebraic simplifications done by the GCC combine phase.

Consider what happens when the expression `(a & 8) != 0 ? 4 : 0` is compiled for the RS/6000 (the first operand of the conditional operator might be the result of testing a single-bit field). Using the transformation discussed above, this expression is equivalent to `4 & -((a & 8) != 0)`. The following transformations are then applied in sequence (we will represent logical right shifts as `l>>` and arithmetic right shifts as `a>>` and assume 32-bit words):

- To obtain a one if a single-bit value is not equal to zero and a zero if it is, we shift the value to the low-order bit. The expression is now `4 & -((a & 8) l>> 3)`.
- A single-bit value can be negated by shifting that bit to the sign bit and then arithmetically shifting it back (to the low-order bit in this case). The expression is now `4 & ((((a & 8) l>> 3) << 31) a>> 31)`.
- The two logical shifts are equivalent to a single right shift of 28 bits, yielding `4 & (((a & 8) << 28) a>> 31)`.
- Logically `and`'ing a sign-extended value with a single-bit constant in the range of the extended sign bits can be done by a logical shift of the sign bit to the desired position. The expression is now `(((a & 8) << 28) l>> 29)`
- Finally, the two logical shifts can be merged into one logical shift and one logical `and` operation. The original expression is thus equivalent to `(a l>> 1) & 4`.

This expression can be evaluated in one instruction on the RS/6000. The `rlinm` instruction rotates a register by a specified constant number of bits and logically `and`'s it with a mask, where a mask is either a single consecutive group of one bits in a word of zeros or vice versa. This single `rlinm` instruction is the code generated by GCC for the original expression. Not only does using these transformations convert what would otherwise be four instructions (which are generated by IBM's compiler) into a single instruction, it has eliminated an expensive branch, yielding an average-case savings of more than a factor of four.

4.3. "scc" Instructions for the RS/6000

Most of the transformations shown above assume the existence of short sequences of instructions that set a register to 1 or 0 depending on the result of a comparison. On the RS/6000, this can be done by doing a compare, possibly performing a logical operation on the condition register bits, copying the condition register into a general register (`mfcr`), and extracting the relevant bit.

Unfortunately, there is a two cycle delay between the compare and the `mfcr` and an additional single cycle delay before the result of the `mfcr` can be accessed to extract the desired bit. Thus, these operations take 6 or 7 cycles, which is more than code using branch instructions would take. (It might be possible to move other instructions to hide the latencies, but these instructions could also be used in the delay between compare and branch.) If we use these code sequences, the advantage of having longer basic blocks would be outweighed by the factor of two cost in cycles. For this reason, it was recommended by researchers at IBM that this method not be used in GCC.

To see if better sequences exist, we had GSO search for the shortest sequences implementing the ten binary comparisons and the six unary comparisons with zero (the unsigned comparisons with zero are degenerate; for `a` unsigned, `a < 0` is always false, `a >= 0` is always true, `a > 0` is equivalent to `a != 0`, and `a <= 0` is equivalent to `a == 0`).

We found that all 16 operations can be done in no more than 3 instructions, three of the comparisons with zero (`==`, `!=`, and `>=`) can be done in two instructions, and one comparison with zero (`<`) can be done in one instruction (the sequences for `>= 0` and `== 0` were shown earlier and all of these sequences are shown in Section 8).

None of the instructions used in these sequences require any communication outside the integer execution unit (such as compare and the `mfcr` instruction discussed earlier); indeed only instructions executed by the integer unit were included in GSO. The fact that such sequences exist was an unexpected result, since discussions with some of the architects of the RS/6000 at IBM led us to believe that no such sequences existed for many of these operations (some of these sequences, such as those for `< 0` and `!=`, were well-known previously).

These sequences enable us to produce code for C statements of the form `a = b` *rel-op* `c;` for all 16 *rel-op*'s that contain at most three instructions and execute in no more than three cycles.

Recall from the previous section that we often need variants of these operations that produce a value of minus one for true and zero for false. One way to obtain such a result is to simply negate the result of the sequences that produce positive one for true and zero for false. However, a close look at the first example in Section 2 suggests that we might be able to find smaller sequences.

In that example, one of the ways we computed `(signed int) a >= 0` was by complementing `A` and shifting the sign bit to the low-order bit. If a logical shift is used, as in that code sequence, this produces a value of positive one for true and zero for false. On the other hand, if an *arithmetic* shift were used, it would produce negative one for true and zero for false, which is the required result. In this case, at least, the cost was the same whether a true value was represented by positive or negative one.

To see if this was the case in general, we used GSO to find the shortest sequences that compute C expressions of the form `-(a` *rel-op* `b)`. The result was that in 14 of the 16 cases, sequences were found of the same length as functions that computed the non-negated conditional value; in the remaining two cases, unsigned `>` and unsigned `<`, the sequences computing the negated result were one instruction *shorter* (two instructions instead of three).

Expressions of the form shown above are rarely encountered in C programs. However, as discussed above, code that conditionally clears a register can be transformed into expressions of the form `a & -(b` *rel-op* `c)`. These can be implemented by using the sequences for the previous set of operations and performing the indicated logical `and` operation. Inspection of some of these sequences showed that they often end with `nand` instructions, so we wondered if it might be possible to perform the required `and` operation without adding more instructions but instead modifying the sequence.

We therefore added code to GSO to search for the shortest sequences of the form `a & -(b` *rel-op* `c)` for all 16 comparison operations. The result was that in two cases, unsigned `>=` and `<=`, the sequences including the `and` had the same length as those without it, namely three instructions. In the other 14 cases, an additional instruction was required, as expected.

The most interesting result was obtained when we looked at the sequences for the 16 basic comparison operations and noticed that there was a sequence for almost all of them that ended with an add or subtract instruction. We were curious whether this instruction could also be used to add another value to the result of the comparison, i.e., how many instructions would be needed to compute `a + (b` *rel-op* `c)`. This operation is rather common, especially when written in its equivalent form as

```
if (b rel-op c)
    a++;
```

After adding code to GSO to search for the shortest sequences implementing these expressions, we discovered that in only two cases (`< 0` and `>= 0`) did the addition lengthen the sequence. Even more surprisingly, in two other cases (unsigned `<=` and unsigned `>=`), the code to compute the sum was *shorter* than that to compute the basic comparison. For example, to compute `a + ((unsigned) b <= (unsigned) c)`, the two instructions

```
sf      r0,r4,r5
aze     r6,r3
```

are used. (`a` is in r3, `b` in r4, `c` in r5, and the result is in r6.) The first instruction subtracts `b` from `c` and the second instructions adds the **carry** flag to zero plus `A` using an `aze` instruction.

The RS/6000 has no single instruction to copy the **carry** flag into a general register, so the sequence for computing the comparison must use an extra instruction to set a register to zero. That is why including the addition produces a shorter code sequence.

To take advantage of the surprising fact that the addition has no cost, we added code to GCC's jump optimization routine to convert the `if` statement to the equivalent conditional expression shown above.

5. Adding GSO-produced Sequences to GCC

Getting GCC to produce the code sequences we presented is a fairly straightforward task. The first step is to choose the appropriate sequence to use, since many of these operations can be implemented by a number of different code sequences. We used three criteria to choose the best sequence:

(1) Some of the instructions on the RS/6000, particularly arithmetic instructions involving the **carry** bit, do not permit immediate operands. Some operands of these functions (such as the second operand being compared and the value added to the comparison result) will often be immediate constants. Sequences that only use these operands in contexts where immediate forms of the instruction exist are preferred to sequences that do not.

(2) The fewer scratch registers a sequence required, the more preferred the sequence.

(3) A sequence that could put its output in the same register as an input is preferred to one that requires the input and output to be in different registers.

The second step is to add the instruction patterns to generate the code sequences. Because of the way GCC's combiner phase operates, this is a straightforward, though sometimes tedious, task. For example, to generate the code for the case shown above, the following pattern was added to the RS/6000 definition file:

```
(define_insn ""
  [(set (match_operand:SI 0 "gen_reg_operand" "=r")
        (plus:SI
          (leu:SI
            (match_operand:SI 1 "gen_reg_operand" "r")
            (match_operand:SI 2 "reg_or_short_operand" "rI"))
        (match_operand:SI 3 "gen_reg_operand" "r")))
   (clobber (match_scratch:SI 4 "=&r"))]
  ""
  "sf%I2 %4,%1,%2;aze %0,%3")
```

This pattern matches the RTL resulting from compiling the expression `a + ((unsigned) b <= (unsigned) c`. Operand 0 (the result), operand 1 (`b`), and operand 3 (`a`) are all required to be in general-purpose registers. Operand 2 (`c`) can be either in a register or be a constant short enough to fit in the immediate field of an arithmetic instruction. One scratch register is needed for this instruction, specified by operand 4. The last line of the pattern lists the assembler instructions this pattern should generate. The string `%`*n* means that the assembler text for operand *n* should be output. `%I2` is replaced by the single letter ''`i`'' if operand 2 is an immediate constant, otherwise nothing is output.

As an example of the use of this pattern, we compiled the function

```
int
sub1 (a, b, c)
     int a;
     unsigned b, c;
{
  if (b <= c)
    a++;

  return a;
}
```

with GCC. This program produced a single insn in GCC's internal representation:

```
(insn 21 13 22 (parallel[
           (set (reg/i:SI 3)
                (plus:SI (leu:SI (reg:SI 4)
                                 (reg:SI 5))
                         (reg:SI 3)))
           (clobber (reg:SI 0))
       ] ) 264 {sleu+30} (nil)
    (expr_list:REG_DEAD (reg:SI 4)
        (expr_list:REG_DEAD (reg:SI 5)
            (expr_list:REG_UNUSED (reg:SI 0)
                (nil)))))
```

The calling sequence on the RS/6000 has input parameters passed in successive registers, starting with register 3; the result is returned in register 3. In this case, register 0 (a normal register on the RS/6000 for all purposes except as a memory address) is used as a scratch register. The generated code for the entire `sub1` function consists of the following three instructions:

```
sf      r0,r4,r5
aze     r3,r3
br
```

The first two instructions were generated by the pattern shown above and the third instruction returns from the function.

6. The doz, abs, and nabs Instructions

One of the more interesting instructions on the RS/6000 is the Difference or Zero (`doz`) instruction. The instruction `doz rt,ra,rb` computes the C expression `rt = (ra > rb) ? 0 : rb - ra`.

This instruction has the potential to eliminate a number of branch instructions. The signed `max` of two values can be obtained by following this instruction with an add of `ra`, computing `rt = (ra > rb) ? ra : rb`. To compute the signed `min` of two values, the result of the `doz` instruction can be subtracted from `rb`, computing `rt = (ra > rb) ? rb : ra`. By having GCC detect the idiom of `a > b ? a : b` and convert it into a `max` operation (similarly for `min`), we can emit this two-instruction sequence, again avoiding branches.

For unsigned `min` and `max`, GSO produced a number of four-instruction sequences, some of which involve the `doz` instruction. These are also generated by GCC. The idiom `a > 0 ? a : -a` is also detected and the `abs` instruction is generated. Similarly `a > 0 ? -a : a` produces the `nabs` instruction, again eliminating potential branches.

We were recently informed that the upcoming RS/6000-based processor being designed by the new IBM/Apple/Motorola consortium will not support the `doz`, `abs`, and `nabs` instructions in hardware (they will trap and be emulated in software) and it was suggested that GCC should therefore avoid these instructions. To evaluate the impact of the absence of these instructions, we created a variant of GSO that did not have these instructions and reran GSO on all the expressions described above.

We reproduced the well-known results that `abs` can be done in three instructions and signed `min` and `max` can be done in four. More surprisingly, we found that all four of the signed comparisons (`>=`, `>`, `<=`, and `<`) use `doz`, `abs`, or `nabs` and require a fourth instruction if these are not available.

7. Operation of the GNU Superoptimizer

Massalin's superoptimizer accepts a sequence of assembler instructions describing a function and exhaustively generates all sequences of instructions of increasing length until one is found that performs the desired computation. Several heuristics prevent testing clearly impossible sequences. His superoptimizer is written in the assembler language for the target machine and operates by executing the sequences on the target. The GNU superoptimizer (GSO) has improvements in the areas of portability, configurability and search strategy.

7.1. Portability and Configurability of GSO

GSO is approximately 3000 lines of C code and is host-independent. Unlike Massalin's superoptimizer, GSO searches for sequences of instructions that compute one of several goal functions that have been compiled into GSO. The desired goal is selected with a command-line option with a mnemonic name.

GSO generates code sequences for many different target machines and is designed so that additional targets can easily be added. Currently, GSO supports the IBM RS/6000, the Sparc, the Motorola 68k and 88k, the AMD 29k, and the Intel 80386. Portability is accomplished by defining generic operations which include the union of all instructions supported by GSO for all supported machines. C code is written to simulate each of these operations.

7.1.1. Goal Functions in GSO

One example of a goal function is `eq0`, which returns the value 1 if its single argument is equal to zero and 0 otherwise. To implement this goal function, the routine `eval_goal_function` in GSO contains:

```
case EQ0:
    r = v0 == 0;
    break;
```

Another goal function discussed above was the result of performing a logical `and` between one value (in this case the third operand) and the negation of the comparison of the first two operands. This goal function for a signed `<=` comparison is called `nales` and is implemented as:

```
case NALES:
    r = (-((signed) v0 <= (signed) v1)) & v2;
    break;
```

Here is a list of some of the goal functions currently supported:

- `eq` and `ne`. Two-operand equality comparisons.
- `les`, `ges`, `lts`, and `gts`. Two-operand signed inequality comparisons.
- `leu`, `geu`, `ltu`, and `gtu`. Two-operand unsigned inequality comparisons.
- `eq0`, `ne0`, `les0`, `ges0`, `lts0`, and `gts0`. Single-operand comparisons against zero. As discussed above, the unsigned comparisons against zero are degenerate.
- `neq`, `nne`, `nles`, `nges`, `nlts`, `ngts`, `nleu`, `ngeu`, `nltu`, `ngtu`, `neq0`, `nne0`, `nles0`, `nges0`, `nlts0`, and `ngts0`. Same as above except that they return negative one for true and zero for false.
- `naeq`, `nane`, `nales`, `nages`, `nalts`, `nagts`, `naleu`, `nageu`, `naltu`, `nagtu`, `naeq0`, `nane0`, `nales0`, `nages0`, `nalts0`, and `nagts0`. Three-operand functions that compute the logical `and` of one operand with the negated result of the comparison of the other two operands. An example was shown at the start of this section.
- `peq`, `pne`, `ples`, `pges`, `plts`, `pgts`, `pleu`, `pgeu`, `pltu`, `pgtu`, `peq0`, `pne0`, `ples0`, `pges0`, `plts0`, and `pgts0`. These functions add one operand to the result of comparing the other two operands. E.g, `plts0(a, b, c)` would be written `((signed) a < (signed) b) + c` in C.
- `mins`, `maxs`, `minu`, and `maxu`. Signed and unsigned `min` and `max` operations.
- `sgn`. Returns positive one if the single operand is positive, zero if the operand is zero, and negative one if the operand is negative.

- abs. Absolute value function.
- nabs. Negated absolute value function.

New goal functions are included by adding a tag to an enum, adding the name and tag to a table used to parse command line options, and adding a case to the switch on goal tags to compute the desired function.

7.1.2. Target Machine Operations in GSO

This version of GSO was written to find instruction sequences for code involving conditional operations. The parts of the machine that are known to GSO are the **carry** bit and a set of registers. All operations manipulate these objects. We do not support operations referencing memory since these will not be part of an optimal sequence of instructions that compute functions on registers. If an input or an output is actually in memory, the sequence produced will normally have to be augmented with load or store instructions on RISC machines. On CISC machines, it may be possible to perform an operation directly on operands in memory. In both cases, the essence of the instruction sequence is not effected.

The operations that GSO uses to create sequences are expressed in terms of generic operations, each of which is available on some subset of the supported machines.

Twelve addition operations are provided, divided into three groups of four. We believe that these operations are general enough to describe the addition operations on all current processors. Within each group, an operation can either use or not use the value of the **carry** bit, and either update the **carry** bit or leave it unchanged. The three groups are addition (ADD), subtraction (SUB), and the addition of one value to the complement of the other (ADC). A typical operation is denoted by ADC_CIO, which computes the sum of the **carry** bit, one operand, and the complement of the other and sets the **carry** bit corresponding to the result of the addition.

Each machine has either ADD and SUB operations or ADD and ADC operations. The distinction between the SUB and ADC operations is in the meaning of the **carry** bit. On machines with an ADC operation, the **carry** bit is the carry out of the high-order bit when the ALU performs the subtraction, which it does by adding the first operand, the one's complement (bit-wise inverse) of the second operand, and the constant 1. An ADC_CI operation computes the sum of the first operand, the one's complement of the second operand, and the **carry** bit.

On machines with a SUB operation, the **carry** bit is negated during subtractions so that it represents "borrow". A SUB_CI operation subtracts the **carry** (really "borrow") from the difference of the two operands.

Of the machines supported by GSO, the Sparc, 68k, and i386 have SUB operations and the remainder have ADC operations. It is interesting to note that this difference in behavior of the i386 and RS/6000 was a surprise to at least one quite proficient assembler language programmer who has written compilers for both machines.

These operations are executed by a block of C code. Here is the code for the ADC_CIO operation, which is the same as the ADC_CI operation mentioned above, except that it also sets the **carry** bit as an output:

```
#define PERFORM_ADC_CIO(d, co, r1, r2, ci)
{ word __d = (r1) + ~(r2) + (ci);
  (co) = (ci) ? __d <= (r1) : __d < (r1);
  (d) = __d;
}
```

The following is the complete list of operations in the current version of GSO:

- COPY. Copy one register to another, or move an immediate value into a register.
- EXCHANGE. Exchange two registers. Used only on two-operand machines.
- ADD, ADD_CI, ADD_CO, ADD_CIO, ADC, ADC_CI, ADC_CO, ADC_CIO, SUB, SUB_CI, SUB_CO, and SUB_CIO. These are the addition and subtraction operations discussed above.
- CMP. Set **carry** bit true if the first operand is less than the second, when interpreted as unsigned numbers.
- COMCY. Complement the **carry** bit.
- AND, IOR, XOR, ANDC, IORC, EQV, NAND, and NOR. Various logical operations. The **carry** bit is not affected.
- AND_RC, IOR_RC, XOR_RC, ANDC_RC, IORC_RC, EQV_RC, NAND_RC, and NOR_RC. Similar, but reset the **carry** bit.
- LSHIFTR. Logical right shift.
- ASHIFTR. Arithmetic right shift.
- LSHIFTR_CO and ASHIFTR_CO. Logical and arithmetic right shift, but copy last bit shifted out into the **carry** bit.
- ASHIFTR_CON. Arithmetic right shift of the RS/6000. Set carry bit if the shifted value is negative and if any bits shifted out were non-zero, otherwise clear the **carry** bit.
- ABS and NABS. Unary absolute value and negative absolute value, respectively.
- DOZ. The RS/6000 doz instruction, described above.
- CPEQ, CPGE, CPGEU, CPGT, CPLE, CPLEU, CPLT, CPLTU, and CPNEQ. If the specified comparison of two operands is true, set the result to a value that contains just the sign bit; otherwise set the result to zero. These instructions are present in the AMD 29k family

processors.

The search routines know which machines have which operations and what operands are supported for each operation. A target-specific (via `ifdef`) function in GSO produces assembler-language output of the sequences for the selected target machine. To add support for a new machine, the following must be done:

- Define generic operations for any instructions present on the new machine but on no previous machine and write C code to emulate them.
- Modify the conditionalization of the search routines to reflect which operations are present in the new machine and add any new operations.
- Write code to output the operations in the assembly language of the target machine.

7.2. Search strategy of GSO

Both Massalin's superoptimizer and GSO search for the shortest sequence by first searching for sequences of length 1, then sequences of length 2 and continuing until a sequence is found, or a specified bound is exceeded. The strategies used when searching for a sequence of a given length differ. Massalin's superoptimizer generates every possible sequence of the desired length. For each sequence it applies a pruning procedure (described in his paper) to eliminate obviously incorrect sequences and then tests the sequence for correctness.

Like Massalin's superoptimizer, GSO initially generates random arguments for all input operands of the goal function. All computations are performed on these values and values computed by instructions GSO has generated for a putative sequence. No symbolic manipulations are performed. GSO searches for instruction sequences using a recursive iterative-deepening method, and avoids generating clearly useless instructions that would otherwise have to be pruned later. Only operands that are either inputs to the sequence or have been generated by previous instructions are tried. Similarly, if the **carry** bit has not yet been set, an instruction that uses it will not be generated. If the iterative-deepening search has reached a leaf node, the ultimately computed value is compared to the value returned by the goal function for the same input operands. If the values are not equal, the generated sequence is immediately discarded.

Initially the sequence consists of no instructions, the **carry** flag is undefined, and the only available operands are the inputs to the sequence. At each level of recursion, the search function, `synth`, scans the list of all available operations for the target machine, adds an operation to the sequence, and makes a recursive call to add more operations if a leaf node is not reached. The operation is also

Goal	Generated Code	Goal	Generated Code

eq	`sf r5,r3,r4`
	`sfe r6,r4,r3`
	`ae r7,r6,r5`
		eq0	`sfi r4,r3,0`
			`ae r5,r4,3`

ges	`doz r5,r3,r4`
	`sfi r6,r5,0`
	`ae r7,r6,r5`
		ges0	`sri r4,r3,31`
			`xoril r5,r4,1`

geu	`sf r5,r4,r3`
	`rlinm r6,r5,0,0,0`
	`ae r7,r6,r6`
		gtu	`sf r5,r3,r4`
			`sfe r6,r6,r6`
			`neg r7,r6`

gts	`doz r5,r4,r3`
	`nabs r6,r5`
	`sri r7,r6,31`
		gts0	`sfi r4,r3,0`
			`ame r5,r4`
			`sri r6,r5,31`

les	`doz r5,r4,r3`
	`sfi r6,r5,0`
	`ae r7,r6,r5`
		les0	`ai r4,r3,-1`
			`aze r5,r4`
			`sri r6,r5,31`

leu	`sf r5,r3,r4`
	`rlinm r6,r5,0,0,0`
	`ae r7,r6,r6`
		ltu	`sf r5,r4,r3`
			`sfe r6,r6,r6`
			`neg r7,r6`

lts	`doz r5,r3,r4`
	`nabs r6,r5`
	`sri r7,r6,31`
		lts0	`sri r4,r3,31`

ne	`xor r5,r4,r3`
	`nabs r6,r5`
	`sri r7,r6,31`
		ne0	`nabs r4,r3`
			`sri r5,r4,31`

Table 1: Sequences for Simple Comparisons, `(A` *rel-op* `B)`

simulated and the resulting value is saved. Two versions of `synth` are provided, one for 2-operand machines (the 68k and i386, of those supported) and one for 3-operand machines. On 3-operand machines, register move instructions are never present in an optimal instruction sequence, so they need never be generated.

At each leaf of the search tree, the result of the last operation is compared with the result of the goal function applied to the random input values. If they agree, a potentially valid sequence has been found and a more exhaustive test will be performed to see if the sequence is most likely to be correct. This test is similar to that used by Massalin: first some typical operand values are tried and then random values are tested. If the sequence passes, it is printed.

To reduce significantly the amount of searching required, the choices of operands are limited to values generated by previous instructions. Operations that accept the **carry** bit as an input will not be generated unless a previous operation set the **carry** bit. For commutative operations, only one ordering of the operands will be tried. The destination of all operations is always the next available register for a 3-operand machine, and one of the input operands for a 2-operand machine. When generating the last instruction even more restrictions are made.

Specifically, the last instruction must use the output or **carry** bit produced by the penultimate instruction, otherwise the penultimate instruction would not have been needed.

These techniques allow for quite rapid generation of sequences. All the sequences shown in this paper were generated in only a few seconds on a modern workstation, although searching for sequences of five instructions for goal functions with three inputs can take a good part of an hour.

7.3. Limitations of Superoptimizers

A fundamental problem with the technique of superoptimization is that the search space is approximately exponential in the sequence length, and that the branching factor, i.e., the number of instruction choices at each point, is relatively large. The approximate number of tested sequences is b^k, where b is the branching factor and k is the number of insns generated in an output sequence. If b is large, the number of tested sequences becomes huge, and the search space will be too large for any longer sequences.

Keeping the branching factor as small as possible is the most important way to make a superoptimizer able to generate longer sequences. GSO's approach is to avoid instructions with constants, with the exceptions of –1, 0, +1, 2^{31}, and 2^{31}–1. As a result, the branching factor lies between 100 and 1000, depending on the target instruction set and the current search depth. If all possible 32-bit constants were used blindly, the branching factor would exceed 2^{32} — and superoptimization would become impractical.

Goal	Generated Code	Goal	Generated Code

`neq`	`xor r5,r4,r3`
	`ai r6,r5,-1`
	`sfe r7,r7,r7`
		`neq0`	`ai r4,r3,-1`
			`sfe r5,r5,r5`

`nges`	`doz r5,r3,r4`
	`ai r6,r5,-1`
	`sfe r7,r7,r7`
		`nges0`	`sfi r4,r3,-1`
			`srai r5,r4,31`

`ngeu`	`sf r5,r4,r3`
	`sfe r6,r6,r6`
	`nand r7,r6,r6`
		`ngtu`	`sf r5,r3,r4`
			`sfe r6,r6,r6`

`ngts`	`doz r5,r4,r3`
	`nabs r6,r5`
	`srai r7,r6,31`
		`ngts0`	`sfi r4,r3,0`
			`ame r5,r4`
			`srai r6,r5,31`

`nles`	`doz r5,r4,r3`
	`ai r6,r5,-1`
	`sfe r7,r7,r7`
		`nles0`	`ai r4,r3,-1`
			`aze r5,r4`
			`srai r6,r5,31`

`nleu`	`sf r5,r3,r4`
	`sfe r6,r6,r6`
	`nand r7,r6,r6`
		`nltu`	`sf r5,r4,r3`
			`sfe r6,r6,r6`

`nlts`	`doz r5,r3,r4`
	`nabs r6,r5`
	`srai r7,r6,31`
		`nlts0`	`srai r4,r3,31`

`nne`	`xor r5,r4,r3`
	`nabs r6,r5`
	`srai r7,r6,31`
		`nne0`	`nabs r4,r3`
			`srai r5,r4,31`

Table 2: Negated Comparisons, `-(A` *rel-op* `B)`

For the kind of goal functions currently defined in GSO, the limited set of constants is not believed to be a problem. For other goal functions, we would have to be smarter. To adequately choose the right set of constants for a particular goal function is an interesting area for future work.

Aside from the intentional omission of constants, it is possible that instructions have been omitted unintentionally, and hence some of the sequences produced may not be optimal.

For example in Massalin's superoptimizer, which tries a significant number of machine instructions, non-optimal sequences have been produced. Massalin shows sequences on the 68020 for computing `d0 *= 29`, `d0 *= 39`, `d0 *= 156`, and `d0 *= 625`. The first three use 5 instructions, while the last uses 7. What was not noticed is that `lea` (load effective address) instructions can be used to perform multiplications by 3, 5, and (sometimes) 9. Since 625 is the fourth power of 5, it can be computed with four consecutive `lea` instructions. Because `lea` only operates on address registers, another two instructions are required to copy between an address register and `d0`.

Thus, the shortest sequence for multiplication by 625 has 6 instructions. However, if the statement of the problem is weakened to the problem of taking a value in an arbitrary register and putting the result into any register, multiplication by 29, 39, and 625 can all be done in four

Goal	Generated Code	Goal	Generated Code

`naeq0`	`ai r5,r3,-1`
	`sfe r6,r6,r6`
	`and r7,r6,r4`
		`nages0`	`srai r5,r3,31`
			`andc r6,r4,r5`

`nageu`	`sf r6,r4,r3`
	`sfe r7,r7,r7`
	`andc r8,r5,r7`
		`nagtu`	`sf r6,r3,r4`
			`sfe r7,r7,r7`
			`and r8,r7,r5`

`naleu`	`sf r6,r3,r4`
	`sfe r7,r7,r7`
	`andc r8,r5,r7`
		`nalts0`	`srai r5,r3,31`
			`and r6,r5,r4`

`naltu`	`sf r6,r4,r3`
	`sfe r7,r7,r7`
	`and r8,r7,r5`
		`nane0`	`nabs r5,r3`
			`srai r6,r5,31`
			`and r7,r6,r4`

Table 3: Negated Comparisons with `and`.

instructions.

If one wishes to include all machine instructions in a superoptimizer, the GSO approach makes it slightly harder to ensure that all instructions are included, because of the introduction of the abstract operations. If actual machine instructions were used, it would be possible to check them off against a list of all valid machine instructions. With GSO, there is a level of indirection that must also be checked.

An early version of GSO demonstrated an interesting case of an omitted operation. That version of GSO did not try operations that set a register to a constant value but it did try logical operations between previous values and the constants listed above. In several sequences, an `and` that cleared everything but the sign bit was generated. However, in the sequences in question, the subsequent use of the result was in a context where the sign bit was irrelevant. A more straightforward sequence would have been to set a register to 0, but this was not one of the operations `synth` tried in that version.

Goal	Generated Code	Goal	Generated Code

peq	`xor r6,r4,r3`
	`sfi r7,r6,0`
	`aze r8,r5`
		peq0	`sfi r5,r3,0`
			`aze r6,r4`

pges	`doz r6,r3,r4`
	`sfi r7,r6,0`
	`aze r8,r5`
		pges0	`dozi r5,r3,0`
			`sfi r6,r5,0`
			`aze r7,r4`

pgeu	`sf r6,r4,r3`
	`aze r7,r5`
		pgtu	`sf r6,r3,r4`
			`sfe r7,r5,r6`
			`sf r8,r7,r6`

pgts	`doz r6,r4,r3`
	`ai r7,r6,-1`
	`aze r8,r5`
		pgts0	`a r5,r3,r3`
			`sfe r6,r3,r5`
			`aze r7,r4`

ples	`doz r6,r4,r3`
	`sfi r7,r6,0`
	`aze r8,r5`
		ples0	`srai r5,r3,31`
			`sf r6,r3,r5`
			`aze r7,r4`

pleu	`sf r6,r3,r4`
	`aze r7,r5`
		pltu	`sf r6,r4,r3`
			`sfe r7,r5,r6`
			`sf r8,r7,r6`

plts	`doz r6,r3,r4`
	`ai r7,r6,-1`
	`aze r8,r5`
		plts0	`a r5,r3,r3`
			`aze r6,r4`

pne	`xor r6,r4,r3`
	`ai r7,r6,-1`
	`aze r8,r5`
		pne0	`ai r5,r3,-1`
			`aze r6,r4`

Table 4: Operations of the form `(A` *rel-op* `B) + C`.

7.4. Correctness of the Sequences

One must be careful in using the results of a superoptimizer, either GSO or Massalin's original work. Neither program exhaustively tests the resulting code sequences. Although it is highly likely that they are correct, and an incorrect sequence has never been found, each sequence should be checked manually to ensure its correctness.

8. Complete Superoptimizer Results for the RS/6000

This section contains tables showing the shortest code sequence for every goal function described in Section 7.1.1. We list only one of multiple sequences, usually the one that GCC will generate.

Table 1 shows the code generated for the 16 simple comparisons. Table 2 shows the same comparisons, but returning a negative one for true and zero for false. In some cases, we can logically `and` the result of the previous operations with another value at no extra cost; Table 3 shows those operations. Entries that are missing cannot be done any cheaper than the code in Table 2 followed by an `and` instruction. Table 4 shows the operations of the form `(A` *rel-op* `B) + C`. Finally, Table 5 shows the code sequence for miscellaneous operations.

9. Conclusions and Future Work

We have described a variation of Massalin's Superoptimizer and shown how it can be used to produce extremely efficient code sequences that do not contain jumps from

Goal	Generated Code
abs	`abs 4,3`
nabs	`nabs 4,3`
maxs	`doz r5,r3,r4` `a r6,r5,r3`

maxu	`xoriu r5,r4,0x8000`
	`xoriu r6,r3,0x8000`
	`doz r7,r5,r6`
	`a r8,r7,r4`

mins	`doz r5,r3,r4` `sf r6,r5,r4`

minu	`xoriu r5,r4,0x8000`
	`xoriu r6,r3,0x8000`
	`doz r7,r5,r6`
	`sf r8,r7,r3`

sgn	`a r4,r3,r3`
	`sfe r5,r3,r4`
	`sfe r6,r5,r3`

Table 5: Code Sequences for Miscellaneous Operations

code that initially has jumps. We have shown that instruction simulation techniques can be used to make a superoptimizer both efficient and easily portable.

There are many possible areas for future work. Clearly, more operations and goal functions can be added to GSO, and this work is currently in progress. Similarly, more machines can be supported.

Another interesting area for future work is the possibility of integrating GSO into the configuration process of GCC. This would allow the compiler to produce these optimal sequences without the manual process of converting GSO-produced code sequences into instruction patterns for the GCC configuration file.

Acknowledgments

Richard Kenner was supported by the U.S. Department of Energy under grant number DE-FG02-88ER25052. Torbjörn Granlund was supported by Sics' research program sponsored by the Swedish National Board for Technical Development (NUTEK), Swedish Telecom, Ericsson Group, ASEA Brown Boveri, IBM Sweden, Nobel Tech System AB, and the Swedish Defence Material Administration (FMV).

This work would not have been possible without the original idea of a superoptimizer suggested by Henry Massalin. We also wish to thank Robert Dewar of New York University for his urging that these results be published. Christopher Fraser, the Program Chair of this conference provided considerable advice on how to improve this paper from the initial extended abstract.

The GNU C compiler was written mostly by Richard Stallman and is being developed and distributed by the Free Software Foundation, to which numerous people and organizations have contributed. The League for Programming Freedom (LPF) is an organization that is fighting user interface copyrights and software patents, both of which would prevent the development of software like GCC. Contact the LPF for more information at `league@prep.ai.mit.edu` or at 1 Kendall Square #143, Cambridge, MA 02139.

References

[1] Henry Massalin, Superoptimizer: A Look at the Smallest Program, in *Proceedings of the Second International Conference on Architectural Support for Programming Languages and Operating Systems* (ASPLOS II), pages 122-126, 1987.

[2] Richard Stallman, *Using and Porting GNU CC*, Free Software Foundation, 1992.

[3] Jack W. Davidson and Christopher W. Fraser, Register Allocation and Exhaustive Peephole Optimization, *Software – Practice and Experience* 14(9):857-865, September 1984.

[4] Henry Warren, Predicting Execution Time on the IBM RISC System/6000, Preliminary Version, IBM, 1991.